TO SERVE WITH GLADNESS

Celebrating One Hundred and Fifty Years
of the Sisters of Mercy, Rochfortbridge

Editor
Danny Dunne

~ TABLE OF CONTENTS ~

DETAIL FROM THE MEDIEVAL STAINED GLASS WINDOW-MEEDIN CHURCH
The stained glass was put in place in this medieval window by Fr. Thomas O'Farrell P.P., in the 1930's. But the iconography displayed is medieval. It depicts Christ as *'Salvator Mundi'* -the Saviour of the world holding the *'Globus Cruciger'* an orb topped with a cross. The orb held by Christ signifies dominion over the whole world. The lily has always been depicted as a symbol of purity, innocence and strength. A lily first appeared in early middle ages art. Mary is often depicted being presented with a lily by the Angel Gabriel as a sign that she would be the Mother of God. In this window, embracing the lily and facing her son, holding the globus cruciger establishes this certainty.

Mercy Sisters – Rochfortbridge

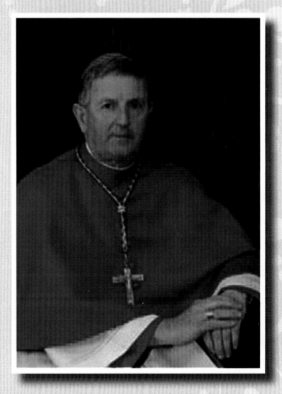

I warmly welcome this book on the history of the Mercy Sisters in Rochfortbridge. When Catherine McAuley began her ministry to the poor and disagvantaged – of which there were many – she could not have imagined that her example would find so many followers, women who, in the name of God, gave their lives to the care and education of others.

The founding of the Convent in Tullamore in 1836 was the third convent she opened. Her second foundation did not survive but that in Tullamore flourished and Mercy Sisters from Tullamore founded numerous Convents both in Ireland and abroad. It was from Tullamore that the Sisters came to Rochfortbridge in 1862.

When the Mercy Sisters arrived in Trim a few years later the parish Priest, Fr. Duncan welcomed them with these words 'I want you to care for the sick and poor and educate the ignorant.' There was little care available for those who needed it and educational opportunity was very limited, especially in some areas. For the past 150 years the Sisters, in all the parishes in which they were located, have fulfilled those words of Fr. Duncan. They have completed what they came to do and undoubtedly other demands and apostolates will unfold over the coming years. They have enhanced the lives of generations of parishioners at many levels, especially in giving them that most essential and precious of gifts – educational opportunity.

They have left a legacy which must be preserved and developed over the coming decades. It is indeed right and just that their dedicated service to this community is recorded and acknowledged.

+*Michael Smith*
  Bishop of Meath

A Message from Anne Eighan
- Principal of the Convent Primary School

I am delighted to welcome the publication of *To Serve With Gladness*, to celebrate 150 years of the Mercy Order in our locality. It has been a pleasure to have been involved in its compilation. I must express my deep gratitude to Danny Dunne, for his tireless work in researching and writing this book. I also want to congratulate the Sisters of Rochfortbridge on the occasion of this anniversary.

Looking back at the history of the Mercy Order in our locality, one can see how the Sisters of Mercy have contributed immeasurably to the advancement of this area. The successive sisters who have resided in Rochfortbridge, devoted their lives to educating the people of this village and beyond. Education is essential to any society, as it passes the knowledge humanity has accumulated, to future generations. After all, most of what we know we learned from someone else. It also allows us to develop our social skills. The Sisters of the Mercy Order nurtured successive generations of children, and inspired them to use their various talents, whether they were in music, sport or other areas.

It cannot be denied that the sisters have been in many ways at the centre of our community for the past 150 years. They have catered greatly for the spiritual and educational needs of the people of this area. They were heavily involved in charitable works which helped the vulnerable members of our community. Eliza Fielding was motivated by the plight of the poor, in setting up the Mercy Convent in Rochfortbridge in 1862. Back then Rochfortbridge was a very poor village. This book will provide a vivid account to the reader of how the Mercy Sisters helped to fight poverty and destitution in this area.

Finally, I wish to thank all those who contributed to this book, by sending in photographs and contributing to the information contained within. Again, I cannot emphasise enough that this book would not have been possible without Danny Dunne. His unceasing efforts in obtaining information and toiling in the archives must be highly commended. He has succeeded in creating a valuable source of information, not only to celebrate this anniversary, but also to inform future generations about the presence of the Mercy Order in Rochfortbridge.

Hopefully you will agree that this book is a fitting testimonial to the contribution that the Mercy Sisters have made to the social and educational life of our community. We can truly say that the Sisters of Rochfortbridge have indeed *"served with gladness"*.

Principal of Convent Primary School, Rochfortbridge.

A Message from Eileen Alford
- Principal of St. Joseph's Secondary School

I am delighted to be sharing in the celebration of this very significant anniversary in the life of our parish and school community. The Mercy Sisters and their work has had a huge influence on the parish of Rochfortbridge. I have always admired the philosophy of Mercy education and viewed it as a much grounded philosophy, very real, very practical and steeped in sound core values of respect, equality and hard work.

As you will see from reading this book the Mercy Sisters who came to Rochfortbridge 150 years ago were great visionaries and since that time have worked very hard in the parish to meet the needs of the people and children in the locality and the wider catchment area. In their work they were never content to remain static but were always reflecting on the needs of the people they lived amongst and how they could best serve those needs. They also then spread their wings and travelled to distant lands setting up a convent in Yass in 1875 and from this convent eight other communies were established in Australia.

We can all learn many lessons from their hard work and the great sacrifices they made in service to our community. We are privileged to be the beneficiaries of their efforts and owe them a huge debt of gratitude for the many opportunities their education afforded the young people of Rochfortbridge.

Each of the Sisters has contributed and are still contributing to our community in different ways and I look forward to their help and advice for many more years.

Finally I say a simple but very sincere Thank you to the Mercy Sisters for their hugely significant work in our community.

Eileen Alford.

Principal of St. Joseph's Secondary School, Rochfortbridge.

Foreword

"Not all of us can do great things. But we can do small things with great love."
–Mother Theresa of Calcutta

The banner displayed on this page is located above the side door of the Convent of Mercy. This is the main access door for the Sisters coming and going every day of their lives from the convent, to the schools, the church, or the village. The words, taken from psalm 99 are a mission statement for them in their labours of serving the Lord. It is a reminder also that this is the purpose of their lives.

Jubilate Deo Domino omnis terra
Servite Domino in laetitia
introite in conspectu
eius in exultatione...

In translation this reads:-

Sing joyfully to God, all the earth
Serve ye the Lord with gladness.
Come in before his presence
With exceeding great joy....

This in fact is the thread that runs through this book, service to the Lord with gladness, and an appropriate title to celebrate one hundred and fifty years of their presence in the Parish of Rochfortbridge.

The Sisters of Mercy are there in our lives, in the lives of the children they have taught, in the community they serve, by quietly taking part in the Social Services that have helped make life better for the poor, the lonely and those in their senior years who may need a helping hand or a welcome smile to brighten up their day. Their work in the Parish can often go unnoticed as the quotation from Mother Theresa above reminds us, no one is looking to do great things, but it is the little things they do with great love that make the difference. This has been their calling card.

Over one hundred and fifty years ago, a young girl from the parish of St. Mary's Castlelost made a conscious decision to leave the comfort of her own Church of Ireland community, and secretly, she studied and was accepted into the Catholic Church unknown to her father and family. The story of Eliza Fielding is the stuff of story-tellers and fiction writers, but in fact her story is true. This remarkable lady, battling against the odds was responsible for the beginning of the Mercy foundation here in this village.

Coupled with the work of local Parish Priest, Fr. Gerald Robbins, his observance of the state of education in the parish and especially the percentage rate of illiteracy among the local women, which was quite low, sought to do something about it. This was a time in Ireland, thirty years after Catholic Emancipation and with the emergence of a growing Catholic middle class in Ireland, something needed to be done to provide basic education for all. During his ministry, National schools were built or upgraded and it was also his vision to establish a Community of the Sisters of Mercy in the village to help educate women and young girls.

This book is the story of Rochfortbridge from ancient times till the midde of the nineteenth century when the story of the Sisters of Mercy begins. It gives an account of Eliza and her work in helping her family to come to terms with her decision to become a member of the Catholic Church, the sale of her house to the parish, her novitiate in Tullamore, the twelve years she spent in Rochfortbridge as Sister Mary Paul and a decision to leave it all behind and to begin a new mission in the Diocese of Goulbourne in New South Wales in 1875. The foundation of the Yass Community and the other sister communities followed from there, and her final destination in the 1890s, led her to establish a house at Wilcannia Forbes, where she died in 1905.

She rests today along the banks of the Darling river beneath the southern cross, far away from her native home. But her name is forever etched in the minds of those she left behind.

The work of the Sisters of Mercy in Rochfortbridge continued at a remarkable pace. The present convent was built by the generosity of Richard Coffey, of Newcastle in 1872. The Deaf and Dumb Institute was established in 1892 and lasted for fifty eight years. The Convent Primary school is still a very important educational establishment in the parish, catering for girls up to twelve years old and for infant boys.

St. Joseph's Secondary school which began in a small way in 1948 as a Secondary Top School under the Department of Education for National Schools, has developed into a strong and vibrant Co-Educational Secondary school, with a total of 815 pupils and a staff of 60 Teachers in 2012.

The faith history of the parish of Rochfortbridge has also been influenced very much by the work of the Sisters of Mercy. Kathleen Wright's book *Light from the Bridge* in 2003 has recorded in great detail, the number of men and women who found their vocations as priests, nuns and brothers, as a result of their education by the Sisters, which has carried on right up to the present day. The light which was lit in this little village has fanned out right across the globe, carrying the message of the gospel, the seed of which was sown at the feet of the Sisters in the little primary school and in modern times at St. Joseph's Secondary School.

In 1912, two past pupils of the Convent Primary School Mother Mary of the Angels(Anne) Wallace, originally from Dalystown and Sister Brigid (Lizzie) Doyle from Esker, Milltownpass, both sisters in the Convent of Mercy, Borris-in-Ossory, Co. Laois were commissioned by members of the parish to create an illuminated address to the Sisters on the occasion of the Golden Jubilee of the foundation of the Convent, their words reflect the gratitude of people and past pupils for their education and subsequent lives.

When you came to the parish fifty years ago, education was at low ebb, owing to circumstances over which there was no control. Some of us can speak on this matter from personal experience and today we recall with thankfulness the brilliant record of your achievements, not only here in our own parish but among our kith and kin in distant lands. 1

Sadly, vocations to religious life are few, but the Sisters who are still with us have indeed served their community with gladness. How does one celebrate these wonderful ladies and all they have done for the community? They have worked diligently and have never asked for anything in return. What can one give back to *them* for all they have done to help the countless people they have taught or helped in any way?

What better way, than to detail the story of their lives, recorded forever in the pages of a book. It *is* indeed a remarkable story and it is now high time to write that down for the future generations who will live and pass through this place.

For me it is a personal journey and one I was glad to have been asked to help out with. A phone call from Eileen Alford, principal of St. Joseph's Secondary School early in the year with a proposal to compile a book for this occassion met with a very definite *yes* on my part.

I was part of all this, a student in St. Joseph's from 1970 to 1975, the era of hippies, rock opera, bell-bottom trousers and platform shoes. It was *their* dedication and commitment to us that set us on the road of life and I have always maintained, I would probably never have become a primary teacher only for their work in sending me off on that journey. For this I will be forever truly grateful and my part in this project, is probably the only way I can pay them back for this, and to say thank you Sisters for being there, when you were needed the most.

But this project would not have been possible if it weren't for a number of people who have helped make this dream a reality. Quite a number of individuals have been very generous with their time and resources to make this happen and to them I say thank you for that. But there were four other people who were the backbone of this project and I just want to acknowledge *their* committment to it. Sister Geraldine Coyne has been a mind of information when it came to photos and other material regarding past pupils, boarders, teachers or anybody who passed through the doors of St. Joseph's. Being a past pupil herself, and a boarder, she has a great insight into the life and development of St. Joseph's for more than forty years.

---

1   The full text of this address can be found in the chapter entitled *Pages from the Annals.*

Eileen Alford, Principal of St. Joseph's Secondary School has left every resource available to us to keep the enthusiasm going. Ann Eighan, Principal of the Convent Primary School also opened the doors for me to access their school archive and to gather material relevant to the primary school.

Noel Foynes, who is a history teacher at St. Joseph's has been a wonderful help in searching the Archives of St. Joseph's and digitizing them for easier access and compilation. Noel has contributed an excellent chapter on the history of Sport in St. Joseph's, as the school has a track record second to none in the area of sport and games, and many of it's pupils have gone on to perform at very high standards both nationally and internationally.

Important sources for this book also are the annual magazine publications *Vox, Involve, X-tra* and *The Leaving Cert Book* which have recorded the life and times of St. Joseph's since the early 1980's. Through the eyes of the students there is another dimension to life within the school, especially in the areas of sport, musicals, school trips, poetry and personal reflection on their lives. A number of articles and poems written by pupils in that time span have been included also.

The backbone of any educational establishment are the personnel, the teachers, Special Needs Assistants, caretakers, secretaries and all other ancillary staff in the schools and in the convent. Without them the work of education would not be possible. I must express also a special thanks to Ann Eighan and her staff from the Convent primary School and to Eileen Alford and the Staff of St. Joseph's for their continued work in the field of education and to continue to carry on with the work, mission and ethos of the Sisters of Mercy.

A special thank you also to the people who have contributed articles and memoirs for the book. They give a first hand account of life within the walls of St. Josephs in its sixty four year history. A mention also to the Sisters themselves who have contributed photographs and material relating to the Deaf and Dumb Institute and to life within the convent walls.

Four of the chapters in the book are taken from the main body of a Thesis submitted by my wife Betty Mimnagh Dunne in 2001 as part fulfillment for her M.A. in Local History at N.U.I., Maynooth. The work, entitled *From Beggarsbridge to the Southern Cross- The Sisters of Mercy, Rochfortbridge and their work in the field of education in Ireland and Australia, 1862-1900*, gives a detailed account of the state of education in the Parish of Rochfortbridge, the circumstances which led to the establishment of the Convent of Mercy, the early years of the Convent Primary School, and the work of education in the mission fields of New South Wales, Australia during the same period. So on behalf of the committee and the Rochfortbridge community a special thanks to Betty to allow us use this material.

Finally, there is a paragraph in a book written in 1925 in the Convent at Broken Hill, New South Wales, when Sister Bernard Grogan(who worked for a number of years with Sister Mary Paul Fielding at Wilcannia Forbes), sat down and wrote a detailed account of the life of it's foundress.

It was written to commemorate the fiftieth anniversary of the Yass Foundation, which was the Mother house of a number of other convents in the Diocese of Goulbourn. The book entitled *The Story of a Valiant Woman*, as well as documenting the life of Mother Mary Paul takes a deeper look at the mindset and the mission of nuns and what attracts them into this world, where they are prepared to leave home and family and to serve the Lord for the rest of their lives. This piece, which I have titled *Sweet Star of Hope*, tells us of their conviction to the life they lead, and the Master they serve:

How strong must be the missionary spirit in the heart of the Irish race? One is at a loss which to admire most—those who bravely face exile in a foreign land, or the bruised and lonely hearts that remain at home to mourn the absent. What heroism in both parents and children to consent to a living death, for such a life-long separation may be called, for from the time they say "good-bye" they have little hope of meeting this side of the grave. This is particularly the case with Nuns. No elusive hope that a gold or diamond or any other gem or mineral mine, will make them millionaires all of a sudden. No dream of the day when as owners of prosperous sheep or cattle stations, they will return in opulence to the green Isle. Their "Sweet Star of Hope" is the joy of sacrifice—the conviction that they are serving a generous Master and winning innumerable graces for those who are dear to them. Their coveted wealth is— Souls-glory for God—this is their dream, the magnet that attracts them.

Danny Dunne
25th August 2012.

THE BOOK COMMITTEE 2012.
From left to right: Eileen Alford, Noel Foynes, Sister Geraldine Coyne,
Danny Dunne and Anne Eighan.

A Message from the Sisters of Mercy

We are very happy with this book – *To Serve With Gladness* written by Danny and the Commitee. It is a wonderful publication and is coming at a good time to celebrate one hundred and fifty years of the Sisters of Mercy in Rochfortbridge. One hundred and fifty years is a long time and many changes have occurred in that period, especially in areas of education, faith and social history. It is now the time to recall and record for further generations, the pathways laid down by many generations of our community. Between 1862 and 2012, it is our privelege to have served the people of this parish.

THE SISTERS OF MERCY, ROCHFORTBRIDGE COMMUNITY
TAKEN IN JULY 2012.
Back row, from left to right, Sister Rosario Shaw, Sister Geraldine Coyne and Sister Pius Doran.
Front row, from left to right, Sister Dolores Carroll, Sister Magdalene Claffey and Sister Maureen O'Brien.

THE CONVENT PRIMARY SCHOOL STAFF, TAKEN IN JUNE 2012

Back row, from left to right, Anne Carey(SNA), Chris Leavy(SNA), Brendan Nolan(Caretaker), Niamh Carty,
Kathleen O'Connor (Secretary), Paula Kilmurray, Ulrika Maher, Lisa Colleary and Grace Brown.
Front row, from left to right, Mary Seery, Thérèse Downey, Ann Eighan(Principal), Helena Farrell,
Thérèse Clarke and Geraldine Gorman

THE CONVENT PRIMARY SCHOOL BOARD OF MANAGEMENT, 2012

Back row from left to right, Helena Farrell, Joan Gorman, Barry Collins and Frank Kelly.
Front row, from left to right, Ann Eighan(Principal), Sr. Pius Doran, Fr. Eamonn O'Brien
and Michael Ó Sullivan(Chairperson).

St. Joseph's Secondary School Staff–2012.

Back row, from left to right, Noel Foynes, Joe Arthur, Cormac Davy, Adrian McCormack, Evelyn Kelly, Ger Markham, Sarah Daly, Susan Hogan, Denis Kelly, Vinnie Rowe, Rita Judge, Mike Flaherty and Dónal Ó Buachalla.

Third row, from left to right, Danny Reddin, Claire O'Connell, Gerard Healion, Julie Duffy, Carmel O Sullivan, Niamh Murray, Yvonne Hession, Liz Shaw, Yvonne Kelly and Adrian Lee.

Second row, from left to right, Mary Fallon, Nicola Honan, Fiona Burke, Helena Heduan, Sarah Crosby, Sandra Nugent, Aoife O'Donoghue, Andrea Treanor, Breda McCormack, Pamela Carroll, Karen Stenson, Caroline Kelliher, Liz O'Reilly, Yvonne O'Mahony, Rosemary Hackett, Sr. Geraldine Coyne, Nuala Flanagan, Claire McCarthy and Niamh Sheridan.

Front row, from left to right, Aoife Carroll, Jean Egan, Niamh Sweeney, Maria Keena, Eamon Scally, Charlotte Holton, Margaret Cole, Eileen Alford(Principal), Anna Kavanagh, Damien Rushe, Luke Dempsey, Martina Croghan, Brigid Currams, Seamus Casey and Cathy Spellman.

ST. JOSEPH'S SECONDARY SCHOOL BOARD OF MANAGEMENT, 2012.

Back row, from left to right, Dónal Ó Buachalla, Una Duggan, Moira Jordan and David Bollard.
Front row, from left to right, Dermot Bennett, Frances Flynn, Liz Shaw, Eileen Alford (Principal)
and Tony Ó Sullivan (Chairperson).

SR. MAUREEN ÓBRIEN CELEBRATED HER 90TH BIRTHDAY ON THE 15TH OF SEPTEMBER, 2012.

She is the oldest member of the Rochfortbridge Community.
She was born in Galway in 1922. She entered the Convent of
Mercy, Rochfortbridge in 1942. She was appointed Principal
of the Convent Primary School in 1959 and retired in 1988.
She has spent the past seventy years of her life as a Sister of
Mercy in Rochfortbridge.

~ CHAPTER 1 ~
THE VILLAGE OF THE FERTILE FIELDS

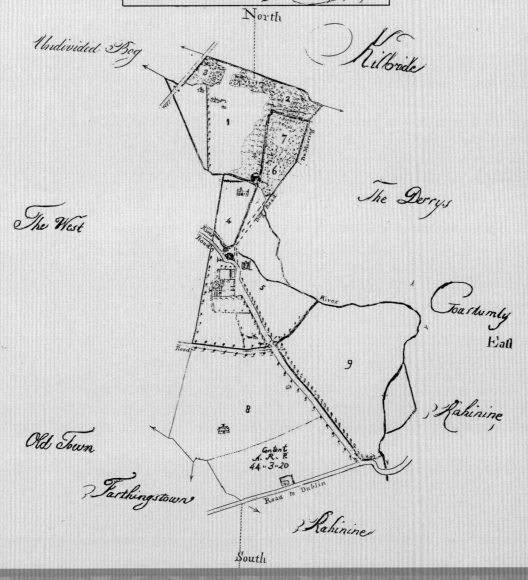

~ CHAPTER 1 ~
THE VILLAGE OF FERTILE FIELDS

Introduction

The village of Rochfortbridge today is a far different place from the village our parents and grandparents knew. Like all villages and towns in Ireland it's origins are a result of circumstances which brought about that development. To describe the village today it is classified as a *'dormitory village'* within the commuter corridor with Dublin. It is mainly residdential with less emphasis on commerce and industry but more on people putting down roots and the services available to accommodate this.

Ireland has been described as young nation compared to other nations of the world. In fact it was one of the first nations to gain independence in the early years of the twentieth century. As well as being decribed as a young nation, it's history reaches back thousands of years as is evident in it's ancient landscape and remnants of the past.

A village like Rochfortbridge whose development is ongoing due to the various parish organisations in sport, social services and tidy towns to name but a few, has done much to enhance the well-being and living conditions of it's people.

The description of Ireland as a young nation can be applied here also, in fact, as a village its development didn't really begin until the end of the 18th century right up to the end of the famine in the 1840's. Thus in the timeline of our past the village is still young.

Take a look around the village, stroll through it's ancient fields, there is a greater feeling of pastness in the place. The rocks, hedges, ringforts, walls, castle, cemeteries, roads and estates reflect that great distance in time, a place where countless generations have

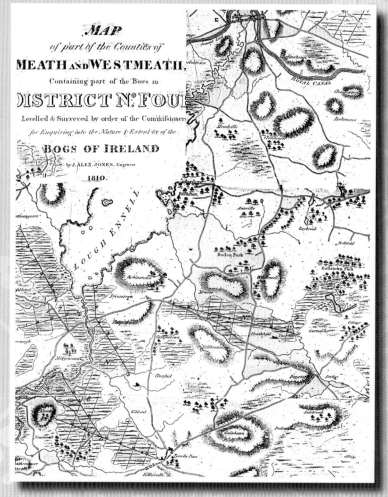

A map of the Barony of Fartullagh in 1810 from a Commissioners Enquiry into the nature and extent of Bogs in Ireland

lived, worked and departed this world quietly, paving the way forward for future generations. We are witnesses to that pastness and the work of people whose foresight and courage have moulded this place and provided for the education, health and indeed better living conditions for those who today bear witness to this work.

The focus of this particular study is not just the village but the influence the Sisters of Mercy have had on the community itself as well as the surrounding districts. People like Eliza Fielding, Father Gerald Robbins and the many other servants of the community, priests, nuns and lay people have contributed selflessly with great zeal and courage to serve the needs of this little rural village and its surrounding districts.

But the coming of the Sisters to the village in 1862 would not have been possible if it weren't for the very existence of the place and the underlying factors of population, poverty and literacy which saw a great need by Father Timothy Robbins Imcumbent Parish Priest for the education of young women in the parish.

The rise of a Catholic Middle class in the nineteenth century and the need to educate the children of the parish, saw the building of the Mercy Convent and the subsequent history of education in the parish. This has been classed as the Fielding Legacy, which celebrates its one hundred and fiftieth anniversary this year.

In order to focus on the impact the Sisters of Mercy have had and continue to have on the village, parish and surrounding districts it is necessary to fold back the layers in the paths of time to explore the factors which influenced the growth of the village and the establishment of the Catholic Parish of Rochfortbridge in the years following the Great Famine.

As a former teacher in the past, I have often used an onion to illustrate to children what history is all about. The outer layer or skin represents us, the people of the present. But peel back that layer, there's another layer underneath. This layer is different. So it is with history. Imagine that this layer represents the people who lived one hundred, two hundred or even five hundred years ago, the people are different, the landscape is different and as each layer unfolds, the place has a different story to tell. A question I was always asked was, what happens when you come to the last layer? Well this is the layer we know very little about, it stretches back to early man and even back to the time of the dinosaurs.

Early People

When one undertakes a study of a group or community of people, there are no specific or clearly defined borders or boundaries. Such divisions are created politically to mark out areas of administration. But when all is said and done, there are no barriers between people and their interaction with one another , and it is for this reason that people studying history reach out beyond those boundaries to tell a story or record events in the everyday lives of people. The study of a village or parish cannot stand alone in its interaction with the environment. It too is a link in the chain, or for that matter becomes part of the jigsaw. Each aspect of our past lives interacts with another and vica versa. People depend on one another to form a true picture of a community.

The Rochfortbridge landscape was indeed a very different one prior to early Christian times.

The central plain of Ireland was a sparsely populated area of dense forest and swampy marsh. Bogs abounded in this landscape. The glacial deposits of esker and drumlin deposited here affected the drainage of the area creating lakes of trapped surface water, which in time acidified due to the accumulation of decaying plant material. This in time developed into fens and eventually the growth of sphagnum moss on the fens resulted in vast tracts of dense bog. The resulting landscape was the deciding factor in the formation of the barony of Fartullagh in it's entirety.[1]

This ancient tuath or territory was the natural location for early population as there were natural defenses there to ensure a relative degree of safety. Fartullagh as we know it today is an island of land surrounded on the northern, southern and eastern sides by large tracts of bog and to the west by Lough Ennel and the Eiscir Riada. At the eastern and western end are two passes between the bogs at the Pass of Kilbride, at Milltownpass to the east, and Tyrrellspass to the west. Passing from north to south and from east to west to these passes ran the Slí Mór or one of the five great roads of Ireland. In ancient times this great road wound its way from Connaught to Clonmacnoise, Clonard and on to Tara.[2]

This Slí Mór ran conveniently along the Eiscir Riada to the Shannon as the countryside at the time was covered in dense dark forests and bogs, making access from place to place quite difficult for travelers. This esker made a very convenient roadway through the midlands. The name Fartullagh is derived from the ancient tribe who lived here the *Fir Tulach* or men of the mounds. This is a reference to a landscape endowed with glacial eskers and drumlins and gentle undulating hills. These Fir Tulach were more than likely part of the two hundred tuatha or tribes in the whole of Ireland at that time. The *tuath* was the smallest political unit in the country with it's own chief and territory. The Kingdom of the Fir Tulach is retained still in the name of the Barony of Fartullagh. It's total area would have been in excess of 60 square miles comprising of dense forest, large areas of bog and cleared land for tillage and the grazing of farm animals.

The landscape of Rochfortbridge focussed also on the course of the river Derry. This river forms in an area known as *The Derries* near Castlelost by two streams, one which rises from a spring at Kilbride and the other, from a spring near Newcastle, Meedin. *The Derries* are named after the great oak woods which covered the landscape locally up until the middle ages and beyond. A section of the river Derry was diverted near Rochfortbridge village in the 1840's to make way for the new section of road from Rochfortbridge to Dunboden, which was completed as a famine relief project commissioned by the Cooper family of Dunboden.

The Derry passes through two bridges- Rochfortbridge and Beggarsbridge and once divided into a series of channels at Sidebrook. Another stream joined it from Farthingstown and when it is joined further on by the Milltown River it becomes the *Mongach* river. It enters the *Yellow* river at Cloneygall bridge near Castlejordan and this river joins the river *Boyne* a few miles above Ballyboggan Bridge in Co. Meath.

To retrace our steps back to the two sources of the Derry river at Kilbride and Newcastle, the landscape of the parish is divided from north to south by a series of drumlins or little hills created as a result of glacial activity in the area during the last ice age. On the western side

---

1   See section on the Barony of Fartullagh
2   Oliver Egan, *Tyrrellspass Past and Present,* (Kildare, 1986), p.2

of these little hills, the surface streams flow at Carrick, Dalystown and Meedin to Lough Ennel, emerging near Lilliput as the river *Brosna,* which flows all the way to the Shannon. This demarcation of the drainage landscape has been described as the middle line or *median* in this division and may be the explanation for the townland of *Meedin* or *An Mídín* in Irish. Today there is no physical evidence of the Derries or oak woods, except for the occasional oak tree growing among the hedgerows, but later we will re-visit them as they formed the boundaries of the fertile fields of Castlelost.

The Fir Tulach who inhabited this area were according to genealogies descended from *Enna Cennselach* King of Leinster who died in 485 A.D. The remote ancestors of these people *the Laigin* were firmly established in the southeastern quarter of the country and were part of the general movement of people from the European mainland populating the area between 500 and 100B.C.

The earliest references we have to the Fir Tulach are to be found in *the Annals of the Four Masters* where under the entry date 759 A.D.

> The battle of Dún Bile was won by Donnchadh, son of Domhnaill, over the Feara Tulach. [3]

We do not know for certain where Dún Bile was it was more than likely some location in Westmeath or one of the surrounding counties.

In some of the early manuscripts the Fir Tulach are referred to as *Telcha Mide* or *Campus Teloch*. [4]

The O'Dooleys of Fartullagh

Within this island fortress surrounded by bog, lake and esker the Fir Tulach found a secure haven in this part of the midlands and as a result was also the location of a few prominent monastic settlements such as Lynn, Kilbride and Clonfad.

But early in the sixth century after a long struggle for power between Meath and Leinster which climaxed with the battle of *Druim Deirg* in 515 A.D., the Leinster Kings yielded control to the overlordship of the southern *Uí Néill* Kingdom of Meath which included the territories of the Fir Tulach.

From then on the Fir Tulach were subject to the control of the *Clann Cholmán* rulers of the western part of Meath from the Hill of Uisneach. They claimed descent from Niall of the Nine Hostages through *Colmán Mór* one of the sons *of Diarmaid Mac Cearbhaill*, a great grandson of Niall.

The Fir Tulach were in fact not driven from their territories but continued to hold their lands under their own leader, but paid tribute to Clann Colmán and acknowledged them as overlords. [5]

---

3   Peter J. Dooley, *The Dooleys of Fartullagh* in *Riocht na Midhe,* Journal of the Meath Archaeological and Historical Society, Vol. III no.4(1992-1993), p.125
4   Paul Walsh, *The placenames of Westmeath,* p. 161.
5   Peter J. Dooley, *The Dooleys of Fartullagh* in *Riocht na Midhe,* Journal of the Meath Archaeological and Historical Society, Vol. III no.4(1992-1993), p. 126

According to the *Book of Rights,* the Fir Tulach were obliged to give as levy or tribute

> 100 wethers[6]
>
> 100 boars
>
> 100 Oxen

every year and would, as gratuity or stipend receive

> 6 horses
>
> 6 swords
>
> 6 shields
>
> 6 foreign slaves

from their overlords.[7]

The name Dooley or *Dubhlaoich* is synonymous with Fartullagh and in the Annals of the Four Masters it is recorded that in 978 A.D. there is an account of a battle between *Maelsechlainn* and the Norse or Viking King of Dublin.

Maelsechlain won the battle but two sons of Dubhlaech two lords of Feara Tulach were killed.[8]

The Ó' Dubhlaoich were readily the principal ruling family in the territory before the Norman invasion. They claimed descent from Brandubh King of Leinster who was slain in the year 605 A.D. and was related to the Ui Felmeda and other Leinster Peoples. It was different blood from the royal Dynasty of Meath and as such was submitted to tribute. [9]The Dooleys were indeed masters of this land towards the end of the first millennium as can be seen again from *the Annals of the Four Masters.* In 1021 A.D. Cucaille son of Dubhlaech, Lord of Feara Tulach died. In the poem by Ó Dubhagain the Dooleys are seen to be successful, prosperous and comfortably established in Fartullagh:

> Ó Dubhlaidhe of great prosperity is King of Feara Tulach of Noble Lords.[10]

In the *The Life of Colmán of Lynn,* we read that Colmán blessed the lands of *Dún na Cairrge.* The people of Carrick asked him to leave a well of fresh water with them. Colmán planted his staff in the meadow of Carrick and twirled it about saying:-

---

6   A castrated ram.
7   Peter J. Dooley, *The Dooleys of Fartullagh.*
8   Paul Walsh, Placenames of Westmeath(Dublin1957), p. 162.
9   *The Placenames of Westmeath,* p.162.
10   ibid.

'This spot is permitted to have in it a famous well till Doomsday'. This Carrick was ever the residence of the kings of Fartullagh until the time of the daughter of the son of Conchubhair, the wife of Conchubhair Ua Maelsechlainn, when the King of Meath wrestled it from Cu Chaille, son of Dublaide, King of Fartullagh, and it was outraged by depriving it of its King and giving it to the queen of Meath.'[11]

Paul Walsh tells us that Conchubhair Ua Maelsechlainn was King of Meath from 1030 till 1073.

He also tells us that there is a pedigree of the Ua Dubhlaoich but it is not accurate in its arrangement. In the book of Ballymote it contains the names *of Flann m Onchon m Saran* (Flann son of Onchon son of Saran) and that from him descended *Ui Flainn*. This Sept is also mentioned in the Life of Colman of Lynn.[12]

Flann son of Onchu is my friend, the flavour of the hyacinth shall never go out of him.Lann of the lands, no feeble remnant what Conall utters does not disturb it. The number of men who rose up before us shall reign of his descendants in the land after Conall. With twelve men, he dared heavy trouble,- the terror of a full hundred upon him with that number. Triumph of the spoil upon you through(?) neither shame nor death shall be his. The judgement of my verse does not come against us, You will die under my cloak. Oh Flann.[13]

The residence of Onchu son of Saran, King of Fartullagh was at Dún na Cairrge -the Fort of Carrick and he died at the Isle of Carrick.[14] We can thus establish that Carrick was a Royal Residence and its ownership was in conflict between the Ó Dooleys and the Kings of Meath around the year 1030.

If the Ó Dooleys were driven out of Carrick they did remain on ruling other areas of their territories as noted in *The Annals of the Four Masters* in 1040. Ua Dubhlaoich, Lord of Feara Tulach was killed by his own people.

It has been recorded also that the Ó Dooleys were still firmly established in Fartullagh over one hundred years later as they were to the forefront of a group of Meath men who killed Conchubhair Mac Toirdhealbhach Ua Conchubhair, the ruler of Meath in 1144. He was killed by the Ua Dubhlaoich at the battle of *Bealach Muine na Stride*. He had come out of Connacht with some degree of success to secure for himself the High Kingship of Ireland. This event was to have serious repercussions for the O'Dooleys as a result.

In revenge for the death of his son, Toirdhealbhach led his army into the disputed territory and, deposed and expelled the reigning king, Murchad Ua Maelsechlainn, ravaged the whole area and divided it into two parts. He granted east Meath to Tieman Ó Rourke of Breffni and Dermot McMurrough, and West Meath to Donagh Mac Muirceartig Ua Maelsechlainn.

---

11   Kuno Meyer, *The Life of Colmán of Lynn*, Ed. Leo Daly, (Dublin 1999), p,38.
12   *Paul Walsh, Placenames of Westmeath* (Dublin *1957), p. 162.*
13   Kuno Meyer, *The Life of Colman of Lynn*, Ed. Leo Daly, (Dublin 1999), p.48.
14   *The Placenames of Westmeath* p. 48.

Their rule of course was subject to Toirdhealbhach. Later that year, following a treaty at Terryglass, other adjustments were made to the kingship of the two divisions of Meath. Murchad Ua Maelsechlainn was reinstated as ruler of that part of Meath from Lough Ennel eastwards, including Fartullagh and installing Muirchearthach Ua Maelsechlainn as king of the remainder of Meath from Lough Ennel westwards. Following these changes in administration the Ó Dooleys are not again mentioned in the *Annals of the Four Masters*. It would appear that they would finally have been overcome and to have lost their power and position as minor Kings of this ancient Tuath, the land of the Fir Tulach or men of the mounds. [15]

Kilbride

The monastery at Kilbride was established by St. Brigid. The earliest reference we have to this establishment is in the Book of Leinster which catalogues *Cath Moin Foichnig la hU Falge for Martinu and for Erna*. This Móin Foichnig has been identified as Boughnagh Bog in the townland of Kilbride.

The following lines in the *Hymn of Broccan on Saint Brigid provides* a basis for the foundation of the monastery established here by Brigid.

> Fo huair congab Mac Caille Caille ós chinn Sanct Brigte

This translates as:

> In a lucky hour Mac Caille held the veil over Brigid's head.

The Franciscan Manuscript of the Book of Hymns has a long marginal comment on these lines.

In translation it runs as follows:

When Brigid desired to have the order of Penitence conferred on her, she went to Cruachan Bri Eile(Croghan) in Uí Fáilge, since she had heard that Bishop Mel Was there, and she had seven nuns with her. And when they arrived the bishop was not there to meet them, but he had gone northward into the district of the *Uí Néill*. So on the morrow, she went with Mac Caille to guide her northward over Móin Faichnigh. And God so wrought it that the bog became a smooth flowing mead. Now, when they drew nigh to the place wherein was Bishop Mel, Brigid bade Mac Caille place a veil over her head. And that would be the veil, which is commemorated in the lines above.

After she had arrived in the house wherein was Bishop Mel, a fiery column flamed out of her head up to the ridgepole of the church, and Bishop Mel beheld that and asked:

---

15   Peter J. Dooley, *The Dooleys of Fartullagh* in *Riocht na Midhe*, Journal of the Meath Archaeological and Historical Society, Vol. III no.4(1992-1993), p. 126

"Who are the nuns?" Mac Caille said to him:

"That," said he "is the famous nun from Leinster even Brigid."

"My welcome to her," said Bishop Mel. "It was I who foretold her when she was in her mother's womb," said he.

"Wherefore have the nuns come hither?" said Bishop Mel.

"To have the order of Penitence conferred," said Mac Caille.

So thereafter the orders were read out over her and it came to pass that Bishop Mel conferred on Brigid the Episcopal order, though it was only the order of penitence she herself desired. And it was then that Mac Caille held the veil over Brigid's head- *ut ferunt periti*, and hence Brigid's successor is always entitled to have Episcopal orders, and the honour due to a Bishop.

While the order was being read over her she was holding the foot of the altar in her hand. And seven churches were burnt over that foot, and the foot was not burnt. Some say the church in which Brigid was ordained was in Fir Tulach, or as other say, it is in Ardagh of Bishop Mel.[16]

The earliest reference to St. Brigid receiving the veil is written by Tigernach, biographer of St. Patrick. He speaks of one of the churches founded by St. Brigid as *Caput Carmelli* and locates it in *Campus Teloch*(Fartullagh). It was in this place that St. Brigid received this veil.

The *Moin Faichnig(Boughnagh Bog)* mentioned previously was the great expanse of bog south of Fartullagh and stretching as far as Croghan. It is in fact part of what we know today as the Bog of Allen. In early Christian times these bogs would have been totally inaccessible even up to modern times and quite dangerous to cross also.

St. Brigid would have to travel many miles round the bog to reach Bishop Mel. Thus we have the miracle of the bog turning into a meadow. Perhaps this is again one of those tales which through time became part of legend but by naming places and giving reasons for the establishment of monasteries etc. puts some of these stories into a historical context for us.

The name Boughnagh has survived to the present day as *Bauna*. The townland which bears this name is in the present Civil Parish of Kilbride. It was in times past a boggy outcrop on the verges of the Bog of Allen, but through the influences of man on the landscape and drainage most of it is grassland today.

Some disagreement often arises as to which parish St. Brigid received her veil. For in Norman times Kilbride became two distinct civil parishes:

Kilbride Escham and *Kilbride* Pilate(Milltownpass).

These parishes were distinct as early the Taxation of 1302-06. Local theories establish the fact that it happened at Milltownpass while others at Kilbride Escham. Another local story

---

16   Paul Walsh, *Placenames of Westmeath*, pp 182-3.

relates to the fact that St. Brigid received her veil from one of Colmcille's monks travelling from Clonfad of St. Etchen to Durrow. The place where this took place was at Kilbride Pilate or as it is known today as Pass of Kilbride. There was also a church founded by St. Brigid here and it was close to this ran the east-west pass through the Barony of Fartullagh. [17]

The old Civil Parish Cemetery of Pass of Kilbride lies very close to the main Dublin Galway road at Milltownpass. In the local folklore this cemetery was much bigger than it is now. It is reputed that Robert Rochfort, first Earl of Belvedere removed part of it to provide for widening the road during the 18th century.

At Kilbride Escham in the townland of Dunboden close to the walled garden of Dunboden Demesne is the site of *TobarBhreedia* or Brigid's well. St. Brigid's day was in times past celebrated as the patron day of the ancient church here.

In 1837 this well was closed in by R.W. Cooper Esq. Local tradition has it that when the well was destroyed it refused to give up. It re-emerged as the cattle pond on the south eastern-end of the wood overlooking Whelehans house. This is highly unlikely as the pond is on higher ground than the well. The old cemetery of Kilbride lie within the walls of the Demesne at Kilbride Crossroads. It has not been used for a long time, but there are many monuments dedicated to the Cooper family within its walls. [18]

In recent years the De Profundis stone was discovered in Kilbride cemetery, where it lay for hundreds of years, placed there in troubled times for safekeeping. The stone which bears a cross resembling a coptic cross indicates the past links in early christian times to the Christians in north Africa through trade and pilgrimage.

Recessed from the present road is a curved stone wall, approximately 3 metres long and 1.2 metres high. At approximately half a metre from the ground is a kind of shelf or seat on which the mourners sat awaiting the burial in the churchyard. It was here they were sympathized by their neighbours and community and quite often offerings of money were made at this spot also.

It has long been customary across Ireland for the entrance of graveyards to be marked by prominent trees or stones, such as the De Profundis Stone at Kilbride beside the Dunboden Estate. This stone is now unique in Ireland as it is the last remaining De Profundis stone in the

The De Profundis Stone at Kilbride

17   A. Doyle and D. Dunne, *Blessing and rededication of the Church of the Sacred Heart Meedin 1983*, pp 14-15
18   *The Meedin Book, 1983, pp 14-15.*

country. As the last remaining stone of its kind in Ireland, it is a unique artefact of great heritage and importance. The slab itself is made of limestone, shaped like a coffin and has a crude cross carved at the top end. On close examination, the cross is not of the celtic type associated with old sites like this, but it is a coptic cross, similar to crosses found across Egypt and the rest of North Africa. The significance of this cross is that it is evidence of very early Christian links from Ireland with the Coptic Church in North Africa. It measures .94m in length, is .44m wide at its widest and 0.22m at its narrowest and is .14m deep. It originally stood on a pedestal.

The second Monastic settlement in Fartullagh was at Clonfad. The Civil Parish of Clonfad is located in the present parish of Rochfortbridge. It is worth mentioning here as it's location in Fartullagh indicates that as well as Kilbride and Lynn, this settlement lay on the main north-south route from Mullingar to Tyrrellspass.

To distinguish it from another monastery of the same name in the nearby Barony of Farbill, this settlement was known as *Cluain Fhada Librán* as distinct from that of *Cluain Fhada Etchen* in Farbill. The Monastery of Clonfad Etchen is named after St. Etchen whose monastery here was important as it provided the early schooling for St. Columba before being trained by St.

Finian at Clonard. Columba was one of the twelve apostles of Ireland trained at Clonard who founded other monasteries and was responsible for carrying the Christian message to Scotland.

The name Clonfad means *the long meadow*. The Clonfad settlement at Fartullagh *Cluain Fhada Librán* is better known as the long meadow of Librán who was one of the early abbots of Clonfad and this foundation was named after him.

From an annate dated 1470 it became known as *Cluain Fhada Fuarán*. Fuarán is the Gaelic word for a spring. This is also the derivation of the name of an area in the townland of Tyrrellstown called *Fuarán* or *Fooraun*. The nearby townland of Templeoran was the parish of ease of Clonfad. All that is left today of the settlement is the cemetery and ruins of the medieval church.

It was in the sixth century that a monastery was founded here by St. Finian of Clonard. St. Senachi was the first Abbot of Clonfad and also of Clonard.

He died on August 21st 587 A.D. It is recorded that in the year 885 A.D., Conor son of Flanagan, Lord of Hy Fáilge was put to death by fire at Clonfad, in the church, and the relics of St. Finian were burned with him. This was done by the men of Fir Tulach. He was on his way to have council with Flann son of Maelsehlainn, King of Ireland.

In 835, Fiachra, Abbot of Clonfad died. There is no record of this monastery after the viking invasions.[19] There is a tradition locally that bad luck would befall anyone that moved the stone from Clonfad graveyard. It is a large round upright stone with the top hollowed out.

A Coptic Cross

It is located inside the gate of the cemetery. One man is believed to have removed the stone to his home, and placed bags of flour on it. Soon all of his animals took sick. As soon as the stone was returned all became well again.

Local men have vied with each other in the past to lift the stone above their heads. Some succeeded they say even to lift it over their heads. Another tradition tells that the stone was carried to Clonfad by St. Colmán of Lynn on his shoulders. There is no documentary evidence for this.

A section of the Dunboden Estate wall at Kilrbide Crossroads. The raised bank was built during the famine so that the coffins of the dead could be laid, before burial in the cemetery.

---

19   *The Meedin Book*, 1983, pp 13-14.

On recent examination of the stone there is a high likelihood that it is actually a capstone for an ancient stone cross, which has long since disappeared. Some early Celtic crosses were capped with a flat-bottomed stone, round at the top. It was probably toppled from the cross during one of the monastic invasions, and this is all that remains. In the recent excavations at Clonfad with the linking of the N52 via Tyrrellspass to the M6 motorway, excavations revealed that there was evidence of bell making at the monastery of Clonfad-hand bells to be used at monasteries across the country. This craft, now long gone and forgotten would have helped fund and maintain the upkeep of the monastery during its lifetime.

Newcastle, a stronghold of the Tyrrells

*Note the gaping holes which were later repaired, the trademark of Cannon fire,
during the Cromwellian Invasion.*

What is a Barony?

Barony: there are 331 barony divisions in Ireland; this is thought be originally a Norman land unit. A county has on average between 7 and 10 baronies, though this may differ in a few cases. There are 17 Baronies in Westmeath. Baronies vary in size and may extend over more than one county on occasion. Baronies are no longer used as a unit for land government. They are in fact important in historical study in relation to land, territory, placenames, medieval ecclesiastical divisions and District Electoral Divisions prior to 1901.

Following the demise of the O Dooley's, the Tyrrells became Lords of Fartullagh, the first being granted by title by Henry II. The Tyrrells would remain in dominance here until the Cromwellian settlement and it is not unusual to to find reference to this particular family in some of the placenames of the area.

Tyrrellstown

Tyrrells-Millton

Tyrrellspass

Simonstown

The division of lands in a county did not stop with the barony. Each barony was sub-divided into townlands.
Each townland was further divided into ploughlands.
Twelve ploughlands was one baile or townland
120 old Irish Acre = one seisreach or ploughland
A ploughland was as much land could be turned up by a single six horse plough in one year.

A baile bisteach, a Victuallers town was the area of land required to provide enough beef for the average clan in an area. The word townland is associated with this division in a country which had no towns or cities prior to the coming of the Vikings, as most communites centred around the monastery.

The Castle of the Kneading Trough

With the coming of the Normans, the Baile Bisteach came into its own as a community unit with the establishment of Castlelost. The name Castlelost came into use when the lands close to the Derries, were denuded of trees, leaving a series of large fields round the Norman enclosure, protected by the further oak woods. This gave the landscape a trough-like appearance, giving rise to the word Losáid, a word coming from the Norman French. In Irish a Losáid is a kneading trough, used to prepare dough for cooking. It was obivous then that the fertile fields provided grain and cattle for this little Baile Bisteach or Victuallers town. Thus with the building of the castle, it became known as The Castle of the Kneading Trough. The kneading trough was the proof that the fertile fields were important to the area. Castlelost in translation is called The Castle of the Fertile Fields.

Rochfortbridge in Irish is known as Droichead Chaisleán Loiste, Translated, it reads as The Bridge of the Castle of the Fertile Fields.

With the creation of Local Authorities in 1898, Baronies were no longer used as political divisions.

Markings on the domed ceiling of the interior of Newcastle...

The remains of a spiral stairs at Newcastle

Castlelost and the Tyrrells

The Norman invasion brought about considerable changes within the Barony. The ruling family of O'Dubhlaoich moved to Offaly, and their lands were granted to various Norman families. When a Norman Knight was granted a Demesne by his Superior, and in this case the famous Hugh De Lacy of Meath, he had to conquer it himself. He first found a place where there was a conspicuous hill, on which was built a, temporary dwelling, surmounting it with a fence forming an enclosed yard or bailey in which he lived with his followers. In time, he built a stone tower or castle and a stone church. More often than not the site chosen had already been there from early christian times. It was the same with Clonfad, Kilbride and Lynn. Having the church close to his demesne, the Norman Knight made it the religious centre of his demesne. This is how a religious unit became as well as a civil unit, the civil parish as it appears on our Ordance Survey maps today. In Rochfortbridge Parish the three early christian settlements of Clonfad, Kilbride and Lynn became civil parishes (Lynn is now in Mullingar Parish). Three new Civil Parishes were formed as well, at this time, and they were Castlelost, Carrick and Enniscoffey, while there were two parishes named Kilbride in the area, *Kilbride Escham* and *Kilbride Pilate*. The Tyrrells were the dominant Norman family in the Barony of Fartullagh for the Next four hundred years or so.

J. H. Tyrrell in his *"Genealogical History of the Tyrrells*, tells us that there are several theories as to the origin of the surname, but as Ralf Sire de Tirel (a small place on the north bank of the Seine, a few miles below Paris in the French Vexin) it would appear he adopted the placename of his Lordship as a surname. The ancient village of *Triel*, a mere transposition of two letters".

They came to Ireland with the Normans, and were Barons of Caslleknock. The earliest reference we have to the parish of Castlelost is in the Taxation of 1302, Caislean Loiste - the Castle of the losset land. The Term *Losset* refers to good rich land, making a comparison with it and a kneading trough. A kneading trough was used to make the dough for baking. The Knight and his low fertile fields, surrounded by the oak woods of the Derries gave the impression of this trough. The fields in close proximity to the motte and bailey and later the tower house or castle produced the corn to make the bread, which named the castle as that of *the Kneading trough*. The grain from the fertile fields made the flour, therefore the kneading trough was symbolic of those fertile fields. Castlelost was named as *The Castle of the Fertile fields*. We will return to the placename once more with the development of the village of Rochfortbridge.

There is also a reference in 1486, granted to Thomas Tyrrell all the country of Fartullagh, with the lands and Manors of Castlelost Perston, Ballefarting (Farthingstown), Ballenmacaill, Gnyrayn[20] (the white ploughland), Rahencoill, Kilwenyn, Rahynyin, Clontytallon, Tyrrell's Mylton and Seanbaile (Oldtown)".

Tyrrells lands were fortified by castles at Tyrrellspass, Newtown, Newcastle, Castlelost, Kilbride, Simonstown and Tyrrellstown. Tradition has it that these castles were so positioned, that in the event of an attack, the alarm was raised by lighting a fire on the roof of the castle being attacked. This was immediately visible to two other castles.

---

20   Gneevebawn

In 1640, Gaelic lands were confined to two townlands in the Barony, Dalystown and Gallstown. In that year, Cochonaght O'Daly was Proprietor of Dalystown and Connla Mac Aodhagan (Keegan) held Gaulstown. It is clear that these two families held official positions under the Tyrrells and later intermarried with them. The Norman custom of fosterage where the children of the Knight were taught Irish customs and educated in the Gaelic traditions ensured that the family remained close to the local Gaelic settlers and peasants. After a few generations, the Normans lost all of their French language and traditions and spoke English and Gaelic.

Castlelost today contains a fort and the ruins of a Castle, and was the earliest centre of local administration for the Tyrrells. The present road from Rochfortbridge to Castlelost was the avenue to the Castle. Further down the fields on the same side of the road, lie the remains of an old church, and a cemetery. Many members of the Tyrrell family sleep here in this cemetery, and there was also an altar tomb, with the recumbant figure of a Knight in Armour, dedicated to the memory of one of the Tyrrells. Sadly this figure disappeared from the cemetery about thirty years ago.

The reason the cemetery and old parish church are located in the distant fields away from the road is that in medieval timesm the road from Mullingar passed this way. Tracts of that road still remain at Whitewell and it continued across country, crossing the Kilbride Stream of the river Derry, through the Derries, past the cemetery and Church, emerging on the present road at Castlelost castle. [21]

---

21   In the 18th century the course of this road was abandoned and a new road was created to accommodate the new landed estates of Dunboden, Kilbride House, Heathfield and West House, turning eastwards at Lamb's crossroads past Castlelost Castle and into Rochfortbridge. A new section of road was created in the 1840's as a famine relief scheme from Rochfortbridge to Dunboden.

Castlelost

Castlelost is the name of a parish in the barony of Fartullagh, County Westmeath. The motte and castle are about a mile north of Rochfortbridge. To the east of the motte is a slightly raised bailey, 61 by 46 yards, and on the edge of this bailey, about 18 yards from the motte, the castle was built with its door facing the motte. It is conjectured that the earthwork was formed out of an esker knoll, that the eastern part of the knoll was cut away to about the height of 6 feet, and that the material thus obtained was used to form the motte, while the denuded part served as a raised bailey. There are traces of another enclosure to the north, and when the stone castle was built, another bailey was added to the south. The road from Rochfortbridge has cut into the motte at one side, and the opposite side has been mutilated, so that the space on the summit, probably originally circular, is now about 23 by 13 yards. The motte rises about 16 feet above the raised bailey.

The church, about 400 yards to the north-east, appears to have been semi-fortified. There are some curious sculptured stones here in the arch of the east window. Others were removed, and have been built into the new chapel at Meedin, where they are preserved. The stone castle was not of very early date.

Little appears to be known about this castle, except that in the sixteenth century it was a castle of the Tirrells. Its very name is a puzzle, and has suggested an obvious pun. I think, however, I can give the true etymology, and show that the place belonged to a Hugh Tirrell, probably the well-known seneschal of the elder Hugh de Lacy, and at any rate was in the hands of the Tirrells from the early years of the thirteenth century.

According to an extract made by Sir James Ware, from the Register of St. Mary's Abbey, Dublin, it would appear that Hugh Tirrell, Lord of Castleknock, was also Lord of Portloman (a parish to the west of Lough Owel), Castlelofty (Castlelost), Knockrath (?), Mastrum (better known now as Edgeworthstown), Rossagh (Russagh, now a parish adjoining Street), and Portshannon (Portnashangan, a parish on the east of Lough Owel). This entry is far from contemporary, being dated 10th May, 1487, but it is under the hand of the Bishop of Ardagh, who was admitting, against his interest, that the churches of these places, so far as they were in his diocese, had been given by Hugh Tirrell to the Prior of Little Malvern.[1] Similarly Hugh is said to have given the church of Castlelost to the same Prior, and this gift was confirmed to the abbot of St. Mary's, Dublin (to whom the Prior of Little Malvern was transferring the Irish property of the Priory), by Maurice Tirrell, then Lord of Castlelost, under date, 25th August, 1486. As the statement agrees with all we know of Castlelost, we may accept it as correct. It may, however, be doubted whether the donor was Hugh Tirrell, the contemporary of Hugh de Lacy the elder, or his grandson (?) Hugh Tirrell, who got seisin of his lands in 1223. The latter Hugh Tirrell was granted a fair at his manor of Neweton in Fertelagh (Newtown, the parish adjoining Castlelost, and including part of the village of Tirrell's Pass) in 1232, a grant which implies a settled manor. So at any rate we find the Tirrells firmly seated in this neighbourhood in the early years of the thirteenth century. Moreover, as it is pretty clear that a Tirrell was the original grantee of Castlelost, we may with probability assign the motte to the elder Hugh Tirrell, and ascribe its erection to about the time when the elder Hugh de Lacy built his motte castle of Durrow, namely, 1186.

The earliest contemporary mention of this place that I have met with is in the Ecclesiastical Taxation of the Deanery of Mullingar (1302-6). Here the name occurs in two forms, as Castellossy and Castell osti. In the Fiants of Elizabeth it occurs as Castelloste, Castellostie, Castelloysty, Castellost, Castellos, and Castleost, while in the Chartulary of St. Mary's Abbey it appears in the obviously corrupt form, Castlelofty. I have not found the name in any Irish text ; but from the above Anglo-Irish forms, and from analogy to other place-names, it would seem to belong to that curious group derived from losáid, genitive loiste, "a kneading-trough." Thus Drumnalost in Co. Donegal is given in the Four Masters as Dún na loiste. According to Dr. Joyce, the word losáid (anglicised "losset") is applied by farmers to fertile land which they see " covered with rich produce, like a kneading-trough filled with dough," and it is in this metaphorical sense it is used in place-names. Caisleán na loiste would thus mean "the Castle of the losset or rich land." Not far off in the parish of Rathconnell is Clonlost, with presumably a similar etymology.

Probably the place was known as "the losset " before the castle was built. There are about a dozen townlands in Ireland called simply "Losset." O'Donovan says, 'In the county of Cavan the farmer calls his well laid out field his fine losset, or table spread with food.'[2]

---

1   The priory of St. Giles of Little Malvern was founded in 1171 by two brothers who were born at Beckford, the name of the one who became the first prior being Jocelin, and that f of the second Edred. They adopted the habit and rule of St. Benedict, and customs from the chapter of Worcester. From the earliest time it was subject to the diocesan and united to the fraternity of the cathedral church in Worcester.

2   G.H. Orpen, The Motte of Castlelost, County Westmeath', *Royal Society of Antiquaries of Ireland*, 1910, pp 226-8.

The arched entrance to Kilbride Castle

The Murder Hole (murthering hole) at Kilbride Castle

The Tyrrells and the nine years war

Castlelost Motte and Castle

The most important event in the story of the Tyrrells relates to the brave deeds of Sir Richard Tyrrell, and his role in the nine year war 1597, during the nine years war, Sir Piers de Petit was killed by the Kerns (rebels) in Westmeath. In revenge of his death, Richard Barnwell, Baron of Trimblestown gathered an amy together to drive the rebels out of Westmeath. The Pale(the area stretching from Louth westward and southward to the Wicklow Mountains, enclosing Dublin and parts of the surrounding counties totally under English control.

In those days it lay within easy reach of the Gaelic and Norman forces, and there were often raids on both sides in revenge for various crimes committted.

The events of the Battle of Tyrrellspass are recorded by poet A.G. Geoghagan in his poem *Tyrrellspass, 1597*. In this account he gives a detailed account of the events leading up to and during the Battle of Tyrrellspass. Barnewell stands in front of his forces and even though Geoghagan is using poetic license in this account it does tell the story of the events at the time.

> *Then started up young Barnewell, all hot with Spanish wine,*
>
> *"Revenge," he cries "for Petit's death, and be that labour mine;*
>
> *For by yhe blessed rood I swear, when I Wat Tyrrell see,*
>
> *I'll hunt to death the rebel bold, and hang him from a tree."*

But Tyrrell,camped on the shores of Lough Ennel, received news of what was going to happen from a spy within Barnewell's ranks. He ordered one of his leaders O'Connor to take a band of men with him

> *....and speed ye to the dell,*
>
> *Where winds the road to Kinegad,*
>
> *You know that togher well.*

He ordered them to lie hidden in the heath and bracken, and to wait until they heard the sound of the bugle. This place was situated in the pass through the bog on the road from Kinnegad to Athlone.

Tyrrell lay in waiting for Barnewell and his band. When Barnewell spotted him, there followed a chase across country until they reached the pass, where a bloody battle ensued, and Tyrrell being the victor. All of Barnwell's men were slaughtered, except for Barnwell himself, who fled the battle on horseback. Where this battle took place gives name to the village of Tyrrellspass today.

Tyrrell was very prominent and was involved in a number of engagements during the nine years war. After the Battle of Kinsale, he left Ireland and spent the rest of his life in Spain.

The Cromellian Invasion And Settlement

The Flight of the Earls from Ireland, following the Battle of Kinsale left the people of Ireland alone and vulnerable and with little or no leadership soon found themselves governed directly from England. The fate of Celtic Ireland and the old order of Brehon rule was gone. The fate of Irish Catholics was on a downward slope and would continue so for the next hundred years or more.

But things were set to change politically where in England, following the death of King James I(1566-1625), his son Charles I came to the throne.

Regarded as a weak ruler and leading an extravagant lifestyle, Charles fought the forces of the English and Scottish parliaments, which challenged his attempts to overrule and negate parliamentary authority, whilst simultaneously using his position as head of the English Church to pursue religious policies which generated the antipathy of reformed groups such as the Puritans. Charles was defeated in the First Civil War (1642–45), after which Parliament expected him to accept its demands for a constitutional monarchy. He instead remained defiant by attempting to forge an alliance with Scotland and escaping to the Isle of Wight. This provoked the Second Civil War (1648–49) and a second defeat for Charles, who was subsequently captured, tried, convicted, and executed for high treason.

In 1641, the Catholics in Ireland had been in revolt and held much of the island. They had generally taken the king's side, although some had seen in England's turmoil a chance to restore Irish independence. Cromwell entered Dublin as Lord Lieutenant with an army of 3,000 battle-hardened Ironsides in 1649. He intended to offer no quarter to papists who had massacred English and Scottish settlers in Ireland. With an army who needed to be paid for their services he could use confiscated lands to pay off the debts of his troops and so-called adventurers who had helped finance the parliamentary cause.

Marching on Drogheda which was defended by an English Catholic and royalist, Sir Arthur Aston, his surrender order ignored, Cromwell's order to kill every man, in the garrison as '*a righteous Judgement of God upon the barbarian wretches*' would ring out over the centuries as *the curse of Cromwell.*

Thus began a sweep across the country with his army moving south from Trim to Wexford and following the massacre there, neighbouring towns submitted. Cromwell's campaign ended with an assault on Clonmel where after stout resistance, the defenders withdrew by cover of darkness.

In 1650, Cromwell returned to England leaving his son-in-law Henry Ireton in command. Within two years, catholic resistance was at an end. Many Irish soldiers were allowed seek their fortune in Europe and some were given the option of settling on less fertile land in Connaught.

The strongholds of the Tyrrells in Fartullagh did not escape the wrath of Cromwell. It is highly unlikely that Cromwell himself passed this way, but his ever-increasing army did.

One by one, each of the tower houses fell. Resistance was a futile exercise as there was no escape. The gaping holes in the remaining walls of Castlelost castle are testimony to the power of the roundhead cannons. Kilbride, Simonstown, Tyrrellstown, Newtown and Newcastle, they too in turn were left abandoned as ruins on the landscape. Tyrrellspass castle was the only fortification left untouched by Cromwell's forces. According to local tradition, the family in residence there pleaded with the forces that if they surrendered they'd let them go. Not a cannon ball was fired at the castle and when the family surrendered they were immediately slaughtered under at the base of its great walls. There is no documentary evidence to this story but it is one of the theories put forward as to the survival of the castle.

In 1680, the Books of Survey and Distribution were compiled as the result of the wars of the mid-seventeenth century after the Cromwellian conquest of Ireland, when the English government needed reliable information on land ownership throughout Ireland to carry out its policy of land confiscation. They were used to impose the acreable rent called the Quit Rent, which was payable yearly on lands granted under terms of the Acts of Settlement and Explanation. It is possible to discover to whom, if anyone, the confiscated lands were granted so that we have a record of landowners for 1641 and 1680. As a result, it is possible to determine the amount of lands lost by the 1641 owners after the Irish Rebellion of 1641 and to discover the names of the new proprietors.

At Castlelost and Ballimolan, Thomas Tyrrell and William Bermingham were dispossessed of their lands and the new incumbents were either Cromwellian soldiers or adventurers ready to make a new start on the vacant townlands. Names like Sir Jerome Alexander, Sir John Rowley, George Fitzgerald, Richard Brinsley, Richard Locke, Mrs. Elizabeth Alexander, Margaret Aggs and Peter Collier appear as new owners of the townlands. One interesting name appears across the country as possessing such lands after the Restoration of the Monarchy in 1660 and it is that of the Duke of York. These lands were then in the possession of the King of England. Parts of the lands of Farthingstown, Kiltotan/Collinstown, Gortumloe and Gneevebawn were the property of the English Monarch. The King was also in possession of lands in Mahonstown in the Parish of Enniscoffey, Rathnure and Templeoran in Newtown Parish and Beggstown in the Parish of Kilbride.

The Parish of Meedin and Milltown

The campaign which resulted in triumph for William of Orange in Ireland, saw the departure for the continent of thousands of Irish soldiers who surrendered at the siege of Limerick. These displaced people known to us in history as the Wild Geese left Ireland a defenceless nation and at the mercy of the Protestant ascendancy who were to become the dominant ruling class in the country for the next two hundred years or so.

The King's advisers now set about devising a series of laws calculated to achieve two objectives:

(1) The prevention of any future rebellion against the crown.

(2) The extermination of the Catholic religion in Ireland.[22]

These laws were passed in the period atler 1691 mainly by the Irish parliament, *in* remained Catholic were denied:

(a) The right to carry arms

(b) Joining all professions except medicine

(c) Involvement in political power at local and national level

(d) The possession of landed property except on a short term lease-held basis.

(e) All education either at home and abroad, except such as was avowedly proselytizing in aim.

The laws were designed, not to make the Catholics good subjects, but to deprive them of the power to be bad ones.[23]

Convinced by experience that most of the Catholic population could not be induced by threats or promises to conform to the King's religion, the legislators decided to extinguish forever the Catholic priesthood in Ireland, and close all Catholic schools. Deprived of priests and the opportunity of a Catholic education they would soon fall prey to the work of Protestant proselytisers whose aim was to provide education for the sake of conversion to their faith. To achieve this and to keep the clergy and laity in the dark about the full extent of their plan, it wasn't fully operational at once. It was done through instalments.

In 1697 all members of religious orders and all bishops, vicars general and other secular clergy exercising papal jurisdiction were ordered to leave the country before lst May 1698. Those who failed to do so would be arrested and transported. The laity were forbidden under dire penalties to harbor any of those who disobeyed the expulsion order. By the end of the year 1698 a total of 424 friars of various orders had been captured and transported. This was a serious blow to the supply of priests available for ministering to the faithful.

---

22   Rev. Dr. *W.Moran, Friarstown, House of Refuge in na Midhe*(1961 Vol II, no.2)p.9
23   Public Record Office of Northern Ireland. Education Facsimiles 101-120, *The Penal Laws.*

There remained at this time the secular priests not covered by the 1697 decree. it was difficult for the government agents to know who was a priest or how many priests remained in the country. To remedy this situation a new decree came into force in 1704. All secular priests were ordered to come into court to be registered. Those who obeyed were to have permission to carry on their ministry work freely in the district they served. Those who refused were threatened with transportation, if and when they were caught.[24]

Meanwhile those priests who registered were issued with another ultimatum in 1709, when another decree was issued which required all licensed priests to come into court before March 25th 1710 to take the dreaded oath of abjuration. This oath called on them to denounce their faith publicly. Of the 1080 priests whose names were recorded in the Government Registers only 37 took the oath.

One quarter of this number belonged to Westmeath, where nine of the thirty seven decided to conform to the law. Among them was Rev. Anthony Coghlan of Castlelost and Ballymollan.[25] The following table lists the names of those who took the oath at this time.

Westmeath Priests registered in 1710	
Name	Parish
Rev. James Dalton, P.P	Ballymacallin
Philip Tyrrell P.P.	Mullingar
Charles Keilry, P.P.	Taghmon
Michael Dillon, P.P	Ballybrickoge
Hugh McDonogh, P.P.	Not Given
John Pierse, P.P	Templeoran
William Cullen, P.P.	Upper Castletown
Thomas Dillon, P.P.	Lacken
Anthony Coughlan, P.P.	Castlelost

Anthony Coughlan was educated in Flanders and was ordained in 1684 by Procopius Wanderberg, Archbishop of Milan. At the time of registration in 1704 he was forty-five years old and lived at Farthingstown. Rev. Bryan Murtagh, aged 55, registered in 1704 it seems, did not take the oath of abjuration, he ministered to the faithful at Carrick, Pass of Kilbride, Clonfad and Enniscoffey. He was ordained in 1619 in Prague by John Waltayne, Archbishop of Prague.

It's not known where Bryan Murtagh resided as he more than likely adopted a low profile to avoid drawing attention to himself.[26] Local tradition has it that this confession of Anthony Coughlans was instrumental in establishing the parish of Meedin and Milltown prior to its later 19th century birth as Rochfortbridge parish. Anthony's acceptance of the oath of abjuration brought the wrath of his parishioners down on him. He was rejected by his

---

24   *Friarstown, House of Refuge*,p.10.
25   W.P.Burke, *Irish Priests in Penal Time, 1660-1760* (1914), p. 464.
26   *Irish Ecclesiastcal Record 1876, Registry of Irish Priests Anno, 1704*, pp 540-41.

relatives and ostracized by his flock. The parishioners of Castlelost sought help elsewhere and attended ceremonies in nearby parishes. The tendency to go specifically to ceremonies in mass houses into neighbouring Milltownpass and Meedin gave rise to a united parish structure which had become an established fact by the end of the 18th century. It is likely the Rev. Anthony Coughlan was in close contact with the authorities and held on to his parish. Therefore on his death of which there is no recorded record, he would not have been replaced. As a named Catholic parish, Castlelost was now defunct and was swallowed up by the new penal parish of Meedin and Milltown.[27]

The House of Refuge and the Dominicans

During the period of their penal history when his flock rejected Rev. Anthony Coughlan was another development, which would have an influence on the future progress of the parish of Meedin and Milltown. It began with the expulsion from the Dominican Friary in Mullingar of the resident friars there who refused to register under the penal code. The friars were expelled in 1698 and continued to minister to the faithful several years later in the vicinity of the town. But this de jure community were not in a position to continue with the conventional life contemplated by their rule. The breaking up of community life over such a long period must have been a source of anxiety to the friars to their superiors and possibly to the bishop of the diocese.

By 1713 during the ministry of Dr. Fagan he sponsored four houses for regulars in the diocese of Meath, they were at Cortown and Donore in the Meath area, and at Multyfarnham and Friarstown in the Mullingar area. The Friarstown foundation was built for the Dominicans of Mullingar. Dr. Moran tells us that the house at Friarstown is the most interesting of the four houses of refuge. It was not just a substitute convent but also a house of refuge, a safe haven for the protection of the priests who resided there.

The site was a good half mile from the nearest public road and a little farther from Lough Ennel. It was protected around half the circumference from any sudden raid. The defence was provided by the lake, the Brosna and and the bog, (the Black Banks as we know it today). The lake provided an escape route to Mullingar for the frars to administer the sacraments. The folklore concerning the penal days in Mullingar recall the work of two men in the town in the protection of the friars in fulfilling their priestly duties. The Nailer Lacey, a nail maker in the town and a Mr. Connell cared for the vessels and altar vestments and hid them in their homes. The town tanners provided a safe haven for mass to be said in the tannery among the skins and hides they were preparing. They also provided a foolhardy way of hiding a priest if they were caught by surprise.

In the dead of night the priest or friar was met at Lynn bog and brought the old coach route - the road from Sean-Bhóthar farm through Ballinderry and into the town. The faithful gathered in the tannery which was located somewhere in the region of the parish community centre today. It is reputed that on at least one occasion the authorities raided such a gathering searching for a priest, as there was a rich bounty on the capture of a priest. £50 was the reward for the capture of a vicar general or a bishop and £20 for an ordinary friar.[28]

---

27   Ann Bennett. A History of the Parish of Rochfortbridge and its people the 19th century- B.A. Thesis 1975, p5.
28   *Friarstown, House of Refuge,*p.10.

In a garrison town like Mullingar where there was sufficient armed forces to provide protection, the priest hunter could carry out his intelligence work in locating his victims. When a discovery was made he was able to seek the help of armed forces and under their protection captured the fugitive priest.

It was a different matter in rural areas where the population was entirely catholic, priest hunting proved to be quite a perilous enterprise. The hunter might find the tables turned on himself and instead of being the hunter he became the hunted.

The tanners provided safe haven for many years for the Catholic priest. Local tridition has it that on a few occasions the gathering to hear mass scattered quickly as warning came that they were going to be raided. The priest was disrobed and taken to the nearly tanning pool and immersed in its foul tanning contents of skins, water and chemicals. The putrid stench from the place was enough to deter the priest hunter from going near it. The priest was safe but very uncomfortable until the coast was clear and then smuggled under cover of darkness to Lynn bog and safely across the lake to the refuge.

The house at Friarstown was built within one of two ring-forts. The reason a ring-fort was chosen was that it contained a Soutterain.[29]

When the friary was built, the soutterain was put to a new use - an escape route to the fields close to the lake. The house was built of stone and mortar. It is likely that the house was built around 1698 just when the persecutions began. A letter written in Latin by Dr. McEgan' Bishop of Meath to the Dominican Superior General in Rome in 1738 reports

> They have neither convents nor houses of refuge, to which to betake themselves especially since 1732, when the whole police force of the country assembled together, demolished and leveled to the ground four houses of regulars.

> One octogenarian father who was unable to run away was captured and after many injuries and tortured, was thrown into prison where he died a few months later.[30]

The friars of Friarstown it seems concealed the soutterain before the friary was leveled and it survived until the 20th century. The friars did not return to the town for at least ten years. In a report on the state of Dominican convents and monasteries in Ireland between the Autumn of 1734 and the Autumn of 1735 it was recorded that:

> The convent of our Lady's Assumption, Mullingar has few sons.
> They are beginning to live in community under the patronage of Mr.
> Matthew Casey.[31]

---

29 A soutterain is an underground chamber leading from a ring fort to an opening some distance away. They were probably used to protect inhabitants in time of trouble. It is a likelihood also that they were used to store food, as they were quite cool. The roof of the chamber was a corbelled roof of interlapping stones, which made the chamber quite strong and waterproof. Some of these chambers are still in perfect condition after a thousand years.

30 *Friarstown, House of Refuge,*p.12.

31 Public Record Office of Northern Ireland. Education Facsimiles 101-120, *The Penal Laws.* Documents found on the person of Fr. John Fotrell, the provincial of the Dominican Order in Ireland when he was arrested at Toome Co. Derry on May 6th 1739.

There are little or no records concerning the operations of the priesthood in the area after the 1740's until the 1780's when the laws which drove the Catholic church under ground began to be relaxed and the priests ministered to the faithful in the open again. In 1788 there were two chapels built at Meedin and Milltown. The chapel at Meedin had a thatched roof and was replaced in 1831 by the *present* Church of the Sacred Heart. The original church was built in a remote rural area away from the nearby villages and out of sight of local big houses and demesnes. Raheenmore is an example of another such church which has survived to the present day. It is recorded that the Dominican order ministered in the parish of Meedin and Milltown from 1784 till 1825. The first of these priests recorded is Rev. Eugene Coffey O.P. who was parish priest from 1784 until his death in 1790. He was born in the area and joined the Dominican order. He served as curate under his predecessor believed to be Rev. Vincent coffey. He was succeeded by Rev. Bernard Coffey in 1790 and remained until his death in 1825.[32]

It is probable ihat they were related to the Coffey family of Newcastle who were later benefactors in the construction of the Meedin Church, Rochfortbrtbridge Church and the Convent of Mercy.

There is an anecdote recorded in Cogan's History of the Diocese of Meath concerning one of the Coffeys, probably Bernard, during an examination he took on the Tractatus De Gratia in Rome. The examiner was a Jesuit and Coffey was a red-haired Irishman. After an excellent display by Coffey the Jesuit asked,

"What was the destiny of Judas?"

"Judas got what was his due," replied Coffey.

The Jesuit said to Coffey,

"was Judas red-haired?"

"Whether Judas had red hair or not," Coffey replied, " is only a matter of conjecture, but it is certain that he was a member of the Society of Jesus".[33] Bernard Coffey was the first priest to take steps into the re-organisation of the parish, in that some of the parish registers begin during his ministry. All of the Dominican Coffeys are interred in Carrick cemetery.

Father Timothy Shanley

With the establishment of Maynooth College in 1795, Irish men were afforded the opportunity to study for the priesthood at home for the first time in hundreds of years. It was a watershed in the relaxation of the penal laws in that these young men could for the first time minister to their flock in the open and set about the development of a parish for the catholic faithful.

In the first years after it's foundation, Maynooth did not have native personnel trained to teach these young men and prepare them for the priesthood.

The first teachers at Maynooth were French and in those early years there was a French influence in the education process there.

---

32   Rev. A.Cogan, *The Diocese of Meath*, (Vo. 3, 1867), p.481.
33   Cogan, p. 483.

Soon native trained priests were being sent out to work in parishes coming to grips with a new found religious freedom and they set about building upon the ruins created by one hundred years of the penal code.

Among these young men was Rev. Timothy Shanley who was the first post penal parish priest of Meedin and Milltown, who was immortalized locally with reference to the ghost of Bobby Bawn and whose grave after his death was and still is a source of pilgrimage for local people every Good Friday.

He was a native of Drumraney, born in 1781 and entered Maynooth in 1800 aged 19. He was ordained by Dr. Troy, Archbishop of Dublin in 1806. He served as curate in Meedin and Milltown under Rev. Bryan Coffey O.P., P.P. and later was curate in Nobber prior to his appointment as parish priest of Meedin and Milltown in 1825.

He took up residence at West Lodge, Castlelost, which remained as parochial house until the 1850's when Father Robbins acquired the parochial house at Rochfortbridge.

While parish priest, Father Shanley befriended Richard Coffey of Newcastle and was a frequent visitor to his house. One day while out on the Coffey farm he noticed a large stone slated shed and said to Richard Coffey,

"I wished I had a church as fine as this building." To which Mr. Coffey replied,

"I'll see to it that you will have your wish."[34]

The present church of the Sacred Heart Meedin is a result of Mr. Coffey's generosity. The previous church was a T-shaped building which stood between the present main door of the church and the church gate. From old maps it seems that it faced in the opposite direction to the present church.

Even though the building of this church brought great joy to the people of Meedin and Rochfortbridge, it brought the following comment in the 1850's in Cogan's History of the Diocese of Meath:

'This parish is particularly blessed in having a gentleman of ample means who takes the liveliest interest in the beauty and decoration of God's house. The church of Meedin is truly a gem, and whoever enters it, will be at once edified."

He is of course referring to Richard Charles Coffey who is also responsible for funding the building of the Convent of Mercy in Rochfortbridge. Meedin church described as a gem was also vilified and by the Westmeath Journal in 1831:

'Some time ago, the Protestant churchyard of Castlelost in this county was entered, a gothic window of the old church were torn down, the stones carried away for the purpose of ornamenting a popish chapel. The matter will shortly be investigated before a bench of magistrates and we shall make it a point to attend."[35]

The main doorway and window overhead which came from Castlelost, date from around 1500 A.D., and the removal of those stones even in 1831 were frowned upon, as it was an offence to deface our ancient monuments.

---

34   *The Meedin Book,* 1983, p. 24. - Also see the chapter on the Coffeys of Newcastle
35   Westmeath Journal, 13th Jan. 1831.

Father Shanley's work in the parish survived this onslaught and the matter was passed over. The only other comment on the matter is recorded in *Cogan's history of the diocese of Meath.*

> No parish priest has the authority vested in him to tear down the ancient monuments of Ireland. If we empart the laity Protestant and Catholic, to respect the consecrated walls of ancient worship, priests ought to show the example.[36]

It is unlikely that Meedin church was completed before Shanley's death. His work was continued by Father Roan who succeeded him.

Father Shanley died aged 54 on the 16th February 1835. He is buried at the east end of the old church in Carrick. There is a monument over his grave shaded by the branches of a large beech tree. It carries the following inscription:

Beati mortu qui in Domino moriuntur
Hic jacent mortales religuae
Rev. Timothei Shanley
Qui per plures annos
Summo religionis zelo paraciaerum
Midin et Milltown
Pastoris munere functus est
Obiit 16 Feb. Anno Domini 1835
Requiescat in pace. Amen.

In translation this reads:-

Blessed are those who die in
the Lord
Here lie the mortal remains of
Rev. Timothy Shanley.
Who for many years performed
the office of Pastor of the Parishes
of Meedin and Milltown with
exemplary zeal.
He died 16 Feb. 1835 A.D.
May he rest in peace.

---

36   Anthony Cogan, *History of the Diocese of Meath,* Vol 3, 1867. p. 481.

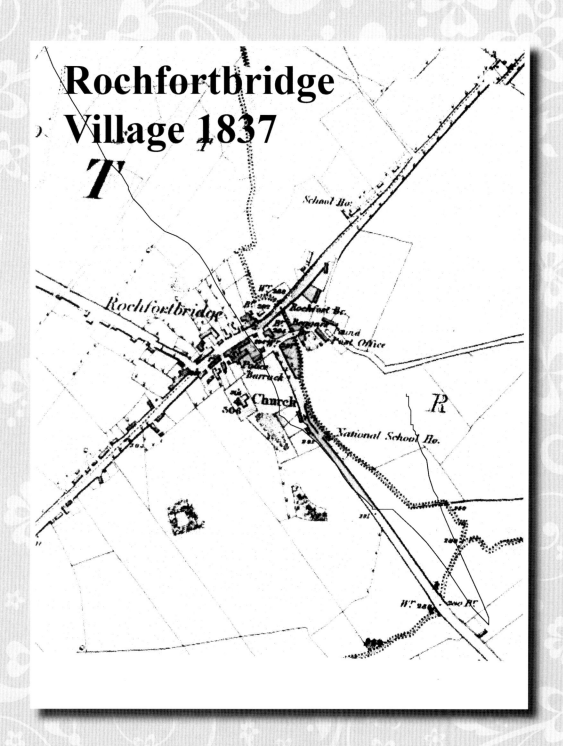

A map of Rochfortbridge village from the
Ordnance Survey map of 1837

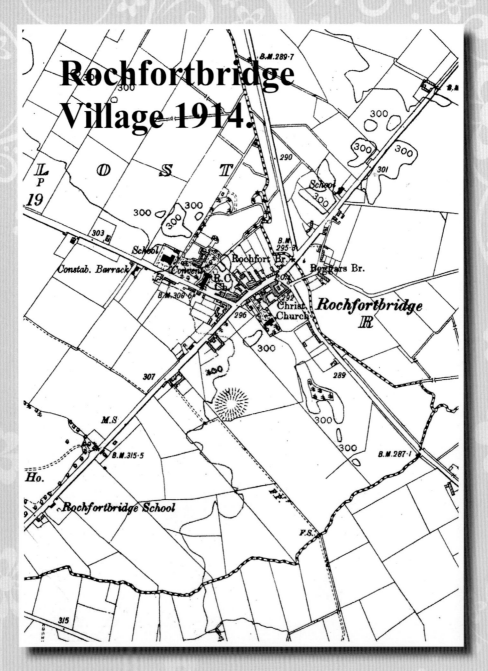

Rochfortbridge Village 1914

*Daly's Licensed premises,
the site of the original
19th century coach house
and inn*

The Parish of Rochfortbridge

Perhaps the most charismatic parish priest in Rochfortbridge during the nineteenth century was Fr. Gerald Robbins. He was a native of Tubber parish, was born in 1809 and was educated at Kilbeggan, Navan and Maynooth, where he was ordained on October 2nd 1833. He officiated as curate in the parish of Meedin and Milltown, Rahan and Ballymore and was promoted to parish priest of Rochfortbridge in 1850. As curate in Rahan, he built the chapel at the Island and was responsible building the Church of the Immaculate Conception at Rochfortbridge. He is responsible also for the introduction of the Sisters of Mercy to Rochfortbridge. During his ministry, national education flourished in the parish with the building of schools in the three villages of Milltownpass, Rochfortbridge and Tyrrellspass.[37]

Into this world of fragmented estates, the parish of Meedin and Milltown, which included Milltown, Rochfortbridge and, half of Tyrrellspass, Father Robbins found himself. confronted with a series hedge schools and a parish recovering from the effects of the famine. He embraced his work with great zeal. The parochial house, which did not belong to the parish, was located at West Lodge and in 1865 he acquired the house on the main street of Rochfortbridge which became the parochial house until the 1980's. His predecessor Father Roan resided in the village during his ministry with relatives who had a business there.

When he moved to Rochfortbridge, he befriended a retired Protestant businessman in the poplin industry. William Fielding gave him a site for a new church in the village on the Castlelost Road. For some time he had difficulty acquiring land to build his church. Being a predominantly Protestant village at the time it was probably frowned upon to see a Catholic chapel erected there.

With the emergence of an overridingly affluent Catholic middle class following Catholic Emancipation in 1829, there was a move among the clergy to establish small ecclesiastical centers in towns and villages. Fr. Robbins sought to achieve this during his ministry. Such a center was in the process of being established in Mullingar with the founding of the Hevey Institute for the Christian Brothers, the Presentation Sisters and later the Loretto Sisters all in close proximity to each other. In 1925 Sister Bernard Grogan, writing on the life of Mother Mary Paul Fielding at Willcannia, Forbes, New South Wales, recalls what Mother Fielding said regarding Father Robbins and the building of his church:-

> The priest of the place was in need of a piece of ground on which to build a little church. He had tried in vain to procure it and was disheartened at failure. The desired gift of land was made to him by Mr. Fielding, an ageing Protestant businesiman resident in the village.[38]

The new church was dedicated to the Immaculate Conception in 1858 and from this point in time on, the Catholic parish of Rochfortbridge, as we know it today was born. The old parish church at Milltownpass - a mud walled building was built in 1794. Stone walls were built, and the roof was replaced in 1825.

---

37   Olive Curran, *History of the Diocese of Meath, 1860-1993* (Dublin 1995) Vol II, p. 805.
38   Sr. M. Gertrude, *A Valiant Woman* (Sydney, 1925), pp 11-17.

In 1879, plans were drawn up and work commenced on an almost new cruciform church. It was dedicated by Dr. Cantwell in 1879 and completed in 1883. The site was donated by George Augustus Boyd Rochfort. With the building of this Church and the Priests serving the parish now residing in the village, the centre of the Parish was now located here. By the time Anthony Cogan published his History of the Diocese of Meath in 1867, the parish was then known as the Parish of Rochfortbridge.

The Village

There was no distinct village of Rochfortbridge until after the year 1800. The area where the village now stands dates from around 1700 onwards and was known as Beggarsbridge. It was named after the original wooden bridge which crossed the river Derry on the road which leads to present day Rahanine.

One of the earliest references to the place refers to the will of John Megawley of Tully, Co. Westmeath, dated the 19th of March 1728, where he left one pound ten shillings to Mr. Coughlan, parish priest of Beggarsbridge.

Another record for the name of the village was recorded in Faulkner's Dublin Journal of 2-5th March 1754 when it states that '*we hear from Beggars Bridge in the County of Westmeath, that the Great Cock Match fought by the gentlemen of that neighbourhood against those of Mullingar was won by the latter.*

The name Beggarsbridge is clouded in mystery and there's no written record as to the meaning or derivation of the name, apart from an account given by Caesar Otway in 1839, in his book *A Tour in Connaught*. The account given by him is based on a story in the local folklore which he recorded and included in his travellers account.

> Our next change of horse took place at a village called Beggarsbridge- a beggarly place, in sooth, as its name imports. The cause of its name is not a little remarkable. In old times, as was the case in most parts of Ireland, the traveller was obliged to ford over the small river that crossed the road, as the wayfaring man slowly picked his passage over the water, from an adjoining bank, asked alms, and invoked all the saints in heaven to aid and bring to his journey's end, *him* that lent to God by showing pity on the poor. It was surely an Irishman who said or sung this stave
>
> *"Of all the trades a-going, a-begging is the best."*
>
> Thus our beggar man throve surpassingly for so ragged, so wretched, so squalid looked he, that no man could pass by, (and it was a great thoroughfare,) without giving him alms, and it so happened that the beggar man died and was buried, and a coffin and winding sheet were provided for him at the expense of the neighbours, and his filthy rags, as altogether offensive and unfit for any use, were cast out on the way-side, to be trodden under foot, and so resolve themselves into the element of dirt and dung they had for years approximated to- but it so happened that some boys were playing by the road-side, one of them gave an unusual toss to the beggars rags, and out fell a piece of money, whereupon a more accurate search

was made, and it was found that the ragged inside waistcoat was quilted with guineas; this money, the young men who found it had the honesty to bring to a neighbouring magistrate, who directed that with it a bridge should be erected over the stream, on whose banks stands the little village *inde derivatur*, Beggar's-Bridge.[39]

By the time Otway heard this tale, it was more than likely one hundred to one hundred and fifty years old and the only recorded record was that which clung to the mouths of the poorer classes and not written down. There is little evidence to prove that the incident ever happened, but there must be some substance of truth there as the name of the bridge implies. At that time, Ireland was thronged with beggars, people trying to eek out an existence by imploring the passing traveller for a halfpenny or a penny to buy bread or alcohol. River crossings were prime places to ply their trade, as it was here that there was a constant movement of people fording the river on foot or on horseback.

The original bridge would not have had a long life as it was made of wood and it was later replaced by Robert Rochfort, first Earl of Belvedere. This would have happened around 1720 as it was at this point that road travel was improving and tolls were being established at villages and river crossings.

From 1729, a network of turnpike roads (charging tolls) were built: "a turnpike was a primitive form of turnstile - a gate across the road, opened on payment of a toll. The toll was usually one farthing.[40] The average length of a turnpike road was 30 miles. Routes to and from Dublin were developed initially and the network spread throughout the country. Turnpikes operated between 1729 and 1858 when the extensive railway network made them increasingly unpopular. Lack of traffic on some routes led to reduced toll income, and maintenance was neglected. However, in the first quarter of the 19th century, mail-coach contracts increased income and the quality of turnpike roads improved. Turnpike roads were also used by horse-drawn carriage services, including the *Bianconi coaches*, established as a form of public transport by Charles Bianconi in 1815. By 1820, there were around 1,500 miles of turnpike roads in Ireland but this had fallen to 300 miles by 1856 when competition from the railways made many turnpike roads unprofitable. By 1858, turnpike roads in Ireland had been abolished. The road from Dublin to Athlone was a turnpike road. There was a turnpike gate on the road at Tyrrellspass at the turn on the Croghan road near the castle. In Beggarsbridge, with the improvement of horse traffic and coach travel to the west in the early nineteenth century, the westward turnpike road was improved and a new bridge was built in 1828. This bridge was called Rochfortbridge, named after the Rochfort family. It was at this point that the newly developing village was called Rochfortbridge.

On the map showing the lands in Castlelost as part of the Estate of George Rochfort Esq. in 1782, the river crossing at Beggarsbridge has no buildings or houses. In fact there is only one building with land on what was then known as *The High Walk Farm*. The main road to Mullingar went through Castlelost and on through Kildbride to Dunboden and Whitewell. As shown on the Boglands map of 1810, there was quite a substantial building

---

39   Caesar Otway, *A Tour in Connaught*, (1839) P.32
40   A farthing was quarter of one old penny. In the old imperial system of money, there were 12 pennies in one shilling and 20 shillings in a pound. There were 240 pennies in a pound and 960 farthings in a pound. The imperial system lasted in Ireland and Britain until the introduction of decimal currency in 1971.

The out-houses at Dalys, this shed was used as the forge

Stables and lofts, used for horses and feedstuffs

The site of the original Beggarsbridge.
The wall was lovingly restored in 2012

Beggarsbridge

development by then. This was all due to the provision of a coach stop, at the corner. On the Gustavus Rochfort map of 1823, there is further development on the western end of the village with holdings belonging to families such as Connells, Kellys, Keegans, Gormans and Eighans, names which are still found in the village and in the parish also. In the 1837 Ordnance Survey Map, the shape of the present-day village was more or less defined. With the building of the new Rochfortbridge in 1828, the present route through the village to Dublin was in place. The earlier village dwellings also would have been fairly ramshackle and quite a lot of them were no more than hovels, a greater interest in tenantry and greater productivity in the use of land and business enterprises led families such as the Kilmaine's at Gallstown and the Coopers of Dunboden to build better housing for the people. By 1850 most of the original houses in the village were replaced with most of those we see today. The oldest building in the village is that of St. Mary's Parish Church Castlelost, which is now a private house. This work of restoration as well as the creation of the new road to Mullingar were done as a famine work project to help sustain the population of the area during this dark period of history.

With the coming of commerce and trade to the village it had for a period mainly a Protestant population. Names such as Austin, Harford, De Boe, Johnston, Yeates, Tims, Wire, Pollard and Fielding appear as residents in the village. By 1850, the village had a school, a police barracks and a post office. From the 1830's onwards there was an Orange Lodge located at the house beside the Beggarsbridge, the early home of the Fielding family. Later when the family moved to the house which would later become St. Joseph's, the Orange Lodge was located there. With the death of William Fielding, there was no Orange Lodge in the village after that. By 1850 also, there was an increasing middle-class Catholic population emerging in the village and in the parish. The need for new Churches, schools and of course the Mercy Convent, was helped by the rise of such families. By 1857, when the new Church of the Immaculate Conception opened and with it the vision Fr. Gerald Robbins had for the place and the growing concern he had for the welfare of the young women of the parish, the time was right for change, coupled with Eliza Fielding's new-found vocation within the Sisters of Mercy, change would take place, a change which would have lasting effect in the development and education of the children of Rochfortbridge and its surroundung districts to the present day, and that was the founding of the Sisters of Mercy in 1862.

Beggarsbridge

The Bóthar and the Slíghe

The ancient roads of Ireland were divided into two classes. They were the *bóthar* and the *slíghe*. The traslation of bóthar means to allow two cows to pass. Another name used in this context was *bóithrín* or boreen. Generally the boreen led to a bog or came to a dead end giving access to various farmsteads. When the Normans divided the lands into townlands and Civil parishes, the only enclosures allowed were between the civil parishes themeslves.

Later in the 1750's the enclosures act saw vast tracts of lands in the townlands divided into fields. The **Inclosure** or **Enclosure Acts** were a series of Acts of Parliament which enclosed open fields and common land in Britain and Ireland. They removed previously existing rights of local people to carry out activities in these areas, such as cultivation, cutting hay, grazing animals or using other resources such as small timber, fish, and turf. "Inclosure" is an old or formal spelling of the word now more usually spelled "enclosure": Therefore the bóthar giving access through the parish followed the borders of townlands, thus giving us the winding country roads we have today. It wasn't till the 1700's that new roads cut through townlands in general straight lines and the roads created during the famine in the famine work schemes did likewise. The road from Whitewell at the the Dunboden junction to Rochfortbridge was a Famine work scheme in the mid-1840's

The *slíghe* was the main road in olden days across Ireland from Tara to Clonmacnoise, Dublin, the Shannon and southwards to the coast. To accommodate vehicular traffic it allowed for an ox and cart to be placed as indicated in the pictures below. The slíghe which went westward to the Shannon followed its course through Rochfortbridge, Farthingstown and Raheenquill into Tyrrellspass. In the early 1700's this road changed to its present location to accommodate coach travel. There are still traces of this road in the Rochfortbridge area.

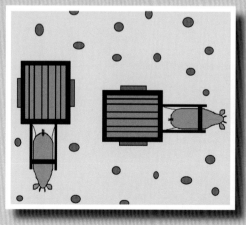

The Width of the Slíghe

The Width of the Bóthar

Survey of the Plantation measure of the estate of George Rochfort in Castlelost in the Barony of Fartullagh in 1783.

No.	Decription	Arable, Meadow & Pasture			Bog			Total		
		Acres	Roods	Sq. Perch	Acres	Roods	Sq. Perch	Acres	Roods	Sq. Perch
1.	Clontitallan arable meadow and pasture	40	2	38				40	2	38
2	Excellent grazing and bog to-ditto				24	0	19	24	0	19
3	Turf bog to ditto				5	1	16	5	1	16
	Total in Clontitallon	40	2	38	29	1	25	70	1	35
4	The church field choice meadow grounds	12	0	26				12	0	26
5	The house holding arable meadow & pastures	76	1	03				76	1	03
6	Good grazing bog to ditto				8	3	16	8	3	16
7	Turf bog to ditto				10	0	8	10	0	08
	Total in house holding	88	1	29	18	03	24	106	4	27
8	The farm called The High walk arable & pasture	125	5	11				125	5	11
9	Mr. William North's holding arable & pasture	102	3	38				102	3	38
	Total, rough and smooth	357	3	36	48	1	19	406	1	15
	By a scale of 40 perches to an inch									

Survey of part of the Town and Lands of Begarsbidge, the estate of Gustavus Rochfort Esq. 1823

Map Reference				
Site No.	Holding	Acres	Roods	Square Perch
1	Thomas Gormans Town Plot	0	1	20
2	Widow Eighan's ditto	0	1	23
3	Walter Connel's ditto	0	1	2
4	William Wilson's ditto	0	0	23
5	William Sheerin's ditto	0	1	28
6	William Keegan's ditto	0	0	24
7	Catherine Kelly's ditto	0	0	32
8	Phillip Wilson's ditto & field	1	1	1
9	William Meres ditto & ditto	1	3	14
10	Patrick Mulkernan's house holding	4	1	0
11	The Widow Eighan's ditto	5	0	5
12	Patrick Mulkernan's Field	3	0	20
13	Thomas Gorman's town park	5	2	2
	Whole Total	22	3	34
	Scale of ten perches to one inch			
	Year 1823			

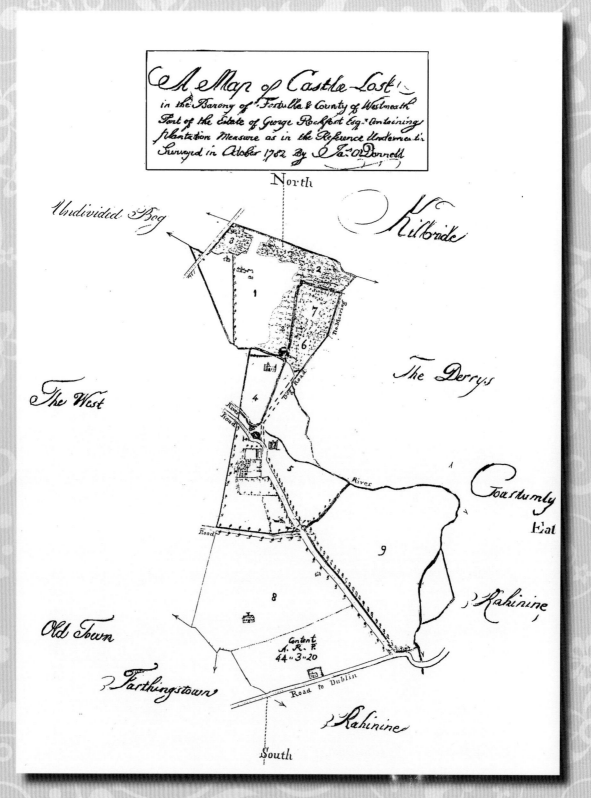

*A map of Castlelost from 1782, showing the holdings
in the Estate of George Rochfort Esq. - Note also there is as yet no village of Beggardsbridge*

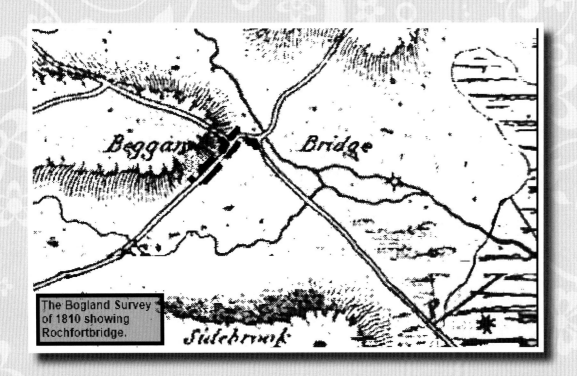

The Bogland Survey of 1810 showing Rochfortbridge.

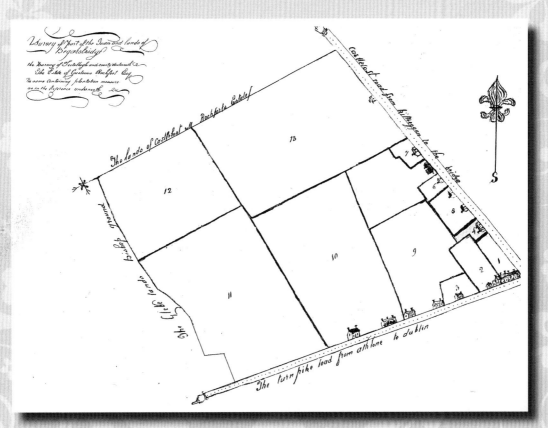

A map of the Western end of Rochfortbridge village from 1823,
showing the holdings in the Estate of Gustavus Rochfort

Church of the Sacred Heart Meedin

The motifs are taken from the stained glass windows in the Church and represent the Litany of the Rosary.

Help of Christians

Gate of Heaven

Tower of David

Queen of Martyrs

House of Gold

Queen of Peace

Queen of the most Holy Rosary

Mother most pure

The Moon

Grove of Olives

Lily

The medieval doorway

Aerial View of Meedin Church

Knot and arrow motif from door

Knot motif from the door

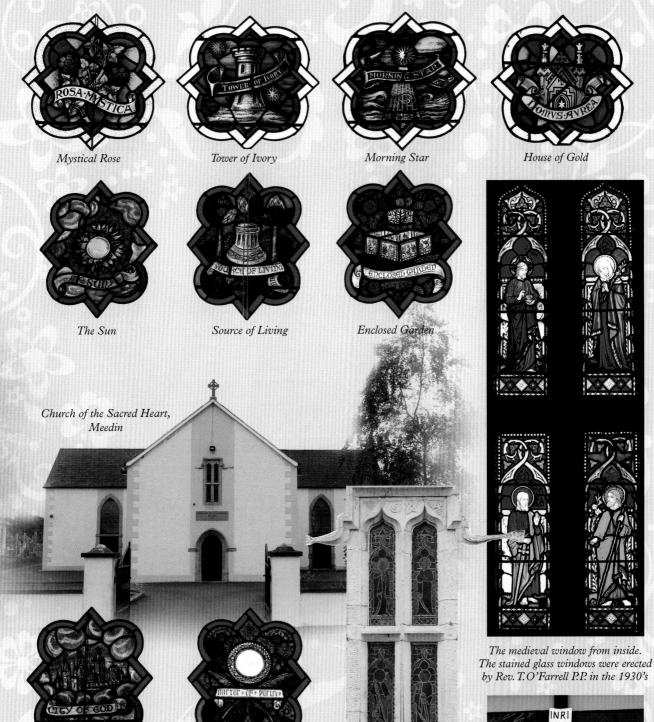

Mystical Rose

Tower of Ivory

Morning Star

House of Gold

The Sun

Source of Living

Enclosed Garden

Church of the Sacred Heart, Meedin

The medieval window from inside. The stained glass windows were erected by Rev. T. O'Farrell P.P. in the 1930's

City of God

Mirror of Purity

The medieval window

Interlocking motif from the front door

The front of the Altar

The Calvary by Lohnergan

The Apostles of Meedin Church

Details from stained glass windows.

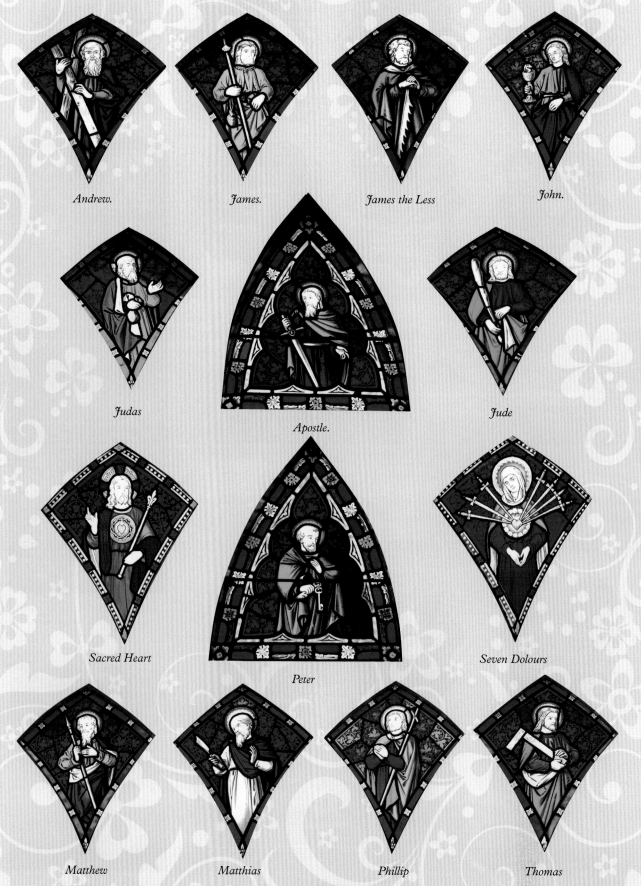

Andrew.

James.

James the Less

John.

Judas

Apostle.

Jude

Sacred Heart

Peter

Seven Dolours

Matthew

Matthias

Phillip

Thomas

~ Chapter 2 ~
Rochfortbridge - the Village and its Educational Needs in the 19th Century.

By Betty Mimnagh Dunne

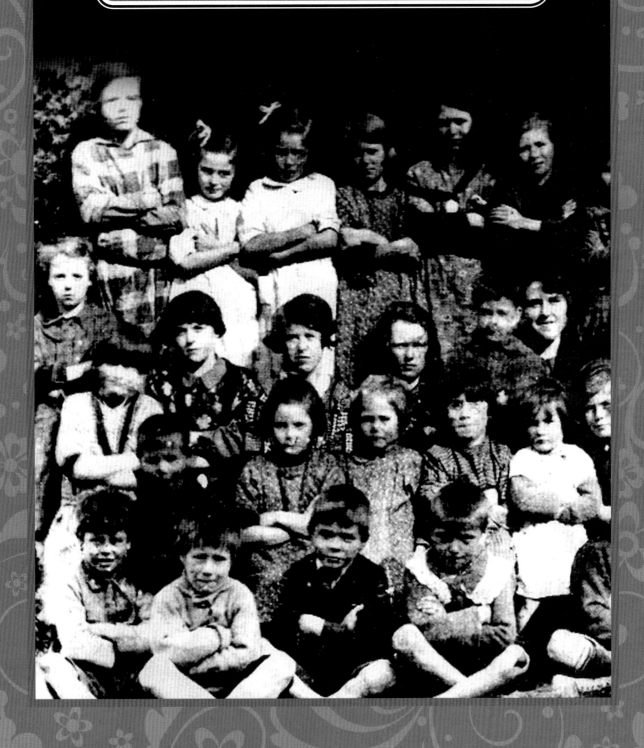

~ CHAPTER 2 ~

ROCHFORTBRIDGE- THE VILLAGE AND ITS EDUCATIONAL NEEDS IN THE 19TH CENTURY

By Betty Mimnagh Dunne

Introduction

As the eighteenth century came to an end, Rochfortbridge was a small village and was not regarded as the centre of the Catholic parish then. Indeed it was only a stopping off point, a place for changing horses and resting for the night. The village's status was to change during the nineteenth century and with this many developments in the social areas. Location is an important factor in any village's development. Rochfortbridge was surrounded on three sides by bog but was not inaccessible in the nineteenth century. It was not cut off from influences of the outside world, as it was a post - town on the road from Dublin to Athlone.[1]

The population of Rochfortbridge varied during the nineteenth century. The first half of the century saw a steep rise in population especially from 1837 to 1841, when it rose from 171[2] to 477.[3] However the next ten years saw a drop to 128 recorded in 1851 and a decline of population in line with the rest of the country due to the famine. The population began to rise slowly again to 164 in 1861[4], When Rochfortbridge saw a marked improvement in educational facilities in its village. As Rochfortbridge was predominantly rural, the vast majority of the people earned their livelihood from the land. Agriculturally the land was good. It was estimated that the best land in the district would feed a bullock to an acre but generally speaking it was capable of maintaining two cattle to three acres.[5] Obviously the

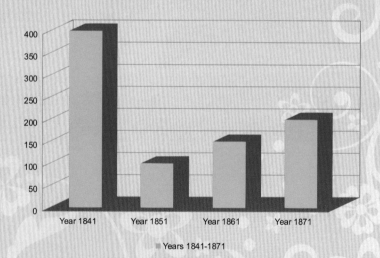

The Population of Rochfortbridge 1841-1871

---

1   Samuel Lewis, *Topographical Dictionary of Ireland* (Baltimore 1837), p. 518.

2   *The census of Ireland for the year 1891: showing the area, population ond the number of houses; Occupations, religion ond education,Vol. 1., Province of Leinster, County of Westmeath*, H.C.1890-1891, (C. 6515), xcv, pp 876-973, (hereafter cited as Census of Ireland,1891).

3   Samuel Lewis, *Topographical Dictionary of Ireland* (Baltimore 1837), p. 518.

4   *The census of Ireland l81: Pt.l. Showing the area, population and number of houses; Occupations, religion and education, Vol II. Province of Leinster County of Westmeath*, H.C.1872, (C.662) lxvii, pp 874-971, hereafter cited as Census of Ireland 1871.

5   Ann Bennett, *A History of the parish af Rochfortbridge and its people in the nineteenth century)*. This minor thesis was submitted in part fulfillment for the requirements of the B.A. examination, Maynooth, 1975. p. 16.

land was suitable for cattle rearing and the majority of larger farmers reared and fattened cattle for the market in England. Much of the land was also under tillage. The principle products were oats, turnips, mangolds and barley. There was also a substantial amount of bog extending along the southen part of the parish as well as some areas of bog in Carrick. The bogs were important for the fuel they provided, but they were also a source of manure for the farmers in the district.[6]

It is fortunate that a report exists which was returned to the Commissioners of Education by the local Church of Ireland clergyman of the area, Rev. Samuel Lewis, in 1832. From this we get a picture of the lifestyle of these people and it can be ascertained whether this community could afford to provide educational facilities and if they would have benefited from a system of free education.

The condition of the houses gives us some idea of the wealth or poverty of this community too. There was a marked growth in house numbers rising from 27[7] houses in 1837 to 74 in 1841.[8] This number dropped again to 24 in 1851 and rose to 29 in 1861 and 43 in 1871.[9]

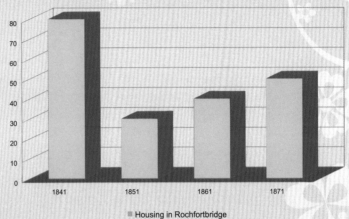

Housing in Rochfortbridge 1841 - 1871

The valuation of these houses varied from seven shillings to £12. An examination of the furnishings of these houses may give us an idea of the poverty of the people at this time. Rev. Lewis describes the type of houses these people lived in. Some were made of clay while others were made of stone. The people generally had bedsteads and the ladies association provided comfortable bedding for some.

There was therefore, it seems, a good community spirit in Rochfortbridge and a tradition where the richer section of the community helped the poorer section. Most people had dressers where they kept a few plates. They also had stools and chairs to sit on. No mention is made of cutlery or tables so this information is unknown. Members of the Church of Ireland, the minority in the community, held most of the wealth of the village. The poorer Catholic class survived on potatoes mostly and sometimes had some oatmeal.[10] The rich on the other hand enjoyed a better diet of meat, poultry, and a variety of fruits produced on their own lands.[11] Rev. Lewis reports that the poor were indifferently clothed. Education in the nineteenth century sometimes included embroidery and needlework especially in schools run by a religious community. Embroidery, needlework, lace work or crochet would also have been an important source of income especially for the female population.

---

6   Ibid

7   Samuel Lewis, *Topographical Dictionary of Ireland* (Baltimore 1837), p. 518.

8   *Census of Ireland 1871*.

9   *Census of Ireland 1891*.

10   *The Royal Commission on the condition of the poorer classes in Ireland. Supplement to Tenantry {E) First Report of the Commissioners*, H.C.1836 xxxii pp 188-285, hereafter cited as *The Royal Commission on the condition of the poorer classes in Ireland*, 1836.

11   *Country LifeMagazine*. June 1961

Students who could pay for education were the only ones who could avail of it. The majority of the people in Rochfortbridge could not afford to pay for it. labourers were not in constant employment. The daily wage for the labouring class in summer was 10d, while in winter it was 8d. The labourer would earn about £12 in the year. His average yearly expense was about £6 during the year for food provisions and the general rent for cabins was with about a rood of land £2 per annum- without it about £1 5s. They were least employed from the middle of November till the middle of February. Additional monies could be obtained when the women were employed during the harvest and in the springtime. Their wages were much lower, about 5d a day.[12] Clearly with irregular and low wages the poorer people could not afford to pay for education on a regular basis. The children were not employed unlike the neighbouring area of Moyliscar where children were employed for 4d per day. Children therefore were free to go to school if a suitable one existed, if they had the money, and if there was a regular supply of teachers.

Looking at the services provided in the village it seems that the community had little or no resources. They had no savings bank or no benefit society. Tyrrellspass, a planned village quite close by, and similar in size however had a savings bank, and a dispensary.[13] Perhaps the better off could have traveled to this village to do business. It seems that they had enough to keep going but nothing extra. Samuel Lewis states that the condition of the poor was stationery neither deteriorating nor getting any worse. They had perhaps a little extra, as there were four public houses in the village. A station of the constabulary police was on the main street but it seemed to be a peaceable place to live. Illicit distillation did not seem to have been a problem.[14] No major crime is recorded when one examines the parliamentary papers of the time. However there seemed to have been some disturbances at a particular time during the year.[15] Education could thrive in such an environment.

The Church of Ireland community was very generous to the Catholic community in at least two instances in the second half of the nineteenth century. William Fielding donated a site for the Catholic Church and his daughter Eliza provided the premises for the local Catholic National school. They wanted to see their poorer neighbours benefit from education. Both communities while working together led two separate and very different lives. The church of Ireland community although in the minority had a church built in a prominent position in the village. It was built in 1812 at the cost of £1,015-7s of which £738-9s was gifted by the board of first Fruits and £276-18s was raised by parochial assessment.[16] It's full title was the Church of St. Mary's, Castlelost.

The Catholic community on the other hand had no Catholic Church in the village itself until mid- century when one was built on a side road, the Castlelost road. Their nearest church was three and a half miles away in Meedin. This church was built in 1831 replacing an earlier thatched church.

---

12   *The Royal Commission on the condition of the poorer classes in Ireland*, 1836.
13   Ibid
14   Ibid
15   Sr. M. Gertrude, *A Valiant Woman* (Sydney, 1925), pp 11-17.
16   *The Parliamentary Gazeteer of Ireland.* (Dublin, London and Edinburgh, 1846), p.366.

A cattle shed built by Mr. Coffey impressed Fr. Shanley so much that on seeing it he exclaimed *'I wish I had as fine a church in Meedin to say Mass in.'* *'I will see to it that you shall have your wish,'* replied Mr. Coffey.

It was not until 1858 that the church of the Immaculate Conception was erected and dedicated in the village of Rochfortbridge itself.[17] The building of the church in the village together with the educational achievements was another step forward in making Rochfortbridge an important focal point in the parish.

Education and Schools in the first half of the nineteenth century

The development of Rochfortbridge as a parish took place in the last half of the nineteenth century during the ministries of Rev. Gerald Robbins and Rev. Peter Fagan. Rev. Gerald Robbins was appointed Parish Preist in 1850, following the death of Fr. Roan. He ministered for twenty five years and when he died in 1875, he was replaced by Rev. Peter Fagan who was transferred from Rathkenny. He died in October 1902 and both men rest in the cemetery in Meedin.[18] These priests played a vital role in Catholic education in Rochfortbridge during the nineteenth century.

They acted as managers to the convent school in Rochfortbridge and other schools in the surrounding areas and corresponded regularly with the education authorities on matters relating to the education of the children. The educational facilities in the parish of Rochfortbridge in the late eighteenth and early nineteenth centuries were continually changing. There were four Catholic schools in the parish in 1788.[19] A report returned to the Board of Commissioners of Education 1826 show that by 1826 there were eleven schools, both Catholic and Protestant with a total of approximately four hundred in attendance. Seven schools were conducted by Catholics and four by Protestants.

The seven Catholic schools were at Carrick, Castlelost, Piercetown, Kilbride, Milltown, Tyrrellspass and Kilbride-Pilate. The four Protestant ones were Castlelost, Tyrrellspass, Templeoran and Gaybrook.[20] The number of children who attended these schools varied according to the returns.

If **Table 1** is examined it will be noted that two schools described as Catholic had children from the established church attending them. These schools were Tyrrellspass and Milltown.

17   Olive Curran, (ed.), *History of the Diocese of Meath 1860-1993* (3 Vols, Dublin, 1995), ii, p.808 'The church was erected in 1857. Dr. Cantwell dedicated it to the Immaculate Conception, 17th October 1858. Dr. Derry, the bishop of Clonfert preached the dedication sermon. The erection of the church was made possible by Richard Coffey of Newcastle, a member of an old Catholic Family in the parish. Renovations costing £500 were carried out during the ministry of Father McKeever.

18   Headstone inscription in Meedin cemetery Westmeath.

19   Olive Curran, (ed.), *History of the Diocese of Meath* 1860-1993 (3 Vols, Dublin, 1995), ii, p.810.

20   *Appendix to the second report to the commissioners of Educational Inquiry (Parochial Abstracts)* H.C. 1826-1827(12), xii, pp 786-789, hereafter cited as *Appendix to the Second Report 1826-1827.*

On the other hand three out of four Protestant schools had Catholics attending. These were Castlelost, Tyrrellspass and Gaybrook.

In 1826 the schools under Catholic control were almost invariably in poor condition, and sometimes the teachers dwellings served as a school as in Piercetown. They were thatched. Kilbride, Castlelost and Tyrrellspass had stone walls. Milltown and Kilbride Pilate were mud cabins. Carrick had neither chimney nor window. Castlelost and Tyrrellspass were rented. The cost of Piercetowm and Carrick was £2. Kilbride was £4 and Tyrrellspass £5 13s 9d.

Table 1 - Catholic Schools				
	Protestant returns		Catholic returns	
	Estab. church	R.C.	Estab. church	R.C.
Castlelost		30		36
Piercetown		8		7
Kilbride		-		27
Tyrrellspass	4	66	3	67
Milltown	8	32	8	22
Kilbride Pilate		20		20
Carrick		20		40

Table 2 - Protestant Schools				
	Protestant returns		Catholic returns	
	Estab. church	R.C.	Estab. church	R.C.
Castlelost	31	14	45	14
Tyrrellspass	73	22	75	22
Templeoran	20			
Gaybrook	10	17	11	12

Catholic and Protestant School Returns for 1826

In contrast to the poor Catholic schools the Protestant run schools were quite different. The Protestant school at Castlelost was built with stone and lime at a cost of £20. The school at Tyrrellspass was a double home, fronted with cut stone; well slated at a cost of £400 of which £112 was granted from the Lord Lieutenants fund. The Protestant school at Gaybrook was built with stone and lime, slated containing apartments for the master. Its cost was £106 of which £35 6s 8d was given by the association for discountenancing Vice. A description of the school in Templeoran is not given.[21] The Protestant schools were in much better condition and better equipped than the predominately Catholic schools.

This was due in part to the fact that they were built by the landlords and were rent free.[22] Another reason for the differences in the conditions of the schools for the differing communities was that some of the Protestant societies such as *the Association for Discountenancing vice, the London Hibernian Society, the Baptist society for Promoting the Gospel in Ireland, and the Sunday School Society for Ireland,* got grants from public funds which was in turn passed on to their schools. Clonfad received £7 from the association for Discountenancing Vice and the *London Hibernian Society* donated books.[23] The school at Castlelost received patronage from the Association for Discountenancing Vice, which amounted to £8 per annum. [24]This discontinued after 1831.

---

21   Ibid.
22   Ann Bennett, *A History of the parish af Rochfortbridge and its people in the nineteenth century).* This minor thesis was submitted in part fulfillment for the requirements of the B.A. examination, Maynooth, 1975. p.29.
23   Ibid. P.30
24   Ibid. P.30

It must be noted too that most schools were pay schools and since the Catholic Community had considerably less wealth than their protestant neighbours this reflected in the condition of their schools. The teachers depended on pupils for subscriptions. Subsequently the income of the teachers depended on the number of pupils and their ability to pay. It varied greatly. Catholic teachers did not earn a high wage. In Piercetown, the smallest school, with only eight pupils, Bridget Kelly, the Catholic teacher, earned £4 per annum. Mr. Darby, teacher in Kilbride Pilate, earned £6. In Kilbride, Denis Brennan, earned £8. In Castlelost school, Thomas Brady earned £10. The teacher in Milltown, Hugh Foy earned £12. A teacher Michael Dunn in Tyrrellspass, earned £3-13s.

Table 3 - Catholic Schools			
Protestant return		Catholic return	Income of teacher
1. Tyrrellspass	66	67	£13-13a
2. Milltown	32	22	£12
3. Castlelost	30	36	£10
4. Kilbride	none	27	£8
5. Carrick	20	40	2d a week from scholars
6. Kilbride Pass	20	20	£61
7. Piercetown	8	7	£4

Table 4 - Protestant Schools			
Protestant return		Catholic return	Income of teacher
1. Tyrrellspass	95	97	£23-11s-6d
2. Castlelost	45	45	£8-12s
3. Templeoran	20	-	£68
4. Gaybrook	27	23	£22-10s

Catholic and Protestant School Returns for 1826

The protestant teachers fared somewhat better. In Castlelost, Protestant school, Abraham Wilson earned £8-12s. In Gaybrook the teacher Robert Strong earned £22-10s. In Tyrrellspass Robert Francis the teacher earned £23-11s-6d. In Templeoran the protestant clergyman Rev. Eames earned £68.

By 1835 the total number of schools had decreased from eleven to eight with only three predominately Catholic schools remaining. Castlelost had an average attendance of eighty, Meedin had twenty and Carrick had thirty students. Garrons established in 1832 with thirty pupils was the only school who had children from the established church attending.

The curriculum in these schools was very basic, but it included the three Rs, as well as Religion. In Piercetown the girls were taught reading, spelling and needlework. The school at Garrons taught bookkeeping, mensuration, and geography as well as the basics.

Educational Conditions

There were many other factors, which contributed to the lack of education of Catholic children. Religion and education were very closely linked in the nineteenth century in Ireland. Catholics were severely curtailed in the practice of their religion because of the Penal Laws.

As long as these laws prevailed Catholics found it very difficult to acquire a basic education. It was not until 1783 that the law allowed a Catholic to open a school and even then it required that an Anglican bishop should license it.[25]

Catholics could not send their children abroad to be educated neither could they teach Catholic children.[26] If they did the parents were penalized and the teacher was liable to suffer the death penalty.[27] Catholics had to depend on hedge schools to quench their thirst for knowledge.[28] For over thirty years successive commissions and enquiries had warned that thedge schools were a threat to peace and social progress, and had categorized their teachers as morally dissolute or politically subversive.[29] This would have to be addressed. A new system of education needed to be put in place.

The educational situation began to improve in the reign of George III, with the relief Acts of 1782,(Gardiner's Act), 1792 and 1793.[30] A summary of these Acts is contained in the papers of John Foster, formerly Speaker of the Irish House of Commons, 1781-2. This Act allowed persons professing the popish religion to teach school.[31] The granting of Catholic Emancipation in 1829 followed these Acts. This was a practical demonstration that catholic demands for favourable treatment could not be suppressed any longer.[32] The hope of education for all was coming clearer. This education work would have to be carried out by catholics and they might not adhere strictly to stipulations set out by any government.

The result of inadequate education meant that a high proportion of the population was illiterate. An official commission in the year 1824 calculated that about two out of every five children of school-going age were actually attending school.[33]

---

25   John Brady, *A short history af the parishes of the diocese of Meath* (Navan, 1937), p. 79.
26   John Coolahan, *Irish Education: Its History and Structure* (Dublin 1981), p. 9.
27   *Irish Monthly,* May 1931. A list of the Poll taken upon an election of Representatives for to serve in Parliament for the county of Westmeath before Thomas Adderly, Esquire, High Sheriff of the county, the 11 May 1761, at Mullingar. Elector No.172. Objected to for being a papist, and for educating his children under the age of fourteen years as papists.
28   Patrick J. Dowling *The hedge schools of lreland* (Cork 1968), p.10.
29   John Coolahan, *Irish Education: Its History and Stucture* (Dublin 1981), p. 9.
30   Timothy Corcoran, *Educational Systems in Ireland from the close of the middle ages,*(Dublin 1928), p.xxii. The purpose of this act was to control the illegal popular schools and their teachers. A system of licenses was set up for teachers. Very few illegal teachers applied for these licenses. The legal requirement for a license was revoked in 1793. However any school that had not a license came under heavy annual taxation. An unlicensed teacher also, had no legal right to school fees.
31   Marquess of Londonderry (ed.), *Memoirs and Correspondence of Viscount Castlereagh*(London, 1848,9), iii, pp 158-60.
32   John Coolahan, *Irish Education: Its History and Structure* (Dublin 1981), p. 4.
33   Graham Balfour, *The Educational System of Great Britain and lreland* (Oxford; Clarendon Press. 1903), P. 79.

Part of the reason was that most schools were pay schools and parents could not afford to send their children to these schools. The buildings were inadequate and the laws prohibited cathotics from receiving a proper education.

Looking at the statistics for the county of Westmeath and Rochfortbridge in 1861, it is possible to get some idea of the percentage of children who could not read or write. Surveys undertaken by the Commissioners of Education from 1861 to the end of the century reveal that a greater percentage of Catholics were illiterate than any other denomination. In Westmeath it is noticed that in 1861 40.5% of Catholics were illiterate. Ten years

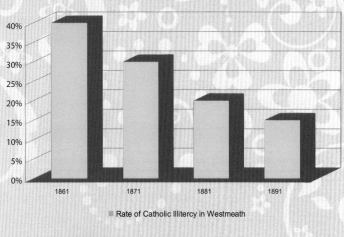

Rate of Catholic Illitercy in Westmeath

Rate of Protestant Illitercy in Westmeath

The Rate of Catholic and Protestant Illiteracy in Rochfortbridge from 1861 to 1891

later it was 33.4%, 25% in 1881 and 17.7% in 1891. The figures for Protestants were lower. In 1861 it was 9%, in 1871 it was 6.5%, 1881 it was 4.7% and in 1891 it was 2.9%.[34]

In Rochfortbridge village in 1861 there were seventy seven females. Thirty of these or 39% could neither read nor write. There were ninety-five males in the village. Seventeen or 18% could not read or write.[35]

These figures show clearly that a greater proportion of the female population were illiterate. If the figures for those who could read only are taken into account it will be noted that seventy eight male or 82% and forty seven females that is 61% could read. Again the males have the advantage. The number of males who could write was sixty-one or 64% and thirty-three females or 43% could write.[36]

Catholic education was badly needed in Rochfortbridge especially for the female population. There is no doubt

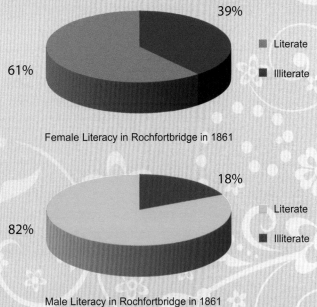

Female Literacy in Rochfortbridge in 1861

Male Literacy in Rochfortbridge in 1861

Female and Male literacy in Rochfortbridge 1861

---

34   *The Census of Ireland 186l, pt. ii, report and tables on ages and education vol. i.* H.C. 1863 (3204-1) lvi, p.262, hereafter cited as *Census of Ireland 1861.*

35   Ibid. pp 284-381.

36   Ibid.

that the Irish people wanted an education for their children. This fact is stated clearly by
Mr. Peel, Secretary in the Westminster Parliament

On 21 February 1816. He said,

> I can state, as a fact within my own knowledge that the greatest eagerness and desire
> prevails, among the lower orders in Ireland, for the benefits of instruction.[37]

As can be seen Catholic education needed to be better organized so as to reach the majority
of children in the village, those who could pay and those who could not. If the conditions
of the poorer classes were to be improved, education had to be provided for all classes and
available for girls as well as boys. Sturdy buildings needed to be put in place instead of the
mud cabins that were being used. Money needed to be available to pay teachers. Society
needed to be convinced that all must attend school regularly and not sporadically.

The Establishment of the National Board of Education

Ireland was frequently used, as a social laboratory where various policy initiatives were tried
out which might be less acceptable in England.[38]

Education was one area where experimentation would prove beneficial. The state at the
turn of the nineteenth century began to take a greater interest in education in Ireland. There
was a

> New and quickening pulse of concern on the part of individual groups and the
> state itself....in relation to education. The great challenge was the provision of mass
> popular education and the significant new depaarture was the involvement of the
> state as an agency providing such an education.[39]

There had been of course a long tradition of state legislation relating to education in Ireland.
The state itself and certain politicians urged the setting up of an educational system in the
early nineteenth century. This system was welcomed by the Sisters and it would help them
in Rochfortbridge. They, unlike the Christian Brothers would try to work within this system
of education.

The Catholic bishops in Ireland too were anxious to improve education. On the 9th. March
1824, *they*, under the auspices of Henry Grattan MP, presented a petition to the House of
Commons enumerating catholic grievances on education. There was also pressure for an
educational system from respected Irish members of parliament, such as Daniel O'Connell,
Thomas Spring-Rice and Thomas Wyse. They realized the urgent need in Ireland for an
organized educational system. Both state and differing religious groups had different aims
in their educational plan.

---

37   Timothy Corcoran, *Education Systems in Ireland from the close of the Middle Ages* (Dublin, 1928), p. xxiv.
38   John Coolahan, *Irish Education: Its History and Stucture* (Dublin 1981), p. 3.
39   Ibid.

In the context of post-union politics the government felt that the schools could serve politicizing and socializing goals, cultivating attitudes of politic loyalty and cultural assimilation. These were not the aspirations of Irish religious in general. The Sisters might not have agreed with all the aspects of the states, handling of education but at least if education was to become more organized and money was available to carry out their work they would try to work within the parameters of this plan. The setting up of an educational system in Ireland was a complicated event and required the work of many commissions. The investigative work of the commissioners is a valuable source of information to us in understanding the educational conditions which prevailed before the coming of the sisters to Rochfortbridge and so gives us some idea of the work they had to do. Using the findings of these commissions it is possible to understand to some extent the progression of education in each village and town in Ireland. In the early nineteenth century Sir John Newport asked that a commission be set up to investigate all aspects of Irish education. This happened in June 1824, which continued in existence until July 1827. The commission would report on measures for extending educational benefits to the people of Ireland.[40] This Royal commission produced nine reports.[41]

The commission's report endorsed the earlier proposal of a goverment board to superintend a state- supported school system. [42] This was a turning point in the education of Catholic children in Ireland. Each one now had a better chance in attaining primary school education. The National Education Board, through the agency of Lord Stanley, chief Secretary for Ireland, was established in 1831. It consisted of seven unpaid Commissioners chosen to represent the different sectors of the community. The Duke of Leinster was the chairman of the Board. Richard Whately the Anglican Archbishop of Dublin, and Francis Sadlier the Anglican provost of Trinity College, Dublin were members of the board. The two Catholics were Dr. Daniel Murray, Catholic Archbishop of Dublin, A. R. Blake, and, a treasury official. The two Presbyterians were Robert Holmes a Dublin Barrister and James Carlile, a minister of the Presbyerian Church of Mary's Abbey in Dublin. The stating of religious denomination of the members is important, because in the Irish context, religion would play a significant role in their work on this board.

It was the earliest such national primary educational system in these islands and it became a model for other countries to follow. The Sisters could not look to another country and follow their footsteps, avoiding educational pitfalls made in England for example. They were in a sense pioneers in education. This Board was instituted for the purpose of administering a fund of £30,000 placed at the disposal of the Lord Lieutenant for the education of the poor. It was empowered to make grants to existing schools for the payment of teachers, for the provision of equipment, to provide for the building of new schools, to appoint and to

---

40   Paul Connell, *Parson, Priest and Master National Education in Co. Meath, 1824-41*(Dublin,1995), p. 9.
41   First report of the commissioners of Irish education inquiry, pp 1-881, H.C.1825 (400) xii, pp l-997. Second report pp 1-133I,H.C. 1826-7 (12), xii; Third report pp 3-32, H.C. 1826-7 (13), xiii, pp 1- 155;Fourth Report... pp 3-202, H.C.1826-7 (89), xiii, pp 156-358; Fifth Report. .pp 3- 26,H.C. 1826-7 (441), xiii, pp 359-84; Sixth Report...pp. 3-116, H.C. 1826-7(442), xiii, pp. 385- 500; Seventh Report...pp.3-36, H.C.1826-7 (443), xiii pp. 501-36; Eight Report...pp 3-461, H.C.1826-7 (509), xiii, pp 537-998; Ninth Cenport...pp 3-138, H.C.1826-7 (516), xiii, pp 1001-113l.
42   John Coolahan, *Irish Education: Its History and Structure* (Dublin 1981), p. 12.

pay Inspectors.[43] The grants afforded to various societies previously, like the Kildare Place Society, for the purpose of education, 1801- 1831, were all diverted to the New Board of State Control, 1831-1832. This is a significant fact. This monetary aspect of education would indeed facilitate a better education for the Catholic children of Rochfortbridge especially in the aftermath of the famine. These other societies were on the whole, non-Catholic. The Sisters would avail of these monies and use them for the education of their children. There was a clear intention of favouring and subsidizing mixed or united education, to the exclusion of schools based on definite religious principles.[44] This however did not happen. There were many factors contributing to the emergence of denominational schools in the nineteenth century. After all, the system proposed by the board of Commissioners in 1831 was to be undenominational. Ireland presented a difficult arena for the success of multi-denominational schooling.[45] It must be noted that in 1831 when the system was founded the country was still heavily influenced politically by the established church. During the century however, a religious revolution occured. Power slipped gradually from the Anglican hands and after disestablishment in 1871, was gone almost entirely.

Denominational Schools

One must examine too the social climate at the time. Ireland was unique as regards the type of community in which the educators of the time had to work. The very demographic pattern of the country saw to it that most schools attended by Catholic children were attended by them exclusively. There was a climate of hostility and suspicion between the churches. Fears of proselytism were rife. The churches view of education differed somewhat from that of the states view. Its intention was that all denominations would be educated together in secular subjects and separate arrangements would be made for doctrinal instruction according to different denominational tenets. The churches both Protestant and Catholic in Ireland on the other hand saw education as an extension of their pastoral care. Educating children in a secular environment was impossible. They also feared the growth of secularism. The Established Church set up its own school system- *the Church Education Society*- in 1839, in opposition to the national system. The Synod of Ulster, representing the Presbyterians, was equally hostile, from 1832 to 1840, when they secured modifications in the rules that enabled them to cooperate with the Board.[46] The Catholic schools though not all of them, on the other hand, worked under the new state sponsored system, This ensured that only Catholics attended most of the national schools. They were not in favour of secular education but the new state system offered them much of what was needed in Catholic education. The non-Catholic schools eventually too came under the National school system.[47]

Another important reason why schools became denominational was that the Commissioners never enforced the rule that managers of one single faith who wished to have their school in connection with the Board would be investigated.

---

43   Ann Bennett, *A History of the parish af Rochfortbridge and its people in the nineteenth century)*. This minor thesis was submitted in part fulfillment for the requirements of the B.A. examination, Maynooth, 1975. p.16.

44   Timothy Corcoran, *Education Systems in Ireland from the close of the Middle Ages* (Dublin, 1928), p. Xxxi.

45   John Coolahan, *Irish Education: Its History and Structure* (Dublin 1981), p. 6.

46   Timothy Corcoran, *Education Systems in Ireland from the close of the Middle Ages* (Dublin, 1928), p. Xxxii.

47   John Coolahan, *Irish Education: Its History and Structure* (Dublin 1981), p. 16.

Of the 4,795 schools in operation in 1852 only 175 were under joint managership.[48] The rules or lack thereof' regulating non-vested schools gave the managers of such schools almost all the freedom possessed by managers of independent denominational schools.[49] The result of all this activity by the various churches in Ireland meant that as early as 1870 approximately 50% of catholic children on the rolls were in schools where there was no Protestant. A further 45% were in schools with an average Protestant enrolment of 7% and only 5% were in what could be regarded as genuinely mixed schools.[50] The schools became more denominational after disestablishment in 1871.

National Education in 1850's Rochfortbridge

By the time the Sisters arrived in Rochfortbridge in mid-century they were to work in a system that had become denominational. The convent schools joined the system with great alacrity. In the late 1850's there were 112 convent schools in connection with the national commissions enrolling 44,116 girls. Only 41 children were non-Catholic.[51]

Prior to the sisters arrival in Rochfortbridge, schools there were trying to work under the new system of education. A church of Ireland school was located in the village of Rochfortbridge under the direction of Rev. Wm. Lucas. As early as 23 July 1835 the parish school, which was a mixed school at Rochfortbridge, referred to as Castlelost, whose principal was Thomas Brady, was recognized by the National Board of Education.[52] This school had been established in 1833 in the townland of Torrybeggan (down the Sidebrook road).

It was built of limestone and thatched and it was in tolerably good repair. This school never received any support from any society. It was a payschool. The parish paid a rent of £3-10.0. It was open from nine until four O'clock each day for moral and literary education. Saturday was set apart for religious instruction.[53] The teacher received £10 per annum from the Board. In July 1836 the inspector visited the school and stated that it was too small. It was 40ft. by 20ft. and the average attendance was seventy six.[54]

It was scantily furnished with only six forms. There were no desks or tables. There was a greater attendance at this school in summer when seventy males and forty females attended. In winter there was a drop in attendance especially among the males. In winter forty males and thirty females attended the school.

These children came from catholic and protestant families. The children purchased the books and while no names were given it was stated that they were those generally used in country schools. The task of teaching such a large number of children of mixed abilities seems a very difficult one. The space was limited and there was only one teacher a Mr. Brady who had not

48   Eighteenth Report of the Commissioners of National Education in Ireland for the year 1851, p.xlvii[1852], H.C. 1852-3, xlii.

49   Donald H. Akenson, *The Irish Education Experiment, The National System of Education in the Nineteenth Century*(London, Toronto,)p.214.

50   Patrick J. Corish, *The Irish Catholic Experience:A Historical Survey*(Dublin, 1985). P.205.

51   Donald H. Akenson, *The Irish Education Experiment, The National System of Education in the Nineteenth Century*(London, Toronto,) p.222.

52   *Appendix to the second report 1826-1827.*

53   N.A. 1/89 folio 17.

54   Ibid.

been educated in any of the model schools. On 11th October 1838 James Gleeson replaced Thomas Brady as principal. On 2 August 1839 Mr. Gleeson was found teaching catechism and the Board sought to replace him. The Board wanted a non-denominational school and enforced the rule on this occasion. He resigned in October 1839. Education was disrupted for a time. It was not until May 1840 that a new teacher was appointed and sent away for training.[55] This type of education could be improved. Continuous education in adequate schoolrooms was needed.

Father Robbins who was manager of this mixed school was anxious to establish a separate girl's school in Rochfortbridge. On 26 October 1852 he made an application to the Commissioners for aid towards the payment of teachers salaries and for the supply of books for a female school, roll number 6674. This school was attached to the male school and established as a separate female school 18 October 1852.[56] It was taken into connection with the Board of Commissioners of Education 17 Decembet 1852 and enlarged.[57] The schoolroom was 20ft. by 12ft.. The furniture consisted of three desks and seven forms each seven-foot in good condition. The teacher Mary Seery was about twenty years old in 1852. She was paid £10 in November 1852 by the commissioners. The patron had verified that she was fit to teach. She had already acted as teacher in Kilbeggan national female school for nearly two months. The average attendance was over thirty.[58] Some records of teachers there have survived. Mary Gaffney taught from 31 January 1859 to 31 Jan 1860.

Imelda English from Kells in Co. Meath taught from 14 January 1859 to 1 April 1861. Anne Pilkington a probationer left the school 31 December 1860. Mary Egan was a monitor February 1862. Sarah and Jane Pilkington became senior monitors 1 March 1863. Bridget Corrigan was appointed senior monitor 1 October 1867.[59] The salary of the teachers varied. In 1856 the salary of the teacher and assistant was £15. In 1857 it was £16. In 1858 it was £12-16-8. In 1859 it was £12-10-0' Money was also supplied by the Board of Commissioners for various requisites. In 1856 it was 10s-3d, 1857, 9s- 9d, 1858, 12s. And in 1859 it was 9s-6d. [60]

The supply of books was adequate in some years and not in others. For example the supply was adequate in 1856, 1859 and 1861. It was however inadequate in 1857, 1858, and 1860.[61] Accounts were accurate in 1856, 1857, and 1858 but incorrect and incomplete in I859, 1860, and 1861.[62] This school admitted visitors freely and was under the management of Fr. Robbins. The school hours were from ten O'clock to three O'clock. Religious instruction was on Saturday and from three O,clock to three thirty each other day. The children who attended were those of farmers, cottiers, shopkeepers, labourers etc. The rector Rev. Warner was favourable to this school.[63] The books used were not those of the National Board. While

55   Ibid. Protestant families were Lewis, Rochfort, David North, William Fielding, Richard Thomas and John Austin. Catholics were John A.Shiel, P.O'Connell, Patrick Geraghty, Tom Kelly, Hugh Summers, Thomas Cunningham, Michael Summers, Christopher Reddy, Walter Connell and James Aughy.
56   N./A. 1/89 folio 122.
57   N.A./2/134 folio 184-185.
58   N./A. 1/89 folio 122.
59   N.A./2/134 folio 184-185.
60   N./A. 1/89 folio 122.
61   Ibid.
62   Ibid.
63   Ibid.

Fr. Robbins had set up this school for the girls in 1852 he was anxious that sisters would come to Rochfortbridge. This opportunity arose in 1862. The state through the National Board maintained control over the curriculum of national schools. They published the textbooks and they could prevent the use of other books. These books contained a lot of factual information. Some would claim these books to be the best text series produced in the English speaking world. At the beginning these books were provided at half price.[64]

Permission was granted to give a stock of free books in October 1833.[65] The free stock was renewed at the end of every four years and, after 1848, every three years. The value granted varied according to the average daily attendance of the school. The free stock was not sufficiently large to suffice for the wants of the entire school.[66] Other ways needed to be found to fill the gap. It can be seen that this small quiet village, Rochfortbrdge in the center of Ireland was slowly emerging as a focal point in the parish. It changed its name taking on that of the wealthy Rochfort family forecasting perhaps a change of fortune especially for the Catholic community there. The population here was divided into two communities-The Church of Ireland and the Catholic Community.

The smaller Church of Ireland Community enjoyed a better lifestyle, better housing, diet and educational facilities than that of their Catholic neighbours. Their church was built in a prominent position in the village. Their wealth meant that they could afford education for their children as schools in the first half of the nineteenth century were mostly pay schools. These schools were mainly sturdy slated buildings and were aided by grants from various societies. The Catholic community on the other hand was described in 1832 by a local clergyman as an agricultural community, working on rich soil as labourers and making use of the surrounding bogland. They lived in low value accommodation and survived on a basic diet. Illiteracy levels were low particularly among the female population due mainly to their own lack of resources to pay for the education of their children. They were not helped by any society. Their schools were in bad repair and their teachers badly paid. Legislation in the eighteenth century deprived them of a basic education. However many factors at the start of the nineteenth century were to change the educational facilities for the Catholic children in Ireland and in this village Rochfortbridge. One important change was the state's attitude to education. It set up various commissions to investigate the state of education in Ireland. As a result of this activity a Board of Education was set up in 1831. Education became more structured. Monies became available to pay teachers salaries which guaranteed a regular supply and grants became available to repair schools. The state intended to establish undenominational schools. It would have control over the teachers and the curriculum of these schools.

At the same time the local Catholic clergy were taking more interest in the schools in their parishes. They became managers and influenced greatly the type of national school in their area. The strong wish of each particular community to attend a school of its own persuasion in Rochfortbridge led to denominational schools here. A need for the education of the female population led to the introduction of the Mercy Sisters to Rochfortbridge.

---

64 Donald H. Akenson, *The Irish Education Experiment, The National System of Education in the Nineteenth Century*(London, Toronto, 1970,)p.154.

65 Ibid. P.228.

66 Ibid.

~ CHAPTER 3 ~
THE FIELDING LEGACY

By Betty Mimnagh Dunne

~ CHAPTER 3 ~

THE FIELDING LEGACY

By Betty Mimnagh Dunne

Philanthropy played a major role in society in nineteenth century Ireland. Organizations and individuals gave of their time and energy voluntarily in many social areas. One of these areas was education. The Catholic Church had neither the resources nor the manpower to achieve its aims with regard to improving the education of the poorer Catholic class. It relied heavily upon help from its members in particular from the activities of middle class men and women, lay and religious.[1]

It was these religious orders who fulfilled the need for human resources needed especially in the field of education. They made an enormous contribution to education, to the history of the Catholic Church in Ireland and to the country as a whole at a time when there was extreme economic poverty in Ireland. As the Catholic revival unfolded its most remarkable feature was the dramatic expansion of these Catholic religious communities in the nineteenth century. In 1800 there were in Ireland a mere 120 nuns based in eleven houses, belonging to six religious orders. By 1900 there were over 8000 women religious in 327 convents, belonging to thirty-seven religious orders. The phenomenal growth in vocational enrolment translated into an equally prodigious output reflected in the provision of educational welfare and health services.[2]

The work of these religious in Ireland certainly quickened the social progress of the poorer class in a remarkable way. The religious order of nuns could be described as pious well to do ladies who were prepared to make considerable sacrifices of material comforts.[3] They renounced rights over their property and their will and voluntarily excluded themselves from social life. Yet they enjoyed especially in Ireland a social standing which was higher than that of an unmarried woman, and a socially approved area of activity which was wider than that allowed the married woman. They too were pioneers. They had to do everything for the first time and had no one else's experience to counsel or direct them. This experience they shared with their fellow nuns in their own immediate environment and with others in convents all over Ireland.

In Rochfortbridge itself it is evident from the Annals that Sisters from other convents regularly visited for short periods of time and sisters often went to other convents to share their experience and to help the Sisters there. This network of communication was indeed very valuable in the development of education in convent schools. The Sisters, as they had no families channeled all their reserves towards providing education, hospital care and welfare services. Their work was also imbued with Christian sentiments. They wanted to give the

---

1   Caitríona Clear, *Walls Within Walls* (Dublin, Washington D.C.), 1987, p.30.
2   Patrick J. Corish, David Sheehy, *Records of the Irish Catholic Church*, (Dublin, 2001), p.41.
3   Norman Atkinson, *A History of Educational Institutions* (Dublin, 1969, p. 74

children under their care a Catholic identity. Religious identity was very important to Catholics and Protestants in nineteenth century Ireland. The sisters taught their children by word and example.

The Mercy Sisters was founded by Catherine McCauley in 1831 in Dublin. She gathered around her a group of ladies anxious to devote themselves to the service of the poor. They decided to form a religious order. These women were primarily religious educators, also anxious to surround their pupils with a religious atmosphere. Catherine McCauley devoted her attention not only to children, but to young female adults as well.[4]

The Mercy congregation was the most widely distributed and rapidly expanding congregation of women religious in Ireland. They lived under a strict constitution with strict rules and regulations. The circumstances leading to the arrival of the Mercy Sisters in Rochfortbridge are very interesting and somewhat unusual. Father Robbins the Catholic parish priest was anxious that a Catholic education would be available for the girls in the village.[5] As cited earlier there was already a female school attached to the male school near the village. Accommodation here was quite limited. The supply of books was often inadequate and accounts were often inaccurate. Attendance was quite low. The average was fifty to sixty in the years prior to the arrival of the Sisters.[6] To improve this situation, it

Mother Catherine McAuley

Catherine McAuley was born in Stormanstown House, Drumcondra, Dublin on September 29, 1778. Her Father, James McAuley was a staunch Catholic and noted for his charity to those less well off than himself. He died when Catherine was only four years old, leaving her Mother Eleanor to raise three children. When Catherine was twenty, her Mother died. Having lived with her Uncle, Owen Conway and then with the Armstrong family for a while, she then moved to Coolock House in 1803 to work with the Callaghan family, an elderly wealthy Protestant-Quaker couple. For the next twenty five years Catherine worked as household manager there. During this time, she grew in her understanding of Catholic faith and practice and her care for those who were poor and destitute.

Catherine proved to be a loving companion and holy example to the Callaghans and on their death beds, they converted to Catholicism, bequeathing their estate to her. With this inheritance, Catherine built a house on Baggot Street in Dublin as a home for poor girls. This first Home of Mercy opened on September 24, 1827, the Feast of Our Lady of Mercy. Her work with the poor and destitute led Catherine to desire a life of total consecration to Our Lord. Encouraged by the Archbishop, Catherine and two other women professed vows on December 12, 1831, and began the Religious Institute of the Sisters of Mercy. Often seen walking the streets to serve the sick and the poor, the "walking nuns" inspired many women to dedicate themselves to Christ and to the service of the Church, causing the Institute to spread rapidly.

By the time of Mother Catherine's death in 1841, there were 100 Sisters of Mercy in ten foundations. In April of 1990 Pope John Paul II declared Catherine McAuley "Venerable".

The legacy of union and charity and tender mercy to Christ's poor left by Mother Catherine to her daughters was kept alive through the Constitutions she wrote, her letters, her poetry, and most of all her prayers. Mother Catherine was gifted with a profound love of God, expressed in a deep love for her Sisters, and a tremendous sense of humor able to help sustain others through difficult times. Her Suscipe expresses her surrender to the loving Mercy of God.

---

4   Ibid. p. 76
5   Olive Curran, (ed.), *History of the Diocese of Meath 1860-1993* (3 Vols, Dublin, 1995), ii, p.805. Fr. Robbins died on 14 April 1875.
6   N./A. Ed 2/134 folio 184/185.

was necessary to provide a bigger building, more teachers, and to have an adequate supply of books, and monetary resources.

Acquiring a new site or building for a national school was a difficult task in the mid-nineteenth century. Church of Ireland wealthy people owned most of the buildings and land in the village of Rochfortbridge.

The national school in a neighbouring village Tyrrellspass was owned by a landlord Charles Brinsley Marley, who had little knowledge and interest in the education of the Catholic community. To have a premises was indeed a great advantage for the Catholic children when they wished to initiate a school. Yet it seemed that since the Catholic people who lived in Rochfortbridge were relatively poor the chances of acquiring a building suitable for a school for the Catholic children was remote.

It was largely through the efforts of one lady Eliza Fielding, that this building became available. She was born in Rochfortbridge 2l November 1834[7] the third child of William and Maria Fielding (nee Payne). She belonged to the Church of Ireland. Eliza had two brothers, Henry and Willie and two sisters Maria and Margaret.[8] By examining her background we get some idea of the qualities she possessed which helped her to carry out the enormous task ahead of her, that of helping to educate the children of Rochfortbridge and setting up schools much further afield. Born into a prosperous home, her father William was from a farming and merchant family. They had a farm and a house of business, a drapery and grocery combined.[9] Her house was a rather large house in this small community next door to the constabulary force with John Kenny and Michael Eighan on one side and Patrick Connell and Rev. Gerald Robbins on the other.[10] The valuation of her house well exceeded that of her neighbours. Wealth and poverty lived in close proximity in Rochfortbridge.[11]

Sister Mary Paul Fielding

Her house was valued at £10 while that of her neighbour Mr. Kenny was £3-5s, Eighan's was £3-13s, and Connell's was £3-5s.[12] Her house was later to become the Convent of the Sisters of Mercy.

---

7   The Register of the Sisters of Mercy, Wilcannia-Forbes Congregation Australia. Supplied by Sister Ryan, Australia.

8   Annals of the Sisters of Mercy, Rochfortbridge, (hereafter cited as Annals, Rochfortbridge), p.204, paginated by author. He entered business in the poplin industry in Dublin in the Co. of Fry-and Fielding, Westmoreland Street. His wife was from Sandymount, Dublin.

9   Annals Rochfortbridge. P.204. Margaret married Mr. Pate a Protestant. A daughter converted to Catholicism and went as a nun to Australia. Maria married Mr.Kellaghan a Catholic farmer in Westmeath. A daughter of Maria's entered the Sisters of Mercy, Navan. Her name was Sister M. Antonia. Willie married a Miss McDonnell from Tullamore.

10   Richard Griffith, *General Valuation of Ratable property in Irelatd, valuation of the several tenements in the Union of Mullingar* (Dublin, 1854), p. 125.

11   When the Fielding family moved to Rochfortbridge they spent their early years in a farmhouse close to the original beggarsbridge, now the Rahanine road. The first Orange lodge was located here. Later they purchased the lands and buildings on the Castlelost road, it was the Fielding house which would become St. Joseph's, the first convent. With this move, the Orange Lodge transferred to here also.

12   Ibid.

In literature written at the end of the century it is stated that her parents were very generous to the poor of the village. She inherited this desire to help others. They were a particularly generous and loved couple, especially her mother Maria Payne[13] whose special care was for the poor of the parish.[14] Eliza herself is described as a bright lovely child who often accompanied her mother on her visits of charity.[15] She would have been very aware of the educational facilities or lack of them in her village. She attended the local school.

Her wish was to provide education for the Catholic children around her. Yet she belonged to another religious community, the Church of Ireland community. Perhaps she would have observed some Catholic practices in school and in her own home, as the servants may have been Catholic. She also may have learned aspects of this religion from visiting the poor in her community. She possibly too was well aware of Catholic observances of the people in her immediate surroundings.

Her mother died when she was thirteen. [16] Her aunt took care of her in her own home. This seemed to mark the turning point in the life of Eliza Fielding. It was around this time that she decided to become a Catholic. This would have required perseverance and steadfastness from her and a firm conviction that she was right. Her father understandably was annoyed and told her to leave home. Yet later it was he who donated a site for the Catholic Church and requested a priest on his death bed. It is said that he too converted to Catholicism.

The ruins of the original Fielding Home beside The Beggarsbridge. The first Orange Lodge was located here also and when the family moved to their new premises (St. Joseph's) to open a grocery and hardware the Orange lodge was located at their new home.

13   The Register of the Sisters of Mercy, Wilcannia-Forbes Congregation Australia. Supplied by Sister Ryan, Australia.

14   *Mount Carmel Centenary Book* 1875-1975, (Australia 1975), p. 21. Article: Extracts from the Records at Rochfortbridge. Book in possession of the Sisters of Mercy Rochfortbridge Westmeath.

15   Ibid.

16   Gravestone inscription of Maria Fielding (Payne). It reads "Erected by Henry Fielding to the sacred memory of his beloved mother Maria Fielding of Rochfortbridge who departed this life 21 August 1847 age 44 yrs. For if we do believe that Jesus died and rose again even then also which sleep in Jesus will God bring with Him".

She, on leaving home became a shop assistant in Tyrrellspass.[17] She stole away to her cousins, the Egans in Moate helped by Miss Catherine and Mr. P. O'Connell and Mr. Thomas Kelly.[18]

In 1858 she entered the Catholic Church and was introduced to Bishop John Cantwell and also to Fr. Nulty later bishop of Meath. Thomas Nulty became one of her geatest friends.[19]

St. Joseph's the Fielding home until 1861. Photo taken in 2000 A.D

Both were deeply interested in education. Bishop Nulty was actively involved in the movement to reform the Irish Education System. He expressed a deep concern in relation to all areas of education, particularly in his own diocese where he encouraged his people to use the educational facilities provided by the clergy and religious.[20]

Eliza was accepted for instruction into the Catholic faith in 1852. She prepared for her future role as a sister and Catholic educator by her involvement in caring for the church and in helping with the choir in the local church.[21] She also taught religion in Rochfortbridge on Sunday, a task she would do often in her new role as a Sister of Mercy. She aimed to lift the people to a standard of existence in keeping with their dignity. [22]

Along with personnel there was also a need for a gift of material wealth to facilitate the Sisters coming to Rochfortbridge. When Eliza had sold her father's estate to the satisfaction of her brothers and sisters her home was purchased by the parishioners for £500 and became the convent for the Sisters of Mercy in Rochfortbridge.[23] Her house was ideally situated being on the main street of the village. It was also very accessible to the village children.

The community in Rochfortbridge acknowledged this lady's contribution to their village by hosting a reception for her in Rochfortbridge[24] before she entered the Mercy Convent in Tullamore about twenty miles from her home to complete her own novitiate.[25] After two years Eliza was permitted to make her vows on 21 November 1864 on the anniversary of her birth.[26] Eliza or Sr. Mary Paul Fielding (her name in religion) returned to Rochfortbridge

---

17   *Mount Carmel Centenary Book* 1875-1975, (Australia 1975), p. 21. Article, Extracts from the Records at Rochfortbridge.

18   Annals, Rochfortbridge, p.204.

19   Letter written by Eliza Fielding to her sister, 9 April 1899. Letter in possession of Mr. Kellaghan, Killucan, Westmeath.

20   Gabriel Flynn, 'Bishop Thomas Nulty and the Irish Land Question' in Ríocht na Midhe, vol. iii, no. 4 1985-86, p.93.

21   Sr. M. Gertrude, *A Valiant Woman* (Sydney, 1925),p. 11.Eliza used to laugh heartily in after years at their rustic choir. A flute played by some country lad, took the place of the organ and the attempt at rendering the vocal music, was equally crude. Still she said that she often shed tears and felt her heart thrilled with devotion when listening to it.

22   *Mount Carmel Centenary Book* 1875-1975, (Australia 1975), p. 24

23   Annals, Rochfortbridge. P.5.

24   Annals of the Sisters of Mercy, Tullamore, Offaly, pp 163 – 172.

25   Ibid. pp 156 -162.

26   Register of the Sisters of Mercy, Wilcannia Forbes Congregation also the Annals of the Sisters of Mercy, Tullamore, p.176.

(by Bishop's order) on 23 August 1865.[27]

On 21 August 1862 the Mercy sisters arrived in Rochfortbridge, from St. Joseph's, Tullamore, accompanied by Rev. G. Robbins P.P. and the superioress of Tullamore, Mother Cantwell.[28] The arrival of the Sisters in Rochfortbridge was a significant social occasion and local newspapers described the event. A leading clergyman most Rev. Dr. John Cantwell drove from Mullingar to greet the Sisters.

The gothic windows formed part of the original convent chapel. The room is now a parlour

Three professed Sisters and one postulant came from Tullamore to found the convent in Rochfortbridge.[29] They were brought by Mr Gavin, (The West), Rochfortbridge.[30] Mother Gertrude Dunne was superioress. Mother Stanislaus O'Neill was assistant and Mistress of Novices and Mother Magdalene Hackett was in charge of the schools. The postulants name was Sr. M. Grennan who later became Sr. M. Bernard Joseph on 23 February 1865.[31] The Sisters also had a bursar who was in charge of the financial matters. According to the Annals of the Sisters of Mercy Rochfortbridge

> The convent is the Fifth Filiation from St. Joseph's Tullamore being founded during the Octave of the Assumption it was dedicated to Our Blessed Lady and received the title of Immaculate Conception, during the Episcopate of His Lordship, Most Rev. Dr. Cantwell. Rev. G. Robbins was parish priest.[32]

The Sisters' Annals give a detailed account of this occasion. The presence of the Blessed Sacrament was very important to the Sisters. Rev. T. OReilly brought the Blessed Sacrament to the chapel and deposited it there. Their preparation work was difficult. Benefactors, the clergy and others helped the Sisters in their work. By researching the lifestyle of the Sisters we can begin to understand why their efforts were so successful. They worked closely with all strands of parish society. They brought an awareness of the plight of the poor to the wealthier class and helped the poorer sections while trying to maintain their dignity. With education people could rise on the social ladder and improve their economic prospects. The Sisters provided not just education but they also tackled the social problems in the community. Right into the twentieth century the Sisters could be confided in with confidentiality, and helped solved problems in many social areas.

Personal comfort was not a priority for these Sisters. One of the hardships that the Sisters had to endure when they came to Rochfortbridge was that the chapel and buildings were

---

27   Annals of the Sisters of Mercy, Tullamore, Offaly, pp 176.
28   Annals, Rochfortbridge. P.4.
29   Ibid.
30   Newspaper cutting dated 1862 in possession of Ml. Curran Gibbonstown, Rochfortbridge, also an interview with Betty Kelly. Mullingar, 16 October 2001.
31   Annals Rochfortbridge, p.10.
32   Ibid. p.4

rough and unfinished. They were incomplete and could not have been very pleasant for the Sisters to enter. Everywhere the Sisters went, there were tradesmen working except in the cells, which were finished and supplied, with the necessities to accommodate six Sisters. They also had only six chairs, which were moved around from place to place.[33] This gives us a glimpse of the poverty as well as the determination and faith of these women. Each Sister also brought a dowry with her when she entered a convent. We can only surmise as to what amount this may be. However Eliza herself suggested that it should be £80 in her letter to her sister Maria 19 July 1897.[34]

Each sister adopted a habit. The Mercy nun also wore a particular ring. Each Sister, on entering the convent, received the 'Cap' from the superior. She made her final profession two years after this, in a public ceremony attended by the bishop and laity. Tickets were sold for this ceremony which raised much needed cash for the Sisters. Every Sister at her profession changed her name and chose a religious name. Eliza took the name Mary Paul Joseph. [35] Each person took a vow of poverty, chastity and obedience. They rose early in the morning for Mass and prayers. Important events were carried out on special Feast days and Catholic observances were strictly adhered to.[36] Mass was said every morning.

The Sisters worked very closely with the clergy. They consulted with them and asked for advice and this perhaps took the form of asking the bishops permission before any major work was commenced. The local clergy met the spiritual needs of the Sisters. The bishop made a special visit to the convent about once a year. The first visitation recorded in the Annals was between 22 February to 24 February 1865.[37] A confessor was appointed to the Sisters. The first record was in December 1865. A priest came from Rahan to hear confessions. The nuns held a retreat usually in July or August. This retreat was under the guidance of a director, a priest from perhaps an order of priests. Sometimes funds could not pay this director and the superioress, as in 1866, directed the retreat. The Sisters also went on retreat before renewing their vows around Christmas time and before they made their final profession.

Sometimes if sisters were ill they traveled to Tullamore or Dublin to see a medical specialist. Another convent accommodated the Sisters if they had to stay overnight. Sometimes the doctor suggested that the sister who was ill should go for a change of air. This was recorded in the Annals and the sister usually arrived home much improved. On the 27 May 1866 Rev Mother Stanislaus went to St. Bridget's convent, Clara, King's County until 3 June, as she was ill.

Their teaching salary and donations given by private individuals financed the sisters. The parishioners were generous to the community and supplied them with vegetables and milk. One benefactor Richard Coffey Newcastle House often sent in a week's supply of meat. Many people regularly visited the convent and donated gifts of land, money, clothes and religious objects to the Sisters. The most notable benefactors were Richard Coffey, Esq., Newcastle House, Lady Kilmaine and Mrs. Shields. Some of these gifts were quite sizeable and without them the work of the sisters would not have been as successful. Mr. Coffey gave the sisters a horse and covered car, to visit the sick and poor who lived at a distance from

33   Annals Rochfortbridge, p.6.
34   S..M. Paul Letter to her sister dated 19 July 1897 in possession of Mr. Kellaghan Killucan.
35   Annals, Rochfortbridge. p. 8.
36   Ibid.
37   Ibid.

the convent. The bishop of the diocese, priests and relations of the sisters donated generously. In June 1866 Rev. J Reynolds (brother of Sr. M. Aloysius) came home from the continent and gave the sisters presents of reliquaries, medals, beads and pictures for the poor.[38]

The Convent of Mercy, built in 1872

Society appreciated the work of the Sisters and the convent flourished taking in new postulants on a regular basis. The ability of the convent to attract numbers of wealthy Sisters was attributed to the high visibility of the congregation and to its secure, established position in Irish Catholic life.[39] The convent in Rochfortbridge soon became congested. The sisters had to devise a plan to enlarge it. A bazaar was determined on and it took place an 22 June 1865. The principal prize on the occasion was the carriage and horses owned by the bishop deceased and given to the community by his nephew Mr. P. Molloy.

The bishop and all the priests of the parish contributed to the cost. Great crowds with many of the surrounding clergy attended on the day of the bazaar. When all expenses were paid the sum of £400 was in hands.[40] The old convent was needed for classrooms at the school. Tickets were sold for a public reception. The monies collected would be used to erect a convent. It was decided to build a new convent in the field adjoining the Parish church. The farmers of the area promised aid for the erection of the convent. After the Bishop's permission had been obtained on 25 October 1870, there was much preliminary work to be done. Details were carefully recorded in the Sisters Annals. This attention to detail as we will see later was one of the criteria demanded by educational authorities.

Rev. Robbins, Mr. Coffey and Mr. Caldbeck met to discuss plans on 30 September 1870 for the convent to be built. 29 December 1870 Mr. Coffey's men drew the first load of stones for the new convent. 26 March 1871 the specification was sent to the convent for the purpose of getting the approval of the Sisters. 28 April 1871 the contract for the new convent was signed by Rev. G. Robbins P.P. and Mr. Coffey of Newcastle vrith the contractor, Mr, Morris, and in the presence of the architect, Mr. Caldbeck. Rev. G. Robbins P.P. laid the foundation stone for the new convent in the presence of the neighbouring clergy. 11 May 1872. The whole lay community took an active part in this ceremony. A large concourse of people, and all the children walked in procession singing the Litany of the Blessed Virgin.

---

38   Annals, Rochfortbridge.

39   Caitríona Clear, *Walls Within Walls* (Dublin, Washington D.C.), 1987, p.141.

40   Annals, Rochfortbridge, p.40, Tullamore, Roscrea, Clara, Drogheda and Tallow sent some fancywork as prizes. A silver snuffbox was also raffled. Rev. Wheller P.P. Balbriggan won the first prize and he gave it to the-sisters of Mercy Drogheda. 20 January 1870, Rev. Robbins gave a beautiful chalice and £50 to be raffled. Another bazaar was held 20 and 21 of May 1872. Convents in Enniskillen and Downpatrick contributed. The sacred Heart Convent in Roscrea and the sisters of Mercy, Tullamore gave fancywork. They made £700. Mr:_ F'razier Dublin won first prize.

Almost the whole community was involved in the building of the new convent. It cost £1650. On 15 August 1872 the Feast of the Assumption of Our Lady, the Sisters took up residence in the new convent. Fr. Robbins celebrated Mass in it for the first time and blessed the whole house.[41] The generosity of the people in Rochfortbridge is evident again when 7 October 1876 a Mr. Cassidy, Castlejordan gave one thousand holly plants to the Sisters to make a hedge around the convent.[42] 10 October 1877 Mr. J Coyne, Dr. Nulty and Mrs. D. Cole gave a donation of £3 towards the erection of an altar in the convent chapel. This was a Sienna marble altar with four pillars very richly carved. It came from Callaghans, in Dublin and was erected 12 April 1878. A laundry and servants quarters were added in 1881.[43] The convent was a landmark in each community. It was open to the public and accessible to all, at all times.

People rich and poor could identify, with the Sisters. The Sisters living together as a community were very approachable both to the poor and the rich. People felt that they could confide in these women with utmost confidence.

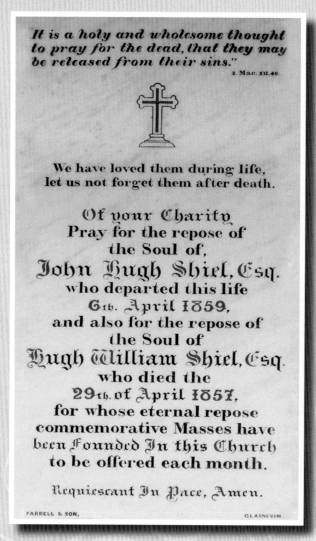

The Shiels family Memorial Plaque in the Church of the Immaculate Conception.
The Shiels family Gortumloe were benefactors of the Church for many years.

---

41   Ibid.
42   Ibid.
43   Ibid. p.190. A Bazaar was held Sep.1887 to clear the debt on the laundry. The prize was a jaunting car.

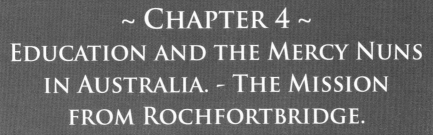

~ CHAPTER 4 ~
EDUCATION AND THE MERCY NUNS IN AUSTRALIA. – THE MISSION FROM ROCHFORTBRIDGE.

By Betty Mimnagh Dunne

~ CHAPTER 4 ~
EDUCATION AND THE MERCY NUNS IN AUSTRALIA.
THE MISSION FROM ROCHFORTBRIDGE.

By Betty Mimnagh Dunne

Irish Sisters were also active in education in Australia. The context for Catholic education there was difficult. Australian Catholics were not content with state run schools, which were for them secular in nature. Education was a unity, not a mechanism that could be put together bit by bit, a little morsel of religious instruction here and of secular instruction there, like separate parcels with as little reciprocal action as have two books on the shelves of a library.[1] They did not want a system in which religious development was not an integral part of the whole educative process.

It was not until Dr. Polding arrived in New South Wales in 1835 that Catholic parishes were being created. Thirty years later in 1865 the Catholic hierarchy were urged to provide Catholic schools by the directive of the Congregation Propaganda Fide in Rome.

> Every effort must be directed towards starting Catholic schools where they are not and where they are, towards enlarging them and providing them with better accommodation and equipment until they have nothing to suffer, as regards teachers or furniture, by comparison with public schools.[2]

Australian bishops of Irish extraction had some experience of the Irish schools system, where schools were managed by religious teaching congregations. The idea therefore emerged to set up a system of education in Australia which would depend entirely on the funds of the Catholic community in which the schools were situated. Staffing and the payment of salaries would be a major problem and most importantly they could not employ lay staff for many reasons.[3] The first being that they could not pay the salaries for the lay teachers certainly not at the rate paid by the state.[4] Many of the best teachers had gone to high salaried positions in state schools. Yet catholics wanted the best teachers available. Thus began a spate of missionary activity to Australia by religious teaching brothers and sisters.

Ireland was the obvious country to look for catholic teachers since the bishops and the great majority of the clergy were Irish. They had been trained in Ireland and most would have had some experience with the National schools. The bulk of the catholic population was Irish and the Australian catholic press gave Irish news a prominent place in its columns, frequently

---

1   Ronald Fogarty, *Catholic Education in Australia 1806-1905* (2 vols. London, New York 1957), p. 188.
2   M. Raphael Consedine, *Listening Journey*(Victoria Australia, 1983), p. 291.
3   F.Byrne, *History of the Catholic Church in South Australia*,(Melbourne. 1896), p 155.
4   Urban Corrigan,*The achievements of Catholic education in Australia*(Sydney., 1937), p. 7.

publishing reports of the educational situation in Ireland.[5] These teachers had a reputation of being very committed and efficient. The idea of religious working in the area of education in the second half of the nineteenth century was not a new one. It had been suggested by Bishop Polding 1839, in Sydney, Bishop Wilson 1847 in Hobart, Bishop Brady in Perth, 1848, Bishop Goold in Merbourne, 1857 and Bishop James Quinn in 1861.[6]

These religious however were working with the richer children in Australia. It was Rev. Tennison Woods (end of 1860's) that diverted the religious to the schools of the Poor. In Goulburn, 1850-1860 it was Bishop Geoghan's efforts at encouraging catholic schools in his diocese in New South Wales that prompted other bishops and clergy to follow his example. He encouraged the setting up of catholic schools. Bishop Lannigan succeeded

Sister Alacoque McLoughlin

him. The catholic countries of Europe therefore and particularly Ireland were visited by bishops recruiting people to teach in their schools.

The religious who came to Australia settled and adapted themselves to Australian conditions. They had to have the ability to stretch slender resources as far as possible. They brought with them the service of their own hands, whatever scholarship they possessed, and their own educational systems.

On the 10th. March 1874 Rev. McAlroy visited the convent in Rochfortbridge requesting Sisters for one of the colonies.[7] In October 1874 the Rev. Mother received a letter from Dr. Nulty (Bishop of Meath) in which was enclosed a letter from Dr. Lannigan applying for a Foundation of Sisters for Yass which was in his Diocese of Goulburn, Australia.[8] The town of Yass was a rising center of industry in 1875. Dr. Thomas Nulty expressed a wish to hear individually from the Sisters who wanted to volunteer.

On the 3rd. November, Sr. M. Paul Fielding, Sr. Bernard Grennan,[9] Mother Alacoque McLoughlin and Sr. Aloysius wrote to Dr. Nulty expressing a wish to work in his diocese.[10] On the 13th. November Dr. Nulty visited and interviewed the four Sisters. He said he would give no decision until he first contacted Dr. Lannigan.[11] Four choir postulants also entered for the mission, Miss Ellen ONeill, Tipperary, (Rev. Mother Stanislaus), Miss Catherine (Kate) Leahy, of Stone house, King's county, (Rev. Mother Zavior), Miss Anastasia Mullaly of Tipperary (Sr. Mary Joseph) and Miss Margaret Nally[12] from Westmeath.[13]

5   Ronald Fogarty, *Cathotic Education in Australia 1806-1905* (2 vols. London, New York 1957), p. 177.
6   Ibid. p.222.
7   Annals, Rochfortbridge, 1874, p. 89.
8   *Mount Carmel Centenary Book 1875-1975*, p.28
9   Ibid. She was from King's County and was later superior of the Tumut Convent Annals, Rochfortbridge, 1874, p. 214.
10   Annals, Rochfortbridge. p. 214.
11   Ibid.
12   Mount Carmel Centenary Book 1875-1975 p 53. She was daughrer of James and Ann Nally from County Westmeath. She was professed in 1880 and was one of the foundation members of the Murrumburrah community. Most of her long life was spent in West Wyalong.
13   Annals, Rochfortbridge. p. 214.

On the 28th December, the bishop advised Rev. Mother to write to Dr. Mullally, All Hallows College, Dublin to arrange for the missionaries. Arrangements were concluded between Dr. Nulty Bishop of Meath and Dr. Lannigan of Goulburn. Dr. Lannigan would pay the passage of all the Sisters and give cash for a supply of school furniture and requisites, a piano and other necessities. The piano was an important piece of equipment. Piano lessons were an important source of income for the Sisters. On the 23rd June 1875 Sr. Stanislaus, Sr. M. Paul and Sr. M. Bernard left for Dublin to make arrangements to travel. On the 8th July 1875 Dr. Molloy, All Hallows College, Dublin, came to Rochfortbridge to arrange with Sr. M. Paul about piano and school requisites. The last arrangements were made when Dr. Gunne and Dr. Mullally visited the convent on the 20th. July 1875. On the 6th August 1875 Sr. M. Paul left for Dublin to select pianos and harmoniums for missions.[14]

Mother Bernard Grennan

The Sisters trunks were sent to Dublin on the 20th August l875. On 21 August 1875, the thirteenth anniversary of the foundation of Rochfortbridge, the Sisters together with four postulants Leahy[15], Mullaly[16], O'Neill[17], and Nally bade farewell to their convent home and set out for Australia. It was a day of general sorrow and lamentation for the Bridge. A local newspaper dated the 3rd September 1875 shows that the people in this village were very attached to the sisters and probably feared for their safety in a foreign land. The departure of these nuns afforded an additional proof of the attachment and love of the people towards them.

> 'For days previous to their leaving, the convent was besieged by anxious and sorrowing crowds asking for permission, which was freely given to them to say farewell and to offer some tribute of affection and gratitude to the Sisters to whom so much was due. Their influence, gently, and charitably exercised had reached to all'.[18]

It must have been very difficult for Eliza herself to leave Rochfortbridge because she had strong ties both to her family and her convent. This convent had also been her childhood home. The journey was detailed by a friend of Eliza's, Sr. Gertrude Grogan and later written in a book *'The Story of a Valiant Woman'*, in Australia in the early nineteen hundreds. They had to go by coach to Killucan Station to get the train for Dublin.

---

14   Annals, Rochfortbridge. p. 122.
15   She was daughter of William and Catherine Leahy, Stone House Kinnegad. She was professed in 1878 and was superior in Murrumburrah and Wyalomg. She was a music teacher and worked with the native Australian children.
16   Her parents were Ml. and Ellen Mullaly. She came from Tipperary.
17   She was daughter of Francis and Judith O'Neill, Queen's County. She was professed in 1878. She taught music.
18   Newspaper cutting dated 3 September 1875, in possession of Ml. Curran, Gibbonstown, Rochfortbridge.

Several young ladies intending to join the Mercy order in Goulburn and a professed sister for the Albury Convent joined them. Records tell us that the Sisters all stayed in a hotel in Dublin. They always tried to attend daily Mass. It was very central in their lives and even while in Dublin they traveled on Sunday morning accompanied by Rev. Fr. McLoughlin, brother of Sr. M. Alacoque, and Rev Fr. Delaney, curate of Rochfortbridge to All Hallows College, where the priests celebrated Mass for them. After Mass they were met, and were courteously entertained by very Rev. Dr. O'Brien late of St. John's Sydney and Rev. Fr. Mullaly. They stayed a few days in Dublin and then left from Kingstown harbour and crossed to Holyhead. They went from Holyhead to London. The nuns had great difficulty in acquiring lodgings. At last they found a noisy place to stay. Eliza talks of the bigotry the Sisters encountered there. They stayed a day in London, and sailed on Thursday the 26th. August 1875 on the Gainsborough for Australia.

Fr. Michael McAlroy

The captain's name was Mr. Carter. Some ship captains declined to accept responsibiliy for lady missionaries as the journey was so hazardous. To appreciate the trauma of travelling to Australia in the second half of the nineteenth century it is important to describe the travelling conditions as recounted by a friend of Eliza.

> The ship's accommodation was wretched. There were no cabins. Partitions were run up to form sleeping rooms for the nuns party but the bunks which served for berths were so narrow that when a mattress was put on it, it hung half over the side and in rough weather keeping off the floor was a problem and to make matters worse, three were put to each

Dr. Lannigan, Archbishop of Goulbourne

box or cabin. When Fr. Delaney and Fr. McLoughlin saw the conditions, they got matresses and bedding that the nuns were bringing out to Australia and made the place more presentable.[19]

Dr. Gunne also had asked Mother Paul to take charge of about a dozen other young girls who were going to enter the Novitiates in his diocese, Bathurst. [20]

---

19   Annals, Rochfortbridge. p. 126.
20   Ibid.

The Sisters took in food at Gravesend. Otherwise Eliza claimed she would have lost some of her party who were not able to eat the rough food provided by the ship.[21] There were six priests on board. Two names are recorded. Rev. P. Delaney, chaplain to the convent, and the Rev. N. McLoughlin, brother to the young mother assistant traveled with them.[22] Three ladies and a gentleman completed the

The Gainsborough

passenger list. The day on the ship resembled that of convent life as much as possible, The day was spent in prayer, spiritual reading, and study. Five masses were celebrated each day. It was a long journey lasting about fourteen weeks.

After the long voyage in the early dawn of the Feast of the Immaculate Conception, the 8th December, the Sisters arrived at Sydney Harbour. Eliza knelt and kissed the soil. Mrs. Casey, Wynyard and Rev. Lannigan met them. He had prepared comfortable accommodation for them. The day after, they left by coach for Goulburn. Eliza speaks of the feeling of vastness and oppressive loneliness when she reached Australia. The mental pictures which the Sisters, like all emigrants, formed of the distant lands, were shaped and coloured by their own usually very limited experience of travel and by the ability of those who contacted them to describe conditions. It is unlikely that the sisters were intentionally misled, but the enthusiasm and the sense of urgency felt by those who contacted them would have perhaps unconsciously distorted the picture. The sisters had to come to terms with a completely different environment and a climate, than that which they were familiar with in Ireland. Having survived the emotional stress of departure and the physical hardships of nineteenth century travel were, after all only the beginning of the new situation that had to be faced.

They had to settle into new surroundings, make contacts, establish friendships, study the particular needs of the area and the distinctive qualities of the children and gain the recognition and acceptance needed for success. All of this had to be done on a shoe string budget. Dr. Lannigan had promised them a proper residence, maintenance, a daily Mass, and that a priest would accompany them when going on long or hazardaus journeys. They would depend on the people for their support. Dr. Lannigan promised 'should anything be wanted I hold myself responsible.'[23]

It is only when one learns that the Yass Plains were discovered in 1821 by Hamilton Hume, John Kennedy-Hume, Willliam Henry Broughton and George Barber that we can begin to understand the courage of these ladies.[24] What type of environment did the sisters work in during the early years? To answer this question one must examine the development of this town.

---

21   *Mount Carmel Centenary Book* 1875-1975, p. 28.
22   Sr. Gertrude Grogan, *A Valiant Woman* (Sydney, Australia 1925). p 65
23   Letter dated 9 Feb. 1875 from Dr Lannigan to Dr. Nulty. A copy in the Annals of the Sisters of Mercy in Rochfortbridge.
24   *Mount Carmel Centenary Book* 1875-1975, p. 5.

It was in its infancy when the Sisters arrived. The census figures taken in 1840 showed that the population was 1281. Law enforcement had been operating since 1832 when the residents of the Yass plains applied to the Colonial Secretary for the establishment of a police force.[25] The Sisters had the facilities of a postal service and were able to keep in contact with home since the first post office was opened on the 1st April 1835. In 1835 Mr. W. H. Dutton, wrote to the colonial secretary on behalf of the residents to have the village reserve laid out as a township. The governor approved the plans of the proposed town of Yass in early 1837. On the 1st October 1837 Mt. John Richard Hardy was appointed police Magistrate of Yass. A new two storey gaol was opened on the old court house site in 1864. Some of the sisters work would entail visiting this jail.

Development of the service type buildings and structures had only started in the 1830s and 40s. In 1843 following representation from the residents of Yass the governor approved the formation of a District Council. In 1856 the N.S.W. Legislative Assembly was introduced. The sisters could avail of the banks in their area- the commercial bank opened in 1858. There was also the oriental, and the Australian Joint stock Bank. Yass had two hotels, the Charles Quail's Globe and Henry Hart's Royal. These included large rooms in them for balls and the entertainment of travelling artists. This indicates perhaps some degree of

wealth. The new Mechanic's Institute was opened in 1869. In 1858 the first telegraph office was opened, first in a room in the Royal Hotel and in 1861 it was moved into new premises in the Court House reserve. The health of the inhabitants was catered for in the hospital whose foundation stone was laid 1849. Some basic facilities therefore were in place for the sisters. However all structures were comparatively new.

Travelling in the country itself still could be very hazardous for the sisters. A wooden three span bridge was built over the Yass River in 1854 and a stronger one made of steel lattice was put in place 1870. It was washed away by a flood when only partially completed and rebuilt in 1872.[26]

The religious situation in Yass was quite different for the sisters from that which existed in Ireland. They would have to assess the situation and develop a program of instruction based on the religious situation of their children. The Catholic Church was not a feature of the early days of Australian history because the church of England was naturally the official religious body and for quite a few years it seemed likely there would be no other.[27] In the early part of the century the residents relied on the ministrations of visiting clergy but later the clergy resided in the town. Many religious organizations existed in Yass when the Sisters arrived and these people contributed financially to the development of parochial buildings. A list of the subscribers to the building of the Catholic Church in Yass 1837-1844 confirms this.[28] It also indicates that all communities lived in relative harmony and were prepared to give assistance to one another.

---

25   Ibid.
26   Ibid.
27   Ibid.
28   Ibid. p.15, List of subscribers, C. O'Brien, Hardwick twenty pounds, H O'Brien Doure, twenty pounds; E. Ryan, Galong twenty pounds; Hamilton Hume, five pounds; W H Broughton five pounds; Y. Dutton, ten-pounds; Moses, ten pounds; Father Terry, five pounds.

The Church of Englands first resident minister was Rev. Charles Ferdinand Brigstock, appointed to Yass December 1838.[29] The population was increasing yet there was no church of any denomination in Yass. Services were shared between denominations in the courthouse until in June 1840 a subscription library was used for a temporary church. In August 1840, services began in a new timber church down by the river. The foundation stone for the existing Church of England was laid 26 November 1847 and the church known as St. Clemens designed by Mr. E.T. Blacket, was opened for service in 1850.[30] This was only fifteen years before the Sisters arrived.

The Presbyterian Church too had come to Yass. It appears that Miss Reid's schoolhouse in Dutton Street was the first place used for services. In 1837 Rev. William Hamilton of Goulburn administered to Yass.[31] The first Presbyterian Church St. Andrews was built behind the present church in 1864 but damaged by a cyclone on 11th November 1891. It was replaced by another church in 1906.

The Methodist minister Rev. William Lightbody ministered in Yass in 1848 but the first resident minister was Rev. Charles Creel 1857. Services were conducted in a schoolroom. The first church was built in Meehan Street in 1859.[32] The Catholic Church had been developing for about forty years when the Sisters arrived in Yass.[33] In early 1837 a collection was organized to begin building a Catholic Church. On 31 March 1838 a site in Meehan Street, containing two acres for a church, Presbytery and school was fixed upon and surveyed by Assistant-Surveyor Thomas Townsend. Catholics now had their own church but they had not sufficient schools.

The accommodation for Eliza's party was not ready when they reached Australia. The Sisters stayed three weeks with a group Sisters of Mercy in Goulburn. The delay was caused because it was not decided where the Sisters were going to stay in Yass. A decision had to be made whether the house the Sisters inhabited would be a cottage that Dr. Morgan O'Connor formerly occupied or whether to use the Presbytery until the new convent, which would be built on church, grounds would be completed. The pattern of building schools quite close to the church as was the custom in Ireland was also used in Australia. Rev. Dean O'Keefe vacated the Presbytery, which was then prepared for the nuns. This was part of the uncertainty endured by the Sisters when they started a new foundation.

On 29 December they started for Yass accompanied by, Dr Lannigan and Rev. Pierce Burke. They reached Gunning for dinner. At four o'clock on 29 December 1875 they saw the Yass plains.[34] As in Ireland the community and the Sisters worked together in harmony.

29   Ibid. p.12. Rev. Thomas Hassell from Cobbitty ministered until 1833.when Rev. John Vincent was ap-
        pointed to Sutton Forest. In March 1838 Rev. Thomas Cartwright was appointed to the southern area.
30   Ibid. The tower was added in 1860 and the church was enlarged by the addition of a similar wing to the
        western side in 1877'
31   Ibid. The Rev. David McKenzie was in residence in 1844 and for a short period between the years 1850
        to 1854. Rev. William Richie was resident until his death. The charge was vacant until 1865 but was
        continuously filled since that.
32   Ibid, p. 13. This building was pulled down in 1870. The new church was built in Rossi St, in 1871.
33   Ibid, p. 14. In 1838 two priests, Father Bermingham and Father McAlroy were appointed to Yass and they
        visited Goulburn periodically.
34   Register, of the Sisters of Mercy, Wilicannia-Forbes, and Congregation supplied by Sr. M. Ryan Australia.

The whole of Yass inhabitants came out to welcome the Sisters when they arrived.[35] The reception for the first Sisters of Mercy in Yass was public and the ceremony was the most enthusiastic and impressive ever in the locality. Some miles outside Yass the nuns were met by people on horseback and in carriages. The grand greeting took place at O'Briens Bridge three miles from the town where an immense throng assembled and *'the little group of pious women were escorted in triumph to the town.'* A band headed the procession to the town playing a variety of irish airs and ended up outside St, Augustine's church with *'Home sweet home.'* The girls under eighteen brought flowers. They lined up either side and put flowers on the ground. Every denomination gathered there –Catholic Presbyerians and others. The people of Yass presented an address.[36]

This welcome must have strengthened the Sisters sense of mission and reminded them of home. However the scene was so different emphasizing to them the culture and way of life led by their new society. So many were on horseback even ladies. They rode side saddle with a double-reined bridle. The school children lined up to be guard of honour. Flowers were strewn along their path to the church door. A grand banquet was prepared. These preparations must have raised the hearts of the Sisters as they started their new life and shows that the Sisters were indeed very welcome in their new home.[37] This show of respect for the Sisters could also be seen in the Irish people as they left lreland.

The Sisters used the same method of organization in their convent here in Australia as they did in lreland. Each Sister had a specific role to play within the small community of Sisters. On the 20th June Dr. Nulty appointed Eliza as Superioress of the Foundation for Yass. Her role was to oversee the life and work of the Sisters. This she did in Yass for nine years.[38] Sr. M. Alacoque McLoughlin aided her as Mother assistant and the same Sister looked after the new novices. Sr. M. Bernard Grennan and Mother Catherine Murphy from St. Bridget's

Convent of Mercy, Yass.

35   Mount Carmel Centenary Book 1875-1975, p. 29. According to the Census there were four hundred and seventy-seven Roman Catholics in Yass at this time.
36   Annals, Rochfortbridge, p. 126.
37   Ibid
38   The Freemans Journal Sydney, 2 December, 1905, p. 19. They founded the convent of Yass, which later was the motherhouse of Murumburrah, Wyalong, Tumut, Junee, West Wyalong, Gunning, Barmedman and Wilcannia.

convent Clara also helped.[39] The provision of a convent and schools were their first concerns. The foundation stone for the convent was laid on the feast of St. Magdalene the 16th July 1876.[40] The new convent itself was detailed in the newspaper The Yass Courier on the 5th February 1878.[41] The Sisters took possession of their convent on the feast of the Immaculate conception 1877.[42] This convent is built of blue stone rubblework, each course well defined. The various openings were surrounded by ornamental brickwork neatly pointed. Letters home to Ireland inform the Sisters that Dr. Lannigan wished Eliza to start a noviceship in Yass.[43]

The sister's work patterns in Yass were in some ways similar to the work being done in Ireland. In Yass their chief work would be in education, spreading the catholic faith, and visiting the hospitals and jails. As in Ireland the Sisters were dependent on donations to keep them going. A local paper states that several handsome subscriptions have been handed over to the Rev. Father O'Keefe for the Yass convent building fund. In March 1876 there were six nuns teaching over one hundred female pupils. Ninety were in regular attendance. The instruction was of a good standard it would appear. The subjects taught were French, German, Italian, Latin, and Music.

The master remained in the old St. Augustine's school and taught the boys for ten years while the Sisters took over the girls and junior boys.[44] In convent schools in Ireland young boys and girls were educated together up to the age of seven years of age. This is still the practice in convent schools today. The children then moved to a boys only or girls only school.

The education given by these Sisters was equaled if not better than that of other Schools. This was the particular wish of the Catholic bishops. To maintain a high standard of efficiency, inspection of a sort had always been imposed upon Catholic schools. Pastors had been obliged since the first provincial Council, in 1844, to see to the erection of schools in their districts and to visit them often, so that they might be in a position to give counsel to the teachers and instruction to the scholars. Not only were the pastors to supervise carefully the teaching of religion, but they were also to assure themselves that the ordinary literary studies were being given all the necessary attention, providing for that purpose only the most suitable teachers. Efficiency had been the theme of many of Pope Leo XIII's letters on education.[45] Inspection had to be more than parochial; it had to be diocesan as well.[46]

---

39   Annals, Rochfortbridge, p. 25.
40   Ibid, p. 141
41   *Mount Carmel Centenary Book 1875-1975*, p. 31. Assembled in St. Augustines's Church was a large congregation including many Catholics from neighbouring towns as well as several persons connected with other religious denominations. The Right Rev. Dr Lannigan the bishop of the diocese was present at Mass, which was celebrated by the Rev. P.J.O'Keefe, the respected clergyman of the district. Rev. Father Dillon of Camden delivered the sermon using as his text the words of Christ 'If thou will be perfect, sell all thou hast, and give to the poor. and thou shalt have treasure in heaven, and come follow me.
42   Annals, Rochfortbridge, p. 30. Also in Mount Carmel Centenary Book (Letters).
43   Annals p. 178, Entry dated 29 July 1879. Eliza wrote to the Rev. Mother looking for well-educated postulants.
44   *Mount Carmel centenary Book,1875-1975*, p.24. Dr. Lovatt built St. Augustine's school of local stone. Mr. Lacey was the first teacher followed by Mr. Gilchrist, Miss Moore, and Thomas Moore. 28 June 1869 Miss McAuliffe and Miss Shannon took charge. In 1875 Mr. and Mrs. Tierney were the teachers, 1876 Mr Holland was headmaster.
45   Ronald Fogarty, *Catholic Education in Australia 1806-1950* (2 vols. London, New York, 1957), ii, p.424.
46   Ibid, p.425.

In 1895 the Second Plenary Council decreed that, in order to promote the efficiency of all schools a priest was to be appointed inspector and examiner in each diocese and this regulation, with the addition that the inspector should submit an annual report to the bishop was later incorporated in the decrees of the Fourth plenary Council.[47] The bishops also requested that the Catholic schools be inspected by government inspectors especially after the schools break with the state in 1875. Bishop Quinn wrote to the minister of education Hon. A.H. Palmer, requesting that Catholic schools be inspected by government inspectors. This request was granted. Bishop Lannigan also made the same request after government subsidies were withdrawn in 1883. This request was granted.[48]

Another important aspect of organization and administration of Catholic education was that of finance. After the Education acts of the eighteen seventies and eighties the full cost of Catholic education –building, equipment, maintenance, staffing, and the like, fell on the Catholic community. Religious teachers were paid very low salaries. Vowed to poverty, these religious were maintained in frugal simplicity. Finance was obtained in many ways. Bazaars, lotteries, raffles, Fancy Fairs and the like were used to provide the necessary monies to run the schools. Records of fund- raising are seen in the records of Wilcannia-Forbes convent and schools. Another source of income was the teaching of music particularly piano.[49]

The Sisters schools went from strength to strength. By the year 1925 a magnificent up to date school had replaced an old building, and was quite an ornament to the town. The girls primary school of those days had also given place to a fine well furnished building, with infant school attached. A counter part of the boys school was erected for a registered high school, perfect in all the latest appointments, science rooms etc. study and recreational halls, and commodious dormitories, dressing rooms, and verandahs for sleeping out purposes. In fact this school had every possible convenience of a modern boarding school which could hold its own with any boarding school in the state. People from the country sent in their children to board with people in the town and the children actually instructed their parents as they had little opportunity to learn themselves.[50] The Sisters worked with the poor in their environment and people at the margins of society.

47   Ibid.
48   Ibid.
49   Ibid. p.445
50   Mount Carmel Centenary Book 1875-1975 p. 34.

Native Australians

When the Sisters were first received by the Yass people in 1875 a group of native Australians assembled. It is interesting to note that they had assembled at the rear of the crowd in the church grounds. The Sisters recorded in detail their meeting with the native Australians. After the Bishops address and the speeches of the notables, the queen of these people dressed in white, stepped forward, and welcomed the *'Sacred Ladies'* on behalf of her people. Both had the same religion.

In the early eighties, the State department of education issued instructions to the Sisters about their schools, forbidding the admission of these Native Australian children among the white pupils. This did not deter the Sisters. They were prepared to give assistance to these people in any way possible. They too would get their chance to be educated. They wanted to help them participate at all levels in society. A separate school was selected for them and a sister selected as their teacher. For a time Sr. M. Alocoque took charge of them. This missionary school was carried on at St. Augustine's former Boy's school. Sr. M. Loretto followed by Mother Xavier carried on the work of teaching these children.

Later, the mission was moved to a new site, when housing had been erected for the various families. Monsignor Leonard built a church so that the spiritual needs of those adults and children could more easily be attended to. This settlement was known as Hollywood. After Hollywood Reserve was established the education department provided a local school and teacher. It was not until 1952, that these children were allowed by the state to enter the convent school.

St. Mary's

As in Ireland when a convent became well established it was common for some of the sisters to start another convent or foundation. The Yass community of 1875 was the nucleus from which developed the autonomous congregations of Murrumburrah, Junee and Tumut. Although Eliza did not go herself, it was from her foundation that sisters traveled to help develop a convent at Murrumburra.

Mother M. Xavier Leahy, Sister Berchmans Nally and two novices, the first two of their own pupils to enter at Yass, made up the foundation. Here it is interesting to note that postulants from Australia were now helping to fulfil the educational needs of the Australian people. They had to occupy a small cottage without the Blessed sacrament. The people were very good to them. Mr. John Bourke gave a fine block of land on which very Rev. Fr. Butler erected a new convent. It had spacious grounds and every convenience. Education was perhaps one of the first priorities of the Sisters. A new school was built at Harden beside Murrumburra. The nuns drove to it every day. In less than a year after Murrumburra Sisters were asked to Tumut. This journey was particularly dangerous.[51] Eliza loved this little convent. Again in Tumut no convent was ready. The Sisters stayed in a rented comfortable stone cottage. The lease expired and again we see the co-operation between Sisters and clergy. The priests gave the Sisters the Presbyery for two months. Dr. Lannigan again appealed to Eliza for nuns for Junee. A colony was sent there in 1888.

Wilcannia

The clergy were continually assessing the needs of the communities in their diocese. A site for the township of Wilcannia was selected in 1863 to provide a service center for surrounding sheep runs, and a port on the Darling River for incoming supplies and outgoing wool. By the mid 1870s it was a busy prosperous town.[52]

The diocese itself was formed in 1887.[53] Right Rev. J. Dunne, a lifelong friend of Eliza was appointed the first bishop.[54] The bishop noted that it had little in the way of religious practice, especially among the men.[55] Again in this area the Catholics were served from Bourke until Fr. Walter Curran was appointed resident priest in 1882. In 1883, Fr. Curran built a stone Presbytery with kitchen annexe. He left the building as a shell so that he could use it as a church and he fitted up the kitchen as living quarters. Father J. Barry succeeded Father Curran.

The average attendance at Sunday Mass was about ninety, with fifty children on the Sunday school roll. There was no Catholic school. Bishop Dunne urged the people to support a bazaar to pay off existing debts, and then to work towards providing a school and convent before inviting Sisters to Wilcannia.[56] Again we see the clergy instigating the building of a Catholic school. In 1888 Bishop Dunne after a Mission given by Vincentian priests urged

---

51   Mount Carmel Centenary Book 1875-1975. p. 42.
52   Research notes supplied by Sr. Mary Ryan, Australia.
53   Patrick Francis Cardinal Moran, *History of the Catholic Church in Australia*(Sydney, no date but circa 1896), pp 403-404.
54   Diary of Bishop Dunne, 1887-1892. Archives of Diocese of Wilcannia-Forbes, copy in the Archives of the Sisters of Mercy, Wilcannia Forbes Congregation. Bishop Dunne was born in Rhode Co. Offaly.
55   Ted McMillan (ed.). *The Wilcannia historical Society Guide Book*, pp 1,6,8. Copy in W.F.M.A.
56   Booklet on the History of Wilcannia and White Cliffs, pp 28-29 (Author and Title Unknown.).

the people to provide a Catholic school. In February 1890 Father P. Davern replaced Father Barry in Wilcannia.[57] He was ordained for the Bathurst Mission and arrived in Australia in 1869. Previous to his arrival in Wilcannia about Feb 1890 he was for several years stationed at Bathurst and Wentworth, He was a man of a very liberal mind a good worker. He worked there from 1887 to 1916.[58] He wanted Sisters to help particularly with instructing the youth. The wishes of the Church were again answered by a group of Mercy nuns. Eliza, now in the twenty sixth year of her profession got permission from Dr Lannigan and she and six Sisters prepared to go to Wilcannia. The Sisters were Sister M. Gertrude Grogan, Sister M. Ignatius Markey,[59] Sister Mary,[60] Sister M. Columba Garry, Sister Millie Cummins, and Sister Minnie Grogan.

The sisters left Yass on the feast of the visitation, the 2nd July 1890 accompanied by Bishop Dunne.[61] They arrived at Wilcannia on the 22d July 1890. The people again cooperated with the Sisters in their work and without them the work of educating the children would have been very difficult if not impossible. They were very generous to the sisters. Mr. E. J. Donnelly of Wagga, who owned properties in the Wilcannia district, loaned the sisters two adjoining stone cottages rent-free. They had been fitted up and supplied with all necessities by the ladies of the town. Bishop John Dunne celebrated Mass for the Sisters on the feast of St. Appolonaris on the 23rd July 1890 and he appointed Eliza Mother Superior, Sister M. Gertrude Grogan as Mother Assistant, and Sister M. Ignatius Martley as Mistress of Novices.[62] The sisters were welcomed by all classes of the community, and, not wishing that the grass should grow under their feet, a high school and primary school were started on the following Monday.[63]

Convent of Mercy, Wilcannia

57   *The Town and Country Journal Sydney*, 18 Aug. 1888, p. 328.
58   Diary of Bishop John Dunne, 1887-1892. Visitation of Willcannia Parish- Auug 5-12, 1888; 27 April,1890; 1 Feb. 1891; 14 Feb. 1892.WFDA
59   *Mount Carmel Centenary Book*.Native of Thurles, Co. Tipperary.
60   Rose Carey came to Australia from Rochfort Bridge on the same boat as Eliza Fielding. However She did not enter the Yass Convent until 1879 There is an entrance record for Rose Carey in the Register of Sisters of Mercy, Yass. Copy in WFMA. As Sr. Mary she was a founding member of the Tumut Congregation in 1883, completing her novitiate and making her profession in that town. She was a lay sister, caring for the needs of the Sisters and boarders and looking after the Convent. She continued this work until her death in 1923.
61   Diary of Bishop John Dunne, 1887-1892.
62   The Freemans Journal, Sydney, 17 March, 1894.
63   Diary of Bishop John Dunne, 1887-1892.

What type of environment did the Sisters live in, in Wilcannia? Wilcannia was referred to as a remote and comparatively unknown part of the country. At that time they would have seen the wool being brought to the port by bullock teams or camel trains. It was then transported to Adelaide or Melbourne by the many paddle steamers that plied the Darling and Murray rivers whenever they were navigable. Mount Brown sent its gold ore through the same bustling port.[64] However life was difficult for the sisters. Their records tell us that they lived for many decades without the convenience of electricity, sewerage or running water in the convent, and through times of terrible dust storms, droughts or floods.

Focussing on the needs of the people, they did what they could to bring them practical help, the comforts of religion, and hope for the future of their children.[65] When the sisters arrived in Wilcannia the schools were not ready. The children were taught in the temporary church until the church and school was completed. The building progress was slow, as it was difficult to get men and materials. Fr. Davern had to act as his own contractor and clerk of works. The school was not opened until Feb. 1892.[66]

By the beginning of 1891, there were sixty children enrolled in the primary School. Protestant squatters and businessmen sent their daughters to the convent High School because of their respect for Eliza and her sisters.[67] Before long plans were drawn up for a new convent, and Bishop Dunne blessed its corner stone in February 1894. The people gave generously, the work progressed well, and the bishop returned to bless and open the building on the 25th Nov. that year. As well as ample provision for the sisters the convent included two High School rooms, music room, and two large dormitories for Boarders.[68]

In 1894 catholic schools both high and primary were flourishing. Bishop Dunne commented in his diary: *'Everything looks promising'*. Bishop Dunne regularly visited the schools and examined the children. The Sisters were receiving cordial support from all, and their schools were highly appreciated. Money was needed in order to do the building work of the convent and schools and to meet the everyday expense of the sisters. A newspaper in March 1894 related that Mr. E. O'Donnel J.P. honorary secretary of the convent building committee complained of the injustice of the law which required catholics to pay a proportion towards an extravagantly administered system of education of which they could not conscientiously avail, while having at the same time to provide and maintain their own schools.

In order to procure a convent a fund raising bazaar was held during the holidays and £230 was raised clear of all expenses. Another bazaar was held in March 1894 that raised £461.[69] The community increased to ten sisters when Mary Tandy (Sr. M. Stanislaus) arrived from Ireland to join them on the 28th October so they would have appreciated their spacious new convent. Sr. M. Stanislaus Tandy later taught bookkeeping, among other subjects. Eliza was superior of the Wilcannia community from the year 1890 until 1902, when failing health

---

64   Notes provided by Sr. M.Ryan, Wilcannia-Forbes Congregation, Australia.
65   Views expressed by Mr. W.J.Taylor, Coolabah, in a letter to Mr. Tony Lawler MHR, 24 Nov. 1898. Notes supplied by Sr. M.Ryan, Australia. Copy given to WFMA by Miss Gwen Rowe, White Cliffs History Group.
66   *The Town and Country Journal,* Sydney, 18 Aug. 1888, p.328.
67   *Catholic Directory of Australia, 1891-1902,* Diocese of Wilcannia, entries for Wilcannia.
68   *The Freemans Journal,* 17 March 1894, p.19, Notes of Bishop Dunne 1892-1907, Entries for 25 Feb. 25 Nov. 1894 WFDA.
69   *The Freemans Journal,* 17 March 1894, p.19

forced her to relinquish that charge. [70]The Rev. Mother Gertrude who was educated by her as a girl succeeded her.[71] The sisters at that time in Wilcannia were twenty-eight professed choir sisters and six professed lay sisters. [72] Her letter dated 1st November 1901 states that she expected to retire in May 1902. She lived until 1905.[73] She had been ailing for a considerable time and died on Thursday the 23rd November 1905. Her remains were taken to the church next day where Mass was celebrated. She is buried in the little cemetery in Wilcannia on the banks of ths Darling River.

The Sisters laboured ungrudgingly training the young, visiting the sick, comforting the afflicted, instructing the ignorant, satisfying themselves and edifying their neighbours.[74] From the point of view of education in general and Catholic education in particular the contribution of the teaching orders was a significant one. But the magnitude of their contribution was not to be measured in terms of education alone. The struggle for education raised the morale of the church itself. Catholic education policy was inevitably influenced by the social composition of the Catholic community itself the largest element of which was the working class. There would have been nothing for these children if the church in particular the Sisters did not provide it. The stance taken by the Catholic schools in Australia to work outside the state run education system, did not coincide with that taken by other churches at the beginning.

The Anglicans later admitted that the stance taken by the Catholics was the correct one.[75] Ten years after the Secular Act had been passed dissatisfaction began to be heard by the state school Boards of Advice. These Boards advocated the introduction of the scripture lessons. Dissatisfaction with the state school system was also evident in the reports of the two big Royal Commissions of 1881 and 1899 and in the press. The 1881 report recommended the introduction of general religious teaching of a non- sectarian character. The 1899 report drew attention to the fact that the purely intellectual aspect of education was in danger of being over emphasized at the expense of the moral and religious. This in turn lead to the setting up of associations called *Bible in School Leagues* who formulated their own manifesto. One of their aims was to have the bible read in schools as part of the normal studies. They were backed by the protestant denominations generally. Wesleyan and non-Anglican groups also supported the Leagues. Catholics were quite opposed to the idea. For them it meant introducing the Protestant principle of private judgement on the bible. This was to them a double injustice-those who had to attend state schools and Catholics who paid taxes to support state schools. Others opposed it too i.e. the Education Defense League. They regarded it as proselytizing. The state schools were teaching the religion of some at the expense of all. When referenda were held in 1896, 1904 and 1910 only in Queensland was there a yes vote to having scripture reading in state schools. Legislation was put through to that effect in state schools and it became law. In South Australia 1940 religious instruction was permissible in state schools.

Schools that were independent from state support could experiment with new courses. The religious question of the nineteenth century became a social and economic question in the

---

70   Notes and Annals of Bishop Dunne, 1892-1902: Entry for Oct. 1894, notes on the arrival in Broken Hill of Mary Tandy, Postulant for Wilcannia. Entry for the 21 June 1897 records her profession. WFDA.
71   Register of the Sisters of Mercy, Wilcannia Forbes Congregation.
72   *The Freemans Journal,* Sydney, 2 Dec. 1902 p.19.
73   Catholic Directory of Australia 1891-1902: Diocese of Wilcannia. Entries for Wilcannia.
74   Freeman's Journal Sydney, 17 March 1894.
75   *The Advocate,* Sydney, 28 July 1894 p.8.

twentieth century. Private schools were not getting grants either and so it became a social or justice problem A certain amount needed to be allocated for each child's education regardless of religion.[76] Catholics in Australia were not content to send their children to state-run schools which they regarded as secular schools. They wanted schools with a religious ethos. Establishing schools without state monies however was difficult. To overcome this problem bishops in Australia looked to religious orders in Ireland and Europe to staff their schools. Sisters from the small village of Rochfortbridge answered the urgent need of providing teachers for a national school in Yass Australia. When preparations were completed, Eliza and a group of sisters made a long dangerous journey to Yass. They were warmly welcomed on their arrival perhaps indicating the urgent need for teachers. Here as in Ireland the sisters were prepared to depend on local contributions to fund their work. The fact that Yass was only discovered some fifty years previous posed problems. Yet the sisters had all the basic facilities of a developing town. Travelling perhaps was still a major difficulty. The religious situation was quite different from that in Ireland. Here in Australia dioceses were only being formed and religious groups were living harmoniously. The sisters with Eliza as superior worked in close contact with the clergy. They organized the building of convents and schools, aided by fund-raising and contributions of the people.

The system of education was similar to that in Ireland. They and the local bishop insisted on regular state inspection and regular visits from the clergy. This ensured that the religious schools were efficient as state run schools. The Sisters paid special attention to the needy in their community, setting up classes for the native Australians since they were not allowed to attend the convent schools until the mid-twentieth century. Sisters from the convent in Yass set up other schools and convents in different parts of Australia. Eliza herself traveled west to Wilcannia. Here she continued her work of educating the youth of Australia until her death in 1905. These Irish Sisters influenced Australian education deeply bringing with them their experience expertise and spirituality.

The Sisters of Mercy, teachers and friends on the Reservation

---

76   Ronald Fogarty, *Cathotic Education in Australia 1806-1905* (2 vols. London, New York 1957), p. 460.

REV. MICHAEL McALROY
(Pastor of Yass 1857-1861)

He was born at Brackler County Westmeath on 4th July 1821 son of John McAlroy and — — Ulyer. He studied at Navan and Maynooth being ordained in1849 for the diocese of Kildare and Leighlin. After working at Carlow Cathedral he responded to Bishop Goold's invitation to come to Melbourne which he reached on 13th February 1855.

After a few months at Geelong and Gippsland he fell out of favour with the Bishop and so in the company of Patrick Bermingham he transferred to Sydney archdiocese. They received a posting together at Yass in May 1857. In June 1861 he moved to Goulburn and was considered a likely appointment as Bishop for the new diocese to be erected at Goulburn. However this post went to

Fr. Michael McAlroy

RevWilliam Lanigan and McAlroy went to Albury as Vicar General to Bishop Lanigan in July 1868. In 1875, Fr. McAlroy was sent to Ireland by Rev. William Lanigan to recruit Sisters from the Mercy and Presentation orders to establish teaching missions in the diocese of Goulbourn.

At Rochfortbridge, Sister Bernard Grennan, Sr. Alocoque McLoughlin and Sr. Mary Paul Fielding and three postulants volunteered to travel with him to New South Wales and it was at Yass that the first mission was established. At Albury he established the Sisters of Mercy also. Father McAlroy died after a protracted illness on 14th July 1880 aged 59. He was revered by friends from Goulburn to Albury being remembered as the pioneer builder of 20 or more churches and convents. He was especially respected by the Sisters of Mercy at Yass, Goulburn and Albury and by the Presentation Sisters at Wagga, being involved in their foundations and developments. His burial place is behind the main altar in St Patrick's Church Albury.

~ Chapter 5 ~
Education and the Sisters of Mercy in Nineteenth Century Rochfortbridge
By Betty Mimnagh Dunne

~ CHAPTER 5 ~
EDUCATION AND THE SISTERS OF MERCY IN NINETEENTH CENTURY ROCHFORTBRIDGE
By Betty Mimnagh Dunne

The Sisters and the Education System

The importance of the Sisters communication with the people of Rochfortbridge is borne out by the fact that when people visited the convent it was recorded in the Annals. People came from Rochfortbridge and even as far as from Mullingar. When the Mercy Sisters came to Rochfortbridge they set about educating the children, They aimed to provide a continuous education for them in suitable accommodation. One of the sentiments of the Sisters of Mercy was that

> no work of charity was more productive of good to society, or more conductive to the happiness of the poor than the careful instruction of women, since whatever the station they are destined to fill, their example and advice will always possess influence...(Rule 2. 5)[1]

Their aim therefore was to teach girls in particular. The Sisters taught boys and girls up to the age of seven or eight and then the boys were transferred to the boys school.

The sisters of Mercy in Rochfortbridge worked under the new system of Education set up by the state in 1831. Under this system each school applied to have itself approved by the board. This meant the school must adhere to a certain set of guidelines and regulations. Most of the religious groups of women chose to work within this system from the beginning whilst the Christian Brothers did not. Almost all of the convent schools at this time joined the New National System of Education set up in 1831 with great alacrity. In the late 1850's there were 112 convent schools in connection with the National Commissioners enrolling 44,116 girls. Only 41 were non-Catholic.[2] Monies were available under this system for the teachers and for repairs of the schools. An independent inspectorate helped them to maintain the highest standard of education for their schools.

The Sisters agreed to take children of any religion into their schools even though in fact no other child from another religion wished to attend it. The Synod of Thurles 1850 presided over by Dr. Cullen issued several decrees warning about dangers in the national school system and stated clearly that the separate education of Catholic youth was in every way, to be preferred to it.[3] In 1853, Richard Whately, the Church of Ireland Archbishop of Dublin,

---

1   Mary C. Sullivan, *Catherine McAuley and the tradition of Mercy* (Cambridge University Press,(1995), p. 5.
2   John Coolahan, *Irish Education: Its History and Structure* (Dublin 1981), p. 9.
3   Ibid. p.18.

protested to the Board of National Educational that his two books, Lessons on the truth of Christianity and Christian Evidences, though sanctioned by the board, were not in use even in Model Schools. The Catholic Archbishop of Dublin Dr. Cullen reacted strongly, and the outcome was that approval for the books was withdrawn and Richard Whately resigned from the board. Religious instruction of Catholic children in the National Schools was henceforth to be based exclusively on the Catholic Catechism.[4]

The Board of Commissioners stated that all schools should be open to all denominations. However it is interesting to note that each religious group were only prepared to attend their own schools. Because of this the Sisters probably found it easier to give a religious education to their children.

The Convent Primary School, built in 1896.

The old Convent Primary school just before it was demolished in the early 1980's following the building of the new Convent primary School. The First School at St. Josephs became overcrowded and on the Feast of St. Joseph, 1894, Father Sherlock laid the foundation stone for a new school. Mr. O'Reilly, Killucan was the contractor and the parishioners helped by subscriptions and by drawing sand and stones free of charge. The new School was opened on the 14th. of September 1896 and Fr. Gaughran said mass there and blessed the building.

There was an altar in the classroom in a press that could be hidden if required. Religion was taught and the children prepared for the sacraments. This had to be done outside school hours to satisfy the Board of Commissioners. The nuns prepared the boys and girls for Holy communion and Confirmation. Many they said even at sixteen and seventeen had not received the sacraments.[5]

The sisters had to work with the trustees and manager of the schools on a regular basis. The legal titles to the schools were vested in trustees. Unfortunately many records have now disappeared but some have survived. This school in Rochfortbridge was vested in the trustees for ninety-nine years from the 10th. December 1894.[6]

4   Patrick J. Corish, *The Irish Catholic Experience:A Historical Survey*(Dublin, 1985). P.208.
5   Annals, Rochfortbridge, pp 28,53,86, 89.
6   N.A. Ed 9/11762.

One surviving record states that the Trustees for Rochfortbridge convent school in 1903 were Mr. James Cole, Kilbride Pass, and Mr. Pat Hughes Castlelost.[7] On 21 January 1914 Rev. James Kelly and Rev. C. Murtagh C.C. Rochfortbridge were appointed trustees in succession to Rev. P. Fagan and Mr. James Cole.[8]

Mr. Hughes had nominated Fr. Murtagh.[9] The trustees nominated a manager for the school. This manager in Catholic Schools was usually a priest. The school manager had the right to hire and dismiss teachers, to distribute teacher salaries, to arrange the timetable, to oversee

As part of the rules for Nationals schools according to the National Board of Education in nineteenth century Ireland, whenever a National School was built, a plaque was erected denoting that the building was being used as a National School. All National Schools displayed this plaque on the school building or on an external wall. In Rochfortbridge, the plaque was contained in one of the panes of glass in the Convent Primary School Building.

the general work of the school and he was also responsible for the general maintenance and equipment of the school. Continuous records are not available.[10] It was usually the manager who corresponded with the commissioners on all matters regarding the schools. This work was done voluntarily.

Even though the sisters of Mercy arrived in Rochfortbridge in August 1862 the schools were not fit for use until the 11th. January 1863. These schools cost £150.[11] The debt on the schools and the convent was defrayed by donations and the generosity again of Mr. Coffey, Newcastle, and Rochfortbridge. Monies were also raised for the schools and for the sisters at the profession ceremonies of the sisters. One such ceremony in 1863 raised £120. The bishop usually officiated at these ceremonies.

Donations were given regularly by these benefactors for the scholars. Mr. Coffey in particular was very generous. He gave money to furnish the schools and sent tradesmen to build out offices and enclose the garden by walls, and sow the garden. He bought the crop then for £10. He also gave the nuns a beautiful piano for the benefit of the school.[12]

The attendance at the school rose sharply as soon as the sisters arrived in Rochfortbridge. This indicates the level of confidence the people in Rochfortbridge had in the ability of

---

7   N.A. Ed9/16178.
8   N.A. Ed 9/23596.
9   N.A. Ed9/23942.
10   N.A.Ed 2/34folio 184/185. 22 July 1875 Rev. Fagan was recognized as manager in succession to Fr. Robbins. On 7 December 1896 the manager was Rev. P. Fagan. In March 1903 the temporary manager was Rev. Thomas Gaughan. N.A.Ed.9/23942..Rev. C. Murray was appointed manager to the convent in succession to Fr. Fagan deceased. 9 June 1903 the trustees nominated him. 2/135. Fr. Kelly was nominated by the trustees 6 July 1913 in succession to Fr.C.Murray. N.A. Ed. 9/23942.
11   Annals, Sisters of Mercy Rochfortbridge, p.8.
12   Ibid. p.8. This school was separate from the other school and was attended by the richer children.

the sisters to educate their children. They were recognized as a group trying to improve the educational facilities in the area. For the twelve years from 1855 to 1862 the number of children present when the inspector visited was usually in the twenties or thirties. The average number of children on rolls is perhaps a better indication of the number of children in school. This number was usually in the fifties or sixties. In 1862 the attendance at the schools was very good. There was about twenty at the benefit school and eighty at the other school. Children of respectful farmers attended this benefit school. French and drawing was taught. The number on rolls in October 1863 rose sharply to one hundred and thirty one. The number dropped to slightly ninety two in October 1865. It rose to one hundred and fifty six in February 1867. This was three times the number up to 1858.[13] On the 14th. November 1875 the attendance was low due to the bad weather. The attendance in Rochfortbridge was very good in January 1877 but it was low again in July 1877 because a lot of the children were working in the fields.[14]

The teacher was not just an educator. The bishops regarded the teacher as the coadjutor of the parish priest in the work of spiritual regeneration. Every aspect of the convent school in Rochfortbridge was run by the Sisters, aided by monitors[15] or assistant teachers. Monitors were appointed according to the number of children on roll and in particular the average attendance of these children. The payment to this monitor could be withheld if the average attendance was too low. An example of this was on the 31st March 1901 when a grant to a second monitor Miss S. King was cancelled from the 31st. March 1901 because of insufficient average.[16] Monitors were observed as to their attention to their duty and effectiveness of their training.[17] Monitors in this school were attentive and regularly trained.[18]

The Pupils and teachers of the Convent Primary School taken around 1910.

---

13   N.A.Ed 2/134 folio 184/ 185.
14   Annals, Sisters of Mercy Rochfortbridge, p. 153.
15   The Kildare Place Society in the early nineteenth century adopted the Lancastrian monitorial teaching method, a scheme which had been designed to teach large numbers of children basic literacy and numeracy with a small teaching force and the use of the older children as monitors. As the number of teachers increased the monitors became teachers aids.
16   N.A. Ed 2/135 folio l60.
17   N.A. Ed. 9/9419.
18   N.A. Ed. 9/12369.

Continuous records were not kept but it is possible to ascertain some of the names of teachers from records held in the National Archives.[19] The Sisters as teachers had to work under the regulations set out by the Commissioners. These rules were very strict and covered the teachers work and behaviour. When one examines the qualities expected in teachers and the workload expected from them perhaps only a group such as the Sisters in Rochfortbndge could best fulfil the criteria expected from teachers at that time. It certainly suited their lifestyle where most of their time was devoted to schoolwork. The Commissioners stated that the teachers should be persons of Christian sentiment. This quality certainly suited the religious Sister. The teacher should have a calm temper and discretion. They should be imbued with a spirit of peace, of obedience to the law, and of loyalty to the sovereign. They were limited in their behavior. They were forbidden to take part in any occupation, which might impair their usefulness as teachers. They were forbidden to attend meetings, fairs, markets and meetings for political purposes or to participate in elections apart from voting. In the execution of their duties the great rule of regularity and order –a time and a place for everything and everything in its proper time and place was enjoined as a basic guideline. Teachers had to be very accurate when completing attendance books, report books and registers. One record shows the teacher being admonished for not calling the roll before noon. [20]They were not alone to be neat and tidy themselves but they also had to carry out inspections of their childrens faces, hair and clothes. They also had to look after the sweeping ventilation and whitewashing of the schoolrooms.[21]

There were many problems with regard to the training of Catholic teachers. However the Sisters would have had an advantage in this area. As they lived together in the same house they could consult with one another and discuss educational matters with other Sisters who were perhaps trained teachers or had some experience in this field. English Catholics had secured a denominational training college at Hammersmith in 1850. Catholics in Ireland on the other hand were forbidden to attend the Model schools. The Catholic hierarchy banned Catholic attendance at the Central Training College in 1863. The bishops pressed for denominational training. A Royal Commission of Inquiry into primary education (Powis Commission) was set up in 1868. This enquiry reported in 1870. Although only one third of teachers were trained teachers the state did not give support for denominational training colleges until the 1880s. The Chief secretary George Trevelyan forced the Board to recognize the denominational training Colleges; St. Patrick's Training College for men and Our Lady of Mercy Training College, Dublin for women.[22]They were finally opened in 1883.[23] By the year 1900, 50% of national teachers were being trained.

Being in connection with the Board meant that teachers were paid a fixed salary. In the nineteenth century male teachers were paid better than female teachers. 1870 teachers were paid, male principal £42, female £34, assistant male £22, female £19. This can be compared

---

19   N.A. Ed. 9/9419. Mary Duncan taught 7 July 1877. 1893 there were seven Sisters teaching, two monitors and one lay temporary assistant. 7 December 1896 there were two monitors.

20   N.A.Ed 2/134 folio 184/ 185.
21   John Coolahan, *Irish Education: Its History and Stucture* (Dublin 1981), p. 31.
22   John Magee, *The Canon Rogers Memorial Lecture*; The Master; A social History of the Irish National Teacher 1831-1921, p.14, delivered at St. Joseph's College of Education Belfast, on 2 November 1982, hereafter cited as Canon Rogers Memorial Lecture.
23   Patrick J. Corish, *The Irish Catholic Experience:A Historical Survey*(Dublin, 1985). P.206

to the laborer earning £16 to £23. Unlike other teachers a certain proportion of the nuns salary would have been used for the upkeep of the school. By living frugally it was possible to have funds to help the poorer sections in the community. Teachers were not entitled to pensions until 1879.

The teaching Sisters in Rochfortbridge would also be aided by the fact that teachers generally began to be more organized as time went by. In January 1868 there were meetings of teachers all over the country, one of which was close to them in Mullingar. There was an emergence of a sense of cohesiveness and of group identity that are the embryonic stage in the creation of a profession.[24] Teacher's conditions of work and payment slowly improved as the century progressed. They now would have a contract of employment with a notice of dismissal clause. All teachers now would have a formal pre-service training of twelve months duration.

Inspectors had a vital role to play in education in the convent of Rochfortbridge. The Sisters ensured that their education was as good if not better than other schools as the Board of Education inspectors independently assessed them. They visited the schools regularly and noted that the Boards rules were observed with regard to religious as well as secular instruction.[25]

The inspector or District Inspector as he was known was instructed to make his visits unexpectedly and his duties were extensive, involving a considerable amount of bureaucratic checking and report writing. He acted as a vital link between the Board and the National school. He examined the house or premises in which the school was situated.[26] The inspector also reported on the suitability and repair of the house, premises offices and furniture.[27]

The Sisters of Mercy Rochfortbridge Convent taken around 1897. Back row, from left to right, Sr. Gertrude Smith, Sister Josephine O'Gorman, Sr. Therése Byrne, Sr. Antonia Kelly and Sr. Alacoque Coffey. Front row, from left to right, Sr. Columba Fitzpatrick, Sr. Agnes Weir, Sr. Magdalene Hackett, Sr. Stanislaus O'Neill and Sr. Agnes Nangle.

24   *Canon* Rogers Memorial Lecture, p. 15.
25   N.A. Ed 9/9419.
26   N.A. Ed 2/134 folio 184-185
27   N.A. Ed. 9/6935.

The pupils and schools were inspected three times a year usually.[28] The inspector also studied the Timetable, its completeness, suitability and observance.[29] It was deemed satisfactory in Rochfortbridge.[30] The school accounts were examined and he commented on their neatness, completeness and fruitfulness.[31] The enrolment, classification, attendance, health, comforts morals, manners, discipline, and personal neatness and punctuality of pupils was inspected.[32] The inspector scrutinized the regularity of attendance and punctuality

Time-table for the Convent Primary School of Education in the 1890's

of the teachers.[33] In Rochfortbridge they were regular in their attendance and efficient. The Inspectors also reported on the children's work.[34]

In the years before the arrival of the Sisters schools did exist but their equipment was very poor and they had not basic essentials. In 1855 a book press was needed and roof and glazing needed to be repaired. The inspector recorded this. Yet In 1856 a book press, a blackboard and a teachers desk was still needed. In 1857 books, presses and a blackboard were still needed. The teachers table was still requested July 1st. 1858.[35]

Finance was available if work had to be carried out at the school. This money was not easily obtained. The Board of Works had to authorize the expenditure on these works and inquired diligently until they were satisfied that the rules governing grant aid was adhered to.[36] Disagreements often took place as to whether work was classified as new work or maintenance. New work was entitled to a grant aid whereas maintenance had to be done by the trustees. Grants were paid in 1894.[37] Sometimes there were problems with regard to giving these grants. A ceiling in the convent school was damaged by a storm on the 3rd. February 1903 and according to the managers letter dated the 7th. September 1907 the Sisters were

---

28   Ibid.
29   N.A. Ed 9/9419.
30   N.A. Ed. 9/12369.
31   Ibid. 1897. The accounts were neat and correct.
32   N.A. Ed 9/9419.
33   Ibid.
34   N.A. Ed. 9/12369.
35   N.A. Ed 2/134 folio 184-185
36   N.A. Ed 9/11762.
37   N.A. Ed.2/135 folio 160. On 31 July 1894 a grant of £532 was paid on £798 expenditure and a grant of £51-18-4- on £77-17-6. Unfortunately the nature of the building was not cited on the records.

in terror of their lives.[38] The manager regarded this as an entirely new work for which monies were expected. This was a serious situation as many of the parents had refused to send their children to school. On the 10th September 1907 the secretary of the office of National education wrote to the manager Rev. C. Murray P.P. Rochfortbridge informing

The Convent of Mercy in 1911

him that the work was maintenance and therefore the trustees were responsible for repairs without State aid. The matter was resolved and on the 1st. October 1907, plans by Anthony Scott & Son Architects 34, Lower Sackville Street, Dublin were forwarded to the secretaries in the Board of Education Dublin. The inspector Mr. J.M. Bradshaw had to make a report and state why the plaster was taken down even though the manager stated that it was falling down. His letter on the 13th. Nov 1907 to the secretaries of education states this. The plaster had come down in large patches and in several instances the lives of the pupils were endangered. The loose portions were consequently removed.

The architect thought it unsafe to replace this ceiling with a plaster one. He suggested that a pitch pine ceiling would be more suitable. Mr. Williams, the Secretary of the Office of National Education, on the 30th. November 1907 informed the secretary of the Board of works that the manager Rev. C. Muray P.P.. had applied for a grant to put up timber ceilings and also to erect a verandah and a water closet for the teachers. Mr. Williams, on the 13th. January 1908 stated that the cost of a plain timber ceiling was £66. The plaster ceiling was removed before the local officer had seen it. This also caused a problem even though it had to be done. The inspector suggested that "the proposed verandah or shelter shed was a desirable improvement and the cost of erecting it £32.18-.9, as estimated by the managers Architect, was reasonable".[39] A grant of £65-19-2 on expenditure of £98-18-9 was granted to provide plain timber ceilings and to erect a verandah at the rear of the school for the children to shelter in on wet days during recreation hours. Mr. Williams secretary to the Commissioners sanctioned this grant on the 16th March 1908. The manager had to provide a third of the cost. A closet for the teachers was refused at this time. H. Williams secretary of the Board of Works informed the Commissioners of National education that the work was completed on the 15th. September 1908. Another stipulation on the payment of grants was that they were not made until all work was completed. A letter written on the 20th July 1908 to Rev. C. Murray, P.P Rochfortbridge, by H. Williams stated that the verandah was not completed. The closet or W.C. for teachers was refused even though there was a room

---

38   N.A. Ed. 9/11762.
39   N.A. Ed. 11762. The architects were Anthony Scott M.S.A.& Son (A. Colman), (Dublin & Navan), 34, Lower Sackville Street, Dublin.

and it had a cistern and a supply pipe. The inspector recommended that it was passed but it was not.[40]

In the 1860s the teaching method used was the simultaneous method, or class group method where all children were taught at the same time. This method did not change until after 1970, when more emphasis was laid on small group learning or individual learning.

Curriculum and Learning

The whole lay community took an active interest in the children's work at school. They were examined both by a goup of influential individuals from the community living in Rochfortbridge and at a different time of the year by the inspector. Earliest records of the children being examined are in the Sisters Annals. In 1866 a public examination of the school children took place at which a number of clergy and gentry with parents of the children were present.

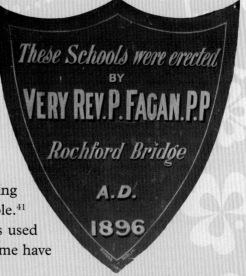

According to the Sisters Annals the children's answering in the various branches taught them was truly credible.[41] Bishop Nulty visited the schools regularly. The books used were those prescribed by the Board of Education, Some have claimed that these books were the best text series produced in the English speaking world.[42]   The grants of free stock were given on condition that the

A plaque, designed by O' Riordans of Dublin

school purchased some books. On the 16th. May 1882 a grant of free stock and school requisites worth £5-10s was given.[43] On the 22nd. December 1896 grants of £7 free stock were given on condition that £2 sale stock was purchased.[44]

The Commissioners published a set of reading books for five different grades, which quickly established a high reputation for themselves in Ireland. Their cheap price and the grants encouraged their use. The board also published texts on arithmetic, geography and agriculture. The religious quality of the books, despite their dogmatic neutrality, gave the teachers of every national school in Ireland an opportunity to mix religious instruction with literary instruction.[45]

---

40   Ibid.
41   Annals, Rochfortbridge, p. 15. Other public examinations cited in the Annals are on the 20th. June 1870 and on the 11th. May l878. The individuals examining the children were impressed by the children's proficiency at piano. The inspections carried out by the inspector were on the 27th October 1873,the 3rd. August 1874,the 28th. October 1875, and on the 6th. October 1879. In 1881 two inspectors spent three days examining the children.
42   Donald H. Akenson, *The Irish Education Experiment, The National System of Education in the Nineteenth Century*(London, Toronto, 1970,)p.229.
43   N.A Ed. 2/134 Folio 160.pp 184-I85.
44   N.A. Ed.2/135 folio 160.
45   Donald H. Akenson, *The Irish Education Experiment, The National System of Education in the Nineteenth Century*(London, Toronto, 1970,)p.237.

Irelands history was not taught. Perhaps the Commissioners thought that it would have been too controversial at this particular time. As the years went by the Sisters had to be aware of educational change and try out new ideas in the field of education. Some of these changes were good. Some were not. The Sisters had no option but to work with new innovations in education if they wanted to stay under the new system of education.

The biggest change came in 1870 when The Powis Commission issued changes in the National school system. In all national schools the National Board discontinued the publication of textbooks but retained the right of sanctioning such books.[46] Compulsory attendance was introduced. The Commissioners also suggested that in any area where there was a large enough number of children belonging to a particular religion a denominational schooling should be permitted in that area. Perhaps the biggest impact came from the introduction of the payment-by-results scheme. Children now would be examined annually by an inspector in reading, writing, spelling and arithmetic. Grammar and geography was added from third class upwards; needlework was taught to girls from first class and agriculture for boys from fourth class. A large number of extra subjects could also be offered provided that the obligatory subjects were satisfactorily taught. A fixed sum was paid for each child who passed in each subject, providing the child had made a given number of attendances during the year preceding the examinations.[47] The inspector examined and tabulated the success of each individual pupil in each subject using his own ingenuity in devising the tests.

It was an attempt to accelerate the acquiring of basic education by young children. If the children did well in examinations the Sisters earned some extra money. This payment by results system came into effect in Ireland 1872. However it was a crude and simplistic

Grattan's Parliament in session 1798

This picture depicting a session of Grattans Parliament in 1798, hung for many years in the Convent Primary School before it closed in 1980.

---

46   John Coolahan, *Irish Education: Its History and Structure* (Dublin 1981), p. 26.
47   Donald H. Akenson, *The Irish Education Experiment, The National System of Education in the Nineteenth Century*(London, Toronto, 1970,)p.317. Vice Regal committee of inquiry into primary education (Ireland), 1913; Final report of the commission, p.3 [Cd 7235], H.C. 1914, xxviii.

mechanism devised to please those who wanted to see results for the money being expended on education. This system probably put teachers under a lot of extra pressure in their teaching. Attendance however at school improved when the payments-by-results was introduced. This scheme gives us an insight into the type of teaching and subjects, which the Sisters did in the latter half of the nineteenth century. They had to work with a precise program in school. This must have led to a very narrow program and an approach, which asked the children to learn by rote without perhaps understanding the content of the subject matter taught. The aim was to be able to answer the inspector whatever questions he might ask. As for the weaker child, he was certainly aware of his failings and self- esteem must have been very low.

The inspectors had to investigate the adequacy of time and the teachers attention devoted to each subject and whether each had been regularly, taught from the opening of the results year. He was asked to pay particular attention to agriculture and needlework and extra subjects.[48]

Obligatory subjects were reading, writing spelling and arithmetic. The book the child was on denoted a child's progression through the school. If the children were successful in the three Rs two extra optional subjects could be taken in the senior class selected from a long list of subjects. This payment by results system while it had a lot of faults it did ensure a wide variety of subjects for the children.

By examining records we get some idea of the extra subjects taught by the sisters in Rochfortbridge. Music both instrumental and vocal was always an important subject taught by the sisters. Vocal Music was taught by Anne Pilkingon in 1861 and 1862.[49] Teaching music was continued in 1863, 1864 and 1865. £5 results fees were received each year for this subject. On the 13th. November 1874 the Annals states that the bishop was impressed with the children playing piano.

In 1877 the Annals record £50 results fees received January 1877 for 1876. This increased to £54 for the year 1877,[50] and £71-10[51] for 1878. On the 21st. November 1873 a work mistress was appointed in the schools under the same conditions as in industrial schools.[52] From 1879 Irish could be taken as an extra subject for which fees would be paid. Records state that classes in instrumental and vocal music, machine sewing, dressmaking bookkeeping drawing and cottage gardening were provided in 1887.[53]

On 23 october 1883 the inspector recommended that physical Geography, girls reading book, machine sewing,drawing and French be taught as extra subjects. Records relating to 1890-1891 gave an idea of the subjects taught these years. On the 28th. July 1890 the Manager made an application for sanction for the teaching of machine sewing, dressmaking, girls reading book, domestic economy, bookkeeping, French, and the new program for vocal music. There were a good variety of subjects and they should have been very useful to the girls in seeking employment. On the 25th. October 1890 the Manager sought to have physical geography

---

48   N.A. Ed. 9/9419.
49   N.A Ed. 2/134 Folio 160.pp 184-185.
50   N.A. Ed. 9/6035.
51   Annals, Rochfortbridge, p. 168.
52   N.A Ed. 2/134 Folio 160.pp 184-185.
53   N.A. Ed 9/12369.

taught instead of French. The Inspector was asked on the 30th. October to inform the Sisters that the commissioners declined to pay results fees for physical Geography. All subjects excluding physical geography were taught from the 1st. July 1890 and Hygiene replaced physical geography. It was taught from the 4th. November 1890.

Convent of Mercy, 1924

On the 21st. April 1891 the inspector reported that extra fees should not be paid for hygiene, as the teacher was not qualified.[54] This decision was overturned on the 23rd. July 1891 the district inspector L. S. Daly reported that hygiene was examined as a subject. The examination was conducted on paper. The pupils had to answer six questions. Records of the answers the children gave to the set six questions have survived together with the children's names and the questions.[55] Answers perhaps give an idea of social conditions of the time.

Table 5: 1891 Pupils who sat the hygiene examination.[56]

Bridget Dinnegan	Maggie Boyhan	Bridie Grehan
Kate North	Nannie Gavin	Mary Nangle
Mary Reynolds	Mary B. Connell	Mary Garr
Anna N. Nangle	Nannie Geraghty	Letitia Delaney
Anna McGarry	Agnes Cole	Annie Noonan
Marcella Flynn	Hetty Egan	Bridget Garry
Hetty Egan	Teresa Duffy	

A letter the 21st. November 1891 from Mr Molloy the inspector to the Commissioners of Education cites that Sister Mary Magdalen Hackett, the Rev. Mother taught this subject and was very competent. He suggested that the results fees should be given for that year. These were subsequently paid on the 8th. December 1891.[57] On the 14th. April 1891 inspector O'Reilly reported the following subjects taught in the convent school.

---

54   N.A. Ed. 9/6935.
55   Ibid.
56   Ibid.
57   Ibid.

Table 6[58]

Children	Subject	Time	Day
14	Machine Sewing Dress Making	11.30-12.30	Friday
14	Domestic Economy	3.00- 3.30	Mon-Fri.
3	French	9.30-10.00	Tues-Thurs.
18	Hygiene	3.30	Tues- Thurs.
6	Instrumental Music	9.30-3.30	Each day
95	Vocal Music	11,00-11.30	Tues- Wed.
75	Drawing	11.00- 11.30	Tues- Thurs.

Teaching extra subjects was not easy for the Sisters. They needed financial aid, which was not always forthcoming from the Board of Commissioners. A letter dated the 20th. May 1891 from Fr. Fagan to the Commissioners stresses that monies earned were urgently needed. The Sisters, he said were very poor and were mainly supported by earnings from the Board.[59]

Convent Primary School, 1928.
Back row from left to right, S. Casey, Rita Walsh, Nancy Walsh, Annie Hyland, unknown, Kathy Hyland, Brigid Gavin, unknown, unknown, Ina Whelehan and Toni Fallon.
Third row, from left to right, Barbara Rowan, Nancy Gavin, Lizzie Leogue, Maggie May Gorman, Mick Gavin, Mary Ignatius Gavin, Katie Gavin, Unkown, Brigid Healy, Mary Cleary and Margaret Cleary.
Second row, from left to right, Unknown, Paddy Cully, Liz Hyland, Mary Quinn, Kay Whelehan, Maureen Whelehan and Unknown. Front row, from left to right, Unknown, Isaac North, Mick Murray, Paddy Keogh, Kevin Geraghty, Mick Whelehan, Lalty Gavin, Unknown and Joe Rowan.

---

58   Ibid.
59   Ibid.

In 1892 the manager wanted the following subjects to be taught for the year ending 1892, hygiene, practical cookery, bookkeeping, machine sewing, domestic economy and girls reading book.[60] Cookery and housekeeping generally would have aided the girls in securing work in the bigger houses, such as West House, West-Lodge, The Cottage. Drumman Lodge, and Heathfield. This would have provided them and their families with much needed income.

Perhaps the children's experience in school in learning these subjects would have been passed on to their parents. Hygiene was discontinued in 1894.[61] Assessment both of the children and the teachers was continual. The inspector J. McMahon stated that the nun who taught agriculture on the 12th. December 1894 was competent.[62]

In 1889 shirt making, a valuable asset to the children when they grew up, was part of the children's experience in school. Records show that a capitation grant was paid to the sisters in l898 and l899.[63] On the 30th. May 1904 permission was sought from Miss Fitzgerald, organizer of cookery and laundry instruction, to open a hole, about 12 inches in diameter in one of the crassrooms for the reception of a stovepipe. This was allowed but the addition of a kitchen for use in connection with cookery classes was not permitted until 14 December 1904. Instead it was suggested that a classroom be divided in two by a partition for this purpose. The commission would be prepared to fund two thirds of the cost of the project. The manager and community would be requested to supply the other third.[64] Another area which would have given the children practical experience for later life was gardening. Some children made a living as gardeners on large estates after their time at school. These children had some valuable experience of basic gardening in school itself and this certainly must have been of great help to them in seeking employment later on.

Records give a map and detailed description of the school garden. It measured one-rood five perches and sixteen yards. The map records the type of vegetables, fruit and shrubs grown and the location of each one. Maybe this information also gives an indication of the diet of the times also.

The inspector Mr. J. McMahon visited the school 1 February 1897. He suggested that the grant be sanctioned on the 6th. February 1897.[65] On the 9th. March 1897 an application for aid to the school garden[66] was refused because the ground allocated was insufficient and inappropriate, and because there was no evidence of suitable and efficient practical instruction of the pupils in garden culture. There was not enough vegetables or livestock. [67]

The manager refuted this and wrote to the commissioners. These letters provide us with very valuable information as to how a group of nuns could teach gardening. Women were not gardeners in the nineteenth century. They also provide us with information as

---

60   Ibid.
61   N.A.Ed 9/9419 also 2/ 134 folio 184/185.
62   N.A.Ed 2/12369.
63   N.A.2/135 folio 160 This states a capitation grant of 12/= was paid for the years 1898-1899.
64   Ibid.
65   Ibid.
66   Ibid. The garden is situated in the plot which surrounds the school It extends for a distance of about 66 yds. long and 7 yds. wide on one side and 5 yds on the other. There are no fences. The garden being entirely enclosed by walls.
67   N.A. Ed 2/135 folio 160 also 9/12369.

to what the garden actually looked like. A letter dated the 13th. March 1897 from Rev. P Fagan stated his disappointment that the school garden was not recognized. He stated that he had spent £22-4s-6d in laying, out plots, excavating for walls, filling in the same with stones and covering with gravel. He had planted shrubs and fruit trees. He also states that the plot was partly in front of the school in an easterly aspect and sufficient distance from the school building. The play area (garden) was at the rear

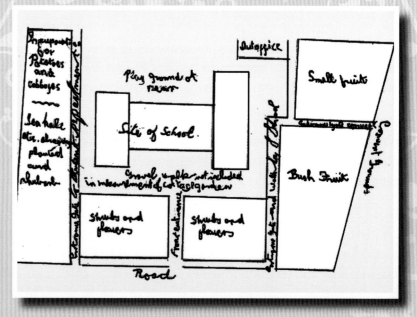

The Plan of the School Graden which was submitted to the National Board of Education in the 1890's.

of the building. He emphasizes that the Sisters had been growing flowers, vegetables and fruit in their own gardens for over twenty years. Interaction between the community and the Sisters is again evident in the help they received in their gardening work.

Here we learn that a Mr. Fox helped them with the garden.[68] This man lived nearby, He had served his apprenticeship as manager for some years in the gardens of a Mr. Smyth, of Gaybrook, Mullingar and afterwards at Castletown House, Celbridge, Co. Kildare. On the death of his father he had returned home to tend livestock etc. This man he stated was always delighted to give his advice and supervision to the Sisters.[69] Pressure was put on the Commissioners even suggesting that the agricultural superintendent could come to Mullingar on the train and make his way to Rochfortbridge. On the 28th. July 1887 the Inspector was advised by telegram not to examine pupils with regard to the school garden.

On the 25th. September 1897 Mr. Carroll, (agricultural superintendent) informed the Commissioners of Education that he had visited the garden in Rochfortbridge Convent School. He reported that it was laid out in most admirable manner for teaching purposes. A large variety of vegetables, flowers and fruits were well cultivated. The fifth class girls were examined and gave accurate answers. He suggested it should be recognized as a model school garden.[70] This garden became a model for other school gardens. Here again is an example of how the sisters were prepared to leave no stone unturned until they had the best for their children.

It was recognized as a model school garden on the 26th. October 1897.[71] A large variety of vegetables, flowers and fruits were well cultivated there, This gardening experience for the

68   N.A. 9/12369.
69   Ibid.
70   Ibid.
71   Ibid.

children would have helped them considerably in their own lives preparing them to supply and expand the variety of their own vegetables, and giving them a better diet. Perhaps the more industrious could sell their surplus thus improving their financial status. Fr. Fagan stated that a lot was being done also in the area of kitchen gardening and window gardening.

Music was another important subject taught by the Sisters. It entailed spending some money on equipment. On the 25th. February 1895 the inspector Mr. McMahon visited Rochfortbridge school, and reported on the suitability of the music room to teach Music. He also had to furnish a sketch of the position and dimensions of the proposed music room. He stated that the room was not used for any other purpose. It was suitably furnished with maps, music sheets, a piano and seats. This room was at the rear of the convent and not directly connected with the school or the convent. The pupils gained access to the room through a door and staircase and did not have to go through the convent. Instrumental music had been taught there since the 1st. September 1895. The Commissioners had no objection to the girls being taught there and the subject being examined for results fees.

Results fees for vocal music were not given to pupils in the infant department. Instruction in Kindergarten could be given for results fees for children enrolled in Infants department.[72] As shown above the education brought by Eliza and the Sisters was different and certainly much better than the previous system. The people of Rochfortbridge recognized this and helped the Sisters in every way possible. Some credit must be taken by the states involvement in education but the difficult work of educating large numbers of poor children involved a lot more than just monetary problems. The Sisters continued to improve and expand their schools. The school-house was enlarged and improved on the 16th. May 1882.[73]

The Convent Primary School 1896

In 1896, Fr. Fagan erected a new school. The date of admission of new pupils was September 1896. The cost was £1,500. The roll number changed from 6674 to 14613, and it was taken in connection with the Board on the 14th. September 1896.[74] The schools were being expanded and improved all the time.

The Sisters too were up to date with educational development. The Superiors, Sr. M. Gertrude Smith wrote to the senior Inspector of National schools J.P. Dalton requesting an organizer for kindergarten on the 29th. May 1913.[75]

Grace E. Austin, 47 Clarendon Street, Derry wrote on the 19th. September 1913 to the secretaries of the National Education Office Dublin saying that Miss Beverage had arranged to come to Rochfortbidge on the 17th. to the 22nd. October to help the Sisters in their work with the children.[76] Convent schools were different than other schools. Various independent people stated this fact in the nineteenth century. Balmer (one of the Powis Commissioners of

---

72   N.A.Ed9/94419.
73   N.A.Ed 2/134 folio 184/185.
74   N.A.Ed 2/134 folio 160
75   N.A.Ed 9/23596.
76   N.A.Ed 9/23596.

1870) states that the Sisters were from comparatively privileged socioeconomic backgrounds and this was evident in their work. He says that '*the refinement of manners which naturally characterizes ladies by birth and education is one of the striking features presented on entering convent schools after leaving a school of any other description*'.[77]

Other commissioners reiterated this opinion. Laurie in 1848 praised the work of the Presentation Sisters attributing their superiority over other National schools to the innate culture of the management staff of the Sisters.[78] The sisters were always ready and willing to take on extra challenges.

Photo taken in the 1930's

Front row, from left to right, Molly Fox, _____, ---Hyland, Eithne Fox, Maggie Keegan, Gertie Kelly, Meta Connell, Mary Bridget Boyhan, Katie Gavin, Biddy Lynch, Nell Eighan and Peter Daly.
Middle row, from left to right, ___Gavigan, Nan Dunne, Nora Fox, Thea Fallon, Maggie May Walshe, Maureen Whelehan, Molly Cleary, Alo Monaghan, Biddy Gavin, Christy Cully and Paddy Curran.
Back row, from left to right, Larry North, Eamonn Duigenam, Larry Duigenam, George Keogh, Tom Geraghty, Jim Treacy, Joe Boyhan, Joe Rowan, Mick Leslie and Nicholas Curran.

---

77   Caitríona Clear, *Walls Within Walls* (Dublin, Washington D.C.), 1987, p.134.
78   Caitríona Clear, *Walls Within Walls* (Dublin, Washington D.C.), 1987, p.134.

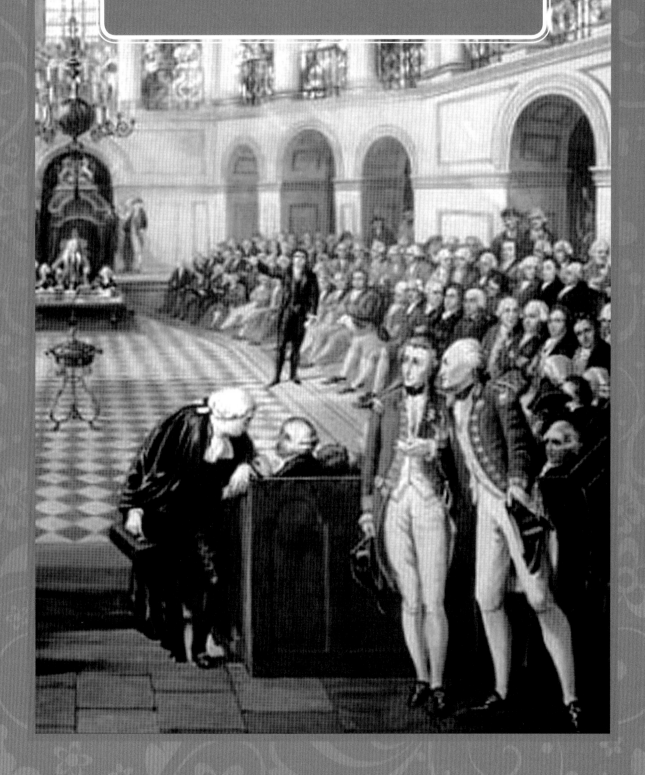

~ CHAPTER 6 ~
'ELIZA THE JESUIT.'

The story of Eliza Fielding's kidnapping incident and the conflicts with her brother Henry

When Mother Mary Paul Fielding established the Convent at Wilcannia Forbes in 1893, one of the sisters, Sister Gertrude Grogan was a member of that community. Sister Gertrude and Sr. Mary Paul, became close friends and in the final twelve years of her life, Mother Mary Paul told her many stories about her early life in Rochfortbridge and the circumstances which led her to convert to Catholicism, her profession as a nun and the decision to follow Fr. Michael McAlroy on the mission to Australia in 1875.

In 1925, Dr. W. Hayden, Bishop of Wilcannia approved the publication of a book dedicated to the six women (two of whom were still alive), who arrived in Australia on the 8th of December 1875 to begin their missionary work there. Two of the sisters, Mother Alacoque McLoughlin and Mother Xavier Leahy were still working in their communities fifty years after the foundation of the Mother house at Yass.

The book entitled *'Life Story of a Valiant Woman,'* was written by Sister Bernard Grogan outlining the story of their foundress, Mother Mary Paul Fielding, twenty years after her death. In a letter to Sister Bernard Grogan Bishop Hayden says:-

> I have read your *'Life Story of a Valiant Woman'* with great interest. Very little is known of Mother M.Paul Fielding except by people who, like yourself, knew her personally. It would be a pity if such an edifying life were lost to Catholic literature; and hence in collecting and publishing the various events of her remarkable career, you have not only done a work for religion, but so also supplied for readers an interesting little volume.[1]

The letter was dated the 21st of November 1924. To meet with the Bishop's approval, the manuscript was submitted to him and returned on that date.

The book itself, a slim volume, all of 110 pages, is filled with many accounts and stories. Some research work would have to have been done also and communication with the Sisters of Mercy at home here, and some of the information recorded in the book tallies also with the Annals of the Sisters of Mercy in Rochfortbridge.

---

[1]   Sister M. Bernard Grogan, *Life Story of a Valian Woman* (1925), The Boys Home, Westmead, Sydney.

The book gives a wonderful account of life in mid-19th century Rochfortbridge, the sailing conditions aboard the Gainsborough on the journey to Australia and the early pioneering years of 19th century New South Wales.

The account, written at first hand gives an accurate description of Mother Mary Paul Fielding's life and is an important source to the local historian.

Events from the lfe of Mother Mary Paul Fielding have been recalled in earlier chapters in this book –especially the factors leading to her conversion, her early years as a Sister in Rochfortbridge and the mission to Yass in Australia.

But there is another very interesting story regarding her early years, recounted in the book and also documented in the Annals of the Sisters of Mercy. Its all to do with her relationship with her brother Henry.

Its the stuff of melodrama and Hollywood movies, an incident recorded by Sister Bernard Grogan and documented in the Annals in Rochfortbridge also. The story spans three chapters in the book and it is worth re-telling it here.

The Fieldings of Rochfortbridge

In Rochfortbridge in the 1840's there was a very strong Protestant population living there. The village, once known as Beggarsbridge, changed to Rochfortbridge in 1828 with the building of a new bridge over the Derry River on the new re-aligned Dublin turnpike road.

The Fielding family who had a thriving business in the poplin industry in Dublin, known as Fry and Fielding moved to a house in the village beside the little Beggars bridge on the Derry river. They lived there for some time and the head of the household, William Fielding who had retired from the poplin industry wished to continue with a trading business in the new thriving village. The village which developed at the end of the 18th century cashed in on the trade resulting in the increase in coach and passenger travel to Athlone and the west. The early buildings, being just of mud wall and thatch were being replaced by local landlords to more comfortable slated buildings. The first Fielding farmhouse(the ruins of which are still standing) housed also the first Orange lodge in the village.

William Fielding was a strong follower of the Orange Order.

Not being contented to live the life of ease in retirement, the Fieldings had moved by the early 1850's to the house and lands which would become the first convent and later, St. Joseph's Deaf and Dumb Institute.

Here he set up a grocer and drapery business and was assisted by his wife and family in running the business there. The Orange lodge moved from the farmhouse by the bridge to the new home also.

From the account given to Sister Bernard Grogan by Sister M. Paul Fielding, she describes the mood of the village as follows:-

The village of Rochfortbridge was peculiarly Protestant, and had a large percentage of admirers of the Dutch Stadth-holder, William of Orange. Many a lively skirmish took place between the 'Orange' and the'Green,' when on the twelfth of July his followers tried to house his statue on the village square. The sight of the 'Hero of the Boyne' roused the frenzy of many a Celt, and his 'Majesty' had generally to beat an undignified retreat, tarred and feathered to boot.[2]

Such were the scenes of feud and unchristian feeling among which Eliza Fielding was reared. They made a lasting impression on her receptive young mind, and perhaps were the cause of the intense dislike that she always manifested towards sectarian strife of every kind. 'Oh, I do detest bigotry,' she would often say, ' it does no good for God or man.'

Within the household, the Fieldings employed servants who were mainly Catholic. Eliza observed their movements, especially their prayer life, the striking of the Angelus bell at 12:00 and at 6:00 each day brought them to stop and spend a few moments reciting the Angelus. Their use of prayerful expressions in everyday conversation was closely observed by the young lady also. From a very young age she found herself drawn to the Catholic way of life.

Apart from the scenes of bigotry witnessed each summer, Eliza had a very happy home life and was educated at the local school. She was one of five children and was the middle child.

Henry was the oldest and took over the family business in Dublin when his Father retired. From the account given by Sr. Bernard Grogan, Henry seems to have established himself as head of the family on his Father's retirement and events at home in Rochfortbridge were constantly monitored by him from a distance. Henry fell in love with and married a Catholic girl and they settled to live in Sandymount Dublin within easy reach of the family poplin business. One would think that by marrying a Catholic, he would be sympathetic to the Catholic way of life and thinking. He was quite the opposite. He loved his wife very much but her Catholic identity was alienated by him and he refused to have any part of it. He loved her as a person but he had a deep hatred of anything Catholic. Eliza befriended Henry's wife and they communicated regularly by letter.

Margaret had moved on also and she married a Mr. Pate, a protestant. Many years later their daughter converted to Catholicism and became a nun, working for many years in the Diocese of Goulbourn in Australia.

The two youngest children were Maria and William.

Eliza was very much influenced by her maternal Grandmother, whom she adored and she was a frequent visitor to her house. Her Grandmother lived with two unmarried daughters and it was on one of her visits that the Aunts complained to the Grandmother that Eliza had contaminated the place with the popish sign, by making the sign of the cross.

But the Grandmother replied, 'that is a good child, Eliza, keep on blessing yourself, for those who bless themselves on earth will be blessed in heaven.'

---

2   *Life Story of a Valiant Woman*, p. 17.

The maiden Aunts of course concluded that their mother was doting and they sent a message to their sister, Mrs. Fielding to guard her daughter from the superstitions of the papists.

In 1848, when Eliza was fourteen years old, her mother died. This event in her life affected her very much, the sadness and loss of losing her mother and thinking about her two younger siblings, Maria and William, losing their mother also would stay with her for many years.

Eliza is accepted into the Catholic Church

Following her mother's death, one of the maiden Aunts came to the Fielding home to care for the children. It was during this period, Eliza began praying to Our Lady and she confided in an old Catholic Gentleman, Mr. P. O'Connell who lived next door of her intentions to become a Catholic. Mr. O'Connell was regarded by the Fieldings as a very good neighbour and was welcome in the Fielding home whenever he called. But the aunt was suspicious of the advice and attention he gave to the young Eliza and she told him he was no longer welcome there.

Some time later, she spoke to him as he passed on the street and he told her not to delay, if she intended to do what she wanted to do. She went to visit Fr. O Reilly, the curate in the village and pleaded with him to instruct her in the Catholic faith. He was reluctant at first as he was afraid that he may not be acting within the law and that she was still quite young. When it was established that she was at an age to decide for herself her preparation began. When it was time for her to be received into the Catholic Church, she stole away from the family home. She left the village by horse and trap and was brought to the house of Mrs. Egan in Kilbeggan by Mr. P O'Connell, his Sister Catherine and a Mr. Thomas Kelly.

She was received into the church in 1858. She was confirmed by Dr. Cantwell, Bishop of Meath and a short time later she received her First Holy Communion.[3]

At this time also, she was introduced to a young priest, who assisted Dr. Cantwell, Fr. Thomas Nulty. Later, as Bishop of Meath, she would become one of his closest friends, a friendship that lasted till the end of his days.

As soon as she was received into the Catholic Church, word reached her father's ears and he was so incensed and angry at what she had done he forbade her to return to the family home. This, she did and she went to work in a shop in Tyrrellspass, where she stayed with relatives.

But time and loneliness softened the old man's heart. Some years prior to her conversion, Henry Fielding took custody of his youngest brother and sister and brought them to Sandymount in Dublin to live with him. He had received his Father's blessing as he felt they would have better opportunities living in the Capital city.

Longing for someone to care for him in his ailing years, William Fielding wrote to Eliza and pleaded with her to return home. She was glad to be reunited with her father again and she

---

3   Annals of the Sisters of Mercy, p. 206.

took charge of the household. Things were changing in the village also as was evident from a very kind gesture her father had made. At the back of the Fielding house, now stood a brand new Catholic Church. Mr. Fielding's gesture of kindness to his Catholic neighbours would change the History of the local Catholic Parish forever.

Fr. Robbins had been seeking a site close to the village to build a Church and he made a request to some of his parishioners for the donation of a site. This didn't happen, but when William Fielding heard of his plight, he donated a site to the parish on his land behind the house. The church opened in 1857 and like a lot of new Catholic Churches of the period, it was dedicated to the Immaculate Conception following the proclamation of the Dogma of the Immaculate Conception in 1854, by Pope Pius IX.

Eliza's conflict with Henry and the kidnapping incident

Back home again and caring for her father, he expressed a wish to have his two youngest children returned to him from Dublin. Henry was very angry with his sister for converting to Catholicism and he made it clear that she would never be welcome in his house. But this didn't stop her communicating with Henry's wife. Occassionally she would call to the house when she was attending to her father's affairs in Dublin. While on these stolen marches, she had befriended her brother and sister once again, as she had not seen them for some years. In time, they looked forward to these secret visits and they longed to return home to Rochfortbridge. William Fielding knew that this might be a difficult task as Sister Bernard Grogan describes in her book:-

> Eliza and Henry Fielding were alike in disposition – impulsive, strong-willed, and determined to overcome all obstacles that might come between them and the carrying out of any project, so there would be sure to be a battle royal over the children.[4]

She planned her strategy carefully. She went to Dublin in disguise and managed to meet the children and they were so excited to be returning to their old home again. She didn't relate to Henry's wife what her intentions were, in case it might bring the wrath of her brother down upon her. The only time she could venture near Henry's house was when he was away on business in the city. Her plan was to snatch the children away and to leave a letter for Mrs. Fielding to relieve her of any anxiety as to the whereabouts of the children. As soon as she had the children with her, pretending to take them for a treat, she had the letter delivered to Mrs. Fielding.

The nearest station to Rochfortbridge was at Killucan and the only train arriving there was late in the evening. She feared she would be pursued if her brother returned at all early from his business. Just as dusk was approaching, she ventured to Broadstone terminus in Phibsboro.

---

4   *Life Story of a Valiant Woman,* p. 30.

When Henry arrived home that evening the explosion of a bomb would not have upset him more than this last performance by '*the traitor*.'

> He fumed and raged, abusing his wife and blaming her for being a party to the conspiracy as he termed it. As soon as he was sane enough to think clearly, the thought of the late train struck him, and away he went full tear to the station, vowing vengeance on all and sundry as he urged on the horses.[5]

Eliza was in dread that he might follow her and her fears were soon confirmed as she heard the thundering sound of the coach and horses. At Broadstone, she found a low stone wall and made the children crouch down behind it until she gave the all clear. She found another spot where she could view any proceedings without being seen. Henry was not alone, he had a number of people with him to help search the train and didn't stop until the train moved off leaving him with the thought that she had changed plans and taken the coach to the country.

Tired and hungry, Eliza took her brother and sister into lodgings for the night. With the children safely in hiding, Eliza felt for Henry's wife and all she had to endure at the hands of her brother and decided the next day to visit her alone at the house in Sandymount to see how she was and what way her brother was taking the affair. When Mrs. Fielding saw her she was upset and concerned that she should have called to the house, as Henry had people watch the place just in case such a thing happened. Eliza entered the house and into the kitchen to speak with her sister-in-law. Mrs. Fielding locked the front door for fear that her husband would make a sudden entrance into the place.

As she expected, someone informed Henry and he came storming back to the house. When he found he could not gain access, he began banging on the door and shouting loudly.

In an instant Eliza was bundled into the coal cellar. Half lying, half sitting, she lay against the coal in fear for her life and as luck would have it, there was a bolt on the inside and she drew it across, just in case Henry decided to open it.

In a fit of rage, Henry went to a locked cabinet and picked up his gun to shoot her. This episode is told with great drama and indeed using some literary license in the story of the Valiant Woman-:

> As soon as the door was opened, he rushed for the gun and swore he would shoot his wife if she did not deliver '*the Jesuit*' up to him. Gun in hand, he searched every room, even the cellar, and Eliza often spoke of the horror she felt when she heard his footsteps so near her. It never struck him to go to the coal hole. When his anger had subsided a little he went away again and he was well out of sight, poor Eliza, black with coal dust and nearly dead with fright, came out of her hiding place and hurried out a back way as fast as she could to some safer place. The horror of this episode never completely left her mind. The thought of her brother staining his hands with murder was a keener agony to her than even her own death. No doubt the prayers

---

5 *Life Story of a Valiant Woman*, p. 31.

of the terrified women drew the protection of the most High upon them as it seemed that the angry man never adverted to the coal hole. She never doubted that had he found her that day he would have shot her, so blinded was he with bigotry and hate, even though he would pay for the rash deed with his own life.[6]

Eliza didn't take the train to Killucan that evening. Instead she enlisted the help of friends who spirited the three fugitives out of the city and in a day or so they were back home safe in Rochfortbridge. William Fielding was thrilled that his two youngest children had been returned to him, but he still feared that the kidnapping episode wasn't over and that Henry would make a further attempt to take them back to Dublin.

In a short few days, a letter arrived from Henry Fielding to his father pointing out to him that he allowed his two youngest children to come under the influence of his infatuated sister. By allowing this to happen, William thought that he might now be estranged from his first-born son whom he cared for so dearly. Then of course, Eliza was also very devoted to her father and was so thoroughly able to manage the household and the family business. He could not live without her and he wrote back to Henry how he felt about both his children.

Henry in turn threatened that if necessary, he would bring armed forces to secure the children. William was advised to refer the matter to the police sergeant Mr. White. He in turn informed Henry that his father would not tolerate any interference with his household and that it would be more prudent if he remained where he was. This cut Henry to the quick and made him more bitter and angry towards anything and everything Catholic.

It was through this anger and hatred that the matter was finally resolved. With no one else to vent his anger on, he turned on his loyal and faithful wife.

> His sister Eliza became his soul obcession, and his conversation night noon and morning were by no means complimentary towards her – *'Eliza the Jesuit'* and *'the traitor.'*[7]

Mrs. Fielding bore his taunts silently for a while until one day she felt she had enough. She dressed herself up while he was in one of his tantrums and she ordered a cab. She told him she was leaving and going home to her mother and would not be returning till certain matters in her household altered.

A number of days elapsed and a message arrived telling her that her husband was very ill and he wanted her to come to him. On her return, she found him very agitated and complaining sadly about his condition. She sat listening to him and sympathizing with him, but she didn't take her coat or hat off. Then he said to her, 'won't you take off that bonnet in your own house?' her reply reflected her unhappiness with his bigotry and would be returning to her mother for the present.

'Take off that bonnet and those gloves and remain with me, and I promise you that the traitor's name will never be mentioned in this house again.'

6   *Life Story of a Valiant Woman*, pp 31-32.
7   *Life Story of a Valiant Woman*, p. 35.

He was as good as his word and life returned to normal in the Fielding house.

Back home in Rochfortbridge with her father's blessing, Eliza brought her two younger siblings to mass in the new Church of the Immaculate Conception and began with the help of Fr. Robbins to instruct them in the Catholic faith, its prayers and practices. In time they were both received into the Catholic Church and received their Holy Communion.

When they grew up, Maria married into a farming family called Kelleghan in Aghamore Killucan.[8] William married Catherine McDonnell from Tullamore and spent most of his life in Dublin.[9]

William Fielding's Conversion

The Fielding house and lands as we know, were to have a different destiny other than a family home and farm. Eliza spent her last years there caring for her ailing father. Eliza herself, now a very staunch Catholic expressed a wish that other members of her family would join her in the Catholic faith. William Fielding in his final days suffered a series of strokes and recovered well enough to communicate with his family. On a number of occassions he was close to death and during these periods, Eliza invited some of her neighbours to pray at his bedside. During some of those lucid moments, she would ask him if he would like to see a priest and he bluntly answered 'No!'

While overcoming one of his turns one day, he called her to his bedside and he requested to see a priest. Fr. O'Reilly, the curate was sent for and he sat by his bedside and had a long conversation with him. On leaving the house Wiliam requested that he return the next day. After a number of visits from the priest, he told Eliza he was receiving instruction and that he was going to be accepted into the Catholic Church. Not long after his conversion, William Fielding died and soon Eliza's life would change forever.

Selling her house to Fr. Robbins for €500 the needs of her younger siblings had to be met. Fr. Robbins then extended an invitiation to the Sisters of Mercy to set up a new foundation at Rochfortbridge, which opened in 1962.

Entering the order of Mercy in Tullamore in 1861, she would later return to the Convent of Mercy in Rochfortbridge in 1864 as Sister Mary Paul Fielding. Working in her community, she helped with the teaching of the young girls now attending the young Convent Primary School and she also taught piano to the girls at the convent. But destiny had shaped a much greater challenge for her which would take her away from her beloved little midland village.

---

8   She had three sons and one daughter. Her daughter Annie later joined the Mercy Order in Navan, taking the name Sr. M. Antonia in religion. She died in 1931. Maria Fielding died in 1902. Maria's descendants the Kelleghan family still live at Aghamore, Killucan.

9   He worked for many years as a Clerk and the family lived at various addresses on the north side of Dublin city. William and Catherine(Kate) had three children, William J., Mary and Lucy. Kate Fielding died in 1896 and William died in 1907. In 1911, the three Fielding children were living at 22.1 Norfolk Road, Phibsboro, Dublin. William J. And Mary never married and both died the same year, 1955 aged 82 and 83 years respectively. The family are buried in Glasnevin cemetery. We have been unable to find details of Lucy Fielding's life after 1911.

In 1875, Fr. Michael McAlroy's mission from the Diocese of Goulbourn in New South Wales to Ireland to seek Sisters who would volunteer to work in the new and vast Australian plains. His mission taking him to Tullamore was stopped in its tracks by a violent storm which led him to take shelter at the Convent of Mercy, Rochfortbridge. This encounter would prompt Sister Mary Paul to be one of the three volunteers to go with him to Australia. Her words to him were

> 'O Father, will you take me; I'll make the sacrifice of all for the conversion of my brother Henry.'[10]

On the 21st of August, 1875, thirteen years after the foundation of the Convent of Mercy, Rochfortridge, Sr. Bernard Grennan, Sister Alacoque McLoughlin and Sister Mary Paul Fielding along with three postulants left Ireland forever. It was a life-long farewell and casting themselves into the arms of a kind providence that has never since forsaken them, they left the shores of Ireland behind.

Many years later, in her final years before she passed away in the little mission in Wilcannia Forbes, Sister Mary Paul was confined to bed due to illness, when a newspaper from Ireland arrived and on it was the death notice announcing the departure of her brother Henry Fielding. The Sisters who cared for her were dumbfounded and reluctant to break the news to her until she had fully recovered from her illness and was strong enough to receive the news. But as they were wondering what to do, there was a commotion from her little room and they ran to investigate what it was all about.

Sister Mary Paul was sitting up in bed and she was in a state of mild hysteria, crying and praising God. Unknown to the other Sisters, a letter had also arrived from Ireland with the news of Henry's death and like her father before her, Henry had been received into the Catholic Church before he died.

He was ailing for some time and he asked his wife to send for a priest. Father Matthew Russell a noted Jesuit priest visited him a number of times and he was received into the Catholic Church.

The request and sacrifice she had made almost thirty years before in Rochfortbridge had come to pass and her prayers were answered. A few short years following Henry's death, she passed away quietly and peacefully in 1905. To sum up this episode in her life the last word is given to Sr. M. Bernard Grogan in the final chapter of her book:-

> After labouring for about fifteen years in the far west, she was called, in her seventy fourth year, to her reward, and died peacefully amidst her sorrowing Sisters, all of whom she had trained to the religious life. In a quiet little cemetery on the banks of the Darling, rest the mortal remains of this valiant woman. Eternity alone will reveal the full extent of the works that follow her.[11]

---

10   *Life Story of a Valiant Woman*, p. 51.
11   Ibid. p.110.

~ CHAPTER 7 ~
THE FIELDING LETTERS

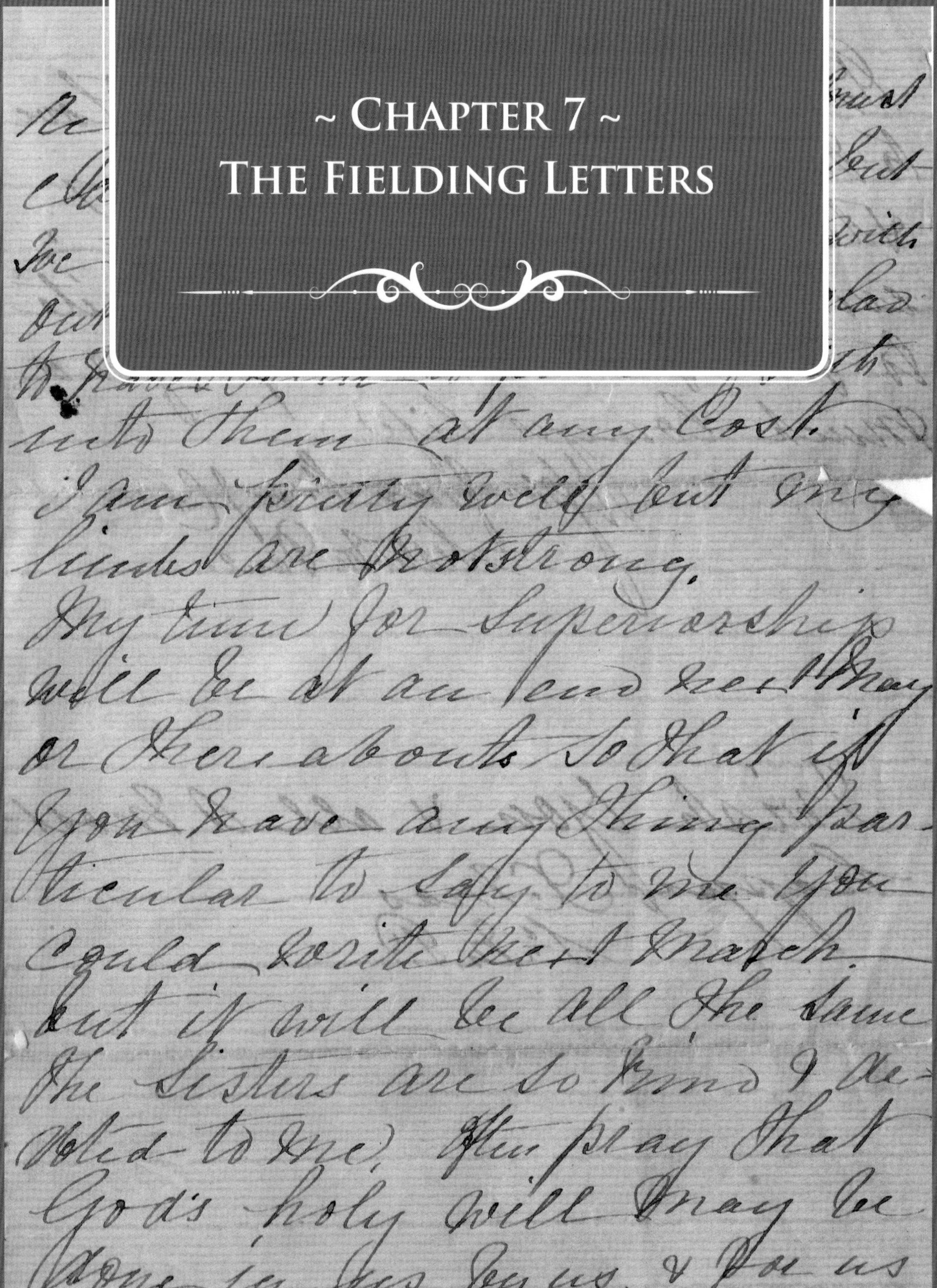

~ CHAPTER 7 ~
THE FIELDING LETTERS

Some letters written by Sr. Mary Paul Felding have survived and give an outline of life at home in Ireland and also in Wilcannia Forbes at the end of the nineteenth century and at the beginning of the twentieth century. Particularly interesting is the advice she gave to her sister Maria Fielding Kelleghan to encourage her daughter Annie later Sister Antonia Kelleghan to become a nun and a later letter she wrote to Sr. Antonia when she received her white veil. Her friendship also with Bishop John Dunne is recorded in one letter when he promised to visit the Kelleghan family while visiting his relatives in Rhode Co. Offaly. Sr. Mary Paul's failing health as well as that of her sister Maria is evident in the letters also. Maria died in June 1902 and Sr. Mary Paul's last letter dated the 9th of November 1901 is more than likely her last correspondence with her sister in Ireland. In the letter, she encourages Maria to write to her the following March, as her term as Superioress was coming to an end and there was an indication that she would have a lot more time to correspond with her sister.

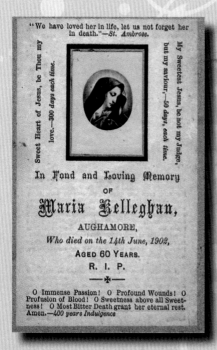

Maria Fielding Kelleghan's memorial card from 1901

The harsh frontier life in those early years in Wilcannia are documented also in the letters, with drought and great loss of cattle and sheep, the high cost of meat due to the scarcity and new taxes imposed on the people also make it impossible for parents to pay for their childrens education, but the Sisters in Wilcannia take them in without any fee, as it is their duty to see that these children as well as being educated academically are also educated properly in the faith.

Sister Mary Paul's close friendship with Dr. Nulty Bishop of Meath is also recorded in the letters as she refers to her dear old friend Dr. Nulty in her letter to Sr. Antonia. Dr. Nulty had died the previous year, but word of his death would not have reached her for months and in the letter she prays that his soul would rest in peace.

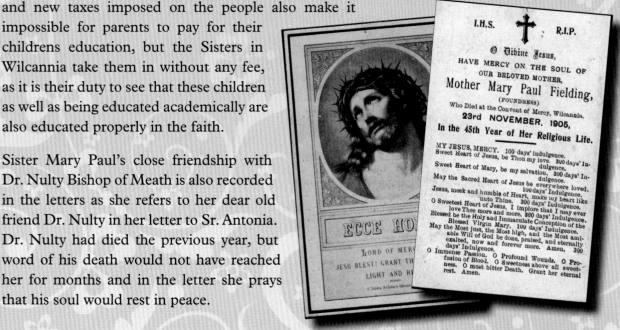

Mother Mary Paul Fielding's Memorial Card 1905.

Convent of Mercy,
Our Lady of the Sacred Heart,
Wilcannia,
July 19th 1897.

My dearest Sister Maria,

Your very welcome letter to hand –I am glad to learn from it that matters are fairly well with you except your poor stiff back. I am so sorry to hear of your suffering in this way and I will pray more than ever that your good God may relieve you if it be His holy will.

If you try to bear your cross well it will add much to your glory in heaven and that is the best place to leave up a store as it will last forever and no one can deprive you of it. We are told that one(Thanks be to God) when we are in pain and trouble are worth more than hundreds of the same when we are in prosperity. So now mind and fill your everlasting store with unfailing riches.

Sister Mary Antonia Kelleghan's Memorial Card from 1931. She was a niece of Sister Mary Paul Fielding.

My health is about the same and I am blessed with kind Sisters who love me and take care of me so that I am very well in my holy religious state provided for thanks be to my good God.

Now about dear Annie, I think if you give her two years education that plenty of convents will be glad to take her with £80, which will pay for her novice ship expenses. It is easy to get into a convent when one is educated but the abscence of this makes matters difficult. I fancy if she likes the order of the Nuns where she is going that they will be glad to get such a subject. I believe Annie is a child of God and that He will remove all difficulties to her giving herself to Him. You need not go to Mullingar to see your friend Fr. Woods. You can write to him at the end of the year and ask him to speak to the Bishop about Annie and tell him who she is, but if you give her another years education, you will be placing more than hundreds in his hands. I will pray that God's will be done in her, for her and by her. I feel as if God has particular designs over her, if so all will go on well.......

Sister Mary Paul Fielding sent prayer cards in letters to her family in Ireland.

(The letter ends there).

Convent of Mercy,
Our Lady of the Sacred Heart,
Wilcannia,
April 9th 1899.

My dearest Sister M.Antonia,

No doubt I was glad to receive your letter which came during the Holy season of Lent and to learn from it that you had received your lovely veil. I presumed your dear Mother was in a great state of delight that the fond wishes of her heart in your regard were so fulfilled.

Please God she will later on see you get your black veil and then her joy and yours shall be full. I sincerely hope your dear Rev. Mother and all her dear children enjoy good health and that she is getting plenty of desirable subjects. You will be glad to hear that we expect a highly educated postulant on the 22nd of this month and I will ask you to pray particularly for her perseverence as I am praying for yours. She was educated by our Sisters and they speak very flatteringly of her abilities.

Sister Mary Antonia Kelleghan as a postulant in Navan 1899

Our schools are splendidly attended and everything is going on well with us thanks be to God for all his care and goodness to us, while a large portion of the surrounding country is quite a desert from the long drought.

I fondly hope that your dear Mother and all at home are well and happy. She does not write often and that is a good sign nothing troubles her besides and give her my warmest love when you are visiting and say that I feel fairly well but I am becoming the old woman fast enough.

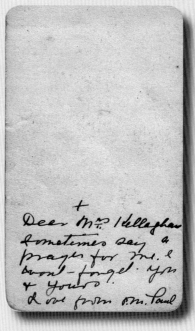

Did you get your new Bishop yet? Poor Dear Dr. Nulty was one of my greatest friends on earth. May his holy soul rest in peace.

Prayer Card

Now I must conclude, as I have no news. With kindest regards for your dear Rev. Mother and Sisters, including your dear self, your fond old Aunt in Jesus Christ,

Sister M. Paul.

Rhode,
King's County,
4th. July 1901.

My dear Mrs. Kelleghan,

I promised your good Sister, my dear old friend, M.M. Paul Fielding, to call to see you and your family.

I hope to have the pleasure of doing so on Monday next(8th July),

With Best Wishes,
I remain,
Yours faithfully in Christ,
+J. Dunne
Bishop of Wilcannia.

Bishop John Dunne

A copy of a note sent by Bishop John Dunne, Bishop of Wilcannia Forbes, Australia to Maria Fielding Kelleghan in 1901.

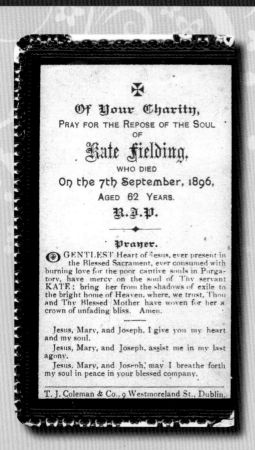

Memorial card for Kate Fielding, wife of William P. Fielding. William died in Dublin in 1907 and is buried in the family plot in Glasnevin along with his wife and two of his children. William J. Fielding and Mary Fielding both died in 1955, aged 82 and 83 years respectively.

A prayer card Sister Mary Paul Fielding sent to Maria Fielding Kelleghan in her last letter to her sister in 1901.

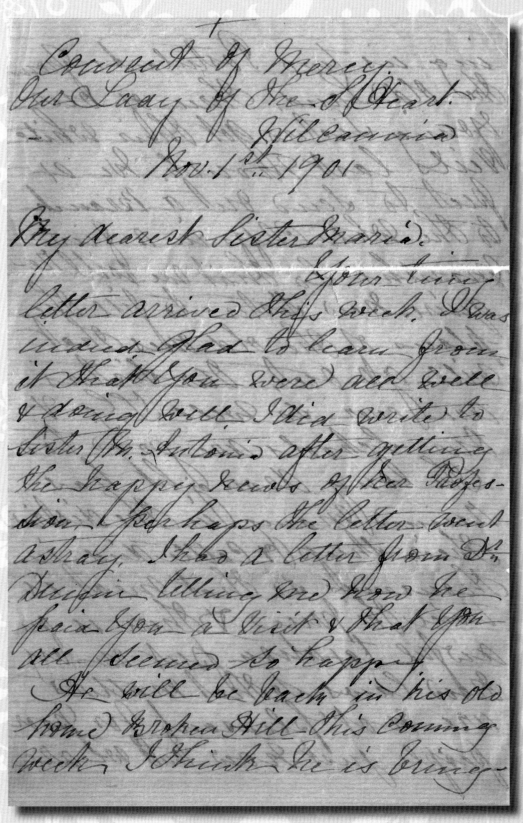

Sister Mary Paul Fielding's last letter to her Sister Maria Fielding Kelleghan.

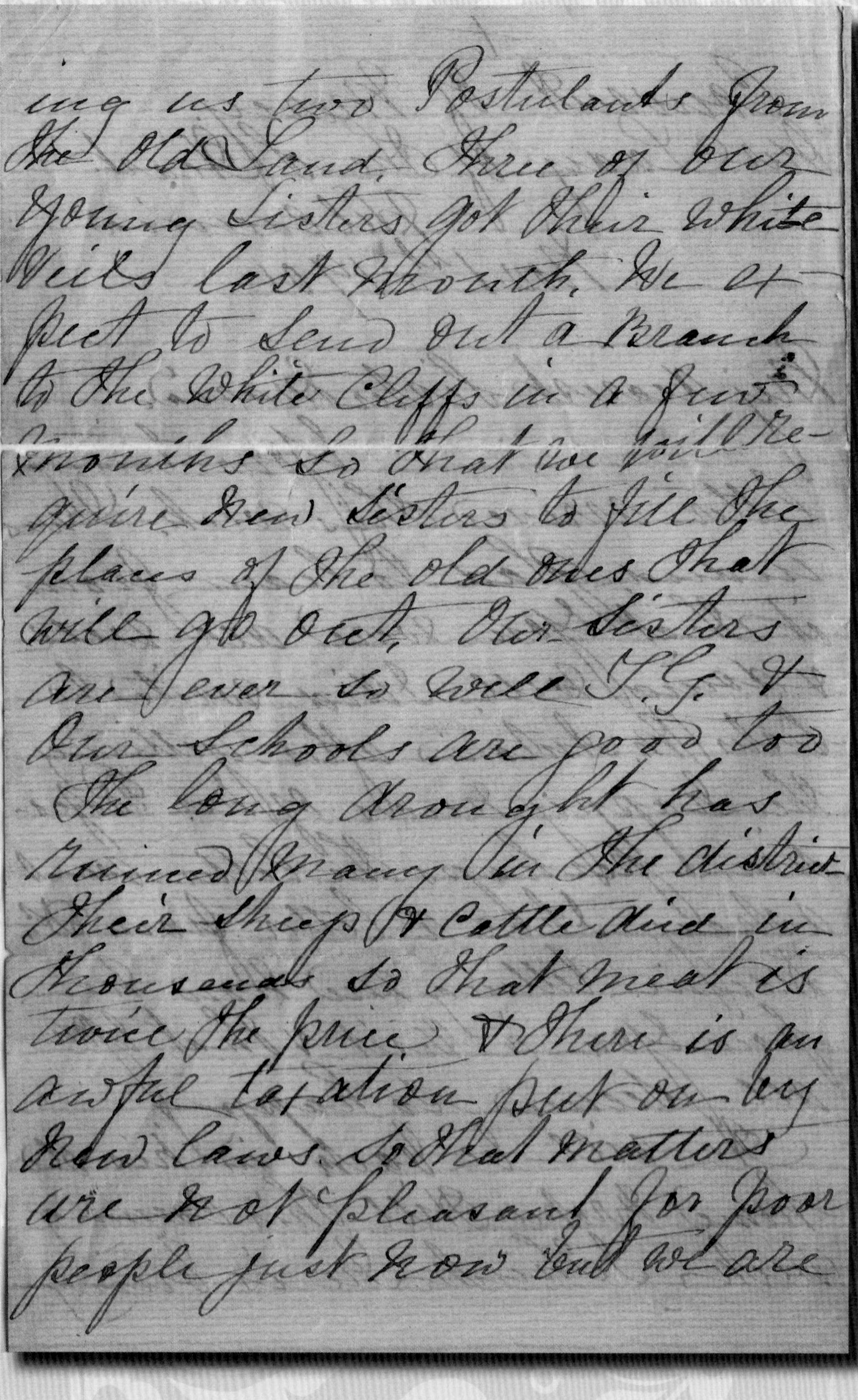

ing us two Postcards from
the Old Land, three of our
young Sisters got their white
Veils last month. We ex-
pect to send out a Branch
to the White Cliffs in a few
months So that we will Require new Sisters to fill the
places of the old ones that
will go out, Our Sisters
are I ever so well T.G. &
Our Schools are good too
The long drought has
Ruined many in the district
Their sheep & cattle died in
thousands so that meat is
twice the price, & there is an
awful taxation put on by
New laws. So that matters
are not pleasant for poor
people just now but we are

Sister Mary Paul Fielding's last letter to her Sister Maria Fielding Kelleghan.

Sister Mary Paul Fielding's last letter to her Sister Maria Fielding Kelleghan.

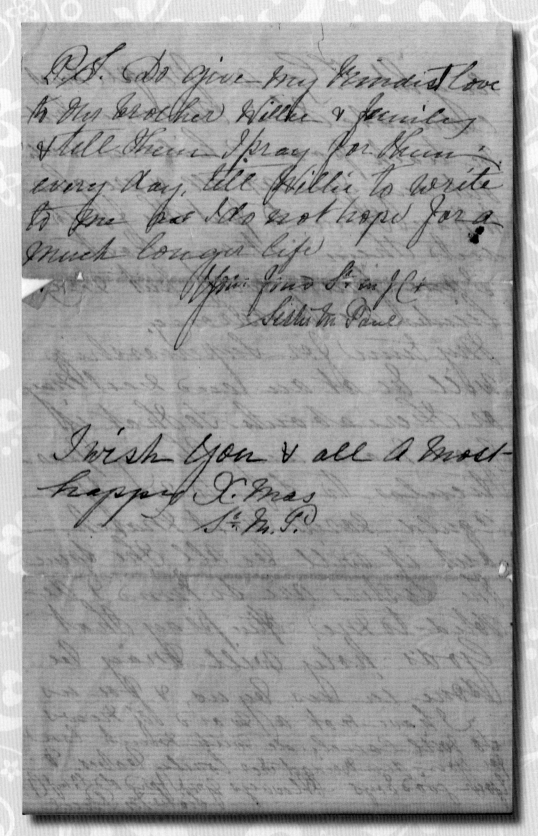

Sister Mary Paul Fielding's last letter to her Sister Maria Fielding Kelleghan.

Convent of Mercy,
Our Lady of the Sacred Heart,
Wilcannia,
Nov. 1st. 1901.

My Dearest Sister Maria,

Your letter arrived this week. I was indeed glad to hear from it that you were all well and doing well. I did write to Sister M. Antonia after getting the happy news of her profession. Perhaps the letter went astray. I had a letter from Dr. Dunne telling me how he paid you a visit and that you all seemed so happy.

Billy Kelleghan and his wife Ruth at their home in Aghamore, Killucan in July 2012. Billy is a Great Grandson of Maria Fielding Kelleghan and a Great Grand Nephew of Sister Mary Paul Fielding.

He will be back in his old home, Broken Hill this coming week. I think he is bringing us two postulants from the old land.

Three of our young Sisters got their white veils. We expect to send on a branch to the White Cliffs in a few months, so we will require new ones to replace the old ones that will go out. Our Sisters are ever-so well T.G. and our schools are good too.

The long drought has ruined many in the district. Their sheep and cattle died in thousands, so that meat is twice the price and there is an awful taxation put on by new laws. So that matters are not pleasant for poor people just now but we are right T.G. as people must educate their children, but we teach poor children without any fee at all and are glad to have them all to put the faith into them at any cost.

I am pretty well, but my limbs are not strong. My time for Superiorship will be at an end next May or thereabouts so that if you have anything particular to say to me you could write next March. But it will be all the same. The Sisters are so kind and devoted to me. We often pray that God's holy will may be done in us, by us and for us.

I have not a word of news so will conclude with much love for your dear Bridget, her lovely babes and your good boys.

Always your fond old Sister in Christ,

Sister M. Paul.

P.S. Do give my kindest love to our brother Willie and family and tell them I pray for them every day. Tell Willie to write to me as I do not hope for a much longer life.

Your fond Sister in Jesus Christ,

Sister M. Paul.

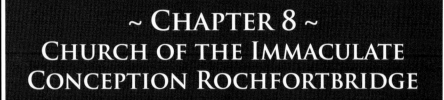

~ CHAPTER 8 ~
CHURCH OF THE IMMACULATE
CONCEPTION ROCHFORTBRIDGE

~ CHAPTER 8 ~

CHURCH OF THE IMMACULATE CONCEPTION ROCHFORTBRIDGE

The Church of the Immaculate Conception, Rochfortbridge was opened in 1857 by Fr. Gerald Robbins on a site donated by Mr. William Fielding. In the 1920's a window was erected behind the main altar, sponsored by Michael Farrelly, Whitewell. The window was designed by Harry Clarke, depicting Mary, the Immaculate Conception as its centre piece. At the main door a smaller window by Clark was erected and by the parents of Bernard Rowan, Farthingsotown who died in 1928. This window was re-installed in the new sacristy when the church was renoved in 1990.

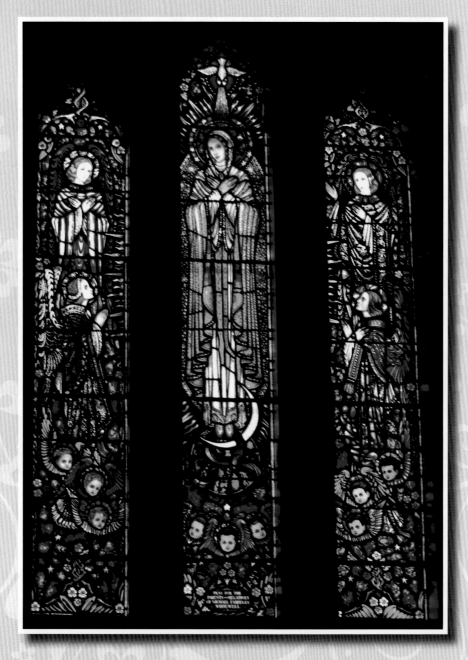

In Memory of
Bernard Rowan, Farthingstown
who Died on 1st August 1928

Erected by his parents

~ CHAPTER 9 ~

THE INSTITUTE FOR THE DEAF AND DUMB

1892 was a landmark year in the history of the Sisters of Mercy in Rochfortbridge, with the creation of the Deaf and Dumb Institute. This establishment played major part in the lives of the Sisters and the village in general until it closed its doors forty eight years later in 1940.

Known affectionately by the local people as '*the Insticute*' this school which was part industrial, was established at the end of a period when the creation of Industrial schools and Institutions was coming to an end.

The establishment of Industrial schools fell into two categories in nineteenth century Ireland:-

   a.   To provide for youthful offenders or in the case of *ragged schools* for children of no fixed abode or vagrants.

   b.   The care of orphans.

In the case of Rochfortbridge, it fell into neither category as the children placed in the care of the Sisters of Mercy were placed there by their families to help provide an education for their children and to help them gain skills which would help them to interact and survive in a world of silence where commnication and understanding were more often than not quite difficult for them.

St. Joseph's Institute for the Deaf and Dumb c. 1900.

During Dr. Nulty's Episcopate in the Diocese of Meath, he was anxious to establish a school for deaf and dumb girls in the diocese. It was said that a close relative of his, was a deaf mute and so that he had a personal interest in this matter. In 1892 he asked, the then Superioress of the Convent of Mercy, Rochfortbridge, Sr. M. Stanislaus O'Neill to undertake this task and she agreed to do so. She began the work in St. Joseph's which had been the Convent, where the sisters resided until the present Convent was built in 1872. Part of this building was also occupied by the Primary School until 1896 when a new Primary School was built. In 1896 the entire building of St. Joseph's was given over to the deaf mutes.

The Bishop secured one third part of the Arthur Smith Bequest, towards the upkeep of the school, which amounted to £50 and the parishioners £132. This with offerings from well wishers brought the total to £300, which completely wiped out the debt. Mother Stanislaus O'Neill wrote to V. Rev. T. Kirby, Archbishop of Ephesus, Irish College Rome, to obtain the blessing of the Holy Father, Leo XIII for the Institute of the deaf and dumb, and this was graciously granted. In 1893 Most Rev. Dr. Kirby sent a piece of marble from the tomb of St. Callistus in the Catacombs given to him by Pope Pius IX which he brought to Pope Leo XIII to be blessed for the Institute.[1] The piece of marble was inserted in one of the class room walls and can now be seen in the classroom still. He also sent a picture of Our Lady of

The Classroom for the Deaf and Dumb c. 1900. It was later the study hall and is now the school library. Note the plaque from the tomb of St. Callistus over the fireplace and the altar press on the far wall *(See the chapter called 'The Sisters and the passing on of the faith in nineteenth century Ireland.*

---

1   The story and history of Saint Callistus. Early in the third century, Callistus, then a deacon, was entrusted by Pope St. Zephyrinus with the rule of the clergy, and set by him over the cemeteries of the Christians at Rome; and, at the death of Zephyrinus, Callistus, according to the Roman usage, succeeded to the Apostolic See. A decree is ascribed to him appointing the four fasts of the Ember seasons, but his name is best known in connection with the old cemetery on the Appian Way, which was enlarged and adorned by him, and is called to this day the Catacomb of St. Callistus. During the persecution under the Emperor Severus, St. Callistus was driven to take shelter in the poor and populous quarters of the city; yet, in spite of these troubles, and of the care of the Church, he made diligent search for the body of Calipodius, one of his clergy who had suffered martyrdom shortly before, by being cast into the Tiber. When he found it he was full of joy, and buried it, with hymns of praise. Callistus was martyred on October 14th. 223A.D. and this day marks his feast day also. St. Callistus is the patron saint of Grave diggers.

Mercy (similar to the one sent to the Mother House, in Baggot Street, by Leo XIII which is a copy of the miraculous picture in the Church of St. Prudentia in Rome) by Fr. Keane to Dr. Nulty for St. Joseph's School. On Christmas Eve 1898 Dr. Nulty died. He had always taken a great interest in St. Joseph's Institute and bequeathed Canal Shares for the upkeep of the Institution.

In 1893 Most Rev. Dr. Kirby sent a piece of marble from the tomb of St. Callistus in the Catacombs given to him by Pope Pius IX which he brought to Pope Leo XIII to be blessed for the Institute.

St. Callistus.

For a short time there were thirty deaf mutes in St. Joseph's, but the number was seldom higher than twenty five. In the beginning a deaf mute teacher who had been governess to Mr. Richard Coffey, Newcastle, Mullingar, (himself a deaf mute, and a brother of Sr. Alacoque Coffey of the Rochfort Bridge Community,) was engaged to teach the deaf mute pupils. When she died about 1898 Miss Browne who had been trained, in Boston Spa, England, and also a Miss Gaynor stayed for a few years. Miss Cronin who had been trained in Cabra came afterwards and remained until 1903. After this Srs. Gertrude Smith, and Antonia Kelly, who had been trained by Miss Cronin took over the charge of the deaf mutes. Sisters Brigid Brady, and Patrick Noone also helped but Sr. Antonia Kelly remained in charge of the deaf mutes until her death in 1947. Two girls who had been trained in the Mercy Convent, Gort, were engaged to teach the deaf mutes lace making and sewing. They were Miss Mary Hayes (1905-1910 – she later married Mr. Michael Eighan and lived in Rochfort Bridge village) and Miss O'Rourke. They did very beautiful work with the pupils and most of it sold well. Knitting machines were also installed in St. Joseph's and stockings were produced to order.

Children from the Deaf and Dumb Institute at the front door of the Convent of Mercy

The Institute and the Manufacture of Drapery.

As an Institution and unlike the pure Industrial units, St Joseph's was constantly in the public view. Running hand-in-hand with the Convent Primary school, there was often interaction between the residents of St. Joseph's and the primary school. In the early years the primary school operated side by side in St. Joseph's, but a greater need for space saw the building of the new convent Primary school building in the convent grounds oppossite the then R.I.C. Police barracks.[2]

Being so close to the community also there was ever a watchful eye on the Institute as is recorded in spoken memory locally. There was an occassion when during the night a fire broke out in one of the outhouses close to the Institute where materials used for the manufacture of clothing was stored. The alarm was raised by the local men in the village and they managed to put the fire out without disturbing the residents of the Institute and the Nuns in the convent. The Sisters didn't know till the next day that there was an emergency during the night and that the local people had prevented a greater tragedy occurring.

Recorded in the Annals also is an incident where the Black and Tans tried to gain access to St. Joseph's one night requesting lodgings for their officers. When it was discovered that it was a school for the deaf and dumb, they went away and the Parish priest gave them lodging for the night.

This picture shows a group of teachers and pupils of the Deaf and Dumb Institute taken between 1905-12.
Teachers: Miss Mary Hayes, Miss O'Rourke, Mother Antonia and Mother Gertrude,
Fr. Murray P.P., Fr. Kane and Fr. Dillon

---

2   Today St.Joseph the Worker Hall is built on the site of the old R.I.C. Barracks.

In 1906, there was a series of articles published in the Westmeath Examiner which give an insight into the work and management of the Institute.

An interesting point to note was the pride of place taken by the Visitors Book, by the Sisters of Mercy, which documented the many visitations and inspections by dignitories and other official visitors to St. Joseph's. The underlying theme of the articles written by the Examiner at the time was to encourage people to visit the cnetre and to purchase the produce created at the hands of the women and girls resident there. The writer justifies the writing of the article by saying

> Toiling away year in year out, in the face of many difficulties the Mercy Sisters at Rochfort Bridge have accomplished work in the interests of society and humanity, that should be chronicled in letters of gold, whilst in the sense of practical useful, industrial labour and work they have achieved a success as which few men of the world would dare hope for with such limited resources and which is only to be appreciated by close observation. In the hope of making these achievements better known and of obtaining for them at least some adequate modicum of public recognition, this article is written and its points and arguments are commended to the careful consideration of one and all, especially to those who are anxious to support that which is of their own country and is done amongst them at their own doors so to.[3]

Furthermore the fate of the deaf mute is described as a sad one which everyone should at once sympathise. Why should that sympathy not be practical and indeed it may be asked to what extent is it sympathy at all, if not practical, where can it be so?

> A profound silence hovers over their young lives which know not the voices of the birds at morn or the lowing of the peaceful herds at eventide. Their ears are never charmed by the sweetness of human speech –and even the voices of loved ones are to them unkown. On the tongue too sits silence and witholds the power to express the many thoughts that fill the human mind. They are helpless indeed, they are saddening to look upon.

> True there are visible in their faces that sweetness and strength and brightness of eye and alertness of mind which no doubt God gives as the complement of affliction borne in Christ-like spirit. But nevertheless, it is sad to think of the mystic stillness of space, that has fallen on their young lives and so to speak cut them off so largely from that 'society' which the dweller on the lonely Island (Selkirk) describes as one of the gifts *divinely bestowed upon men* .[4]

---

3   **A Practical Industrial Object-** A Westmeath Examiner Special, 31st. March 1906.
4   **Alexander Selkirk** (1676 – 13 December 1721) was a Scottish sailor who spent four years as a castaway after being marooned on an uninhabited island. An unruly youth, Selkirk joined several buccaneering expeditions to the South Seas, including one commanded by William Dampier, which called in for provisions at the Juan Fernández Islands off Chile. Selkirk judged correctly that his craft, the *Cinque Ports*, was unseaworthy, and was given the choice of being left ashore on his own. He was eventually rescued by Dampier after four years, in which he had developed hunting and woodcraft skills to a high degree. Selkirk's story aroused great interest at home, and Daniel Defoe's fictional character Robinson Crusoe was almost certainly based in part on him.

But though the poor deaf mutes may lack generally speaking the society of the denizens of the world in general in the Institute at Rochfort Bridge they are not deprived of that *'friendship and love'* of which the exile also spoke for the zeal affection and devotion of the good Nuns, wields them into a little community where all is peace and cheerfulness and mutual affection and mutual helpfulness. Therefore it is clear that to assist the Nuns in this task is an action of the highest practical Christianity and humanity and is real sympathy worthy of the name. This is all the more apparent as is also the moral aspect when it is remembered that these poor girls are necessarily, owing to their affliction –of a diminished usefulness to the outer world, whilst within the Institute they are in many respects more useful members of society than a large proportion of toilers in the business of the world. Unfortunately, also the dangers that beset girlhood and young womanhood in the world – especially the world of today, would be in their case very much increased – defenceless as they are to hear what the world says or to know what might be to others a warning –helpless to protest or to speak in their own behalf or for their own protection. This must assuredly be a great and a potent consideration with any Irishman deeming himself worthy of the name who does not forget the tradition and the pride of this country in the defence and championship of the honour and safety of its women. The almost insurmountable difficulties in providing situations for girls of this class thought excellently trained as skilled workers must be at once apparent on a glance at a commercial and industrial modern world in which ears, eyes and tongue are so much required. Their affliction debars them in many places and on the other hand many of their parents could not afford to keep them at home. They must like other human beings work and be useful members of society and they must be protected meanwhile against the numerous dangers material and moral that follow on their affliction where can these things be done so well as in an Institute such as that at Rochfortbridge.[5]

The only negative remark made by the author was that the place at the disposal of the community and inmates was all too small for the requirements of the work carried on, especially for any further development of it. There was space available to make a site for at least some of the needed extension, but the institute was lacking in funds to enable the work to be started.

The Institute provided an education for the girls, but also it trained them to be useful in the work place by developing skills in knitting, sewing and lace-making, which resulted in the production of fine garments for use by people of all ages. These were displayed and sold at the Institute and the type of garment was listed by the author.

---

5   **A Practical Industrial Object-** 31st. March 1906.

The following table lists some of the garments produced at Rochfortbridge:-

Clothes and Garments manufactured at the Deaf and Dumb Institute	
Lace work	Limerick
Irish Hosiery	Socks,stockings and tights
Linen Work	
Handkerchiefs	Cambric[6]
Altar Cloths	Ornamented
Football Jerseys	
Gentlemen's Underwear	
Vests	
Drawers	
Ladies Underwear	
Childrens Underwear	

Miss Mary Hayes taught at the Institute from 1905 till 1910. She later married local man Michael Eighan and the lived for many years in the village.

The lace work described as Limerick lace, developed into its own particular pattern and style and became known as Rochfortbridge lace. It was hugely sought after and quite often pieces of work were commissioned by private individuals also.

Miss Hayes was in charge of the lace making and Miss O'Rourke looked after the linen work. They were both excellent teachers as the result of their skill and training shown in their pupils work could testify. In their work of course they were always and most successfully assisted by the Nuns and indeed, were it not for their wonderful patience, perseverance and judgement by which the Sisters train the mind and educate the faculties of their pupils in ordinary educational subjects, it would be imposible for the children in their care to acquire a technical knowledge.

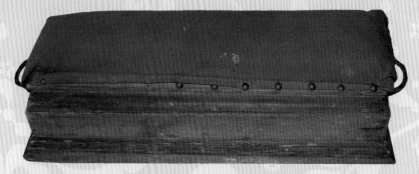

Quite a varied array of garments were made and sold at the Institute. This appararus was used for socks or other garments. It was used also for ironing habits

6   Kind of fine white linen, originally made at Cambray in Flanders (also applied to an imitation made of hard-spun cotton yarn).

The author continues to encourage local people and people from around the adjoining counties to come to Rochfortbridge and purchase some of the goods there. He says that :-

It is surely becoming and worthy that Irishmen should wear, when they can get them at reasonable price, Irish manufactured shirts etc. linen or otherwise made too from Irish materials. It may be mentioned too that the articles, including so many things of everyday need, are sold by the Sisters, with no effort to obtain large prices, or to add on on account of the work being done at the Institute. On the contrary, they merely ask a fair, reasonable price, comparing most favourably with the prices in some of the largest shops.[7]

The prices charged by the Nuns were fair and reasonable with a view to maintain the workers and schoolchildren resident there. The Institute depended on donations and endowments which helped provide for the upkeep of the place as can be seen from the will of the Rev. Matthew Hynes who died in 1903 as C.C. Collinstown. The will is dated the 28th. of December 1900.

I, the Rev. Matthew Hynes, at present residing in Moynalty, in the county of Meath, do hereby bequeath the effects of my property of whatsoever kind I may possess at death, my lawful debts being paid, and eight Masses being said in public churches in Ireland for the repose of my soul, to St. Joseph's Institution for the Deaf and Dumb at Rochfort Bridge, in the county of Westmeath, Ireland.[8]

Letters of Administration, with the will and effects of the estate were on the 2nd of December 1904, granted forth at the Mullingar district Registry of the King's bench Division, Probate of the the High Court of Justice in Ireland to Sister Mary Stanislaus, Superioress of St. Joseph's Institute for the Deaf and Dumb at Rochfortbridge. Solicitors for Sister Mary Stanislaus were N. J. Downes, Mullingar.[9]

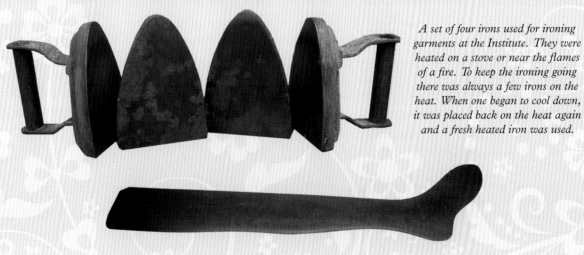

A set of four irons used for ironing garments at the Institute. They were heated on a stove or near the flames of a fire. To keep the ironing going there was always a few irons on the heat. When one began to cool down, it was placed back on the heat again and a fresh heated iron was used.

This long wooden sock shaped implement was used for pressing newly knitted football socks which were sold at the Institute.

---

7   **A Practical Industrial Object-** 31st. March 1906.
8   Rev. Matthew Hynes was a native of Tyrrellspass. He was educated at Navan and Maynooth and ordained in June 1900. He served as C.C. in Moynalty (1900-1901), Castletown-Kilpatrick(1901-1902), Dunderry (1902-1903). He died as C.C. Collinstown on the 5th of December 1903 and is buried in Meedin Cemetery.
9   The Westmeath Examiner, 25th Feb. 1905.

The Institute and the Education of Young Deaf Girls

A second aspect highlighted in the work of the Institute for the deaf and dumb was the education provided for the girls at Rochfortbridge. Unlike the other forms of Industrial Instutions, namely, the Reform schools, orphanages and ragged schools, the children were neither, orphans,offenders or vagrants, but were placed there by their families who hadn't the skills or resources to educate these children.

At the end of their education years they were returned to their families, but some of the girls remained on working at the Institute. They provided the skills and labour necessary for the manufacture of the various garments listed earlier.

A large metal medallion was worn round the neck by pupils of the Institute when they travelled home for their Christmas or Summer Holidays. Provision was made to write their names and destinations on the medallion.

Therefore educating these girls was not an easy task. According to the second Examiner report on the 14th of April 1906 it pointed out that no one, except those who had attempted the task, could conceive an adequate idea of the difficulties of teaching even elementary matters to the children. One can tell them nothing by the mouth, for they would not hear, and they could not, on the other hand, tell what it was they knew or would like explained, because they were unable to speak. They could write down questions certainly. But then who was going to instruct them how to write, and tell them what the different letters were and what their many combinations were? How was this knowledge to be conveyed to them, and long would it require to impart it and make sure they had made their own of it? The writer explains as follows:-

> By means of objects, observance of the motions of the lips and mouth, facial expression, pictures etc.. by degrees patience and kindness and love are rewarded, and the poor deaf and dumb girl begins to be able to write questions or frame answers on a piece of paper, or a blackboard or a slate.

> Prayers are taught, and religious instructions imparted, also a difficult and extra onerous undertaking in the case of deaf mutes. But after a time, labour and patience have conquered all; and once well on the road they learn quickly.

> Indeed some of the answers given on religious literary and other subjects by most of the inmates on the occassion of a recent visit surprised and astounded the writer of this article, and gave him a feeling of great satisfaction, that so much would be done for the poor children and that the good Nuns knew so well how to do it.

> Some of those answers would put to shame many a school child in the full possession of the blessings of all her senses. Of course the answers are written, but they teem

with direct, clear and extremely intelligent conception of the subjects dealt with. One of the most painful things in the task of training the children is to observe the freshness and brilliancy of intelligence that beams from every eye and radiates from every feature of the face –seeking striving, yearning to express itself quickly and to ask the formative process of educational training and reflection. All else is bright, vivid, and instinct of intelligence except the afflicted senses –the ears and the tongue. Around them alone hangs the '*cold chain of silence*' – all else, eyes, gestures, features –*speak* blessed and beloved of God and man must surely be the tender patience, love, forbearance and care that day after day toils on with drudgery and care and often monotony to educate those afflicted ones, these crippled birds that at length they may be able to soar into the realms of thought and expression and speak, if not with the tongue in written words, of things human and divine.

And the day comes, and the good Nuns feel how sweet it is to have helped the more or less helpless. The visitor calls and he is delighted, thunderstruck at what can –be what has been done to educate the deaf mutes. It is when he examines into the work it implies that he realises the full significance and value of achievement.[10]

Letters and words, parts of speech and grammar once learned, then syntax, composition, mathematics, literature –all the stores of learning were largely opened up and the pupils who were witnessed by the author in various school subjects were quite marvellous and even better than many of those who could hear, see and speak. As the training advanced the pupils could begin to crystallise thought and express either acquired knowledge or something original of their own creation in the form of essays and composition.

One sample of such work survives and was given as an example in the article. It was from one of the girls exercise books and written in copper-plate style.

'*The Autumn months are August, September and October. The daylight gradually shortens, the flowers fade, the fruit ripens, the leaves assume various tints, and fall from the trees. We may now gather blackberries, acorns, nuts, chestnuts and walnuts.*

The farmer is very busy harvesting his wheat, barley, oats, peas and beans. He takes advantage of the fine weather to get crops carried from the fields. Some of the corn is threshed out by the threshing machine and sent to market. Sometimes the sheaves are built up in stacks on a dry foundation, carefully thatched and are preserved from the damp until required by the farmer for market.

When the wheat fields are cleared, the women and children glean the scattered ears of corn. Then the ground is ploughed up in preparation for another seeding. Some seed is sown in Autumn with the drill, but much more is sown in the spring.

The gardener gathers the apples, pears and plums, and digs up the potatoes. The sportsman with his dog, goes out to shoot partridges. Thousands of people are engaged in some counties hop picking. Late in the Autumn we are glad to wear our thickest coats and jackets.'

---

10   **An Interesting Institution-Practical Industrial Effort,** Westmeath Examiner Special, 14th April 1906.

It is interesting to note that the girl who wrote the essay referred to the harvesting of hops and hop picking. This is not a crop synonymous with Westmeath, but once carried out on a large scale in Kent in the south of England. This reference tells us two things,

1. the girl who wrote the piece had probably read about hop growing and in her own creative world referred to it in her essay.

2. There is a hint also that she may have been English, as there were some children who came to the Institute from England.

The second aspect of their education as pointed out by the writer of the article, was that the education of girls such as these should not continue indefinitely on a literary basis, but the next step was to initiate them into the mysteries of technical work of various industrial descriptions. How successful this was, was evident on the excellence of craftsmanship on the articles on display and it was a sound inducement to the encouragement of Irish made work in the future.

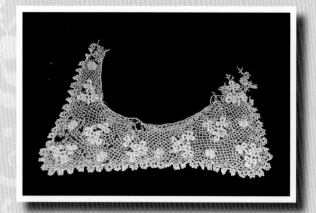
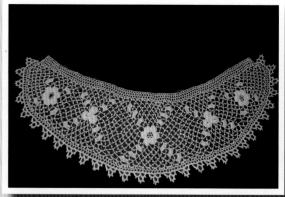

Samples of Irish lace which were made at the Institute. The shamrock motifs were very popular at the time.
Local people called the lace manufactured at the Institute *Rochfortbridge Lace*.

The Institute and its Departments

In the final section of the article, the author paid a visit to the various departments in the Institute. In addition to the school room and work rooms, there was a reception room, a well-fitted kitchen, a clean, bright dormitory with a number of windows and well-ventillated, a smaller dormitory, lavatories, a small infirmary compartment(seldom required), as good health was always enjoyed by the inmates. He noticed also that in all departments there was a great scarcity of room and that the requirements of the place and the excellent work carried out there demanded further extension.

Mary Ellen Geraghty was the last pupil of the Institute. She remained on the staff of the convent of Mercy till she died in 1991. She was the first person to be buried in the new cemetery in Rochfortbridge. Pictured with Mary Ellen is Chrissie McNamara her friend and co-worker. Chrissie worked for many years as the cook in St. Josephs providing meals for the boarders. She has now retired to Santa Maria Nursing Home Kinnegad.

As an example, he gave, that every day it was necessary to clear out one of the workrooms, disturb the workers and their materials, and lose time in order to convert the apartment into a temporary diningroom for some of the inmates. In a final plea to the public, he hopes that they will come to the aid of the sisters to make more space available to extend the Institute further.

It seems that the writer was very taken by the Institute and how it was operating, so much so that it warranted two very long articles in the local paper at the time, a time also, when such local papers not only printed local news but international news also. So there was a very narrow corridor of space available to the inclusion of local news, so the extent of space given by the paper was evidence of the regard and esteem the author held for the place.

In his conclusion, the writer again urged the importance to Irish people generally of supporting Irish manufacture, and in this case study, the duty which the people of Westmeath and other midland counties owe to give earnest practical help to industrial effort:-

> But in the case of the Rochfort Bridge Institute it would be forgetful of the character of the Irish people if the writer did not express the view that the fact that at the Institute, the best of work of a most practical character is done by poor afflicted Irish girls, will be a potent additional reason why the hearts of the people will expand towards them and towards the good Nuns who live and labour for them, and that they will order in future, their stockings, underwear, and a hundred and one other things from Rochfort Bridge Institute, and at least give a fair trial to what is the work of their own race and is done so to speak at their doors.[11]

---

11   **An Interesting Institution-Practical Industrial Effort,** 14th April 1906.

As a result of this article, there must have been a response to the plea given by the Examiner author as in 1912 the paling around St. Joseph's was erected with permission from the rural District court, at a cost of £10. In 1915, the long room in St. Joseph's was built where the entrance from the road to the yard was. For a short time there were thirty deaf mutes in St. Joseph's and this number seldom rose higher than twenty five.

The number of deaf mutes in St. Joseph's were gradually decreasing, and although the Sisters wrote to all the Councils, very few new pupils were procured. The following is a copy of an advertisement inserted in the paper on the 30th June, 1925.

"Do not neglect the Afflicted"
There is at Rochfort Bridge,
Mullingar
A School for the teaching
and training
of Deaf Mutes.
Any person knowing of uneducated
deaf mute girls should write to
The Superioreress,
Convent of Mercy,
Rochfort Bridge,
Co. Westmeath

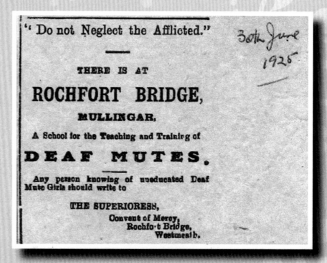

Newspaper ad. from 1925.

Between 1920 and 1940 the number decreased. Better facilities were available in Cabra, Dublin and it was more central for most people. By 1940 the school was closed. Some stayed on the staff of the Convent. The last surviving person was Mary Ellen Geraghty who died on the 4th. of August 1991 and was the first to be buried in the new cemetery Rochfortbridge.[12]

The grave in Meedin Cemetery of members of the Deaf and Dumb Institute who died between the years 1892 and 1947

The Grave of Mary Ellen Geraghty who died in 1991

---

12   Information from the Sisters of Mercy, Rochfortbridge.

MOTHER STANISLAS O'NEILL
1841-1917

Mother Stanislas O'Neill one of the founding Sisters was born in Dublin in 1841 and entered the Novitiate in Tullamore in 1858. She was sent on the Foundation to Rochfortbridge as Mistress of Novices at the early age of twenty one. (A position she filled till her death, when not in the capacity of Superior). After three years she was elected Superior. Few knew the poverty and hardships she and her infant community had to fight with, but her trust in God brought her through all her trials.

Later, the Institute for the Deaf and Dumb was opened by Most Rev. Dr. Nulty and the charge of this big undertaking given to M.M. Stanislas. While undertaking this project, she enlarged the old convent and fitted it up to educate the deaf children

The new convent is also the work of her industry, with its beautiful grounds, not to speak of the National Schools, so much admired.

Gentle, holy and humble possessed of an unusually cultured holy mind, she developed the intelligence of her pupils always, with the view to make them thrifty, refined members of society.

Mother M.Stanislas O Neill

Today the sisters can count over seventy professed nuns sent from their schools to all quarters of the globe to spread the knowledge of the Gospel.

Quite recently, she prepared very young pupils for the London College of Music; all obtained honours.

To the bereaved members of her Community we tender our sympathy. Her death was the echo of her saintly life, one of close union with God, and perfect resignation to His will under very severe pain. The funeral obsequies testify to the esteem in which deceased was held, and were largely represented by leading gentlemen of Mullingar, Rhode, Kilbeggan and the three parishes of Rochfortbridge. The Office of High Mass was held on Friday after which the internment took place. May she rest in peace.[1]

---

1   Un-dated newspaper article from 1917.

~ CHAPTER 10 ~
THE SISTERS OF MERCY AND THE PASSING ON OF THE FAITH IN THE NINETEENTH CENTURY

When the Natonal Board of Education established the National School System in Ireland in 1831, one of its main objectives was that the education provided was to be of a secular nature and the teaching of religion and the displaying of religious objects in the classroom was forbidden. There was a climate of hostility and suspicion between the churches at this time. Fears of proselytism were rife. The churches view of education differed somewhat from that of the states view. Its intention was that all denominations would be educated together in secular subjects and separate arrangements would be made for doctrinal instruction according to different denominational tenets. The churches both Protestant and Catholic in Ireland on the other hand saw education as an extension of their pastoral care. Educating children in a secular environment was impossible. They also feared the growth of secularism.

The Established Church set up its own school system- *the Church Education Society*- in 1839, in opposition to the national system. The Synod of Ulster, representing the Presbyterians, was equally hostile, from 1832 to 1840, when they secured modifications in the rules that enabled them to cooperate with the Board. The Catholic schools though not all of them, on the other hand, worked under the new state sponsored system, This ensured that only Catholics attended most of the national schools. Bishop John McHale of Tuam would not allow the National School System into his diocese and it wasn't until after his death that the national school system took root in the diocese. The Bishops were not in favour of secular education but the new state system offered them much of what was needed in Catholic education. The non-Catholic schools eventually too came under the National school system.

The Sisters on the other hand looked to mainland Britain and elswhere for a system to meet their educational needs also and the closest model to meet their requirements was the National Education System and they were prepared to work within its parameters. The Christian Brothers did not. With the teaching of religion being left outside the new secular model, the Sisters looked to find ways to stay within the secular model and yet and to quote the way Sister M. Paul Fielding put it in a letter to her Sister Maria Kelleghan in 1901,

> *'... we teach poor children without any fee at all and are glad to have them all to put the faith into them at any cost.'*

There were many cases where the teacher was dismissed from his post for teaching religion and in the case of the first National School in Rochfortbridge, there was an incident in the Torrybeggan school.

Father Shanley established the first National School in Rochfortbridge in 1833 in the townland of Torrybeggan which was located close to the village down the Sidebrook road on the banks of the Derry river. Prior to the sisters arrival in Rochfortbridge, schools there were trying to work under the new system of education. A church of Ireland school was located in the village of Rochfortbridge under the direction of Rev. Wm. Lucas at this time.

The new Parish School established by Fr, Shanley on the 23rd. of July 1835 was a mixed school and was known as Castlelost. The principal, Thomas Brady, was recognized by the National Board of Education.

It was built of limestone and thatched and it was in tolerably good repair. This school never received any support from any society. It was a payschool. The parish paid a rent of £3-10-0.

It was open from nine until four O'clock each day for moral and literary education. Saturday was set apart for religious instruction. Therefore on examination by the National Board of Education this school was granted salary for the teacher due to its committment to the National Education System and its ethos.

The teacher received £10 per annum from the Board. In July 1836 the inspector visited the school and stated that it was too small. It was 40ft. by 20ft. and the average attendance was seventy six. It was scantily furnished with only six forms. There were no desks or tables. There was a greater attendance at this school in summer when seventy males and forty females were present. In winter there was a drop in attendance especially among the males. In winter forty males and thirty females attended the school. These children came from catholic and protestant families. The children purchased the books and while no names were given it was stated that they were those generally used in country schools. The task of teaching such a large number of children of mixed abilities seems a very difficult one. The space was limited and there was only one teacher. Mr. Brady had not been educated in any of the model schools. On the 11th of October 1838 James Gleeson replaced Thomas Brady as principal. On the 2nd of August 1839 Mr. Gleeson was found teaching catechism and the Board sought to replace him. The Board wanted a non-denominational school and enforced the rule on this occasion. He resigned in October 1839. Education was disrupted for a time. It was not until May 1840 that a new teacher was appointed and sent away for training.

To ensure that the children under their care were educated academically as well as in their faith, the Sisters found ingenious ways to work round this system of education so that the faith could be passed on through the school day as well as through the time allotted outside the secular system for religious instruction. This would include the inclusion of religious and pious objects as part of school life as well as prayer and reciting the angelus.

If an inspector visited the school and children were reciting their prayers the school was in breach of the rules for National Schools, but if the children stood up and recited their prayers silently, no rule was broken according to the Inspectors. More often than not as the nineteenth century wore on, quite a lot of inspectors were prepared to ignore these rules and breaches such as these, were not written into their reports.

Perhaps the most daring move made by the Sisters was the provision of altars in the classroom which defied the rules of the National System and The Sisters at Rochfortbridge were among the schools who defied this rule also. A fine example of this furniture is to be found at the

Convent primary School in Rochfortbridge. At a glance these fine pieces of furniture which comprised of a large press not unlike a Welsh Dresser, but with wooden doors and not glass doors on the top half. They were finely finished, ornately decorated, turned and finished with a coat of varnish. The top half, when the doors were opened out revealed a series of pedestals usually three where statues could be placed, the centre pedestal higher than the others. With their great devotion to Mary, a large statue of Our Lady of Mercy was placed on the centre pedestal. The other pedestals allowed the statuary of other saints to be placed there, or vases of flowers. The background was painted light blue and in the case of the Convent Primary School Altar, the words *Holy Mary Pray For Us* is written on a banner which fitted just over the head of the statue. The banner is written in gold lettering with a sky blue background.

The design allowed for the doors to close at the end of the day. Therefore when the Inspector called, the Sister on hearing of his arrival, closed the doors and locking the press with a key, placed it in her pocket. The Sister would also have the children trained to keep this secret, therefore finding no evidence of religious or pious objects in the classroom the school was obeying the rules for National Education.

From the end of the nineteenth century, the displaying of pious or religious objects in the class were ignored and they became part and parcel of Catholic Primary schools as well as Convent Schools. But the beautiful altar presses remained on and were used right up until modern times. In the chapter in this book dealing with the Deaf and Dumb Institute, the picture of the school room taken around 1900 shows an altar press in the classroom with its doors opened out revealing the altar and its contents inside. This press remained in that room until the late nineteen seventies when the room was divided to provide for two classroom spaces in the Secondary School.

The Alter Press

~ CHAPTER 11 ~

THE COFFEYS OF NEWCASTLE

NON·VICTORIA·SED·PROVIDENTIA

~ CHAPTER 11 ~
THE COFFEYS OF NEWCASTLE

Over the past 800 years the history of the parish which contains most of the barony of Fartullagh is closely connected with the fortunes of three families, the Tyrrells, the Norths and the Coffeys.

The Tyrrells came from Triel — a little place outside Paris. They came to England with William the Conquerer. Sir Hugh Tyrrell came to Ireland with his cousin Strongbow in 1167. In 1173 when Hugh De Lacy was given the Lordship of Meath by Henry II— he appointed Sir Hugh Tyrrell, Baron of Castleknock. Sir Hugh went on the third crusade and his son Gerald was appointed Lord of Fartullagh. For many generations the descendants of this man were rulers of much of this part of Westmeath.

Emily Coffey, Sister Alacoque in religion, spent many years in the Rochfortbridge Community. She died in 1934.

For many centuries the Barony of Fartullagh, containing 39,000 Irish acres was known as "*Tyrrells country*" and the head of that family was called "*Captain of his nation*". Castlelost was the chief stronghold of the Tyrrells — the present road from Rochfortbridge to Castlelost was the front avenue to the castle. Sir Thomas Tyrrell was Lord of Castlelost in 1585 — he was a supporter of English rule as was his son Sir John Tyrrell who was visited in Castlelost by the Lord Deputy Lord Mountjoy 27th February 1601 according to Fynes Morrison an English traveller in Ireland in the early 1600's.

The most famous of all the Tyrrells was Captain Richard Tyrrell of Tyrrellspass - the leading Irish chief after O'Neill during the nine years war. With only 400 men he ambushed and wiped out an English force of 1,000 under Barnwall which was about to invade O'Neill territory. So complete was his victory that only one man escaped to Mullingar to tell the story.

Captain Richard fought alongside O'Neill at the ill-fated Battle of Kinsale and later went to Spain with the Earls.

In 1651 Tyrrell had castles at Newcastle commanded by Thomas Tyrrell, Kilbride commanded by Walter Tyrrell, Gaybrook commanded by Richard Tyrrell, Tyrrellspass commanded by Thomas Tyrrell and Castlelost also commanded by Thomas Tyrrell. All of these castles were taken by the Cromwellians in 1650-51 when the land and possessions of the Irish chiefs who opposed Cromwell were forfeited and given to the soldiers in Cromwells army or to "Adventurers" i.e. people who adventured or loaned money to help in the conquest of Ireland. It is recorded that "a castle of the Tyrrells in Kilbride after an obstinate resistance on the part of its proprietor Walter Tyrrell was surrendered to the Cromwellian forces under General Heuson in 1651". All of Tyrrells castles were destroyed except Tyrrellspass castle. The only way this can be explained is by the fact that one member of the Tyrrell family living in Tyrrellspass must have supported the English in the war. The names of Frances Tyrrell and Peter Tyrrell appear in the list of people who got lands in the area from Cromwell.

The Norths of Fartullagh

In the Act of Settlement and Explanation 1660 the lands of Newcastle were given to Sir Jerome Alexander and Thomas Hooke. It is most unlikely that either of these men ever lived here. In the division of the lands of the Irish chiefs forty nine Cromwellian officers got no land — they rebelled and some of them later got land in Fartullagh. One of them was Mr. John North. The North family were Earls of Guilford in Surrey in England. In 1660s and 1670's we find John North in Kilbride, his son Roger who died in 1701 was in Newcastle and his other son, John was in Clooneen in Kings County(Offaly).

The Norths lived in Newcastle until around 1780. They were very industrious and with the help of money from the English branch of the family they developed their land and soon there were Norths in Tyrrellspass, Clonfad, Whitewell and Guilford. There was also a Dr. North living in Farview. They had large families and soon they were too numerous for the available land. Many of them emigrated to the United States in the 18th century where North is a common name today. The last member of the family to live in Newcastle was Ulysses North Esq. High Sheriff of Westmeath. He died around 1780 leaving no heir. They left Guilford around the same time. The Clonfad branch of the family continued into the nineteenth century when Barbara North, only child of Peter of Clonfad, married Rev. James Croften a rather unpopular landlord in the 1830's. The name of North died out also in Kilbride when Mary, only child of Roger North, married Capt. A. Pilkington of Toar. Many members of the North family are buried in Newtown cemetery.

The Coffeys of Newcastle

In the 1780's Mr. Christopher Coffey a prominent Catholic farmer from the Curragh of Kildare bought Newcastle, an estate of 505 acres. The Coffeys were an old Irish bardic family. The bards or "*Aos dána*" were prominent in Ireland from the death of Christ until the disaster at Kinsale. In Gaelic Ireland various families or clans specialised in various disciplines — law, medicine, poetry, etc. The bards or poets had a strong influence on kings and nobles. They preserved the Gaelic civilization because it was they who recorded the exploits of the ruling classes. A king or noble acted as patron to a bard or bardic clan by supporting them financially and providing for their needs.

The Coffey Coat of Arms, depicted on a stained glass window in Meedin Church. Arms: "Vert(centre band, a fess of ermine, between three coons or Irish cups." Crest: A man riding on a dolphin, proper. Motto: "Non prudentia sed victoria" 'No Forethought, Except Victory.'

It was the duty of the poet to record the special events in the life of the local chieftain and patron e.g. birth, marriage, battle adventures etc. The poets were trained in special bardic schools.

The Coffeys were prominent Gaelic Poets in Westmeath living close to the Hill of Uisneach. There are several references in the Annals to various members of the family — Hugh O Coffie, Eoin O Coffie, Domhnall O Coffie, who were prominent bards during the 14th and 15th centuries. In the Barony of Fartullagh there is a civil parish called Coffeys Island –*Inis Chofaigh*. In English it is Enniscoffey, between Milltownpass and Gaybrook.

The Coffeys held extensive lands around Mount Temple, Ballymore, Killare and Dysart all of which they lost in the Cromwellian Confiscations 1660.

Some years after, Mr. Christopher Coffey bought Newcastle he also bought 400 acres at Cruhill, Loughnavalley and 190 acres at Calverstown. The 1st reference we have to Mr. Coffeys presence in the parish is in Dr. Plunketts diary of his Visitations. He tells us that after visiting the Parish of Midin and Milltown on September 17th 1795 he spent the following day at the home of Mr. Christopher Coffey.

The Coffey family seem to have been closely involved with the life of the Church in this area. Four Fr. Coffeys all Domnicans and all related, and according, to Cogan, natives of the area ministered in the the parish for over fifty years 1767-1825. Frs. Vincent and Dionysius Coffey were in charge of the parish during the 1770's and 80's. Fr. Eugene Coffey nephew of Fr. Dionysius succeeded 1784-90 and Fr. Bernard, brother of the preceding Pastor was parish priest from 1790-1825. Some of them were members of the Dominican House of Newbridge, which is near the Curragh, the former residence of Mr. Christopher Coffey. Priests were scarce during the 2nd half of the 18th century because of the rigours of the penal laws and these Fr. Coffeys may have been introduced into the area by Mr. Coffey with Dr. Plunkett's approval or they may have been attached to the Dominican House in Mullingar.

Christophers son, Richard Charles Coffey took over Newcastle on his father's death in the early 1800's. He developed the farm giving employment to many in the area. He was regarded as a good employer and a generous man. Many came from other parts of the country to work for Mr. Coffey, as jockeys, stewards, herds, masons etc. People named Ryan, Leech, Hale, Davis, Grainery all worked in Newcastle and Noonans, Connors, Langans, Leogues,

Newcastle House today.

Keegans, Flynns, Duffys and Hannigans all lived in Newcastle estate in 1851.

Newcastle soon became famous for its bloodstock. The Grand National winner of 1855 "*The Wanderer*" was bred there. Other class horses owned bred and trained by Mr. Coffey were *Fear-a-tulla*, *Theodora* and *Yaller Girl* which won the Mullingar Handicap 1862. The impressive house and beautifully laid out garden and Orchard was visited by many of the hunting and racing fraternity from Dublin and even from England. Mr. Winston Churchill is believed to have spent summer holidays here as a child. Up to thirty horses and riders often came up the back avenue to exercise or to follow the Westmeath Hunt. Three jockeys were killed while working in Newcastle and are buried in Meedin. One called O'Reilly was killed on the Rochfortbridge side of Gneevebawn hill, another called Burke was killed in a fall in Bellewstown racecourse and a third called Langan was killed when he fell from a horse in Mullingar town.

There are a number of references in "History of Westmeath Hunt" by Dease 1898 to the involvement of the Coffey family in bloodstock. "Richard Coffey of Newcastle kept harriers in 1853 and for some years after many a good steeple chaser made his debut with this pack".

Anthony Cogan in his history of the "Diocese of Meath" 1862 gave lavish praise to Mr. Coffey for his generosity in building the Church in Meedin and the Convent in Rochfortbridge for the Sisters of Mercy.

The parish is singularly blessed in having a gentleman of ample means who takes the liveliest interest in the beauty and decoration of God's house. The Chapel in Meedin is truly a gem and whoever enters it will at once be edified. A fortune has

The stable yard and part of the Tyrrell Tower House Stronghold

The Stable Yard.

Father Shanley befriended Richard Coffey of Newcastle and was a frequent visitor to his house. One day while out on the Coffey farm he noticed a large stone slated shed and said to Richard Coffey, "I wished I had a church as fine as this building." To which Mr. Coffey replied, "I'll see to it that you will have your wish." The present church of the Sacred Heart Meedin is a result of Mr. Coffey's generosity. The Meedin Book, 1983, p. 24

been expended in ornamenting the Chapels supplying them with church furniture and in the foundation of a Convent for the Sisters of Mercy. To Richard Charles Coffey Esq., Newcastle House, all this is due, and to him religion is deeply indebted for the laudable and meritorious use he makes of his position and property.[1]

The Coffey family had their own Gallery in the east aisle of Meedin Church. It was removed in the renovations of 1982-83. The Coffey coat of arms is on the small stain glass window in the sanctuary on the east side of the altar. The motto is *Non Victoria sed Providentia* — not in victory but in providence. The window on the opposite side bears the Rochfort coat of arms — an old Anglo Irish Catholic branch of the Rochfort family who lived in Kilbride from the 14th century to the 16th century. The motto is: *"je ne change quun mourant"*, "I will not change until I die".

Richard married Penelope Rathbourne a Protestant, who became a Catholic a few years later. They had three children. Christy, Emily and Richard. Christy took over the family business in the 1870's . Emily entered the Sisters of Mercy in Rochfortbridge as Sr. Alacoque where she died on November 24th 1934, and Richard was a deaf mute, losing his speech at the age of seven after a serious illness. There is a story told locally regarding Penelopes conversion to the Catholic faith. She was on her way to her weekly Sunday service in Tyrrellspass when the horse took fright, the carriage was overturned and she was hurt. Her husband, Richard immediately suggested that this was a sign that she should not go again to Sunday service. She then became a Catholic.

The recession of the 1870's and 80's had a severe effect on the Coffey farming enterprise and the family were soon in financial difficulties. Christy was now in charge, and the lifestyle which included lavish entertainment and gambling did not help. Dease comments as follows regarding his love of hunting and his wit.

"In 1876 and for some years Mr. Christopher Coffey kept a smart pack of harriers at Newcastle hunting hares carted deer and occasionally an outlying fox".

He once hunted a respectable member of the R.I.C. who came to count his hounds around dog tax time. Mr. Coffey instructed his kennel boy while "Robert" was counting the hounds, to paint the heels of his well folded regulation trousers with aniseed. They gave the peeler ten minutes start, and then laid the pack which ran like fury until they got up with the policeman and then, devoted more time to his trousers than he cared for. He never counted Master Christy's hounds again.

Poor Christy whether hunting, racing, shooting or fishing he had at his command an endless fund of wit and good humour which made him a most amusing companion. He was a neat horseman and rode a few good races in his time".

The family business went from bad to worse. Tragedy also visited them in 1882 when Theodora, Christy's young wife, died tragically in a riding accident, aged 22. There used be a portrait of her hanging in the sacristy in Meedin.

Soon after this Christy, who had always associated with the hunting fraternity and landed class signed the *"Coercian Act"*[2] and as a result was boycotted. He could not sell cattle or do

---

1   Anthony Cogan, *History of the Diocese of Meath*(1867). Vol 2, P.481.
2   The Protection of Person and Property Act 1881 was the first of over a hundred such Acts that aimed to suppress the increasing discontent in Ireland with British rule. England was seen in Ireland as responsible for having turned the failures of the potato crop into the Great Famine and the loss of 20% of its population. The Irish National Land League and the Fenian Brotherhood were part of the dissent in Ireland in the years from the Famine to the Irish War of Independence.

business. People refused to work for him and soon he was bankrupt.

The sad end for the family came when they had to leave Newcastle. The family who had so generously endowed the parish now had nowhere to go. They stayed for a short time in the West and later moved to a house in Gneevebawn, where old Mr. Richard Coffey died in 1893. He is buried in the family plot in Meedin alongside Theodora. Richard the deaf-mute lived on for many years, frequently visiting his sister, Sister Alocoque in Rochfortbridge with whom he was always very close. Emily was born in 1858. She was educated at the Convent in Roscrea and she entered religion on the 24th of February 1876 aged 17 years. She was professed on the 7th of January 1879. She spent the greater part of her life and labours at Rochfortbridge. She taught in the school for many years and and she taught music. She was also a very gifted organ player. Part of her duties was to prepare the young girls for First holy communion. In her final years she had problems with her heart which left her quite ill on many occassions. During this period of her life, she was recommended to rest, but it didn't stop her from doing her community duties. She died on the 10th of November 1934. Her brother Richard died a few years later. It has not been possible to discover the later fortunes of Christy. Some say he lived near Mullingar for a time and later went to India. Another relative of the family, also called Richard, emigrated to New Zealand around 1908. He returned to Europe as a soldier during the First World War and was killed at the Battle of the Somme in 1916.

On this sad note ended the history of a remarkable family who made a significant contribution to life in this parish.

10. The final resting place at the Convent of Mercy Cemetery, Rochfortbridge of Emily, Sister Alacoque Coffey who died in 1934. In the background is an ornate metal garden seat which was given to the Sisters of Mercy by the Coffey family, Newcastle.

A Statue of St. Patrick in Meedin Cemetery keeps guard over the resting place of members of the Coffey Family, Newcastle.

LETTER OF THANKS- 1871

In 1871 Mr. William Noonan from Massachussetts, U.S.A. was visiting Ireland when his daughter met with an accident and was tenderly cared for by the nuns at Rochfortbridge. On his return to the U.S.A., Mr. Noonan did not foget the kindness his daughter had received from the Sisters of Mercy.

Lennox Terrace,
Massachussetts,
United States of America,
August 28, 1871.

Mrs. Richard Coffey –Madame

While on a visit to Ireland in the month of June last, and as I was going through my native county of Westmeath, to see again after the expiration of thirty one years, those green fields where long ago I spent my younger days, but which now made lonely and desolate by death and emigration, on my way I happened to pass by the little town of Rochfortbridge with my daughter who was then with me, fell from the jaunting car in front of the Convent of that place, but the good Sisters of Mercy who are always on the watch to do good, saw my daughter falling, and immediately brought her into their good house, where she was tenderly cared for, and where she soon recovered.

While waiting in the Convent, I could not help noticing the good order which everything denoted in and about that good place. All was respectful and silent, and that stillness was only broken by the sweet voices of little children singing praises to God. I came away, however, after a short time, contenting myself with only thanking the good ladies for their kindness, and indeed, I shall not soon forget my unexpected visit to the good Sisters of Mercy of Rochfortbridge.

In a few days after my return home to America I received a letter from my brother Thomas Noonan, now living in Ireland in which he reminded me of my neglect in not offering something to the convent , when I was there, besides thanks. Well now, I must confess that I did not think of doing so, because I did not then know anything about the rules of the Sisters, much less about their necessities.

On my arrival home I determined to raise a contribution for the Sisters as they were poor. I therefore opened a subscription, and made application to the working men of the Iron Works of Coffinge Church, and Taylor, of this place, who have freely given. Please find enclosed two drafts, amounting to six pounds, which I know you will forward to the Convent of Rochfortbridge, and perhaps we will again, at some future time, send you another donation for the same good place, which we hope will be better than the present one.

For the information of the Sisters, I give the names of those who have subscribed to this little fund:- William Noonan and John O'Toole, two dollars each:
Mrs. Noonan, Peter Shea, John Boyle, James Wigman, Daniel O'Brien, Thomas O'Brien, William Coleman, John Manion, Edward Bossidy, James Donivan, James Toole, Daniel Hogan, Patrick Hickey, James Brown, William Woodlock, Mark Carey, Patrick Ford, Patrick Shea, Thomas Berry, Michael Payne, John McCabe, Richard Cowher, John Bartley, Thomas McGrein, Jeremiah Keefe, James Wickham, Jeremiah Lawlor, Timothy Fahey, Timothy Bartley, and Nicholas Shea, one dollar each. Total, 34 dollars,

–Yours respectfully & c,
William Noonan.
Promotions and Appointments
(By Irish Times Wire)
(From Last Nights London Gazette)

~ CHAPTER 12 ~
PAGES FROM THE ANNALS

~ CHAPTER 12 ~
PAGES FROM THE ANNALS

The following extracts are taken from the Annals of the Sisters of Mercy Rochfortbridge. The Convent Annals are an annual account giving details of the work the Sisters engage in within the convent, the schools, the parish and with other convents in the diocese and around the country. They outline also their interaction socially among themselves, with the Bishop and clergy as well as documenting progress in the development of schools and buildings. Outside events impact on their lives also, such as *the Troubles* in 1920, *the Emergency* during the years 1939-1945, the opening of schools, the 1966 celebrations of the Easter Rising. They document the comings and goings of the Sisters, holidays, school, accidents, illness, tragedy and the passing of the Sisters to their just reward. Most religious orders keep and record their annals and today they have become a very important source historically, especially in social, religious, local and faith history. The Rochfortbridge Annals have been kept meticulously since 1862. There are gaps in places, and depending who the keeper of the Annals was, depended on the amount of detail recorded also. This chapter stops in the year 1970 as it is felt that other records in relation to the convent, the schools and the community are so numerous since that time. To follow on from that period would result in another book. But lets keep that for another time.

Some events are not recorded here, as they have been documented in earlier or subsequent chapters. This chapter tries to focus on events that don't relate in any way to earlier events in the book. Each year during parish visitation the annals are presented to the Bishop of the diocese. He registers his examination of them by signing his name and the date at the end of each annual record.

A.M.D.G.[1]

This Convent is the fifth filiation from St. Joseph's, Tullamore. Being founded during the octave of the Assumption was dedicated to Our Blessed Lady, and received the title of *Immaculate Conception*, during the episcopate of His Lordhip, Most Rev. Dr. Cantwell, Rev. G. Robbins being P.P.

The foundation came from St. Joseph's Tullamore to Rochfortbridge Co. Westmeath on the 21st of August 1862, accompanied by Rev. G. Robbins and the Superioress of Tullamore, Mrs. Cantwell.

The Convent was dedicated to the Conception, 4 Sisters formed the new community, being three professed and one postulant of which Mrs. Dunne was Superioress and Sr. M. Stanislaus Ó Neill assistant and Mother of Novices. Our late and much beloved and deeply

---

1   *Ad Maiorem Dei Gloriam –For the greater Glory of God.*

honoured Bishop Dr. Cantwell drove from Mullingar to welcome the filiation here, with the gracious P.P. Rev. G. Robbins and worthy curate Fr. T. O'Reilly, received the Sisters with much affection and respect. Fr. T.Ó Reilly brought the Most Holy Sacrament and deposited it in the choir, which like all other parts of the house was rough and unfinished....

1865 – A carriage and horses

The community increasing very much, the house became quite uncommodious. It was therefore agreed to strike on some plan to enlarge it. A Bazaar was determined on and our good Bishop Most Rev. Dr. Nulty gave permission for it to take place on the 22nd of June 1865. The principal prize on the occassion was the carriage and horses of our late beloved Bishop –given to the community by his nephew Rev. P. Molloy.

The zealous parish priest of Rochfortbridge left nothing undone to spur on the parishioners to take up the affair and work in earnest. They did so and each according to means acted most liberally, especially the warm-hearted benefactors Mr. Coffey, Newcastle. The Bishop and all the Diocese of Meath were generous in sending donations.

Great crowds with many of the surrounding clergy attended on the day of the bazaar. After all expenses had been paid, the sum of £400 was in hands.

1866 – Sr. Margaret Hackett was clothed taking in religion the name of Sr. M. T. Xavier Joseph, the ceremony being performed by Dr. Cantwell, a member of the neighbouring clergy attended. At the dejeuner the Bishop expressed his joy at being able to officiate as he was for some time before in delicate health predicting everything good in the future for the community. On the same day he kindly ordered Rev. Mother Stainslaus to take change of air for some time in Clara or elswhere, she, Rev. Mother being rather delicate.

1868 – Bazaar

Our bazaar was held on the 22nd and 23rd of June. It realized £500, expenses amounting to £100 reduced the amount to £400. Nearly every priest in the diocese contributed generously towards this charitable object. The principal prizes were the carriage and horses, a beautiful cameo given by Fr. Purcell to Sr. M. Stanislaus and given to him by Cardinal Cullen, a hamper of wine, a gold watch, a sheep, a Limerick lace shawl, a beautiful gold bracelet, with many other valuable things, amongst those who gave donations were

Most Rev Dr. Nulty £10

Rev. G. Robbins £5

Rev. G. Horan C.C., Rochfortbridge £5

Richard Coffey, Newcastle, £10

Rev. M. Higgins, Tullamore £3

Nearly each priest in the diocese gave £1. The ladies who furnished tables were Miss Shiel, Gurtomloe, with Miss Digan, Mullingar. Miss Nangle, Castlepollard with Miss McLoughlin. Miss Reynolds, Guilford with Miss Geoghagan, Athlone. Miss Kelly, Milltown, with Miss Byrne, Woodville. Miss Farrell, Mullingar with Miss Glynn, Mullingar.

A beautiful silver snuff box, two cakes, together with many other valuable things were raffled for.

The following convents sent some beautiful fancy work. –Tullamore, Clara, Drogheda, Tullow. There were also many amusements intended for the people such as the wheel of fortune at the post office. A band from Clara attended. The drawing of prizes took place on the 2nd day conducted by G. Petit Esq. Who took an active part in the business(shortly after he became a Christian Brother).

1st. Prize, a carriage and horses won by Rev. G. Wheeler P.P., Stamullen, Ballbriggan,who gave it to the Sisters of Mercy, Drogheda.

1872 – The new Convent
On the 3rd of August the first day the furniture was removed from the old to the new convent was passed very joyfuly by us.

10th. Aug. Mr.H. Fielding and Mrs. W. Fielding, Phillipstown visited the convent.

15th Aug. On the Feast of the Assumption the 15th of August 1872 we took up residence in our new convent. It was a day of general rejoicing and gratitude to God. Fr. Robbins said mass in it for the first time and blessed the whole house and the Sisters, Mrs. Coffey, The Misses Coffey and Master Coffey, Newcastle assisted at mass.

1875 – The Mission to Yass
Mr. L. Trimble came to say 'farewell' to the Sisters; it was a sad parting felt very lonely by us all. He gave Sr. M.Paul £3. Mrs. Locke, Kilbeggan came to see the Sisters and presented them with a beautiful statue of the Sacred Heart nicely packed in a case for travelling.

1875 – Extract from 'The Nation.'

On the 21st of last month the thirteenth anniversary of the foundation of the Convent of Our Lady of Mercy Rochfortbridge, County Westmeath four nuns of that Community left to form a house of their Institute in Australia. The immediate sense of their future labor is Yass in the Diocese of Goulbourn, where resides that distinguished prelate and Irishman Dr. Lanigan.

It is doing but scant justice to the zeal of that good Bishop to say that he spared neither time nor trouble and least of all expense to secure for his people the ministrations of the good Nuns who are now on their long journey.

The Sisters who form this little band of missionaries are Mother Paul Fielding Superioress of the foundation, Mother Alacoque McLoughlin, Mother Assistant, Sister Bernard Grennan and Sister Catherine Murphy. They are accompanied by four young ladies, Miss Leahy, Miss Mullaly, Miss O' Neill and Miss Nally, who have thus given up friends and home and severed every tie that bound them to the world. For days previous to the departure of the Sisters, the Convent was besieged by anxious and sorrowing crowds, seeking permission(which was freely accorded) to say farewell and to offer some tribute of affection to the good Sisters to whom so much was due.

Well indeed had they carried such manifestations of regret as accompanied their departure. They had labored and toiled amongst them for long years in the most unselfish spirit. They trained the children how to love and serve God. They taught the young how to live and the aged how to die. Wherever sorrow and affliction had fallen, there was the gentle Sisters to soothe the sufferers and like the Divine Master whose spouses they are, they went about doing good to all, and hence it was within the veil of their influence.

To Mother Paul, this separation from all association must indeed have been painful. Here was the greatest sacrifice of all. For she left not alone the convent home –she left her father's house –for within the walls of what is now the Convent of Rochfortbridge, Mother Paul spent her early years.

The noble little band of which she is the heroic leader was accompanied to London by Mr. N. McLoughlin, brother to the Mother Assistant and Mr. P. Delaney, chaplain to the Convent. The Sisters with six priests for the same mission sailed from London on the 28th in the ship, Gainsborough. May God protect them on their long and perilous journey.

20th Aug. The trunks and boxes belonging to the Sisters was sent on to Dublin this morning and our loved Sisters will follow them tomorrow.

21st Aug. Our loved Sisters are gone and have left many sad hearts after them. I will pass over the parting and write the extract from the 'Freemans' describing their leaving here and Ireland. [2]

1879 - Mission to Kilbeggan

The opening of the new Convent of Mercy, Kilbeggan took place on the 8th of December 1879. The Sisters forming the foundation came from Rochfortbridge and were received by the Most Rev. Dr. Nulty, Bishop of the Diocese of Meath., the very Rev. Dr. McAlroy and all the priests from the surrounding parishes. On the arrival of the Sisters, solemn High Mass was celebrated in the beautiful little Church of St. James. A most impressive sermon on the duties of the Sisters of Mercy by Rev. J.Nicole O.M.

The Church was crowded, the parishioners being most anxious to give a warm welcome to the Sisters who had come to labour amongst them. Immediately on the conclusion of the sermon the instalment of the Nuns in their little house took place. The ceremony was performed by Most Rev. Dr. Nulty, the zealous pastor of Kilbeggan, the Rev. W. Hope left nothing undone that might contribute to the comfort and happiness of the Sisters. In this he found willing co-operators in the Kilbeggan people all of whom were most generous and attentive to the Sisters.

On the 10th of January, the Sisters opened their schools. The children from the surrounding districts came in large numbers the parents being most anxious to secure for their 'little ones' the advantages of the religious harmony given by the Sisters. Before the end of the month of January there were over 200 children in the poor schools and 40 in the pension schools.

The Sisters had one great difficulty to contend with – the obtaining of the 'National Education Grant' for their schools. Owing to the existence of a vested school in the parish, the commissioners of Education refused the grant to the Convent Schools. Every effort was made by the Bishop of the Diocese and the priests to obtain the government aid but could not scceed until the sum of £250 had been paid. This sum being the amount which the Commissioners had contributed towards the erection of the vested National Schools in Kilbeggan.

The Convent of Mercy, Kilbeggan

2   See the extract attached to this chapter also. Even though the Sister who was keeper of the annals said that the extract was taken from *The Freemans Journal*, the extract came from *The Nation*.

The raising of the money necessarily involved the Sisters as they had to confront this debt, but a bazaar brought up most warmly by the people more than realized funds to pay off the debt.

Amongst the generous benefactors of the Kilbeggan Convent the names of M. Devereux, Wexford and his niece Mrs. Locke of Adrnagher, Kilbeggan may be specially mentioned as having taken an active part in the establishment of the convent. Mr. Devereux contributed the sum of £300, Mrs. Locke £100.

1886 - A bazaar for the laundry
In September a bazaar was held in the Convent grounds the object of which was to liquidate the debt due on the new laundry commenced some years before. Our beloved Bishop gave £10 as a prize. Fr. McCormick our chaplain at the time gave a jaunting car and a £5 note.

Many others gave nice prizes also and were most generous in taking tickets. The supervisor of Philipstown Reformatory Fr. Quested, kindly allowed the boys to attend with the brass band during the day and to give a dramatic entertainment in the evening, this attracted the people and afforded much amusement.

1892 – The Deaf and Dumb Institute
Dr. Nulty was anxious to start an Institute for the Deaf and Dumb girls in his diocese. He asked Rev. Mother Stanislaus to begin the work, to which she agreed. He secured the third part of the Arthur Smith Bequest towards the upkeep of the Institution. Rev. M. Stanislaus wrote to Very Rev. T Kirby, Archbishop of Ephesus, Irish College, Rome, to obtain the blessing of the Holy Father Leo XIII for the Institute for the Deaf and Dumb and also for the foundations sent to Kilbeggan and Yass, Diocese of Goulbourne, which was graciously granted.

1893 - Father Fagan arranged for a charity sermon to be preached by Most Rey Dr McCormick, Bishop of Galway, to clear off the debt on the Institution. The Pope gave a medal of his Episcopal Jubilee to be placed first in the box that it might bring a blessing on the work. Most Rev. Dr Nulty gave £50, and parishioners £132. This, with offerings from well-wishers brought the total to £300, which completely wiped out the debt. Dr Kirby also sent a piece of marble from the tomb of Saint Callistus in the Catacombs given to him by Pope Pus IX which he brought to Pope Leo XIII to be blessed for the Institute.

He also sent a picture of Our Lady of Mercy (similar to the one sent to Our Mother House, in Baggot Street, by Leo XIII which is a copy of the miraculous picture in the Church of St Prudentia in Rome) by Fr Keane to Dr Nulty for St Joseph's school. A Deaf-mute teacher was engaged to teach the deaf mutes who came to St Joseph's.

1897 & 1898 - When the new schools were opened, the entire building of St Joseph's was given over to the Deaf Mutes who had occupied part of it since

1898 - On Christmas Eve, Dr Nulty died RIP. He always took a great interest in St Joseph's Institute and bequeathed Canal Shares for the upkeep of the Institution.

1899 - In 1899 a public Concert was given. The Deaf Mutes acted "The Babes in The Wood" in signs. They also danced the Skirt Dance, Tarantella and Jig.

1909 - In this year the garden at the back of the Convent was made and fruit trees were planted. The Sisters in St Joseph's took over the garden beside the house and gave £200 to the Convent for it. The Bishop gave permission for two men to be appointed to collect for the Institution, but it was not a success and after a few years was abandoned.

1910 – A fire in St. Josephs

A fire broke out in the turf shed in St Joseph's. Some of the children saw the blaze and came to tell the Sisters about it at 2 am. The Sisters arose immediately, roused the teacher and sent her out to rouse the people to come to help. A number of them came immediately, M. Egan, N Boyhan, Fraynes, Bradleys, etc. The children kept a chain of buckets of water to them. The men broke down the roof of the shed with hatchets etc., between the fire and the coal-shed, where there was about 15 tons of coal and a cask of paraffin oil. In a short time they had the fire extinguished and all was safe again. The Sisters in the Convent knew nothing of what had happened till the next morning. The people can always be counted on to help when needed.

1912 – Convent of Mercy Golden Jubilee

The Jubilee of the house was celebrated on August 21st. Rev. Mother wished to have a great celebration, but the parishioners wished to show their appreciation of the Sisters work for them and their children. They formed a committee to make a collection through the parish and have an illuminated address prepared. The committee assembled in the Infant School. When the Sisters arrived, they congratulated them and read the address. They then presented Rev. Mother with a purse contianing £147-17/= and the illuminated address prepared by Rev. Mother Mary of the Angels Wallace and Sister M. Brigid Doyle, Borris-in-Ossory(natives of the Parish). Mr. Larry Gavin proposed and Mr. J. Boyhan seconded a vote of thanks to Rev. M. Mary and Sister M. Brigid for the artistic way they prepared the address.

After this there was an impromptu concert and many vocal items were contributed by the priests and the Sisters.

The committee were entertained to a sumptuous luncheon in St. Mary's School.

In the afternoon, the priests had dinner in the refectory. When dinner was over, we had a very enjoyable evening of music and song.

Rev. C. Murray P.P. was absent on holidays but gave a present of a carpet to Rev. Mother. Fr. Dillon C.C. said the mass and presided in the school and refectory. Also present were Fr. J. Lynam, Rev. T. Seale, Rec. P. Smith and Rev. J. Russel C.M.

The ladies of the committee were entertained next day in the refectory.

1913 – Death of Fr. Murray

On Feb. 18th Fr. Murray went to Navan after singing a requiem mass for Miss Catherine Connell R.I.P. he told the Rev. Mother he would be back on Wednesday. On Monday evening he went with Fr. Poland to look at the field where the Boyne Valley coursing match was to be held next day. On their return they paid a visit to Mr. W. Smith, Church View, and then went to the parochial house. Fr. Murray retired early to his room to say his office. Next morning Fr. Poland went to the room to call him. He found him dead in his chair with the office book in his hand, R.I.P. Evidently he had got a stroke and died off.

When Fr. Dillon received word next morning, he came to the convent and told Rev. Mother the sad news. She communicated it to the Sisters who all got a shock. The remains were brought by road to Rochfortbridge and the following day a solemn requiem was held, at which the Bishops presided and there were about 50 priests present.

The following text is transcribed from the Illuminated Address presented to the Sisters of Mercy on the 21st of August 1912 by the People of the Parish of Rochfortbridge. The address was prepared by Rev. Mother Mary of the Angels Wallace and Sr. M. Brigid Doyle, Borris-in-Ossory. They were both natives of the parish and past pupils of the Convent Primary School. The Address reflects their gratitude also to the Sisters for their education in Rochfortbridge.

Address to Rev. Mother & Community, Rochfortbridge

On the occassion of the Golden Jubilee of the Convent

On behalf of the priests and people of the united parishes of Rochfortbridge, Meedin and Milltownpass, we beg to offer you our heartiest congratulations on the occassion of the celebration of your Golden Jubilee. In doing so we wish to associate in our tribute of love and gratitude the venerable names of Mother Stanislaus and Magdalene who were pioneers of the work which, under your fostering care and inspiration, has produced results far beyond our most sanguine expectations.

When you came to the parish fifty years ago, education was at low ebb, owing to circumstances over which there was no control. Some of us can speak on this matter from personal experience and today we recall with thankfulness the brilliant record of your achievements, not only here in our own parish but among our kith and kin in distant lands.

You prepared many of us for the Sacraments of Penance , the Blessed Eucharist, and Confirmation and we look back with tender feelings to those happy days when gathered in a circle around the good Sisters, we listened to the instruction or the simple story with the moral, that was intended to take root in our very young minds, and help and safeguard us in after years.

The sick and dying have always had your sympathy and help, and it is only they who can really understand the peace and consolation your mere presence imparts. God's little afflicted ones have also been taken under your charge, and their misfortunes greatly alleviated by your gentleness, courtesy and admirable system of teaching.

In conclusion we pray God may continue to pour His special favours on you, for the many blessings we derive from your bright example and christian charity. Hoping you will accept the accompanying presentation as a tribute of esteem from your grateful friends whose names are on the appended list.

21st August 1912

Illuminated address given to the Sisters of Mercy from the people of the Parish in 1912 on the occassion of their Golden Jubilee.

Apostolic Blessing sent by Fr. P.V. Rowan O.P. to the Sisters of Mercy in October 1912 commemmorating the 50th anniversary of their house in Rochfortbridge.

The funeral which took place to Meedin immediately adterwards was largely attended by the parishioners. By his will he left us £85.

In Febrary, Fr. James Kelly P.P. Dysart was transferred to Rochfortbridge. In April Rev. M Dillon was appointed P.P. Curraha and Rev. C. Murtagh C.C. replaced him.

1917 – The Death of Mother Stanislaus O'Neill.
On August 14th. Rev. M. Stanislaus , M. Gertrude and Sr. M. Patrick went to Trim to bring home M.M. Brigid who was on retreat there. M.Stanislaus insisted on going to Navan also and then visited the Sisters friends. On August 16th she went to Glasson to see Fr. Gaughran who was very ill. On the 18th she was practising sacred music for Sunday, when she got a pain and had to retire.

Dr. Keelan was sent for. He considered her bad and was out every day to her, and sometimes spent hours with her trying to give relief. After a week she was changed to Novitiate where she lingered on in great pain till September 12th feast of the Holy Name of Mary, when she peacefully passed away R.I.P. She was one of the foundresses of the community and a very gifted Sister. She was an accomplished musician and scholar, and always tried to keep the schools and everything connected with them up-to-date. She had most to do with the building of the Convent and with M.Magdalen and Fr. Delaney got the trees and shrubs planted around the convent. Then later on, she and mother Magdalen with the help of Fathers Fagan and Gaughran got the schools built and the Institute for the Deaf and Dumb opened.

On September 14th there was a very nice requiem Mass celebrated and the Church was crowded with parishoners, who afterwards accompanied the remains to the grave preceded by the priests, Sisters and children R.I.P.

1918 – The Conscription Act.[3]
In April, the British Government decided to apply the Conscription Act to Ireland. The Irish headed by Mr. De Valera were determined to resist, but prayer was a powerful weapon

---

3   From early 1918, the British Army was dangerously short of troops for the Western Front. In the German Spring Offensive of 1918, German troops broke through the Allied lines in several sectors of the front in France, with a local advantage in numbers of four to one, putting severe strain on the Allied armies. The British Army, in one day, suffered a stunning setback, with the enemy overrunning ninety-eight square miles of territory, and penetrating, at the furthest point, to a depth of four and a half miles.

In addressing this grave military situation, the British Government decided to extend conscription to Ireland (conscription in Great Britain having started in January 1916), as an untapped reservoir of manpower for the front through a new Military Service Bill, as well as proposing a new Home Rule Bill. This had the effect of alienating both nationalists and unionists in Ireland. Despite opposition from the entire Irish Parliamentary Party, conscription for Ireland was voted through at Westminster.

Though large numbers of Irishmen had willingly joined Irish regiments and divisions of the New British Army at the outbreak of war in 1914, the likelihood of enforced conscription created a backlash. The reaction was based particularly on the fact that implementation of the Government of Ireland Act 1914 (as previously recommended in March by the Irish Convention) was controversially linked with a "dual policy" enactment of the Military Service Bill. The linking of conscription and Home Rule outraged the Irish nationalist parties at Westminster, who walked out in protest and returned to Ireland to organise opposition.

Rev. John McManus P.P. who was appointed to Rochfortbridge in 1949 celebrated the Golden Jubilee of his ordination in 1968. As a student priest in Maynooth, some ordinations were brought forward as a result of the Conscription Act, as there was a risk of some of them being conscripted into the army. For this reason he was ordained in 1918, almost a year before he was due to be ordained to the priesthood.

in the hands of the Irish people. During Our Lady's Month of May, the devotions were offered every evening by the order of the Bishops of Ireland, consisting of rosary, Benediction and hymn to Our Lady of Lourdes that the evil might be averted. There was also a jubilee procession of the Blessed Sacrament round our grounds with Benediction of the Blessed Sacrament at an altar erected on the hill at the back of the trees in our field. There was a very large attendance of the parishioners and some people from neighbouring parishes.

1920 –Busy and Troubled Times

Gaulstown House Greenhouse
During the summer, everything in Gaulstown was put put up for sale. We got word the greenhouse would be sold for £10. Mother Gertrude and Sister Theresa were talking to Fr. Kane about it. He said it would be a very good thing to get it and handed £10 to Sister Theresa for it to have flowers for the chapel.

Mr. Symonds, Gardener at Gaulstown house in 1899. The Greenhouse in the background was purchased by the Sisters of Mercy in 1920 for £10 and installed beside the Convent.

Black and Tan Activities
During 1919 and 1920 the Black and Tans were guilty of great cruelty through the country. Many were shot without any reason, and many more imprisoned without cause. In other parts of the country people suffered much more than around here. Lorry loads of Black and Tans with rifles were constantly passing and many shots were fired.

On a few occassions, the Sisters who were in the grounds narrowly escaped being hit by bullets, and often shots were fired from the barracks and very light sent out.

The Sisters in St. Joseph's were terrified one night, a number of lorries stopped in the village and a number of Black and Tans came to the door and hammered on it to get in. Fortunately someone told them it was a convent and got them away.

On another occassion there was a round up of the district when the military were searching for the IRA men who were wanted. People who had come in for confession at a big station[4] were not allowed and they were examined and the officers gave them leave.

---

4   Stations were an Irish tradition quite common across Ireland. Today the tradition is still carried on in the west of Ireland. A number of families each year volunteered to hold a station in their homes. The parish was divided into districts for this. A station was a mass celebrated in the home and all the neighbours of the district attended. Confessions were held beforehand and then mass was celebrated in the house. At the end of the station, the host family provided the priest and neighbours with breakfast.
The tradition grew up during the Penal days, when people moved secretly from house to hear mass celebrated or at mass rocks or bushes at remote locations around the country. This Mass became known as the "station Mass" because of the random movement from place to place. In some areas, some houses became known locally as regular venues for Mass and became known as Mass houses. More of these emerged as the Penal Laws were repealed but the Catholic community still did not have resources to build enough churches. With the relaxation of the penal code, mass moved indoors into little chapels and later following Catholic Emancipation when there was a huge growth in church building, mass rocks and bushes were abandoned, to be remembered only in folklore, although today such places are cherished as places and emblems for the preservation of the past in a very dark historical period. The station tradition remained and became very much part of Irish faith culture. The social changes of recent decades have forced change on many aspects of the tradition around the Station Mass. However, the tradition remains strong in may parishes esecially in the west and south of Ireland.

Colonel Cooper, a retired British Officer and his wife had to remain with all the others. The soldiers camped for the night in the field oppossite St. Joseph's and the officers examined the school and St. Joseph's to see would they suit for them. Fr. Kelly very kindly came along and allowed them to stay in the parochial house. They left the next day after a fruitless search. Some of the soldiers actually jumped their horses over the ditch where the men were hiding near Croghan Hill.

Many houses in the parish were raided and four parishioners were imprisoned in a tiny cell in the barracks for a considerable time. We supplied a dinner to them each day. Rev. Mother spoke to Dr. Keelan about their condition. He reported the matter to the military authorities who had them removed to Athlone and afterwards to other prisons.

Things were so bad that the bishops issued a statement setting forth some of the atrocities committed, and directed that a novena be held in all churches in preparation for the feast of the Irish Saints, Nov. 6th. And that the litany of the Blessed Virgin Queen of Peace be recited on Sundays after mass and on other days to obtain from the Divine Mercy, peace, freedom and every blessing spiritual and temporal for our beloved country.

The Convent Chapel Project
Since 21st november 1917 the Sisters had collected £100 for the chapel.

In January Most Rev. Dr. Gaughran held visitation and was asked by Rev. Mother Gertrude for permission to make a public collection for funds towards the new chapel. He granted the request, and next day's post brought a cheque for £200 from His Lordship *'For your New Chapel'*.

On September 5th, Most Rev. Dr. Gaughran Rev. W Bracken P.P. V.F., Kinnegad received Sr. M. Cecilia's vows. For the occassion there was a charity sermon preached by Rev. Malachy Gavin Provincial C.P., Fr. F. Rowan C.C., Longwood celebrated the Mass. Fr's Murtagh and Clavin were C.C.'s at the time and Rev. James Kelly P.P. The Charity Sermon realized £118 + £7 and £125. By the end of December there were £2000 on hands, the principal sources being:

<u>Parish Collection</u> for which Rev. C. Murtagh was responsible. He appointed collectors: Messrs. Hugh O'Neill, Michael Kilmurray, M. Frayne, T. Dunne, P. Daly, (Tyrrellspass), P. Gavin and P. Casey(Dalystown), W. Carey and P. Geraghty(Oldtown). This realized £379-7/=

<u>A fete</u> was held during the summer. One of the principal organizers being Miss Kate Mullaly, Mullingar. These were half hour concerts, dances, fortune-telling, tea room, cock fights etc, etc. In all it realized £254 -9-0.[5]

Death of Fr. Kelly
On the morning of February 21st, our P.P., Rev. T. Kelly got suddenly ill and before his C.C. Rev. C. Murtagh, who had gone on sick calls could be got, he was dead. Fr. Downes C.C. Tyrrellspass was sent for, but he also was late. Rev. Mother and some of the Sisters said the prayers for the dying. He was a great priest and a wonderful preacher. He reached the great age of eighty four years.

One of our former C.C.'s Rev. J. O'Callaghan C.C. Kells who was suffering from phlebitis got suddenly very bad on the 25th of February. His fellow curate Rev. P. Casey had only time to anoint him when he breathed his last, R.I.P.

---

5   See Appendices for breakdown of funds raised in the Summer of 1920-1923

Rev. Fr. T. O'Farrell, President of St. Finian's College was appointed P.P. Rochfortbridge and took up duty on April 2nd.

Death of M.M. Magdalen Hackett

On July 28th. Rev. W. Bracken P.P.V.F., Kinnegad received Sr. M. Imelda's vows, soon after the close of the annual retreat which was conducted by Fr. Nolan C.S.S.R. On the same day about 3.00 p.m. Mother Mary Magdalen died a very holy death, having got absolution from several priests who were present at the ceremony.[6]

She had been confined to bed for more than ten years and though not suffering much, was very helpless. An attendant was always with her, and for some weeks before she died a Bon Secour nun was in attendance. She was unable to speak for a few days, but was conscious till the last moment.

She was one of the foundresses of the Convent, having come from Tullamore in 1862 with Sr. M. Stanislaus and Rev. M. Gertrude Dunne. She did great work through the parish among the poor and the sick, and prepared many, even big men for the sacraments. She did splendid work in the schools also and having a great love for plants and flowers, she did much to adorn the grounds with them. She, M.M. Gertrude and Fr. Delaney laid out the grounds and got the trees planted. The older generation revered her, the younger people did not know her as she was so long an invalid.

She was laid to rest in the Convent cemetery on July 30th after Solemn Requiem Mass at which a great number of priests were present. The rain poured all day and the edge of the grave slipped in. This had to be settled during the office. In spite of wind and rain, the singing at the graveside was heavenly. R.I.P.

1921 – The Gibbonstown Races.

This year again, the people organized a race which realized £87-10/=. The Gavins(all branches), Careys, Fraynes, Haffords, T. Dunne and Mr. Maher Newcastle were some of the principal organizers.

1922 – The Third Race Meeting.

The building of the new chapel was begun in June.... For the third time races were organized by the same zealous committee and £105 was handed to Rev. Mother for the chapel fund as the result...

On Christmas Eve, the Sisters went into the new Chapel. At about 11.45 p.m. they assembled on the gallery and there sang the *Te Deum*, Adeste and hymn to Our Lady. Afterwards they went to choir for morning office and retired at 2.00 a.m.

1923 – The New Convent Chapel

In January, Rev. T. O'Farrell P.P. assisted by Rev. M.Moore C.C. consecrated our new chapel...

The Bishop was very pleased with the chapel. Fr. Herbert C.P. gave the annual retreat in July.

A concert was organized for funds to clear off the debt on chapel and realized £98-10/=.

---

6   Mother Mary Magdalene Hackett, was the last of the founder members of the House at Rochfortbridge.

Final payment of £56-12/= was paid to Mr. Murphy on 11th June and to Mr. Cullen of £58-8/= on 26th July. The £3500 collected was expended as follows:-

Furniture	Cost
Stalls	£180
Stations	£70
Carpet	£65
Repair Harmonium	£15
Brass Goods	£30
Vestment Press	£40
Prie Dieux [7]	£20
Total	**£410**

Furniture	Cost
Mr. Murphy	£2500
Mr. Cullen	£160
Mr. Early(Windows)	£300
Mr. Mullaly(Heating)	£120
Furniture	£420
Total	**£3500**

1924 – On October 21st. Fr. O'Farrell received Sr. M. Attracta's first vows. This was the first ceremony in the new chapel.

1926 – The Grotto

This year Mr. And Mrs. Mullaly had a grotto erected in our grounds as a thanksgiving to Our Lady for favours received. It was solemnly blessed by Fr. O'Farrell.

1932 – The Eucharistic Congress

This year is memorable for the magnificent display of faith at the Eucharistic Congress in Dublin. In common with other places, Rochfortbridge was artistically decorated. Fr. Callary with a number of parishioners assisting had festoons of laurels, bunting, banners, pictures etc. through the village. The convent also displayed Congress flags from the roof, also from

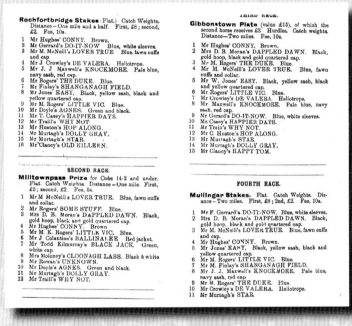

The front and rear pages of the the Gibbonstown Race card, 1921. This event was held in 1921, 1922 and 1923, the funds raised were donated to a fund to finance the building of the Convent Chapel.

The inside pages of the race card

---

7   A narrow, desk like kneeling bench with space above for a book or the elbows, for use by a person at prayer.

the chapel and schools and bunting all through the grounds.

As there was no provision for Nuns attending any of the ceremonies, even on children's day, we had not the pleasure of seeing the splendid decoration in Dublin or the Park.

The Confessional and the Hall
Our Bishop Dr. Mulvaney told us to have a confessional erected in the chapel. This was purchesed from Mr. Nolan for £36. Some years ago we appealed for a grant to build a

The Convent Chapel in the 1990's

play shed, but we got no acknoeldgement of our communication. As we needed it badly, we started the work ourselves. Mr. Kelly who built the hall suggested having it enclosed and eventually it was decided to erect the present structure at a cost of £340 for recreation hall and cookery room.

1934 –The Death of Sr. M. Alacoque Coffey
Sr. M. Alacoque suffered from disease of the heart for years, and during the early part of the year was not very strong, and required a good deal of rest. Later she got much better and was able to attend all the community duties, and during the year was in better health than she had been for a long time.

On Nov. 10th she got a bad heart attack and had to remain in bed. Dr. Keelan attended her and considered her case serious. He advised us to have her attended and she received the last Sacraments from Rev. M. Troy C.C. on the day of her death, Saturday November 24th, Dr. Keelan saw her, and said she was somewhat improved, and he would send medicine.

M. Brigid remained with her most of the day until 2 O'Clock, when she went to spend some time with Miss D. Morris who had come to pay a visit to Sr. M. Attracta. One or other of the Sisters stayed with her all day until recreation time when we left her for a short time.

Fr. Donegan who was staying in the Parish collecting for the new Cathedral paid her a visit, heard her confession and gave her Holy Viaticum at 10 O'Clock.

At 5 O'Clock p.m. as we were going to the chapel to prepare for Confession, we heard her knocking. M.M. Gertrude went to her cell and took her out. When she had been out a moment, she gave a little cry and her head fell forward. Her pure soul had gone to God without a struggle. M.M. Gertrude, who did not know at the time Sr. M. Alacoque was dead, could not stir and it was some time before she could attact the Sisters attention. When they came up and got her into bed, it was plain to be seen her soul had winged its way to the great white throne. Word was at once sent to the priests and to her brother Dick. He, being a deaf mute would not come near the remains, though they had always been devoted to each other.

On Sunday morning at 7 O'clock her remains were brought to the convent Chapel, where the parishioners came all day to pay their respects to the dear departed , who had always taken such an interest in them. Her remains were removed on Sunday evening to the Parish Church, accompanied by a great number of people and neighbouring clergy. On Monday there was a Solemn Office and requiem Mass for the repose of her soul at 11 O'Clock. His Lordship Most Rev. Dr. Mulvaney presided and there were 23 priests present. After the last absolution was given by the Bishop, the funeral took place to the convent Cemetery R.I.P.

Sr. M. Alacoque was the daughter of Mr. Richard Coffey, Newcastle, who was such a generous benefactor to the Sisters when they first came to Rochfortbridge. She entered at the age of seventeen and taught in the school for many years. She also taght music and played the organ. She was specially gifted in preparing for First Communion....

Funds for the new Cathedral in Mullingar
During the year Dr. Mulvaney sent a letter to each Convent, striking a flat rate of £300 for each Convent to be paid in instalments for the Cathedral. Some had subscribed liberally when collections were first made and others, little or nothing –that the latter were in a better position to give a share now. We had already given £50 in 1933 and this year gave £150. Balance will be paid later.

Death of Fr. O'Farrell

1937 - In January Fr. O'Farrell got a very bad flu cold, and could not be persuaded to mind himself. He developed pneumonia, and was very ill for a long time, having a nurse to mind him. He got somewhat better but did not recover. On Sept. 8th he went to a private nursing home, and returned for Christmas not much improved..

Photo taken in Lysters yard in 1932. The building in the background is Rowans. The village is dcorated with bunting to celebrate the Eucharistic Congress in that year.
Pictured are the Lyster family, with Fr. Dineen. Back row, from left to Right, James Lyster, Bridie Quinn and Fr. Dineen. Middle row from left to right, Jim Lyster, Attracta Feely (Mullingar), Nell Lyster and Christina Lyster with baby Essie on her knee. In front from left to right are, Una, Monica and Jack Lyster.

1938 - Fr. O' Farrell remained an invalid, and had two nurses to mind him. He got much worse in June, and died on July 14th. he was much regretted by all his parishioners to whom he was a real father, and to young boys preparing for the priesthood, and young girls who wished to enter the Convents. R.I.P...

Fr. McKeever was appointed P.P. in August and took up duty first Friday in September.

1941 – Fr. McKeever was changed to Castlepollard as P.P. on Jan. 17th the community and the parishioners missed him very much. He did grat work in the parish during his few years here.

1947 – Mother Attracta appointed Mother Superior

In the election of the 18th January. Sr. M. Attracta Duffy was duly elected Mother Superior. Rev. Monsignor Flynn P.P. V.G., Tullamore presided at the election assisted by Very Rev. Fr. Kilmartin P.P., Rochfortbridge. The following council were then elected by the votes of the community:-

Mother M. Antonia O' Kelly	Mother Assistant
Mother M. Catherine Healy	Mother Bursar
Mother Brigid Brady	Mistress of Novices

Mother M. Gertrude Smith at her own request retired from office –that of novice mistress.

A Great Snow Storm

The following week a snow storm commenced and lasted over a period of six weeks during which the National School was closed. Necessary certificates beig produced.

Sr. Agnes knocked down by a vehicle

On Tuesday of Easter week, when Sisters were putting things in order after funeral,[8] Sr. M. Agnes was on her way to the Parish Church was knocked down by English's bread van and her left leg badly broken and mangled. Doctors Fox and Keelan were sent for and the same evening she was removed by ambulance to Mullingar hospital, where she remained over a period of eleven weeks.

1948 – St. Joseph's Secondary School began (See chapter on the History of St. Josephs.

1949. – The New Boys National School –Scoil Bhríde

On March 7th Feast of St. Thomas Aquinas, the new boys School was officially opened. Bishop and Vicars Forane attended.[9] Our P.P. Very Rev. J. Kilmartin requested that boarders

---

8   On the 5th of April 1947, Sr. M. Bernadette who had been suffering from TB for a number of years passed away. She died in Mullingar hospital . Her remains were accompanied to Rochfortbridge by Fr. Delaney C.C., four Sisters from the Rochfortbridge Community, four Sisters from the Mullingar Community and Dr. Peter Fox. After Solemn High Office and High Mass on Easter Monday, she was laid to rest in the company of six Sisters of Charity, a large gathering of relatives and laity and at least 28 Diocesan priests attended.

9   **Vicar Forane** A priest who by a bishop's appointment exercises limited jurisdiction over the clergy in a district of a diocese.

and pupils of Convent School should walk in procession to the official opening ceremony. Sisters accompanied children.

1951 – Card Drive

In March a card drive was organized by Rev. P. Delaney C.C., ably assisted by Mr. V. Foley N.T. and local committee to defray parochial expenses, principally to reduce debt on teachers residence. The running was on lines of monster drive previous year, but crowd and receipts did not come up to their expectations, however after paying off all expenses, Fr. Delaney gave £100 to Rev. Mother to lessen debt incurred by E.S.B. and also lodged £100 credit in Parochial Funds. .

Sale of Work

A Sale of Work –the proceeds of which were to go to Convent funds was organized by Sisters and Children of Mary. During the year, wool and materials were distributed and tasty and seviceable garments made. Many acceptable gifts were received and in all there was a magnificent display in St. Mary's School, Dec. 9th. Children of Mary attended at counters, while school children sold raffle tickets. In the Infant School, Mick Frayne took charge of Mens Dept. Later in the evening he acted as auctioneer for jumble sale. The sale was a huge success and realized the proud sum of £240.

1953 – Monster Raffle

It was decided by the Sisters to get up a raffle to help cear off the debt for the electric light. The following provided the prizes.

Rev. J. McMAnus	£10
Mr. T. Gavin	Fat Lamb or £6
Michael Egan, John Carey, and Mrs Julia Daly(M. Gertrude's Sister	£5 each
Mr. Fallon	£2
Mrs. O'Neill	Silver Coffee pot

We got the tickets from the Westmeath Examiner Office and Mr. Cox very kindly provided them free of charge. The tickets were distributed among the children, neighbouring teachers and Sister's friends before the holidays...

On September 24th, the raffle draw took place in the Convent Hall. Dr. Fox presided with Fr. McManus. One of the children drew the ticket. Prizes went to Dublin, Meath, Longford, Galway, Leitrim and five to Westmeath. It realized £146 after all expenses were paid.

The Mikado

On December 16th the Sisters were invited to St. Finian's College for the opera 'The Mikado.' Mothers M.Catherine and Agnes, Sr. M. Joseph, Aquin, Magdalen, Stanislas, Rosario and Dolores attended it.

1955 – Sr. M. Brigid's Golden Jubilee

On May 24th Mother M. Brigid celebated the Golden Jubilee of Profession. She wished to have a quiet celebration with her own friends, but M. M. Attracta and the community were anxious to mark the occassion with High Mass etc. The Bishop very kindly consented to preside at the mass which was celebrated by Fr. Fallon, Kinnegad, Fr. Kennedy was deacon, Fr. Carey Sub Deacon and Fr. McManus Master of Ceremonies. With the exception of Fr. Delaney who was on holidays, Fr. M. Moore and Fr. J.F. Murphy who were ill all the former curates joined in the celebrations –also present were Fr. Farrelly P.P.V.F., Killucan, Fr. P. Gaughran P.P. Curraha(cousin), and former P.P. Fr. McKeever P.P.V.F.(Trim). The jubilarian's brother, sister and a number of nieces and nephews were also present. After the mass all were entertained to a beautiful lunch by the community. In the evening a picture was shown in St. Joseph's and an address read by P. Cunningham. Afterwards, tea was served in the Convent and the guests dispersed after a pleasant day. Five Sisters from Navan were present and Rev. Mother and two Sisters came over from Kilbeggan in the evening.

1956 – New Dormitory

Much needed reconstruction was undertaken by Mr. Roarty, contractor in the month of May. A large open dromitory in St. Joseph's was divided into cubicles, and cost in the region of £300. Senior pupils were allocated separate compartments to the great satisfaction of all. A sister occuppies one cubicle. Thus ensuring safety and supervision during the night.

1957 – February Storm

On February 4th there was a severe storm of wind, which did damage all through the country. Many slates were blown off the Convent, St. Martha's, St. Joseph's and a ridge tile was blown off the Infant school which broke six slates. Six trees were blown down, and one of the boarders narrowly escaped being struck by one as it fell.

1958 – New Convent Hall

Rev. Mother M. Attracta went to Mullingar to get Dr. Kyne's permission to secure loan to build assembly hall in St. Joseph's. The leave was got and Mr. Ginnell, Architect drew up plans which were sanctioned by His Lordship. The contract was signed and work was started in July. Mr. O'Reilly, Mullingar was Contractor.

Death of Mother M. Attracta, following car accident.

On December 4th, M.M. Attracta went to the city by bus to visit a nose specialist, Mr. O'Dogherty, who was attending her. She was travelling with her aunt and brother in his car, when they were in collision with a high powered car driven by a lady and they met with a very serious accident, which in M.M. Attracta's case proved fatal. They were taken to Jervis Street and treated there. She suffered very much from shock and she had broken ribs which pierced the lungs causing haemmorrhage which weakened the heart and she died as a result before leaving the theatre, on evening of December 8th, R.I.P. Fr. Daniel, her brother was with her. We got word of the accident on Sunday about noon –a wee notice on the paper. We phoned the hospital and sister answered and said patient was resting, she was suffering from shock and there was no cause for alarm. She had just a broken rib and some bruises.

Next morning Revd. Mother and Sr. M. Carmel visited her and found her very weak but conscious and able to say a few words to them. She was later anointed and then taken to the theatre and was there for a few hours, brought back and again taken to the theatre, but the heart gave out.

The two Sisters had gone home(left the city) when we got a phone to say 'she was very low and to pray for her.' We said the rosary and when finished, we came out of the choir. Rev. Mother and Sr. M. Carmel had just come in. We phoned again and got word , 'no hope!'

Revd. Mother, Srs. Joseph and Magdalen went up with Dr. Fox. They met Fr. Dan when they arrived and he said she was dead about an hour. We got a phone at about 11p.m.

We contacted the mason to prepare and build the grave and sent the coffin and hearse up next day at 3.30.

The remains arrived at about 5.30 accompanied by a very large funeral. The friends were in the convent for tea afterwards. The sisters of Mercy from Kilbeggan and Mullingar county hospital, were here and the neighbouring clergy.

Office and High Mass at 11 a.m. on the following day Dec. 10th the Sisters of Mercy from Drogheda, Navan, Ardee and the Franciscans from Bloomfield were present at Office and funeral.

The priests with His Lordship Dr. Kyne, Sisters and relations were entertained to lunch in Convent after funeral.

1960 – The First Concert *Pearl the Fisher Maiden performed on 17th March*. See the chapter *Shows and Musicals*

1962 – Centenary of the house celebrated. See *History of the Secondary School*

1963 – St. Joseph's becomes Co-Ed.
March 29th was Confirmation day. 100 children were confirmed. There was a big attendance to welcome the Bishop and the children answered very well. His Lordship announced the extension of St. Joseph's Secondary School to accommodate the boys of the district. Mr. Ginnell drew up the plans and Mr. Ledwith, Longford started work in the building on June 4th. When school reopened in September, the work was not finished but pupils were taken into old building. Ten boys attended. On Sunday September 15th Dr. Kyne blessed the extension, afterwards parishioners who were present attended rosary and benediction in parish church. Very Rev. J. McManus P.P., Rev. J. Conlon C.C. P.Fallon W.J. and very Revd. W Clarke P.P., Eglish were present. Also present were P. Ginnell, Architect, Ledwith Brothers, contractor, Dr. Fox and Mr. McAuliffe, Senator. On 7th October, classes were able to move into the new building.

1965 – Mother Brigid's Diamond Jubilee
On 24th May, Mother Brigid celebrated the Diamond Jubilee of her profession. Mass was celebrated in Convent Chapel on that day by Very Rev. Fr. McManus P.P. and the jubilarian with the community celebrated the occassion with fitting ceremonial. On 23rd May, the

previous Sunday, the friends of the Jubilarian were entertained to lunch by Rev. Mother and Community, and later in the evening, Benediction was given by Very Rev. T. Brady P.P. On the following Sunday, Feast of the Ascension, 27th May, the Sisters from Kilbeggan were entertained to lunch and in the afternoon, they, with the pupils of St Joseph's were entertained in St. Joseph's Hall to a very pleasant film. The celebraations continued all that week, during the course of which His Lordship paid a visit on the 28th May.

1966 – St. Loman's Pantomime/ The Sisters from LoughGlynn/Leaving Cert and Confirmation
On the 12th of March, St. Loman's Hospital put on their annual pantomime in the County Buildings and Fr. Cleary, the Chaplain invited the Sisters to a matinee.

Rev. Mother, Sr. M.Joseph, Concepta and Philomena enjoyed the show.

The sisters from LoughGlynn stayed in the convent for over a week during the close of Marchand beginning of April.

During those days, they collected in the parish and also in the neighbouring parishes.

On the 30th of March Mr. McCanna, a secondary Inspector from Dublin examined the oral Irish of the Leaving Certificate.

On the 25th of April, Confirmation was held in the parish. The bishop was very well though he had been of indifferent health for some time previously. He examined the accounts of the convent, and did visitation of the Sisters.

Sale of Work
A Sale of Work was held to reduce debt on St. Joseph's during the week 20th-27th. March. It was well supported and the people of the parish and the children's friends came along with gifts and bought tickets and so helped make it a financial success.

The Easter Rising
This year being the golden jubilee of the Easter Rising, the event was comemmorated in the parish. Mass was said in Irish by Fr. Conlon C.C. and afterwards the children of the parish and the teachers, people and clergy assembled in the Hall where a tribute was paid to the men who fought in 1916. Very Rev. Fr. McManus P.P., spoke, as did Mr. Ó Riordáin N.T.. Afterwards the National Anthem was sung and the proclamation of Independance read.

1970 – Nuns on Bikes
In July of this year, two bicycles were purchased for the Sisters. They are to be used for visitation of the sick, and Sisters also go out together to take the fresh air. In July Srs. M. Concepta and Columba took part in a charity ride in the neighbouring parish of Cstletown Geoghagan and brought in £40 in funds.

NUNS ON BIKES.

The Annals record in 1970 the purchase of two bikes to take the sisters out on visits into the community. In the first photo, Sister Concepta shows everyone how it is done. In the second picture, Sister Magdalene and Sister Geraldine get stuck in with great enthusiasm. In the first photo Sister Concepta's handling of the bike is witnessed by Sister's Columba, Genevieve, Maureen and Aquin. In the second picture Siser Pius and friends show their approval.

~ CONVENT CELEBRATIONS ~

Celebrations in the Convent, from left to right, Eileen
McMahon, Breda O'Connell, Tess Geraghty,
Mary Meehan and Chrissie McNamara.

Chrissie McNamara, happy in retirement

Back row, from left to right Sr. Magdalene, Kathleen McMahon, Chrissie McNamara,
Kathleen Farrell, Eileen McMahon, Breda Daly, Mary Pearse and Sr. Maureen.
In front, from left to right, Jean Arthur and Sr. Annunciata.

~ CHAPTER 13 ~
ST. JOSEPHS CHURCH, MILLTOWNPASS

~ CHAPTER 13 ~
ST. JOSEPH'S CHURCH, MILLTOWNPASS

The first Catholic church in Milltownpass was built in 1794 and was a mud-walled building. In 1825 the mud walls were replaced with stone and a new roof was put on the building. In 1867, during the ministry of Fr. Robbins, extensive renovations were carried out, then in 1879 plans were drawn up and work commenced on a new cruciform church. It was dedicated by Most Rev. Dr. Cantwell to St. Joseph in 1879, but was not completed until 1833. Mr. William

St. Joseph's Church
Foundation Stone Was Laid And Blessed
On May 1st 1977
By Most Reverend John McCormack DD
Bishop Of Meath
Rededicated By
Bishop Michael Smith
On February 3rd 2008
Following Renovations

Haue was the architect and the site was donated by the Boyd Rochfort family. The second chapel at Milltownpass was probably erected towards the close of the eighteenth century. It was almost entirely rebuilt by Fr. Fagan in 1879 and was dedicated to St. Joseph.

In 1977 another new church was erected in Milltownpass, also dedicated to St. Joseph. The old church was closed in December 1976 and was demolished to provide space for the new building. The foundation stone for the new building was laid on the 1st. May 1977 and it was concecrated on the 4th December 1977 by Most Rev. John McCormack and Rev. Patrick Fallon preached the homily. The architect was Mr. Kelly of Galway and the contractor was Christopher Bennett and Son, of Milltownpass. The site was extended to provide car parking facilities and part of the site was donated by Mr. Tom Coyne of Milltownpass. Rev. Colm Murtagh C.C. was responsible for the work.

In 1989 the Abbey Stained Glass Company provided new windows in Milltownpass church at a cost of £5,010. The old statue of St. Joseph which rested at the apex of old St. Joseph's Church now stands in the grounds of the present Church.

~ THE CONVENT OF MERCY ~

The Convent of Mercy, taken from
St. Joseph's Secondary School

The Entrance to the Convent of Mercy

The Convent Chapel

Our Lady of Mercy
keeps vigil over the
Convent Grounds

The front Facade of the Convent of Mercy

The Entrance Hall

The upstairs corridor leading to the Sisters Sleeping quarters.

The Dining room

The main corridor downstairs

The kitchen

The main stairs

The back stairs

Stop and Pray

Gardian angel look over us

St. Anthony and the Christ Child

The prayer chapel

Holy Spirit guide us

The Nun's Chapel

The Altar Window, sponsored by Rev. T. Masterson

Chapel Window, sponsored by Miss E. Garry

Chapel Window, sponsored by Patrick Leogue

The Grotto was erected in 1926 by Mr. And Mrs. Mullaly as a thanksgiving for favours received. It was solemnly blessed by Fr. O'Farrell P.P. –The Annals of the Sisters of Mercy, Rochfortbridge

A landmark tree in the convent grounds –the weeping ash

The grounds, at the front of the Convent

~ CHAPTER 14 ~
ROCHFORTBRIDGE
IN THE 1940'S

~ CHAPTER 14 ~
ROCHFORTBRIDGE IN THE 1940's

Introduction

The coming of the Sisters of Mercy in 1862 was a milestone in the history of Rochfortbridge and the establishment of the Convent Primary school at St. Joseph's and later in the new school in 1896 was the completion of a vision initiated by Fr. Gerald Robbins who saw a great need for the education of women in the parish and later in the century Dr. Nulty's request to establish an Institute for the Deaf and Dumb saw the Sisters of Mercy take on new challenges and were not afraid to do so. To provide for these challenges, they upskilled and received training to meet those needs or employed personnel who were trained in the field of education at primary level or in the area of special needs. The demise of the Institute was not as a result of it failing to function, but greater and more

Taken in the Park in the 1940's, at the back from left to right are Kate Coroon, Malachy(Mal) Gavin and Michael Coroon. In front are May Gallagher, Catherine Donoghue(Gainstown), Kathleen Gallagher, Dodie Gallagher, Deirdre Saunders(Mullingar) and Bridie Gallagher. The Gallagher children went to the Convent Primary school until 1949, when they moved to Clontarf in Dublin.

modern facilities at a more central location in Cabra in Dublin meant that it was more difficult to acquire pupils for the school. It finally closed its doors in 1940 and it would be another eight years until the Sisters of Mercy would take on a new venture and perhaps its most challenging one to date, the establishment of a Secondary school at St. Josephs. The story of St. Josephs can be compared to the little proverb *Great oaks from little acorns grow.* It would begin in a small way and over the next fifty years would expand into one of the largest secondary co-ed schools in the midlands with over 800 pupils. In order to set the scene for it's early beginnings it is important to take another look at life in the village and the parish in general to look at the lives of the people and the Sisters and how through this interaction with each other their vision for their commnity would take on a new life which would change the fabric of the village and the school would become a focal point in the social and educational development of the students who passed throught its doors.

When the Deaf and Dumb Institute finally closed its doors, St. Joseph's lay idle, apart from a small number of boarders attending the National School. It was a time when it appeared that there was very little happening in the village apart from the daily routines of buying and selling in the shops and pubs, or the residents with land adjacent, who brought their animals twice daily to the byres and sheds for milking.

It was the period where ration books were issued and commodities such as sugar and tea were in short supply. The Sisters of Mercy have recorded also their difficulties in acquiring certain goods which prior to 1939, were quite readily available:-

May Gallagher on the street of Rochfortbridge in 1947. St. Joseph's is visible in the background

> During the war years there was great difficulty in getting goods and the prices were exorbitant. We could get no veiling, apron or handkerchief check and it was almost impossible to get serge or calico. Butter, tea, sugar, flour bread, soap and clothes were rationed and coupons had to be produced for each. Part of the time people were only allowed ½ lb of sugar, ½ ozs. of tea ¼ lb. of butter and 2 ozs. margarine per week. Later this was increased to ¾ lb. of sugar, ¾ ozs. of tea, 6 oz. of butter and ¼ lb of margarine. 6 ozs. of soap was allowed per person per month and during a strike which lasted some months, the 6 ozs. had to do for two months. Serge was about £1 a yard and calico four shillings to four and sixpence and not good at that price.[1]

So the problems encountered by the Sisters in acquiring goods for the convent as well as the boarders at the school were the same for the families living in the parish also.

Ireland's neutrality in the war coupled with our location out in the Atlantic set the scene again for possible famine in the country, but the government introduced a scheme that ensured that people would not starve.

Each farmer was obliged to provide space on their lands for compulsory tillage. With the scarcity of petroleum products, the carriage and trap were taken out and dusted down, the axels greased and the horse drawn vehicles travelled the roads again. Transtport reverted back to the status it had in 1900, except for emergency vehicles such as the doctor, the Guards and the army. Some people managed to get fuel on the black market, but it was an expensive commodity and only those who were well off managed to keep a vehicle on the road.

---

1   Annals of the Sisters of Mercy, p.311.

The coming of the wireless, Paddy Dowd and all that...

Despite the difficulties of the time, new innovations like the wireless were coming on stream and it soon became a regular chore for a young boy or girl to bring the wet battery for re-charging at Paddy Dowd's Garage. Even though things were quiet in Rochfortbridge, Paddy Dowd still mended punctures on bicycles and cars and provided a hackney service for people who neded to get places in an emergency. He was always available to the Sisters in the convent for those sometimes urgent calls in the night for a doctor or visit to the hospital.

On Sundays, people gathered to listen to Mícheál O'Hehir broadcast commentaries from the G.A.A. matches at Croke Park. Michael O'Hehir gave his first commentary when Galway defeated Monaghan in the All-Ireland Senior Football Semi-Final at Cusack Park in Mullingar on the14th of August, 1938. It was at this local venue that this distinctive voice which became part and parcel of Irish life for many years on radio was heard for the first time.

Paddy Dowd was the heart and soul of the village in the 1940's and 1950's. His garage was located where Michael Cooney's garage is now. His wit and quiet spoken ways endeared him to many people and a few incidents relating to his time in Rochfortbridge are recounted in this chapter.

At night the dials were adjusted to listen to hear the words broadcast across Europe *'Germany Calling! Germany Calling!'*[2] William Joyce, or Lord Haw Haw as he was nicknamed found an audience in Ireland and Britain, broadcasting propaganda to the English Speaking world. Being of Irish-American stock by possessing a British passport, he would later hang for treason.

The wireless became a very important social event in people's lives and it too was the forerunner to the quiet revolution of rural electrification which would reach Rochfortbridge in 1949.

One funny story from this early period of Irish radio relates to a farmer's wife in the Rochfortbridge area who was one of the lucky people to possess one of the first wireless sets. It was mounted on the wall in the kitchen and the thin narrow aerial wire was directed

---

2   William Joyce (24 April 1906 – 3 January 1946), nicknamed *Lord Haw-Haw*, was an Irish-American fascist politician and Nazi propaganda broadcaster to the United Kingdom during the Second World War. He was controversially hanged for treason by the British as a result of his wartime activities, being taken to owe allegiance to the UK by his possession of a British passport.

out the window and fastened to the eave gutter outside. She was crossing the kitchen floor with a bundle of plates when the wireless beeped and the announcer spoke, *'This is Radio Éireann!* She got such a fright, she jumped, crossing the kitchen floor carrying a bundle of dinner plates.

'Oh God bless us!' she shouted.

At the same time, the plates fell on the cement floor, smashing in to tiny fragments. The husband, sitting in the corner shouted and laughed at the same time,

'Begob Mary, chaineys!'[3]

Dr. Peter Fox from Milltownpass is recorded many times in the Annals of the Sisters of Mercy as he was often called upon to attend the convent during times of illness. He was also a member of the company established in Milltownpass in 1941 to provide electricity in the village for the first time, by harnessing the waters of the local river to operate a turbine to generate electricity.

One other tale relates to the funny and often easy-going world of Paddy Dowd. From his garage, there were many tales told of his drawl comments on life and his remarks became part and parcel of the local folklore. For example, when pumping up a wheel one day, it was pumped up too far and when the tyre blew, Paddy said in his own calm way, *'that will howld no more!'* When driving his car through the village one day, the back wheel came off and it passed him out down the street and seeing the wheel pass him by, and the car travelling on three wheels, he said, *'that looks like wan of ours!'* Later on in the fifties when the fuse went at a concert in the Convent hall, he was called upon to hold a torch for an electrician who was present to change the fuse. When the electrician cried out after getting an electric shock, Paddy remarked, *'Is the crow at home?'*

But one of his finest gems relates to an incident with a lady from the Dalystown area. Lets call this lady Mary for the sake of the story. Mary travelled occassionally to Mullingar with the pony and trap to buy provisions for the house. This would include sacks of flour, oatmeal and meal to feed a pig. As well as that she was not a small person herself. On one occassion she decided to buy her first wireless and this was transported on the trap also. Travelling up Carrick hill, with the weight of goods as well as herself in the trap, the belly strap on the harness broke and the trap tipped over, throwing her and all her goods out on the road. On this occassion, she was lucky to get away with a cut on her forehead. Everything was scattered over the road and upset and angry she was trying to retrieve everything when Paddy came along in the car. The new wireless was in pieces all over the grass verge and the gravelled road and seeing this Paddy said, *'What station were you lookin' for Mary?'* Upset and angry she wasn't ready for Paddy's comments and seeing that it was better to go, Paddy got into the car and drove off. None the worse for her ordeal, she got home safe with all her goods. Next day, peace was made with Paddy, as he arrived at the door with a brand new wireless and all was forgiven. Such was his generosty also.

---

3   Chaineys were broken fragments of crockery used by children as plates and saucers when they played house in the garden. At a time when children had little or no toys, they improvised by using what they could find. Locally, when children played house it was known as *'Babby House.'*

It was during this period also that the recordings of John McCormack were first aired and in 1932, his historic rendition of *Panis Angelicus* at the Eucharistic Congress in the Phoenix Park has never been equalled. Delia Murphy made a name for herself also, paving the way for a revival in Irish folk songs which would later cross the Atlantic in the early sixties with the Clancys. *Two lovely lassies from Bannion* and *The Spinning Wheel* were among her favourites on the wireless. The wirelesss also began the tradition of ringing the angelus bell at twelve noon and at six O' Clock each day to call the people to prayer. Living close to the village, Paddy Frayne rang the bell each day at these times and anyone within earshot were aware that a few minutes should be set aside to pray. For people living in the country, unless there was a chiming clock in the house, the angelus on the wireless became part of the household daily call to pray also.

The electricity works at Milltownpass

The Emergency

This period in our not too distant past was known of course as *The Emergency* and local men volunteered to join the LDF or the local Defence Force to train as a volunteer army to protect the country. The army set up barricades in the sky called barrage balloons which help provide a barrier to low flying aircraft to make bombing of towns and villages much more difficult. Long poles were placed in fields also to discourage aircraft landing and everyone was issued with a gas mask in case of gas attacks. Any road vehicles had to have shades on their lights to diffuse light downwards and each

Mrs Fox reading a book under the electric light.

house put blackout blinds in the windows to hide any visible signs of population. All street lighting was switched off in towns where electricity was installed. Travelling at night also, the carbide lamp became an important source of light in the abscence of battery torches.

But life continued as normal. Like previous generations who lived in the Rochfortbridge area, it was still a very rural environment and farming was the life-blood of the people.

Farming Life

The year began with the birth of lambs and calves and the preparation of sheds for the spring milking. Nature awakened slowly on the farm. The hens began to lay again and after the feast of St. Brigid the potato pit was opened to separate the seed potatoes from the larger eaters. Turf banks were cleaned and readied for the new season in Rahanine, Raheenquill, Kilbride and Moorow. The top layer of spoil was dug away and toppled into an awaiting boghole. The sleán was sharpened and a number of days were spent in some back-breaking work, cutting catching the turf and wheeling it on to a dry windy area and left to dry. The turf was later turned, piled into wind rows and dried. It was hard back-breaking work, but the tea made on the bog and the brown bread and buttermilk provided some sustenance from the hungry days labouring to provide fuel for the winter.

When the cows calved and milk became more plentiful, the churning began. The buttermilk was drawn off into a bucket and kept for baking and for drinking also on a hot summer day. The butter was taken out, salt added and clapped with wooden pats, not unlike table tennis bats to extract the last of the water out of it. It was finished in quantities of about a pound weight and used at home, shared with neighbours or often sold in the market in Mullingar. The money created by the sale of butter and eggs to the local shops and market was often used to buy boots and clothes for the new school year.

After St. Patrick's day the early potatoes were planted and the late or maincrop were planted any time up to the midle of May. The oats was sown and when it was a few inches above ground it was rolled to secure the young plants in the soil. The hay harvest began at the end of June and into July. People pooled resources by helping one another to save the crop, which was always weather driven.

The Summer of 1946 brought the country close to starvation as the very wet year left the much needed corn harvest at risk. People from towns and cities were brought by bus into the country to help save the harvest. The quality of flour produced at home during these years was not of a very high standard of refinement and the bread that was for sale from the bakeries was known as black bread. It wasn't very popular and when the more high quality refined flour came back on the market, people were glad to see its return. Ironically, this black bread was high in fibre and better for the human condition that the bread manufactured with the finer white flour.

During the war years, Milltownpass had it's own private electricity service. A turbine was built on the river flowing through the village and homes in the village had the benefit of electric light for a number of years until the ESB electrical scheme took over.

As the war drew to a close, the emergency was not over as rationing would still continue into the 1950's. But farmers were embracing change and the tractor began to take over from horse power on the farm. It was a common sight every Autumn so see Tom Geraghty's Mill, trundling slowly along the country roads, drawn by a tractor and it was making its way from farm to farm to thresh the oats and corn. The mill was powered by a belt attached to the tractor and the area where the tractor and belt operated was a no-go area for everyone as it was quite a dangerous operation.

It was a time when children took the day off school and their job was to have the terrier dog at the ready to watch for rats escaping from the ricks of straw. It was a busy time for the women also as the visitng group of helpers or *meitheal* as it was known in Irish had to be fed. Dinner had to be prepared and socially, it was a time to open the bottles of stout or anything stronger if required. In some places it was a barrel of porter and it was filled into a large jug which was passed around to fill the mugs or glasses. The oats was later brought to the mill and crushed to make porridge meal and cracked to provide winter feed for sheep and horses.

It was a time also of abscence from school for a period in October. Children were required to help out with the potato picking harvest or to snag turnips. By November the harvest was saved and the house dance attracted people on bikes from far and wide. During the summer months football and hurling matches were very popular and the rivalry between Rochfortbridge and Gibbonstown on the field has become part of local folk history. Pitch and toss was a popular game on Sundays when the GAA season was over. Sadly the conversation at such gatherings turned to emigration and the boat to England. Work was plentiful following the Blitz on London, Manchester and Birmingham. It was common also to hear of a young man or woman whose health had failed due to the dreaded epidemic of TB which ravaged Ireland during the early decades of the 20th century. The sanatorium was often their only option and many didn't return.

The Christmas Season and card playing

November brought the first heavy frosts of winter and most farm activity slowed down, apart from milking the cows and foddering the animals. But soon thoughts of Christmas entered each household and preparations were made to welcome the new Church year with the approach of Advent and Christmas.

Ingredients for Christmas cakes were in short supply during the 1940's but many people often acquired the necessary raisins and spices on the black market or for some lucky families they arrived by parcel from relatives in America.

A feature of life leading up to the Christmas season in Rochfortbridge parish were the card plays. Here, a faithful following of local people gathered on Friday nights to play twenty five, paying a small fee to the head of the household, the prize was a turkey or a goose. In later years the faithful card players continued the tradition at Whelehans on the main Street and prizes included hams, turkeys and hampers. When Fr. Eamonn O'Brien renovated Meedin Church in the early 1980's the weekly card play at the new meeting room became a very popular social event for many people.

The Tilly lamp, using methylated spirits produced a beautiful bright light and shone down on the table. The oil lamp in some homes was placed in the centre of the table and everyone was careful not to touch the tall glass globe as it could inflict a severe burn to the hand. Through the night, smokers placed a cigarette between the lips and placed the top of the cigarette over the opening on the top of the globe. The heat emanating from the globe was hot enough to light the cigarette, causing it to glow into life. Many a Christmas's dinner was won at a card plays and they became some of the great social events of the winter season.

Always thinking ahead to raise funds to pay off debts or to fund some new project for the convent or the schools, the Sisters of Mercy have recorded in their annals many card playing events during the 1940's and 1950's as fund raisers.

In 1950, the Convent was furnished with a bill from the ESB to pay for the cost of wiring and installing electricity in the Convent, St. Josephs, the school and out-buildings.[4]The annals recorded details of a monster card drive in the Convent hall to help pay for this work.

> To help defray some of the cost of installing E.S.B., Rev. P. Delaney C.C. organised a monster card drive in Convent Schools. It was an outstanding success and realised the grand sum of £340. Apart from its financial success it was *'a red letter'* night for all who participated –free supper was served in the convent hall and it was estimated over 700 were amply provided for. Special tribute is due to Fr. Delaney and his well organised committee.[5]

In preparation for Christmas day, the traditional red Christmas candle, secured in a two pound jam jar full of sand and decorated with crepe paper was placed in each window. It is a beautiful Irish tradition which is still practised today. The gentle light reminding us that Joseph and Mary needed light to guide their journey to the stable at Bethlehem. Fasting began from midnight for anyone who would be receiving holy Communion and mass at dawn brought the ponies and traps from across the parish to the church of the Immaculate Conception. The church, lit by pale candlelight gave it a warm feeling, but the twinkling stars in the sky and the cold air meant that the top coat was buttoned well to keep the cold out even in the church.

On the journey to and from the village, rugs were placed around the legs and waist and people prayed that it wouldn't rain on that early morning journey. It was a time of year also when people everywhere had some form of cough or cold and quite often the drone of coughing and sneezing in the church often brought the priest to stop in his tracks during the mass till the noise caused by the coughing ceased.

Home again, the chores had to be done and in the dingy little cattle sheds a storm lantern was used to give some light before the dim mid-winter light brightened up the day. The postman delivered letters on Christmas day during those years and travelling from house to house he was often offered a little drop to drink and by the time his journey had finished, he was often a little the worse for wear.

When Christmas dinner was over, towards dusk, the animals had to be cared for and come nightfall the deck of cards was taken down for some more card playing, quietly drawing Christmas day to a close. The wrenboys arrived on St. Stephen's day and there was great merriment and cheer as they stepped around the floor and played their music, requesing the good lady of the house *to rise up and give them a trait.*

---

4   See Appendices at the end of this book.
5   Annals of the Sisters of Mercy, p. 340.

Soon the Christmas season passed and the new year approached. For the Sisters of Mercy, their annual retreat took place in the early days of January as they prepared for another year in their ministry. Schools opened and the cycle of life continued.

Winter was a tough time, especially for the sick and the elderly, and more so the winter of 1947, when the snow came with a vengeance –a repeat of the winter of 1932. The world ground to a halt and snowdrifts blocked the roads. Animals died in the fields and men spent days trying to lure them through the drifts to the safety of outhouses where at least they could be kept alive. It took a long time for the snow to clear and on May day there were still mounds of snow melting away in the ditches.

The 1940's were tough and so indeed were the 1950's. But times were changing once more and the hungry years of the Second World War were now faded to memory. The number of cars increased on the roads again, and the pony and trap slowly faded back to memory. Times were changing in the convent also as plans were being made to open a new Secondary School for girls.

Taken in the convent grounds are at the back, Patrick Healy, John and Bernie McCarthy.
In front are Maggie and Eilish McCarthy with Michael Frayne in the centre.

~ CHAPTER 15 ~
CHRISTMAS IN ROCHFORTBRIDGE
By Danny Dunne

At Christmas when the dinner is over and all the hype associated with the season becomes just a memory Christmas is as far away as ever and we leave midwinter behind and look forward to longer days and the impending arrival of Spring. Its at this time that one remembers the days in the distant past when Christmas was so special and it was a magical time for us all.

Living in the country we were all in the same boat, a time when it was hard to make ends meet and we relied on the few dollars from America or a pound from a Great Aunt in Dublin to bring home the Christmas for a family of nine children.

It all began around the 17th of December when Master McEngeggart closed the school door at Dalystown and we ran the three miles home through puddles on stony roads or frosty fields, not a care in the world for the wet or the cold.

The first job was to gather the holly in Dunboden wood and take it to all the neighbours. The sash windows were adorned with holly and it was also placed behind the pictures on the walls.

Then my mother and Father spent a day in Mullingar. We stayed at home and took care of the younger ones and we were not allowed venture into the town on that occassion.

We spent our time making patterns on the frosty grass in the fields pretending that were were ploughing the land for the spring.

Christmas Eve arrived and it was the longest day of our lives. We didn't want to eat anything. Darkness arrived and having washed, we were dispatched off to bed.

In the early years of our lives there was no electricity and there was a little oil lamp flickering on the mantlepiece. Outside we could hear my father doing the evening jobs like foddering the animals and milking the cows.

He carried a storm lantern or yard lamp to give him light and we watched the moving glow in the back yard through the curtains.

Of all nights of the year, sleep was the last thing on our minds. We called for drinks of water or requested to go to the toilet many times. Our father would occassionally peep in and say that he could hear bells over Dunboden wood.

This was the worst thing of all to say as we were frightened that Santa Claus would pass us by and not make any deliveries at all.

It certainly was the longest night of the year and we all felt it, but suddenly and out of the blue, sleep came and we would wake up at some unearthly hour of the morning.

We'd sneak down through the darkness to find a stack of brown parcels tied with string on the kitchen table. Mother followed at our heels, and lighting a tilly lamp she distributed the parcels to us all.

Back up to bed and the excitement was terrific. My first memory of this morning was opening a parcel to find a little wooden box of bricks. It had little windows with red see-through cellophane. They fitted into the little box like a jigsaw and and it had a sliding lid. There were also the trimmings, balloons, sweets, a toy watch, handkerchiefs with pictures of Santa going down the chimney and sometimes a Christmas stocking with allsorts of goodies from whistles to colouring books. Depending on the time of the morning my mother returned to bed, but at 6.00 a.m. we were all called to get ready for dawn mass mass in Rochfortbridge.

In those years, my father had a pick-up truck as he cut and sold timber for fuel to people in Mullingar. On Christmas morning there was a gathering of neighbours who hitched a ride to mass on the back of the truck, rain, hail or snow.

The village of Rochfortbridge was a busy place and it was lit up with bright electric lights. The rural electrification took place in the 1940's and 1950's in phases, as the villages and towns were lit first. We didn't get the electricity until the early sixties, but thats another story.

Our first excitement of Christmas was to visit the crib. We knelt at the altar rails and watched with great excitement at the infant in the cradle lit up by a red star over the crib. The crib looked as if it was made of stone and the statues were huge. To the right of the crib there was another room overlooking the altar and we could see nuns praying. The Sisters of Mercy attended mass in a little side-chapel looking on to the altar and in those years prior to Vatican II they did not mix with the community at all.

The church came alive with the most beautiful music and singing as Christmas Carols eased us into prayer and soon mass began.

It was a long wait as we were thinking of getting home and playing with the toys we got from Santa Claus. Mass was said in those early mornings by Father John Conlon, a native of Ballinabrackey Parish. He was curate in the parish for many years assisting Parish Priest Fr. John McManus, who was a native of Collinstown, Co. Westmeath. Father McManus preferred to say the morning mass in Meedin Church as it was a place close to his heart, being one of the earliest churches in the parish with links back to the penal days of the 18th century.

It was always at this mass that Fr. Conlon announced the date of the annual Children's Christmas party. It was usually held in early January around the time we returned back to school, but it was something we really looked forward to.

At home, the table was dragged up to the fire and we sat down to a hearty breakfast. We were hungry after the cold early morning trip to mass. After breakfast we were dispatched off to the rooms to play with the toys as my father and older brothers did the outside chores and my mother began to make preparations for the dinner. Around midday, Uncle Tom my fathers brother called and he would share in the excitement with us all. He came to visit Grandfather Joe, who lived with us and spent most of his time in bed. If the day was fine, we went out to play or visit our neighbours to show them our toys. But the day passed quickly and we were tired going to bed that night.

On Stephens day the wrenboys came by. The story goes that when St. Stephen was trying to escape from those who were trying to kill him, he hid in the bushes and would have escaped only a little wren flew out alerting his captors to the fact that he was there and finding poor Stephen, they stoned him to death. It was tradition in Ireland to catch and kill a little wren and carry it from house to house chanting the rhyme

The Wren, the Wren
The King of all birds
On Stephens day
Was caught in the furze
Although he was little
His family was great
So rise up good lady and
Give us a trate
Up with the kittle
And down with the pan
And give us a penny to
Bury the wran(wren)

As I rose up with my hat so tall
I saw a wren upon the wall
I took a stick and knocked him down
And brought him in to Dalystown.
I dipped his head in a barrel of beer,
I wish you a Merry Christmas
And a happy new year.

The wrenboys who came to our door carried no wren as it was impossible to catch one. Such a practise is outlawed today, but I have seen people carry little plastic birds such as Christmas robins, re-painted to represent the wren.

The children who came to our door were usually local children, with their coats turned inside out, their faces blackened by a cork which was placed in the fire or coloured with lipstick. My mother in her jovial way always tried to chase them to get a kiss from them and they ran screaming lest she would succeed. My father then called them back and threw a few copper coins into their little sweet can. As we grew older we all hunted the wren and we headed for Rochfortbridge. Our destination was the Bórd na Móna Houses(Derrygreenagh Park) or the three pubs, Lysters, Rowans and Whelehans. There were always plenty of people in those establishments on the day and in their high-spirited seasonal way were very generous in throwing money into our cans. The songs we sang were usually those learned at School, and at that time in the lead-up to the 50th Anniversary of the 1916 rising there was a plethera of Patriotic songs on the curriculum, *The Foggy Dew, Roddy McCorley, The Three Flowers, God Save Ireland* etc. They always went down a treat. Then we were asked to sing something Christmassy and we finished *Jingle Bells*.

Tired and weary we returned home near dark to count our money and divide it up among ourselves.

Just as we were about to return to school we were driven to The children's Party in the convent Hall in Rochfortbridge.

The convent hall was the venue for many parish functions during the fifties and sixties until Fr. John Conlon built *St. Joseph the Worker Hall* using local volunteer labour. It became the focal point for many a Parish Dance during the Showband era but the Convent hall was a great venue for local drama as well as functions such as the childrens Christmas Party.

It was a world then where the plastic cup and plastic bag were non-existant. We arrived at the hall and put sitting at long tables on forms, and the noise was deafening. Fr. Conlon had a whole team of workers at the back of the stage in what was known as the cookery room and it wasn't long until the proceedings began.

Down the steps they came carrying buckets of paper bags filled with boiled sweets from the cans sold in the shops. The wise ones put the bags in their pockets as the sweets began to melt away and the hands became sticky and wet. They were left for another day and on a few occasions some of the children didn't want them and they were going to throw them away, so I ended up with a few bags of sweets going home.

As I have said already, there were no plastic cups and people came from the cookery room with tin baths full of cups, volunteered from houses all over the village to feed the multitude of children. This was followed by buckets of Pak Orange diluted in water and the cups which were being banged off the tables, became quiet as they were filled to the brim. There were sandwiches, plates of Christmas cake, buns and biscuits brought to the tables. Amongst all the noise Father Conlon addressed the crowd of children and announced that everyone go out to play while the hall was cleaned up for the entertainment. On a number of occassions there was a film show. This was the first time I had ever seen moving pictures and my memory of them were of short stories, or fillers used between movies as children wouldn't have the staying power to watch a full movie(or so they thought).

On other occassions there was a concert of music and singing. Here my three oldest brothers played a part. Together with a few local lads from around the Rochfortbridge area, everyone was entertained by *The Dalystown Juvenile Band*. For a few years during the early sixties they entertained at local functions and they were taught music every Friday night at Dalystown School by Tony Lynch from Castletown Geoghagan and later by Larry Arthur.

As the Sowband era drew in a group of young lads from Edendery called *the Hoot'n Nannies* sang and entertained us. Wearing cowboy hats and carrying guns and holsters they rocked the house away and it was magic.

As the sixties progressed, the popularity of the Christmas Party began to wane as there were other attractions coming on stream, namely, television. But for a very short while Fr. Conloin's Christmas party was the highlight of our lives and something that stayed with us for a very long time after Christmas.

Sadly that great season of childhood ended very quickly and we returned to school. Christmas today, I suppose is different, but the magic is still there, but it has different dimensions in a more high-tech world. The only thing that has not changed are the children who have made this time of year their own with memories they too will cherish forever.

~ CHAPTERS 16 to 21 ~
THE CONVENT PRIMARY SCHOOL

~ CHAPTER 16 ~
1960'S NATIONAL SCHOOL

1. Mary Doherty	22. Mary B. Byrne
2. Mary Dunne	23. Anne Dowdall
3. Margaret Farrell	24. Genevieve Doherty
4. Eithne McEnroe	25. Anne Healy
5. Ursula Geraghty	26. Mary B. Tormey
6. Teresa Baker	27. Mary Baker
7. Veronica Austin	28. Claire Gavin
8. Rita Doody	29. Mary P. Egan
9. Mary Browne	30. Patricia Fallon
10. Rose Hickey	31. Pauine McGrath
11. Bernadette Gaye	32. Mary O'Brien
12. Evelyn Donoghue	33. Dorothy Smyth
13. Anne Hope	34. Annette Cribbin
14. Mary Carey	35. Anne Tormey
15. Eileen Doody	36. Margaret Dunne
16. Claire Gillespie	37. Mary Ryan
17. Catherine Molloy	38. Anne Cully
18. Cecil Corbett	39. Mary Naughton
19. Frances Baker	40. Sheila McCabe
20. Vera Fox	41. Kathleen Gouldsberry
21. Elizabeth Egan	

This photo was taken in 1961.
Sr. Aquin taught 5th, 6th and 7th class. Because of the angle the photo was taken it is difficult to name the children by row, so follow the names from the numbers in the following table:

Key to Sr. Aquin's 5th, 6th and 7th Class 1961.

*Photo taken in Sr. Maureen's class in 1961. Front row from left to right, Patricia Baker, Anne Carey and Eileen Carey.
Second row from left to right, Mary Hannon, Mary Daly, Nora Gouldsberry and Kathleen Dunne.
Third Row, from left to right, Carmel Gilsenan, Madeleine Kenny, Ann Dunne, Marie Cleary and Margaret Bligh.
Fourth Row, from left to right, Teresa Flynn, Mary Cully, Betty Healy, Mary McCarthy, Mary O'Riordan and Mary
Mullarkey. Fifth Row from left to right, Rosemary Hyland, Mary Jane Gouldsberry, Margaret Geraghty, Maureen Carey
and Margaret Dunne. Sixth row from left to right, Maura Malone, Carmel Mullarkey and Sr. Maureen.*

*Convent Primary School Staff, 1969. Sister Concepta,
Sister Maureen, Mary Alford and Sister Assumpta.*

*Eileen and Ann Whelehan share a
Christmas moment in the Convent
Primary School.*

Geraldine and Ann Reidy, taken in the Convent Primary School in the 1960's

~ CHAPTER 17 ~
1970's NATIONAL SCHOOL

PHOTO TAKEN OF THE SCHOOL BAND IN 1968 WITH SR. MARIE THERÉSE IN ATHLONE.
Included in the photo are Margaret Murphy, Lelia Gavigan, Kathleen McCarthy, Camilla Gavigan, Anne Reidy, Moya Mulroy, Ita Flynn, Jackie Gilsenan, Margaret Cleary, Noeleen Keogh, Marie Malone, Bernie Fitzpatrick, Eileen Lynam, Deirdre Walsh, Liz Dunne, Margaret Keegan, Sheila Gavin, Kathleen Rhattigan, Geraldine Cully, Eileen Whelehan, Colleen Walsh

FÉILE NA SCOILEANNA, 1969. *Back row, from left to right,* *Ann Earley, Kathleen McCarthy, Dolores Cleary, Patricia Donovan, Maureen Frances, Lz Dunne, Geraldine Carey, Margaret Cleary, Mary Murphy, _____ and Mary Byrne. **Third row, from left to right,*** *Teresa Mulroy, Mary Cleary, Lelia Gavigan,_____, Anne Peppard, Bernadette Cully, Geraldine Baker, Geraldine Moran, Jackie Gilsenan, Mary Davy and Bernadette Walsh. **Second row, from left to right,*** *Jean Newman, _____, Geraldine Lynam, Catherine Swords, Kathleen Rhattigan, Colleen Walsh, Geraldine Whelehan, Bernadette Hannon, Bernadette Carey, Deirdre Walsh, Eileen Whelehan, Geraldine Cully, Marie Malone and Margaret Murphy. **Front row from left to right,*** *Ann Whelehan, Kay Hanlon, Pauline Murphy, Ann Murphy, Annette Carroll, Jeanette Curran, Noeleen Keogh, Joan Nolan, Maura Nolan, Eileen Lynam, Nora Frances and Margaret Swords.*

223

FÉILE NA SCOILEANNA 1970. *Back row from left to right,* Bernadette Earley, Mary Cleary, Jacqueline Gilsenan, Ann Peppard, Josie Coleman, Liz Dunne, Maureen Francis, Patricia Donovan, Mary Murphy, Margaret Cleary, Teresa Mulroy and Lelia Gavigan. *Fifth row, from left to right,* Patricia Gilsenan, Catherine Swords, Kathleen Mulroy, Kathleen Rhattigan, Brigid Newman, Bernie Carey, Josephine Cleary, Cepta Henry, Mary Davy, Bernadette Walsh, Geraldine Mangan and Sheila Newe. *Fourth row, from left to right,* Phil Ryan, Geraldine Lynam, Coleen Walsh, Kathleen Geraghty, Bernadette Fitzpatrick, Margaret Murphy, Margaret Swords, Mary Leavy, Marie Murphy, Deirdre Walsh, Eileen Whelehan and Breda Usher. *Third row, from left to right,* Jean Newman, Rosemary Grennan, Geraldine Cully, Ann Murphy, Ellen Rhattigan, Ann Curran, Annette Carroll, Marie Malone, Jeanette Curran, Noeleen Keogh, Marina Daly and Joan Nolan. *Second row, from left to right,* Brid McDermott, Ann Cleary, Maura Nolan, Eileen Lynam, Frances Cully, Síobhán Malone, Bernadette McCarthy, Pauline Murphy, Therese Byrne, Tina Francis, Kay Hanlon and Dolores Murphy. *Front row, from left to right,* Patricia Gavin, Ann Glennon, Kathleen McCarthy, Regina Kelly, Bernadette Hannon, Colette Alford, Marian Doonan and Nora Francis.

CONVENT PRIMARY SCHOOL BAND 1971, *Back row, from left to right,* Bernadette Walsh, Catherine Swords, Margaret Murphy, Katheen Mulroy, Carmel Mulroy, Jean Newman, Brigid Newman, Josephine Cleary, Marie Murphy, Cepta Henry and _____. *Fifth row, from left to right,* Geraldine Lynam, Margaret Swords, Pauline Murphy, Marie Malone, Rosemary Grennan, Patricia Gavin, Stephanie Dunne, Patricia Cleary, Kathleen Rhattigan, Helen Henry and Kathleen Geraghty. *Fourth row, from left to right,* Coleen Walsh, Nora Francis, Dolores Murphy, Síobhán Malone, Caitríona McDermott, Annette Carroll, Fionnuala Seery, Eileen Whelehan, Ellen Burke, Mary Leavy and Bernadette Fitzpatrick. *Third row, from left to right,* Maura Nolan, Tina Francis, Ann Ennis, Breda Morgan, Marina Daly, Mary Flanagan, Kathleen Earley, Ann Whelehan, Ann Murphy, Jacintha Henry and Mary Hyland. *Second row, from left to right,* Dympna Carey, Bernadette Casey, Caroline Mooney, Deirdre Walsh, Geraldine Cully, Jeanette Curran, Ellen Rhattigan, Ann Curran and Noeleen Keogh. *Front row, from left to right,* Claire Nolan, Theresa Carey, Mary Bollard, Carol Baker, Frances Cully, Bernadette McCarthy, Therese Byrne, Margaret Morgan, Mary Whelehan, Eileen Lynam, Pauline Henry and Florrie Hyland.

CÓR NA N-ÓG SCHOOL CHOIR 1972. *Back row, from left to right,* Margaret Murphy, Rosemary Grennan, Lorna Kenny, Jean Newman, Carmel Mulroy, Kathleen Rhattigan, Deirdre Grace, Bernadette Carey, Margaret Judge, Eilen Whelehan, Kathleen Geraghty and Bernie Campbell. *Sixth row, from left to right,* Pauline Murphy, Chris Fitzpatrick, Jacintha Henry, Margaret Bradley, Ellen Burke, Margaret Swords, Patricia Cleary, Kathleen Coleman, Kathleen Earley, Ann Whelehan and Noeleen Keogh. *Fifth row, from left to right,* Jeanette Curran, Patricia Tone, Helen Henry, Annette Carroll, Ann Ennis, Nora Francis, Mary McCabe, Patricia Gavin, Fionnuala Seery , Florrie Hyland and Mary Flanagan. *Fourth row, from left to right,* Frances Cully, Dolores Murphy, Thérése Byrne Angela Carrol, Tina Francis, Ann Cleary, Catríona McDermot, Lorna Kenny, Kathleen Bradley, Kay Hanlon, Maire Hanlon. *Third row, from left to right,* Bernadette Casey, Betty Carey, Teresa Carey, Maura Nolan, Mary Carter, Ellen Rhattigan, Caroline Mooney, Ann Bradley, Mary Whelehan , Marina Daly and Marie Murphy. *Second row, from left to right,* Marie Malone, Stephanie Dunne, Deirdre Walsh, Pat Gilsenan, Geraldine Cully, Marie Byrne, Bernie Fitzpatrick Coleen Walsh, Ann Murphy and Attracta Coyne. *Front row, from left to right,* Theresa Carey, Siobhán Malone, Claire Nolan, Mary Bollard, Margaret Morgan, Ann Curran, Caroline Byrne, Finola Usher, Pat Mangan and Eileen Lynam.

FÉILE NA SCOILEANNA, BAND 1973. *Back row, from left to right,* Eileen Mulroy, Ann Cleary, Nora Francis, Margaret Swords, Pauline Murphy, Bernie Carey, Kathleen Earley, Mary Hyland, Patricia Gavin, Fionnuala Seery and Marie Hanlon *Fifth row, from left to right,* Thérése Byrne, Dolores Murphy, Caitríona McDermott, Annette Carroll, Ann Murphy, Catherine Judge, Finola Usher, Florrie Hyland, Marina Daly, Mary Whelehan and Geraldine Walsh. *Fourth row, from left to right,* Tina Francis, Frances Cully, Siobhán Malone, Caroline Mooney, Teresa Carey Patricia Tone, Dympna Carey, Caroline Byrne and Bernadette Casey. *Third row, from left to right,* Kathleen Bradley, Mary Ennis, Margaret Morgan, Ann Ennis, Jeanette Bollard, Mary Whelehan Geraldine Walshe, Ann Marie Denehan, Alberta Malone, Pauline _____, Finola Usher and Ellen Rhattigan. *Second row, from left to right,* Eileen Lynam, Claire Nolan, Bridget Walsh, Mary Bollard, Finola Usher, Attracta Coyne, Marie Byrne, Jeanette Curran, Deirdre Grace, Pauline Henry, Teresa Carey, Rosemary Keegan and Mary Carter. *Front row, from left to right,* Concepta Flanagan, Ramona Lyster, Fiona Conlon, Marie Keogh, Ann Marie Daly, Dolores Daly, Cepta Coyne, Ann Curran, Eilis Cocoman, Bernie Morgan, Rosario Whelehan, Geraldine Tone _____, Ann Flynn and Mary Flynn.

FÉILE NA SCOILEANNA BAND 1974, *Back row, from left to right,* Dolores Murphy, Ann Cleary, Eileen Mulroy, Kathleen Bradley, Florrie Hyland, Margaret Earley, Thérèse Byrne, Patricia Gavin, Marie Hanlon, Mary Flanagan, Marina Daly, _____ and Caroline Mooney. **Fourth row, from left to right,** Marie Malone, Frances Cully, Bernadette Casey, Tina Francis, _____, Josephine Cooney, Ann Marie Daly, Dolores Daly, Janette Bollard, Ann Curran and Mary Whelehan. **Third row, from left to right,** Judy Rhattigan, Dympna Carey, Fiona Conlon, Alberta Malone, Finola Usher, Margaret Hyland, Theresa Carey, Geraldine Walshe, Margaret Morgan, Rosemary Keegan, Mona Lyster, Siobhán Malone, Ann Marie Denehan and Mary Bollard. **Second row, from left to right,** Cora Earley, Cepta Lyster, Brigid Walsh, Marie Keogh, Pauline Henry, Ann Bradley, Geraldine Tone, Eilís Cocoman, Jacinta Davitt, Annette Byrne, Mary Flynn, Caroline Murphy, Cepta Flanagan, Catherine Cooney and Ann Ennis. **Front row, from left to right,** Theresa Leavy, Patricia Arthur, Carmel Hanlon, Rosario Whelehan, Deirdre Whelehan, Majella Usher, Rosanna Delaney, Eileen Morgan, Joan Gunning, Ann Flynn, Calire Nolan, Patricia Slattery and Linda Lynam.

FÉILE NA SCOILEANNA, BAND 1975, *Back row, from left to right,* Jeanette Bollard, Antoinette Daly, Mary Bollard, Fiona Conlon, Josephine Cooney, Ann Marie Deneghan, Caroline Mooney, Mary Whelehan, Caroline Byrne, Bernadette Casey, Margaret Early, and Kathleen Bradley. **Third row, from left to right,** Marie Keogh, Claire Nolan, Pauline Henry, Ann Ennis, Alberta Malone, Judy Rhattigan, Ann Bradley, Rosario Whelehan, Rosemary Keegan, Dympna Carey, Margaret Hyland, Dolores Daly, Geraldine Walshe, Geraldine Tone, Ann Ennis and Pauline Cleary. **Second row, from left to right,** Linda Lynam, Concepta Flanagan, Finola Usher, Geraldine Walsh, Mary Flynn, Annette Byrne, Veronica Dunne, Carmel Hanlon, Martina Fennelly, Martina Arthur, Theresa Leavy, Deirdre Whelehan, Patricia Arthur, Patricia Slattery, Eilís Cocoman and Bridget Walsh. **Front row, from left to right,** Cora Early, Cepta Lyster, Ann Flynn, Mandy Yates, Genevieve McCormack. Mary Mooney, Joan Gunning, Therese Duigenan, Ann Quirke, Fionnuala Cleary, Majella Usher, Mary Quirke, Cepta Coyne, Noreen Walsh and Nuala Curran.

Mary Alford in 1972

Mary and Ann Alford on the Staff of the Convent Primary School in 1973

First Communion day in the early seventies

*Convent Primary School Staff, 1972.
Back row from left to right, Sister Concepta
O'Brien, Ann Alford, Mary Alford and
Sister Assumpta Heavey. Seated in front is
Principal, Sister Maureen O'Brien.*

*Convent Primary School Staff 1973, from left to right, Ann Fagan,
Mary Alford, Sr. Maureen O'Brien (Principal) and Ann Alford.*

Heading off on the school tour are Mary Gavin, Sister Maureen, Mrs. Smyth and Sister Freda.

Ready for Lough Key are at the back, from left to right, Ann Quirke, Linda Lynam, Sr. Maureen, Linda Boyle, Jacinta Davitt, Caroline Murphy, Deirdre Whelehan and Patricia Arthur. Front row, from left to right, Jacqueline Quirke. Veronica Dunne, Majella Usher and Caroline Darby.

Sister Assumpta taught in the United States at the Convent of Mercy, Berlin, New Jersey for a period in the 1970's. While she was there she arranged for pupils from the Convent Primary School to become pen friends with children from fifth and sixth class. Joan Gunning became a pen friend with Lisa Bisaga, from West Berlin, New Jersey and when Joan was in sixth class, Lisa Bisaga came to Ireland for a number of weeks in the Summer of 1978. She joined Joan and her class each day at the Convent Primary School. In this photo are at the back, from left to right, Caroline Murphy, Lisa Bisaga, Annette Byrne and Caroline Darby. In front are Jacintha Davitt, Veronica Dunne and Deirdre Whelehan.

Sixth Class group from 1978. At the back, from left to right, Linda Lynam, Jacintha Davitt, Linda Boyle, Sister Maureen, Mary Plunkett, Sister Freda, Mary Gavin, Ann Reidy, Sister Concepta and Ann Bradley. Second row, from left to right, Lisa Bisaga, Annette Byrne, Caroline Darby, Thérése Duigenam, Veronica Dunne, Caroline Murphy, Theresa Leavy, Judy Rhattigan and Majella Usher. In front, from left to right are Patricia Arthur, Deirdre Whelehan, Sheila Gavin and Eileen Morgan.

Taken on a school tour to Lough Key Forest park in 1977, from left to right, Carmel Boyle (O'Sullivan) and Linda Boyle (Allen).

<< *Summer 1978 at the Convent Primary School, back row, from left to right, Annette Byrne, Deirdre Whelehan, Mary Plunkett, Judy Rhattigan, Linda Boyle, Ann Bradley and Patricia Arthur.*
Middle row, from left to right, Jacintha Davitt, Linda Lynam, Caroline Murphy, Theresa Leavy, Joan Gunning and Theresa Duigenam. Front row, from left to right, Caroline Darby, Veronica Dunne, Eileen Morgan and Majella Usher.

Caught in the jump, Theresa Duigenam, Joan Gunning and Deirdre Whelehan.

Back Row, Teresa Duigenan, Ann Bradley, Patricia Arthur, and Judy Rhattigan. Front Row, Linda Lynam, Wileen Morgan, Siobháin Lynam and Teresa Leavy.

Jacintha Davitt and Joan Gunning in the old Cookery Room at the Convent Primary School

Theresa Duigenan & Deidre Whelehan

Sister Maureen and Joan Gunning in 1978

Patricia Daly, pictured with Sr. Concepta on her First Holy Communion Day.

Bishop McCormack arrives for Confirmation in the village in the early 1970's

All ready for the school band, are Nora, Maureen and Tina Francis

John Daly on his First holy Communion Day

30. Three little boarders who attended the Convent Primary school are photographed on Confirmation day. Caroline McCluskey, centre, made her Confirmation in Rochfortbridge Church. Also in the picture are left, Iris Williams and right, Siobhán O'Connell.

Bishop McCormack and Fr. John McManus P.P. in conversation outside St. Joseph's

~ CHAPTER 18 ~
CONVENT PRIMARY SCHOOL
1980's AND 1990's

Patricia and Brigid Daly 1980

The Bingo Committee who raised funds for the building of the new convent primary school. Back Row from left to right, Bill Swords, Tom Hanlon, Tom Dunne, Ann Alford and Brendan Arthur. Front row from left to right, Sister Maureen O'Brien, Marie Dunne and Mary Alford.

The children, parents, teachers and friends of the Convent Primary School, taken on the 24th of January 1980 at the official opening and blessing of the new Convent Primary School by Bishop John McCormack, Bishop of Meath.

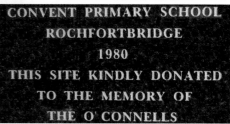

The Sisters of Mercy, pictured in 1983, back row, from left to right, Sister Freda Farrelly and Sister Kathleen Daly. Front row, from left to right, Sister Dolores Carroll, Sister Maureen O'Brien, Sister Magdalene Claffey, Sister Pius Doran and Sister Dympna Lynch.

Plaque dedicated to the memory of the O'Connells which was erected in 1980 to commemmorate the opening of the new primary school. The site was donated by Mary Jo Murphy.

The Board of Management of the Convent Primary school, taken on the 24th of January 1980 on the occassion of the official opening and blessing of the new Convent Primary School. Pictured from left to right are, Sister Imelda, Michael Gavin, Breda O'Connell, Bishop John McCormack, Sister Maureen (Principal), Tom Hanlon and Rev. Colm Murtagh C.C. (Chairperson).

Sister Kathleen Daly, taken during her term as Principal of the Convent Primary School during the 1980's and 1990's

Apostolic Blessing sent by His Holiness, Pope John Paul II, to the Sisters, Staff and Children of the Convent Primary School in 1980 on the occassion of the official opening and blessing of the new school by Bishop John McCormack, Bishop of Meath.

A very special occassion in the life of the Convent Primary School and St. Joseph's Secondary school in 1985, when two teachers, past pupils of both schools celebrated their wedding in the Church of the Immaculate Conception, Rochfortbridge. Anne Reidy from the Convent Primary School and Pat Eighan from St. Joseph's Secondary School were married.
Pictured on the occasion with the couple are the Sisters of Mercy, from left to right, Sister Freda Farrelly, Sister Dolores Carroll, Sister Finian Larisy, Sister Concepta O'Brien, Pat Eigan(Groom), Anne Reidy(Bride), Sister Maureen O'Brien, Sister Kathleen Daly, Sister Dympna Lynch, Sister Pius Doran and Sister Magdalene Claffey.

Senior Infants 1984. In front are Caroline Byrne, Jenny Eighan, Lisa Cusack, John Daly and Colin Pearse. Second row, from left to right, Maria Doyle, Caitriona Tone, Mary Sheeran, Sharon Dunne, Caroline McNamara, Edwina Tone and Patrick Brogan. At the back include, Eoin Daly, Brian Kenny, Paul O'Connor, Damian Gavin and Leonard Malone. and Tommy Daly.

May 26th 1984 was also a very special day for Dympna Gavin when she received her First holy Communion, from left to right are Anne Reidy(Teacher), Dympna Alford, Angie Hyland, Dympna Gavin, sister Kathleen Daly and Mary Gavin, holding her baby son John Gavin.

11. Saturday 26th May 1984 was a very special day for Brian Horgan, Rochfortbridge when he received his First Holy Communion. He is pictured here with his teacher Anne Reidy and Sister Kathleen Daly, Principal.

Watched over by the statue of Jesus - the convent primary school staff, Mary Gavin, Sister Freda Farrelly, Ann Reidy, Sister Maureen O'Brien and Sister Kathleen Daly.

CONVENT PRIMARY SCHOOL
1990's

The new Sisters of Mercy at the Convent Primary School Fancy Dress competition, Rebecca McCabe, Rebecca Nolan and Sarah Flanagan.

Holding the cup in 1999, from left to right, Leanne Carroll, Aisling Dunne, Ruth Heaney, Megan Glennon, Shauna Coyne, James Eighan, Aoife Beglin and Michelle O'Sullivan.

Bringing home the cup in 1999, from left to right, Jennifer Cully, Sarah Brady, Alice Doyle, Rachel Farrell, Orla Eighan, Claire Judge, Louise Peppard, Sally Alford, Deirdre Eighan, Leanne Carroll, Callie Daly, Emma Gavin, Sharon Hyland and Martha Gavin.

Three future hopefuls, Jason Carroll, Jamie Gonoud and Kieran Gill

Photo taken at a First Holy Communion Mass, from left to right are, Sister Maeve, Sister Kathleen Daly and Anne Eighan.

Celebrating with smiles all round, Gemma Dolan, Ruth Heaney, Shauna Coyne, Megan Glennon, Laura Heavey, Laurna Dunne, Emma Gavin and Leanne Carroll.

This picture was taken on the occassion of Sister Kathleen Daly's retirement as Principal of the Convent Primary School. Back row L-R, Laura Heavey, Áine Cooney, Jacqueline Kelly, Lorna Dunne, Niamh Broderick, Patrice Nolan, Deirdre Kelly, Mary Maguire, Yvonne Palmer. Middle row L-R, Sr. Kathleen, Olivia Gorman, Breda Daly, Jeanette Brogan, Olwynn Cleary, _____, Maria Keegan, Jane Alford, Louise Peppard and Fr. Eamonn O'Brian P.P. Front row L-R, Ciara Byrne, Claire Heduan, Michelle Gonoud, Jill Mangan, Siobhán Kiernan, Denise Brady and Grainne Breslin.

Little Eddie Alford in Senior Infants

Victorious Convent Primary School Team.

Members of a 1990's Board of Management, from left to right, Declan Downey, Anne Eighan, Sister Pius and Fr. Eamonn O'Brien P.P., chairperson of the Board of Management.

Nicola Judge, Luke Dempsey and Michaela Brady share the winning trophy.

The Cumann na mBunscoil team present teacher Miss Ulrika Maher with a bouquet of flowers.

Sheila Lyster and Anne Eighan pictured with the school team at the Cumann na mBunscoil County final.

Ann Eighan (Principal) and Miss Lisa Colleary with children who raised money for the Zambian mission fund.

Fr. Eamonn O'Brien, Sister Maureen O'Brien and Ann Eighan with children who raised money for the Zambian mission fund.

Sister Kathleen Daly on the occassion of her retirement in 1998.

School staff taken in 1998 on the occassion of Sister Kathleen Daly's retirement, from left to right, Yvonne Brady, Anne Eighan, Sister Kathleen Daly, Ann Murphy, Sister Maeve, Marie Carroll and Mary Gavin.

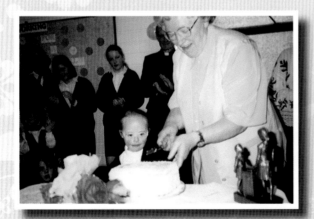

Sister Kathleen Daly cuts a cake on the occassion of her retirement in 1998, watched by Niamh Maguire, Olwyn Cleary, Jane Alford and little Shauna Cully.

Sister Kathleen Daly is presented with bronze sculpture called The Teacher. Also in the picture is Chris Palmer.

Cumann na mbunscoil Semi-final

The Presentation of new Jerseys to the Convent Primary School, by G.M.S., Windows in 1992, from left to right, Cliona Duigenan, Emma Gavin, Colleen Gill, Sinéad Whelehan, Mrs. Anne Eighan (Principal), Mr. Gerry Sheridan, Dawn Wallace, Laurie Byrne and Niamh Morgan.

Back row, left to right, Mrs. Anne Eighan (Principal), Gillian Gonoud, Tara Duigenan, Rita Cleary, Grace Gavin, Lisa Kelly, Siobhán Jessop, Claire Heduan, Xenia Wallace, Andrea Gorman, Kate Nugent, Claire Judge and Mary Kate Wille. Front row, from left to right, Bayleigh O'Flynn, Aoife Hyland, Janice McHugh, Orla Hanrahan, Niamh McGuire, Colleen Gill, Lisa McDonnell, Dawn Wallace, Sinéad Whelehan, Ciara Lowry, Michelle O'Sullivan and Shirley Heaney.

CHAPTER 19
CONVENT PRIMARY SCHOOL, FACES AND EVENTS

The first girl mass servers from the Convent Primary school in 1997-1998, Back row, from left to right, Donna Kiernan, Maria Keegan, Michelle Plunkett, Áine Cooney, Jeanette Brogan, Deirdre Kelly and Denise Brady. Second row, from left to right, Jane Alford, Yvonne Palmer, Denise Peppard, Annette Gunning, Michelle O'Sullivan and Niamh Maguire. Front row, from left to right, Mary McGuire, Patrice Nolan, Jill Mangan, Niamh Broderick and Olwyn Cleary.

All Ireland Finalists in the Irish Credit Union Quiz, from left to right, Sarah Smith, Aoife Beglin, Colleen Gill, Dawn Wallace and Erin Tormey

In 1999, the Convent Primary School were Westmeath Cumann na mBunscoil Football champions. Back row, from left to right, Sheila Lyster(Coach), Gemma Dolan, Ruth Heaney, Laura Heavey, Megan Glennon, Charlene Judge, Lisa Kelly, Laurna Dunne, Rachel Farrell, Orla Eighan and Mrs. Anne Eighan(Principal).
Front row, from left to right, Anne Marie Curran(Coach), Leanne Carroll, Bernie Jessop, Ciara Dunne, Maria Bagnall, Ann Peppard, Callie Daly and Claire Judge.

The Convent primary School girls, who won the under thirteen schools quiz, organised by Castlelost Credit Union in the year 2000, from left to right are Rachel Farrell, Sally Alford, Claire Keegan and Alice Doyle. At the back are Frances Gillespie, Manageress, Castlelost Credit Union, Mrs. Anne Eighan(Principal) and Bill Swords, Chairman, Castlelost Credit Union.

The Convent primary School girls, who won the under eleven schools quiz, organised by Castlelost Credit Union in the year 2000, from left to right are, from left to right, Dawn Wallace, Erin Tormey, Claire Judge and Colleen Gill. At the back are Frances Gillespie, Manageress, Castlelost Credit Union, Therese Clarke(teacher) and Bill Swords, Chairman, Castlelost Credit Union.

2011, Danni Malone(left) and Emily Bollard(right), representing Sixth Class at the Convent Primary School, handing over a cheque for €933.64, the proceeds raised at a jumble /cake sale, to Esther L'Estrange of Cystic Fibrosis, Ireland. Also Pictured are Mrs. Therese Downey, sixth class teacher and Mrs. Anne Eighan(Principal).

Ceili Coyne with teacher Helena Farrell

Claire Bagnall, Colleen Conlon, Gemma Gorman, Anne Peppard, Ceili Coyne, Deidre Seery.

The Bothar organisation, provides practical help for Third World countries, by sending livestock there on a regular basis thanks to the generosity of Irish people. Three young students from the Convent Primary School, Rochfortbridge, assist in the Bothar effort. From Left, Sarah Jane Fox, Alice Doyle and Jennifer Cully

Sinead Whelehan, Captain of Rochfortbridge N.S. shows her delight on receiving winners cup

Convent Primary School Staff, 2002, From left to right, Mary McCormack, Mary Gavin, Thérèse Clarke, Emma MacWeeney, Anne Eighan (Principal) Helena Farrell and Joan Heduan.

Exchange visit to Hanhinevan Koulu School, Finland in 2004. At the back, from left to right, Michael O' Sullivan, The Principal of Hanhinevan Koulu School, Anne Eighan (Principal), Tony Hartnett and Thérèse Clarke. In front are Caitriona MacNioclás and the music teacher in the Finnish school.

Exchange visit to Hanhinevan Koulu School, Finland in 2004.

The Principal of Hanhinevan School makes a return visit to Rochfortbridge in 2005.

Holding their certificates for the Write a Book Project in 2001 are from left to right, Aoife Hyland, Mary Kate Wille, Amy Daly, Ailish Maguire, Lillian Gonoud and Rita Cleary.

Ailish Maguire with her medal for the Write a Book Project in 2001

Emer and Alex Evans Pictured at the second Green Flag Awards ceremony in 2009

Lisa O'Kelly and Zara Hamada enjoy the music at the 2009 Green Flag Awards.

Back row (l-r) Noelle Byrnes, Therese Downey, Rachel Kelly, Crona Kenny, Hanna Farrell, Fiona Coyle, Tara Rogers, Laura O'Sullivan, Nicole Lonican, Becky Lawlor, Lisa Flanagan. Front row (l-r) Michaela Brady, Cora Nugent, Marty Whelan, Carmel Kenny and Jean Henry.

On Monday the 23rd of June 2009, the Convent Primary school in Rochfortbridge celebrated the raising of their second Green Flag, with celebrity guest Marty Whelan in attendance.

Pictured are back row, from left to right, Therése Clarke, Joan Gorman, Grace Brown, Ulrika Maher, Geraldine Gorman, Mary Seery, Marie Carroll, Lisa Colleary, Molly Rafferty, Paula Kilmurray, Anne Carey and Helena Farrell. Front row, from left to right, Dermot Murphy (Westmeath County Council), Marty Whelan, Anne Eighan (Principal), Therése Downey and Fr. Eamonn O'Brien.

Marty Whelan raises the Green Flag for the Convent Primary School, together with at the back row, Eoin Duffy, Therése Downey, Rachel Kelly, Anne Eighan, Nicole Lonican, Fr. Eamonn O'Brien, Fr. Liam Carey, and in front are Lisa O'Kelly, Faye Gorman and Jason Groome.

Mass Servers from the Convent Primary School, back row, from left to right, Maria Keegan, Charlene Dunne, Michelle Plunkett, Jane Alford, Yvonne Palmer, Olwyn Cleary, Niamh Broderick and Áine Cooney. Middle row, from left to right, Deirdre Kelly, Jill Mangan, Éadoin Brady, Ciara Dunne, Alice Doyle, Louise Peppard, Sharon Hyland and Donna Kiernan. Front row, from left to right, Gillian Gonoud, Rachel Farrell, Michelle Gonoud, Sally Alford, Sarah Brady and Tara Duigenan.

~ CHAPTER 20 ~
CONVENT PRIMARY SCHOOL GROUPS

1984-1985. SIXTH CLASS,
Back row, from left to right, Tanya Ennis, Miriam Curran, Bernadette Mulvin,
Kathleen Collins, Paula Ennis and Maeve Wright. ***Front row, from left to right,*** Fiona Flynn,
Ann Gavin, Elaine Loughrey, Janet Farrell and Martina McGrath.

1985-1986. SIXTH CLASS.
Front row, from left to right, Violet Carter, Monica Gavin, Aoife Bradley, Caroline Conroy, Linda
Plunkett and Tara Brogan. ***Second row, from left to right,*** Patricia Whelehan, Margaret Conroy,
Lorraine Healy, Frances Murphy and Sr. Maureen O'Brien (Teacher).
Third row, from left to right, Martina Byrne, Dympna Gavin, Bernadette Mulvin and Cleo Byrne.

1986-1987 SIXTH CLASS,
Back row, from left to right, *Catherine Walsh, Shirley McCormack, Imelda Geraghty,*
Niamh Bollard, Martina Gahan, Bridget Daly and Lorna Bollard.
Front row, from left to right, *Ursula Heaney, Eilish O'Connell, Ann Marie Curran,*
Jennifer Scully, Caitríona Arthur, Elaine Eighan and Fidelma Brogan

1987- 1988. SIXTH CLASS.
Front row from left to right, *Arlene Farrell, Niamh Gallagher, Josie Campbell, Vicky Henry,*
Marilyn McNamara and Rhona Daly. ***Second row, from left to right,*** *Sr. Maureen O'Brien,*
(Teacher,) Olivia Gorman, Olwyn Scully, Laura Mulligan, Olive----------
Back row, from left to right, *Siobhán Tone, Gráinne Breslin, Olivia O'Gorman and Sinéad Kennedy.*

1987-1988. SIXTH CLASS.
Front row, from left to right, Jacqueline McNamara, Catherine Mulvin, Lisa Heavey, Sharon McNevin and Aisling Dunne. *Second row, from left to right,* Margaret Lambert, Kerrie Hogan, Finola O'Neill, Sheila Gavin, Michelle Ward, Johanna Palmer and Sister Kathleen Daly (Teacher). *Third row, from left to right,* Shirley Heaney, Sandra Delaney, Caroline Whelton, Joanne Gallagher and Gillian Brogan.

1988-1989. SIXTH CLASS.
Back row, from left to right, Sharon Dunne, Mary Sheerin, Olivia Campbell, Niamh Coyne, Aisling Donnelly and Colette Palmer *Middle row, from left to right,* Maria Doyle, Helen Cooney, Caroline Byrne, Fiona Dunning, Sonya Fennelly and Sister Kathleen Daly(Principal) *Front row, from left to right,* Breda Daly, Aileen Kennedy, Edwina Tone, Caitriona Tone, Jenny Eighan and Caroline McNamara.

1989-1990. SIXTH CLASS.
Front row, from left to right, Elaine Cully, Shirley Poynton, Carol Gately, Priscilla Gahan
Elaine Newman, Jeanette Brennan and Therese Martin.
Second Row, from left to right, Carol Byrne, Jennifer Plunkett, Lisa Whelton, Joan Heaney,
Helen Munnelly, Sister Kathleen Daly (Teacher) **and absent from photo,** Nicola McCormack.

1991-1992. SIXTH CLASS.
Front row, from left to right, Linda Cully, Elaine Oxley, Catherine Smyth, Celine Colgan,
Áine Dunne, Fiona McGuire, Nicola Maher and Hazel Malone.
Second row, from left to right, Maeve McGuire, Triona Whelehan, Bernie O'Neill,
Margo O'Reilly, Alma Fennelly, Tara Broderick, Karen Farrell, Emily Griffin and Martha Boland.
Third row, from left to right, Katherine Meehan, Celine Sheridan, Edel Gavin, Pam O'Neill,
Ann Palmer, Olwyn Corrigan, Cora Wright and Laura Sheridan.

1992-1993. SIXTH CLASS.
Front row from left to right, Ann Kenny, Carol Ann Boland, Sharon Gunning,
Debbie Sheridan, Linda Poynton and Ann O'Reilly.
Middle row from left to right, *Jennifer Daly, Aisling Griffin, Karen Healy, Sarah Cully, Nollaig
Daly, Valerie Palmer and Siobhán McNamara. Charmaine Corrigan, Niamh Quirke, Eileen Heaney,
Irene Byrne* **and absent from Photo** *Elaine Conroy.*

1993-1994. SIXTH CLASS.
Front row, from left to right, Fiona Murphy, Siobhán Kiernan, Katrina Leogue
and Treacy Maher.
Second row, from left to right, *Sharon O'Reilly, Denise Heavey, Sinéad Griffin, Joan Keegan,
Caitríona Quirke, Ann Marie Fox and Sister Kathleen Daly (Teacher).*

1994-1995. SIXTH CLASS.
Front row, from left to right, Andrea Burke, Tracey Quirke, Andrea Bollard, Emer Martin,
Alicia Gammell, Caroline Horgan and Rita Doyle. *Second row, from left to right*, Lisa Irwin,
Linda Oxley, Mairéad Mulvin, Caitríona Burke, Rachelle Whelehan, and Sharon Lambert.
Third row, from left to right, Ann O'Reilly, Ciara McGuire, Alison Plunkett, Mairéad Smyth,
Sinéad Bagnall, and Elaine Gavin. *Absent from photo,* Carol O'Reilly.

1995-1996. SIXTH CLASS.
Front row, from left to right, Edel McGuire, Patricia Meehan, Michelle Meehan,
Carmen O'Sullivan, Jenna Bagnall and Siobhán Sheridan.
Second row, from left to right, Sarah Duncan, Lesle Kelleher, Michaela Mangan, Tara Colgan,
Denise Peppard and Maeve Nea.

1996-1997. SIXTH CLASS.
Back row, from left to right, Rosemary Gavin, Mary McGuire, Catherine Heduan, Annette Gunning, and Lorraine Mulvin.
Front row, from left to right, Natasha Glennon, Ailish Maguire, Catherine Gavin, Mary Conroy and Noeleen Meehan.

1997-1998. SIXTH CLASS.
Front row, from left to right, Róisín Breslin, Claire Heduan, and Janette Brogan.
Second row, from left to right, Yvonne Palmer, Michaela Gonoud, Donna Kiernan, Denise Brady. Jill Mangan and Jacqueline Kelly.
Third row, from left to right, Laurna Dunne, Alwynne Cleary, Niamh Broderick, Ciara Byrne, Ciara Heavey, Deirdre Kelly and Áine Cooney.
Fourth row, from left to right, Róisín Breslin, Claire Heduan and Jeanette Brogan.

1998-1999. SIXTH CLASS.
*Front row, from left to right, Helen Metcalfe, Leanne Carrol, Ciara Dunne
and Deirdre Eighan.   Second row, from left to right, Mrs. Anne Eighan (Teacher),
Shauna Coyne, Jennifer Sweeney, Ruth Heaney, Yvonne McAteer, Megan Glennon, Emma Gavin,
Laura Heavey and Gemma Dolan.*

1999-2000. SIXTH CLASS.
*Front row, from left to right, Sharon Hyland, Orla Gallagher, Sally Alford, Sarah Fox, and
Sarah Brady. Second row, from left to right, Mairéad Metcalfe, Serena McGuire,
Jennifer Cully, Louise Peppard, Bernadette Jessop, Orla Eighan and Claire Keegan.
Third row, from left to right, Marie Bagnall, Rachel Farrell, Alice Doyle, Charlene Dunne,
Callie Daly and Martha Gavin.*

2000-2001. SIXTH CLASS.

Front row, from left to right, Tara, Duigenan, Katie Nugent, Ciara Lowry, Amanda Stapleton, Gillian Gonoud, Grace Gavin, and Xenia Wallace. *Second row, from left to right,* Amy Daly, Rita Cleary, Ursula Gavin, Andrea Gorman, Ailish Maguire, Lisa Kelly, Hannah Larkin, Siobhán Jessop, Vivienne Floody, Mary Kate Wille and Mrs. Anne Eighan (Teacher).

2001-2002. SIXTH CLASS.

Front row, from left to right, Emma Hayes, Jennifer Lumsden, Orla Hanrahan, Claire Judge, Michelle O'Sullivan and Nadine Carroll.
Second row, from left to right, Lisa McDonnell, Siobhán Dolan, Niamh McGuire, Aoife Hyland, Martina Mealiffe, Janice McHugh and Mrs. Anne Eighan (Teacher).

2002-2003. SIXTH CLASS.
Front row, from left to right, Emma Williams, Mary Seery, Ciara Bagnall, Louise Byrne,
Debbie Wilson, Erin Tormey, Kelly O'Neill, and Maria Morgan.
Second row, from left to right, Mrs. Therése Downey (Teacher), Sarah Smyth, Nicola Bradley,
Emma Whelehan, Cliona Duigenan, Laurie Byrne, Aoife Beglin, Colleen Gill, Maria Timmins,
Sinéad Whelehan, Niamh Morgan, Dawn Wallace and Mrs. Anne Eighan, Principal.

2003-2004. SIXTH CLASS.
Front row, from left to right, Emma Cleary, Shauna Jones, Darien Gandia, Amy Mahony, Sinéad Lowry,
Nicola McCabe, and Monica Seery. *Second row, from left to right,* Mrs. Therése Downey (Teacher),
Nicole Milmoe, Ciara Floody, Olivia Keegan, Wendy Carpenter, Chloe Gavin, Jennifer Lonican,
Naomi Plunkett, Rachel Gallagher, Angela Bradley, Natasha Jessop and Mrs. Anne Eighan (Principal).
Third row, from left to right, Lauren Thompson, Rachel Duggan, Sinéad Doyle, Sarah Hogan,
Caitlin Mangan, Karen Treacy, Clodagh Gill, Leanne Hendley and Asling Dunne.

2004-2005. SIXTH CLASS.
Front row, from left to right, Clare Geraghty, Tori Gandia, Aoife Brady, Mary Metcalfe, Ciara Farrell, and Karen Hopkins. *Second row, from left to right,* Mrs. Therése Downey (Teacher), Rebecca Cleary, Jessica Adams, Fiona McHugh, Laura Sweeney, Laura Bagnall, and Mrs. Anne Eighan (Principal).

2005-2006. SIXTH CLASS.
Front row, from left to right, Sinéad O Neill, Rebecca Williams, Cassie Whelehan, Emma Treacey, Róisín Farrell, and Jodi Henry.
Second row, from left to right, Mrs. Therése Downey (Teacher), Tracey Jessop, Lauren Phelan, Siofra Fennelly, Elaine Geraghty, Mary Gavin, and Mrs. Anne Eighan(Principal). *Third row, from left to right,* Frances Fallon, Laura Walsh, Jean Kelly, Sarah Jane McCabe and Jade Wallace.

2006-2007. SIXTH CLASS.
Front row, from left to right, Ciara Duffy, Louise Judge, Rebecca Rooney, Tamara Nolan, Gemma Gorman, Colleen Condron and Aoife Whelehan. *Second row, from left to right,* Miss Ulrika Maher(Teacher), Courtney Jessop, Lisa Byrne, Sally Gorman, Anne Peppard, Deirdre Seery, Claire Bagnall, Céile Coyne and Mrs. Anne Eighan (Principal) . *Third row, from left to right,* Shannon O'Reilly, Jennifer Connolly, Emma Diggin, Rita Fitzgerald, Hannah Byrne, Rachel Cully and Keeva Daly.

2007-2008. SIXTH CLASS.
Front row, from left to right, Lauren O'Reilly, Noelle Burns, Aoife Jenkins, Laura O'Sullivan, Jane Kinsella, Chloe Renshaw, Tara Condron and Maria Redmond.
Second row, from left to right, Miss Ulrika Maher(Teacher), Crona Kenny, Fiona Coyle, Rachel Kelly, Nicole Lonican, Collette Kenny and Mrs. Anne Eighan (Principal).
Third row, from left to right, Stacey Milmoe, Rebecca Lawlor, Emer Kelly, Selina Bradley, Temi Obilana and Sarah Timmins.

2008 - 2009. SIXTH CLASS.
Front row, from left to right, Tara Rogers, Lisa Cully, Jean Henry, Michaela Brady, Michelle Groome, Leah Kenny and Ciara Cox. *Second row, from left to right,* Mrs. Anne Eighan(Principal), Katie Downey, Carmel Kenny, Jennifer Judge, Bayeigh O'Flynn, Ailish O'Neill, Ciara Nugent, Clodagh Jessop and Miss Ulrika Maher(Teacher). *Third row, from left to right,* Vicky O'Reilly, Kelly Gahan, Chloe Bagnall, Esther Amedu, Nicola Judge, Hannah Farrell, Lisa Flanagan.

2009-2010. SIXTH CLASS.
Front row, from left to right, Éadaoine Brady, Emma Bradley, Chloe Travers, Aoibheann Gorman, Orla Hyland, Alex Grenham, Clare O'Sullivan, Amy Cully and missing from photo –Eimear Daly. *Second row from left to right,* Mrs. Therése Downey (Teacher), Bobbie O'Neill, Megan Davitt, Natalia Lüber, Anu Soile, Geraldine Morgan, Christine McSparron, Erica Redmond and Mrs. Anne Eighan (Principal).

2010-2011. SIXTH CLASS.
Front row, from left to right, Éadaoin Coyle, Sarah Fox, Emily Bollard,
Charity Musasa, Niamh Cully, Lauren Buckley and Danni Malone.
Second row, from left to right, Mrs. Therése Downey(Teacher), Tori Maher, Hannah Amedu,
Priscilla Obilana, Kathleen Lonican, Ellen Kiernan, Sarah-Jane O'Connor, Kym Maher
and Mrs. Anne Eighan (Principal).

2011-2012. SIXTH CLASS
Front row, from left to right, Bláithín Downey, Amy Smith, Amy Hogan Gill, Emer Lyster,
Lauren Doyle, Ciara Forde, Melissa Cully, Leah Harris and Jennifer Cunningham.
Second Row, from left to right, Mrs. Therése Downey (Teacher), Eithne Coyle, Rebecca McCabe,
Mollie Reid, Ava Balfe, Lauren Malone, Emily O'Sullivan, Róisín Fay, Emma Kennedy and Mrs. Anne
Eighan (Principal). *Third row, from left to right,* Justyna Lüber, Nadine Walsh, Rebecca Nolan,
Michelle Malone, Rebecca Joyce, Sarah Flanagan, Katie Doyle and Ciara Cox.

~ CHAPTER 21 ~
GREEN SCHOOLS 2012

In June 2012, the Convent Primary School, celebrated the hoisting of it's third Green Schools Environmental Awareness flag. The theme of their project was water conservation and their meticulous monitoring of water use in the school resulted in Westmeath County Council crediting the School €500. The flag was raised at the ceremony by Brendan Keeley from Tullamore, who was one of the finalists in *The Voice of Ireland* competition on RTE Television in 2011-2012. Entertainment was provided by past Pupil Chris Loughrey and

The Green Flag Celebration Cake, by Johanne Arthur.

the *Southsun Band*. A great day was had by all, and parents, friends, teachers and pupils were provided with refreshments in the school assembly hall afterwards. To mark the occassion, a beautiful cake was provided by Mrs. Johanne Arthur displaying the green flag. Mrs. Thérése Downey and her sixth class pupils who monitored the Green Flags project during the school year cut the cake. The girls were all decked out in their new purple fleeces, signed by all the members of the class.

Pictured with the Green Flags Cake are from left to right, Chris Loughrey, Thérése Downey (Teacher) Ann Eighan(Principal) and Brendan Nolan(School Caretaker).

Enjoying the Green Flag celebrations from left to right are, Chloe Gavin, Elaine Nolan, Kathleen Loughrey, Catherine Walsh and Betty Walsh.

Majella Farrell and her Granddaughter.

Yoyo Cheuk and friends.

Aoife Flanagan, Róisín Lyster and Clodagh Cully.

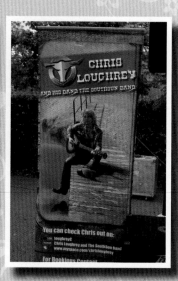

Barry and Orlan Collins.

Fr. William Coleman P.P. and Geraldine Gorman.

Chris Loughrey and his Southsun Band.

Chris and the band in action.

Chris and the band in action.

Brianna O'Reilly and Kelsey Poynton

Aaron Scott and Finnian Carroll.

Sylvia Love and Laura Doyle

Jenny Cunningham

Michael O'Sullivan (Chairperson of the Board of Management) and Ann Eighan (Principal).

Ann Eighan (Principal) and Pattie Heavey.

Catherine, Geraldine and Betty Walsh.

Ms. Mary Love

Ann Eighan (Principal), pictured with members of the Community of the Sisters of Mercy, Sister Maureen (Retired Principal of the Convent Primary School), Sister Dolores and Sister Rosario.

Brendan Keeley and Ulrika Maher.

Justinä Lüber addresses the gatherins on behalf of the pupils of the Convent Primary School.

The back of the Class of 2012 Sweatshirt, worn by the Sixth class pupils and signed by each member of the class.

Therése Downey and the sixth class pupils cut the celebration cake.

The flag is raised by Brendan Keeley and the sixth class pupils.

Therése Downey (sixth class Teacher), Brendan Keeley and Ann Eighan (Principal) with the newly raised green flag.

~ Chapter 22 ~
St. Joseph's Secondary School

~ CHAPTER 22 ~
ST. JOSEPH'S SECONDARY SCHOOL

For the duration of the war years, St. Joseph's lay dormant apart from the accommodation provided for the junior boarders at the Convent Primary School. As shown earlier, life was quiet in Rochfortbridge but things were changing in the latter half of the decade. Following the great snowfall of 1947, a welcome visit to Laytown Co. Meath for the sisters and visits to the convents in Navan and Trim saw the emergence of a new proposal for a project to further develop the buildings known as St. Josephs.

Sister of Mercy, in the 1950's. Back row from left to right, Sr. Joseph McAuley, Sr. Attracta Duffy and Sr. Rosario Shaw. Front row, from left to right, Sr. Magdalene Claffey, Sr. Pius Doran and Sr. Dolores Carroll.

With agriculture undergoing change in post-emergency Ireland, there was a greater demand from farming communities, professional people and families who owned their own business in the surrounding areas to provide access to Secondary Education for their children.

It was seen that the Sisters of Mercy could provide the answer, as families in the Rochfortbridge area had to send their girls away to towns like Mullingar, Athlone or Navan for their secondary education.

With this in mind, the Sisters of Mercy made an application to Dr. John Kyne, Bishop of Meath to put St. Josephs school on a secondary basis. The Diocesan Council considered the matter and with certain stipulations permission was granted.

Funds were needed to set this project up and shares belonging to the former St. Joseph's School for the Deaf and Dumb were sold to facilitate matters. Christopher Bennett was engaged to do the necessary repairs to the building.

By October 1947, the repair work was in full swing and Martin Bennett began to wainscot the work room and passage and to repair the abandoned dormitory. This work took three months. When this was complete, Larry Ward painted the school, rooms, passages dormitory and parlour.

By the end of June 1948 the place looked as good as new. Extra books and school equipment were needed and some of this was provided on loan from the Convent Primary School.

To fulfil the Board of Education requirements for secondary schools, a certified secondary teacher was needed. The first selection made were not sanctioned by the Department authorities. Their recommendation was that a secondary trained nun take up the post and that they should apply to other convents for a teaching nun to be loaned to meet the requirements. The Rev.

Aerial view of Rochfortbridge, taken around 1959.

Mother from the Convent of Mercy in Kells took it upon herself to find a suitable candidate and tried convents as far away as Macroom in Cork. Replies from Convents posted letters of regret, being unable to send the required help.

Permission was made to Bishop Kyne to advertize for the post. A number of applicants applied, but they withdrew when it was discovered that the school was only at proposal stage and not yet established.

When no one from the Rochfortbridge community was quaified to take up a post at the new school, Rev. W. Conlon, headmaster at Navan Classical School recommended that the school begin as a Secondary Top. This meant that the school would work in conjunction with the Convent Primary School but still entirely disinct in its own premises and teaching. The Rochfortridge community approved the idea and another ad was placed in the national papers. Two applications were received and Maureen Doyle B.A. H.Dip. took up the post and her subesquent work in the school proved very successful in those early years.

When the Convent Primary School opened on September 7th 1948 for the new school year, St. Joseph's Secondary Top School opened its doors for the first time. In this new school year, there were 32 boarders housed. 14 of them were the first pupils of St. Josephs and the rest attended the Convent Primary School.

The First pupils were:

Breda McCoy	Patricia Hope	Lily Whelehan.	Eileen Whelehan
Genevieve McCardle.	Frances Ennis,	Betty Hayes,	Ursula Marry.
Mary Berry	M. Finnegan	Mary McLoughlin	Margaret Buckley
Bernie McGearty			

- In October Rev. J.H. Kilmartin P.P. celebrated mass in the classroom and it was attended by the community of Sisters as well as the pupils attending the school. He imparted a special blessing to the work and all concerned in making it a success.

- Before Christmas, a Miss Fox, a music and dance mistress gave the children in both schools lessons in music and dance and according to the Annals of the Sisters of Mercy

Before Christmas recess they brought off a most successful and creditable concert, consisting of singing, dancing, and drill, a most humorous sketch and juvenile recitations. Rev. J. Kilmartin, Delaney, Jennings, Plunkett, J.Byrne –Chinese Mission attended. Also Dr. P. Fox, the Sisters and staff in Convent, St. Josephs and parochial house. All children went home in excellent form and spirit to their Christmas vacation.[1]

- On the 7th of March 1949, a Mr. Finlay, schools Inspector made his first official visit to the school and was very pleased with the efficiency of the teacher and the progress of the pupils.

The Lighting of the Village

With the establishment of the ESB to provide electricity for the country in 1927, they took control of the Shannon electrical Scheme, which had been passed in the Shannon Electrical Act in 1925. The project was at an advanced stage in 1927and the work of the ESB was to manage the scheme and control electricity supply and generation generally.[2] By the 1940's the scheme was being rolled across the country with electricity reaching most cities and towns.[3]

Milltownpass village had its own supply of Electrical power long before other Westmeath villages. Not alone that but power came to the village during the war years.

A number of attempts had been made in the early nineteen forties to have electricity brought to Rochfortbridge village, but nothing came of it.

A delegation of the Sisters of Mercy journeyed to Athlone and interviewed the District Engineer of the ESB, Mr. W. Callanan regarding an electrification project.

---

1   The Annals of the Sisters of Mercy.
2   At the time, the Shannon Scheme at Ardnacrusha was the largest hydro-electric station in the world, though this was soon superseded by the Hoover Dam which commenced construction in 1930.
3   It was during World War II that the village of Milltownpass took it upon themselves to have electricity brought to the village. Encouraged by local man Dr. Peter Fox, a local company was formed to harness the river to produce power. Christopher Bennett, William Dardis, P.J. Beglin, L.J. Lawless and John O'Donoghue were some of the local people who lead the project. P. J. Beglin, was appointed Secretary and Managing Director, while Dr. Peter Fox, was appointed Chairman. A turbine and 16 horse power generator which was designed to give 4 kilowatts of electricity allowing for a five foot fall in the river was purchased for £160 from a company in Dundrum, Dublin. It was estimated that 10 kilowatts of electricity could be generated if there was a ten foot fall in the river. The scheme in total cost £700. Trees were felled in the local woods to provide poles to carry the cables to all the houses and local electricians as well as people from Tullamore wired the village for power. Local man Billy Beglin was the local resident engineer who supervised the project. It was a very proud moment when the village was lit for the first time and the power provided was generated locally. There was a novel way to pay for the use of the power as there was no metering of electricity usage in the homes, a fee of £2 per point per house was charged and it varied from £2/10= to £20 per annum for each household.

He went into the matter carefully with them and promised his sympathy and assistance. Contact was made with Mr. R.Brown, chairman of the Board of the ESB and with the help of Brother Noonan, a native of Clonfad, Dalystown, he was sympathetic to their request also.

Their main argument for the importance of electricity for the area was with the new Secondary School and the children had to study at night under *'injurious conditions.'* Never to be stuck for a reason, this statement of course set the alarm bells ringing with the ESB as at this point in time, most Secondary schools were centered in large towns and most of these had already received electricity. The safety element alone, with so many young people in a changing and modern Ireland, having to still study using lamplight or candlelight posed a serious problem indeed.

The local area was canvassed in the meantime to see how interested the community would be in having their area electrified and the returns to the ESB were fairly satisfactory.

Pretty soon, the Board of the ESB decided to bring power to Rochfortbridge and a letter was sent to the Rev. Mother confirming this.

The scheme commenced in early September 1949, and in November, the first electricians arrived to wire the convent, St. Josephs and the Domestic classroom. The contract had been given to the ESB to carry out this work at a cost of £760 – fittings to be supplied independently. Mr. G. Russell was the main electrical contractor assisted by P.Carey and a Mr. Liam. By 1950, electricity had arrived in Rochfortbridge and without much fanfare, the standard of living for most homes changed overnight. Light, heat, radio, power for cookers, fridges, irons, washing machines, kettles, radios and later television were now controlled at the flick of a switch. Living conditions improved greatly and even though this changeover was quick and sudden, it is still known as the quiet revolution. Like every other parish and district in the country, Rochfortbridge had become part of this quiet revolution also.

Further Developments

- When St. Josephs opened its doors for their second year in 1949, it was found necessary to employ a second teacher and Miss B.Galvin was appointed. She came from the Marist College, Tubbercurry, Sligo. In addition to teaching first years, she taught art to the boarders on Saturday. The salary to pay the teachers came from St. Josephs funds.

- In 1950, there was still an outstanding bill to be paid for the wiring of the convent and secondary school buildings. To help defray the cost, Rev. P. Delaney C.C. organised a monster card drive in the convent hall. It was very well attended by all the local card enthusiasts and it realised the sum of £340. According to the annals, it was a red letter night for all who participated. Free supper was served in the convent hall and it was estimated that over 700 were amply provided for.[4]

- In June 1950, the first pupils from St. Josephs sat their Inter Cert exam in Loreto College, Mullingar. They were transported there each day by car for the duration

---

4   There were a number of other card drives recorded in the Annals up until the mid-nineteen fifties, as it took some time to pay off all the expenses of this project.

of the exam and the first pupils, there were three of them received their results in September. They were Bernadette, McGearty, Breda McCoy and Mary Berry.

- With Rural electrification now well established in the village, it was possible to show *'interesting and instructional films'* in the convent hall. Among them was the life of the Holy Father, which according to the annals were fully appreciated by the sisters and pupils, both primary and secondary.

The First Principal and full recognition as a Secondary School

Sister M. Magdalene Claffey entered the Convent of Mercy in 1942 and together with Sr. M. Stanislaus O' Brien, received their habits on the 1st.of September. On September 11th 1946, she was informed that she had received a place at Carysfort College of Education in Blackrock, Dublin to train as a primary teacher. Having completed her primary training, she returned to college in 1949 to study for an arts degree. In 1951, she completed her B.A. at the National University of Ireland and obtained a Higher Diploma with Honours.

At this point, the Sisters of Mercy decided to discontinue with the Secondary Top arrangement with the National School and to become a Secondary school proper with Sister Magdalene as Principal.

In September 1951, there were 26, pupils attending the secondary school and the number of pupils having almost doubled in three years sounded that the school was running quite successfully and as there was a possibility also that this number would increase even more, it was time to create a more stable educational establishement and to ensure that it would grow and flourish in future years.

At the beginning of the school year, Sr. Carmel and Sr. Magdalene were teaching in the Secondary School. A new lay teacher was also appointed –Miss B. Smith, Oldcastle and as a teacher she also relieved the Sisters on several occassions at evening study time.

- It became obvious that the Department of Education was monitoring the progress of the new school with a view to its future proposed status. A number of inspections were carried out between October and December 1951 in various subjects

Name	Subject
Mr. KcKeown	Geography and Maths
Mr. Sugrue	Irish and History
Mr. Fitzgerald	Latin and History
Mr. Duane	General
Miss Cleary	Cookery

All gave satisfactory reports and following this, Sister Magdalene applied to have the secondary school registered.

In February 1952, the Department furnished the results of their reports carried out between October and December 1951 and the the following letter was enclosed:

The Manager,
Convent of Mercy,
Rochfortbridge,
Co. Westmeath.

A Bhean Uasal,
I am to inform you that the Department has decided to grant provisional recognition to your school as a Secondary School in respect of the school year 1951/52.

The reports of the Inspectors on the work of your school in the current school year are enclosed herewith

Mise
S. Ó Conchubhair

Letter from the Department of Education granting provisional status to St. Josephs Secondary school.

As part of this procedure and provisional recognition, Sr. Magdalene and Mother Attracta visited Department of Education Secondary Headquarters at Hume Street, Dublin to meet with officials on the matter.

The main topic for discussion was the recognition of the school as an exam centre for Intermediate Certiificate for the coming year. This application was successful also and in June 1952 the first Intermediate Certificate Examinations were held at the school, supervised by a Mr. Joyce B.A. Hdip from Malahide. Twelve candidates sat the first exams and all were successful, some of them receiving honours.

In 1953, the centre was upgraded to include Leaving Certificate as well as Intermediate Certificate exams.

On the 16th of March 1954, the Secondary School was granted full status by the Department of Education and four students were presented for the Leaving Certificate Examination in 1954.

- In 1956, the school re-opened in September with 52 boarders. A graduate from Galway was engaged to teach for the year – Miss Angela Costello. The increase in pupils also meant an increase in teaching staff to meet the demand and the following table lists the number teachers for that year:-

Teacher	Status
Sr. Magdalene	Principal
Sr. Dolores	
Sr. Pius	
Mother Agnes	Part-Time
Sr. M. Stanislaus	Part-Time
Miss Angela Costello	

- To comply with pressing demands for outdoor games, a bulldozer levelled a sloping field in the convent grounds with a view to building a tennis court. This work was done at a cost of £55. The tennis court took some time to get off the ground and it wasn't till 1961, that the project was finally carried out.

- September to Christmas 1956, was a very busy time at the school as the pupils had entertainment in the form of films and whist drives. Fr. Kirly C.C. kindly gave the use of his 16mm projector, showing films and pictures for the benefit of the children and staff, while at Halloween there were festivities and games to celebrate the end of Autumn and the approach of winter.

St. Josephs Secondary School Hall

- In 1958, the number of boarders had risen to 72

This of course did not take into account also the number of day pupils on rolls. There were 20 day pupils on rolls in 1958, taking the total number of pupils up to 92.

The number of boarders increased more than five-fold in the ten years since the Secondary School opened its doors and in reviewing their space requirements also and to provide accommodation for Physical Education as

Photo of the Sisters of Mercy, taken before 1958. Back row, from left to right, Sr. Maureen O'Brien, Sr. Magdalene Claffey, Sr. Attracta Duffy.
Sr. Aquin Geraghty, Sr. Catherine Healy, Sr. Dolores Carroll and Sr. Rosario Shaw.
Front row, from left to right, Sr. Columba Gargan, Sr. Pius Doran, Sr. Agnes Farrell, Sr. Concepta O'Brien, Sr. Brigid Brady, Sr. Assumpta Heavy, Sr. Carmel Brennan and Sr. Joseph McCauley.

well as other recreational activities, assemblies, concerts etc. the Sisters visited Dr. Kyne, Bishop of Meath to secure a loan to build a new assembly hall.

This request was granted by the Bishop and Phillip Ginnell, Architect, from Mullingar prepared the plans.

By early 1960, the new hall was ready and the first concert was produced there on the 17th of March. The operetta performed was *'Pearl, the Fisher Maiden,'* Mr.Halett, a violin master, conducted and Sr. Dolores was at the piano. The opening night was specially provided for the children, parents and friends of the school. On the following Sunday night, the doors were opened to the general public to attend.

Bishop Kyne attended, as did twelve priests from the neighbouring parishes. In an address at the end of the show, the Bishop complimented the children and the Sisters on a very creditable performance. The funds raised at the concert and a card drive on the 27th of March were used to help pay off the debt on the new hall at St. Josephs.

- Following the success of *'Pearl the Fisher Maiden,'* another concert was held on the 8th of December 1960 comprising of a Nativity Play called *'Wonder Night!'* and a short operetta entitled *'The Stranger.'* On Sunday the 11th of December the concert was open to the public and despite the cold and very frosty weather which left the roads icy and dangerous to travel on, there was a large attendance at the production.

The Centenary Celebrations 1962

The 21st of August, 1962 recorded the centenary of the foundation of the Convent of Mercy at Rochfortbridge, but the occassion was not celebrated until the 2nd of October as schools were closed during the month of August. The Westmeath Examiner covered the event and on the 30th of June 1962 in an article,

Sr. Dolores and Bishop John Kyne pictured with the pupils from St. Joseph's who sang at the High Mass to commemorate the centenary of the Sisters of Mercy in 1962.

outlined the history of the Sisters of Mercy from its foundation till the present time of 1962. Reflecting back fifty years they gave an account also of the Golden Jubilee celebrations and the work of the Sisters subsequently:

On the occassion of the Golden Jubilee of the Convent, in 1912, the people of the Rochfortbridge area presented the nuns with an address, paying a fitting tribute to the work of the members of the order there. The centenary of the Order of Mercy was also marked in the convent in 1931 by appropriate ceremonies. Today the work of the Sisters continues to expand. In their primary school, they have from 150 to 160 pupils

and there are over 90 girls in the Secondary School. Year after year, pupils of the school join various Orders and many of them today are working in various parts of the world, France, Rome, South Africa, Australia, etc. Three past pupils are at

The Rochfortbridge community of the Sisters of Mercy pictured with Bishop John Kyne on the occassion of the centenary of the foundation of the Rochfortbridge Community in 1962.

present members of the community in Rochfortbridge. The examination results from the Convent are adequate testimony, if such were needed, of the good work being done. Numerous scholarships have been won by students from the school and quite a number have been called to training as teachers. Excellent results are also obtained in the music examinations each year. A century of achievement, especially in the things that really matter; a steady development from small beginnings; a fountain from which other foundations for the glory of God have strung up –these are but some of the achievements of the Convent of Mercy in Rochfortbridge. That it may long continue to flourish in its good work is the prayer of the people of the area and of the many past pupils who have passed through its doors.[5]

On Wednesday October 3rd, the celebrations were in full swing and there were a number of events to mark the occassion. Pontifical High Mass was celebrated in the Parish Church by Dr. Kyne. The sermon was preached by very Rev. John Gavin, P.P. Huyton, Liverpool, a native of the Parish. His sister Mother Ignatius (Poor Servants Order) accompanied him from Liverpool for the occasion. Many well deserved tributes were paid to the members of the Community on their good work and a comment was made to the local press stating that they conduct a Primary and Secondary School and the results of the annual examinations bear testimony –if such is needed –to the excellence of the education imparted.

There was a large attendance of clergy to mark the occasion and the following table lists all those who were present.

Title	Name	Place
Deacon	Rev. F. O'Connor C.C.	Mullingar
Sub-Deacon	Rev. J.Carey C.C.	Tullamore
Assistant Deacons	Very Rev. H. Conlon P.P. V.F.	Killucan
	Rev. John McManus P.P.	Rochfortbridge
	Rev. E. Crinion P.P.	Kinnegad
Assistant Priest	Rev. P.J. Regan C.C.	Mullingar
Master of Ceremonies	Very Rev. P.J. McGahey P.P.	Castletown Geo.
	Rev. F. O Reilly C.C.	Tyrrellspass

5   Westmeath Examiner, June 30th 1962.

In attendance also	Rev. Fr. Martin C.P.	
	Rev. J. Conlon C.C.	Rochfortbridge
	Rev. J. Troy C.C.	Castletown Geo.
	Rev. J. Abbott C.C.	Ballinabrackey
	Rev. P. Delaney C.C.	Killucan
	Rev. A. McCauley C.C.	Liverpool
	Rev. J. Healy C.C.	Ballivor
	Rev. P. Cuffe C.C.[6]	Duleek
	Rev. P. Reilly C.C.	Kinnegad
	Rev. W. Kirley C.C.	Rathoath
	Rev. P. Bartley C.C.	Tubber
	Rev. D. Crilley C.C.	Kells
	Rev. A. Farrell C.C.	Enfield
	Rev. P. Claffey C.C.	Carrick-on-Shannon
	Rev. M. Murchin C.C.	Longwood
	Rev. W. Cleary, Chaplain. St. Lomans	Mullingar

Also present were members of the Irish Christian Brothers,
Rev. Brother Maloney, Bursar, Marino
Rev. Brother O' Farrell, Trim
Rev. Brother Geraghty, Superior, Tullamore

The following Mercy Order Houses were represented, Trim, Drogheda, Navan, Clara, Kilbeggan, Tullamore, Moate, Mullingar as well as members of the Presentation Convent, Mullingar.

Sr. M. Brigid Leogue a member of the Poor Servants Order and a native of the parish was present, as were Dr. And Mrs. P. Fox, Mr. P. Ginnell, Architect and Mr. J.Dowling, manager of the Hibernian bank, Mullingar.

The Church ceremony concluded with a Te Deum and Benediction.

Afterwards, the pupils of the Secondary School staged the opera 'Blossom Time,' The opera and music by Franz Schubert was according to the Westmeath Examiner

> Was one of the best productions in St. Josephs since the school started putting on annual performances. This was only as it should be in the centenary year. The production, orchestra, lighting, scenery, make-up and all the very essential ingredients that go into a production like this were excellent.[7]

Blossom Time' traces Schubert's own battle for recognition as a composer. It has many romantic scenes and a good sprinkling of sparkling comedy. It brought many a laugh in the crowded hall and the audience enjoyed the production very well.

Visiting clergy and seculars were later entertained to luncheon in St. Joseph's Study Hall and the Sisters in the Boarders Refectory.

6   Rev. P. Cuffe conducted the choir at the ceremonies.
7   Westmeath Examiner 11th October 1962.

'*Blossom Time*' was presented in the parish three times during early October. On October 6th, Mr. J. Gavin and M. Egan on behalf ot the parish committee presented Mother Agnes with a cheque for £700. This was added to with another cheque for £136-10-0. On this date also the opera was performed for a second time for members of the children of Mary Sodality and they later presented the community with a cheque for £141.

The final production took place on Sunday October 7th for friends of the community and past pupils. Supper was provided in St. Josephs for the visitors and it was on this occassion that a past pupils Union was formed and Very Rev. Fr. J. McManus P.P., Rochfortbridge Miss B. McGearty N.T. was elected president. Mary Flanagan presented Mother Agnes with a spiritual bouquet and a cheque for £42 on behalf of the Union.

Miss McGearty paid a tribute to the pupils and members of the Community on the excellent presentation of '*Blossom time.*' She spoke of the wonderful work of the nuns in Rochfortbridge during the past one hundred years and paid a special tribute to the late Mother Attracta for her achievements.

The centenary celebrations concluded on the 8th and 9th of December when the Convent Primary School presented their concert in St. Joseph's Hall.

Grace Delaney and Jane Treacy, taken at the centenary celebrations for the Sisters of Mercy in 1962.

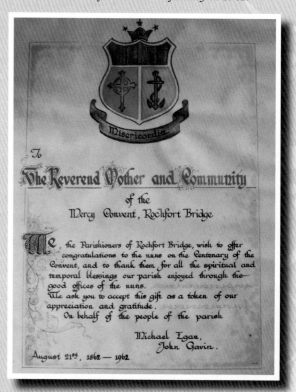

An Address presented as part of the centenary celebrations of the Convent of Mercy in 1962 by representatives of the people of the Parish.

St. Joseph's Co-Educational School - 1963

In 1955, Bórd na Móna built Derrygreenagh Park to accommodate its workers at the Derrygreenagh works, Rochfortbridge.[8] Following the establishment of rural electrification in Ireland in the late 1950's the national grid was expanding rapidly too and there was an increasing demand to produce more electricity to feed industry, school, town and city lighting, farming and domestic use. The objective of Bord na Móna was to harvest the vast quantities of peat on Irish bogs which was then later sold to the E.S.B. to feed peat burning power stations to create additional electricity.

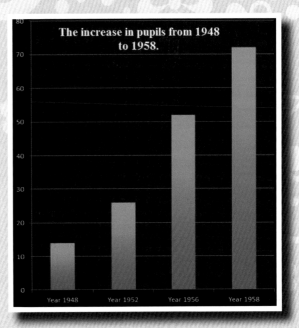

Statistic showing the growth in the student population at St. Joseph's from 1948 to 1958.

In the midlands, power stations were built at Rhode, Allenwood, Ferbane and Portarlington on the fringes of the bog of Allen to make the transportation of milled peat through a network of narrow gauge railways easier across the bogs.

The increase in population in a number of midland villages due to the employment created by the E.S.B. and Bord na Móna saw many young families settle in the new custom-built village. Derrygreenagh park comprised of 100 houses meant that there was a need to put in place further educational infrastructures to meet future demands for primary and secondary education. A new boys National School opened in 1949, replacing an earlier building in the village. The Convent Primary School had ample space for the present, to meet the educational needs for young girls. St. Joseph's Secondary school, opening in 1948 accommodated boarders mainly with some day pupil girls from the parish attending as well.

By 1962, there was a large increase in the number of boys in the village requiring secondary education and many parents expressed concerns that the educational needs of boys were not being met locally. Traditionally, local boys who went forward into second level education were sent away to boarding schools like St. Finians in Mullingar and Ballyfin, College in Co. Laois. The only other option would be to cycle the ten miles into Mullingar to the Vocational School or the C.B.S. Secondary School.

---

8   The state agency, Bórd na Móna began harvesting peat in the 1950's, establishing a works centre nearby at Derrygreenagh. This attracted great employment in the area and as a result there were not enough houses in the village to accommodate this influx of workers and their families.
Bord na Móna built Derrygreenagh Park around 1955 as housing for its employees. Due to it's unusual architecture it is regarded as a heritage village. Comprising of one hundred houses it is laid out in a crescent, facing the main Dublin road and the remaining houses surround a circular green to the rear of the crescent. Derrygreenagh Park was one of a small number of housing estates built to a particular design. This Bord na Móna village has won awards for its tidiness as well as its neatly manicured and landscaped grounds. It also has the added attraction of a local community pitch-and-putt course.

Stationed in the village at this time, was Garda Patrick O'Reilly, who resided in the village of Tyrrellspass. Garda O'Reilly's daughters were pupils of St. Joseph's Secondary School. Hearing the sentiments of young parents with regard to the dilemma of seeking secondary education for their boys, he decided to take it upon himself to do something about it. He wrote to His Lordship Dr. Kyne about the matter and he received a prompt reply:

Clonard House,
Mullingar,
Co. Westmeath.
31 July 1962.

Dear Mr. O'Reilly,
I have given your letter much consideration and I must say I admire your enterprise.
Have you got in touch with the Nuns Federation of Catholic Unions of Ireland, 39, Kildare Street, Dublin 2. The Secretary is Mr. Aidan Williams.

I could see you for a chat on Thursday 9 August at 1.30 or 3.00 to discuss the matter

+ John Kyne[9]

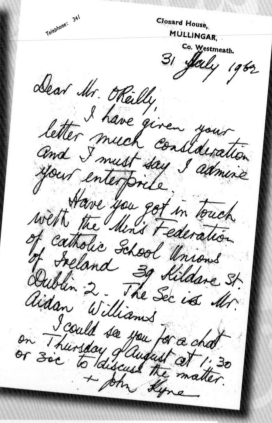

A letter written by Dr. Kyne to Garda Patrick O'Reilly, Rochfortbridge, July 1962.

School group taken with Sister Columba in 1960. Back row, from left to right, Betty Corcoran, Teresa Treacy, Mary Harte, Moira Duffy, Mary Bollard, Nuala McGibney, Marjorie Ring, Patricia O'Reilly, Mary Padian, Mary Maher and Mary Clonan. Middle row, from eft to right, Margaret Maher, Marcella McCabe, Pauline Byrne, Cepta Bradley, Theresa O'Connell, Frances Byrne, May Gunning, Geraldine Coyne, Christine Tyson, Ann Dardis, Moira Duffy and Mary Murphy. Front row, form left to right, Helen Corcoran, Eileen Molloy, Maureen O'Reilly, Margaret Doyle, Sr. Columba Gargan, Maureen McEnroe, Joan Murtagh, Grace Walshe, Margaret Brennan and Mary Briody.

---

9   Letter in the possession of Sr. Regina O'Reilly, Convent of Mercy, Trim.

Dr. Kyne consulted with the Rochfortbridge Community on the matter. But it was put on the long finger due to the up and coming centenary celebrations.

On Confirmation day, 1963 Bishop Kyne announced that St. Josephs would be taking in boys for the first time in September 1963.

This announcement received a great welcome from local families and the Sisters looked forward to this new venture into the field of Second Level Education. It was a new and innovative breakthrough in the Diocese to establish a Co-Educational Secondary School. Concerns of course were expressed in some quarters regarding the implications of educating adolescent boys and girls together. In general the idea received a warm welcome and a meeting was held at the school by the Sisters outlining their future plans.[10]

To accommodate the reception of boys, an extension was needed at St. Joseph's and three new classrooms and a boys toilet unit were built over St. Joseph's hall. These were linked via corridors and a boys cloakroom with the hall and the main part of the St. Joseph's building creating one contained building unit.[11]

The architect was Mr. Phillip Ginnell, Mullingar. A unique feature of this building unit also was that it was roofed with copper, adding to the architectural appearance of the building which opened on to the main Street and a large white statue of St. Joseph over the front door. Ledwith Brothers of Longford were the main contractors and work commenced on the 4th of June 1963 when the school closed its doors for the Summer break, apart from the exam classes who had to remain for the duration of the State Examinations.

When St. Joseph's opened its doors in September, the building was not complete, but pupils were accommodated for a while in other convent buildings.

Ten boys were enrolled in first year:

Pat Eighan	Joseph Peppard	James O'Brien
Phillip O Reilly	Thomas Cole	Peter Daly
Pat Joe Martin	Richard Flynn	Malachy Gavin
	Seán Kane	

On Sunday the 15th of September, Dr. Kyne blessed the new building and afterwards, parishioners who were present attended Rosary and Benediction in the Parish Church. The ceremonies were attended by Rev. J. McManus P.P., Rev. J. Conlon C.C., Rev. P. Fallon, Very Rev. D. Clarke P.P., Eglish. Also present were Mr. Phillip Ginnell(Architect), Ledwith Brothers(Contractors), Dr. Peter Fox and Mr. Tim McAuliffe(Senator). On the 7th of October, classes moved into the new extension for the first time.

---

10   The Convent of Mercy, Trim opened a Co.Educational Secondary School in Athboy in 1949 and a house was purchased also to provide accommodation for the Sisters residing there. The School lasted until 2004, when it was amalgamated with the Vocational School to form the Athboy, Community School.
      In 1948, the same year as St. Joseph's Secondary Top School opened in Rochfortbridge, a similar school opened in Kilbeggan by Sr. Philomena McDonald. The first Leaving Cert Examinations took place there in 1952. In 1964, the Secondary part of the school became Co.Educational.
11   This new building was popularly known as the extension.

- On the 13th of October 1966, a meeting was held in the convent at which was discussed the possibility of the erection of a Technical School at Tyrrellspass. Representatives of the two Secondary Schools at Kilbeggan and Rochfortbridge were present. Mr. O'Lochlainn CEO, Mullingar and Mr. Tim McAulliffe, Chairman of the Vocational Education Committee put forward the claims of the committee and the need for such a school in the area. Mr. O'Súilleabháin, Vocational Education Inspector represented the Dept. Of Education. Mother Magdalene, Rochfortbridge and Mother Philomena, Kilbeggan, recognised the need for technical Education in the area. They felt that this need could be best met by making provision at the existing schools at Kilbeggan and Rochfortbridge. Extensions were needed at the schools and this could also include technical subjects for the boys and girls of the area rather than erecting a new building and school in competition with existing ones. Mr. Ó Súilleabháin gave an account of his role at the meeting as his function was to report back to the Dept. the views of both parties.

Bishop Kyne visited the Rochfortbridge community on the 25th of November to discuss this new proposal and he promised to give it his full support when the later county meetings took place in April of the following year. Bishop Kyne would not attend this meeting and in fact this was his last visit to the Rochfortbridge, community as he died suddenly on the 23rd of December 1966.[12]

The proposed Technical School project at Tyrrellspass was later abandoned by the Dept. Of Education as it was more cost-effective to make the provision of such Education available at the two schools at Kilbeggan and Rochfortbridge.[13] As there had been a recent building programme in Rochfortbridge, a new extension was not forthcoming, but three pre-fabs were erected to accommodate, Metalwork, woodwork and science. The V.E.C. also supplied teachers to accommodate the two schools on a part-time basis for woodwork, metalwork and mechanical drawing. Mr. Liam Corcoran was appointed to teach Metalwork and Mr. Pat Cooney was allocated hours to teach woodwork. Later Jim Harte and Ciarán Gavin taught woodwork and mechanical drawing at the school.

---

12   When Dr. John D'Alton was appointed Archbishop of Armagh in August 1946, it was announced that Dr. John Kyne, replace him on the 20th of May 1947. Dr. Kyne was Vice-Rector of the Irish College in Rome and his consecration took place in the Church of St. Ignatius on the 29th of June 1947. The following day he proadcast a message to the people of his new Diocese on Vatican Radio and this was in turn broadcast by Radio Éireann. A native of Longwood, where he was born in 1903, he attended Longwood National School and later St. Finian's N.S., Clonard, where his mother was a teacher. He was awarded a scholarship to St. Finian's College Mullingar and following his secondary education, he studied in Rome and was ordained in 1927. He returned to Ireland to serve as curate in Navan before joining the staff of St. Finian's College. He returned to Rome in 1930 to take up his role as Vice-Rector of the Irish College. During World War II, his skills as a negotiator ensured the safety and well-being of the students at the college. As Bishop of Meath he was very much involved in the building and replacement of Churches within the diocese as well as the building and renovations of schools. He was a keen supporter of the G.A.A., amateur dramatics and was patron of the Meath Historical Society. He was especially supportive of *Muintir na Tíre*, looking at it as a means of *'curing the festering sores of emigration and unemployment.'* He purchased Clonard House on the Dublin road, Mullingar in the early 1950's as a new Bishop's residence, turning over the Cathedral House in Mullingar to the Priests of the parish. He is buried in the Cathedral Grounds. *Beneath Cathedral Towers-* Mullinagr(2009) p. 174.

13   At Kilbeggan, the inclusion of the Technical School project co-incided with a building programme at the school. In 1966, Gus Marshall, was employed to build new classrooms, a Science lab and a metal-work room. Bantile Ltd. in Banagher were the builders employed for this project. Later in 1970, Fabricast, the local Kilbeggan company were engeged to build a new woodwork room.

The Green Isle

In the early 1970's the number of pupils attending St. Joseph's began to increase rapidly as a result of an increase in the numbers of children from Derrygreenagh and the extenion of bus routes to accommodate areas such as Knockdrin, Rhode and Croghan. Not only was further classroom space required, but but new ground was necded also to accommodate classrooms and sports facilities. Connell's house and garden which opened on to the main Street of the village and adjacent to St. Joseph's became available and the house and garden were purchased by the Sisters of Mercy. During this period, new classrooms were built when the area known as the boot room was demolished. Connells House was renovated and a canteen and music room were provided. The shed attached to the house was upgraded to provide indoor football for the boys on wet days.

In Connell's garden, the boundary wall and apple trees were removed and replaced by a prefab, comprising of three classrooms, cloakrooms, girls toilets and a Geography room. This space was urgently needed and by the mid 1970's all classrooms were occuppied as each year the school had to provide for two classes of first years rather than one. The new pre-fab was affectionately known as *'The Green Isle,'* due to the green colour on the plaster render finish on parts of the building.

A New Secondary School

The need for a new school was obvious and in January 1977 negotiations commenced with the Department of Education re sanctioning same, Eventually the Department agreed to grant-aid a school to cater for 315 students, though it later increased this number to 375 when they realised that the numbers were growing fast.

Papal Blessing presented to the Sisters of Mercy in 1975 on the occassion of the establishment of the Union of the Mercy Communities of Clara, Drogheda, Kells, Kilbeggan, Navan, Rochforbridge, Trim and Tullamore on the 29th of July, 1975.

The firm of Architects Robinson, Keeffe & Devane were recommended for the Work. Mr. R.P.McCaffrey was approached and he agreed to take on the planning of the new school. Boyd &Creed were accepted as the Quantity Surveyors and Varming Mulcahy Reilly Associates as Consultant Engineers. In the original schedule of accommodation given by the Depeartment a Metalwork room was not included. This was a cause of concern to all, pupils, parents and teachers. The idea of dropping a subject which had been on the curriculum for ten years was not acceptable, especially in a Bord na Mona, E.S.B. area. Negotiations at Department level by public representetives, members from the National and local Parents Council were unsuccessful. Eventually a letter to the then Minister for Education, John Wilson, brought a positive response and sanction was given for the inclusion of a Metalwork room at the expense of general classrooms.

> **St. Joseph's School, Rochfortbridge**
>
> ---
>
> **SCHOOL YEAR 1987/1988**
> ENROLMENT AND MEASUREMENT
> FOR UNIFORM AT 9.30 A.M.
> ASSESSMENT AT 10.00 A.M.
> **Saturday, 2nd May, 1987**
>
> Westmeath Examiner, Sat April 25th 1987

The cost of the proposed building which the Department of Education was prepared to grant aid, was in the region of £600,000. The Department would pay 85% of this and the School Authorities 15%. Certain items which the school manager considered necessary were not grant-aided, so this had to be met at local level leaving a rather heavy financial burden on the school community. The school went to tender in 1981 and the Lowest tender, that of, C. Bennett & Son, was accepted by the Department of Education. Work commenced on the site in March 1982. The contract was due to expire in December 1983, but thanks to the efforts of Christopher Bennett and his workmen, the school was ready for occupation in September 1983, even though final work was not completed until the end of that year.

The overall cost of the school, between buildings, equipment, and furnishing was well over £1,000,000. The local contribution to the school was over £350 ,000. Fund-raising had been carried out over a period of years by the Parents' Council and their work in this area must be commended and congratulated on their efforts and achievement.

The new school consisted of a total floor area of 1,637.70 square metres which included:
5 General Classrooms,
1 General Classroom cum Art Room,
1 Demonstration room,
1 Science Laboratory,
1 Woodwork Room,
1 Metalwork Room,
1 Social Studies Room,
1 Library,
1 Canteen,
2 Music Rooms,
1 Career Guidance Office,
1 Needlework Room,
1 Religious Instruction Room

In addition to this, other accommodation included social areas, pastoral areas, cloakrooms, locker areas, administration, staff accommodation, toilets and general stores.
The enrolment in 1984 was 437, which included 70 boarders and 170 boys.

The school catered for Religious Education and the usual academic subjects included Home Economics, the different branches of Science, Music, Art, Commerce and Physical Education. In addition, the students had the option of taking Woodwork, Metalwork and Technical Drawing to Intermediate level, and Engineering Workshop Theory & Practice and Technical Drawing to Leaving Cert level.

Opening of the New School

Tuesday May 15, 1984 was a very historic day for Rochfortbridge, when the new school was officially opened and blessed. Rochfortbridge could now boast of one the finest schools in the country with a wide range of facilities for subjects both academic and practical. The day itself was a triumph for all the hard work and efficient organisation that preceded it for weeks. Concelebrated Mass began at 11 o'clock and was relayed to the whole school, thanks to the the morning rigging up the amplification system. The Mass was concelebrated by the Most Rev. Dr. Michael. Smith, Auxiliary Bishop of Meath with Most Rev. Dr. J. McCormack presiding.

In his homily Dr. Smith spoke of the excellent work the Sisters of Mercy had done since their arrival in Rochfortbridge and praised their courage and determination in deciding to extend the secondary school. He praised the community of Rochfortbridge for all their assistance and hoped that the new school might produce students who would dedicate their lives to God, both at home and abroad. The school was blessed after the homily, and Mass continued with the school choir at its best throughout. Add to this the nicely sung responsorial psalm by Miss Mary Hayes and Mr. Eugene Dunbar, both teachers in the school ; the appropriately

The Staff of St. Joseph's Secondary School taken in 1984, on the occassion of the opening of the new Secondary School. Back row from left to right, Noel Foynes, Tony O'Sullivan, Tony Hartnett, Seamus Casey, Luke Dempsey, Chris Cole, Pat Eighan, Dermot Bennett, Sr. Dympna, Sr. Geraldine, Ellen Murray, Mary Fallon, and Marie O'Callaghan. Front row from left to right, Eugene Dunbar, Sr. Magdalene, Veronica O'Donoghue, Kathy Spellman, Nuala Lawlor, Sr. Finian, Bridget Currams, Phil Fallon, Sr. Pius, Liz O'Reilly, Mary Hayes, Nuala Flanagan and Sr. Dolores.

chosen prayers of the faithful read by Breda and John McCormack, Camilla Beglan, Marina Hughes, Aidan Nolan, Padraic Arthur, Michelle Whelehan and Pat Dowdall, all in all, a very memorable occasion.

After Mass the school was officially opened by Most Rev. Dr. Michael. Smith, Auxiliary Bishop of Meath. Students from the school formed a guard of honour along the entrance and were complimented on their excellent behaviour.

The guests then proceeded to the canteen where Mr. Noel Foynes, P.R.O., invited speakers forward. Mr. O'Sullivan spoke about the difficult conditions that existed for both teachers and students before the new school was built and he praised the high standard of achievement that always existed in the school.

Mr. Foynes then invited Mr. O'Nualain to speak on behalf of the Department of Education, informing guests that Mr. O'Nualain's wife Mona, was a past teacher in the school.

Despite Mr. O'Nualain's insistence that Most Rev. Dr. Smith had covered most points of his prepared speech during the homily, he still managed to "hold the floor" for quite a long time! Fr. O'Brien was then invited to speak and he mentioned the high moral and academic standards that existed in the school. He was followed by Sr. Camillus O'Reilly, Mother General of Meath Mercy Sisters, who spoke of the great team spirit that went into building such a beautiful building. She singled out the school choir for special praise, resulting in a great ovation from all the guests.

Mr. R. P. McCaffrey, the chief architect, was then called on to speak and he praised the motivation and determination of his clients, both former Principal Sr. Columba and the present principal Sr. Dympna, stating that these qualities made it easy for him in a professional sense.

Joe Murray then spoke on behalf of the Parents Council and his plea to the Department for another grant was again greeted with a great ovation. He asked for parity of funding for Voluntary Secondary Schools with other schools in the State. With rumbling noises echoing from the stomachs of different guests Mr. Foynes invited the last speaker forward - Sr. Dympna, School Principal. She thanked everyone associated with the building of the new school and left out nobody. She praised the attentiveness to details by the architects; the helpfulness of Bennetts, Pat Fox the foreman; Jim Ruane; Lynskey/ Slaney etc., the clergy in surrounding parishes, the Department of Education Building Unit, the parents,who deserved special recognition; the Parents' Council; the people of the area, the staff, both teaching and maintenance in the school and finally the Sisters of Mercy in Rochfortbridge.

It was now time for Grace before meals and members of the Parents' Council served a beautiful meal. The remarkable rapidity of bread-rolls disappearing during the first course, together with the empty bowls and clean plates after the main course suggested that all the guests enjoyed their meal. The guests were then shown around the new school and as the last one left for home a great feeling of satisfaction must have been felt by all those connected with making the official opening day a great one indeed.

Sr. Dympna Lynch/The Sports Hall and the New Building

In 1995, Sr. Dympna Lynch who had been Principal at St. Joseph's since 1982, retired as Principal of St. Joseph's. She continued working in the school in a teaching capacity for another fifteen years. On the occassion of her retirement she gave a small personal interview to the student council which was included in the annual Vox magazine. In this interview she expressed her thoughts with regard to teaching and her role as Principal:

The old Parochial House on the main Street of Rochfortbridge, taken in the late 1980's before the front part of the building was incorporated into the new Sports Hall which was opened in 1990.

> Just going into a classroom, closing the door and shutting off the outside world is enough to keep her happy. Being able to educate bright young things and making them concentrate is something that Sr. Dympna delights in[14]

The best thing about being principal according to Sr. Dympna was having young people around her all the time. Their vibrant personalities, and the energy they have, left her in a (reasonably) good mood. The worst thing about being principal was the alienation from pupils because of the authority she held. When asked exactly why she wanted to retire, Sr. Dympna replied in her good humoured nature, that she *was "sick of giving out."*

Sr. Dympna left a great legacy of work behind her also, as the school population rose rapidly in the 1990's. The building of the Sports Hall which was completed in 1990 was a follow on from her earlier work with the new Secondary school. The Sports Hall project opened new doors for the school and provided state of the art facilities for physical Education and games. The ever-increasing popularity of many other non-field games which required indoor facilities, flourished. [15]

---

14   *Vox*(1995), p.4
15   See Chapter on Sport.

The work which was the brainchild of Sr. Columba in the 1970's, which resulted in the new Secondary school ran into difficulty in the early 1990's as there was no adequate space once again to accommodate the increasing student population. The resulting project which was opened in 1992 and known as *The New building* comprised of seven classrooms and a science lab.

First Male Principal – Tony O'Sullivan

In 1994, Tony O'Sullivan was appointed Principal of St. Joseph's. He was the first male principal of the school. He joined the staff of St. Joseph's in September 1969. Tony taught a number of Subjects during his career, but his major subjects were Latin and Irish in the early years. He was later appointed Vice-Principal and worked alongside Sr. Dympna Lynch in the school building programmes. During his career, Tony's daughters attended St. Joseph's and completed their Secondary Education there. Before he retired in 1994, Tony was interviewed by members of the Student Council for the Leaving Cert Year book and he reflected on his teaching career at St. Joseph's.

The Staff of St. Joseph's Secondary School pictured with Tony O'Sullivan on the occassion of his retirement from St. Joseph's as Principal in 2002.
Back row, from left to right, *Noel Foynes, Lyndsey Brunton, Denis Kelly, Joe Arthur, Nuala Flanagan, Sheila Coyne, Breda McCormack, Evelyn Kelly and Adrian Lee.* ***Fourth row, from left to right,*** *Luke Dempsey, Helen Lennon, Sarah Butler, Miriam O'Lochlainn, Margaret Cole, Liz Shaw, Mary Fallon, Ellen Murray, Susan Hogan, Niamh Maloney, Dympna Quinn, Veronica O'Donoghue, Jane Treanor and Dermot Bennett.* ***Third row, from left to right,*** *Phil Fallon, Liz O'Reilly, Brigid Currams, Sr. Dympna Lynch, Fiona Burke, Carmel O'Sullivan, Marie Callaghan, Calre McCarthy and Eugene Dunbar.* ***Second row, from left to right,*** *Martin Kiernan, Ellen McMahon, Charlotte Holton, Cathy Spellman, Eamonn Scally, Johanna Walsh, Catherine McNichols, Caroline Kelleher and Danny Reddin.* ***Front row, from left to right,*** *Pat Eighan, Eileen Alford, Tony O'Sullivan, Tony Hartnett and Anna Kavanagh.*

In 1969, St. Joseph's was a community of about 150 pupils, many of whom were boarders. When asked what the funniest thing he ever confiscated was, he replied, that they were many and varied from notes written by the pupils to cigarettes. Tony witnessed many changes during his teaching career, especially the large increase in pupil members, especially among the boys. Most pupils now stayed on to do Leaving Cert and that there were a lot more subjects made available to the students and a huge expansion in extra-curricular activities. The one concern he had was that too many pupils had part-time jobs which meant that they were not having enough time for school work. Among highlights of his teaching career was the building of the new school and the Sports Hall, but his greatest memories were the two All Ireland Finals won by the Boys and Girls basketball teams. The formulation of the student charter on bullying was a wonderful achievement as it ensured that troublesome pupils sorted themselves out. When asked about how he viewed the future of the school he said:

> I see it as a lively place, where pupils are challenged and where a vibrant educational service is provided.[16]

When asked would he still maintain links with the school, Tony's reply was that it would not be possible to remove St. Joseph's from his system. He promised to always have a keen interest in the progress of the school, to be associated with its activities and to support them in as far as appropriate. In 2012, Tony still maintains that contact as he is now Chairperson of the Board of Management at St. Joseph's.

The last of the Boarders and Mr. Tony Hartnett as Principal

There is a chapter included in this book which looks at the life of the Boarders at St. Joseph's. Boarders were very much the backbone of the school for many years, even with the admission of boys, boarder numbers increased and St. Joseph's remained a very popular boarding school all through its first forty years or more. But with the decline in vocations to the Sisters of Mercy personnel to run and manage the boarding school grew less and less. Local people were employed in the evenings to supervise study and other management work, but it didn't prove successful and it was expensive to run. So it was decided to phase out the boarders altogether. From about 1996 onwards, no first year boarders were admitted and by 2001, the last of the boarders, sat their leaving certs and the dormitories closed forever.

By then, Mr. Tony Hartnett, was principal, replacing Tony O'Sullivan. Tony once again, met with the problems of lack of space for increasing subject matters as well as changes in the Revised Curriculum, which required more teaching staff and personnel. The increasing student population remained a problem also, as with the era of the Celtic Tiger, the village of Rochfortbridge expanded rapidly and there was a large increase in population in the area due to the construction industry which fanned a rapid economic growth. Families sold their homes in the suburbs of the cities and moved down to new accommodation in a line from Dublin to Athlone, Mullingar and Tullamore. This new shift in population became known

16   2004-Leaving Cert Book

as, the commuter corridor, saw people who were employed in the city commute from these areas every day. The M4 motorway was a deciding factor in the movement of people also. This shift in the demographics changed the status of the village, where it was once central to the commerce and industry of the area. The resulting change sparked new classification as in the Geography of the area, as that of a dormitory village. The population rise saw the two primary schools expand rapidly as did the secondary school.

By 2007, St. Joseph's had reached a crisis point and Tony Hartnett expressed his concerns to Westmeath Examiner about the lack of space at St. Joseph's and the need to redress this situation. The dormitories and other ancillary rooms which were used as the living space for the boarders had been converted into classrooms, cloakrooms, storage etc. And even at that, the problem wasn't solved. In 2009 a block of pre-fab buildings were erected at the front of the school, but this wasn't enough to solve the accommodation problem. Finally in 2012, a new building programme began, the canteen space which was far too small for the student population was expanded and all buildings are in the process of being linked via corridors, so that the whole school space is contained under one roof. As this book goes to press, four new classrooms are being built as well as a science lab.

Mr. Tony Hartnett retired in 2009 and Eileen Alford was appointed Principal of the school. Eileen is the first female lay principal of St. Joseph's. The work of the school continues and today with a teaching staff of sixty teachers as well as ancillary staff, comprising of Special Needs Assistants, Lab technicians, secretary and caretaker, the personnel too are increasing annually to meet the rapid increase of pupils. In September 2012, eight hundred and fifteen students are on the rolls at St. Joseph's.

The success of St. Joseph's is testament to the talents and skills of their teacing staff, who not alone have achieved great results academically, but have pooled their other talents as well into the school's long list of extra curricular activities from sport to music, science, environmental projects, student exchange etc. The following table lists some of the projects which were and still are part and parcel of the education process of St. Joseph's:

The Young Scientists Exhibition
European Studies
The Bog Studies in the 1990's
Co-operation North
All Ireland Schools Choirs, North and South
Musicals (see Separate Chapter)
Young social Innovators
Green Schools

The Success of St. Joseph's Secondary also, is due to their sound and well-prepared Prospectus which is distributed annually to parents at enrolment and it's vision and ethos documented therein is carried out to the letter of the book.

The vision the school has today in 2012 will of course in the future be changed and reviewed to match the needs of a changing society. It is important therefore to record its status today in 2012 on the occassion of the one hundred and fiftieth anniversary of the founcation of the Sisters of Mercy here.

At present St Joseph's offers 5 programmes, Junior Certificate, Leaving Certificate, Leaving Certificate Applied Programme, Leaving Cert Vocational Programme and Transition Year Programme which incorporate the subjects listed below. In the provision of subjects it is important to understand that there are restrictions on the number of places that can be provided in a subject. This can arise due to staff shortages in certain subject areas and as a consequence of the recent budget cuts in spending on education.

Subjects For Junior Certificate
- Irish, English, French and German
- Science
- Mathematics
- Technical Graphics
- Materials Technology (wood)
- Materials Technology (metal)
- Geograph
- History
- Art
- Music
- Home Economics
- Business Studies
- Religious Education
- Physical Education
- Civics, Social and Political Education
- Social, Personal and Health Education
- Choir
- Career Guidance

Subjects for Leaving Certificate
- Irish, English
- French or German
- Mathematics
- Chemistry
- Physics
- Biology
- Design and Communication Graphics
- Engineering
- Business
- History
- Geography
- Art
- Music
- Home Economics
- Religious Education
- Physical Education
- Career Guidance
- Choir
- Construction Studies
- Link Modules

First Year Students
The core subjects covered by all first year students are Irish, English, German, French, Mathematics, History, Geography, Science, Social Personal and Health Education (SPHE), Civics, Social and Political Education (CSPE), Physical Education and Religious Education.

In addition, in the First term, all students are given the opportunity to sample other subjects on a rotational basis.

The subjects involved are Materials Technology (wood), Materials Technology (metal), Technical Graphics, Art, Business Studies, Home Economics and Music. This gives students a better insight into the value and content of each subject and allows them to make a more infomed decision about which subjects to take for Junior Certificate.

At the end of October, the students are asked to select three subjects from these seven and the school endeavours to offer two of the three subjects which they will study in addition to the other set subjects for their Junior Cetificate.

There are restrictions in the numbers that some subjects can take especially Materials Technology (wood/metal), Art and Home Economics. Every reasonable effort is made to facilitate each student's preferences. In case of over subscription for a subject a lottery system operates.

Students of St. Joseph's are offered the opportunity to pursue the Transition Year Programme rather than go directly into Fifth Year. This progmmme is optional.

The purpose of the programme is to promote self-directed learning, communication skills and self-confidence.

With its emphasis on maturity and development, all young people can benefit from the programme. It is especially suited to:

• Students who are too young to go directly into Fifth Year.
• Students who are finding it difficult to decide on subjects for Leaving Certificate.
• Students who want to develop skills in Thinking Teamwork and Technology.

The programme is designed to strike a balance between the core academic subjects such as Irish, English, Maths, Languages and other Non-Leaving Cettificate subjects like Information Technology, Life Skills, Mini-Company,

Work Experience, Career Guidance and Environmental Studies

While the programme has a definite content in each subject area, the emphasis is always on the process of learning so that students can approach Fifth Year confident that they have selected the correct subjects and developed the

skills to pursue their studies successfully to Leaving Certificate level. Subjects are taught using varied active learning methodologies. Students participate in project work and also engage in 2 weeks work experience.

Leaving Certificate Applied

This is a two year progrmme for students who have completed the Junior Certificate. It is certified by the Department of Education and Science and is designed primarily for students who do not intend to go direcly to third level education.

Having completed the Leaving Certificate Applied programme students may go straight into the world of work or continue with their studies in a Post Leaving Certificate course, Apprenticeship, Fáilte Ireland course etc.

The subjects covered are: Vocational Preparation and Guidance; Social Education; English and Communication; Mathematical Applications; Craft and Design; Construction and Manufacturing; Information Technology; French; German; Irish; Leisure and Recreation; Drama and Music.

Leaving Cert Vocational Programme

This is a Leaving Cert Programme designed to give a strong vocational dimension to Leaving Cert. The Programme combines the traditional Leaving Cert with a new and dynamic focus on self-directed learning, enterprise work and community. A meeting for parents of Third Year Students is held to give information on these courses. There are a limited number of places in this programme and they are allocated on a first come first come first served basis.

School Facilities

- Career Guidance - Counselling Office
- Computer Room
- 2 Science Laboratories
- Demonstration Room
- Woodwork Room
- Metalwork Room
- Music Room
- Gymnasium
- Canteen/Assembly Hall
- Art Room
- Home Economics kitchen
- Needlework Room
- Dark Room
- Basketball Court
- Playing Pitches
- Specialist Rooms e.g. Geography room
- Technology Room
- Broadband access in each classroom

Students are encouraged to participate in Extra Curricular Activities. The school offers many opportunities for students to participate and to develop skill competencies in many areas. The list of Extra Curricular activites in 2012 include:

Gaisce- The President's Award	School Choir
Outdoor Pursuits	Musical Production(bi-annually)
Foreign Tour	Public Speaking –Debating, Quizzes
Charity fundraising activities	School orchestra
Art Exhibition/Art Competitions	Traditional Music Groups

Sporting activities include:

Athletics	Badminton	Basketball
Equestrian	Gaelic Football	Golf
Hurling	Soccer	Swimming

Supplementary teaching is available for pupils who experience learning difficulties in accordance with the Education Act, 1998. It is offered to pupils, in particular in the areas of literacy and numeracy, in collaboration with subject teachers.

To conclude this chapter which explored the history of the school for its sixty four year history leaves an education legacy of a very superior quality. It's past pupils are engaged in every walk of life right across Ireland and in every corner of the globe. St. Joseph's Secondary

school is committed to creating and developing conditions for learning in a caring and safe environment, where everyone is respected, listened to and enabled to approach life with confidence.

The school's ethos and vision is that of a Voluntary Catholic School which is non-selective in its intake of pupils. It supports the Mercy philosophy of edcation, which calls for a system that is based on justice and equal esteem for all. It is committed to the holistic development of its students as informed Christian People.

School Management aim to create an atmosphere of trust and good communication where students, staff and parents work together as a community by fostering respect for others and respect for the environment. It provides a good, broad-based education in which students get the opportunity and the encouragement to realise their potential in the best educational facilities that management can afford. They aim to meet and adapt to the changing needs in education as effectively and efficiently as possible.

To conclude then, I will leave the last word with the good lady

Mother Catherine McCauley who founded the Mercy Order in the early nineteenth century. Those words then, which were directed at the poor of Ireland, in a different context today, pretty much sum up the vision she had for the mission she established for her followers, this mission is still being fulfilled today at both schools, the Convent Primary School and St. Joseph's:

> *There are three things the poor prize more highly than gold, tho' they cost the donor nothing; among these are the kind word, the gentle, compassionate look and the patient hearing of their sorrows.* – Mother Catherine McCauley.

Former principals pictured when her Excellency President Mary McAleese visited St. Joseph's Secondary school. From Left Tony O'Sullivan, Sr. Columba, Martin McAleese, President Mary McAleese, Tony Hartnett, Sr. Magdalene and Sr Dympna.

SR. MAGDALENE CLAFFEY

In 1988, Sister Magdalene Claffey said farewell to a long career of service to the people of Rochfortbridge as teacher and Principal of St. Joseph's secondary school. A native of Moydrum, Athlone, she entered the convent in 1942 on the same day as Sister Stanislaus or Sister Maureen as we know her today. In 1946, she made her final vows and at the time, there was talk of the possibility of the establishment of a Secondary School at St. Joseph's. Sister Magdalene didn't wait on ceremoney and received a place at Carysfort College to train as a primary Teacher. With the establishment of St. Joseph's as a Secondary Top School under the umbrella of the Department of Education Primary Section, St. Joseph's had no qualified secondary teacher among the community. As soon as she was trained as a primary teacher she wasted no time and returned to the National University of Ireland to study for her B.A. In 1951, she qualified with a B.A. degree and Higher Diploma and the process of establishing St. Joseph's as a secondary school began with her at the helm as Principal. Having attained it's status as a Secondary School under the umbrella of the Department of Education, Secondary Branch, Hume Street, the school went from strength to strength, with the development of the tennis court and assembly hall, the extension of St. Joseph's in 1963 to receive boys into the school, thus establishing the school as a co-educational school for the first time. In 1967, prefab buildings were added to accommodate the teaching of technical subjects such as woodwork, metalwork and mechanical drawing as well as a science lab.

Sister Magdalene Claffey, July 2012.

Pictured on the occassion of Sr. Magdalene's retirement in 1988 are, from left to right, Sr. Pius Doran, Sr. Magdalene Claffey and Sr. Dolores Carroll.

In 1972, the refurbishment of Connells old house and the building of further prefabs known as 'The Green Isle' helped to alleviate an ever-increasing student population. In 1948 St. Joseph's opened with a total of fourteen pupils. Forty years later in 1988, there were 550 pupils attending the school. Retiring from her role as Principal in the mid-seventies, Sister Magdalene continued teaching at St. Joseph's and in 1988, she decided to call it a day. She was replaced as principal by Sr. Columba Gargan who was principal until 1982, when she transferred to Tullamore.

But Sister Magdalene was a person who never said no and she continued working in the parish social service area as well as sacristan to the parish church. She was one of the founding members of Rochfortbridge Social Services and worked for many years as a committee member in helping the elderly, the poor and the needy of the parish. In the 1950's, she established the Pioneer Total Abstinence Association at St. Joseph's and led the organization at parish level for many years also. In 2012, she is celebrating seventy years as a member of the Rochfortbridge community of the sisters of Mercy. Now in quiet retirement, she is in her 90th year and her record of service can only be equalled by her legacy of work and success in the field of education.

Sr. Dympna Lynch, Principal of St. Joseph's Secondary School and Luke Dempsey make a presentation to Sr. Magdalene on the occassion of her retirement in 1988.

Photo taken in the 1980's at the presentation of pins and certificates to Golden Jubilarians of the Pioneer Total Abstinence Association. Back row, from left to right, Francis McCarthy, Fr. Eamonn O'Brien P.P. and Jimmy Heaney. Front row, from left to right, Lilian Curran, Kathleen Dunne and Sr. Magdalene.

~ CHAPTERS 23 TO 30 ~
ST. JOSEPH'S SECONDARY SCHOOL
1950's - 1980's

~ CHAPTER 23 ~
ST. JOSEPH'S SECONDARY SCHOOL
IN THE 1950'S

Sr. Carmel Brennan in 1952.

Exam Time in 1956. From left to right, Maureen McGearty, Ann Fitzimons, Mary Creagh and Dympna Flynn.

Sr. Magdalene, Miss Costello and Mother Attracta.

Josie McGearty and Kay Hope outside St. Annes Summer House in 1955.

Picture taken around 1952/53. Back row from left to right, M.Clarke, B.McGearty, G.Hiney, C. Bruton, M.O'Connor, K. McLoughlin, M.Creagh and F. Flynn. Front row from left to right, --, K. McLoughlin, J. McGearty, E. Purcell, Mgt. Buckley and F.Sloan.

Inter-Cert Class 1957. Back row from left to right, Bernadette Costello, Rose Dardis, Bernadette Byrne, Bridie O'Neill, Jo Murray, Ursula Clavin and Kay Newman. Middle row, from left to right, Irene O'Connor, Mary Creagh, Josephine Berry, Eithne Lawlor, Philomena Heaney, Maureen McGearty, Kay Fitzimons and Olive Carey. Front row from left to right, Kay Mulvin, Mary Dermody, Marcella Murtagh, Liz O'Reilly, Rena Flynn, Mary Bradley and Una Keegan.

Postulants in 1953, Kathleen Doran, now Sr. Pius and Mary O'Brien, now Sr. Concepta.

Sr. Stanislaus in 1953, later known as Sr. Maureen was for many years, Principal of the Convent Primary School.

Leaving Cert. Class 1955. Back row from left to right, Kathleen Hope, Miss Burke and Josie McGearty. Front row from left to right, Pauline Cunningham, Francis Shanahan, Sr. Magdalene, Gertie Hiney and Una Fitzpatrick.

National School Boarders out playing in May 1955. Back row from left to right, Mary Glynn, Mary Barry, Sadie Lawler and Enda Molphy. Middle row from left to right, Eileen Keegan, Anna Kena and Jenny Creagh. The little girl in front is Grace Walsh.

Josephine Monaghan and Bridie McGearty in 1956.

Last day for three McGearty Sisters together in St. Joseph's, May 1955, from left to right, Maureen, Bridie and Josephine.

Class group 1950's

Outing to Lough Ennell in Bennett's Lorry, back row from left to right, Frances Shanahan, Gertie Clarke, Imelda Murtagh and Margaret Buckley.
Front row from left to right, Josephine McGearty, Mary Casey and Angela Buckley.

Josephine McGearty, a child of Mary at the garden arch in 1955.

Angela and Margaret Buckley at the Grotto in 1953

Sr. Magdalene in 1953.

Vera Cunningham and Maureen McGearty in the big Study Hall in 1957.

*School year 1952/53, back row from left to right, Bernie McGearty, Mary Casey(Mullingar), Patricia Hope and Margaret Buckley.
Front row from left to right, Mary Casey(Meedin), Josephine Monaghan and Maura Lawlor.*

19. Inter Cert Exam time in 1956, outside the Parish Church gate, Eithne Lawler, Mary Creagh, Maureen McGearty and Dympna Flynn.

In the school year 1954/55 a retreat was given by
the Passionist Fathers. Taken during the retreat at
St. Anne's Summer House are Jo McGearty
and Kay Hope.

Back row from left to right, Rita O'Donoghue, Annette Roche,
Frances Corrigan and Sadie Lawlor.
Front row, from left to right, Gretta Bradley, Anne Fallon, Teresa
Dennigan and Mary Ellen O' Hara.

May 1955 at Our Lady's Grotto beside the Nun's Graveyard at
the side of the Parish Church, Bridie, Jo and Maureen McGearty.

The Big Study Hall in 1957, Olive Carey and
Maureen McGearty.

Anne Fallon and Gretta Bradley.

Back row, from left to right, Josie Monaghan, Maire Lawlor, Bridie
McGearty and Fionnuala Byrne.
Front row, from left to right, Gabriel Donoghue, Marie Farrell, Dympna
Flynn and Ann Fitzimons.

*Rita O'Donoghue, Annette Roche
and Gretta Bradley.*

*Taken in 1953, Back row, from left to right, Josie Monaghan, Fionnuala
Byrne, Angela Buckley and Kathleen Fitzimons. Middle rfow, from left to
right, Marian Lynch, Mary Cox, Bridie McGearty, Maura O'Connor,
Gabriel Donoghue, Maura Lawler, Marie Clarke and Margaret Purcell.
Front row, from left to right, Josie Monaghan, Fionnuala Byrne,
Angela Buckley and Kathleen Fitzsimons.*

*Taken with Sister Magdalene in 1954, from left to right, Joan Gunning,
Kathleen McLoughlin, Sister Magdalene, Gertie Clarke and Eileen Purcell.*

*Mary Murphy from Whitehall,
Castlepollard.*

*First year students in 1956, Rita O'Donoghue
and Dolly Mooney.*

*< St. Joseph's in 1957, standing at the back, Nuala Casey,
Seated are Rita O'Donoghue and Pattie Reynolds.*

< Inter Cert Class, 1957-58.
Back row, from left to right, Dolly
Mooney, Rosemary Keegan, Anne
Cross, Patricia Reynolds, Angela
Reynolds, Mary Mahon, Helen Cooney,
Patricia Corrigan, Patricia Murtagh
and Mary Ellen O'Hara.
Middle row, from left to right,
Frances Corrigan, Kathleen Bannon,
Mary Barry, Nuala Casey, Rita
O'Donoghue, Elma Peppard, Evelyn
Casey, Sadie Lawler and Gretta
Bradley.
Front row, from left to right, Sheila
Tyson, Annette Roche, Doreen Dargan,
Mary McDonnell, Mary Fay, Anne
Fallon and Pauline Cunningham.

First years 1957, Front, row, from left to right,
Gretta Bradley, Pauline Cunningham andMary
Ellen O'Hara
Second row, from left to right, Anne Fallon, Mary
Barry, Rita O'Donoghue and Dolly Mooney.
Third row, from left to right, Annette Roche, Sadie
Lawler, Sheila Tyson and Nuala Casey.
Fourth row, from left to right, Pauline O'Connor,
Evelyn Casey, Philomena Murtagh and Frances
Corrigan.
Fifth row, from left to right, Jane Tracey and
Doreen Dargan

St. Joseph's in 1959, Gretta Bradley
and Anne Fallon.

Leaving Cert Class, 1960, 1961, back row, from left to right,
Rita O'Donoghue, Anne Fallon, Teresa Dennigan and Mary Ellen
O'Hara. Front row, from left to right, Gretta Bradley, Anne Fallon,
Teresa Dennigan and Mary Ellen O'Hara.

School Group taken on the 13th March 1958.
Back row, from left to right, Gretta Bradley, Joy Smith, Nuala Casey, Mary McDonnell, Mary Fay, Annette Roche, Kathleen Bannon, Angela Reynolds, Bernadette Byrne, Rita O'Donoghue, Anne Fallon and Patricia Reynolds. **Fourth row, from left to right,** Frances Corrigan, Patricia Corrigan, Lily Bagnall, Noreen Traynor, Dolly Mooney, Rena Flynn, Eithne Lawler, Phil Heaney, Maureen McGearty, Sadie Lawler, Phyllis Cuffe, Rose Dardis, Brighdin Lawler and Josie Berry. **Third row, from left to right,** Enda Molphy, Margaret Allen, Roseanne Kealaghan, Rosaleen Dargan, Attracta McArdle, Annette Kilmurray, Mary Murphy, Mary Doyle, Phyllis Ahearne, Elma Peppard, Helen Cooney, Rosemary Keegan and Shelagh Tyson.
Second row, from left to right, Anne Crosse, Doreen Dargan, Mary Barry, Mary Ellen O'Hara, Dolores Cooney, Mary Flynn, Rita Connolly, Bridie McCabe, Myra Duignan, Margaret Murtagh, Pauline Cunningham, Evelyn Casey and Mona Murray. **Front row, from left to right,** Shelagh Hayes, Ethel Menton, Tess Arthur, Mary Dunne, Mary Wiley, Betty Carey, ____Mooney, Josie Dargan, Mary Lacey and Patricia Murtagh.

Back row, from left to right,
Kathleen Bannon, Frances Corrigan,
Dolly Mooney, Mona Murray and
Ethel Menton.
Middle row, from left to right,
Sadie Lawler, Rita O'Donoghue,
Gretta Bradley, Anne Fallon,
Annette Roche, Myra Duigenan and
Mary Ellen O'Hara.
Front row, from left to right,
Mary Dunne, Mary Murphy,
Bridie McCabe, Attracta McArdle,
Mary Wiley. Shelagh Hayes and
Mary Doyle.

Taken on the day of the Music Exam in 1958 are Annie Fallon and Elma Peppard

Gretta Bradley in 1958

Mother Brigid Brady, Sister Magdalene Claffey and Sister Aquin Geraghty.

~ CHAPTER 24 ~
EDUCATION – THE KEY
By Bernie Grier

Ireland in the late forties was recovering from the difficulties caused to the country during the Emergency. Times were hard for most families. Our family of eight children lived on a small farm in Ballivor. It must have being hard work to eke out a living in such austere times. Strange as it may seem I was blissfully unaware of hard times. Looking back I consider that I had an idyllic childhood though lacking many of today's must haves (*cf* J Quinn: Goodnight Ballivor I'll Sleep in Trim). We all enjoyed the blessing of good health and our hungry appetites were satisfied by home grown produce. Recycling was the Xpose of the day. We wore hand knitted jumpers, coats were remade and vintage clothes were always in vogue. We were also blessed with good intelligence and our parents believed that this was a gift to be used for the betterment of others and our own good - but how would we achieve our potential. Two decades would pass before free Second Level Education would become a reality.

My three older brothers attended St. Finian's College in Mullingar. They won County Council scholarships which paid for their school fees. Una, my older sister, was a day pupil in the Mercy Convent Secondary School in Trim. She rode her 'High Nellie Bicycle' 18 miles per day in all weathers. She was accompanied by two other cyclists, Carmel and Bernie. The were often swathed in oil-skin capes and pull-ups having battled wind and rain to arrive at the school dripping wet and chilled to the marrow. Their journey improved if the wind "was on their backs from Drinnadaly. Such were the hardships endured by the lucky few availing of Second Level Education. Many other pupils from Ballivor N.S. took the boat to England or to other far off places when the "scattering came". At that time pupils in sixth class sat their Primary Cert. I was lucky to pass this exam. Now it was my turn to leave primary school.

My father and mother considered my future options. In those days weak spelling and poor penmanship were considered to be the hallmarks of a poor scholar. I was weak in both skills. The fact that I had poor eyesight was not considered a contributing factor. I was not regarded robust enough to cycle the 18 miles daily trip to Trim. A Station Wagon collected pupils from outlying areas - the word catchment was not in use then. The nearest collection point to us was Bagnall's Cross approx. 4 miles from the village. Mother queried could the Station Wagon come as far as the village. No such luck. I'd be the only passenger so it wasn't considered viable to do the detour. I was quite enthusiastic to continue my schooling. I had read all about schools in Girls Crystals and in other books that I got from Marie Dempsey. School life in these books was full of all exciting adventures, midnight feasts and other thrilling escapades, study and exams were never mentioned.

The Sisters of Mercy in Trim told my mother that a new Secondary Boarding School would be opened in Rochfort Bridge that year - but where was Rochfort Bridge I wondered? Mother remembered that Teresa Cunningham from Coolronan Ballivor went to that school as she had special needs (Deaf and Dumb). Enquiries were made as to the best and shortest route to travel to see the school and find out necessary details.

On a glorious sunny day we set off on two bicycles and we made the forty-mile round trip to Rochfort Bridge and home again. There were many rest stops on the way and "are we there yet?" was often asked. Flowers in a front garden were so attractive that we dismounted to see and smell the roses. That was the garden of Bernie and Maggie Donnellan, Coralstown. Further on we stopped at another house and asked for a drink of water - a common practice in those times.

The Arrival

At long last Mother and I arrived at the Convent door and were greeted by a smiling nun who volunteered to show us the way to St Joseph's School. We were brought into the Big Study Hall. Mother Attracta was on her knees painting the rostrum. She was enveloped in a huge blue apron. What a welcome she gave us. She actually gave me a hug and said she would be delighted to have me as a boarder. I was smitten by such a charming welcome. Later, I told my mother I wouldn't go anywhere if I didn't go there not realising how limited my options were. A prospectus was given to my mother and fees were discussed. Was it a coincidence that the fees could be paid in April and October – months when cattle fairs were held in Ballivor? The list of clothes that was needed would have daunted many a parent but not the resourcefulness of my mother. The school blazer was bought in Goravans, Dublin. It came complete with the school crest and the motto Laborare est Orare – to work is to pray, was emblazoned on the breast pocket. Our local dressmaker Jenny measured me for the gymslip and left generous seams and hems for further growth. A long full-length white coat was obligatory for cookery class as Sister Agnes insisted on a proper dress code. My Aunt Esther, before she emigrated to America, made this garment for me. My dressing gown was once my mother's summer coat. It was shortened and lined with pink flannette and bands of plaitted wool were attached to the edges and used as a tie belt. It wasn't as eye catching as the black and red kimono style dressing gown worn by Betty complete with multi coloured dragon on the back. At last my case was packed but unlike my brothers there was no "tuck – box" included. A hackney car was hired and I set off on a new adventure. This was my first time leaving home. What I didn't fully realise then was that I'd only be back home for holidays ever again.

First Impressions

St. Joseph's was a noisy, busy place and I didn't know anyone. I didn't know my way around to such places as dormitories, big and small, refectory or study hall. Sister Joseph was in charge. She asked some of the girls to look after me. Not all the girls were new comers. Some boarders were already attending the National School. The Lawler Sisters, Máire and Eithne, from Dublin were enrolled due to teachers' strikes in Dublin. They looked so young to be away from home. Miss Evens was in charge of the "little ones". The Rural Electrification Scheme for Rockfort Bridge had taken place and St. Joseph's had 'the light'. We were warned by Sister Joseph not to be switching on and off lights as it wasted too much electricity. Bed time came at last and lights out. In the dark I wondered if I had made the right decision but knowing deep down I was one of the lucky ones given the chance to further my education.

The Old School

Traces could still be seen of the many skills of the pupils who had attended the earlier school. There were framed samplers of cross-stitching and of Rochfort Bridge lace hanging in the main hallway. The white cotton quilts in the small dormitory had all been done by girls in their "silent world". A storage room was full of huge metal knitting machines that were once used to teach girls how to knit socks and jumpers. A blackboard, complete with alphabet and fingers drawn in various positions, leaned against the wall of the study hall – a discarded, and unnecessary teaching aid. Sign language would no longer be taught. A marble slab containing a relic from the Collosseum in Rome had been presented by the Pope and held pride of place in the big study. A huge painting hung in the big dormitory. It also had been presented in 1892, by Pope Leo XIII in recognition of the good work being undertaken by the Sisters, for girls with special needs. The most obvious reminder to all of the school's previous status was the presence of former pupils Mary Connor and Mary Ellen Geraghty. When the Institute finally closed, there were three girls, who for reasons now unknown were unclaimed by their families. They were now gainfully employed as housekeepers. Mary was forever busy in and out of the various rooms at the back of the school. She shook her head, nodded vigorously and shrugged at those who could not use sign language. Patricia Hope could communicate with her and make her smile and laugh. Mary Ellen was a tall elegant lady with beautiful golden curly hair. Her time was mostly spent in the Convent. She always wore lovely clothes with great style for she had "the walk of a queen". Chrissie McNamara was Sister Joseph's right hand person. She had all her faculties and often threatened, in her strong Clare accent, to report any misdemeanour to Sister Mary Joseph. Of course there were stories told and retold about these good ladies and nothing was lost in the telling. However, these people shared their lives with us and I hope we showed them respect and kindness.

A Snapshot in Black and White

In the days prior to Vatican II, the nuns dressed in black serge full-length habits. They wore long leather belts, from which large Rosary beads rattled when they walked and a bunch of keys often jingled. A white linen coif encircled their heads and a black veil was pinned to the coif. A gamp was like a large white stiff celluloid bib. How uncomfortable it must have been to be encased in such a fashion. In winter they wore black woollen shawls, which were referred to as "our shawl". In church they wore floor length trains that looked very elegant. Because of the sameness of the habit it was difficult to tell the sisters apart. Some could be identified by the staccato sound of their footsteps. Young aspiring postulants wore lace caps which some months later were exchanged for white veils. William Leech captures this beautifully in his painting "A Convent Garden".

A New Beginning

So many years have passed since that September morning that it is now difficult for me to recall the names of all the girls who commenced their Secondary school days with me. This class of First Years was made up of thirteen boarders and some day girls and we all sat in the small study hall for class. The Roll was called and answered by Ursula Marry, Patricia Hope, Margaret Buckley, Mary McLoughlin, Breda McCoy, Betty Hayes, Marie T O'Brien, Mary Berry, Frieda Crean, Lily Whelan, Betty Clarke, Frances Ennis, Mary Nea and Eileen Whelehan.

I remember the day-girls arriving on bicycles, often wet and windblown, from Milltown Pass, Meedin and Tyrellpass. Their bicycles were stored in the shed under the watchful eye of Mary Connor. Just before class began a smiling Eileen could saunter to the Emergency door, perfectly groomed unhurried from her three minute stroll. Homesick boarders often envied the day girls as they returned home to their own fireside.

Our teachers were nuns with the exception of Ms Doyle. She taught English and Latin. I can still recall some Latin phrases and also how much she detested the use of the word "Nice". One year when we returned from our summer holidays, Ms Doyle was no longer on the staff. We heard on the grape vine that she had entered an enclosed order of nuns in Co. Wicklow. I remember her as a hard working and diligent teacher. Gradually I got to know each nun. Mother Attracta was my favourite and her presence seemed to fill a room. Sr. Agnes taught the finer points of cookery and I can clearly recall sieving potatoes for soup, watched by the beady eye of an Inspector. Sr. Magdalene taught Latin, History and English. The local P. P. offered a prize to whoever could translate a Latin quotation. Sister smiled and said that we had not read that section in Virgil. Perhaps I saved the day by answering, "I fear the Greeks even when they come bearing gifts". I won a box of chocolate bars - what a luxury to share.

There was a predictable routine to our day. We were wakened by the loud sound of a bell being vigorously rung by Sr. Joseph as she reminded us we were late. We said sleepy prayers, washed, dressed and went to the Emergency door still sleepwalking. The cold woke us up on our way to church. Breakfast was eaten in silence. Spiritual reading took place at meal times. We all had chores to do before class. Class ended at four o clock followed by recreation outdoors, then supervised study and perhaps later some dancing and so to bed. Any variation in the routine was welcome. Boarders did not travel home at weekends One fine Sunday afternoon in September 1949 Ursula Marry from Slane and myself were invited by Fr. Kilmartin P.P. to the Parochial house. Here we listened to the All Ireland Football Final and were delighted when Meath won. We were also treated to a lovely meal. There was no radio in St. Joseph's School but we listened to music eminating from a pianolo, which was a type of an automatic piano, which was carefully fed with perforated music scrolls. Great care also needed to be taken when placing the heavy wax records onto the wind up gramophone complete with its large brass horn.

At Halloween we were allowed parcels from home. These were much appreciated. We played all the old games; snap apple, ducking for coins and two royal visitors came in full regalia from Morocco. This game was played only on gullible first years. Life had other lighter moments. A Christmas concert was mooted and under the direction of Mother Attracta we took to the stage. Miss Fox showed us how to do a Scarf Dance and a song and dance routine to the tune "The Little White Horse". My rendering of the monologues 'The Old Violin' and 'Little Boy Blue' needed long practising until I was word perfect. I am sure our parents thought it was wonderful entertainment but did it lack the X Factor?

Home for Christmas only to find the rooms had shrunken. How small everywhere was, even the family teapot seemed tiny. It was wonderful to be home and a family again. Some of the girls I had known at National School weren't so friendly. Years later that they talked about how grand and swanky we looked in school blazers, not realising that it was the only coat we had. Friendship rekindled, and style worn by friends was not an issue. January came. Back to the familiar routine. School was cold and we danced to keep warm. Chillblains were on hands and feet we were hungry for every meal. It was advantageous to be on good terms with whichever girl was helping Chrissie in the kitchen. We often augmented our bosoms with extra bread for best friends – Come dine with me, 50s style. My sister Jo or Josephine as the Nuns insisted in calling her had joined the boarders and it looked as if the routine of our life would continue unchanged.

We went home for our Easter Holidays delighted to be back in the family circle. Daddy, who was in his sixties and never known to be sick, was confined to bed. I felt sure that my newly acquired cookery skills would work wonders. But that was not to be. He died suddenly on Easter Sunday morning. The world as we once knew it was gone forever. In the turmoil, grief and sadness that followed the Nuns came to console the stricken family, to encourage us to return to education and to assure mother of their support. This great back up convinced my mother that she would find the money for the fees somehow. We returned to school brokenhearted. We were not alone in our grief. Many other girls had also suffered the loss of a loved one. The Hope sisters had lost both parents and Marie Therese O Briens' brother, Tommy, had died while a student in St. Finians.

Secondary Top

St. Joseph's was not recognised by the Department of Education as a secondary school. It was classed as a Secondary Top. The school would need to prove itself before it could claim its proper status. One big draw back to a Secondary Top was the issue of school holidays. We had the same arrangements as a National School - shorter holidays than other Secondary students. Our school did not qualify as an exam centre, so the students taking the Intermediate Certificate were transported to Loreto Convent Mullingar in order to sit the exam. There I met a girl named Nuala who was particularly friendly to me. Years later I realised she was even more friendly with my brother Patsy in St. Finians College.

As the years passed, my sister Bridie joined Jo, me and two others girls from Ballivor, Gertie Hiney and Carmel Ging. We were very kindly allowed sleep in Room 1, which was then called the Ballivor Room. Here we talked, laughed, shared goodies, and even had singsongs, so life was good. Then the unexpected happened. One bright moonlight night we were awakened by loud demanding knocking sounds. It seemed to be coming from both the front and back of the building. Gertie grabbed her dressing gown and rushed down to let in whichever nun had been locked out. Though that night was bright Gertie failed to see who was knocking. Then the clock struck three and all was quiet again. Sr. Joseph arrived into our room and reassured us that there was no need to be afraid and told us we could sleep together for the remainder of the night. That was a night of shocks – the shock of hearing loud knocking, the shock of seeing Sister Joseph barefoot and in her night attire, the shock of Gertie using an expletive, the shock of the impromptu sleeping arrangement, even the shock of being allowed waste electricity. Next day there was an aftershock tinged with relief - we were evacuated bag and baggage back to the big dorm. No satisfactory explanation was ever given for the weird sounds in the night.

During my time in school we walked the walks, passed rows and rows of identical white crosses inscribed with the names of deceased Sisters. We talked the talk, exchanged stories of families and relations to the second or third degree. Longer walks were undertaken on fine Sunday afternoons. A long line of girls walked two by two out the school gates, be-hatted, be-gloved and in ladder-less black stockings. Girlish giggles were suppressed and walking with eyes cast down we went as far as "Mary Lamb's and home by the West". Another Sunday the walk included a visit to the ruins of a castle, which had been the home of the important Rochfort family. Once we walked all the way to Tyrellspass to see the film "Quo Vadis". En route we topped the summit of Gneeve Bawn Hill and viewed that part of the old kingdom of Meath with the hill of Croghan in the distance. This panoramic view may have compensated for the pain of blistered feet as we trudged our weary way back to base. I imagine there was no talking in the dorm that night.

Camogie was played with great enthusiasm. We wore our school uniforms and outdoor shoes, as sports gear was not in vogue. I broke a bone in my arm at a crucial moment in a game. This may have hastened the end of my career as a camogie player, and left me out of the running at prize giving.

Extra Curricular Achievements

Many extra curricular achievements were also recognised. I was enrolled as a Child of Mary and still have the silver medal with my name engraved on it. Fr Kenny Religious Examiner awarded me a prize for Christian Doctrine – a picture of Our Lady of Fatima. Christian Doctrine was taught by Sister Attracta but practiced by all. I was one of the many girls enrolled in the Pioneer Association by Sr. Magdalene. Silver Fáinnes were much prized by those who excelled at the oral Irish exam. Some girls were taught how to play the piano. They reached high grades and also entertained the rest of us with their music. I still recall the Hope sisters playing duets especially The Skaters Waltz.

A sewing circle of girls embroidered numerous large linen tablecloths. We learned how to combine various colours in order to achieve the best effect. These cloths were sold at Sales of Work at Christmas in aid of the Missions. Sr. Joseph was an enthusiastic supporter of the Foreign Missions.

Girls were given the opportunity by Sister Mary Stanislaus to learn short hand and typing. This was an optional subject. I have since regretted not availing of this opportunity. It would have been no load to carry and a great help to me even compiling these "ramblings". Sr. Stanislaus, a full time teacher in the National School, gave up her Saturdays to lay the foundation for a choir. We were introduced to the concept of part singing. Sr. Dolores joined the Congregation. She is a gifted pianist. I can recall her youthful complexion and white veil as she graciously played music for our delight. She gave of her great gifts and with endless patience she assisted with the school choir. Two of the songs I recall were "Whispering Hope" and "Juanita". Therese Clarkson and Mary Cox delighted all with their solo singing of October Winds and Alice Blue Gown. From such small beginnings the choir has continued to flourish. It now has an impressive repertoire and has been seen and heard on national television. "Well Done."

Secondary School Status

Changes in the number of boarders occurred following the results of the Intermediate Exam. Entrance to the Civil Service and other positions could be attained with this Certificate. Many girls opted to begin their life in the work place. Three students, Mary Mc Loughlin Kinnegad, Margaret Buckley, Rosemount and I, soldiered on to the Leaving Cert. We studied and revised the work that had been done and wondered what questions would be set that year. We were given extra tuition by Sr. Carmel in the intricacies of Maths. Sr. Stanilaus prepared us for the Easter Orals and taught me how to sing Fainne Geal an Lae as a soloist. Our family had no car. Fr. Colm Murtagh drove me to the centre in Mullingar. Once again I knew no one. I sat the orals, sang my solo piece and wondered was it too late to consider a Plan B.

"Five years had passed five summers and the length of five long winters" and so it was time to 'face' the Leaving Cert. We did revision at the most unusual hours, said all the right prayers, especially to St Joseph of Cupertino. As it had at last been recognised as a Secondary School, there was now a centre for the Exam in Rochfort Bridge and that was a major milestone in the Annals of the school. The exam and all its tension that June, is now a blur. Exams at that time did not merit the attention of the media and went unnoticed outside the family circle.

Exams over, suitcases packed, extra space found for heavy books and hard backed copies, our time in Rochfort Bridge was nearly over. Heartfelt messages were written on the backs of small holy pictures and given to friends to be stored in their prayer books. We were sad to bid farewell to nuns, teachers, Mary Ellen and Chrissie. Parting with best friends was not easy. Of course we promised to stay in touch and to write and even to meet in Mullingar. Twitter, Facebook, texts, or emails had not been envisaged but the silken thread of shared memories would bind us together in our unchartered future where hopefully we would follow our school motto "To Work is to Pray".

~ CHAPTER 27 ~
ST. JOSEPH'S SECONDARY SCHOOL
IN THE 1960'S

1. Second Year Class of 1967. Back row from left to right, Patricia Moore, Marie Coffey, Patricia Glennon, Ann Johnson, Mary Troy and Josephine Corcoran.
Middle row from left to right, Eileen Cleary, Goretti Brown, Mary J. Gouldsberry, Margaret Bradley, Thérèse Cavanagh, Kathleen Donoghue and Barbara Smyth.
Front row, from left to right, Annette Cully, Nora Gouldsberry, Patricia Baker, Mary Fox, Mary Costigan, Catherine Dardis, Margaret Boyle and Esther Kiernan.

1965. Back: Mary Naughton.
Front from left: Mary and Ann Alford

At the grotto, Marie Harte and Marie Coffey.

Back row from left to right, Agnes Whelehan, Philomena Geraghty, Lily Abbot, S. McCabe, M.Brennan, Dolores Heaney, Helen Geraghty, Mary Fallon, Ursula Gaffney, Mary Fallon, Mary Baker and missing from the photo is M.Flood. Middle row from left to right, K.Coyne, S. McEnteggart, P.Gavin, Hilda Clabby, N.Ryan, Anne Cooney, Maura O'Rourke, K.Dunne, M.Fitzpatrick, Thérese Flynn and Eileen Abbott. Front row, from left to right, Mary Doody, K.Reynolds, D. Kerkpatrick, C.Crosse, A.Cowley, Cath. O'Rourke, Helen Cole, Nancy McGrath, Mary Daly, Doreen Egan and Frances Gavin.

Taken in the school year 1963/64, Back row from left to right, K.Fox, M.Harte, E.W. Whelehan, A. Campbell, O. Molphy and C. Flynn. Front row left to right, Margaret Cross, Louise Leavy, Margaret O'Connor, Mary McCauley, Mary Murphy and Anne Leech.

Goretti Brown

Back row from left to right, M.McEnroe, M.O'Reilly, G. Coyne, T. O'Connell, J.Murtagh,
P.O'Reilly, N. MacGibney, Mary Bollard and M.Clonan.
Front row from left to right, Mary Briody, Margaret Doyle, G.Walshe, M.Gaffney,
B.Reynolds, Moira Duffy, ---Gaffney.

Taken around 1968, in front Clare Lynch, Second
row, Marie Harte, Goretti Brown, and Nuala
Brennan. At the back are Josephine McKeon and
Connie Whelehan.

1966: Choir for Sr. Regina's Profession
Back: Mary Baker, Mary Doody, Ann Cooney, Mary Alford,
Patricia O'Reilly. Front: Liz Egan, Eileen Carey, Ann Carey,
Ann Alford.

Eithne McEnroe.

M. Clonan, C. Bradley, M. Daly and A. O'Dowd.

Mary Briody.

St. Joseph's in 1961, Back row, from left to right, Sadie Lawler, Rita O'Donoghue and Frances Corrigan. Front row, from left to right, Teresa Dennigan, Annette Roche, Anne Fallon, Gretta Bradley and Mary Ellen O'Hara.

Rita O'Donoghue and Gretta Badley in 1960.

Sadie Lawler, Mary Ellen O'Hara and Rita O'Donoghue.

Sister Dolores tries her hand at photography.

Theresa O'Connell.

Class Photo, 1961. Back row, from left to right, Teresa Cunningham, Triona Murray, Carmel Flynn, , Ann Lynch, Kathleen Hyland and Margaret Cross Front row, from left to right, Mary McCauley, Evelyn Whelehan, Ann Leech, Olive Molphy, Louis Leavy, Kathleen Fox, Teresa Carey, Anne Campbell and Nora Curran.

ST. JOSEPH'S SCHOOL, ROCHFORTBRIDGE
Entrance Examination
SATURDAY, 17th MAY, 1969

SCHOLARSHIPS AVAILABLE
FOR FULL PARTICULARS APPLY SUPERIOR

Westmeath Examiner, Sat May 3rd 1969

First Years, 1964-65. Back row from left to right, M. Whelehan, M. Glynn, M. Murphy, R. Gilsenan and M. Cross.
Middle row, from left to right, H. Hand. S. Martin, Judy Geraghty, B. Tierney, G. O'Rourke, J. O'Rourke and P. Doherty.
Front row, from left to right, L. Wrght, Maura McEnteggart, G. Reynolds, Gret Dunne and Maura Dunne.

Grace Walsh, Anne O'Dowd and Eithne McEnroe.

Back row, from left to right, Marie Murphy, Eile O'Rourke, Sheila Martin and Mary Keating. Front row, from left to right, Judy Geraghty, Jean O'Rourke, Olive Flynn and Monica Coyne.

Back row, from left to right, H. Geraghty, N. Ryan, C. O'Rourke, Eileen Abbott, M. Alford, Anne Cooney, Dolores Heeney, Hilda Clabby and Alacoque Dolan. Middle row, from left to right, M. Brennan, F. Gavin, M. Flavin, C. Cross, D. Eighan, Agnes Whelehan, M. Maher, M. Baker, Phil McCabe, P. Geraghty and Lily Abbott. Front row, from left to right, R. Jones, S. O'Dowd, D. Kirk, T. Flynn, C. Coyne, M. O'Rourke, H. Cole, N. McGrath, M. Leggett, M. Fitzgibbon and G. Gavin.

Back row, from left to right, Mary Baker, Rosemary Kelly, Ann Alford, Philomena Cooney and Eithne Lenehan. Front row, from left to right, Genevieve Doherty, Brid Lynch, Anne Martin and Elizabeth Egan. Missing from the photo are two boys, Richard Flynn and Phillip O'Reilly.

Back row, from left to right, Phil Cooney, Ann Alford, Loreto Abbott, Eithne Lenehan and Rosemary Kelly. Front row, from left to right, Mary Baker, Dorothy Smith, Genevieve Doherty, Ann Martin and Brid Lynch.

First Years, 1963-64. Back row, from left to right, M. Boland, Mary Nolan, B. Bligh, G. Wiley, P. Flynn, E. Boyle and R. Kelly. Middle row, from left to right, Ann Alford, F. Baker, G. Cawley, B. Lynch, D. Smyth, A. Shanahan, and M. Mckeon. Front row, from left to right, C. Corbett, M.P. Egan, L. Abbott, P. McGrath, E. Lenihan, A, Martin, L. Egan, M. Baker and G. Doherty.

Photo taken around 1965. Back row, from left to right, Detta Gaye, Esther Reynolds, Margaret Glynn, Olive Flynn, Mary Keating, Margaret Cross, M. Whelehan and Ann Dunne. Third row, from left to right, Marie Murphy, E. O' Rourke, Monica Coyne, Hilda Hand, Sheila Martin, Judy Geraghty, Jean O' Rourke, Anne O' Neill and Pauline Doherty. Second row, from left to right, R. Gilsenan, Maura Dunne, Marie Cleary, Ann Dunne, Mary Mullarkey, Madeleine Kenny, Maura McEnteggart, Mary Boyle and Lucy Wright. Front row, from left to right, Michael Ryan, Michael Peppard, Jim Mulroy, Vinny Bagnall, Joe Kelly, Finian Dardis, Laurence Gavin and Pat Bradley.

Siobhán Smith, Marie Reilly , Marian Glennon, Mary Duncan, Anne Hannon, Ann Whelehan, Rose Tormey, Marian Dunne and Eithne Cleary. Middle row, from left to right, Sheila Keating, _____, Mary Maguire, Marion Gayton, Gerardine Reidy, Catherine Moore, Kathleen Earley, Dympna Dunne, Pauline Hyland and Clare Donovan. Front row, from left to right, Kathleen Gavin, _____, Marian Cully, Anne Carey, Dympna Mullarkey, Marie Deegan, Alice Donoghue, Róisín Harte, Róisín Gaffney and Brigid Eggerton.

Back row, from left to right, Olive Flynn,_____,_____,_____, Marie Murphy, Judy Geraghty,
Sheila Martin, _____, Hilda Hand, Margaret Glynn and Ann O'Neill.
Front row, from left to right, Anne Dunne, _____, Róisín Gilsenan, Mary Boyle, _____,
Madeleine Kelly, Mary Mullarkey, Sheila Keating and Jean O' Rourke.

Dorothy Smith.

Liz Deegan, Mary Doherty and friend.

13. Back row, from left to right, Collette Keogh, Mary Alford, Anne O'Dowd,
Peggy Mulroy, Ursula Geraghty, and Mary Doherty.
Front row, from left to right, Bernadette Gaye, Renee Gaffney, Patricia O'Reilly,
Pauline Farrell, Kathleen Casey and Áine Kelly.

Mary Deegan and Liz Deegan

School group taken around 1967, back row, from left to right, Liz Deegan, Kathleen Duffy, Valerie Darby, Dorothy Oakes,
Christina O'Dowd, Mary O'Dowd and Mary Duffy. Middle row, from left to right, Ann Ganly, Ann Mulroy, Ann Glennon,
_____ Glennon, Margaret Geraghty, Patricia Kenny, Theresa Reilly, Maura Curran and Mary Ganley.
Front row, from left to right, Anne Doherty, Olive Gray, Ann Fagan, Moira Lynch, Esther Mahon, Rosaleen Neery,
Catherine Kelly and Carmel Mullarkey.

~ CHAPTER 26 ~
ST. JOSEPH'S ROCHFORTBRIDGE.
By Frances Shanahan (Flynn)

Come with me on a trip down memory lane to St. Joseph's school Rochfortbridge, as it was in 1950.

The visitor's entrance to the school was the front door on the main street. As you entered on either side of the hallway were the two parlours. To the rear of the parlours were the kitchen, the scullery, the pantry, the wash- up area, and a delph storage area. Continuing back one came to the refectory on the road side, and parallel to the refectory was the big study hall.

Having closed the refectory door behind one there was the emergency door (it is still there), and opposite that door was the back stairs, which led to the dormitories. The big dormitory was over the big study hall, and the small dormitory was directly over the refectory.

Moving on through the small dormitory one came to a large washroom on the left hand side, and along the corridor were rooms number one to number six, and at the end of this corridor was the front stairs which brought one back down to the front hall.

Back to the ground floor and continuing on from the back stairs there was a small room which was later used as a classroom and to the right of this was the small study hall.

Taken at Lambe's Crossroads on the first of June 1953, back row from left to right, M. Lawler, Ber Purcell, M. McLoughlin, M. Buckley and M.O'Connor. 2nd row from left to right, Una Fitzpatrick, M. Clarke, M.Keane, J. Monaghan, B.Ryan and Frances Shanahan. 1st. Row from left to right, C. Bruton, A. Purcell, D. McLoughlin and Angie Buckley.

At the back of the building there were cloakrooms, bathrooms, toilets and storage spaces. Outside there was a vegetable garden, the nuns graveyard, and the parish church. On the right hand side of the gravel path there was a high wall surrounding Mossy Connell's orchard.

Leaving Cert Students in the Science Hall, 1955, Frances Shanahan, Jo McGearty and Kathleen Hope.

The *"Boarders"* as we were called attended morning mass in the parish church After mass we had breakfast. Then everyone had a chore to do before class. Sister Joseph cared for the Boarders, ably assisted by Chrissie.

Teachers at that time were Sister Carmel ,who taught Maths, English, History and Geography, Miss Doyle who lived in St. Joseph's and taught Latin, Mother Agnes who taught Domestic Science, Sister Stanislaus who taught Art, and also trained the choir, Mother Attracta who taught Christian Doctrine, and Sister Rosario who gave piano lessons in the front parlour.

Cookery lessons were held in the kitchen which was part of the primary school. Here Mother Agnes taught us many culinary skills, producing first class potato and lentil soups, Irish stew, shortcrust pastry, and bread and butter pudding.

There Was no Art room so Sister Stanislaus took art classes on Saturday mornings in the big study hall. Each student had a couple of containers of water on her desk,and these would often topple over causing quite a mess.

During my first year in St Joseph's Sister Aquin came down from the primary school for one hour on Friday evenings to teach us Irish grammar -a memory to cherish!

Recreation meant camogie in the field by the river,-walks to Mary Lambe's and back or the occasional Sunday afternoon walk out the Milltownpass road.The highlight of the return from this walk was the forbidden stop at O'Rourke's shop which was located near the present Credit Union office. Here one could buy a *"dinky bar"* which was hard toffee with coconut pieces, for one penny. A real treat!

At this time St Joseph's was what was known as a *"Secondary Top."* There was no centre for state examinations. The pupils who sat Intermediate Cert prior to 1952 and Leaving Cert prior to 1955 had to travel to a centre in Mullingar daily by taxi owned and driven by local man Paddy Dowd.

In 1952 Sister Magdalene having completed her studies in U.C.D.returned to St Joseph's to teach Irish, Latin, English, History and Geography. Miss Burke who taught Maths and Latin joined the staff in 1953.

By this time the new postulants Sister Pius, Sister Concepta, and shortly afterwards Sister Dolores and Sister Assumpta had joined the Mercy Order. They took turns supervising first study session from five o'clock until seven.

Our science subject for Leaving Cert was Physiology and Hygiene. In those days there was no science laboratory in St. Joseph's. I can recall a large glass case standing at the top of the room which was well stocked with test tubes, Bunsen burners, litmus paper, methylated spirit, asbestos mats, and little else. Experiments were carried out on the long classroom table, around which the Leaving Cert girls sat for class.

At some stage during our final year in St. Joseph's, Father Dargan, who was a prominent member of the Pioneer Total Abstinence Association visited the school. Following his visit Sister Magdalene set up a branch of the P.T.A.A. in the school.

Leaving Cert Class, 1955, from left to right, Kathleen Hope, Gertie Hiney, Frances Flynn, Una Fitzpatrick, Josie McGearty and Pauline Cunningham.

~ CHAPTER 28 ~
THE HUB OF THE UNIVERSE

By Danny Dunne

In 1985, ten years after I left St. Joseph's, I was asked to contribute an article to the school's magazine *Vox*, to document the story of the Leaving Cert Class of 1975. The article entitled *The Green Isle,* referred to the long prefabricated building built in the early seventies to accommodate the ever-increasing numbers at the school. By 1983 with the opening of a new Secondary School building, the Green Isle was just a memory.

Ten years after I had left the school I was teaching at Dalystown National School and still a bachelor. The very last sentence in that article read, *'for me St. Joseph's Secondary School was for a few short years-the hub of the Universe.'*

Danny

I still stand by that statement. Twenty seven years later, circumstances have changed, marriage, children, illness and retirement, all in a nutshell. Thus with a lot of time on my hands its time to stand back, take stock and maybe update that article which Noel Foynes had retrieved from the school archives.

During my days at St. Joseph's I was older than most of my classmates by one year as I didn't start National School till I was nearly seven years old due to a series of childhood illnesses. Subsequently I spent only one year in the infant classes, beginning in the spring of 1963. Instead of spending the required eight year primary school cycle, I was ready for Secondary School in the Summer of 1970.

My two oldest brothers Joe and Mick spent a few years at Mullingar Technical School, now the Community College and attained careers in the Air Corpse and Bórd na Móna. My brother Tommy went to the C.B.S. Secondary School in Mullingar.

I was destined to follow him to the Christian Brothers and my Mother wrote to the Principal Brother McGrath to have me enrolled there.

She received a short letter by return post telling her that he would be unable to accommodate me, as parents were being encouraged to send their children to secondary schools in their own catchment area. In the letter he said, *'theres a fine Secondary School down there in the Bridge, you can send him there.'*

Soon after that the ad. appeared in the Westmeath Examiner, which required that all intending students should attend for Examination and registration at the school at 1.30 p.m. on a certain Saturday in early May.

The Examination was held in the afternoon as St. Joseph's Secondary school was open for five and a half days per week. At the end of my first year there, Saturday School ceased. Shorter lunch breaks and later closure in the evening meant that the required hours were spent from Monday to Friday. Students and teachers were very pleased at the time with this result.

My Mother was very apprehensive about sending me there as she thought that being in class alongside girls was not a suitabe environment for a boy. She had heard that the girls were writing notes to the boys and the boys were making dates with the girls. On top of that how would the nuns be able to have any control over the boys? I had received countless lectures and tellings off from her if I ever over-stepped the mark.

Well, the upshot of it all was and I say it amusingly, *how wrong she was?*

The nuns were indeed a force to be reckoned with and we young mavericks from the country would soon settle down into a strict, but caring environment.

I was enrolled for September 1970 and my remaining five younger siblings spent their Secondary School years at St. Joseph's also.

Dalystown N.S. closed for the summer holidays in those years around the 15th of July-St. Swithen's day. According to folklore and tradition, if it rained on that day, it rained for forty days and forty nights, the whole duration of the summer holiday.

But the sixth class were released early around the first of July when classes changed for the coming year. So four boys bade farewell to Dalystown that year, Joe Martin, Gerry Gavin, Adrian Keegan and I. Adrian parted company with us and spent his Secondary School years at St. Finian's College, Mullingar and the remaining trio were ready for the new challenges St. Joseph's had to offer.

Beginning in July, we had a long summer holiday and to our delight, Secondary School didn't start until near the end of September as there was a Secondary School Teachers Strike that year.

This was the season also, I had begun working in my spare time at Ginnell's Farm at Kilbride. My Dad worked there and James Ginnell asked me to do some part-time work, gardening, mowing lawns, clipping hedges etc.

Something happened that summer that made me hope that a certain dream would come true for me.

One afternoon in August, I was raking the chippings on the driveway at the front of the house, when I heard some piano music coming from the drawingroom.

James Ginnell's Aunt, Madeleine King O'Farrelly had travelled up from her home in Limerick to stay at Kilbride, her childhood home. She was a very accomplished piano player and in fact she it was, who composed the music to the poem, *The Old Bog Road*, by Meath Poet Theresa Brayton. The song went on to become established among one of the most popular songs in the Irish Ballad tradition.

The music I heard was Madeleine playing *The Irish Washerwoman* and the sound resounded out into the August air across the lawn and echoed off the walls of the old Norman Castle or tower house.

It was then I said to myself, 'I would love to be able to to that.' This was a dream that would later be fulfilled for me at St. Joseph's.

So with great excitement, tinged with a little fear and anxiety, I headed off walking the short mile to Carrick Crossroads to get the big yellow bus to Rochfortbridge and local man Sheamus Berry was our driver. Later as numbers increased further at the school, a second bus was placed on the Bridge route and our driver then was Tom Giles. The bus hadn't the comforts of modern bus travel, but it was rickety, noisy, smelled of diesel and was freezing cold in winter.

The first shock to the system was that having been the oldest and biggest at National School, were now the youngest, smallest and most vulnerable with older pupils towering over us like a collossus.

The school was enormous, as we were used to only two small classrooms in National School and little else.

The morning began with assembly, when Sister Pius greeted us all, said some prayers and *we* first years were escorted to our new classroom upstairs over the assembly hall.

It was a bright cheery room, with walls painted a magnolia or creamy colour, two big blackboards and plenty of windows with venetian blinds. I had never seen venetian blinds before except on some of the American comedy shows on Teilifís Éireann.

The end windows over-looked Connells orchard and in September the apple trees were laden down with fruit. In the spring they were alive with blossom and the sound of bees humming in the branches. Within a few short years they were gone, as the property was purchased by the Nuns and the pre-fab we christened *The Green Isle* was built on it.

Most subjects were new to us except, the core subjects of English, Irish and Maths. Geography and history were familiar to us also from National School. We were introduced to

• Office Procedure and Business Knowledge
• Book Keeping and Accounts
• Civics
• Christian Doctrine
• General Musicianship
• Woodwork (Boys only)
• Metalwork (Boys only)
• Mechanical Drawing (Boys only)
• Latin
• French
• Domestic Science (Girls only)
• Science
• P.E. (Girls only)

In choosing our subjects for first year, they boys were advised to take Latin rather than French as Latin was a requirement for any young man contemplating joining the priesthood. None of our class ever became a priest but Latin came in very useful many years later when I researched Local History at N.U.I. Maynooth for my M.A.

So we were all dispatched to our various subjects. We stayed in our own classroom for most subjects, except, music, woodwork, metalwork, mechanical rawing, science and domestic science.

Not all boys opted for the technical subjects, but followed the academic course. If the nuns saw that you had a certain talent for a subject you were advised to follow that course. It wasn't long till Sr. Columba approached me and recommended that I join the science class. Six boys from my class followed the science programme for Inter-Cert.

The upshot of this move for me into this world of academia soon earned me a nickname which stuck to me right through Secondary School. In those years I wore the typical free brown County Clinic Glasses and I was soon known by all and sundry as *The Professor*.

Soon after this, Sister Genevieve discovered my great interest in music and I was asked if I would like to take piano lessons. This was an answer to that dream I had earlier that Summer on the front drive of Kilbride House. The only snag was that we had no piano at home. The problem was solved very quickly when I was told I could practise on the piano in the parlour in St. Joseph's at lunch time or when the girls were at P.E.

Little did I know then that the little parlour with the Gothic windows was used by the nuns in the early years from 1862 as the convent oratory.

So began my great interest in music and I took to it like a duck to water. At the end of the 2nd year, I sat the Grade 1, Royal Irish Academy Practical exam.

There was no exam centre for piano in St. Joseph's that year and we were driven to the Greville Arms Hotel Mullingar by Jack Lawrence from Sidebrook House. His daughter Eileen who was a pupil in the school was sitting piano exams also. When I was in fifth year, Eileen Lawrence taught piano for a year and I was one of her students. General and Practical Musicianship was one of the subjects I chose for Leaving Cert and I had reached Grade 5 Royal Irish Academy by then. Later it formed part of my Academic Qualification as a Primary Teacher. Over the years, I have played the church organ on Sundays, something I was glad to do.

From second year onwards, Sr. Dolores who taught music and choir was my piano teacher. In all those years, she was on of the people who fostered and nurtured that love of music and it is great to see her still at the helm, playing at Sunday masses and accompanying the choir. Having had such an opportunity in your education to study a subject like music, follows on into your life beyond school. It is now part and parcel of our home life in Gaybrook and our love of music has passed on to our children also. This is something you can never pay back, but all you can do is be ever so thankful for the opportunity to have done so.

In those years also, the girls wore uniform, but the boys were exempt. Hair was getting longer for boys. It was the era of bell-bottom trousers and platform shoes. It was a time also where the boys had their hair styled and layered. The girls adopted the gypsy style as well as long flowing hair. It was the seventies and the pop culture of the time was our guideline. Abba's appearance at the Eurovision Song contest singing *Waterloo* in 1974 dictated how we dressed over the next few years. As far as we were concerned we were the bees knees and and every bit as cool as the rest of the world. Forty years later our children cannot imagine that we dressed like this. In fact, they cannot imagine that we had a childhood at all.

There were huge changes across our faith also. A few years previously the format of the mass changed with Latin taking the back door and more involvement by the community in readings and liturgy as right across the Catholic world, mass was celebrated in the language of the people, or as it was termed, celebration in the vernacular.

So we were greeted in the spring of first year by the annual retreat, where a priest visited the school for a few days of prayer and contemplation. The big surprise in our lives was the introduction to the folk mass and the lively hymns asociated with it. Quite a lot of them taken from the American Spiritual, African and West Indian folk traditions. It was fresh and new to our lives and attractive to a young modern receptive audience. The sounds of

Someone's crying Lord Kumbaya

resonated through the assembly hall each day during mass, but perhaps one of the most popular hymns was

> *Brothers, Sisters, we are one*
> *And our life has just begun*
> *In the Spirit we are one*
> *We can live forever.*
> *Sons of God, Hear His holy Word*
> *Gather round the table of the Lord*
> *Eat His body drink His Blood*
> *And we'll sing a song of love*
> *Allelu, Allelu, Allelu, Alleluia.*

There were talks and discussions and times for reflection and the greatest temptation to us all was to break the silence requested when we were out on the walks. Visits to the church to do the stations of the cross followed by walking silently through the convent grounds. Need I say that such a request for a bunch of boys was to say the least bordering on the impossible. Whatever attempt the girls made, this was not possible for the boys. Did the Sisters of Mercy overlook this? You bet they didn't! We were all shepherded together and the sisters took turns in herding us like cattle round the walks, reciting the rosary, when Sister Magdalene finished her turn, Sister Genevieve took over. In hindsight, this was part and parcel of our faith formation. We were the same at home when our parents allocated the nightly ten minutes for the rosary. We were often up to our antics also, to be chastized by our parents for disrespecting that holy reflective time. But the apple never falls far from the tree, we are now the parents who are bringing our children and grandchildren for baptism and passing on those things we learned from our parents and teachers at a time, when there was nothing in our heads but fun and frivolity in a new and unexplored world.

The formal dress adopted by the Sisters of Mercy since it's foundation by Mother Catherine McAuley was undergoing change also. When I started in St. Joseph's most of the nuns were wearing the long flowing habit as set out by the order. Then the school Principal Sister Magdalene went on a trip to Rome. When she returned she was wearing the more modern shorter outfit we all became familiar with. Sister Magdalene taught us history that year and she brought back books and brochures all about the Vatican, the Sistene Chapel and the great Roman architecture of the Eternal City.

Within the convent walls also, they were making arrangements for the future. School numbers were on the increase and as a result, more teaching personnel were needed to meet this demand. In our first year Sister Geraldine went away to college to study for her degree. At the beginning of second year, Sister Genevieve went to college and Sister Regina returned and she was our Geography Teacher for Inter Cert.

There were a number of lay teachers employed in the school, Tony O'Sullivan taught Irish and Latin and in time, became the first Lay Principal. Pat Cosgrave taught English and History. He fostered a great love of English and encouraged creativity in us all. Pat would eventually leave teaching to follow a different career and I have always maintained that he was a loss to the teaching profession.

At the beginning of our second year, Nuala Lawlor replaced Miss Earl as P.E. Teacher and two young graduates, Eugene Dunbar from Limerick and Tony Hartnett from Dublin began their teaching careers. Tony Hartnett would later replace Tony O Sullivan as Principal when he retired from teaching.

With all these young teachers involved in our lives they encouraged us to use our talents. Tony O Sullivan and Sister Columba would become very much involved in the Local Youth Club and the annual three Act play in the Hall, became a highlight of the school year.

The first production I remember was, *The Year of the Hiker* by John B. Keane.

Phillip Brady, Tom Byrne, Mary Fox, Johnny Fox and Geraldine Baker were among the cast. One of the finest moments from the play was the cast singing the Jimmy Kennedy song, *Red sails in the Sunset*. This play was performed in the old Convent Primary School hall. I think this might have been the last play staged there as it was later demolished to make way for the new Convent Primary School. Subsequent plays were performed in the *St. Joseph the Worker* Parish hall. Further productions followed into the seventies, *Home is the Hero, Many Young Men of Twenty* and *Sive*, all by John B.Keane, Walter Macken and another production of Brian Friel's *Philadelphia Here I Come*, which was also one of the prescribed plays in the Leaving Cert Programme.

Eugene Dunbar could also play the guitar and on our fifth year trip to Kerry, he played and sang many of the Simon and Garfunkel hits, *Bridge over Troubled Water, The Boxer* and *Scarborough Fair* and introduced us to Folk singers like Tom Paxton and Don McLean. Whenever I hear *American Pie* and *Vincent* on the airwaves I recall those very happy times. Sister Regina on occassion, brought the guitar to class and played quirky amusing little songs like:

The Worm Song and *She sat on the Verandah:*
She sat on the verandah and played her guitar
Played her guitar, played her guitar
She sat on the verandah and played her guitar,
Played her guit-a-a-a-ar

It was a story of betrayed love. A young lady falls madly in love, but her intendent leaves her to marry another. At the end of their lives, she goes to heaven, but he is sent down below, the moral of the story being never to lie.

When we were in fifth and sixth year we went away on Geography and History tours. The first one was to Kerry. We stayed near Glenbeigh, the girls in the hotel and the boys in a B&B nearby. It was the first time some of us had ever been up the mountains to see corrie lakes and waterfalls in the wind and the rain.

We travelled to the Dingle Peninsula also and retraced the footsteps of Peig Sayers. *Peig* was the main prescribed text on the Leaving Cert course and we lived, ate and drank the book for the two years leading up to the Leaving Cert.

We were accompanied on our trip by a student from the Mercy Convent in Dingle, who was our guide for the day. But first, the bus took a detour to the County Home to meet Peig's Son Mícheal Ó Guithín, the *file* or poet who made the trip with us round the Dingle peninsula.

In our Leaving Cert Year, Sister Regina and Eugene Dunbar brought us to the Burren in Co. Clare to experience this strange limestone moonscape. We stayed in the Liscannor hotel and all I remember most is the howling wind at the Cliffs of Moher and each of the hotel rooms had its own ensuite - such luxury!

In October 1973, something happened that would change my life forever, my father died suddenly at the age of fifty seven. This was a very traumatic time for my family. My mother was left to rear her family alone and some of them still very young. The kindness and encouragement of the Sisters of Mercy at this point in my life is something I will never forget. It was a very difficult time and it wasn't easy settling back to school, having to take on extra duties and responsibilities at home. Time is a great healer, but the Sisters were excellent in encouraging me to follow my dream to make a better life for myself and my family.

During those years also, Pat Cosgrave set up a film club and there was a movie shown once a month during school term at night after school. The film was projected from the stage in the Assembly Hall on to the gable wall. Some of the productions were on the Leaving Cert Course or were important film adaptions of the time.

- Lord Jim
- Dr. Strangelove
- Lord of the Flies
- To Sir with Love
- The Yellow Rolls Royce
- The Good, the Bad and the Ugly

It was always something to look forward to. For me, it meant returning to the school at night on the bike and quite often without a flashlight. I fell into a heap of nettles on the Kilbride road on one occassion. Thankfully I didn't get stung as I was wrapped up in an anorak. On another occassion I hit the wall of the bridge on the Derry River, but I lived to tell the tale.

In time Sister Geraldine and Sister Genevieve returned from College to teach at St. Joseph's and in the Spring of 1975, our Leaving Cert. year it was decided to stage a school musical. Popular at the time was Andrew Lloyd Webber's *Joseph and his Amazing Technicolor Dreamcoat*.

Sister Genevieve, Sister Geraldine, Nuala Lawlor, Eugene Dunbar and Tony Hartnett were at the helm. It was a spectacular production with plenty of glitzy pop costumes and bell bottom trousers. My brother Pascal played the part of Joseph and Paddy Gavin took on the role of Pharoah. Pascal suffered from a bout of larynxgitis a few days before the show. Sister Genevieve kept him dosed with honey and lemon drinks and throat lozenges- *Zubes* and *Fisherman's friends*. One Sunday afternoon, a week before the show, Pascal had no way of getting to a rehearsal when Sister Genevieve arrived on the bike at the house to collect him. She took him on the carrier of the bike to the Bridge. It was do or die, as the show had to go on. It was staged on a weekend shortly before the end of the school year and it brought light relief to us Leaving Certs. Our whole time was taken up with the Leaving Cert exam just a short time away.

As a pupil, you got to know most of the pupils senior to you and some who followed behind you also. There was a great track record in the school of students following into the few careers available at the time, medicine, teaching, the Civil Service, the Garda Síochana, the Army, Nursing, Bórd na Móna, the E.S.B., and careers like Engineering were becoming popular also.

Among those who followed a teaching career from my time at St. Joseph's, Ann Fagan returned to the Convent Primary School for a short while. Ann Reidy was appointed to the school in the late seventies and now as Mrs. Eighan, she's the first lay Principal of the Convent Primary School. Camilla Gavigan and Phil Ryan were appointed to Miltownpas and Tyrrellspass National Schools respectively. Camilla would later be appointed Principal of Milltownpass N.S. Dympna Alford began her teaching Career at Tyrrellspass and is now principal of Dalystown N.S. Noleen Keogh taught in Kinnegad for a number of years before moving to Donegal. Mary O' Rourke and Nuala Gorman were appointed to the staff of St. Joseph's and are currently on the teaching staff in the school. When I graduated in 1978 from St. Patrick's College in Drumcondra, I spent two years teaching in *O'Growney N.S.*, Athboy, thirteen years at Dalystown N.S. and and my final eighteen years as Principal of *St. Finian's N.S.* Clonard. Since its early years in 1948, to the present day there has been a great track record in students following careers in teaching. Quite a number of them are currently on the teaching staff of St. St. Joseph's and the Convent Primary School.

The Leaving Cert came and went and we went our separate ways. There was no Debs night out in those days. Today, the Leaving Cert Students are able to get together for that final farewell before college life begins. But we went our separate ways and began following our dreams. I meet some of them on occassion and we are always drawn back to those years. It is a part of our lives we will always share and something we will always have in common.

The place described as *The Hub of the Universe*, was for me only part of our lives for five short years. It was an eventful and influential time for us. As a teacher myself, we were told in our training that ones role in this chosen career meant that you were 'in loco parentis,' and even though we were no longer small children, we still needed guidance, nurturing and encouragement to steer us on our journey. Like the *Mary Stevenson* poem, *Footsteps in the Sand,* where the Lord walks beside you on your journey at difficult moments in your life, there are times when there are only one set of footprints.

So I said to the Lord,
"You promised me Lord,
that if I followed you,
you would walk with me always.
But I have noticed that during
the most trying periods of my life
there have only been one
set of footprints in the sand.
Why, when I needed you most,
you have not been there for me?"

The Lord replied,
"The times when you have
seen only one set of footprints,
is when I carried you."

There *were* such moments in our lives and we needed help also. The Sisters of Mercy really lived out their vocation as servants of the community and carried us on that journey when the need arose. They gave of their time, even out of school without pay or recognition especially during exam time. At those times we returned to school on Saturdays to attend extra classes in the core subjects of Maths, English and Irish in preparation for the exams. But living in our adolescent world, we grumbled about having to attend those classes, but the Sisters as well as the lay teachers who gave of their free time, I wonder did they ever get thanks for it. Our youthful minds could not see that they were fulfilling their vocations by giving of themselves to the children of the community. They were moments also, recorded like the footsteps in the sand where like the Lord on our journey of life, they carried us also.

One hundred and fifty years is a very long service record to the village of Rochfortbridge. Father Robbins, seeing a need to improve the literacy of women in his parish, coupled with Eliza Fielding's legacy and her vision and missionary zeal, would ring out to the four corners of the world, to Australia and beyond, where past Pupils of St. Josephs have ventured and taken root. The Sisters have worked selflessly and quietly for the people of Rochfortbridge doing something marvellous and wonderful, preparing their pupils and giving them the life skills needed for survival. I was part of this process for a few short years, something I am ever so thankful for and will cherish for the rest of my life.

~ CHAPTER 28 ~
ST. JOSEPH'S SECONDARY SCHOOL
IN THE 1970's

Down the walks in the early seventies, from left to right, Imelda Coyne, Ann Dunne, Áine Morgan, Mary Raleigh and Theresa Cunningham.

Outside 'The Green Isle,' from left to right, Theresa Cunningham, Janette Curran, Ann Dunne, Catherine Judge and Áine Morgan. Standing in front is Mary Glynn.

Anyone for tennis?

Imelda and Angela Gorman.

From left to right, Patricia Rawlings, Geraldine Mangan, Patricia Mulligan, Emer_____, _____ and Annette Keogh.

Taken around 1975, enjoying the flowers are Deirdre Grace and Mary Raleigh.

The Convent Grounds in 1977, back row from left to right, Thomas Coleman(R.I.P.), Ann Ennis, Margaret Earley, Imelda Gorman, Marie Byrne and Tony Maguire, Next row from left to right, _____, _____, Angela Gorman, Mary England, Pauline Kelleghan, Ann Dunne(Moorow) and Siobhán Gorman. Seated in front, Deirdre Grace.

Mary and Carmel Raleigh in 1975.

Aidan Dunne, Breda Smith and Jimmy Keegan.

Taken in 1973/74, Back row, from left to right, Imelda Gorman, Angela Gorman, _____, Kathleen Earley, _____ and Margaret Keegan. Front row, from left to right, Elizabeth Newman, Caroline Ronan and Betty Carey.

Back row, from left to right, Geraldine Walsh, Theresa Cunningham, Margaret Judge, _____ and Mary Raleigh. Front row from left to right, Elizabeth Behan, Anne Quinn and Marina Daly.

Summer picnic in the field.

Sunny days on the steps neat St. Joseph's.

< Terence Murray, Paddy Gavin and Edward Nugent.

Back row from left to right, Elizabeth Newman, Caroline Ronan,_____ and _____.
Front row from left to right, Angela Gorman, Betty Carey and Imelda Gorman.

Sister Columba. and friends

Tony Maguire, Terence Murray and Paddy Gavin

Catherine Judge, Nuala Doyle, Attracta Coyne and Breda Smyth in 1975.

Valerie Mangan in 1975.

Competitors in the Inter Schools Debating Championships in 1973, from left to right, Nuala Moran, Kathleen O'Mahoney, Josephine McKeown and Mary O'Rourke.

Debating Team 1974, from left to right, Emer Gavin, Ann Reidy, Johnny Fox and Mary Byrne.

Patricia Foy and John Nolan

Joan Gunning and Eamon Gorman.

Sister Columba as we remember her in the old science lab.

Kathleen Gavin and Eithne Cleary

Liz Deegan and Ann Doherty on retreat in 1970.

Eugene Dunbar practising Hamlet's speech 'Alas! Poor Yorick, I knew him well, Horatio! The only problem was there was no skull to practise with, but the football stopped a gap there.

St. Anne's 1970, at the back, Robina Gavin, Emer Gavin and Eileen Lawrence. Middle, Eithne Cleary and Rose Tormey. Front, Theresa Deegan and Kathleen Gavin.

At first glance one suspects it to be film star Donald Sutherland. In fact he's more famous than that, former Principal Tony Hartnett in 1974.

Mary Walsh

When this photo appeared in Involve magazine in 1984, this photo from 1974 was given the caption 'Hands off, he's mine!' The rest can be left to the imagination.

Patricia Donovan, Maureen Frances, Mary Cleary and Liz Dunne.

Big Sister, Elizabeth Behan, Caroline O'Connor and Siobhán O'Connell.

Pauline O'Brien, Imelda Coyne and Mary Hevey.

Pascal Dunne and Paddy Gavin as Joseph and Pharoah, in the 1975 production of Joseph and His Amazing Technicolor Dreamcoat.

Mary Hyland & Deirdre Grace.

Paul Fox and Caroline Murphy

At Back Catherine Judge. Marie Malone, Imelda Coyne, Pauline Murphy, Angela Gorman and Margaret Swords. Middle Row Nora Frances, Aine Morgan and Marie Byrne Front Row Mary Hyland, Rosaleen Dunne and Noeleen Keogh

Back Row Imelda Gorman, Camilla Bermingham, Angela Gorman and Mary Hyland. Middle Row Imelda Coyne, Brigetta Giles, Margaret Bradley and Jeanette Curran. Front Row Bernadette Carey, Rosaleen Dunne, Anne Dunne and Marie Byrne.

Noeleen Keogh, Rosaleen Dunne, Camila Bermingham, Miriam Ward, Brigetta Giles, Deirdre Grace, Angela Gorman, Janette Curran, Front Row Marie Byrne, Sheila Kennedy and Mary Hyland.

Angela Gorman, Imelda Gorman, Bernadette Carey, Mary Hyland, Jeanette Curran, Noeleen Keogh, Sheila Kennedy and Marie Byrne.

Bernadette Carey, Imelda Coyne, Deirdre Grace, Marie Malone, Nora Frances, Marie Byrne, Angela Gorman, Margaret Bradley, Mary Hyland and Imelda Gorman.

Deirdre Grace and Patricia Mulligan.

Jeanette Coyne, Imelda Gorman, Mary Hyland, Mary England
and Marie Byrne.

Ann Griffin, Noelle Lynam, Ann Doran, Regina Gorman
and Collette Doyle.

Included in this group are Máiréad Dardis, Caitríona
Donlon, Dolores Burke, Loretto Loran and Patricia Tone.

Geraldine Walsh, Ann Marie Denehan, Fiona Conlon,
Jeanette Bollard and Noeleen Lynam.

Patricia Mulligan, Gráinne O'Neill and Annette Keogh.

Up to their tricks are Mary England, Deirdre Coyne and Fiona Kirby.

Joan Dargan

Mary Kirby impersonating Sister Geraldine.

Mary Young, impersonating Sister Geraldine.

Back row, Annette McDonnell, Ann Marie Denehan and Marie Keogh. In front are, Regina Gorman, Edel Corcoran, Ann Doran, Eilish Cocoman, Mary Darby and Esther Giles.

ST. JOSEPH'S SCHOOL,
ROCHFORTBRIDGE
ENROLMENT FOR SESSION
1971-'72

FULL TIME COURSES LEADING TO GROUP,
INTERMEDIATE AND LEAVING CERTIFICATE
EXAMINATIONS.

ALL INTENDING STUDENTS SHOULD ATTEND FOR
INTERVIEW AND REGISTRATION AT THE SCHOOL
AT 1.30 P.M. ON SATURDAY, 8th MAY, 1971.

Westmeath Examiner, Sat May 8th 1971

CONVENT OF MERCY
ST. JOSEPH'S SCHOOL,
ROCHFORTBRIDGE
ENTRANCE EXAMINATION
FOR RESIDENTIAL PUPILS TO THE ABOVE
SCHOOL
SATURDAY, 22nd MAY, 1971
HOURS OF EXAMINATION: 2—6 P.M.
Pupils who intend to sit for Examination please notify
Superior.

Westmeath Examiner Sat May 15th 1971

THE SISTERS

The Summer Picnic and other photos

The following group of photos were taken at the Convent of Mercy Rochfortbridge during a 1970's Summer and at some other functions. Some of them have gone to their just reward and others have been transferred to other Convents in the Diocese of Meath.

Sr. Pius Doran and Sr. Regina O'Reilly

Picnic on the lawn, at the back, Sr. Freda Farrelly, Sr. Magdalene Claffey, Sr. Assumpta, Sister Concepta O Brien, Sister Genevieve Doherty, Sister Sacred Heart, Sister Regina O Reilly and Sr. Maureen O Brien. In front are Sister Gemma, Sister Annunciata and Sr. Rosario Shaw.

On holiday, Sr. Magdalene Claffey, Sr. Columba Gargan, Sr. Concepta O Brien and Sr. Regina O Reilly.

Sr. Concepta O'Brien

Sr. Freda Farrelly

Enjoying a cuppa in the sun.

THE FIRST YOUTH CLUB

The First Youth Club in Rochfortbridge began as a result of an initiative set up by Sister Columba and Tony O'Sullivan. Apart from the work of the GAA and Macra na Feirme in encouraging young people into sport and other activities there was little else in the Rochfortbridge area at the time to encourage and challenge the minds of young people into sport, drama and other projects to encourage their talents and to develop other social skills

The 1971 production of The Year of the Hiker, by John B. Keane in the old Convent Hall. From left to right are Geraldine Baker, Johnny Fox, Thomas Byrne, Phillip Brady, Geraldine Whelehan, Dick Maher and Mary Fox.

as part of their learning process. The youth club began in a small way with discos, public speaking, games and drama. Drama was a very popular medium to encourage the talents of young people and the work of Playwrights like John B. Keane and Walter Macken were very popular in the club.

Their first production began in 1971 in the old Convent hall. It was John B.Keane's *The Year of the Hiker*. Ironically this location was probably one of the last productions in this old building as within a few short years it was demolished to make way for the new Convent Primary School building which opened in 1980.

Other popular productions followed,

• *Home is the Hero*
• *Sive*
• *Many Young men of Twenty*
• *Philadelphia Here I Come*

They played to packed houses with each production and the club grew from strength to strength competing in all competitions and projects across the midlands. Unfortunately, other committments led Sister Columba and Tony O'Sullivan away from the club. Sister Columba became principal of the Secondary School and Tony was appointed vice-principal. As the 1980's approached the youth club phased out due to changes in the social lives of young people as well as access to other sports and activities.

The programme from the Youth Club Production of Many Young Men of Twenty,
by John B. Keane.

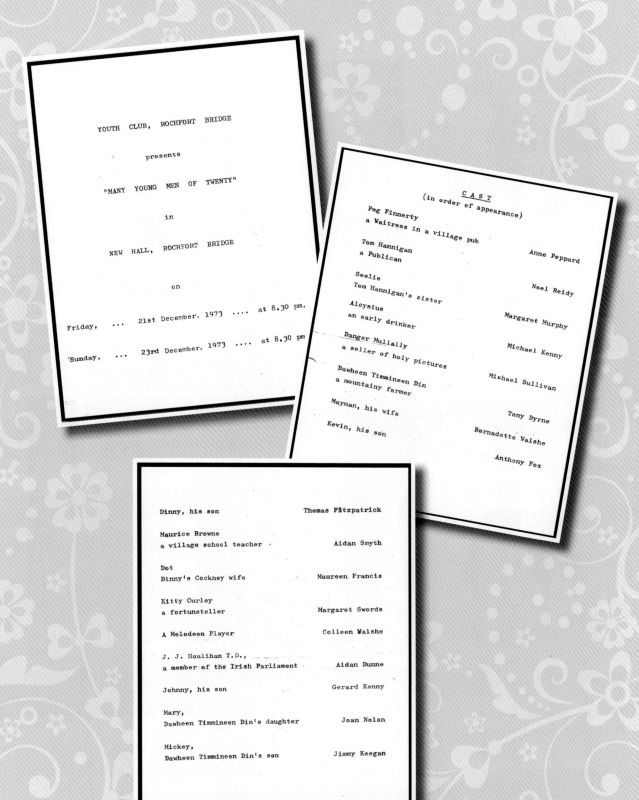

YOUTH CLUB, ROCHFORT BRIDGE

presents

"MANY YOUNG MEN OF TWENTY"

in

NEW HALL, ROCHFORT BRIDGE

on

Friday, ... 21st December. 1973 .... at 8.30 pm.

Sunday, ... 23rd December. 1973 .... at 8.30 pm

C A S T
(in order of appearance)

Peg Finnerty a Waitress in a village pub	
Tom Hannigan a Publican	Anne Peppard
Seelie Tom Hannigan's sister	Noel Reidy
Aloysius an early drinker	Margaret Murphy
Danger Mullally a seller of holy pictures	Michael Kenny
Dawheen Timmineen Din a mountainy farmer	Michael Sullivan
Maynan, his wife	Tony Byrne
Kevin, his son	Bernadette Walshe
	Anthony Fox

Dinny, his son	Thomas Fitzpatrick
Maurice Browne a village school teacher	Aidan Smyth
Dot Dinny's Cockney wife	Maureen Francis
Kitty Curley a fortuneteller	Margaret Swords
A Melodeon Player	Colleen Walshe
J. J. Houlihan T.D., a member of the Irish Parliament	Aidan Dunne
Johnny, his son	Gerard Kenny
Mary, Dawheen Timmineen Din's daughter	Joan Nolan
Mickey, Dawheen Timmineen Din's son	Jimmy Keegan

~ CHAPTER 29 ~
A VIEW FROM THE OTHER SIDE

By Marie Therése Kilmartin

Marie Therese is a past pupil who returned to St. Joseph's to teach for one year as part of her Higher Diploma in teaching

First Published in Vox Student Year Book 1990

What's it like in the staff room? Was it hard to settle in? Was it difficult to teach people who were at school with you? These are just a few of the many questions which I have been asked during the year. Most of my own school friends were dying to hear about "the staff room", most people wanted to know whether the teachers are the same in the staff room and the classroom.

Marie Therése is now principal of Coláiste Bríde Secondary School, Clondalkin

At first it was weird to walk into the staffroom and chat to people who taught me for five years, but after a while it no longer bothered me and it seemed as though I never left the place except that there were a lot of new faces on the staff and nearly two hundred more pupils.

As the year progressed 1 got to know more and more students and I could see many changes in them happening under my own nose. I was reminded a lot of my own class as I looked at the different classes, the way in which we all developed as young people during the five years. At different stages I felt so sorry for the manner in which we treated some of our teachers, but being on the other side you suddenly develop an empathy and understanding.

Teaching is no easy job but it does have its moments!!! It was great to identify the faces of brothers or sisters of people which I knew while at school. It made it much easier to learn everyone's name. Even walking into different classrooms reminded me of incidents in my own class and here I was seeing things from a new angle for the first time.

It is also interesting to see how the school itself had changed so little except for new classrooms and more photos and trophies in the cabinet. The teachers themselves haven't changed a bit however I remember the first day I met Mrs. Alford I didn't recognise her, even though I spent five years in her class she'd cut her hair and got contact lenses. I was so embarrassed at not recognising her!

This year I was in the position of seeing all the hard work that goes on behind the scenes, planning classes, modules for the European studies, correcting copies and exams, organising all the extra-curricular activities.

I never knew that the teachers carried schoolbags too!!Did you?

I remember standing outside the staff-room door and wondering why the teachers never answered but now I do!! Lunchtime provides the precious time we need to recuperate from the morning's activities and the endless series of knocks on the door can be rather annoying when it's 12.50 and you still haven't sat down.

The staff room is a refuge in a sense, at times a place-of serious discussion, at other times a place of laughter and provides an ideal stage for comedy and jokes.

A certain corner in the room is most likely to initiate a lot of the crack (I wonder can you guess which teachers though!!). The slagging is good natured and nobody can get away with a thing. I definitely think that everyone would be surprised to know the real truth of what goes on. It's not really like what I always thought it would be like much better crack* altogether. Being a student teacher also leaves one open to a lot of wise cracks but all in good nature (I hope!!!).

Supervising at the school Ceili and the Irish Tour reminded me a lot of my own time in class, the many friends I had, and what we used to do!! It was great to hear such comments as *"Sure you're only a young one Miss"* when the B4 pupils found out my age and the way that the fifth years read old copies of *"VOX"* to find a few slags· on me!!!! I never thought I'd return to the school but I've had an extremely enjoyable experience and writing in the school magazine seems to be a natural progression.

As a teacher I've had my share of funny moments in the classroom, but I've enjoyed meeting everyone and working with them. This year has shown me that I really do enjoy teaching and the challenge it offers. In the beginning it was a bit nerve-wrecking to stand in front of students who are by nature a critical audience but I soon got over it and began to enjoy my work and meeting everyone.

The staff were extremely supportive when the supervisors arrived to watch us teach and it certainly helped when teachers slipped out to send a message to the class in question. Finally I'd like to wish everyone well and I hope that everyone enjoys their days in school as much as I did, that Rochfortbridge will be a place of happy memories and finally don't be too hard on the poor teachers - they are doing a great job.

Go n-eírí libh go léir!**

* Crack has nothing to do with the consumption of illicit substances. It is a term used in Ireland to describe fun, laughter and enjoyment associated with entertainment.

· To slag someone in Ireland is to tease or joke with them in good faith without causing offence.

** Success to you all.

Coláiste Bríde, Clondalkin

~ CHAPTER 30 ~
ST. JOSEPH'S SECONDARY SCHOOL
IN THE 1980'S

J.J. Fynn, Hilary Gaffney, Peter Deegan and Claire Dillon.

*Gráinne O'Neill, Claire Byrne,
Ann Delamere.*

*Avril Kirwan, Geraldine Nolan,
Gerry Brennan, Ger Hannon,
Sinéad Slevin, James Gavin,
Sandra Lyng, Pauline O' Grady,
Paul McCabe, Jane Mangan,
Eamon Cleary, Seán Corrigan and
Brendan Nugent.*

*Paul Manning, James Gavin, Jamie McMahon and Eugene
Dunbar talk to Dick Hogan at the Topic office*

Joan Gunning, Thomas McDonagh and Patricia Foy.

Caroline Murphy and Joan Gunning

On a trip to Dublin Zoo, from left to right, Paul Fox, John Nolan, Dermot Gorman and Eamon Gorman.

At the metalwork room. Inside at the back, Tommy Byrne and Paul Fox. At the back, Maura L'Estrange, Mary Plunkett, Gráinne Smith, Linda Lynam, Caroline Murphy, Pat Kelly and Colette Rathbourne. Next row, Eileen Morgan, Majella Usher, Vincent Tone, John Cocoman and Phillip O'Grady.

On the Zoo trip also from left to right, John Nolan, Ita Finnegan, Patricia Foy, Paul Fox, Caroline Murphy, William Tone, Eamon Gorman, Paul Cocoman and Eleanor McDonagh

Mary Hayes and Luke Dempsey

On the trip to the Isle of Man, from left to right, Dermot Gorman, John Nolan, Caroline Murphy and Enda Cully.

Caroline Murphy bringing home the goodies from the Isle of Man.

Caroline Murphy and John Nolan.

Homeward bound, from left to right, Mary McGovern, Patricia Foy, Joan McDonald, Joan Gunning and Jacintha Davitt.

On a Geography trip to the Dingle peninsula from the top of the signpost down, Mark O'Connell, Joan McDonald, Mary McGovern, Patricia Foy, Jacintha Davitt, Caroline Brennan and Margaret Doran.

Making waves in Kerry, at the back, Mark O'Connell, Pauric Nolan and John Denehan. In front Jacintha Davitt, Patricia Foy, Joan Gunning, Joan McDonald and Mary McGovern.

Enjoying the party are Joan Gunning and John Denehan.

*Patricia Foy, Mark O Connell and
Joan Gunning, all set for the debs in 1983.*

*A group from the Inter- Cert Class 1989. Back row, from left to right,
Eamonn Farrell, Pat Jessopp, Declan Whelehan, Vincent Daly, Thomas
Hyland, Niall Dunne and Dermot Connell. Middle row, from left to right,
Paula Ennis, Breda Curran, Sharon Kane, Deirdre Martin and Emma
McLoughlin. Front row, from left to right, Tara Brogan, Tanya Ennis, Ann
Gavin, Martina McGrath and Violet Carter.*

Patricia Foy and Eamonn Gorman

The future of Irish farming assured.

October 1987, Laurence McDonnell, Billy Byrne and Declan Rogers.

Class leaders, 1988/89, Back row, from left to right, Niall Dunne, Camilla McGurran, Lorna Bradley, Aedín O' Rafferty, Frances Murphy and Rebecca Maslin. Front row, from left to right, Emma Byrne, Alma Gavin, Willie Murphy, Geraldine Flynn, Lorraine Tormey, Imelda Geraghty and Denise Farrell.

Back row, from left to right, Joe Giles, Colm Arthur, Jim Arthur, John Healy and Michael Kilmartin. Middle row, from left to right, Shirley McGovern, Rachel Mooney and Maeve Pearson. Front row, from left to right, Tracey McDermott and Ursula O'Brien

Class leaders, 1989/90. Back row, from left to right, Lorraine Kelly, Catherine McDonnell, Rebecca Maslin, Sharon Kane and Helene Keegan. Third row, from left to right, Maurice Eighan, Emma Smith, Dominic Sheehy, Olivia Sherry and Tommy Farrell. Second row, from left to right, Caroline Feery, Tracey Fanning, Mark Malone, Camilla Lynam and Helena Farrell. Front row, from left to right, Ciara Muldoon, Ken Berry, Sinead Twomey and Kevin Brennan.

Kicking along and feelin' groovy, From left to right, Gerard Noonan, Brendan Murtagh, Jonathan Geraghty and Enda Carey.

Some members of the magazine Committee, from left to right, John Healy, Josephine Kiernan, David Moore, Emma Cash, Mark Malone, Yvonne Callaghan and Barry Kilmartin.

Class leaders 1986, Back row from left to right, Gráinne Walsh, Geraldine Farrell, Mary Gorman, Aedamar Nolan, James Gunning, Declan Whelehan, June Murphy, Thomas McDermott, Joseph Giles, Aidan Dunne and Julie Mahony. Front row, from left to right, Valerie O'Neill, Jacinta O'Reilly, Tanya Ennis, Patricia Bollard, Catherine McDonagh, Anthony Gillard and Brendan Sheehy. Absent from the picture are Martin Daly and Damian Foy.

Aidan, did you hear the one about …

Sr. Dympna, school Principal.

Aidan Dunne and Deirdre O'Brien.

Students council 1985-86. From left to right, Julie Mahony, Mary Gorman, Aidan Dunne and Geraldine Farrell.

School production of A Christmas Carol, by Charles Dickens

Magazine Committee. Back row, from left to right, Doreen Geoghan, Sheila Casey, Joan Heduan, Patricia Daly, Marie-Thérése Kilmartin (editor), Deirdre O'Brien (sub-editor) and Breda McCormack. Front Row, from left to right, Karen Clyne, Michael Kilmartin, Brendan Sheehy, Pat Costello, Voncent Daly, Martin Daly and Michael Carley.

Patrick Dowdall and Frances Kelly.

Noel Moodey, David Aughey, Gerry Brennan and Joe Doyle.

Irish Residential Course, European Study Module, from left to right, Enda Heavey, Damien Brennan, Liam Hussey, Cathal Nugent and Joe Earley.

From left to right, Finian Curran, Dessie Gorman, Noel Moody, Brendan Nugent, David Aughey, John Scully and Gerry Brennan.

Back row, from left to right, C. Smullen, A. Wright, S. McDonnell, E. Corrigan, K. Farrell, C. Colgan, T. Saunders, M. Dunne, D. Bradley and J. O'Connor.
Front row, from left to right, A. Colgan, G. McNamee, M. Geoghan, A. Mitchell, J. Fallon, D. Gavigan, D. Muldoon, P. Kenny, A. Corcoran, J. Drinan, G. Gibney and J. Glennon.

The 1986 Debs dance took place in the Greville Arms Hotel Mullingar and this photo was taken at this event. Back row, from left to right, Damien Nolan, Michael Glennon, Tommy Byrne, John Hanlon, Kevin Murray, Damien Foy, Des Maguire, Declan Whelehan, Pat Costello, Conor Delaney, Peter Deegan, Ciaran Kenny, James Gunning and Aidan Dunne.
Third row, from left to right, Joe Gorman, Deirdre O'Brien, Olive Manning, Shirley Griffith, _____, Sheila Casey, _____, Claire Dillon, Marie-Thérése Kilmartin, Carmel Reid and Rosaleen McDonagh.
Second row, from left to right, Frances Kelly, Doreen Geoghagan, Jackie Doonan, Claire Byrne, Aideen Donlon, Lisa Ennis, _____, Deirdre Conroy, _____, Bernie Conlon, Lelia Newe, Niamh O'Brien and Helen Keogh.
Front row, from left to right, Breda Moore, Pamela Eighan, Miriam Curran, Louise Dunne, Annette Clarke, Nessa McDermot, _____, Mary Curran, Breda Deegan, Yvonne Gunning, Julie Mahoney and Roseanne Kellaghan.

School tour to Trim Castle 1982, Back row, from left to right, Pat Costello, Aidan Dunne, Joe Gorman, Damien Foy, Robert(Bob) Dunne, and Ciarán Kenny. Front row, from left to right, Damien Nolan, Kevin Murray, Mary Curran and Louise Dunne.

Homeward bound on the Dingle Tour, 1985, from left to right, Michael Glennon, Vivian Henry, Tommy Byrne, Aidan Dunne, Muireann Cunningham and Briga Clarke.

School Basketball Team, 1985, back row, from left to right, Mary Kenny, Louise Dunne and Marie Therése Kilmartin. Front row, from left to right, Yvonne Gunning, Lorna O'Brien and Mary Curran.

Student Council 1984, from left to right, A Leahy, Noeleen Raleigh, M. Hughes and B. Leahy.

Fancy Dress fanatics, Declan Fennelly and Kevin Murray.

Competitors in the 1989, Young Ireland Programme, Regional Table Quiz, Joan Heduan, Lorraine Farrell, Elaine Leavy and Audrey McDermott.

Nuala Quinn, Patrick Gorman and Rachel Reid.

Briga Clarke and Fiona Garry, a night out at the theatre in 1986.

Ann Kavanagh, Mary McGovern, Gráinne Ó Neill, Angela Leahy, Theresa Martin and Mary Ó Brien.

Night at the debs!

David Nolan, Vincent Tone, Dermot Mooney_____, Tomás McDonagh and Michael Kane.

ST. JOSEPH'S SECONDARY SCHOOL, ROCHFORTBRIDGE, PARENTS COUNCIL

ANNUAL ST. PATRICK'S NIGHT BUFFET SUPPER DANCE

IN WHELEHAN'S LOUNGE, ROCHFORTBRIDGE

MUSIC BY THE RANGERS

HOURS 11—2 A.M.   ADMISSION £2.50.

PROCEEDS IN AID OF SECONDARY SCHOOL BUILDING FUND

Adrian Lee, Aishling Herraty, Emma Smith and Emma Byrne enjoying the Viking Boat at Ferrycarrig in Wexford.

Leaving Cert Class 1988. Back row, from left to right, Anthony Casey, Michael Carley, Gordon Eighan, _____, Camillus Fennelly, Colin Yeates, Bernard McCabe, _____, Gerard Hussey and Nial O Riordan.
Fourth row, from left to right, Sandra Lynge, Linda Malone, Irene Malone, _____, Yvonne Smullen, Regina Dunne, Breda McCormack, _____, Lilian Curran, Valerie Berry, Siobhán Garry and Anita Farrell.
Third row, from left to right, Linda Murphy, Imalda Kavanagh, _____, _____, Orla Gane, Carmel Wallace, Deirdre Flynn, Linda Davis, _____, Marie Giles and Sandra Campbell.
Second row, from left to right, _____, Fiona Joyce, Ruth Shortt, _____, Orla Gavigan, _____, Suzanne Walsh, _____, Fiona Walsh, Emer McCormack, Hilda Reid and Tara McCormack.
Front row, from left to right, James Clarke, Colin Cunningham, Elaine Clyne, _____, Margaret Hannon, Olivia Curran, Michelle Hayes, Mary Gavin, Helen Daly, Ann Dunne, Sheila Giles, Joseph Giles and Declan Feery.

~ CHAPTER 31 ~
SOCIAL SERVICES

Members of the organising committee of the Rochfortbridge and District Social Services Party in Harrys, Kinnegad, Dec. 1991, Back row from left to right, Sr. Magdalene Claffey, Mrs. Josephine Duignam and Caroline Kelleher. Front row, from left to right, Mrs. Anne Byrne, Mrs. Una Malone, Mrs. Margaret Nolan and Sr. Maureen O'Brien.

Mrs. Hill and Mike McCabe, the two oldest citizens in Rochfortbridge Parish in 1991 preparing to cut the Christmas cake at the Rochfortbridge and District Social Services Party. With them are Fr. Hugh Roche C.C. and Fr. Eamonn O'Brien P.P.

Mary Murphy, Eileen Medford, Ann Cooney and Mrs. Lynch Social Services Christmas Party, 1992.

Patricia Carey, Ann Gavin, Mary Kenny and Matt Walsh, Social Services Christmas Party 1992.

Johnny Whelehan, Dinny Cleary and Millie Brennan, Social Services Christmas Party 1992.

Paddy Keogh, Ellen Delamere and Pat Delamere, Social Services Christmas Party 1992

Kathleen Dunne, Kathleen Coleman, and Maggie Daly, Social Services Christmas Party 1992.

Christopher Duignam, Nancy Duignam and Nicholas Curran, Social Services Christmas Party 1993.

Mrs. Edwards, Maura Fox, Patricia Mangan, Kathleen Corrigan, Tommy Clarke and Denis Corrigan, Social Services Christmas Party 1992.

Michael Curran, Dolores Wright Sheila Swords, Bridget Keegan and Mary Murphy, Social Services Christmas Party 1993.

Margaret Nolan and Mrs. Conroy, Social Services Christmas Party 1993.

Mary Francis, Sr. Maureen O'Brien, Margaret Nolan, Miriam Gavin, Mary Arthur, Anne Byrne and Sr. Magdalene Claffey at the Social Services Christmas Party 1993.

Kitty McCarthy and Kathleen Dunne, Social Services Christmas Party 1993.

George Bagnall, Jack Keogh and Paddy McCabe enjoy the entertainment at the Social Service Christmas Party.

Members of the 1996 organising Committee of the Rochfortbridge and District Social Services Christmas party which was held in Harrys Kinnegad. Back row, Mary Murphy and Michael Curran. Front row from left to right, Mary Francis, Sheila Swords and Maisie Whelehan.

Joe Keegan, Castlelost sings a song for the new Millennium in 2000 A.D. He is accompanied by Kit Loughrey on Accordeon.

Social Services Committee group from the 1980's. Back row, from left to right, Mary Arthur, Brigid Keegan, Agnes Mooney, Oliver Manning, Danny Dunne, Anne Byrne, Mary Murphy, Chris Bollard, Michael Curran, Maisie Whelehan and Dolores Wright.
Second row, Hannah Gavin, Sister Conrad Lynam, Fr. Eamonn O'Brien P.P., Mrs. Beglin, Eily Duignam and Sister Magdalene Claffey. In front are Sheila Swords, Miriam Bagnall and Mary Francis.

~ CHAPTER 32 ~
THE BOARDERS

In 1831, the British Government in Ireland established the National Education System as an experiment to find a means of providing an education for everyone including the poorer classes and it was an overwhelming success. In earlier chapters in this book we saw how the system was established nationally and the knock-on effect of such a system was to resound downwards through the years even to the present day, even after the the foundation of the Irish Free State in 1922 following the War of Independence and the subsequent Civil War. It's effectiveness and success in the new-found State was as a result of a full working Civil Service which was in situ following the ending of British rule in Ireland. This education model was of course copied in other countries also within the British Empire and proved to be a very effective system of education.

National education for children finished at the age of twelve or thirteen and for some children at fourteen. The standard of education reached in the system provided proficiency in the three R's –reading, writing and arithmetic as well as other disciplines in the humanities, but little else to provide for further education.

The progress to further education to prepare for work in careers such as the Civil Service, Medicine, Nursing, etc. needed further study to prepare for University and other centres of learning. This was provided by Secondary Education and later in the newly established State by the Vocational Education Programme which saw the establishment of Vocational Education Schools in some of the larger towns and cities.

Unlike the National School system, greater specialization was needed and there was a wider range of subjects to cater for. As well as that the state did not provide a free Secondary education system. Therefore secondary education became available to those who were prepared to pay for it.

The religious orders who had embraced the new National Education System and adapted to its rules and regulations of governance set about providing Secondary Education also for the children of Ireland. Schools were established in cities, towns and villages to cater for these needs. The only successful way to achieve this successfully was through Boarding schools, where families sent their children to be educated on a fee basis. Some of the schools became feeder schools for the seminaries and Convents where students were enccouraged to enter religious life by their parents and by the school also.

In nineteenth century Ireland and indeed into the first half of the twentieth century there was such an upsurge in vocations that many young men and women left the country as priests and Nuns to work on the missions helping to establish foundations of their religious orders in other countries. The example of course in the case of Rochfortbridge was the mission to Yass in New South Wales in 1875 and its subsequent sister foundations beneath the southern cross.

Since the Convent of Mercy at Rochfortbridge was founded in 1862 its first project was the establishment of a National School. It was common practise with some families to send their children at a very young age to the Sisters as boarders until their primary years were complete and they they transferred to a Secondary Boarding school in towns like Tullamore, Navan and even Dublin.

When the Institute for the Deaf and Dumb was opened in 1892, the Convent still provided accommodation for children attending the National School. In fact, boarders continued to attend the National School until 1980's.

Boarders attending the National school was also an important source of income for the Sisters to help maintain the Deaf and Dumb Institute. With the decline in numbers, the pension money supplied for the upkeep of the Institute was not enough and the funds received from keeping National School boarders helped to alleviate this shortfall.

With the closure of the Deaf and Dumb Institute in 1940, the Sisters of Mercy were left with a near empty building, except for the National School boarders. The war years, or the emergency as it was known as here held up any further development of the premises and it wasn't until 1946 that the idea of a Secondary Boarding school for girls was proposed. It was a development that was welcomed also by the local community as there was provision made for local girls to attend as day pupils. The main classroom of the Deaf and Dumb Institute became the Study Hall, and other smaller rooms became classrooms and with an already fitted kitchen, refectory and dormitories, the school was up and running as a Secondary Tops school in 1948.

The Boarding School was organised and competely managed by the Sisters of Mercy and the pupils school day was catered for hour per hour from early morning mass to breakfast, school, dinner, recreation, study, evening tea, study and then to bed. Within that structure also was time for games and those early years camogie was very popular. Hockey then took over as the main games activity for the boarders. It was later superceded by other games such as tennis, basketball and badminton.

The lives of the boarders also centred around drama and musical shows. As the 1950's progressed, pupils prepared an annual musical and shows such as *Pearl the Fisher Maiden,* and *Blossom Time* played to packed houses at the school.

As the 1960's approached and the school accepted boys for the first time, the number of boarders remained steady and as the 1970's arrived, past boarding pupils of the school who were now married began sending their children as boarders as well. It was a reflection in the education the girls received that they were prepared to send their children, following in their footsteps to Rochfortbridg to be educated.

In the late nineteen sixties and early seventies the world was changing fast. Vocations to the priesthood and to the Convents dropped drastically. There was a problem in maintaining boarding schools, as the personnel available within the Religious Orders were not there to manage, supervise and run the boarding schools. Many schools such as Ballyfin College, Bloomfield and Clara closed their doors altogether. In some towns such as Kells, families living a long distance from the school continued to send their children to school there and they boarded with families in the town.

In Rochfortbridge, the life of the boarder changed also and it became a Monday to Friday affair, returning to school on Sunday evening and home again on Friday night.

In the final years of the boarding school at Rochfortbridge, local people were employed to supervise night study and also evening time supervision. The continuation of the school as a boarding school was getting more difficult to manage and towards the end of the nineteen nineties it was decided to phase out the Boarding School altogether. No first years were enrolled and as each year passed, the number of boarders reduced. The boarding school finally closed its doors in 2001 for the last time when the boarders who sat their Leaving Cert that year left St. Josephs.

The building which was originally a family home, an orange lodge, a convent, a primary school, an Institute for the Deaf and Dumb and a boarding school found a new lease of life as additional classrooms for the Secondary School.

The death knell of boarding schools was also sounded with the establishment of free education by the Minister for Education Donagh O'Malley in the 1960's. The introduction of school transport opened new corridors where pupils could be collected and delivered to schools and returned to their family homes in the evening. Accessibility to Secondary Schools was thus made easier.

There are always those questions one can ask in hindsight, *what if?* What if vocations to the Religious Orders continued at a steady pace would boarding schools have survived? The answer is probably yes! Their success as educational establishments was reflected in the willingness of past pupils to send their children to follow in their footsteps to be educated there. Going to a certain school became a family tradition also.

It was here too that life-long friendships were made. A pupil had to adjust to a new life away from the comfort and security of a family unit. The loneliness of these early days and the parting from the family home was a grief shared and within this change, new bonds of friendhips were made. Young men and women on the cusp of adulthood were being prepared to move on to seek further education and to carve out a new career or indeed vocation for themselves. It was a means as well where they learned to organise and manage their own lives and they knew that they could always return to the security of their home. For some people they could never adjust to boarding school, for others it was the making of them and as the years rolled by they were always drawn back to the old alma mater to share for a brief moment some time with friends and to re-live again, the memories of those early days when they first realised there was another world outside the family home.

The Life of a Boarder

In a boarding school life is very different from being at home especially for first years. It is hard to settle in. I myself found it very hard, but now I like it and I've made a lot of new friends and I get a lot more study done.

Here is a story about what we do all day. I get up every morning at half past seven, except Wednesdays, when we get up at ten to eight. We all get up when the bell goes, at least we're supposed to! We make our beds, get washed, put on our clothes and go downstairs to get our blazers and shoes to go to Mass. At about twenty five past eight we come in from Mass and then we go to breakfast.

When breakfast is over we do our morning charge (duty) if we are unlucky enough to have one. Then we go into the study hall and get our books out for that day in school. We then go out and put them in our bag and at five to nine we go to our class. At twenty-past ten we can come down to the locker room if we want to. At half past twelve we all come down to the refectory for dinner.

When Grace after Meals is said, we do our charge if we have one that week.

If we haven't we can either go into the locker room or go around the walks.

After fhat it is time to go back to school until four o'clock when we get tea, bread and cake. Then we are free until five-thirty. Then we all study hard until a quarter past seven when we get our tea.

After tea we do our charge and then we are free until eight O' clock when it's back to study again until half nine. We all go upstairs. Then we get ready for bed. As soon as the lights go out there is supposed to be no more talking although that rarely happens.

Anita Farrell
First Year Journal 1982.

Snack time, with Jenny Larissey and Niamh Smith

Sister Geraldine will you tell us all a bedtime story?

Will ye go away with that camera? Lisa Scanlon and Niamh Smyth enjoying a photographic moment.

Barbara Coyne, all in a haze!

Recreation time for Mary England and Martina Keogh.

Emer Daly and Niamh Coyne.

Sarah Galligan, Niamh Coyne and Barbara Coyne just chillin' out before bedtime.

'No we were not planning a midnight feast Sister!' Sarah Galligan and Maeve Coyne in jovial mood.

The two Niamhs –Niamh Coyne and Niamh Smith.

Christmas Party time for the boarders.

Did ye hear the one about....?' Lisa Fagan, Jenny Larissey, Ethel McKnight, Niamh Coyne and Hazel Scanlon enjoying some free time in the evening.

Picnic time for Lorraine Gorman and Friends.

Fun and frolics in the Study Hall under the watchful eye of Sister Pius, Pauline Loughrey, Helen Keogh, Fiona Smith, Michelle Hayes, Marie Thérése Kilmartin, Mary Curran, Gráinne Walsh, Louise Dunne, Roseanne Kelleghan and Nessa McDermott.

Martina Keogh, Bernadette Plunkett and Mary Young enjoying the fresh air.

Nice badges girls, John Travolta and all that! Mary Greene, Bernadette Flynn and Elizabeth Behan out in the sunshine.

Boarder Geraldine Coyne taking it easy.

Included in this photo are Therese Flynn, Katherine Coyne Helen Cole and Darina Walsh.

Loretto Jones, Catherine O'Rourke and Catherine Cross.

Bridie Reynolds.

Nellie Ryan and Grace Walsh

Geraldine Coyne during her Boarder days.

Geraldine Kelleghan and Bernie Coyne, trying to escape.

Sleeping Beauty, Edel Corcoran.

Bernie Coyne, ready to attack but Geraldine Kellaghan is amused by it all.

Leaders of the sock parade, Rosario Coyne, Geraldine Kellaghan, Majella Coyne and Noeleen Lynam.

The Coyne Factor, Majella Coyne, Sister Geraldine Coyne and Bernie Coyne discuss grave matters, Sr. Geraldine looks so worried.

Noeleen Lynam and Bernie Coyne, make a bid to escape from St. Joseph's.

~ CHAPTER 33 ~
ST. JOSEPH'S SECONDARY SCHOOL
IN THE 1990'S

~ CHAPTER 33 ~
ST. JOSEPH'S SECONDARY SCHOOL
IN THE 1990'S

< *The 1997 Magazine Committee. Front row, left to right: Ciara Devine, Kathleen Hickey, Siobhán Smyth and Naomi O'Farrell. Second row. from left, Paula Garry, Pamela Feery, Claire Halligan, Emer Tomkins and Eleanor Doyle. Third row, from left, Fiona Fagan, Niamh Fitzsimons, Denise Cully, Joan Brogan and Eithne Spellman. Back row, from left, Sinead Curtis and Pauline Walsh. Missing from photo: Pamela Clinton, Claire Broderick and Helen Weir.*

Miss Cavanaugh

Winners of 1st Year Table Quiz 1993 from left to right, Oonagh Donoghue, Derek O'Reilly, Louise Graham and David Horgan.

Student's Council 1992-'93. First row, Caroline Coffey, Sinead Glennon, Anne-Marie Kenny. Second row, Orla Carroll, Sinead Murtagh, Nuala Healy, Fionnuala Dunne and Mary Coghlan. (standing), Jonathan Geraghty and Christopher Lacey.

Students wo took part in the co-operation north project with Killicomaine School in Northern Ireland are form left to right, Sinéad Sherwin, Ciarán Leech, Carmel Rice Ciarán Wright, Martin Reidy, Andy Glennon, Fiona Kenny, _____, Caroline Lynch, Keith Lenehan and Emma Jane Farrelly.

Minor Basketball Team, back row, from left to right, Eileen Coroon, Serena Gavin, Angela Kelly, Nicola Thornton and Tracey Fanning. Middle row, from left to right, Majella McGuane, Ruth Murray, Anne-Marie Kenny and Yvonne Martin. Front row, Linda Mulligan and Shona McCourt.

From left to right, Marina McWalter, Catherine Smith, Ulrika Maher, Linda Cully, Koran Larkin, Martina Croghan (Teacher) Lorna Dunne Eugene Dunbar (Teacher) and Christina from Denmark, who was on a student exchange programme It was a transition year trip to Derry as part of the course, staying in a hostel. The visit included The Derry walls, the Giants Causeway and the Carickareed Bridge!.

Laura Jordan, Raharney and Rosita Carroll from Kildalkey-Navan area got full 600 points in the Leaving Certificate in 1999. They were both pupils of St. Joseph's Secondary School, Rochfortbridge.

Caroline Byrne, Caroline McNamara, Lorraine McNicholas and Jill McQuaid who qualified for the Leinster Final of the 4x100 m senior relay in Santry.

Sr. Dympna welcoming students from Northern Ireland who were hosted by twelve second year students in a Co-operation North Exchange Programme.

Jonathan O'Connor and Alan Gavin aged 16 from Rochfortbtidge. When this photo appeared in Vox, the caption was that they were both better known for their kicking skills on the football field and were compulsive eaters of Milky Mints.

Students Council 1990/1991, from left to right, David Moore, Josephine Kiernan, Raymond Gorman, Yvonne Callaghan, Aisling Donoghue, Suzanne Clarke and Mark Malone. Missing from the photo is Jason Croash.

Helping Sr. Finian and Sister Dympna with some planting and landscaping.

Students from Dronninglund Gymnasium, Gronninglund, Denmark pictured with students from St. Joseph's undertaking a two week exchange programme studying energy and energy conservation in Ireland and Denmark.

Taking a break for tha camera are Caroline Moran, Olive Hyland, Edwina Cleary, Camilla Burke and Tina Owens.

Tony O'Sullivan and Fr. Eamonn O'Brien P.P.

Sister Finian, busy looking after things.

Senior Gaelic Football Team, Back row from left to right, Barry Pierce, Ian Jones, Darren Meehan, Keith Oxley, Mark Dunne, David Mitchell, Alan Gavin, Alan Wright and Adrian Egan. Front row, from left to right, Enda O'Rafferty, Mark Geoghan, Paul Briody, Alan Jones, Roy Malone, Jonathan O'Connor (Capt.) David Muldoon and Patrick Kenny.

Hilda McQuaid and Louise McCauley with their collage work for Crannóg construction.

Under 14, Cross Country Team, back row from left to right, Emma McDermott, Nessa O'Sullivan and Orla McNevin. Middle row, from left to right, Jacqueline McNamara and Linda Mulligan. Front row, Lisa Heavey.

Cadet B Basketball Team. Back row, from left to right, Claire Dardis, Michelle Dardis and Olga Wright. Middle row, from left to right, Ursula Heeney, Anne Carroll and Catherine Maher. Front row, Denise Garry and Anne-Marie Curran.

Junior Boys Tennis Team. Back row, left to right, Michael Carroll, Thomas Larkin, Frank Gorman and John Driver. Front row, from left to right, James Carroll, Clifford Flynn and Eddie Doyle.

Back row left to right, Patrick Gunning, Patrick Cooney, Francy Jessop, Thomas Murphy, Grainne Lynch, John Hyland, Roy Brennan. Front row left to right Kevin Brennan, Tara Kelly, Regina Brennan, Barbara Jones, Fionnuala Dunne and Claire Reid.

On third year Residential in Tiglinn are Camilla Gahan and Patricia Moran.

Jill McQuaid and Karen Corcoran.

Leonie Maher and Rosita Carroll.

Carl Moore, Joe Arthur, Keith Kavanagh and Sinéad Curtis.

Carmel O'Sullivan, Joe Arthur and Adrian Lee on tour.

Project 2000 Competition sponsored by Wrights, Milltownpass, Back row form left to right, Conor McDermott, Olga Scully, C. Leonard, Karen Hawkshaw, Emma Smith, Johanna Giles, C. Duncan, Fiachra Daly and Margaret Giles. Third row, from eft to right, Niamh Casey, Cathy Timlin, Clare Heavy, Siobhán Tone, Catherine McCarthy and Lisa Scanlon. Second row, from left to right, Declan Carey, Marie Harnett, Sr. Geraldine, Leo Wright, Rose Wright and Lorna Bradley. First row, from left to right, O. Geoghagan, L. Kilmurray, M.Casey, Fiona Moody, Louise Gavin, Mr. Kingston, Sinéad Kennedy, Marina Casey, Marina Casey, Pauline Swords and Irene Nugent.

Sharon Leech and Linda Poynton Standing guard over the second year book binding.

Business Awareness Awards 1990, award-winning study of Local Business, The Wright Group, Milltownpass. Back row, left to right, C. McDermott, M.Mea, Olwyn Scully, J. Giles, E. Smith, C. Duncan, C. Timlin and C. Leonard. Third row, from left to right, F. Leavey, M.Harnett, L. Bradley, S. Tone and M. Casey. Second row, from left to right, M. Geoghagan, L.Kilmurray, L. Scanlon, M. Giles and Irene. Nugent. Front row, from left to right, M.Casey, Louise Gavin, F. Murphy, P. Swords and C.McCarthy.

Catherine and Mairéad Smyth, 1996.

Carmel Rice shares a moment with one of the Students from Killicommaine Northern Ireland in the Co-operation North, Student Exchange Programme 1993.

Watchful eyes over busy students.

On tour in Denmark.

Fiona Nally and Caroline Byrne at the local Art Exhibition in 1992.

President's Awards, 1995.
Back row, left to right: Nicola Roundtree, Sinead Sherwin, Carmel Rice, Helen Jordan, Michelle O'Gorman, Sophie McEntee, Christine Ryder and Craig Scully.
Front row, left to right: Carol Gately, Jacinta Feery, Sharon Dardis, Heather Dolan, Gillian Murtagh, Eimear Dunne, Audrey Treacy, Karen Corcoran and Helen Munnelly.

Left to right, Ms. Johanna Walshe, Lisa Whelton, Carol Gately, Jacinta Feery, Therese Martin and Ms. Martina Croghan pictured at the Youth Enterprise Exhibition in Athlone in 1995.

Last minute checking before the exam, Olwyn Scully, deep in thought.

Back row, left to right, Teacher, Sarah Egan, Lisa McCormack, Sharon Leech, Alan Gavigan, Hugh Byrne, David Nugent and Leonie Maher.
Front row (left to right): Valerie Feery, Tracey, Claire Broderick, Rosita Carroll, Francis Heavey and Patrick Kiernan.

The 1997 Magazine Committee. Front row, left to right: Ciara Devine, Kathleen Hickey, Siobhán Smyth and Naomi O'Farrell. Second row.from left, Paula Garry, Pamela Feery, Claire Halligan, Emer Tomkins and Eleanor Doyle. Third row,from left, Fiona Fagan, Niamh Fitzsimons, Denise Cully, Joan Brogan and Eithne Spellman. Back row, from left, Sinead Curtis and Pauline Walsh. Missing from photo: Pamela Clinton, Claire Broderick and Helen Weir.

The Great Radio Debate, 1997. Back row, left to right: Francis Heavy, Claire Broderick, Don Delaney and Breda McCormack. Front row, left to right: Leonie Maher, Derry Kilroy and Roseita Carroll.

Students Council 1997. Left to right: Karen Galligan, Audrey Byrne, Michelle Bardon, David Cleary, Fiona Dardis and Celine Doran. Missing from photo: Iason Leech and Amanda Gavin.

The Coventry Trip - "We sent them to Coventry" and they enjoyed every minute of it. Front row, left to right, Ciara Garry, Liam Croash, John Alford, Jade Milburn and Niall Judge. Back row, left to right: Helen Moore, Philip Sheridan, Caroline Duffy and Derek Keaney.

Editorial Committee Vox 1998- Back row, from left: Fiona Dardis, Celine Doran, Noelle Hawkshaw, Gemma Dardis, Isolde Keaney, Amanda Gavin, Barbara Hynes, middle row, from left, David Cleary, Caoimhe Morris, Elaine Leavy, Gearoid Reidy, Maura Reagan, Christopher Galvin, front row, from left, Lorraine Lenehan, Sonya Quinn, Karen Galligan. (Missing from photo – Lesley Kellegher and Daniel Cahill).

1998. A show took place at Cavan Equestrian center on the 25th of April. This show concerns showmanship. Essentially, this relates to how well the calf is prepared and presented for the show. The calf we entered was not our own but we figured we had a good chance. I was very optimistic about leading the calf. My task involved were (a) grooming the calf, (b) leading the calf before the judge. My job was to lead the calf calmly and efficently. I also had to stand the calf straight in a line and to make sure that the calf was totally relaxed.

The judge asked me some questions concerening the age of the calf and about my method of handling the calf. The judge made the decisions that I was the winner and gave the reasons accordingly. I was delighted with my cup, rosette and cheque. Later on that day, I emerged the Champion of the show. I was very happy with this distinction.

John Kelly.

At the Leaving Cert Mass in 1998, from left to right, Brian Horgan, Brian Fallon, Mark Bagnall and Jim Bollard.

Transition Year April 1996, from left to right, Linda Cully, Lorna Dunne, Catherine Smith and Dolores Flynn.

On tour with Martina Croghan

St. Josepeh's Secondary School, Rochfortbridge Presents
"CINDERELLA"
In The Parish Hall, Rochfortbridge
ON FRIDAY, 13th, SATURDAY, 14th & SUNDAY 15th DECEMBER
At 8 p.m.
MATINEE SUNDAY, 15th AT 3 p.m.
Tickets £4 :: Matinee £2
Booking St Joseph's Secondary School Tel.: (044) 22176

THE GREAT RADIO DEBATE

Back row, left to right: Frances Heavy, Claire Broderick, Don Delaney and Breda McCormack. Front row, left to right: Leonie Maher, Derry Kilroy and Roseita Carroll.

Debating has not been one of the strong points of the Bridge, but when Ms. McCormack asked her transition year class if anyone was interested in debating on radio, four students volunteered, just enough for a team. Leonie Maher, with a gift of the gab, Francis Heavy, our budding journalist, Claire Brodrick, noted for her interesting movements on the court in Tallaght, and well, me, proved to make quite a good combination.

After our substitute was decided on (poor Francis had to wait his turn), we received our motion. After momentary horror at the idea of opposing that "Ireland is a nation of bedgrudgers", we got to work, grateful to Sister Dympna and many others for allowing us to be excused from the 'odd' class. The first round on the 16/02/97 against the three girls from Mount Mellick, chaired by Don Delaney, was an enjoyable and interesting experience. We all found radio microphones, headphones and rooms carpeted from floor to ceiling quite a novelty, (not to mention Don's tie, Claire!). To our delight we won and indulged ourselves in Supermacs.

A month later the whole process started again with Claire taking a rest and Francis stepping in. Once again we were opposing the motion, against three girls from the Sacred Heart in Tullamore, and proved that "a united Ireland is not the answer to all our troubles".

Alas no rest for the wicked. Soon after Easter we received

our motion for the semi-final and set to work, opposing the motion that "The travelling community are 2nd class citizens in this country". Thanks to Mr. Dunbar and Mr. Bennett for filling in for a few days while Ms. McCormack was enjoying herself in Coventry. This proved to be a more interesting debate, nothing to do with the fact that we were pitted against three lads (Michael, Mark and John), from the Cistercian College in Roscrea! It was here unfortunately that our crusade to victory and to getting a decent computer came to an end. On a two to one majority from the three adjudicators, we resigned ourselves to coming in the top four, while the 'socialising' helped to compensate for some of us, and of course, Supermacs!

The final was held on the 7/5/97 with a school from Clara winning the competition. However, Kilroys had generously supplied all semi-finalists with plaques which we received at lunch time that day. While seeing the trophies and computer that might have been ours was rather sad, it wasn't all bad. Claire got to see Don's tie again while Francis admired the shirts, ties and Oakley sunglasses of the lads from Roscrea. Leonie and I make no comment! We finished up in ... yes, you've guessed in Supermacs. All in all it was an excellent experience, educational and enjoyable.

ROSEITA CARROLL

SR. PIUS'S RETIREMENT

*Sister Pius Doran plants a tree in the school grounds on the
occassion of her retirement from teaching in 1990.*

Pat Eighan and Sister Pius share a moment.

Sister Pius cuts the cake at her retirement function in 1990.

BOG STUDIES - 1996

Left ot right, Pádraig Leavy, Damien Duffy, Gordon McDonnell, and Fergal Dardis. May 1996.

Damien Molloy, Jennifer Conroy, Aoife, Fitzimons and Niall Plunkett.

Niall McAteer, Francis Kenny, Barry Dully and Liam Byrne.

Martin Dowdall, Gary Lusk, Owen Miller and Barry O'Farrell.

Grace Kelly and Caitríona Leogue.

Aoibheann Gavigan, Aishling Sheridan, Michelle Hernes and Sinead Barrett.

*Dearbhla O'Sullivan, Sarah Graham, Paul Connolly
and Ronan Hogan.*

*Brendan Cullen, Christopher Glennon, Alan McGuire,
Conor Daly and Joe Lynch.*

Lorna Hoye, Fiona Dardis, Heather Flanagan and Lorraine Lenehan.

~ CHAPTER 34 ~
THE TRADITION OF MUSIC AT ST. JOSEPH'S

~ CHAPTER 34 ~
THE TRADITION OF MUSIC
AT ST. JOSEPH'S

"Music, of all the arts, stands in a special region, unlit by any star but its own,
and utterly without meaning ... except its own."
Leonard Bernstein

From the very beginning music and things musical became part and parcel of the curriculum at the Convent of Mercy, Rochfortbridge. One of the earliest pieces of furniture supplied to the Sisters was a piano donated by the Coffey family, Newcastle. There are countless references in the annals to the sisters providing a little light entertainment for their own amusement on occassions such as Christmas night, as well as concerts at Christmas provided by the children of the national school for family and friends.

In the book *The Story of a Valiant Woman,* Sister Bernard Grogan records how Mother Mary Paul Fielding in her Autumn years recalled times in Rochfortbridge during the twelve years she served with the Sisters of Mercy from 1863 to 1865. During those years she taught piano at the convent. She was a gifted piano player and she taught some of the children on the new convent piano. She recalled also those early years when the new parish church was in its infancy and the attempts made by the parishioners to provide a choir and some singing at the Sunday masses and other ceremonies throughout the Church year. The music was of a poor quality, but their hearts were in the right place. She recalls also a young lad who provided accompaniment rather poorly on a flute or tin whistle.

It was from these early beginnings the Sisters of Mercy nurtured music in their schools and they recorded meticulously in the Annals, the examinations and the number of children who sat the exams annually. The grades received were recorded also and in time, this became a good reason to advertize the school and the standard of education provided at the national School. An example of this is the publication of the annual results in the local paper shown on the table, from the Westmeath Examiner dated the 5th of May 1928. It displays the high standard achieved by the children who underwent these examinations.

RESULT OF MUSIC EXAMINATIONS CONVENT OF MERCY, ROCHFORTBRIDGE

At the recent examinations held at the above Convent, Miss Congreve of Leinster College of music examined. Thirteen pupils were presented, all obtained first class honours.

Primary Grade

Maureen Bradley	First Class Honours
Eamon Gavin	First Class Honours

Preparatory Grade

Theckla Rowan	First Class Honours
Nan Kelly	First Class Honours
Kitty Fallon	First Class Honours
Nuala O'Farrell	First Class Honours (And a Prize)

Junior Grade I

Barbara Rowan	First Class Honours
Rosemary Smith	First Class Honours
M.M. Gorman	First Class Honours
Agnes Rowan	First Class Honours
Nancy Gavin	First Class Honours
Moira O'Farrell	First Class Honours

Junior Grade II

Mary B. Egan	First Class Honours

Violin

Agnes Rowan	First Class Honours

It was not until the opening of St. Joseph's Secondary School that music took on a new dimension. When the school was first recognised as a Secondary School in 1952 a school choir entered for the Department of Education Examinations and each succeeding year since, the school choirs have performed with distinction, even reaching such heights as the RTE School Choir Competitions held annually.

When Sister Dolores Carroll entered the Convent of Mercy as a young postulant in the 1950's, she brought with her a great passion for music and everything musical. She has served the community for many years at Sunday masses and ceremonies throughout the Church year by playing the church organ and directing the choir from the choir gallery, and accompanying the singing on the fine Church Organ. In this year 2012, she continues her work with the choir, and her work is very much appreciated in the parish.

As a young nun, she too was sent away for further studies and taking all that knowledge back with her to St. Josephs, she taught music for many years. But it was in the mid 1950's that a new chapter opened in the musical life of the school.

The venue for many of the concerts produced at the National School was the convent hall and in the early years of St. Joseph's Secondary School it was used for their productions also. On the 18th of March 1956, a variety show was produced at the Convent Hall and performed by the girls from St. Josephs. Comprising of songs and dances, highland flings, scarf dances, dutch dances, and reels, they were joined on stage by *the Brownies*. These were the little boarders who attended the Primary school. The second half of the concert was a performance of the courtroom scene from *The Merchant of Venice*, by William Shakespeare.

In 1958, a new assembly hall was built at St. Joseph's with a large stage and open theatre lay-out which provided greater facilities for the production of shows and concerts.

On the 17th and 20th of March 1960, St. Joseph's produced its first great musical *'Pearl the Fisher Maiden.'* It played to a packed house each night, with very colourful dance routines, singing and a great array of costumes.

This was followed at Christmas 1960 with the performance of two productions *The Stranger* and a nativity based play *Wonder Night*.

St. Josephs was now beginning to shine as a school for musical productions. Under the guidance of Sister Dolores another show was in preparation to correspond with the centenary of the Sisters of Mercy at Rochfortbridge in 1962. *Blossom Time* by Franz Schubert is an account of Schubert's early life and his attempts to *break* into music as a composer. There was a play on the words *Blossom Time* which was read by one of the students in the citation at the beginning of the production, which reflected the work and the blossoming of the Convent of Mercy and its achievements in the years from 1862 to 1962.

> *My Lord, very Reverend and Reverend Fathers, Sisters, Ladies and Gentlemen.*
>
> *On behalf of the students of St. Joseph's Secondary School at Rochfortbridge, I bid you welcome to this entertainment which is part of the celebrations that mark the Centenary year of the founding of our Convent.*
>
> *A hundred years ago the Sisters of Mercy were invited by the then Parish Priest, Fr. Robbins, to make a foundation in his Parish to look after the poor, to nurse the sick and to give elementary education. From the moment of their arrival they became part of the organization known as the Diocese of Meath and as such received encouragement and help from Bishop, Priests and Laity. To such good effect was this help and encouragement given, in times of poverty famine and ignorance, that the community then established, has from small beginnings grown to its present stature.*
>
> *We as Students, are fully conscious of the benefits we enjoy here, thanks to the continued encouragement and help of successive Bishops, Priests and Sisters of the Diocese. Many of these have long since passed to their reward, but you are still with us and through you, we thank you all.*
>
> *Hence with grateful hearts, we welcome you to this establishment, which, under the guidance of the good Sisters, we have prepared for your amusement. A hundred years ago, the seed was sown. Since then the tree has grown and now, it is **BLOSSOM TIME**.*

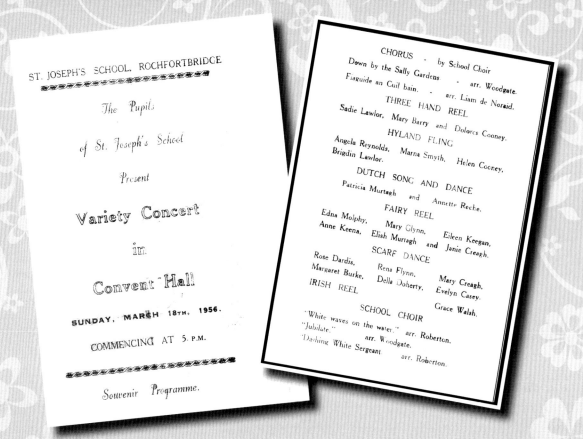

ST. JOSEPH'S SCHOOL, ROCHFORTBRIDGE

The Pupils

of St. Joseph's School

Present

Variety Concert

in

Convent Hall

SUNDAY, MARCH 18TH, 1956.

COMMENCING AT 5. P.M.

Souvenir Programme.

CHORUS - by School Choir
Down by the Sally Gardens - arr. Woodgate.
Fiaguide an Cuil bain. - arr. Liam de Noraid.
THREE HAND REEL
Sadie Lawlor, Mary Barry and Dolores Cooney.
HYLAND FLING
Angela Reynolds, Marna Smyth, Helen Cooney,
Brigdin Lawlor.
DUTCH SONG AND DANCE
Patricia Murtagh and Annette Roche.
FAIRY REEL
Edna Molphy, Mary Glynn, Eileen Keegan,
Anne Keena, Elish Murtagh and Janie Creagh.
SCARF DANCE
Rose Dardis, Rena Flynn, Mary Creagh.
Margaret Burke, Della Doherty, Evelyn Casey.
IRISH REEL Grace Walsh.
SCHOOL CHOIR
"White waves on the water." arr. Roberton.
"Jubilate." arr. Woodgate.
"Dashing White Sergeant arr. Roberton.

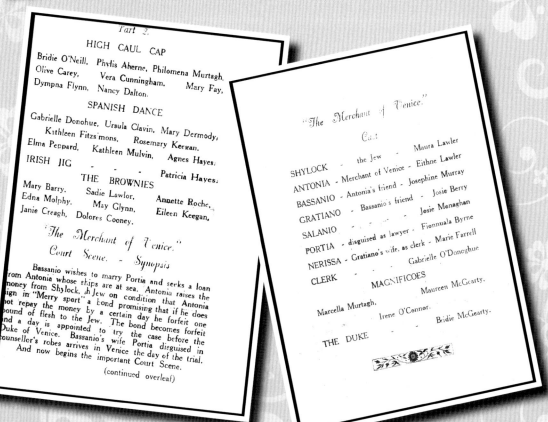

Part 2.
HIGH CAUL CAP
Bridie O'Neill, Phylis Aherne, Philomena Murtagh,
Olive Carey, Vera Cunningham, Mary Fay,
Dympna Flynn, Nancy Dalton.
SPANISH DANCE
Gabrielle Donohue, Ursula Clavin, Mary Dermody,
Kathleen Fitzs'mons, Rosemary Keegan.
Elma Peppard, Kathleen Mulvin, Agnes Hayes.
IRISH JIG - - -
Patricia Hayes.
THE BROWNIES
Mary Barry, Sadie Lawlor, Annette Roche.
Edna Molphy, May Glynn, Eileen Keegan,
Janie Creagh, Dolores Cooney.
"The Merchant of Venice."
Court Scene. - Synopsis
Bassanio wishes to marry Portia and seeks a loan
from Antonia whose ships are at sea. Antonia raises the
money from Shylock, ih Jew on condition that Antonia
sign in "Merry sport" a bond promising that if he does
not repay the money by a certain day he forfeit one
pound of flesh to the Jew. The bond becomes forfeit
and a day is appointed to try the case before the
Duke of Venice. Bassanio's wife Portia disguised in
counsellor's robes arrives in Venice the day of the trial.
And now begins the important Court Scene.
(continued overleaf)

"The Merchant of Venice."
Cast
SHYLOCK - the Jew - Maura Lawler
ANTONIA - Merchant of Venice - Eithne Lawler
BASSANIO - Antonia's friend - Josephine Murray
GRATIANO - Bassanio's friend - Josie Berry
SALANIO - Josie Monaghan
PORTIA - disguised as lawyer - Fionnuala Byrne
NERISSA - Gratiano's wife, as clerk - Marie Farrell
CLERK - Gabrielle O'Donoghue
MAGNIFICOES
Maureen McGearty,
Marcella Murtagh,
Irene O'Connor.
THE DUKE - Bridie McGearty.

Programme from Show in 1956

The show played to great acclaim and there were a number of performances during the month of October 1962. It was also given great mention in the Westmeath Examiner:

> The pupils of the Convent gave a sparkling performance of that lively, lilting opera, "Blossom.Time," with the music of Franz Schubert. It was one of the best productions in St. Joseph's since the school started putting on annual performances.
>
> This was only as it should be, in the centenary year.
>
> The production, orchestra, lighting, scenery, make-up and all the very essential ingredients that go into a production like this were excellent.
>
> The dance numbers, especially the ballet received a very well-deserved encore as did some of the beautiful duets in this well-performed opera.
>
> Apart from the splendid music, the story itself is a moving one, tracing Schubert's battle for recognition as a composer. It has many romantic scenes and a good sprinkling of sparkling comedy.
>
> What a sweet voice Miss S. Tyson(Vicki) has, and this gift was well appreciated by the audience; she received quite a number of encores. Miss M. Murphy as Schubert gave the right touch of docility and hope that the part called for, while Miss V. O'Reilly(how difficult it is to write Miss before the names of those playing the roles of young gentlemen –they looked their parts) as Wimpassinger the dancing teacher, was the perfect happy fond of the brandy tutor of the light fantastic with the first class manner of getting 'his' witty lines across. He had an excellent accomplice in the romantic scenes in the bright vivacious Countess –Miss A. Campbell. Miss C. Flynn as Lafont gave dignified and very human characterization that her part demanded, while Miss S. Lawler as the Count was a properly military-looking and acting 'Gentleman.'
>
> Miss A. Lynch took the role of the Archduchess and quite regal she looked. This was a charming performance.[1]

Other productions, followed, most notably, *The Message of Fatima* which took place in 1964, a year following the admission of boys for the first time.

Following this there was a lull in show production as Sister Dolores went away to further studies in Music. The school put on a number of annual concerts under the direction of Sr. Regina O'Reilly, who as a student played the part of Wimpassinger in *Blossom Time*.

In 1968, Fr. John McManus P.P. celebrated the golden Jubilee of his ordination and there were events in the parish to mark this occassion. A gala concert co-production between the Convent Primary School and St. Joseph's Secondary school was organised and a Sunday Matinee performance and a night show took place in the spring of that year.

---

1   Westmeath Examiner 11th October 1962

With the advent of free education and school transport it had become more difficult for schools to indulge in extra curricular activities. School buses were now the norm and pupils were quickly whisked away homeward at the end of the school day. In later years, examinations and points systems were uppermost in the minds of parents and pupils alike.

But under the surface, music and concerts continued at St. Joseph's into the 1970's. Annual carol concerts took place within the school and performed at times to allow school buses to take pupils home on time.

When Father Colm Murtagh C.C. was appointed to the Parish in the early 1970's he began a series of fund-raising events such as sports and parish walks to raise funds to build a new Church at Milltownpass. During the winter he organised weekly quizzes among the various parish organizations and to go along with that there were some song and dance routines prepared by Sister Dolores mainly among the boarders. They were available to practise after school each evening and the girls performed on stage in St. Joseph's Hall, which added greatly to the variety and entertainment and enjoyed by everyone.

During the late 1960's and early 1970's some members of the Sisters of Mercy were sent off to college to study for their degrees in various subjects and disciplines and when they returned to St. Joseph's they brought back with them, skills they acquired at Secondary School as well as at University. Sr. Geraldine Coyne has over the years been at the helm of musicals and shows within the school. As a student, she took part in those earlier productions at St. Josephs and it was such memorable performances that nurtured a great love of music and stage among many past pupils. In the Spring of 1975, Sr. Geraldine, along with Sr. Genevieve Doherty, Eugene Dunbar, Nuala Lawlor and Tony Hartnett - all new teachers at the school entered into the realms of the new phenomenon of the modern era *the Rock Opera*.

Andrew Lloyd Webber's *Joseph and His Amazing Technicolor Dreamcoat* had made its way all the way from the World Stage in London and New York to Rochfortbridge. It was an excellent production with limited resources. The main characters of Joseph and Pharoah were played by first years Pascal Dunne and Paddy Gavin. It was the talking point among many people, young an old for a long time in the parish.

For a number of years after that St. Joseph's continued producing shows and concerts organised by the students under the guidance of some of the teachers right into the 1980's. One of the most memorable productions was *Scrooge* with Patrick Dowdall playing the part of Scrooge and Aidan Dunne as Bob Cratchitt. Louise Dunne played his wife. Michael Kilmartin acted the part of Tiny Time very well also. It was a daunting task for Aidan to carry tiny Tim round the stage. But it was work well done. They went their separate ways, Aidan a member of the Garda Síochána and Fr. Michael is a curate in Mullingar parish.

But it was in 1984, that St. Joseph's returned big time to the stage in a co-production with St. Finian's College Mullingar. St. Finian's had for most of it's history a tradition of producing many of the Savoy operas or more popularly known as the operas of Gilbert and Sullivan.

Like St. Joseph's in the early sixties, where girls had to play male parts, in the St. Finian's productions, female parts were played by the boys. It was recorded at one of the productions that there were some very beautiful maidens on stage giggling with a flurry of fans, but following that the next day, the same maidens were fit to knock another fellow to the ground in a football tackle.

Under the baton of Shane Brennan, *Patience* was brought to the stage in St. Finian's College, Mullingar with the female parts provided by the girls from St. Joseph's Rochfortbridge. Sister Geraldine Coyne took on the role of directing the girls in their musical numbers at St. Joseph's and then rehearsals began in full swing at St. Finian's college. The show played to packed houses from the 29th of November till the 2nd of December 1984. This show was such a success that a further production *The Mikado* followed in 1986 and St. Joseph's was making its mark as a school where stage production was of an excellent standard.

As the 1990's approached the school began putting on annual pantomime productions such as *Jack and The Beanstalk* and *Cinderella*. These shows were staged in St. Joseph the worker hall and the productions included as many pupils from the school as were willing to take part.

In 1998, Niamh Moloney, decided to produce the show *Oliver* loosely based on the Dickens Classic *Oliver Twist*, but adapted for the stage by Lionel Bart. Such big productions were now possible as with the opening of the Sports Hall in 1992, there was no shortage of space, to erect a large stage and to seat comfortably large audiences, as the school population was rising fast and reaching levels as high as eight hundred.

The subsequent productions were of mammoth proportions and of excellent professional quality. Quite a number of past pupils from these productions have gone further afield in stage and theatre production as a result of their performances and experience at these shows. The pictorial record of these productions speak multitudes in relation to these events and this article will just give a brief account of them.

Joseph and His Amazing and Technicolor Dreamcoat 2005

Oklahoma 2007

Back to the Eighties 2008

Les Miserables 2011

There is something in music that lights the soul. It begins at a very early age and the child is attracted to it. So when the little child starts school, the little nursery rhymes and songs are the first learnings off by heart they have and become embedded deeply in memory. The lasting joy of listening to or performing music, whether it be instrument or voice is probably a force that bring people together. The guiding hand of the teacher whether at junior level, second or even third level holds the minds and hearts of those who are willing to perform and enjoy this medium which we have inherited from the Lord God above. It is the little seed sown by Eliza Fielding when she taught piano or listened to the simple sounds of a boy playing a simple flute accompanying a choir in the new parish church. This seed has indeed flourished and just as the citation read in 1962 on the centenary of the Sisters of Mercy, the Tree has grown it is now blossom time. Now the blossoms have borne fruit. This can be seen in the continuing advancement of Education in Rochfortbridge in both the Primary and the Secondary School. Music has played a very important part in that bossoming and to conclude this chapter I'll finish as I began with a quotation from Leonard Bernstein with his thoughts on the art of Music.

"Any great art work ... revives and readapts time and space, and the measure of its success is the extent to which it makes you an inhabitant of that world - the extent to which it invites you in and lets you breathe its strange, special air."

EARLY MUSICALS

PEARL THE FISHER MAIDEN
1960

Back row, from left to right, Betty Carey, Ann Coughlan, Kathleen Hyland, Patricia Corrigan, Mary McAuley, Teresa Cunningham, Eileen Dardis, Kathleen O'Reilly, Rosaleen Gunning, Patricia Gouldsberry, Mary Wiley, Margaret Allen, Louie Leavy, Margaret Clabby, Teresa O'Connor, Margaret Murtaghand Rita Connolly.
Fourth row, from left to right, Eithne McArdle, Mary Cross, Mary Greville, Frances Corrigan, Sadie Lawler, Elma Pappard, Annette Roche, Shelagh Tyson, Mary Dunne, Attracta McArdle, Avril Kirkpatrick, Ann Leach, Triona Murray, Anne Cross, Rosemary Keegan and Anne Fallon.
Third row, from left to right, Doreen wiley, Anne Campbell, Angela Reynolds, Patricia Reynolds, Joy Smith, Rita O'Donoghue, Mary Ellen O'Hara, Sally Troy, Sheila Hayes, Anne Conroy, Olive Molphy and Margaret Cross.
Second row, from left to right, Catherine Molloy, Veronica Austin, Daphne Kirkpatrick, Joan Murtagh, Rose Coleman, Geraldine Gavin, Grace Walshe and Dorothy Smith.
Front row, from left to right, Gretta Bradley, Josie Austin, Mary Murphy, Mona Murray, Bernadette Cooney, Mary Doyle, Bridie McCabe, Kathleen Fox, Teresa Dennigan, Mary Flynn and Anne Lynch.

Back row, from left to right, Margaret Cross, _____, Rosie Gunning, Ann Leech, Sadie Lawlor,
Mary Dunne, Elma Peppard, Louie Leavey, Margaret Clabby and_____.
Middle row, from left to right, Kathleen O'Reilly, Olive Molphy, Mary Cross, Mary Wiley, Eileen Dardis,
Margaret Allen, Rita Connolly, Rosemary Keegan, Ann Fallon and Greta Bradley.
Front row, from left to right, Patricia Gouldsberry, _____, Avril Kirkpatrick, _____, Ann Campbell,
Enda Molphy, Mary B. Murphy and Ann Cross.

From left to right, Angela Reynolds, Patricia Reynolds, Joy Smith, Rita O'Donoghue, Sheila Tyson, M.E. O Hara,
Sally Troy, Sheila Hayes and Ann Conroy.

The Floral Dance. From left to right, Daphne Kirkpatrick, Joan Murtagh, Geraldine Gavin, Rosie Coleman, Grace Walshe and Veronica Austin.

Sheila Tyson, Mary Dunne, Annette Roche, Elma Peppard and Sadie Lawler.

SYNOPSIS

Act 1 opens with Pearl and her companions assembled outside Daddy Whelk's cottage celebrating Pearl's birthday. Lorenzo (a Brigand Chief) enters with his companions, all disguised as Spanish merchantmen. Lorenzo, who has fallen in love with Pearl, promises to give up his bringandage if she will consent to marry him. She learns of his identity and goes to plead with the king for her lover's pardon. If her request is refused Lorenzo's only hope of freedom is a paper which he possesses and which holds some secret concerning the King.

INTERVAL

Act II.

Pearl is presented to the King at his palace and there she begs the Royal pardon for her lover. The King refuses to grant liberty to the "traitor chief" and pronounces the death sentence.

Act III.

Lorenzo appears before the court and produces the precious document which reveals the real identity of the Brigand Chief. Lorenzo is, in reality, the King's long lost son. The document also holds good news for Pearl, and all ends happily with bridal bells.

We wish to thank sincerely our patrons and all who helped to produce this performance.

THE PUPILS

OF

ST. JOSEPH'S SCHOOL,

ROCHFORTBRIDGE

present

"PEARL, THE FISHERMAIDEN"

IN ST. JOSEPH'S HALL

ON 17th & 20th MARCH, 1960

Programme ———————— 3d.

WESTMEATH EXAMINER LTD., MULLINGAR.

PRINCIPALS

(In order of appearance).

PEARL (Fishermaiden)	Mary Dunne
FILLETTE (Fishermaiden)	Anne Leech
DADDY WHELK (Retired Sailor)	Sadie Lawler
DAME WHELK (His wife)	Elma Peppard
LORENZO (Brigand Chief)	Shelagh Tyson
PETRUARCH (Lorenzo's friend)	Rita O'Donoghue
KING ALPHONSO	Annette Roche
LORD CHAMBERLAIN	Attrfacta McArdle
JESTER	Avril Kirkpatrick
MISTRESS OF BEDCHAMBER	Patricia Corrigan
1st OFFICER	Margaret Cross
2nd OFFICER	Doreen Wiley
1st FOOTMAN	Triona Murray
2nd FOOTMAN	Frances Corrigan
ATTENDANTS	Dorothy Smyth and Catherine Molloy.

CONDUCTOR .... MR. HALLETT.

BRIGANDS:

Sally Troy, Patricia Reynolds, Angela Reynolds, Mary E. O'Hara, Sheila Hayes, Joy Smith, Anne Conroy.

CHORUS OF FISHERMAIDENS AND COURTIERS

Rosemary Keegan, Anne Cross, Anne Fallon, Gretta Bradley, Teresa Dennigan, Margaret Clabby, Mary Murphy, Rita Connolly, Margaret Allen, Enda Molphy, Margaret Murtagh, Bridie McCabe, Mary Cross, Mary Flynn, Mary Wiley, Mona Murray, Anne Coghlan, Mary Doyle, Bernadette Cooney, Kathleen Hyland, Josie Austin, Kathleen Fox, Teresa O'Connor, Eileen Dardis, Patricia Gouldsbury, Teresa Cunningham, Rosaleen Gunning, Anne Campbell, Kathleen O'Reilly, Eithne McArdle, Maura Greville, Anne Lynch, Olive Molphy, Mary McAuley, Louie Leavy.

DANCE OF MERMAIDS AND FLORAL DANCE

Geraldine Gavin, Grace Walshe, Joan Murtagh, Daphne Kirkpatrick, Veronica Austin, Rose Coleman.

EARLY MUSICALS

BLOSSOM TIME - 1962

THE STORY

The story of "Blossom Time" is a story of the gay Vienna a century before it was to experience the desolation of two World Wars. It is a story also of Franz Schubert and his immortal music.

It is the Spring of 1826 and the trees are laden with blossoms. Schubert, a young musician, is as yet unknown outside the circle of a few friends. In an effort to gain recognition he has written his "Marche Militaire" for the Imperial Court but without result. His friends arrange a concert of his songs and engage a famous opera singer to sing them, but this is a failure too. He is in love with Vicki, the daughter of Wimpassinger, a dancing teacher, but he is too timid, to reveal it until it is too late. Vicki has fallen in love with Rudi Von Hohenberg, a young officer in the Imperial Guard. Schubert is annoyed with the Archduchess because she has ignored his music, and he writes a lampoon about her. Vicki, afraid she is going to lose Rudi, confides in Lafont, and at his suggestion she sings the lampoon in the public street. It has the desired effect. She is arrested and then demands to be taken before the Archduchess herself. Schubert, as the author of the lampoon, is also arrested. In the course of the proceedings they are amazed to learn that the Archduchess herself was crossed in love in her youth. Schubert appeals for Vickie and Rudi in his now famous "Once there lived a Lady Fair." Her Imperial Highness softens and the young lovers are united. Schubert is commissioned to write music for the Court, and so begins his rapid climb to fame.

Schubert died at the early age of thirty-six, but his music is still ringing round the world of our own day.

DEO GRATIAS
1862 ✠ 1962
Convent of Our Lady of Mercy,
Rochfortbridge
OCTOBER, 1962

●

CENTENARY
CELEBRATIONS

●

THE PUPILS OF THE SECONDARY SCHOOL

PRESENT

"BLOSSOM TIME"

(MUSIC BY FRANZ SCHUBERT)

WESTMEATH EXAMINER LTD., MULLINGAR

The 'Blossom Time' Centenary Programme.

DRAMATIS PERSONÆ

Franz Schubert	M. MURPHY
Mayrhofer)	(C. BRADLEY
Schwindt) Friends of	(MGT. CROSS
Lulu) Schubert	(M. DALY
Elsa)	(M. CROSS
Lafont (An Antique Dealer)	C. FLYNN
Wimpassinger (Dancing Teacher)	V. O'REILLY
Vicki (His Daughter)	S. TYSON
Count Rudi Von Hohenberg	S. LAWLER
Wili (His Friend)	C. TYSON
Archduchess Maria Viktoria	A. LYNCH
Therese (Her Ward)	G. GAVIN
Lucie) Ladies in	(G. COYNE
Wilhemina) Waiting	(P. GERAGHTY
Countess Fritzi Frangipani	A. CAMPBELL
Vogl (An Opera Singer)	U. GAFFNEY
Colonel of the Imperial Guard	M. CLONAN
Major of the Imperial Guard	A. DOWD
	(B. BOLLARD
Gendarmes	(
	(D. WILEY

OFFICERS OF THE IMPERIAL GUARD:

B. Cooney, M. Meagher, M. O'Rourke, K. Coyne,
M. Bollard, M. Clabby, M. Ring.

LADIES OF THE COURT:

J. McManus, H. Cole, M. Doyle, N. Ryan, M. O'Connor,
E. McEnroe, A. Leech, K. Fox, C. Cross.

CITIZENS:

P. O'Reilly, A. Cooney, T. Flynn, H. Clabby, T. O'Connell,
M. Flood, M. O'Connor, E. McEnroe, K. Fox, D. Smyth,
C. Cross, R. Gunning, C. O'Reilly, A. Leech.

BALLET GIRLS:

A. Dardis, O. Molphy, K. O'Reilly, N. McGrath,
P. McGrath, M. McEnroe, C. O'Rourke.

SYNOPSIS OF SCENES

ACT I.

Scene I: The Courtyard and street outside Wimpassinger's House.

Scene II: An Anteroom at the Archduchess's Palace.

Scene III.: Wimpassinger's Studio (five minutes later).

Scene IV.: The same as Scene II. (twenty minutes later).

Scene V.: The same as Scene I. (a week later).

ACT II.

Scene I.: The Ballroom at the Palace.

Scene II.: Behind the Stage at the Alexandra Concert Hall.

Scene III.: The Stage at the Alexandra Concert Hall

Scene IV.: The same as Scene I. (half an hour later).

The play is set in Vienna in the Spring of 1826

*The Citation which was read to the guests at the Centenary
Celebrations on the 2nd of October 1962.*

*The Cast of 'Blossom Time', Back row, from left to right, Helen Cole, Ann Leech, Geraldine Coyne, Thérése Flynn, Jean
McManus, _____, _____, Margaret Clabby, _____, _____, _____ and Therese
O'Connell.*
*Third row, from left to right, _____, Dorothy Smith, Catherine Cross, _____, Margaret Doyle, Katherine
Coyne, Margaret Meagher, Marjorie Ring, Mary Bollard, Doreen Wiley, Nellie Ryan, Mary O'Rourke, _____,
_____ and Rosie Gunning.*
*Second row, from left to right, Cepta Bradley, Mary Clonan, Anne Lynch, Carmel Flynn, Christine Tyson, Sadie Lawler,
Sheila Tyson, Mary Murphy, Vera O'Reilly, Ann Campbell, Ursula Gaffney, Margaret Cross and Anne O'Dowd.*
*Front row, from left to right, Mary Daly, Olive Molphy, Ann Dardis, Maureen McEnroe, Catherin O'Rourke, Kathleen
O'Reilly, Nancy McGrath, Pauline McGrath and Mary Cross.*

Members of the cast of 'Blossom Time' 1962. Back row from left to right, Geraldine Coyne, Philomena Geraghty, _____, Margaret Maher, Maura O'Rourke, Marjorie Ring, Christine Tyson, Mary Bollard, Margaret Clabby, Catherine Coyne and Bernadette Cooney.
Front row, from left to right, Ann O'Dowd, Carmel Flynn, Ann Lynch, Mary Clonan, Nelly Ryan, Ann Leech, Catherine Cross, Margaret Connel, Margaret Doyle, Kathleen Fox, Eithne McEnroe, Jean McManus and Mary Flood.

The Gallant soldiers, from left to right, Ann O'Dowd, Margaret Maher, Marjorie Ring, Maura O'Rourke, Bernadette Cooney, Christine Tyson, Margaret Clabby, Mary Bollard, Catherine Coyne and Mary Clonan.

Sadie Lawlor and Sheila Tyson.

Vera O'Reilly and Ann Campbell.

Back row, from left to right, Geraldine Coyne, Nelly Ryan, Jean McManus, Vera O' Reilly, Margaret Doyle, Eithne McEnroe and Philomena Geraghty.
Front row, from left to right, Ann Lynch, Helen Cole, Ann Leech, Kathleen Fox and Catherine Cross.

EARLY MUSICALS

THE STRANGER & WONDER NIGHT - 1960

"THE STRANGER"

The curtain rises on a field at harvest time. We meet the Merry Peasant and his friends. The Wild Rider announces the arrival of the soldiers. The Colonel orders that all the reapers leave their work to search for the lost Princess Rosalie. The Merry Peasant refuses to leave his work and is threatened with arrest when the local Squire arrives and saves the situation. The Poet gives a description of the Princess and is applauded by a Tinker who brings with him a ragged little waif. The latter is frightened by the entrance of a Stranger who claims to have wonderful magical powers. By this power the Princess is found and the scene concludes with a public holiday for all the workers.

WESTMEATH EXAMINER LTD., MULLINGAR

THE PUPILS OF ST. JOSEPH'S SCHOOL,
ROCHFORTBRIDGE

PRESENT

"THE STRANGER"

AND

NATIVITY PLAY

"WONDER NIGHT"

IN ST. JOSEPH'S HALL.

Christmas ———— 1960

PROGRAMME .... 3d.

The Progamme for 'The Stanger' and 'Wonder Night.

"THE STRANGER"

(Characters in order of appearance)

THE MERRY PEASANT .... Sadie Lawler
HIS WIFE .... Ann Campbell
THE WILD RIDER .... Margaret Cross
THE COLONEL .... Mary C. Murphy
THE HUNTER .... Ann Lynch
THE POET .... Margaret Allen
THE TINKER .... Christine Tyson
THE ORPHAN .... Geraldine Coyne
THE STRANGER .... Annette Roche

THE PEASANT REAPERS:

A. Fallon, M. Clabby, K. O'Reilly, R. Gunning, K. Keegan, Mary Cross, A. Kirkpatrick, O. Molphy, G. Walshe, A. Dardis, C. Bradley, M. Doyle, V. O'Reilly, C. O'Reilly, M. Ring, M. Clonan, M. Mahon, J. McManus, O. Bruton, P. O'Reilly.

SOLDIERS:

G. Bradley, D. Wiley, T. Cunningham, A. Conroy.

NATIVITY PLAY

"WONDER NIGHT"

OUR BLESSED LADY .... Bernadette Cooney
ST. JOSEPH .... Margaret Murtagh
ST. ELIZABETH .... Mary E. O'Hara
THE ANGEL GABRIEL .... Eileen Dardis
MYRA .... Mary Dunne
INNKEEPER .... Rita O'Donoghue
GRANDMOTHER .... Mary Flynn
SILAS .... Carmel Flynn
DANIEL .... Ann Campbell
EZRA .... Ann Leech
FIRST GUARD .... A. Roche
SECOND GUARD .... S. Lawier
GAOLER .... Maria Maher

CHILD ANGELS:

G. Gavin, J. Murtagh, M. McEnroe, R. Coleman, V. Austin, E. McEnroe, D. Kirkpatrick, C. Molloy, D. Smith.

GUESTS:

T. O'Connell, T. Dennigan, M. B. Murphy, T. Murray, N. Curran, J. Austin, C. Fay, L. Leavy, M. Wiley, M. O'Reilly, M. Harte, M. Briody, M. Brennan, M. Gunning, P. Gouldsbury, T. Treacy.

The cast of 'The Stranger' and 'Wonder Night.' Front row, from left to right, Mary Wiley, Maureen O'Reilly, May Gunning, Mary B. Murphy, Teresa Treacy, Louie Leavy, Triona Murray, Teresa O'Connell, Mary Hart, Nora Curran, Teresa Dennigan and Josie Austin.
Second row, from left to right, Margaret Brennan, Veronica Austen, Joan Murtagh, Maureen McEnroe, Catherine Molloy, Dorothy Smith, Rosie Coleman, Eithne McEnroe, Daphne Kirkpatrick, Geraldine Gavin and Patricia Gouldsberry.
Third row, from left to right, Ann Leech, Eileen Dardis, Mary Ellen O'Hara, _____, Sadie Lawlor, Bernadette Cooney, Geraldine Coyne, Annette Roche, Rita O'Donoghue, Mary Flynn, Mary Dunne and Carmel Flynn.
Fourth row, from left to right, Teresa Cunningham, Ann Conroy, Margaret Allen, Marjorie Ring, Cepta Bradley, Ann Lynch, Patricia O'Reilly, Sadie Lawlor, Cann Campbell, Margaret Doyne, _____, Margaret Cross, Mary Murphy, Doreen Wiley and Gretta Bradley.
Fifth row, from left to right, Grace Walsh, Mary Cross, Teresa O'Connell, Margaret Mahon, Avril Kirkpatrick, Kathleen O'Reilly, Kathleen Keegan, Christine Tyson, C. O'Reilly, Vera O'Reilly, Ann Fallon, Olive Molphy, Mary Clonan, Jean McManus, Margaret Clabby, Ann Dardis and Olive Bruton.

From left to right, Sadie Lawlor, Ann Campbell, Anne Lynch, Margaret Cross, Geraldine Coyne, Annette Roche Margaret Allen and Christine Tyson.

THE PUPILS OF ST. JOSEPH'S
SCHOOL, ROCHFORTBRIDGE
— PRESENT —
THE STRANGER AND
NATIVITY PLAY, WONDER
NIGHT
ON
SUNDAY, 11th DECEMBER, 1960
AT 8 P.M.
ADMISSION 3/6, 3/-
MATINEE 3 P.M. SUNDAY, 11th
CHILDREN 1/-
1—10—12.

*Bernadette Cooney and
Mary Ellen O'Hara.*

*The Guards, from left to right, Doreen Wiley, Gretta Bradley, Mary Murphy,
Teresa O'Connell and Ann Conroy.*

*From left to right, Carmel Flynn, Maureen McEnroe, Ann Campbell, Joan Murtagh, Catherine Molloy,
Bernadette Cooney, Dorothy Smith, Veronica Austen, Margaret Murtagh, eithne McEnroe, Ann Leech,
Geraldine Gavin and Rose Coleman.*

Mary Flynn, Rita O'Donoghue and Mary Dunne

Hilda Hand, Nuala McGibney, Margaret Glynn, Mary Hart and Mary Doherty.

Early Musicals

THE STORY OF FATIMA - 1964

A scene from The Story of Fatima.

Back row from left to right, Pauline Doherty, Ann Cooney, _____ and Philomena Geraghty.
Third row, from left to right, Loreto Jones, Therese Flynn, Loretto Abbott, Ann Molphy, Patricia O'
Reilly. Mary Alford, Doreen Eighan, Ann Kelly, Mary Clonan, Nancy McGrath and Katherine Coyne.
Front row, from left to right, _____, Breeda Tierney, Sheila Martin, Ann Alford, Olive Flynn,
Geraldine Coyne, Phil Cooney, Mary McKeon, Catherine Cross and Mary Flood.

The Cast of The Story of Fatima

Members of the cast of The Story of Fatima, from left to right, Ursula Gaffney, Bridie Reynolds, Eileen Abbot, Moira Duffy, Ann Molphy, Joan Murtagh, _____, Geraldine Wiley, Patricia O'Reilly, Betty Bligh and Renee Gaffney.

JOSEPH 1975

PROGRAMME

for

MIDLAND REGION OF YOUTH CLUBS'

DRAMA FESTIVAL 1975

to be officially opened
on
Sunday Night, 13th April
by

Patrick Cooney T.D., Minister for Justice

St Joseph's Hall, Rochfort Bridge

Venue:

For three nights: 13th, 16th and 27th April

Adjudicator: Capt. Harry Smith (Athlone)

Winners announced and prizes presented
on
Final Night, 27th April

***   ***   ***   ***   ***

Sunday, 13th April

Rochfort Bridge Youth Club
presents
"Home is the Hero" (a 3-act play)
by Walter Macken

Cast:

Paddo O'Reilly
Daylia, his wife
Willie, his son
Josie, his daughter   Noel Reidy
Trapper O'Flynn   Ann Peppard
Dovetail, the tenant   Michael O'Sullivan
Bid, his wife   Pauline Murphy
Mrs Green   Anthony Fox
Lily Green, her daughter   Peter Carter
Manchester Monaghan   Gerard Kenny
                                       Thomas Fitzpatrick
                                       Stephanie Dunne
                                       Tony Byrne

Wednesday, 16th April

8.00 pm "Riders to the Sea": By John M. Synge (1-act)
Presented by Kilcormac Youth Club

Cast:

Maurya
Cachleen (her daughter)
Nora (her younger daughter)
Women Keening: Patricia Murray
                                       Anne Heffernan
                                       Teresa Dooley
                                 Barbera Nolan, Mary Bracken,
Bartley (Maurya's son)   Cathleen Bergin, Bernadette Deegan
Men (neighbours)
                                       Tom Finnerty, Pat Buckley,
                                 Liam Corboy, Gerard Nolan,
                                       Stephen Barrett

9.00 pm   "The Pawnshop" by Brian Kenny (1-act)
Presented by Birr Youth Club

Cast:

Pawnbroker
Mulcahy
Cassidy   William Murdock
O'Rourke   Delia Egan
Mrs Flynn   Christine Rosney
Mrs Mulvaney   Catherine Lally
Jamsie   Ann Dunphy
Guard   Beverly Rosney
                                       Kieran McCarthy
                                       Catherine Lally

9.30 pm   "O ! Lawsey Me!" by Thomas K. Moylan (1-act)
Presented by Clara Youth Club

Cast:

Lizzie Byrne (a charwoman)
Mrs Digby Dix (wife)
Guard 99E D.M.G.   Martina Hackett
Paddy Duffy (un-handyman and gardener) Susan Fitzsimons
Frederick Digby Dix   Johnny Bracken
Dr Bunny (neighbour)   Brendan Egan
                                       Tom Fallon
                                       Joseph Bracken.

Sunday, 27th April

8.00 pm "The Yank Outsider" by Brian Drumm (1-act)
Presented by Mullingar Youth Club

Cast

Jane O'Grady
Mrs O'Hare
Lily Cunneen   Siobhan Donnelly
Patsy O'Dowd   Katherine Gavin
Mr O'Hare   Therese Leslie
Agnes Flaherty   Muirish Moynihan
                                       Louis Kenny
                                       Joan Ryan

9.00 pm: Joseph and his Amazing Technicolour Dreamcoat
presented by
Pupils of St Joseph's, Rochfort Bridge

Cast in order of appearance:

Narrators   Annette Keogh, Patricia Mulligan
                                   Gerry Mooney
Jacob   Imelda Muldowney
Jacob's Wife
Brothers: Ann Quinn, Jimmy Slattery, Ina Kelly, Michael
          Cooney, Mairead Dardis, Denis Brady,
          Mary Coyne, Frankie Wallace, Frances Cully,
          Eileen Mulroy, Caitriona Donlon.
Joseph   Pascal Dunne
Slave   Tina Francis
Ishamaelites: Mary Carter, Mariena Daly, Dolores Burke,
              Patricia Mangan, Anne Curran, Anne Cleary,
              Loretto Loran, Mary Lynam.
                           Jimmy Gallagher, Laurence Ennis
Camel   Dolores Burke
Goat and Sheep   Therese Byrne
Potiphar   Dolores Murphy
Potiphar's Wife   Teresa Carey, Tina Francis
Potiphar's slaves   Carmel Raleigh, Gerardine Mangan
Guards   Siobhan Malone
Butler   Terence Murray
Baker   Paddy Gavin
Pharaoh   Patricia Rawlins
Lively Lad   Leo Murphy, Patrick Walsh, Thomas Coleman.
Guards   Anne Curran, Mary Carter,
Fan Girls   Tina Franci   Mary Lynam
                            Pauline Brennan, Anne Cleary,
Adoring Girls   Dolores Murphy, Tina Francis
                            Loretto Loran, Florry Hyland,
Pharaoh's Slaves   Ellen Rattigan
Choir: Breda Smith, Irene Mangan, Bernadette McCormack,
       Nuala Doyle, Breda Delamere, Patricia Tone,
       Mary Flanagan, Carmel Kenny, Christina Deegan,
              Geraldine Burke.
                                       Ann Peppard
Piano   Bernadette Troy
Stage Manager

PATIENCE
NEWSPAPER ARTICLE FROM 1984.

Rehearsals are in full swing for the production of the Gilbert and Sullivan comic opera "Patience" at St. Finian's College, Mullingar from November 29th to December 2nd. It is a co-production between the boys of St. Finian's College and the girls of St. Joseph's Secondary School, Rochfortbridge.

Richard O'Keefe, Fiona Garry, Teddy Flaherty and Nessa McDermott

This is not the first time that "real girls" have taken part in an opera at St. Finian's - that "honour" was achieved in the 1982 production of "H.M.S. Pinafore" by Loreto College, Mullingar. However, it promises to be a great step forward in colour, spectacle and musical enthusiasm. The stage has been totally reconstructed and special lighting and amplification are to be introduced. It is a first venture into Gilbert and Sullivan for the Rochfortbridge School who have certainly gone in at the deep end, "Patience" being an opera where the

Matthew Lalor, Ronan Nugent, Lorna O'Brien and Muireann Cunningham.

"twenty love sick maidens" have to bear a major share of the action. However, it should be no bother to them. Under the eager tutelege of Sr. Geraldine Coyne the girls have been rehearsing their parts since September. " Patience" the dairymaid, whom everybody loves, is played by Lorna O' Brien from Dalystown, Lady Angela is played by Claire Dillon fromTyrrellspass, Lady Sapher is played by Roisin Grier from Granard, Lady Ella is played by Fiona Garry and the part of Lady Jane is played by Nessa McDermott, both from the Mullingar area.

The leading parts on the St.Finian's side are Ronan Nugent played Colonel Calverley. Ronan is from Ballinlough, County Meath and has appeared already in *Trial by Jury* by Gilbert and Sullivan. Major Murgatroyd is played by Teddy Flaherty from Athenry, who has also appeared in "Trial by Jury" and in "H.M.S. Pinafore".

Richard O'Keeffe from Killucan is the Duke of Dunstable and he formerly played a "young lad" in "Trial by Jury". Reginald Bunthorne is played by Morgan Cooke. Morgan is from Dublin, appropriately enough since the character he plays, Bunthorne, is meant to represent the Dublin born playwright Oscar Wilde. Archibald Grosvenor is played by Matthew Lalor from Dunsany, County Meath who has already appeared in "Trial by Jury" and "H.M.S. Pinafore". And finally the solicitor is played by Dunshaughlin Boy Niall McDonnell, who previously played in "Trial by Jury".

Musical Director of "Patience" is Mr. Shane Brennan who has succeeded Fr. Frank McNamara as director of the Scola Cantorum at St. Finian's College. Mr. Brennan is also Musical Director of Mullingar Cathedral choir. The Producer is Mrs. Pat Flood from Dublin.

Sr. Geraldine Coyne, at the piano for rehearsals.

It is over one hundred years since "Patience" was produced in the Savoy Theatre, London (1881). It holds the distinction of being the first theatre production in Britain to be lit by electricity.

St. Finian's have a long tradition of Gilbert and Sullivan, being the first to stage their famous "Pirates of Penzance" in the Navan School as far back as 1900.

"Patience" is about snobbery and it satirises the ridiculous style of life of people such as Oscar Wilde, author of "The Importance of Being Earnest" and the painter, Whistler who painted his "Mother". The wit of Gilbert did not do Oscar Wilde any harm, it made him more popular, if anything, especially in America where "Patience" was a great hit. .

*Lorna O. Brien and Morgan Cooke
on stage in Patience.*

"Patience" as presented by St. Joseph's and St. Finian's, is also bound to be a great "hit" too. By the time the "twenty love sick maidens" have reduced the poets and dragoons to "matter of fact young men" you will have surrendered too, to the charm and delight of Sullivan's music and the wit and cleverness of Gilbert's dialogue.

CAST

Officers of Dragoon:
COLONEL CALVERLEY .... Ronan Nugent
MAJOR MURGATROYD .... Edward Flaherty
LIEUT. THE DUKE OF DUNSTABLE .... Richard O'Keeffe

REGINALD BUNTHORNE (a Fleshly Poet) .... Morgan Cooke.
ARCHIBALD GROSVENOR (an Idyllic Poet) .... Matthew Lalor
MR. BUNTHORNE'S SOLICITOR .... Niall McDonnell

Rapturous Maidens
THE LADY ANGELA .... Clare Dillon
THE LADY SAPHIR .... Roisin Grier
THE LADY ELLA .... Fiona Garry
THE LADY JANE .... Nessa McDermott
PATIENCE (a Dairy Maid) .... Lorna O'Brien

CHORUS OF RAPTUROUS MAIDENS

Ann Arthur, Clare Byrne, Shelagh Casey, Briga Clarke, Deirdre Conroy, Marie Cully, Muireann Cunningham, Mary Curran, Aedin Donlon, Jacqueline Doonan, Louise Dunne, Ita Fletcher, Rachel Gaffney, Marie Therese Kilmartin, Sharon Loughrey, Rosaleen McDonough, Aedamar Nolan.

CHORUS OF DRAGOON GUARDS

Cathal Brady, Cathal Daly, Sean De Burca, Kevin Dodd, Gerard Duffy, Derek Egan, John Fleming, Declan Kilmartin, John Kinirons, Ian McNamara, Jim Noctor, John O'Brien, Bernard O'Reilly, David Sheridan, Andrew Smith.

ORCHESTRA

Niamh Ballance .... 1st Violin
Aingeala De Burca .... 1st Violin
Jean Donaghy .... 2nd Violin
Declan Daly .... 2nd Violin
Tiernan O'Cleirigh .... Cello
Sean Gormley .... Double Bass
Hubert Magee .... Clarinet
Seamus Macken .... Flute
Mary Daly .... Oboe
Petrina Mills .... French Horn
David Tracey and Cambell Grant .... Trumpets
Fergal Collier .... Percussion
Francis Coll and Terence Sheridan .... Piano

SCENE

A Glade Outside Bunthorne's Castle

LIGHTING by Fr. Michael Murchan and Sean Lynch

SET DESIGN by Kevin Flood

SET CONSTRUCTION by Jack Reilly

MUSICAL DIRECTORS:
Shane Brennan and Sr. Geraldine Coyne

CONDUCTOR — Shane Brennan

PRODUCTION by Mrs. Pat Flood

THE MIKADO

The Mikado played to full houses for four nights last week at St. Finian's College, Mullingar, and was highly praised by very knowledgeable audiences. A lively cast, made up of boys from St. Finian's and girls from St. Joseph's Secondary School, Rochfortbridge, turned the tables on the audience for the encore by inviting them to a singalong of Tit willow, a subtle ending to an altogether highly satisfying night's entertainment.

All credit to the musical directors of both schools, Mr. Shane Brennan of St. Finian's and Sr Geraldine Coyne of St. Joseph's for the all round excellence of the singing. Both choruses sang well and looked well on stage. The boys, every inch gentlemen of Japan, with their clear diction fine footwork and fanwork, got the show off to a lively start, while the girls, looking suitably youthful and charming, carried out some very light and intricate movements, especially memorable being the *'Three Little Maids from School'* scene.

Here a special tribute must be paid to the Producer, Mr. Andy O'Loughlin, who obviously has great experience in getting the best out of a youthful cast collectively, as in the stunning finale to Act I and individually, in bringing out the best qualities of the principal actors.

The leading male character, Ko-Ko, was played in a rascally manner, by Morgan Cooke who has clearly a great understanding of the Gilbert and Sullivan comic genre. He danced about the stage at lightning pace, singing flawlessly even while in full flight when he said to his partner in comedy played by JohnKeegan, *"There's another nice mess you got us into"*, I was reminded of' Laurel and Hardy. John was very much the Oliver Hardy, large and pompous. But again singing and moving with real style.

The audience favourite was the brilliant little actress who played Pitti-Sing, Celine Kearney. This bubbling "little imp" literally throws , herself at one point risking life and limb when she is rolled upon by Pooh-Ba into the part. The little dance she gives across the stage as she sings *"He's going to marry Yum-Yum"* is a delight, her every gesture and expression are perfection. .

Celine was also in the quartet, which provided what for many was the higilight of the night, the Madrigal, *"Brightly dawns our Wedding Day",* at the start of Act II. The others were Rachel Mooney, who played Yum-Yum, and Synnott brothers Andrew and Cathal, who played Nanki-Poo and Pish-Tush respectively. The Madrigal is a very diifficult piece and this group handled it with near professional ease, full credit to their singing teachers.

Rachel Mooney as Yum-Yum has a very pleasing voice and stage presence with her romantic partner her darling Nanki-Poo. played by Andrew Slnnott were excellent.

Andrew looked very well in the part of Nanki-Poo and had an attractive tenor voice which he used to great effect. His brother, Cathal, also, sang well in the part of Pish-Tush and managed to put across well the look of disdain for the antics of Pooh-Bah.

The two very difficult parts of the Mikado and Kitisha were splendidly played by James Noctor ana Caroline Lyng. The Mikado has to be a menacing individual with a bizarre sense of humour. James Noctor's roaring laugh and his very powerful voice certainly caught the mood.

Caroline Lyng had the unenviable task of playing the aging Katisha from whom men flee in horror. She played the part with feeling and dignity leaving us in no doubt that she really had a heart.

Caroline Glennon as Peep- Bo, the third little maid and Donel Hennessy as a Noble Lord complete an excellent set of principal actors. Little Michael Curran as Ko-Ko's Boy, obviously enjoyed carrying the axe for his master.

All told this show was a great night's value. It looked well in its delightful Kevin Flood stage design. The amplification and lighting worked well.

The playing of the large orchestra under the baton of Mr. Shane Brennan never drowned out the voices, but constantly added every nuance and detail of the glorious Sullivan melody. The local members of this large orchestra were in no way outshone by their professional R.T.E. counterparts. This was a show in which all the parts worked in close harmony and for which all concerned can take a deep bow.

- Un-named Newspaper Article from 1986

Ladies of the Chorus: Lillian Curran, Olivia Curran, Dympna Duigenan, Anita Farrell, Deirdre Flynn, lmelda Kavanagh, Noelle Kenny, Breda McCormack, Emer McCormack, Irene Malone, Lynda Malone, Linda Murphy, Maeve Pearson, Carmel Wallace.

Gentlemen of the Chorus: Francis Coll, Fergal Collier, Aonghus De Burcan, John Donlon, Thomas Doyle, Malachy Dunne, James Elliffe, Leo Foyle, Campbell Grant, Paul Halpin, Aidan Higgins, Barry Higgins, Gerard Lillis, Eoin Lorrigan, Paul Ryan and Cian Ryle.

Guards: Paul Eiffe, Thomas Farrell, Kevin Martin and Dermot Neary.

Orchestra: String, Members of RTE Concert Orchestra

Oboe: Peter Healy, RTE Concert Orchestra

French Horn: Fergus O'Carroll, RTE Concert Orchestra

Basoon: Arthur Fallon

Flutes: Angela Cummins and Helen Smith

Clarinet: Hubert Magee

Trumpet: David Treacy

Timpani: Danny Murray

Piano: Leonard Dorrian.

Make-up: Mr. And Mrs. Joe Lane

Lighting: Fr. Michael Murchan and Seán Lynch

Set Design: Kevin Flood

Set Construction: Jack Reilly

Musical Direction: Shane Brennan and Sr. Geraldine Coyne

Conductor: Shane Brennan

Production: Andy O'Loughlin

Set Team: Damian Callaghan, John Donlon, Paul Eiffe, Damien Everard, Jim Farrell, Colman Jarrett, Fergus Keegan, Thomas Kelly, Edward Lyons. Fergus Mulvany, David Murphy, Daragh Nugent, Patrick Nugent, John Smith, Stephen Smith and Michael Walshe.

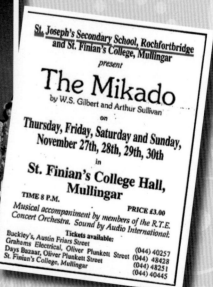

St. Joseph's Secondary School, Rochfortbridge
and St. Finian's College, Mullingar
present

The Mikado
by W.S. Gilbert and Arthur Sullivan
on

Thursday, Friday, Saturday and Sunday,
November 27th, 28th, 29th, 30th
in

St. Finian's College Hall, Mullingar

TIME 8 P.M.   PRICE £3.00

Musical accompaniment by members of the R.T.E.
Concert Orchestra. Sound by Audio International.

Tickets available:

Buckley's, Austin Friars Street	
Grahams Electrical, Oliver Plunkett Street	(044) 40257
Days Bazaar, Oliver Plunkett Street	(044) 48428
St. Finian's College, Mullingar	(044) 48251
	(044) 40445

PANTO'S

ST. JOSEPH'S SECONDARY SCHOOL, ROCHFORTBRIDGE

G5

— PRESENTS —

JACK AND THE BEANSTALK

in The Parish Hall, Rochfortbridge
on Saturday, 15th December, 1990
At 8 p.m.

Admission: Adults £3;   Students £1.50

(Booking St. Joseph's (044) 22176).

Nᵒ ¯¯.067   Westmeath Examiner Ltd. 044/48426

Joyce, Owen and himself who did excellent work with the dancers and singers.

Watching intently during Dancers' Rehearsals

PIERROT	Helena Farrell
DANCERS	Linda Murray, Aideen O'Rafferty, Lisa Doran, Lorraine Kelly, Carol O'Meara, Lorna Bradley, Olivia Corcoran, Monica Nea, Monica McQuaid, Caroline Holdwright, Lorcan O'Brien, Keith Oxley, Sharon Scanlon, Christine Scanlon, Tracy Purcell, Catherine McCormack, Anne Hussey, Noelle Walsh, Carol Dowdall, Edel Smith, Regina O'Meara, Mary Coughlan, Leslie Smith, Nessa O'Sullivan, Jackie McNamara, Helen Arthur, Lorraine Healy, Bernadine Rooney, Elva Dunbar, Karen Egan, Ciara Muldoon, Lisa Heavey, Lorraine Leogue, Antoinette Andrews, Claire Maher, Anne-Marie Kenny, Averil Swords, Sinead Tuomey, Jennifer Doyle, Grainne Breslin, Jennifer Eighan, Marlyn McNamara, Johanna Palmer.
LITTLE PEOPLE	Niamh Muldoon, Marcella Branagan, Aine Rooney, Elaine McQuaid, Caroline McNamara, Ciara Reidy, Breda Daly, Sharon Dunne, Colette Palmer, Louise Curran, Amy Wallace, Caroline Byrne, Olga Maher, Sharon Buckley.
PIT SINGERS	Maggie Kirby, Shirley, McCormack, Tara Brogan, Eilish O'Connell, Lorna Bollard, Cleo Byrne, Fiona Murphy.
SINGING TEACHERS	Mary Hayes, Lynda Ahearne, Mary Fallon, Nuala Flanagan, Eugene Dunbar, Luke Dempsey.
CHILDREN	Ronan Dunbar, Fergal Kelly, Martin Dowdall, Andrea Maher.
BREAK-DANCER	Mark Daly
BAMBA DANCER	Sinead Tuomey

6

The Pantomime Committee would like in particular to thank the patrons, the majority of whom are mentioned below:

JOHNNY HEALY, ROCHFORTBRIDGE
RAY BRADLEY, ROCHFORTBRIDGE
SHEILA LYSTER, ROCHFORTBRIDGE
JOE DELANEY, ROCHFORTBRIDGE
MICK COONEY, ROCHFORTBRIDGE
TOM WARD, ROCHFORTBRIDGE
MAL GAVIN, ROCHFORTBRIDGE

LEO & ROSE WRIGHT, MILLTOWNPASS
BENNETTS, MILLTOWNPASS

BERNARD TROY, TYRRELLSPASS
ERNEST ALFORD, TYRRELLSPASS
PETER KEEGAN, TYRRELLSPASS
THE VILLAGE INN, TYRRELLSPASS

THE GREVILLE ARMS, MULLINGAR
PAT MONTGOMERY, MULLINGAR
THE BLOOMFIELD HOUSE HOTEL, MULLINGAR
BANK OF IRELAND, MULLINGAR
ALLIED IRISH BANK, MULLINGAR
OLIVER BRENNAN, MULLINGAR
DENIS MCDERMOTT, MULLINGAR
DATA PACKAGING, MULLINGAR
GALAXY, PROP., TINA EARLY, MULLINGAR
TEMPTATIONS, PROP., JOAN MCLOUGHLIN, MULLINGAR
BLATHANNA, PROP., CAROLINE KELLY, MULLINGAR
HAMILLS GARAGE, MULLINGAR
THE BODY SHOP, MULLINGAR
BOBBY BEGLEY, MULLINGAR
DECLAN FITZSIMONS, MULLINGAR
MATT BUCKLEY, MULLINGAR
JIMMY ANDREWS, MULLINGAR
GRANGE MOTORS, MULLINGAR
CLAIRE FOX, MULLINGAR
BIJOU BOUTIQUE, MULLINGAR

MIDLAND BOOK SHOP, TULLAMORE

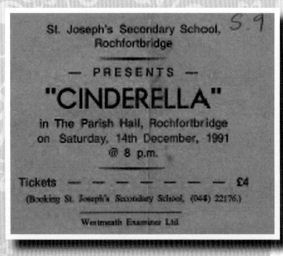

St. Joseph's Secondary School, Rochfortbridge

— PRESENTS —

"CINDERELLA"

in The Parish Hall, Rochfortbridge
on Saturday, 14th December, 1991
@ 8 p.m.

Tickets — — — — — — £4

(Booking St. Joseph's Secondary School, (044) 22176.)

Westmeath Examiner Ltd.

CINDERELLA

St. Joseph's Secondary School, Rochfortbridge
Friday 13th — Sunday 15th December 1991.
PRICE 30p.

CINDERELLA

ACT I

SCENE 1	THE VILLAGE SQUARE
SCENE 2	IN THE WOODS
SCENE 3	ROYAL COURT
SCENE 4	BACK IN THE WOODS
SCENE 5	THE KITCHEN

ACT II

SCENE 6	THE PALACE GATES
SCENE 7	THE BALLROOM
SCENE 8	THE KITCHEN
SCENE 9	FINALE

✱✱✱✱✱✱✱✱✱✱✱✱✱✱✱✱✱✱✱✱

PRODUCER .... Tom Dempsey
DIRECTOR .... Luke Dempsey
CHOREOGRAPHY .... Jenny Perry
MUSICAL DIRECTOR .... Eoin Lynch
COSTUMES .... Claire McCarthy
MAKE-UP .... Mary Hartnett and Josephine Dunbar
FRONT OF HOUSE .... Noel Foynes
LIGHTING .... Sean Lynch, Mervin Cunningham and Barry O'Brien
SOUND .... Mongey Cummunications
MUSIC .. Deirdre McLoughlin (piano/keyboards), Jackie O'Hare (electric guitar), Frank Rooney (trumpet), Gerard O'Dell (drums) Jonathan Mills (trombone), Jennifer Cleary (clarinet), Pauline O'Neill (flute), Canny Bruton (base guitar), Ray McDonnell (saxophone)
STAGE MANAGER .... Joe Arthur
ASSISTANT STAGE MANAGER .... Adrian Lee
SETS .... Dermot Bennett, Kevin Brennan, Simon Mooney and David McDonnell
SALES .... Eileen Alford and Marie O'Callaghan
SHOP .... Alan Wright and Laurence Arthur

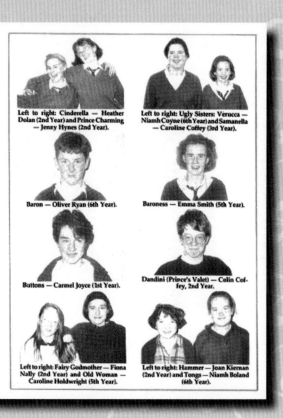

Left to right: Cinderella — Heather Dolan (2nd Year) and Prince Charming — Jenny Hynes (2nd Year).

Left to right: Ugly Sisters: Verucca — Niamh Coyne (6th Year) and Samanella — Caroline Coffey (3rd Year).

Baron — Oliver Ryan (6th Year).

Baroness — Emma Smith (5th Year).

Buttons — Carmel Joyce (1st Year).

Dandini (Prince's Valet) — Colin Coffey, 2nd Year.

Left to right: Fairy Godmother — Fiona Nally (2nd Year) and Old Woman — Caroline Holdwright (5th Year).

Left to right: Hammer — Joan Kiernan (2nd Year) and Tongs — Niamh Boland (6th Year).

OLIVER 1998

Last May, Miss Moloney announced the possibility of staging the production of a musical. "Promises, promises", we all thought, raising our eyes to heaven in disbelief. Well, for once a promise was kept, and lo and behold, 7 months later saw the production of "OLIVER", which turned out to be quite an "Oscar winning performance". However, it didn't happen just like that. Long hours of slog were spent auditioning, rehearsing and plenty of shouting to get everything perfect.

St. Joseph's Secondary School
Rochfortbridge
presents
OLIVER
IN THE SCHOOL GYM
on MONDAY 15th DECEMBER
Commencing at 8p.m.
Tickets - £5
0218

Eventually everything came together - acting, dancing and singing, and about time too! With the help of all our budding artists, the set was made which was truly indescribable. On entering the gym, students gasped at the transformation which had taken place. It was no longer a torturing chamber for lazy people(!) but the next best thing to The Gaiety! Many compliments are owed to the woodwork teachers and classes and to Miss O'Brien and her crew. The stage organisers were very efficient in their task of changing the set and are currently holding a record for their swiftness! Costumes looked good on stage, comfortable to wear and looking flattering i.e. Matthew Rice with his sexy jodhpurs and knee high boots. A big thanks is owed to the Home-Economics teachers for their needlework.

It has to be said that Miss Moloney did an absolutely fantastic job of selecting the cast. It would be unfair to single out any particular person because truly all the acting was of the utmost quality.

She seems to pick out people with the same traits as their characters. Everybody worked hard, extending themselves beyond the call of duty, even when fatigue threatened to overcome them.

All were determined to make it succeed and that was what mattered. Over the long period of working together there was a great feeling of intimacy and closeness between the cast.

Sunday night - the opening night came upon us all too soon and all backstage were very nervous. Mark Greville, playing *"Dodger"* paced up and down trying to ease his nerves, but they were instantly forgotten. It seemed that all the actors, once they hit the stage became totally immersed in the magic of acting, quite oblivious to the audience, just like real pro's. (You never know, first stop Rochfortbridge sportshall, next stop Broadway)!

All the cast seemed to be natural born entertainers. Backstage, the atmosphere was electric. Strange looking characters, running all over the place complete with costumes and bearing quite a resemblance to the Oompa Loompa's, (particularly orange stage make up). At this stage it seems necessary to thank Mrs. Hartnett and her helpers for making us look perfect under the stage lights.

There were two changing rooms. The "boys" and the "girls" of course, and lo and behold if any poor unfortunate male or female was found trespassing in the wrong room there was hell to pay. Certain girls, who will remain nameless, found that there was a tremendous, inexplicable force pulling them to the lads room, where they could flirt quite shamelessly with Jason Leech, playing Fagin, or any other unsuspecting male who tickled their fancy.

Well anyway, we made it to Wednesday night - the night of The Finale, without any (many!!) major hitches (members of choir falling faint). This was the night to remember. Another spectacular performance was made and then came a truly meaningful speech from our dear principal, the one and only "Mr. O'Sullivan". The first 5 minutes were great, but the next 5, 10, 15 minutes tried our patience ever so slightly. Standing under the bright lights with stupid smiles fixed upon our faces 'C'mon sir, we don't want the audience to nod off, so get off'.

The musical, which turned out to be such a success, wouldn't have been the same without the help and co-operation of the following people:

- The Woodwork Class
  - The Art Class
  - The Choirs
  - The Dancers
  - Miss Moloney
  - Mr. Hartnett
  - Mrs. Hartnett
  - Miss Hogan
- Choreographer, and all the staff who helped so earnestly, - THANKS!!!
- Written by Elaine Leavy and Celine Doran. with the help of Mark Prior.

AN INTERVIEW WITH MR. HARTNETT

Q: Why did you decide to get so deeply involved in Oliver?

A: I feel that doing musicals is very important in the learning process in a school. I have a great love of musicals and lastly I feel it gives the cast an opportunity to mix with other age groups that they may not have had a chance to get to know during school.

Principal Tony O'Sullivan addresses the audience on the final night..

Q: Did you find the pupils enthusiastic?

A: Yes, they were fantastic. I think the response was so good because Oliver was for some their first chance to perform and also because lots of people love acting and singing. The musical gave everyone a chance to try different activities outside of the school curriculum.

Q: Did you find it difficult to find suitable people for the parts?

A: It was difficult to narrow the choices down because so many people could have done the single parts.

Q: Was there a high level of acting in the school?

A: Yes, exceptionally high. Very few schools could have put on such a performance.

Q: Was the organisation of the show difficult?

A: Yes. A lot of co-operation was needed from teachers, pupils, parents etc. and we had to try to cut class disruption to a minimum. It meant that myself and Miss Moloney had to stay back late some evenings. On such occasions parents were very helpful in picking up their children - often quite late. The staff of the school also gave great co-operation.

Q: Would you do it again?

A: Yes. It would be an honour to do it again. During the show I was so tense I didn't know if I was enjoying it or not, but the aftermath was truly euphoric.

AN INTERVIEW WITH MISS MOLONEY

Q: Why did you decide on Oliver as the musical?

A: We chose Oliver because we wanted to include as many people as possible from the junior and senior years of the school. The musical Oliver can be adapted to have a huge cast and chorus.

Q: Were you met with enthusiasm?

A: Yes. The enthusiasm which I encountered from the first auditions right through to the opening night was wonderful. It was great to work in an atmosphere of willingness and must I commend all those involved for their co-operation.

Q: Was it difficult to find suitable people for the parts?

A: With most characters no it wasn't difficult, but I was getting worried about the part of Oliver himself until John Cully showed up and he was perfect for the role.

Q: Was the organisation of the show on the whole difficult?

A: All the teachers involved were so helpful and supportive, but it was really Mr. Hartnett who oversaw everything and it must be said he did a wonderful job.

Q: Were you apprehensive that it wouldn't come together for the opening night?

A: No. I knew it would come together but I wasn't quite sure how good it would be. I think everyone was delighted with the result.

Josephine Dunbar and Niamh Moloney.

Q: Were you thrilled with the overall success of the show?

A: Yes, I think it was a great achievement for everybody, the cast, the chorus, the dancers, the crew and all who were involved and who worked so hard. I felt proud of being part of such a major success in the school.

Q: Would you do it again?

A: Yes of course, but first let me get my breath!!!

AN INTERVIEW WITH LEONIE MAHER (NANCY)

Q: What attracted you to the part of Nancy?

A: I want to pursue acting as a future career and any parts available in productions, I am only too happy to avail of.

Q: How did you get the part?

A: Miss Moloney auditioned approximately 20 girls from all years for the part and I was fortunate enough to get it.

Q: How did you feel on the opening night?

A: I was a bag of nerves!!! There was chaos backstage with over 300 members of the cast, and trying to get my costume and make-up done was hell!!!

Q: How did you feel at the 'Grand Finale'?

A: I was extremely relieved and overjoyed that the whole performance had gone so well. To see the audiences reaction was overwhelming.

Q: Do you have any regrets in taking part in the musical?

A: Not at all!! It was a great experience and the rest of the cast and organisers were a pleasure to work with.

AN INTERVIEW WITH MATTHEW RICE (BILL SYKES)

Q: What attracted you to your part in "Oliver"?

A: it wasn't planned. I just went along to an audition for the crack and ended up getting the part of "Bill Sykes".

Q: What did you think of your costume - kneehigh boots, jodhpurs, top-hat, etc.?

A: it wasn't that comfortable, but it was bearable. It was all good fun and a good laugh.

Q: How did you feel on the opening night?

A: I have to say I was a bit nervous but after a while I was totally immersed in the part of Bill Sykes.

Q: Were there any mistakes, to your memory?

A: The technical rehearsal on Friday night didn't go too well, but thankfully, everything went right when it mattered.

Written by Celine Doran and Elaine Leavy.
Vox 1998

JOSEPH AND THE AMAZING TECHNICOLOR DREAMCOAT 2005.

Last year, St Joseph's Rochfortbridge decided that *"a bit of an 'auld' musical"* was in order. After all, being a school, which for years was renowned for its spectacular musicals, it was about time that we reclaimed that status. So, after a very hushed six-year gap, the musically inclined management of our school sat down, for what must have been hours and discussed what would be the most suitable musical to attempt to produce. Eventually, they choose **"Joseph and the Amazing Technicolor Dreamcoat"**. A decision, which 'conveniently' tied in with our school's name. (More than a little suspicious if you ask me!)

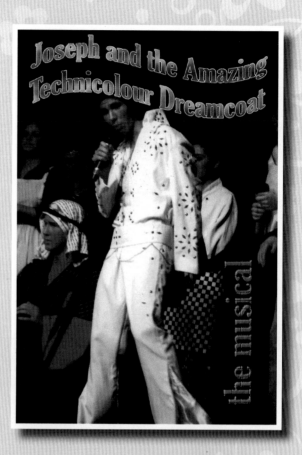

The new school year rang in and within days the plans had leaked; the girls showed an expected enthusiasm and eagerly awaited the auditions whilst the lads vowed that such an extra curricular activity would be overly feminine for their tastes. We were all made aware of their complete lack of interest in the school's production, except on a purely non-musical level and yet, when the auditions came around, there was quite a few familiar male faces present, ready to sing, dance and act their little hearts out, 'Bless em!

Soon enough the roles were posted outside the assembly hall (conjuring up scenes reminiscent of Fame; Darren Price danced, skipped and pirouetted through the school corridors upon discovering that he had acquired the role of Gad). The rehearsals got under way, as did the

preparations for every other aspect of the musical, including the 'artsy' side of things and nobody dared question Ms Sweeny's demand for *"fluff an lots of it"* but admittedly, after seeing the end product and the sheer impressiveness of her fake sheep, it's safe to say that she was justified in her fluffy requests.

Ah, but what about those rehearsals? Unforgettable is what they were, Every Tuesday after school, the assembly hall was filled by what can only be described as a choir of angelic proportions! The lads kept to themselves in their designated corner issuing noises as Ms Muldoon produced melodic harmonies on the *'old Susanna'*. Meanwhile some girl led the singing … she had a minor role; Narrator or something? Laura Bracken, was it? Unforgettable, isn't that what I said?! And of course, what Tuesday rehearsal would be complete without an impromptu piano recital from Brendan O'Rourke. I can still hear him playing Robbie William's "Angels", complimented perfectly by an off key chorus led by none other than the uber talented Chris Cole. Strangely enough those recitals came to cease with the arrival of Ann Marie (dance instructor extraordinaire) and the unfeasibly talented Greg (the piano man or the English guy).

After school on Thursdays was reserved for dance rehearsals. There was the Western one, the Calypso one, the Rock n' Roll one and the incredibly annoying Go, Go, Go, Joseph one (dances that is), which Ann Marie insisted on repeating an unhealthy number of times every Thursday. Which was more disturbing though I'm not sure; the lads' eagerness to learn or Ann Marie's whole hearted faith in our ability to dance. All the same, cartwheels were perfected (as were some painful looking three-quarter splits), limbs were stretched to their maximum potential (and some) and the jive just went from strength to strength as opening night edged ever closer. Weekend rehearsals became a necessity if the dances were to be of an acceptable standard to Ann Marie. Still, even the odd visit from Sr Dympna's Saturday Maths Class (and with them the occasion high pitched outburst of; 'queers! Giggle giggle') couldn't deter the dancers, or hamper their professionalism.

Coming closer to Even class time would have to play second fiddle to what was hotting up to be one of the most exciting developments in the school's recent history. It had everything from flash dance routines, to humour, massively talented voices (from some unexpected sources), not to mention controversy. Oh, the controversy! But we won't mention that, we're and friends now, after all.

Things were beginning to get hectic and just in time for the dress rehearsal, which actually turned out to be somewhat of a double dress rehearsal, showing the sheer dedication of the entire cast and crew. Still, the stage was built, costumes were fitted, scenery was touched up (including one eerily lifelike camel), tickets were sold, some important last minute decisions were debated (to wear the afros or not to wear the afros?) and all in time for opening night. Apparently the cast were nervous stepping out into the limelight on the 11th of December. A nervousness, which was completely absent from their amazing performances.

The show itself was spectacular to say the least. And completely devoid of any mistakes too! Not a single mistake in any of the five performances! Nobody had a slight slip of the tongue during the safety message on the first night (but what a disaster it would have been if people in the audience hadn't turned off their mobile phones. Nobody tripped up during the Western dance. Nobody had a brief memory lapse and decided to ad lib a bit. None of the brothers (played by a first year) sang when they weren't supposed to during the reprise. Nobody caught the 'Chariot of Gold' on the 'green and red decoration thingies'. None of the 'backstage teachers' had to run out under Joseph's coat to fix the stool (yes, he was standing on a stool). And definitely; nobody's skirt fell off at a most inappropriate stage (despite the fact that video evidence may say otherwise). But besides the mistakes, which most definitely never happened, the standing innovations were well deserved. On the

nights, the singing was superb. The dancing was a pleasure to watch. The musicians, as always, played to perfection.

Backstage, a team of specialists prevented any wardrobe malfunctions from happening (the 'skirt falling' incident was strictly Gillian's fault... oops). The stagehands were extremely handy. Chucky ensured that all things in the sound department went soundly (excuse the pun). The ushers excelled at whatever it is they did.

No seat was left unfilled; a testimony to the stellar work put in by Ms Muldoon, Mr Hartnett, Ms Stenson, Ms McNicholas.

Vox 2005.

OKLAHOMA 2007

The Cast of Oklahoma

The Cast of Les Miserables

LES MISERABLES 2011

BACK TO THE EIGHTIES
TUES. 21ST-SAT. 25TH OCTOBER 2008.

The following text and information is based on the programme for the show when it was staged in 2008.

Corey Palmer Senior:	Eoin Rigney
Corey Palmer Junior:	Conor Walsh
Alf Bueller:	Eoin Nugent
Kirk Keaton:	Jamie Shields
Tiffany Houston:	Francis Fallon
Cyndi Gibson:	Leanne Quinn
Mel Easton:	Emma Kerrigan
Kim Easton:	Christina Gahan
Michael Feldman:	Cayman Power
Billy Arnold: .	Shal Osiadi
Lionel Astley:	Jamie Gonoud
Huey Jackson:	Jack Colgan
Fergal McFerrin:	Gavin Kirwan
Eileen Reagan:	Jean Kelly
Laura Wilde:	Shauna Wilson
Debbie Fox:	Niamh McAdden
Sheena Brannigan:	Hannah Mulroy
Mr Stevie Cocker:	Jake Byrne
Featured Female Singers:	Sinead Doyle, Meekness Musasa, Claire Flanagan, Ellis Jobson
Featured Male Singer:	Daniel Cooney

Choir
Aileen Moore, Andrea Wright, Angela Bradley, Aoife Geraghty. Ciara Moran, Clare Geraghty Cliona Gallagher, Elaine Geraghty, Eimeair Treacy, Emma Hyland, Emma Treacy, Fiona Creamer, Janet Flood, Jennifer Gavin, Karla Stynes, Lorna Moore, Meekness Musasa, Michelle Monaghan, Miriam Wynne, Naomi Plunkett, Niamh McEnteggert, Niamh Spellman, Nicola McCabe, Oisin Murphy, Paul Plunkett, Rachael Gallagher, Sarah Brannock, Shannon Tone, Shauna Naughton, Shayne Tone, Sinead Doyle, Sinead Lowry, Sinead McGuirk, Tanya Lee Forde, Jennifer Lonnigan, Joanne Fox, Katie Kennedy, Niamh McCarthy, Nicole Burke, Nicole Milmoe, Roisfn Farrell, Sarah Gahan, Sarah Kiernan, Sarah McCabe, Shauna Stynes, Sinead O' Neill, Stacey Geoghegan, Jennifer Gavin.

Dancers
AmeeDunne, Aisling Geraghty, Amy Mahony, Ashleen Minaguchi, Avril Byrne, Brian Duignan, Cian Burke, Cian Flynn, Clare Flanagan, Deana Weir, Dermot Judge, Donal Hickey, Eddie Alford, Eibhlin Fitzpatrick, Ellis Jobson, Eoin Gorman, Finbar Murphy, Fiona McHugh, Hannah Mullin, Jane Sleator, Karen Tracey

Jake Byrne *(Mr. Cocker)*
When Jake steps on stage he becomes the teacher Mr Cocker. He is very passionate about sports and is more accustomed to shining on the race track. Jake may be a novice on stage but he gives an outstanding performance.

Jack Colgan *(Hughie)*
Jack is very interested in music and his guitar rarely leaves his hands. His previous acting experience includes playing Jack, in Jack and the Beanstalk! He admits to not relating to his goofy character much but as he says himself "a good character will always make it work!!. Jack gives a great performance as Hughie, the Michael Jackson fanatic. Watch out for that signature move!

Frances Fallon *(Tiffany)*
Frances plays the part of Tiffany, the popular girl next door. This pint sized girl is hugely talented and has sung solo twice in the National Concert Hall in the High Achievers awards, winning a Special achievement award for her singing. She is also a violinist with the Midlands Youth Orchestra. Frances plays both violin and piano. She is also passionate about football and plays for her club and county.

Christina Gahan *(Kim)*
This Sixth year student is very passionate about dancing. She has performed in the West End Shaftsbury Theatre. Christina plays the part of Kim, the twin with attitude.

Jamie Gonoud *(Lionel)*
Jamie tells us that his good looks and charms won him the part of Lionel!! He hails from Tyrellspass and is an avid sports person. Jamie is funny both in person and in character. This is Jamie's first experience in musicals and we are sure that it won't be his last.

Jean Kelly (Eileen)
Jean plays the new girl Eileen Regan in her stage debut. She has a passion for music, guitar, piano and also sings in Scór. Jean is a member of the School Choir. She describes herself as "a traditional farm girl who loves her home comforts".

Gavin Kirwan *(Fergal)*
Gavin's previous acting experience includes a part in his primary school's production of The Emperor's New Clothes. He's into rock music and he plays the drums. He relates to his character and believes there's a Fergal in all of us!

Eoin Nugent *(Alf)*
Sixth year Eoin from Gaybrook plays the part of "geeky guy" Alf with great enthusiasm and aplomb. Eoin likes singing and dancing and is counting this as his stage debut even though he played the part of Joseph in the Nativity play in primary school.

Shal Osiadi(Billy)
Shal plays the part of cool sidekick Billy. This is Shal's stage debut although he has previous experience on television having appeared as an extra in Fair City and on Den 2!! Shal loves acting and has said that the show 'will be an experience never to be forgotten.'

Kymann Power *(Michael)*
Kymann is a singer and song-writer who enjoys music and dancing. He plays football and soccer for Kinnegad. "I'm a normal everyday kinda guy but when I hit the stage I'm brought to life". He is also a member of the band 'Bottoms Up'. Kymann delivers an excellent performance as Corey's arch rival, Michael.

Leanne Quinn *(Cyndi)*
Leanne plays Cyndi, a material girl with attitude. She is no stranger to the stage having sung solo in Scór. She loves dancing and has previous experience in drama. Her hobbies include football & basketball.

Emma Kerrigan *(Mel)*
This bubbly Rhode girl plays one of the "not so identical twins". She has some previous experience dancing in Tullamore but her true love is football whether it be playing it or supporting the Rhode senior team. She is sure to give an energetic performance.

Niamh Me Adden(Laura)
Niamh plays the part of Laura, Fergal's friend and Eileen's sidekick with great enthusiasm. Niamh is no stranger to our stage as she was a dancer and sung solo in 'Oklahoma'. She is a member of the school choir. Niamh is known for being as lovely in person as she is in character.

Hannah Mulroy *(Ms. Brannigan)*
Hannah is no stranger to our stage here in St Joseph's. She performed as a dancer in 'Joseph' the Musical here in the school in 2004 and was also in the choir for Oklahoma in 2006. She has also sung with the Mullingar Youth Choir and sings with the school choir. Hannah who has been having her voice trained for a number of years plays the enigmatic teacher Ms. Brannigan this time round.

Eoin Rigney *(Corey Snr.)*
Eoin plays Corey Senior, the narrator of the show. Eoin began his acting career when he played Joseph in his primary school nativity play but he tells us that he is equally as interested in sports and the ladies, as he is in acting. He plays corner back on the schools Senior Football Team and also plays for his local club Rhode.

Jamie Shiels *(Kirk)*
Jamie plays the part of geeky sidekick Kirk to perfection. As a Rahamey man, Jamie is of course interested in sports as well as music and wrestling! He believes he can relate to his character as apparently he admits to also being "idiotic and goofy" from time to time!

Conor Walsh *(Carey Jnr)*
Conor plays the part of the hero of the musical. Conor is very musical and plays guitar, drums, piano and French horn He is also passionate about rugby, golf and football. Conor played in the Orchestra for our last musical, Oklahoma. He is a member of the band "The Big Fat Avocado". Conor delivers an excellent performance as Corey Junior.

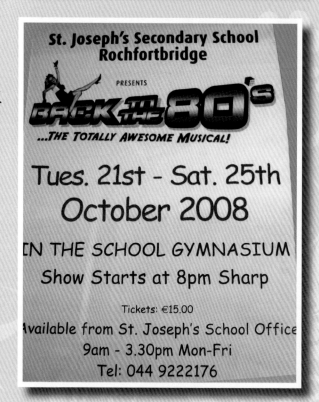

St. Joseph's Secondary School
Rochfortbridge

PRESENTS

BACK TO THE 80's

...THE TOTALLY AWESOME MUSICAL!

Tues. 21st - Sat. 25th
October 2008

IN THE SCHOOL GYMNASIUM

Show Starts at 8pm Sharp

Tickets: €15.00
Available from St. Joseph's School Office
9am - 3.30pm Mon-Fri
Tel: 044 9222176

Shauna Wilson *(Debbie)*
Shauna represented Ireland in an Irish dancing competition in America and has also been in numerous productions with Shockwaves Stage School. She is very excited about strutting her stuff on the stage!

Band

Trumpet:	Paul Hensey
Trombone:	Brendan Kennedy
Lead Guitar:	Pat Ennis
Bass Guitar:	Darragh Caffrey
Drums:	Ricky Byrne
Piano /Keyboards:	Petrina Mills, Gerard Lillis

Musical director:	Yvonne Muldoon
Drama and Production:	Yvonne Muldoon, Niamh Sheridan, Margaret Cole
Choreography:	Anne Marie Bentick

Art and set design: Niamh Sweeney, Assisted by TYO Group 1, Jessica Adams, Jack Colgan, Avril Corroon, Jason Cully, Katie Deegan, Emma Doyle, David Fleming, Niamh Hannon, Leanne Hendley, Conor Kavanagh, Dean Mc Enteggart, Brian Mc Gearty, Hannah Mullen, Sarah Nolan, Laura Sweeney, Shauna Wilson, Simone Kennedy

Stage Construction: Ray McDonnell, Pat Eighan

Assisted by: Christopher Timmons, Eoin O'Donoghue, Jake Hobby Royale, Diarmuid Coughlan, Cian Flynn, Brian Duigan, Shane Keegan, Jamie Gonoud, Adam Boardman, Sean Geraghty

Costume:	Yvonne Hession, Liz Shaw
Props:	Susan Hogan, Fiona Burke
Assisted by:	Adam Boardman, Kevin Ronan, Aaron Coughlan, David O'Keefe
Sound:	Reeks Sound, Clara
Lighting:	Pascal Gough, Adrian McCormack
Assisted by:	Eoin O'Donoghue, Jake Hobby Royale
Programme:	Ms Sheridan's LCVP Class
P.R.O:	Niamh Sheridan
Sponsorship:	Margaret Cole
Ticket administrator:	Evelyn Kelly

Raffle & Front of house: Eileen Alford, Adrian Mc Cormack, Helena Heduan, Liz O'Reilly, Claire Mc Carthy, Rita Judge, Martina Croghan, Breda Mc Cormack, Bridget Currams, Edel Enright, Jean Egan, Yvonne Kelly, Eamonn Scally, Nuala Lawlor, Mary Fallon, Margaret Treacy, Anna Kavanagh, Chris Cole

Ushers: Colm Muldoon, Katie Deegan, Diarmuid Coughlan, Dan Riggs, Laura Kelleghan, Aoife Brady

Video: Tom Shaw

The Transition Year Students
of
St Joseph's Secondary School,
Rochfortbridge,
are pleased to announce their production of

Macbeth

Thursday March 22nd
Parish Hall
Rochfortbridge
8.00pm

Tickets available from Evelyn in the School
Office @ 0449222176

€8

JOSEPH AND THE AMAZING TECHNICOLOR DREAMCOAT

In this retelling of the Biblical story, Joseph is a handsome man who is his father's favourite son, able to interpret dreams, and the bearer of an amazing coat. These facts lead Joseph's eleven brothers to become insatiably jealous. Therefore, they sell Joseph into slavery to some passing Ishmaelites. After refusing the advances of his owner's wife, Joseph is sent to jail. Once in jail, he becomes popular due to his ability to interpret dreams. The Pharaoh soon hears of Joseph's ability and appoints him to the post of Number Two man in Egypt. Years later, Joseph's now starving brothers arrive in Egypt and ask Joseph, whom they don't recognize, for assistance. Joseph, in turn, gives his brothers a scare, but eventually grants them all they desire, reveals his identity, and reunites the family.

St. Joseph's Secondary School
Rochfortbridge Co. Westmeath present

Joseph and the Amazing Technicolor Dreamcoat

Monday December 13th at 8pm

Venue: School Gym
Doors open at 7.30pm
Tickets: €12.50

Cast

Kevin Mains is fourteen years old and he is a third year student He is originally from Glasgow. His. Granddad taught him how to play the guitar. He plays in a band called The Arrows. In addition he played Danny in the musical *Grease* during' a holiday vacation in Spain. Kevin wishes to pursue a career in acting and/or music.

Laura Bracken is from Mullingar and is eighteen years old. This is her first acting experience. She studies Voice with Dorothy Horan in Mullingar. In addition she plays the Clarinet with the Mullingar Town Band.

Narrator:	Laura Bracken
Jacob:	Aidan Wright
Pharaoh:	Brendan O'Rourke
Potfphar:	Fintan O'Reilly
Potiphar's Wife:	Gillian Gonoud
Butler and Baker:	Niamh Molloy and Grainne Callaghan
Young Child:	Lisa Kirwan
Brothers:	Daniel Mooney , Christopher Cole, Brendan 0 Rourke, Darryl Marron Philip O' Connell, Alan Hannon, Alan Mc Cormack, Ricki Byrne, Mark Walsh, Darren Price, James O' Connor
Wives:	Gillian Gonoud, Joanne Harney, Kerri Smith, Sarah Monaghan, Catherina Murph, Laura Dunne, Laura Hutchinso, Amanda Corcoran, Claire Keegan, Karen McDonnell, Orla Eighan
Dancers:	Sandra Muldoon, Grace Gavin, Hannah Mulroy, Amanda Stapleton, Miriam Wynne, Nichola O' Keeffe, Amy Lynch, Louise Dunne, Martina Burke, Janine Heavy, Niamh Molloy
Guards:	Jonathan Hickey, Kevin Me Dermott, Colm Dardis, Ben Palmer, Stephen McKiernan, Patrick Harney, Noel O'Reilly, Andrew Cunningham

Orchestra

Flute: Helen Glennon and Rebecca Walsh
Clarinet: Sharon Barrett and Fiona O'Callaghan
Saxophone: Danielle Smith
Trumpet: Paul Kiernan
Lillis
Electric Guitar: Jonathan Hartnett
Rehearsal Accompanist: Greg Bentick

Oboe: Mary Mulligan
Bassoon: Arthur Fallon
French Horn: Petrina Mills
Keyboards: Greg Bentick and Gerard

Percussion: Danny Murray

Choir:

Natalie Cooney, Sarah Mooney, Yvonne O'Reilly, Kirstie Mc Donnell, Kelly O'Neill, April Baker, Amee Dunne, Mary Seery, Cliona Duignan, Sarah Gavin, Niamh McEntegart, Louise Flynn, Rita Cleary, Sally Alford, Colleen Gill, Emma Hyland, Michelle Murtagh, Aisling Leonard, Niamh Spellman, Sarah Kiernan, Louise Lynch, Aisling Maher, Tanya Brickland, Ciara O' Connor, Sharon Dale, Vanessa Dardis, Claire Temple, Claire Kenny, Tara Henry, Kirstie Finn, Tanya Flynn, Laurie Dunne, Claire Flanagan, Debbie Wilson, Aisling Hyland, Niamh Morgan, Niamh McCarthy, Alice Doyle, Jennifer Fox, Dawn Wallace, Mary Delaney, Erin Tormey, Niamh McAdden, Carina Hardy, Ailish Burke, Ciara Bagnall, Megan Barr, Sinead McDermott, Louise Darby, Jenny Geraghty, Emma Williams, Danielle Trimble, Karen McDermott, Sinead Lynam, Ciara Floody, Lauren Thompson, Ruth Hannon, Mary Grennan, Laura Reid, Lyndsey McGlynn, Maria Timmons, Ciara Moore, Amy Quinn, Stacey Glynn, Joanne Pimley.

Credits:

Musical Director: Yvonne Muldoon.
Stage Directors: Caitriona Mc Nicholas, Karen Stenson and Anthony Hartnett.
Choreographer: Anne-Marie Bentick.
Set and Props Design: Niamh Sweeney and Celine Sheridan.
Set Construction: Joe Arthur and Pat Eighan.
Assisted by: Jack Hanrahan, Noel Kilmurray, Brian Lannigan, James Leogue, Thomas Maher, Barry Morgan, Alan Ryan and Brendan Sheridan.
Set Painting: Niamh Sweeney and Celine Sheridan.
Assisted by: David Kelleghan, Karen McDermott, Jackie Glennon, Sinead Loran, Serena Maguire, Karl Gammell, Francis Kelly, Joe Kelly, Patrick Carlisle, Ross Geoghegan, Seán Murray, Claire Moore, Ciara O'Connor, Orla Gallagher, Niamh Maguire, Amy Daly, Patrick Kelly and Fifth Year Art Students.
Stage Management: Karen Stenson.
Props: Margaret Cole and Susan Hogan.
Lighting: Darren Brick and Sean Casement.
Sound: Aidan O'Rourke and Eoin Kavanagh.
Costume Design: Johanna Walshe.
Costume Making: Johanna Walshe, Elizabeth Shaw and Helen Maguire.
Raffle and Posters: Sarah Butler and Charlotte Holton.
Programme: Miriam O'Loughlin.
Cover Design: David Kelleghan.
Ticket Administration: Evelyn Kelly.
Front of House Management: Breda McConnack, Sheila Coyne, Martina Croghan, Michelle Keogh and Margaret Cole.

~ CHAPTER 35 ~
A NEW CENTURY

~ CHAPTER 35 ~
A NEW CENTURY

Jonathan Polsinelli, Monica Seery and Jordan Reid, represented St. Joseph's in the Games (Maths Quiz), which took place at Maynooth Post-Primary School in 2006.

St Joseph's Junior Cert students beat off teams from 15 schools in five counties to win a table quiz organised by the Midlands Branch of the History Teachers' Association of Ireland in Moate Community School. The members of the winning team (from left). are: Dwayne Leavy, Monica Seery, Lorna Moore and Eoin Rigney.

2006 Equestrian members, Lorna Moore, Emma Wright, Clodagh Gill and Jane Sleator.

A second St Joseph's team tied for third place in the history quiz with questions drawn mainly from the Junior Certificate History syllabus. They are (from left): Colm Muldoon, Laura Kellaghan, Aishling Geraghty and Gavin Kirwan.

Kevin Metcalfe, John Fagan, Andrew Cunningham and Garry Shaw. The golfing team from St. Joseph's School in Rochfortbridge emerged as provincial U-19 champions, after winning the Leinster finals at Killeen Golf Club, near Kill, Co. Kildare.

The 2006 Vox magazine committee.

From left to right, Caroline Flynn, Lisa Kirwan,
Niamh McAdden, Sarah Anne Smith, Niamh McEnteggart
and Chloe Gill.

Off to the Debs in 2011, Sr. Geraldine
wishes Aimee Dunne well.

Back row from left to right, Dan Riggs,
Claire Flanagan, Niamh McCarthy,
Cian Flynn and Brian Dignan.
Third row from left to right,
_____, Jade O Brien, Sharon
Dale, Cliona Duigenan, Miriam Wynne,
Diarmaid Coghlan and John Gorman.
Second row, from left to right, Lisa
Kirwan, Amee Dunne, Michelle Murtagh
and Emma Hyland.
Front row, from left to right, Niamh
Spealáin, Caroline Flynn,_____
and Sarah Anne Smith.

On Monday January 26th 2009 a notable success was achieved by four Leaving Cert Students from St. Joseph's Secondary School, when they won the annual Senior history Table Quiz and perpetual Cuchulainn Trophy. The event was organised by the History Teachers Association of Ireland and was held in St. Conleth's College Ballsbridge, Dublin with a total of 32 schools from around the country participating.

After a very close fought and difficult contest over ten rounds the St. Joseph's team emerged victorious by a slender one point winning margin which saw them bringing in an excellent final score of 37 points out of a possible total of 60 points. The victorious St. Joseph's team were from left to right, James Eighan, Sarah Smyth, Monica Seery and Dwayne Leavy.

Cliodhna Duigenan all set for the Debs in 2011, Sr. Geraldine, Jennie Gavin and Jennifer Lonican are there to wish her well.

Class Prefects 2011, back row from left to right, Jake Hobby Royle, Joanne Fox, Robert Grey, Cillian Duggan, Adam Boardman and Amie Giles. Front row from left to right, Robert Gray, Jodie Lewis, _____, Sarah Kiernan, Orla Judge, Jean Kelly and Jacob Cairns.

James Gallagher, Karl Wilson, Glen O'Reilly, Conor Raleigh, Richard Harris and Martin Daly. Front Row: Shannon Garry, Mikayla Fivey, Emma Coffey, Shannon Carney and Louisa Judge Not in photo: Ruth Shields, Emily Hughes, Kyle Conway, Brandon Darcy.

Prefects for 2012 include Frances Fallon, Conor Walsh, Kymann Power, Janet Flood, Sinead O'Neill, Emilie Holton, Adam Flanagan, Robbie Greville, Eimear Noonan Treacy, Sean Hanaway, Elaine Geraghty, Mark Glennon, Cian Burke, Niamh McDermott and Aoife Boyle

Lions Club, table quiz runners up in 2012 held in Mullingar, St. Joseph's were represented by Cian Burke, Gemma Gorman, Seán Downey and Christopher Kirwan.

Junior Councillors, Christopher Cole and David Kellegher.

Students from St. Joseph's Sec. School, Rochfortbridge who were presented with a special parchment by Athlone Institute of Technology in recognition of their having achieved an A in the Business Studies (Higher) exam in the Junior Certificate 2010. Pictured here (L-R) Mary O'Sullivan President of BSTAI,Cliona Spellman, Rebecca Smyth, Charlotte Holton (teacher) Mairead Lynam, Niamh Lynch and Prof. Ciaran O'Cathain President of AIT.

Young Social Innovators.

The School choir rehearsing for the later competitions which were held in Dublin.

One of the many faces of Adrian Maguire.

Team Theatre

On the 5th and 6th of October, a youth theatre group from Dublin were performing at Rochfortbridge parish hall. The crew of five performed for the fifth year students of the local secondary school. The play is centred around a group of four friends, who are each faced with life-changing choices, questioning their careers, friendship and commitments.

The play begins at the youngest of the four sitting her Leaving Cert English, Paper one. As she reads through the paper she sees a preferable essay titled, "A turning point in my life". She chooses to write about when she went to the Fusion festival with three friends last summer. Basically the play is based on her memories of the events leading up to and the festival. From here the play follows the path of each of the characters.

Overall, I think this is a very good play, executed brilliantly in such a confined space. The actors interacted very well with the audience, made easy by the fact the audience was on the same level as the actors. The play has its extremely funny moments and never fails to tackle the issue of making serious choices. In the end this play lets us, the audience, wonder what paths the characters are going to take. It keeps the audience guessing. That is what makes it so enjoyable. This play definitely targets senior secondary school students, who have to make decisions for the future. I don't think it would appeal to any other age group. Older people have already made the hard decisions and younger people aren't bothered about the future. I would recommend this play to any T.Y.O., fifth or sixth year students who have yet to start thinking about the future.

Adrian Maguire
Vox 2005

Outdoor Pursuits 2005

The Changing of the Guard. In 2002, Tony O'Sullivan retired as Principal. In an exchange, he handed the keys of St. Joseph's to his successor Tony Hartnett. In return, Tony Hartnett gave him with a golf ball, something he could use a lot, now that he had plenty of time to play the game.

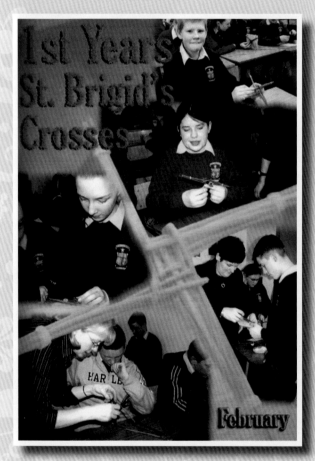

First years St. Brigids crosses, 2005.

Sister Geraldine and friends.

~ CHAPTER 36 ~
THE VOICE OF THE STUDENT

POETRY

The following poems represent a sample of submissions to the school magazines from the early 1980's to 2011.

THE BONFIRE

The flames are rising up and up
I wish that fire would never stop
Lovely colours in all the flames
And everyone playing brilliant games.
And when at last it seems to die down
Everyone's face begins to frown
"Let's throw on another branch"
And everyone begins to dance.
At last - the finish spark goes out
And everyone begins to shout
"Let's have another fire next week"
But that coming true looks quite bleak.

Linda Byrne
Fom 'Vox' 1989

GOODBYE

Goodbye for now,
But not forever.
Hearts may change
But mine will never.

Amanda Woods
Fom 'Vox' 1989

PEACE

Peace is immaculate, Peace is great.
Peace is the opposite of war and hate.
Peace is unique in all its ways,
Peace we hope will not just last for days.
Peace is happiness. Peace is grace,
Peace will bring joy to Ethiopia's face.
May peace last, dear God we ask,
And this poem wasn't such a hard
task.

John Healy
From 'Vox' 1986

SOUNDS OF SCHOOL

Whats first? History!
Everyone groans through Roman civilisation
moan, moan, moan,
Then there's break everyone eats
Crisps, chocolate and all types of treats!
Then there's maths trying to divide by 4
That's it! times up, theres a rush for the door.
Ding! Dong! there goes the bell for lunch
Everybodys gone ....rush, rush, rush
Pencils, copies, everything drops
When the bell for 4 goes nothing stops.
The rustle and bustle as the teachers stare
As people cram and all down the stairs
And the reason of course is too good to be
true,
Because its four o'clock, times up, thats the
end of school.

By Louise McCauley
From 'Vox' 1988

GIRLS

Some girls wear make-up, they like to have
charm,
Others are punctual with a watch on their arm,
Some girls are scruffy with torn hems and
greasy hair,
Others are loving and like to care.
Some girls are shopkeepers, they like to sell,
Others are gossips with a tale to tell,
Some girls are brainy and good at sums,
Others are religious and soon become nuns.
Some girls are weak, some girls are strong,
Others are always humming a song,
No matter how bad some girls are,
Boys are always worse by far!

Olive Manning
From 'Involve' 1984

BUY IRISH

A man looked into his fridge one day,
the sight he saw caused him dismay,
The goods had labels from many a land,
but not even a chip said *"Made In Ireland"*.
So he said to his wife "Now see here Bess
no wonder our country's in such a mess.
We are buying this stuff in from afar,
We even drive a foreign car!
From this day on let me explain
I'm starting my own *Buy Irish Campaign*.
Buy Irish potatoes, cheese, cod or coal,
Help create a new job and
Get a man off the DOLE.

John O'Brien
From 'Involve' 1984.

SOUNDS OF HATE

First thing in the morning
How I hate that sound!
The buzz of the clock
Time to hit town.
As the morning wears on
On my way into school
"Ding-a-ling" goes the bell
Wish I could change that rule.
I sit in my classroom
With my friends all around
Teacher squeak loudly
I wish I could go.
Then home in the evening,
At the end of the day,
The donkey brays loudly,
He'll be wanting some hay.
When dinner is over
And all are fed,
Then mother yells loudly
"Get up to bed. "
And then I crawl under
The covers once more,
Once again to discover
My sister, she snores.

By Karen Gavigan
From Extra 1997.

ST. JOSEPH'S SCHOOL

In the middle of the bogland
Far away from the town,
St. Joseph 's lies sheltered
In peat and so brown.
Why such a monastery was
Built so remote
And what is the purpose,
Of this oversized "motte"?
It was built by the sisters
Who came to the place
With a mission from God
To pray for our race.
They built their big nest
And weaved it so well
And now it's a centre
For learning as well.
It caters for girls and also for boys
From 12 to 18
They came in their droves.
On buses and bikes
With britches and tights.
A fair minded, fun loving, frolicking lot
Some are determined, while others are not,
To prepare for tomorrow Or let it all drop.
When five years are over
And the foundations are down
They will go on their way
To find fame and renown.
Whatever they do, Wherever they go,
St. Joseph's and the bogland,
Will have shaped them so.

BY CATHERINE LONDON.
From Extra 1997.

SHARING YOUR FRIENDSHIP

Sharing your friendship means so much to me
For I think its as close as a friendship can be.
We've shared dreams together and seen them
come true.
We've experienced sorrow and emptiness too.
But to feel these emotions and share them
together,
Can bring out the sun in the stormiest weather.
So always hold on to the love that I send and
thank you for
being such wonderful *Friends*.

Written By: Therese Daly
For: The 6th Years of 2001
Vox 2001

ALWAYSTOGETHER NEVER APART

As I step out into the world
I feel so alone,
I feel like I'm the only one
I just want to go home,
I want to have more confidence
To be a stronger me,
I never want you to go
We'll be alone, why can't you see,
But this is what we have to do
We have to move on,
To go our separate ways alone
And sing our own song,
To make our own path in life
But never forget this please,
Our paths will join again someday
We will all reunite,
Because nothing in the world could break
The bond we have in life

Samantha Kirby
2003 Leaving Cert Book.

TEACHERS

Our many thanks, the countless smiles
So teachers, my advice to you is:
You blessed us with for so long;
Be assured we treasure them still in our hearts,
Even though we will be gone.
Our many thanks, the kindest words
You shared with us in our pleasure and pain;
Know each one of them win be remembered
and returned
When, in time, we meet again.
And our many thanks, the freely love given -
Without condition - you gave to each of us;
Of all the gifts you've given,
None other means quite as much.

The Leaving Cert Book 2003.

ODE TO THE SIXTH YEAR FRIENDS

A Circle of friends, that's what we are,
We've come so close and yet so far.
Throughout the years we've helped each other
To come so close like sister and brother.
A simple word, a little sigh
Can easily bring a tear to your eye.
Scarcity of words, fear of the unknown,
What will we do when we are fully grown?
And now it's time to say goodbye
As we all thank each other for years gone by.
Some will mourn, and some will jump with
delight
But for me, I'll try to fight the pain of
something that's not quite right.
I'll miss you all loads and I wish you well
And maybe sometime we could give each
other a bell.
So take my advice that someone once said,
'Don't cry because it's over,
Smile because it happened'.

Aoife O' Neill
From Vox 1999

LIFE

The field of dreams,
The sound of silence,
The cheer of teams
Is wrecked by violence
The expectation
Yielded by concentration
The sound of drums,
The screaming Mums
The heartbreak of loss,
The joys of winning,
The coming together,
The manager grinning
Life is a cycle
Of regret and despair,
But our time will pass,
If we don't aim to dare
And when we remember
The times that we had,
We will not feel guilty,
But rejoice and be glad.

By: L. Gallagher
Vox. 2011

A tribute to the 6th years: Class 2002

So another year comes to an end,
We say goodbye to all our friends.
As we part along our different ways,
And reminisce on our old school days -
We think of those we met in first year
And all the friends who are so dear,
The times spent down 'behind the gym'
And some inside trying to win.

Moving on and gaining power
Some friendships known have now turned sour.
From Junior Cert to 5th year doss
And our famous year not doing a toss.
Losing some to T.Y.O.
And more into the bad world go.
While others thought of exams and sighed,
And opted for the Leaving Cert Applied.

So now our year, reduced by many,
Trundles on without a penny.

And heads into the final year,
With nothing less than joyful cheer.
And welcomes back some of last year's crowd,
Who've proved they are quiet well - endowed!
And have so far survived with grace,
To keep up with the rigorous pace.

So another year is over now
Will we sigh and wonder how -
We could've made all the mistakes we did,
Instead of just trying to get rid
Of any bad memories that we have,
And anything that has made us sad?
For think we're out of the land of torture,
No more work or teacher's slaughter.
We're free from the judgmental eye,
And all of those who made us cry.
So thank the teachers' and the rest,
For they tried to do their best -
With a year that was doomed from the 1st year mass,
Who has now become a year with class.

So 5th years, we are your guides,
Wear our 6th year badge with pride.

Mary Mcguire.

~ CHAPTER 37 ~
A TRUE HEROINE

Proud and happy 16-year old Delvin student Deirdre Manny delighted organisers of this years 58th Texaco Children's Art Competition when she arrived back in Ireland after undergorng major surgery in London just one day before she was due to receive her first prize award from Minister for Arts, Heritage and the Gaeltacht, Jimmy Deenihan.

Accompanied by by her parents Lonan and Lena sister Mary and brother Lonan-Francis (also a special merit award winner), Deirdre displayed all the courage and determination that helped her through difficult surgery and made her first prize winner in Category G of the competition for the third year in succession.

In Early March 2012, Deirdre underwent an intricate eight hour operation at Great Ormond Street Children's Hospital in London, where surgeons worked to correct a neurological condition that had affected her since early childhood.

After a period of recovery at Great ormond Street, Deirdre transferred to a special rehabilitation unit in Surrey, where she remained for twelve weeks before heading home to attend the prize ceremony and collect her €450 prize.

Describing her as a *'a true heroine,'* Enda Riney, country chairman of Texaco brand owners Valero (Ireland) Limited said Deirdre was *'a highly talented young artist and a wonderful example to every young person.'*

A student at St. Joseph's Secondary School, Rochfortbrige, Deirdre won first prize for her entry, *White Wild Roses.*

This wasn't the first time Deirdre was successful in this competition

- 2008, Merit Summer Morning 12 Years

- 2010 Still Life- Fruit of unusual colours 14 years

- 2011 First Prize- Welsh Poppies- 15 years

- 2012 First Prize-Category G White Wild Roses 16 years

Deirdre always had an eye from an early age for colour. Her artistic talent was greatly encouraged in St. Joseph's and continues to blossom there. Artistic talent runs in the family also, Deirdre's brother Lonan Francis received a merit award in 2010 and again in 2012 in the Texaco Children's Art Competition.

~ CHAPTER 38 ~
SNAPSHOT FROM 1984

The opening of the new secondary school in 1984 produced an interesting archive of staff photos. The following are but a few.

Chris Cole and Sheamus Casey enjoying dessert.

Relaxing with a pint after a busy day, Eugene Dunbar, Sheamus Casey, Chris Cole and Noel Foynes.

Tony O' Sullivan observing the proceedings.

Sister Geraldine checking that all the delphware is in order.

Sister Columba, posing for the camera

Sister Pius in deep conversation.

'Is the cake all for me?' asks Tony.

'What next?' asks Noel.

Deep in conversation, Dermot Bennett and Nuala Lawlor.

It's Ok Eugene, it was the days before the smoking ban.

Luke Dempsey and Mary Hayes, pose for the camera.

~ CHAPTER 39 ~
FACES

Cathy Spellman

Eugene Dunbar

John Drumey

Damian Rushe

Eamonn Gallagher

Mary Grogan

Eileen Alford

Brian Smyth.

Let me out!

Nuala Lawlor- 1997

Aoife Sweeney

Laura Kelleghan

Matthew Rice -1998

Ronan Dunbar-1997

Stephen Kirwan

Tommy Byrne- 1984

~ CHAPTER 40 ~

PAST PUPILS OF ST. JOSEPH'S WHOSE VOCATION LED TO THE PRIESTHOOD.

Fr. Liam Carey.

Fr. Kiam Carey was born in the village of Rochfortbridge in 1949. His late parents Edward and Mary reared a large family in the street of the village quite close to St. Joseph's and the parochial house. He attended the Convent of Mercy Primary school and later the Boys National School and received his Secondary education at St. Joseph's Secondary School. As a young boy he served mass in the local Church of the Immaculate Conception and together with his brother Jimmy served at the mass to commemmorate the centenary of the foundation of the Sisters of Mercy in 1962.

He completed his secondary education at Galbaly Park, Ballinasloe.

Liam followed a career in the butchering trade and for many years, he owned shops at Kilcormac and Daingean.

His life moved in an entirely different direction in 1978 when he joined the Columban Fathers at Dalgan Park. During his time as a seminarian in Maynooth, he spent two years working in parishes in Peru, from 1982 to 1984.

On completing his studies in Maynooth, he was ordained in Meedin Church by Bishop Michael Smith on the 5th of December 1987 and celebrated his first mass in St. Joseph the Worker Hall on the 6th of December 1987. At this time the Church of the Immaculate Conception was undergoing renovations. He later spent some time in Portugal learning Portuguese and worked at his first mission in Bahia in Northern Brazil for four years. His work continues tirelessly on the mission fields and he returns every three years to Rochfortbridge to stay with family and relatives.

Fr. Liam is pictured with his nephew Conor Wall holding the cake at the celebrations to mark his ordination in December 1987.

Rev. Raymond Kelly

Rev. Raymon Kelly was born in Tyrrellspass in 1953. His home at Church Road, Tyrrellspass was very well known by the many families in the Tyrrellspass, Rochfortbride and Kilbeggan areas for many years as is Mother, Mona served as Mid-wife to the locality for many years. He attended Primary school at Tyrrellspass N.S. and later at St. Joseph's Secondary School, Rochfortbridge. On leaving Secondary school he worked for ten years in the Civil Service and then entered St Patrick's Missionary Society, Kiltegan in 1980.

He was ordained in St. Stephen's Church Tyrrellspass by Bishop Michael Smith on the 19th of June 1989. He worked for a time in Aughnacloy on the Monaghan, Armagh Boarder, the Curragh, Kildare and in England, when he was transferred as C.C. to Navan in 2002. Fr. Ray now serves as P.P. in Oldcastle, Co. Meath. Fr. Ray comes from a very musical background and many of his close family and extended family are involved in the music industry. He is often called upon to sing at functions and has indeed been into the recording studio also. In this photo he is pictured with his Mother Mona and his Father Joe on the occassion of his ordination in 1989.

Rev. Michael Kilmartin

Rev. Michael Kilmartin was born in Mulingar Regional Hospital on the 14th of January 1972. He was the first son of Brendan and the late Noeleen Kilmartin, Kinnegad. He was the middle child of three. His sister MareTherése, being the oldest and his brother Barry, the youngest. He attended Kinnegad National School from 1976 to 1984 and St. Joseph's school from 1984 to 1989. While at St. Joseph's Fr. Michael was very active in drama and sport and was a shared prizewinner at the Aer Lingus Young Scientist Competition. He entered St. Patrick's College, Maynooth in 1989 and qualified with an arts degree in 1992. He completed his Degree in Theology in 1995, and went to Rome as Deacon to take a Masters Degree in biblical Theology at the Gregorian University. He was ordained in Kinnegad Church by Dr. Michael Smith, Bishop of Meath on the 21st of July. He was appointed C.C. Mullingar in September 1997, but did not take up the position until February 1998.

Rev. Michael comes from a family who have a history of serving the church over the years. Three Grand Uncles were priests of the Diocese of Meath during the 20th century and all hailed from Kinnegad.

Rev. John Kilmartin was appointed Parish Priest of Rochortbridge in 1941 and served there until 1949, he died P.P., Drogheda in 1952.

Rev. Joseph Kilmartin was appointed P.P., Kilcloon in 1943 and died in 1973.

Rev. Michael Kilmartin was appointed P.P., Ballynacargy in 1942 and died in 1990.

Rev. Michael Kilmartin has in his possession the oil stock used by his Grand Uncle Michael when he was P.P. Ballynacargy which he carries with him today when administering the sacraments to the sick.

Since coming to Mullingar parish Fr. Michael has worked in the Gainstown area and was one of the driving forces in the refurbishment and re-building of Gainstown National School, now known as St. Colmcille's National school.

~ CHAPTER 41 ~
INTERESTING IMAGES

Car Parking in the 1980's

The Convent Garden and tennis court.

A neatly manicured garden.

The convent taken from the Secondary School

Construction work begins and Gavin's hay is saved.

This little friend appeared in one of the Vox School magazines and the students gave it the title, 'Mr. Bennett's new car.'

Up the bare stairs to a classroom at the back of the convent.

Rochfortbridge village in the 1980's.

The entrance to the nuns chapel which was attached to the Parish church of the Immaculate Conception. The chapel was removed when the church was renovated in the late 1980's.

Rochfortbridge village in 1981. Note the standard paint colour on the walls of St. Joseph's and the rest of the street. Chris Cole and Tony Harnett review the situation.

Oh when the Saints..... The crib figures from the parish Church are being taken in Joe Carthy's blue Volkswagen truck into storage for another year at the end of the Christmas season in the 1980's.

Tony Hartnett outside St. Joseph's in 1981.   *Tony Hartnett and Eugene Dunbar outside St. Joseph's.*

The Green Isle with the convent in the background, just before it was demolished in 1981.

Fr. John McManus P.P. taken in the garden in the 1970's.

< Connell's house and shed which were converted into a canteen, music room and games shed in the early 1970's.

~ CHAPTER 42 ~
THE STAFFROOM

Enjoying a cuppa

Saying farewell to German exchange student.

'I'm wondering what the Examiner have to say about St. Joseph's this week?'

'Does anyone know where the toilet is?'

Pat Eighan, striking a pose!

Sheamus and Noel joining the lifeboats!

Sheamus the boat builder.

At the opening of the new Secondary school in 1984, Sister Finian directs traffic while Sister Pius carries the bread for the sandwiches.

Sheamus McHugh and Dermot Bennett.

Wishing you well on your retirement Sister!'

'Watchful eyes keep an eye on things!'

Staff and teachers at Sister Magdalene's retirement in 1988.

'New fashions for principals!'

'Lights, camera, action!'

'Sheamus's new car!'

'Entertaining Mr. Foynes!'

Teachers on tour.

Stopping for the camera, Adrian Lee, Eamonn Scally, Susan Hogan and Eileen Alford.

'Why are you holding the camera the wrong way?'

'Deep thinker!'

'Another squeeze and I'm through.'

'Go away with that camera!'

'A man! I've got a man all of my own!'

'One sandwich, cheese and ham, forget the Mayo!'

Teachers on tour again!'

'Getting ready to walk the plank!'

Pupil parade, Break is over!

Bringing it all back home to Rochfortbridge!

Staff photo from the 1970's.

Oh Sorry! The engine is on the other end.'

'Tony handing over to Tony! Farewell Mr. O'Sullivan!'

Denis Kelly and Sr. Pius.

~ CHAPTER 43 ~
YOUNG SCIENTISTS

Young Scientists Exhibition: 1983

This was the schools first year ever to take part and it received a highly commended prize for one of two projects entered. Five students in all took part and were assisted by Miss O'Rourke and Mr. Bennett.

Our project examined the effects of preservatives on a number of foods. It also determined the presence of sulphur dioxide in named foods and its effect on human consumers. We found that sulphur dioxide protects Vitamins A and C while it kills Vitamin B which is necessary for normal growth, carbohydrate metabolism, functioning of the heart nerves and muscles. We discovered that this could be rectified by eating green vegetables, however, if they are over-cooked they become dehydrated and sulphur dioxide would be formed. This project received a highly

Barry Kilmartin, pictured with Minister for Education Mary O'Rourke, discussing his entry in the Young Scientists Exhibition.

commended prize for research into the food preservative, sulphur dioxide, which the E.E.C. has talked about banning.

The second project titled Water Fluoridation - How Good, did a large survey of two areas in the locality, one having, fluoride in the water supply the other not. We found a large difference between the number of teeth missing, filled and decayed in both areas thus showing that Fluoridation of water supplies is a means of preventing dental caries up to even 30% .

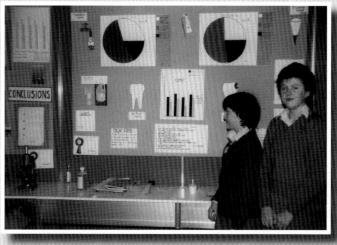

1983, Aer Lingus Young Scientists Competition held at the RDS in Dublin, with a project entitled 'Water Fluoridation-how good?" Exhibitors, Frances Kelly and Marie Therése Kilmartin.

Young Scientists Exhibition: 1984

On Wednesday, January 4th all exhibitors assembled their projects as judging was due to commence that evening. On arrival all received exhibitors badges, a pencil and a catalogue. Once our projects were assembled we were free to stroll around viewing the other exhibits. The range of topics included Accoustic Braille and Silage Effluent.

Official judging began on Thursday and Friday, all exhibitors were interviewed by three judges. Many leading politicans visited the exhibition including the Taoiseach, the Tanaiste, Gemma Hussey and the President. Every day we received a copy of the Young Citizen magazine which contained interesting facts and details of the exhibition. We became friendly with many exhibitors especially Aileen Ivory and Mary Lou McDonald who exhibited a Project on Pollution and the Dodder River.

On Friday the major award winners were announced, these included projects on Ohms Law, Silage Effluent, Mussels in Bantry Bay and the Five Liffeys. Over a hundred prizes were awarded that night and on Saturday a hundred more received sweat-shirts. The following days were open to the public and the exhibitors answered any queries that arose about the projects.

One of the funny occurrences was the story of how three boys were charged double to bring a barrel of manure in a taxi through Dublin. Also we heard stories of how others broke equipment needed for demonstrations. On Sunday evening as we were taking down our projcts we were all told to leave quickly, this was due to a bomb scare as we found out later.

At the end of the day we left Dublin after making many new friends and discovering very interesting facts about shampoos, milk, rivers, food, fungi and computers. We all hope to exhibit again next year, we also hope that others shall accompany us.

Marie Therese Kilmartin D2
Geraldine Giles 5B
Colette Gaffney 5A

From left, Geraldine Giles, Collette Gaffney and Mary Clarke - highly commended for their project on Food Chemistry and Preservatives in 1984.

YOUNG SCIENTISTS 1995

Joseph Corcoran, Audrey Daly, Danny Culligan Aoife Smyth, exhibitors in 1995.

Last October four Rochfortbridge students were faced with the challenge of constructing a project which would win us a place at the RDS in January '95. We were Joseph Corcoran, Audrey Daly, Danny Culligan and myself Aoife Smyth as group leader.

Our entry was successful and the preparation and hard work was underway. We got lots of help from our class, 3.3 and teacher, Mr. O'Rourke. Eventually on December 22nd our project entitled *"Gummys not funny – preventative factors"* was ready.

On January 3rd we set up our stand in the RDS numbered 372. While setting up our stand we met a newspaper reporter from the "Irish Times". He asked us questions on our project. This got us off to a brilliant start.

On January 4th we were excited and nervous while we waited for our first judge. She soon arrived and we all felt the judging was fine. She congratulated us on our project as it was our first time entering.

On January 5th we met our second judge who also seemed to enjoy our project. Around lunch time we received a note inviting us to be on radio 103.5 FM, which is our local station. It was a wonderful experience. That afternoon we had our last and final adjudication.

Unfortunately this did not go as well as the other two. Friday, January 6th was a day of tours which we enjoyed. Our class also came and they enjoyed looking at all the different stands on the different topics that ranged from "the bog" to things like "bats" and "safety".

Saturday the RDS was open to the public. It was a fantastic experience. Sunday, the big day arrived for the announcement of the Young Scientists '95. This day was filled with mixed emotion. Some people were excited, others were sad as they had to say goodbye to the people they had made friends with over that week. Ray D'Arcy was the special guest who presented the "ending party", which was the presenting of awards and some fun and games. President Mary Robinson and Gerry Ryan and Pat Kenny were others who also attended. We unfortunately did not succeed in winning a prize but we received a certificate and most of all the memory of the friends we made and the fun we had in that one week.

AOIFE SMYTH
Vox 1995

Jenifer Nolan, Marina McWalter, Ulrika Maher, Transition Year 1995/96 who were highly comended at Young Scientist Exhibition '95/96

~ CHAPTER 44 ~
YOUNG SOCIAL INNOVATORS 2008

Over 5000 transition year and fifth year students participated this year in some 450 projects throughout the country in The Young Social Innovators Competition 2008. The responses from each of the YSI projects were impressive and inspiring and show how Young people's ideas, work and passion are making differences to real issues affecting local communities.

Saint Joseph's Secondary school's project entitled *"Feeling Low? Let Someone Know .. *is a step up challenge for Making The World A Healthier Place. This project dealt with depression and the awareness of suicide among young people. It is an ongoing project which began in September 2006. With initial sponsorship from The Health Service Executive, they redesigned their helpline card. This year they received further funding from our local Soroptimists International group and once again redesigned the helpline card into a wallet sized card with numbers of the main organisations that are relevant to young people. They also ran a poster campaign through local establishments such as The Greville Arms Hotel, Mojo's Nightclub and The Final Fence. The group were one of the 365 chosen projects to showcase our project in the RDS for The Young Social Innovators Competition 2008. The project members were also invited to present their Speak out piece which was a short play entitled *"Dear Diary"* to a selection of special guests and also during the two day showcase for the students present. They were also chosen to pitch an idea to a panel of judges, to apply for further funding. The Opening Ceremony was presented by PJ Gallagher, comedian and TV personality of *Naked Camera*. It was very humorous as he introduced an array of guests including our President, Mary McAleese, Sister Stan, Rachel Collier and Elaine Higgins. Incidentally, one of the group made her way through security to personally hand Mary Mc Aleese a *"Feeling Low, Let Someone Know"* Helpline card.

Three students Amée Dunne, John Gorman and Miriam Wynne represented their project in the YSI Den. They applied for funding to place their poster campaign on the back cover of *Faceup*, which is a monthly magazine distributed to schools nationwide. The students were awarded €2,400 to put this campaign into action so their posters will appear on the back cover of *Face Up* for a year and thus will be seen by every student in Ireland. A huge achievement. Mary Kennedy an RTE Presenter hosted the Closing Ceremony, with entertainment by popular Irish band *The Coronas.*

The real excitement came when the awards were announced and given and after a long wait the amazing news that St Joseph's Secondary School, Rochfortbridge had won the Silver Award Overall among the projects in the competition.

This was a huge achievement and well deserved as the students involved have worked tirelessly to promote their message and raise awareness.

Their work doesn't stop there. The group have been offered sponsorship by both the Mullingar and Tullamore Lions Clubs to continue the project next year. On Saturday next the group have been invited to meet with **Dáil na nÓg** by the Office of the Minster for children and have been approached by *The National Office for Suicide Prevention* who wish to support the group in making the project a national concern. So it looks like things are only just beginning... So watch this space ...

Young Social Innovators Project
S.0.S - Save Our Schools

In September Ms Sheridan introduced us to *the Young Social Innovators Project.* She arranged for Ms McCarthy, who works in India during the summer months teaching disadvantaged children, to visit our Transition Year class. She informed us that there are four schools in North East India, who are in dire need of funds so that they can remain open for another year. Our class were very moved by what she had to tell us, and we immediately decided to do whatever we could to help these children. Fr. Anthony Vallurain, an Indian priest who works with these schools, later visited us and gave us more of a realistic idea of the troubles that these schools face. He said that the teachers get paid a mere €20 a month and that the children have no desks, and must sit on the floor. These children have not got much but really value their education, which makes you appreciate our great way of life, and the many opportunities available to us in the Western World.

Fr. Anthony said that just to keep these schools open, we would have to raise at least €3000. And so we set this amount as our initial target and, with this goal in mind, we were spurred into action.

We began to "brainstorm" ideas to raise the funds, and an idea we came up with was a sponsored sleepover in the school. So we slept over in the school on Friday, 23rd November and raised a staggering €1500!! This amount far exceeded all our expectations, pushing us up to the half way mark.

Following on from the success of the sleepover, we organised a number of other fundraising events, including carol singing, a carol service, and a raffle and along with donations, we managed to reach our target of €3000 just before Christmas. It was an amazing achievement, made all the more special by the knowledge that we were doing so much good for the four schools, and that they would benefit enormously from this money.

After Christmas, our class began to prepare for our YSI *Speak Out Forum* at the end of January- a chance to explain our project and the motives behind it. We decided to stage a play showing the differences between our school life and that of Indian students. The play was a success and we had a great time performing it! from both staff and fellow students, which was very much appreciated. We were kept busy, trying to prepare our proposal for the YSI Showcase in May, while at the same time trying to come up with possible fund raising events, as we wanted to raise as much money as possible. A fashion show was suggested, and immediately our group knew it would be a success. We, along with Ms Sheridan and indeed many other teachers, began making preparations straightaway.

We approached clothes shops in Mullingar to ask for their support and we received a very positive response, with a total of eleven shops coming on board, ranging from Wilf's to Wisteria and Cocoon, from Hugh Daniels to Sassy. Throughout the project we had overwhelming support.

Overall we have raised a massive € 10,000 euro, €7,000 from our fashion show and €3,000 from our other ventures. We cannot believe that we have achieved above and beyond our initial target of €3,000.

We are so happy to think of the good that will be done for those children far away in India.

~ CHAPTER 45 ~
THE VALUE OF SPORT AT ST. JOSEPH'S 1948-2012
By Noel Foynes

~ CHAPTER 45 ~

THE VALUE OF SPORT AT ST. JOSEPH'S 1948-2012

By Noel Foynes

"The lessons we learn from sport can help us to live our lives off the sports fields. Team games show us the value of team work. The selfish player who refuses to co-operate is of no great benefit to their side In the same way in our daily lives we can achieve much more if we accept the help of others. In sport we learn the way to accept defeat with good humour and be generous when we win".

Ruth Coffey, Vox Magazine, 1985

In this prize winning and very perceptive essay published in Vox the student magazine from 1985 and titled, *"The Value of Sport"*, Ruth Coffey, a pupil in St. Joseph's at that time best described the values of the give and take of participation in sport. In this she advised that acceptance and generosity ought to be part of the emotions that are generated by success and failure in competition and offered very positive advice on how to greet both of these sporting challenges in equal measure.

Sport has always been an integral part of school life in St. Joseph's. From the foundation of the Secondary School in 1948, there has always been an encouragement of physical exercise in some form or another, even though it may not have been in the structured and formalised organisation and of such a variety of activities that are on offer to present day students, nevertheless, the facilities provided by the Sisters in these early years laid the foundations in every sense of what was to be achieved in the years to come.

An early Hockey Team c.1968. Back Row: Left to Right: Valerie Darby, Olive Gray, Ann O'Dowd, Maura Curran, Rosemary Hyland, Bernadette Harte, Mary Duffy, Theresa O'Reilly, Mary O'Dowd. Middle Row: Left to Right: Ann Doherty, Mary Donoghue, Margaret Geraghty, Patricia Kenny, Anne Mulroy, Mary Glennon.
Front Row: Left to Right: Elizabeth Deegan, Dorothy Oakes, Carmel Mullarkey, Mary Ganly, Rosaleen Neary, Catherine Kelly, Ann Fagan, Ann Ganly.

Not surprisingly we read about these early efforts from the Annals of the Convent which stated in 1956:- *"School re-opened in Sept. with fifty two boarders. A graduate from Galway was engaged to teach for the coming year – Miss Angela Costello – so with Sr. M. Magdalene, Dolores and Pius, and M.M. Agnes and Sr. M. Stanislaus part time, school work sprang into life for another year. To comply with pressing demands for further outdoor games, a bulldozer levelled a playing field in preparation for a tennis court. This cost £55."*

Deirdre Grace with St. Anne's in the background.

In the earlier years as the school was a boarding school for girls, hockey and tennis seemed to have been the major activities, though competitions were not entered into in that era and Sr. Geraldine would supervise games of Tennis on the *"new"* courts. Photographic evidence from the time seems to portray a more leisurely approach to sport in comparison to the commotion created by modern day competitive action. This idyllic setting in the *"convent field"* being ever more enhanced by the presence of St. Anne's an American-styled summer house belonging to the Sisters that formed the backdrop to the tennis courts. St. Anne's with its enchanting green roof and its timber framed structure was then a place for rest and reflection and seemed to be more in keeping with a scene from *"The Little House on the Prairie"* rather than as at the centre of what was to become a bustling school yard as time went by. Physical Education as such was unknown in the early years and it was not until the mid 1970's when it was introduced into the Schools time-table that the competitive elements on offer began to be looked into more seriously and the story of sport at St. Joseph's was about to begin.

Imelda Coyne with St. Anne's in the background.

Mid 1960's: "On the Steps of St. Anne's"
Marie Hart, Josephine Corcoran, Goretti Brown.

Athletics

Athletics has been very much to the forefront in recent years, but there is earlier evidence to suggest that talented athletes were always in the school. In 1979, the school competed in the Leinster Cross Country Championship Finals for the first time and Thomas Cully represented the school with great distinction here. In the Leinster Cross Country Finals held in Santry on the 1st. March, 1983, Pat Costello came home first in the Under 15 event with Eileen Morgan also doing the school proud finishing in fifth position at Under 19 level.

Pat Costello.

An edition of Forum, the School's newsletter dated March 1983, best summed up their achievements:- *"the best performance of the year by a student of St. Joseph's in any sport was given by Pat Costello in the Leinster Schools Finals held in Santry, Dublin on March 1st. Pat came first in a very strong field of runners – a just reward for a very dedicated and committed athlete. Eileen Morgan also did the school proud when she came in a very respectable fifth position and qualified along with Pat for the All-Ireland schools finals in Belfast"*. Eileen and Pat went on to represent the school with distinction in the All-Ireland Schools Finals in Belfast later that year. It is also worth noting that in the North Leinster Championships held earlier that year, Aedemar Nolan, Tommy Byrne, Louise Dunne, Olive Manning and Mervyn Daly finished well up the field in their age groups

The 15th. February, 1984, saw the school's Cross Country teams travelling to Malahide Park to compete in the North Leinster Championships, the conditions on the day were described as excellent for running and the standards in each race was very high. In the girl's Under 20, Audrey Brennan qualified for the North Leinster final in Santry a few weeks later where she finished well up the field. Other notable performances from Malahide Park were Cera Nolan and Michael Nugent at Under 17 level, and at Under 15 level Anthony Casey and Aidan Dunne deserve special mention for their great efforts over a challenging course.

In the North Leinster Track and Field that year, Audrey Brennan threw an outstanding 21 metres in the javelin; Cera Nolan won her heat of the 80 metres hurdles, with Louise Dunne making it to the final of the junior hurdles with great times also achieved in the hurdles by Noelle Kenny, Marie Giles and Olive Mangan. In the 100 and 200 metres, Rosanne Kelleghan and Nessa McDermott reached the semi-finals in their events respectively. Both Helen Keogh and Yvonne Gunning competed in the shot putt, Bernie Maher fought to the finish in the 1500 metres, Fiona Walsh the same in the 800 metres, the team that day was completed by Theresa Feery, Colette Farrell, Niamh O'Brien, Martina Hannon, Avril Kirwan and Anne Marie McGearty. Towards the end of the 1980's, the concept of individual sports awards began to be introduced into the school and it was described thus at the time:- *"as an award for the most outstanding junior and senior girl and boy who has shown excellence on the field and inspires others"*. In 1989, the Junior girls award went to Ann Marie Curran for her commitment to training in cross-country, basketball and hockey, the Senior girl's award went to Denise Farrell, not just as an athlete but for her assistance to the junior teams in the school. The Junior boy's award that year went to Jonathon O'Connor, and the Senior boy's award went to Noel Gavin. In more recent years the Sports Awards became more wide ranging and formed part of a school day usually towards the end of May when the entire school assembled in the Sports Hall for the presentation ceremonies. This in turn has also being replaced by a Gala Night now held in a local hotel where the Awards are presented by an invited personality from the world of sport to the worthy recipients each year.

2012 Sports Awards Night: "Ned happy to be here"
From Left: Dessie Dolan, Ned Cully, Shane Corcoran,
Joseph Hyland.

The 1990's began with success in the North Leinster Track and Field Championships held in Malahide Park where Jacqueline McNamara finished third in the Cross Country event and Yvonne McCormack did excellently well finishing first in the 100 metres and later finished second in the Leinster Colleges held in Santry later that year equalling her own best time of 12.63 seconds in the process. In 1993 an Intermediate girl's team comprising of Jackie and Caroline McNamara, Sonya Fennelly and Caroline Byrne won the North Leinster Cross Country Championship. That same year a strong boys team competed in the same event and had outstanding performers

Yvonne McCormack
Winner of the 100 Metres
Under 15 Sprint in the
North Leinster Track and
Field, Santry, Dublin 1990.

2001: Louise Moore:
Member of the successful
Leinster Under 16 Girls
Cross Country Team.

at Under 14 level with Brendan Mulvin and Shane Rafferty at Under 15 level with Derek Griffin, Emmett Brennan, Jacko Healy and Paul Dempsey, the Under 17's being represented by Andrew Glennon, Denis McElroy and Sean Drinan and the Under 19 team featuring Patrick Cooney and Roberto Mezzapelle. In 1995, a team containing Caroline Byrne, Caroline McNamara, Lorraine McNicholas and Jill McQuaid qualified for the 4 X 100 Metres Senior Relay. Also that year John Gavin qualified for the finals of both the Under 14 100 and 200 Metres held in Santry. In 1997, at the Leinster Track and Field Finals, both Lorraine McNicholas and Justin Murtagh agonisingly failed to qualify for the All-Ireland Cross Country Championships by just one place. The following year saw Stephen Burke picking up a Silver medal for the Junior Shot Putt in the North Leinster Championships and Caroline Harney picking up Bronze for the 200 Metres at the same event. In 1999, Caroline Harney continued to shine by taking Gold in the 1500 Metres at the North Leinster Championships held in Santry with Marie Duffy a strong athlete winning Bronze in the 800 Metres, other members of that team were Verona McQuaid, Emer Fox and Bridie O'Sullivan. In the early part of the 2000's, Louise Moore as a cross country runner represented her school, her club, her county and Ireland and in 2003 was a recipient in the Westmeath Annual Athletics Sports Stars Awards. In 2006, Adam Boardman, a new star in St. Joseph's won an Under 14 Leinster Cross Country Title.

Saturday 8th March, 2008 has become a red letter day in the history of Athletics in the School as Jake Byrne outsprinted Ryan Creech of Cork in the final 600 Metres to take the All-Ireland Intermediate Cross Country Championship held in Loughrea Co Galway. Jake then became the first pupil from St. Joseph's to win a national title and in doing so won his first international singlet as he was selected for the Irish Schools Team. At that same meeting, Amie Giles battled very hard in the Intermediate Cross Country race and later that year was greatly compensated when she won an All-Ireland indoors title in Nenagh. In June 2009, Jake Byrne won another gold medal when finishing first in the 3,000 Metres in the All-Ireland Secondary Schools Track and Field Championships held in Tullamore. Other successes were soon to follow and in 2011 five students qualified for the Leinster Championships that took place in the DCU sports grounds, they were Jake Byrne, Shane Fitzsimons, Jack Reid (who came first), Liam O'Reilly and Aisling Moody (who finished second). Also as a first for the School, the Girl's Junior Cross Country Team finished second to take Silver on the Podium, this team for the record was:- Aisling Moody, Jill Booker, Amy Foran, Dawn Hannon, Aoife Holton, Lauren Creamer and Clare O'Sullivan. By the end of the 2010-2011 season athletics had such a high profile in the School that it could claim three International athletes in Jack Reid, Shane Fitzsimons and Jake Byrne who for his many achievements would later go on to secure an Athletics Scholarship to Iona College, New York. The 2011-2012 season began on a high when thirty-eight students from the School took part in the Westmeath County Schools Cross Country Championships taking home seventeen medals. In the North Leinster Cross Country Championships, five students progressed to the Leinster Final, Cormac Dalton, Aisling Moody, Eoin O'Brien, Lorna Moody and Jack Reid, from here Cormac and Aisling progressed to the All-Ireland Cross Country Championships held in Galway where Cormac came in fourth place and was just pipped on the line for the bronze medal, Aisling came eleventh and earned a reserve place for the international team. Success came early in 2012 at the North Leinster Track and Field with:- Emma-Jude Lyons (1st. Year) gold for javelin, Méabh McNulty (1st.

Jake Byrne on his way to victory again.

Jack Reid powers home yet again.

2009 All-Ireland Schools 3000 Metres Final. From Left: Liam Brady, St. Brendan's Birr (Silver), Jake Byrne, St. Joseph's Rochfortbridge (Gold), Tommy Casey, Sligo Grammar School (Bronze).

Athletics Coach: Susan Hogan.

Year) silver for 500M, Cormac Dalton (1st. Year) bronze for 1,100M, Jack Reid (3rd. Year) bronze for 1500M and Shane Fitzsimons (TY) gold for 1500M. Indeed Shane Fitzsimons eventually went on to capture the All-Ireland title in the Senior Boys 1500M at the Aviva All-Ireland Schools Track and Field Championships held in Tullamore in June 2012 with a blistering fifty six second final lap that burned off all opposition and saw him literally leaping over the line with joy. Jack Reid also claimed silver for the Under 16 mile, illness robbing him of

Shane Fitzsimons crosses the line first in the All-Ireland Schools 1500 Metres Final in Tullamore 2012.

6th. June 2012: Gerald Killeen: "The enduring honour of a Torch Bearer"

his best form which saw him being passed just 50 metres from the line. Very bright futures in store. Another highlight has to be for 2007 Rehab Young Person of the Year Gerald Killeen who has the enduring honour of being part of the Olympic Torch Run when on the 6th. June 2012 he carried the famous flame along the Grand Canal from Clanbrassil Street to Harold's Cross on its way to London 2012.

Basketball

Basketball has always been a central and very successful part of school life in St. Joseph's. The first evidence of competitive Basketball came in November 1979 when the School took part in the Meath Leagues for girls competing against Loreto Mullingar, Mercy Navan and Scoil Mhuire Trim. St. Joseph's then entered four teams comprising of Seniors \ Cadettes \ Juniors and Minors, and of these the Cadettes were the most successful with this particular team being powered by a combination of Joan Mc Donnell's speed and Adrienne Corcoran's accurate shooting. A 1980 edition of the then student magazine known

A Rochfortbridge Under 16 Basketball Team from 1997.
Back Row: Left to Right: David Horan, Brian Broderick, Eoin Miller. Middle Row: Left to Right: Damian Gilligan, Vincent Doherty, John Shaw, Tomás Doyle. Front Row: Left to Right: Darren Kavanagh, Fergal Dardis, Matthew Rice, David Cleary, Ronan Dunbar.

as *"Joe's Journal"* described quite colourfully the ups and downs in the lives of the above mentioned Junior and Minor basketballers thus:- *"The Juniors started off the season badly by losing their first two games, but after Christmas, they won their following two games. They will be playing in the future without Bernie Coyne; presumably the odds for a win will be against them. The Minors had an excellent season and had a lot going for them, Mary Kenny the experienced player from Rhode, the natural advantage of Cathleen Coakley's height and the very accurate shooting of Theresa Feery. However, in all fairness to them, they practised hard, deserved their wins and were unfortunate to lose two games. Keep up the interest girls".*

There was also around this time a great revival of Basketball at lunchtime and prominent student captains of note from these league teams were Frieda Ward and Dympna Maloney, however, it was Fiona Langan's team that won this first *"internal"* league competition and Fiona and her team were presented with their medals before Christmas 1981. A particular highlight from the Meath Leagues occurred in 1983 when Junior A and B and Minor A all contested finals. The Junior A team had Louise Dunne as Captain along with Julie

"Joe singing the Blues in Tallaght"

Daly, June Murphy, Michelle Gunning, Carmel McGovern, Yvonne Gunning, Jacinta Hannon and Olive Manning. The Junior B team was captained by Patricia Hannon and also on that team were Concepta Earley, Geraldine Nolan, Rosaleen McDonough, Marie-Therese Kilmartin and Mary Curran. The Minor A team that year had Mary Gorman as their captain and also included Mary Murtagh, Theresa McCormack, Ann-Marie Bollard, Aedemar Nolan, Lily Garry and Rachel Gaffney. The following year, the most noteworthy achievement was the bringing home of the Junior A League Trophy with the help of Anne Marie Bollard and Geraldine Dunne. The Cadettes were not as successful, but were well served nonetheless by Niamh O'Brien, Clare Mulrooney and Margaret Bollard. For the first time ever the Senior Boy's played competitive matches in 1984 when they were beaten by St. Finian's in Rochfortbridge and also defeat was their lot at a one-day Blitz in Mullingar.

This group of *"pioneers"* for boy's basketball in the School was made up of Brendan Leahy, Joe Arthur, Joe Ennis, Ciaran Kenny, James Gunning and Tommy Newe. This new found interest may have stemmed from the visit earlier that year to the school of U.S.A. basketball star Bobby Lee Ford who at the time was representing The Hawks, a semi-professional team operating in Portarlington.

In 1985, St. Joseph's entered the Midland Leagues for the first time and success came immediately when the Girls Senior Team won their final defeating Moate on a scoreline of 25-15 in Athlone, a new star to emerge in this victory was Lorna O'Brien. The Junior team also won their final the same day defeating Mullingar Vocational School on a scoreline of 26-18, starring for Rochfortbridge in this victory were the Malones, Irene and Linda, Breda McCormack contributed significantly to this victory with some excellent rebound catching and although Josie Garry missed this final, she did receive a trophy. The next success in the Midland Schools League came in 1988 when a group of Fifth Years inspired by Fiona Walsh defeated Kilbeggan. A feature of this final was the excellent contributions by both Patricia McCormack who played with a badly sprained ankle and Tona O'Rafferty who was recovering from a recent operation, others to shine were Mairead Tuomey, Breda Daly, Fiona Davis and Claire Corcoran.

In 1989, a Junior B basketball team secured a North Leinster League title when defeating Mercy Secondary School Ballymahon in Newtownforbes by 20 points to 16. This team was captained by Anne-Marie Curran and also included Sharon Longe, Olga Wright, Geraldine Dardis Ann Connell, Eileen Flynn, Catherine Maher, Claire Dardis, Sharon McDonnell and Carol Dowdall.

Of most importance, 1990 saw the opening of the new Sports Hall as the Assembly Hall although marked out for basketball and was often the scene of many a good duel in badminton was now no longer practical as a venue for sport. All credit for this new change of direction was due to the hard work and forward planning of Sr. Dympna, and while the old outdoor courts may have been better for developing lower body strength in basketball players, this bright and exciting new building allowed for all weather participation, it was also a venue where St. Joseph's would now become proud hosts. Vox, the student magazine of that year clearly captured the prevailing optimism:- *"all years in the School contributed to wooing success and this should even increase as our new gymnasium is now in the process of being built and our playing fields being developed further with new goal posts going up"*. 1990 also saw the capture of the Minor A North Leinster League Title in Girl's basketball with a team captained by Nessa O'Sullivan which also included Karen Egan, Regina O'Meara, Lorraine Farrell, Lesley Smith, Bernadine Rooney, Caroline Shaw and mascot Orla Carroll. More serious moves were now also being made in the area

1988 Midland Schools League Winners.
From Left: Patricia McCormack, Claire Corcoran, Fiona Walsh, Fiona Davis, Mairead Twomey, Denise Farrell, Breda Daly, Orla Geoghegan.

1989 Junior B North Leinster League Champions.
From Left: Catherine Maher, Sharon Longe, Geraldine Dardis, Olga Wright, Ann-Marie Curran, Claire Dardis, Eileen Flynn.

ST. JOSEPH'S PARENTS COUNCIL
ROCHFORTBRIDGE SECONDARY SCHOOL

GALA OPENING OF NEW SPORTS HALL

on Friday, 5th October, 1990

GREAT 2 BAND SESSION
The Rangers & The Glenside Ceili-Band
AND GUEST ARTISTS
DANCING 11 - 2

Admission   (Including Supper)   £3

№ 0352   Westmeath Examiner Ltd., 044/48426

1990 Gala Opening organised by the Parents Council.

of boy's basketball. The Senior Team that year was led by Enda Corrigan; it also saw the beginnings of sponsorship when Mr. Gerry Sheridan provided singlets for the Under 16 boy's team. With new state of the art facilities in Rochfortbridge, it was now possible to invite schools to participate in what were to become a series of annual one-day blitzes, unfortunately, the first ever Under 16 A Blitz Final was an outside affair when Pobail Scoil Rosmini defeated Athboy Convent of Mercy.

1990 Minor A Basketball Team.
Back Row: Left to Right: Karen Egan, Ciara Muldoon, Regina O'Meara, Claire Corcoran, Lorraine Farrell.
Front Row: Left to Right: Lesley Smith, Bernadine Rooney, Nessa O'Sullivan (Captain), Caroline Shaw. Mascot: Orla Carroll.

The 1991/1992 school year was particularly noteworthy as a very talented group of students represented the school with distinction in the various age levels of girl's basketball. On the 11th. February 1992, three teams from the school played in the finals of the Midlands Inter-School League. In the first game St. Joseph's defeated Mullingar Community College by 17 points to 14 in the Cadet B and starring for Rochfortbridge were Linda Mulligan, Nicola Thornton and Ciara Muldoon. Next the Cadet A's defeated the Bower Athlone by 22 points to 20 powered by Claire Corcoran, Joanne Grogan and Lorraine Leogue. Not to be outdone, the youngest team of the day, the Minor A's defeated Loretto, Mullingar quite comfortably on a scoreline of 16-5 with future stars Aoife Donoghue, Elizabeth Shaw and Eimear Dunne in their ranks. A memorable day.

1992 Cadet A Basketball Team.
Back Row: Left to Right: Bernardine Rooney, Josephine Giles, Joanne Grogan, Sandra Delaney, Karen Egan.
Front Row: Left to Right: Jacqueline McNamara, Nessa O'Sullivan, Claire Corcoran, Lorraine Leogue.

The years 1993 and 1994 saw more success for basketball in the school. In 1993, the Girl's First Year A won the Midland League, this team included Alma Fennelly, Niamh Fitzsimons, Denise Maguire, Lisa Connaughton and Aoife O'Sullivan. Also that year, a great victory was recorded by the Senior B team in the Midland League Final against Newtownforbes with the winning basket coming in the dying seconds from Sandra Delaney. On the boy's front, 1994 will be remembered for the success of the Under 16 team who defeated St. Mary's Drogheda in the Provincial Leinster Final on a scoreline of 54-45. They then went on to defeat Drimnagh Castle Dublin in the full Leinster Final in the National Basketball

Arena with a buzzer beater from Trevor Thornton decisive Four members of the Under 15 team, Cathal Malone, Derek Griffin, Cathal Donoghue and Paul O'Connor also represented the school at the Reebok-Blacktop Eurochallenge held in Templeogue in May of that year.

The girl's game in 1995 was mainly dominated by the success of the Cadet A team who won the Midland League and were runners-up in the S.B.A.I. Leinster Final; this team had stars in Avril Collier, Maria Carroll, Sinead Masterson, Ulrika Maher and Sinead Barrett. Undoubtedly pride of place in 1995 must go to the winning of the Boys Under 19 B Cup Final in the National

1992 Senior A Basketball Team.
Back Row: Left to Right: Claire Dardis, Thérése Grogan, Joanne Grogan, Josephine Giles, Emma Smith.
Front Row: Left to Right: Anne-Marie Curran, Niamh Bollard, Niamh Coyne, Lorna Bollard, Lorraine Kilmurray.

Basketball Arena in Tallaght on February 1st. defeating Tramore C.B.S. on a scoreline of 73 points to 56. Central to this first All-Ireland Title for the School was M.V.P. Cathal Malone (who later represented Ireland in Portugal at Junior Men's Level) along with Shane Donoghue, Patrick Gunning, Michael Carroll, Damien Gavin and Damien Healy. A convoy of buses from the school made up of colourful teachers, students \ cheerleaders descended on Tallaght to greatly add to what was already a festive occasion and later became a fruitful visit.

The years 1996-1998 were mainly characterised by high and lows and this was nowhere more apparent than with the performances of the Senior Girls Team proving *"that you often have to lose one to win one"*, and defeat may have been a bitter pill for them to swallow in the semi-final of

1995 All-Ireland Under 19B Basketball Cup Winners.
Back Row: Left to Right: Joe Arthur (Coach), Damien Gavin, Shane Donoghue, Fergal McWalter, Patrick Gunning Michael Carroll, Damien Healy, Derek Griffin, Adrian Lee (Coach). Front Row: Left to Right: Johnny Morgan, Niall Broderick, John Hearns, Emmet Brennan, Cathal Malone (Captain), Cathal Donoghue, Paschal Kelleghan, Leonard Malone.

1997 Under 14 Midland League Basketball Winners.
Back Row: Left to Right: Mr. Eamonn Scally (Coach), Ronan Dunbar, David Cleary, Derek Keaney, Brian Broderick, Eoin Miller, Declan Gavin, Mr. Adrian Lee (Coach). Front Row: Left to Right: Dermot Bradley, Darren Kavanagh, Andrew Cannon (Captain), Mark Cole, Tomás Doyle, John Alford.

1998 Bank of Ireland Senior Cup Winners.
Back Row: Left to Right: Ms. Nuala Lawlor, (BOI Representative), Louise Byrne, Sarah Graham, Aoife Donoghue (Captain), Sarah Corcoran, Denise Maguire, Sharon Barrett, Andrea Maher, (BOI Representative). Front Row: Left to Right: Niamh Fitzsimons, Ulrika Maher, Ciara Malone, Yvonne Weldon, Anna Barrett, Roisin Conlon.

1996 and the final of 1997 both against Ard Scoil Mhuire Bruff Co Limerick. However, February 11th, 1998 saw a different outcome, Vox 1998 rightly proclaimed it *"a day to remember"*, as after many years of hard work and dissapointments, the Rochfortbridge Rockets triumphed in the Bank of Ireland Senior Cup Final defeating Community College, Killarney by 62 points to 49 again at the Basketball Arena in Tallaght. This success was due to the excellence of captain and M.V.P. Aoife Donoghue along with Ulrika Maher, Sharon Barrett, Niamh Fitzsimons, Sarah Corcoran and Roisín Conlon.

International Basketballers.
Sarah Healy, Patrick Horan, Mark O'Callaghan

The step up to A league basketball in 1999 proved difficult, and after a good win over now familiar Ard Schoil Mhuire Bruff Co Limerick, games were lost to Sacred Heart Secondary School Tullamore, Mercy Secondary School Ballymahon, Presentation College Portlaoise and Presentation Convent Thurles. The first round of the A Cup was lost to Presentation Convent Listowel, Co Kerry, despite the best efforts of newcomers to the panel, Aoife Maguire, Sarah Graham, Aisling Curley, Nicole Farrell, Ciara Maguire, Diane Fuller and Lesley Kelleher. Other highlights in basketball have seen the School being recognised for some of its outstanding players over the years; in 1999 both Alwynne Cleary and Mary McGuire were selected as part of an Under 15 Midlands Development Squad. Other players from the School to be selected at Midlands and International levels have included Sarah Healy, David Byrne, Patrick Horan, Mark O'Callaghan, John Gavin, Barry Murphy, Stephen Cole, Darren Price, David Horan and Matthew Rice, with Byrne, Patrick Horan and O'Callaghan all making their full international debuts against England abroad. Unfortunately for Patrick Horan and Mark O'Callaghan, the Foot and Mouth ban on organised sport in 2001 robbed them of the dream opportunity of representing Ireland in the Four Countries International Tournament that was to be held in Galway that year. The Senior Boys basketballers started 1999 well with a win in the League over St. Finian's Mullingar, but there followed losses then to Portlaoise C.B.S., Cnoc Mhuire Granard, and a loss in the Cup to St. Patrick's College Dungannon Co Tyrone. This team was well served all year by David Tormey, Brian Broderick, Niall Cole, John Alford, Vincent Doherty, Tomás Doyle and Darren Kavanagh. A very talented Second Year team that year with Cup medals in sight found themselves in a very difficult three way play off with Rockwell College Cashel Co Tipperary and St. Mel's Longford in which they narrowly lost both games through no fault of the efforts of Barry Murphy, David Flynn, Fergus McCarrick, Kevin O'Rourke, Niall Daly, Richard Coughlan and Mark Price.

The 2000's started on a high note for basketball when an Under 16 Boys team captained by John Gavin reached the All-Ireland A League semi-final held in Waterford with wins over St. Mel's Longford and De la Salle Waterford on the way, this team included Mark Cole, Mark Harte, Darren Corcoran, Enda Leonard, Patrick Jones, Fiachra O'Loughlin, Aidan

Ward, Aaron Morris and Dylan O'Neill. The following year with some of this squad still available the Under 16 Midland League won the previous year was easily retained with Thomas Byrne, Christopher Cole and Martin Dunne new to this level. Interestingly, in 2001 the four boy's basketball teams from the School won the four A titles available to them in the Midland region which was unparalled in any other region that year. The Senior Boys team that year although eventually beaten in the All-Ireland A Cup competition by Coláiste Eanna Dublin did manage to secure the Midland League Title with a victory over old rivals St. Mel's of Longford, this team included Larry Poynton, John Farrell, David Newman and Tomás Doyle. The Senior Girls also had a very good run in the Bank of Ireland Schools Cup with wins over Ballinrobe Community School Co Mayo and Pobalscoil Falcarragh Co Donegal before losing in the semi-final to Our Lady's Secondary School Castleblayney Co Monaghan with Susan Buckley and Sarah Healy being selected as the Most Valuable Player in these games.

In 2003, the Senior Boys basketball team did well in the All-Ireland League with wins over St. Brendan's Killarney and Moyle Park College Clondalkin before eventually going under to St. Fintan's Sutton in the semi-final with a buzzer beater from Michael Westbrooks being the killer punch.

Undoubtedly, Thursday 1st February 2007 will go down as a major date for basketball in the School in recent times because twelve years after their first All-Ireland win the Under 16 Boys team scaled the heights when defeating Summerhill College Sligo 33-30 to claim the Under 16 Cup. It was to be a bitter sweet day as the Girl's Under 16 team just failed to make it a memorable double when they went down to Presentation Convent Tralee Co Kerry 46-29. The Westmeath Examiner that week accurately painted the scene:- *"with over five hundred pupils from the school present, all kitted out in the school's colours and supported by friends and past*

2007 Robert Leavy, Captain of the Under 16 Winning Cup Team.

2007 Under 16 Winning Cup Team, National Basketball Arena, Tallaght.
Back Row: Left to Right: Mr. Adrian Lee (Coach), Wayne Fox, Cian Flynn, Adam Boardman, Adam Browne, Evan Hughes, Mark Conroy (Assistant Coach).
Back Row: Left to Right: Stephen Cooney, Robert Leavy (Captain), Shane Brogan, Gary Conroy

pupils, *the noise, atmosphere and resulting tension ensured a real "Field of Dreams feeling about the occasion"*. After the game, the Cup was presented to victorious captain Robert Leavy and the Most Valuable Player went to Cian Flynn for an outstanding performance scoring thirteen points in the process, the other members of this memorable success being Shane Brogan, Wayne Fox, Stephen Cooney, Adam Boardman, Evan Hughes, Thomas Dowling, Gary Conroy and Adam Browne whose memorable three pointer won the game with only minutes to go and was rightfully referred to in that week's Westmeath Examiner as *"the shot of the century"*. In the Under 16 Girls Final, the Tralee team were described in

2007 Basketball Ireland Girls School of the Year.
Ms. Nuala Lawlor receives the honour from Ardene
O'Neill and Tony Colgan President of Basketball Ireland

one of the local papers that week as being *"physically stronger in all areas"*. The panel that represented the school that day with great honour included Cliona Duigenan, Maud-Annie Foley, Niamh Spellman, Jodie Lewis, Fiona McHugh, Joanne Fox, Louise Darby, Aisling Dolan, Amie Giles, Amie Dunne, Aoife Brady, Ciara Brannock, Leanne Quinn, Cliona Gallagher and Ciara McGuinness. Nevertheless, between 2002 and 2008 this particular group of girls had been very successful on the basketball courts and as a result of winning four Midlands Titles from 2002 were voted "Basketball Ireland's Girls School of the Year in 2007", a just reward to compensate for the loss in the Cup Final of that year.

Other members of those successful panels included Clodagh Gill, Shauna Hogan, Tanya-Lee Ford and Laura Nugent. The Under 19 Boys Team found life very difficult in 2008 while operating in the All-Ireland A series and despite losses against Coláiste Eanna Dublin,

An Under 14 All-Ireland Basketball Tournament, Waterford from the early 2000's.
Back Row: Left to Right: Ms. Margaret Cole, Mr. Eamonn Scally (Coach), David Glennon, Keith Mooney, T.P. Fallon, Thomas Byrne, Christopher Cole, Shay Hannon, Mark Conroy, David Byrne, Mr. Adrian Lee (Coach).
Front Row: Left to Right: Danny Mooney, David Wright, Garreth Hickey, Alan Hannon, Mark Price, Bryan Smith.

Knockbeg College Carlow and St. Mel's Longford, this team with Alo Gavigan, Finbarr Murphy Sean Cody Baker and Tony Finn put in great work in a very difficult competition. In 2011 the Senior Ladies Team got off to a winning start in the Cup with a great victory over Holy Family Secondary School Newbridge Co Kildare before eventually giving way to a very strong St. Leo's College Carlow in the next round through no fault of the great efforts of Niamh O'Reilly, Sally Gorman, Emer Kelly, Deirdre Seery, Anne Peppard and Sarah Timmins. At present boys basketball is very strong in the school and the introduction of breakfast basketball where students get to school by 8am on Fridays for games between 8am-8.45am will ensure that the future is safe in the hands of younger players like Jamie Rooney, Cian Flood, James Quinn, Lee Kilbane, Lucas Radziunas and Eoin Fallon. The Under 16 team will have Shaun Moran, Josh Dowler, Patryk Krzyzak, Brian Lynam, Kevin Giles, Dean Core and Fionn Daly. The Senior team will look to Kyle Fox, Conor Briscoe, Ryan Fox, Stephen Mulvin, Adam Whelehan, Darren Giles, Shea Murphy, Senan Murphy, John Fox, Matthew Darcy, Tadhg Flynn and Brendan Keaveney.

Equestrian Sports

Over the years a number of students have been interested and have represented the School with great honour in Equestrian Sports. On Sunday 10th. May, 1992, the first Show Jumping Team from the school competed in an inter-schools competition in Greenhills, Naas, Co Kildare. This involved show jumping and a parade, and although Elaine McQuaid and Carmel Joyce were forced to retire early, Joseph Rice and Thomas Larkin earned a place in the "jump off" where they finished in a very credible third place.

Sarah McNamee goes clear.

Sunday April 9th. 1995, St. Joseph's fielded three teams at the Inter-Schools Show Jumping Championships held at the Mullingar Equestrian Centre. The participants from Rochfortbridge included, Gillian Murtagh, Ciara Timlin, Niamh Kelly, Louise Graham, Brian Fallon, Elaine Gavin, and Gillian Murphy. One of the teams from Rochfortbridge which included Maria

Catherine Lundon on the way to victory.

Carroll, Joseph Rice, Matthew Duane-Rice and team captain Thomas Larkin eventually emerged victorious on the day. Again in 1998 the School was very successful at the All-Ireland Hunter Trials staged at Clonshire Equestrian Centre, Adare, Co Limerick with 125 teams from all over Ireland competing. St. Joseph's finished in an excellent third place overall with a team that was made up of Jane Swarbrigg, Catherine Lundon and Emer Curley. In 1999, the school squad in equestrian disciplines was the largest on record including, Hannah Evans, John Gavin, Doreen Dowdall, Ciara Cahill, Anna Kiernan, Aishling Sheridan, Karen Flood, Sarah Troy and Michelle Gilmore. In 2000, a Show Jumping team made up of Laura McAuliffe, Mary-Ellen Rice, Orlaith Farrelly, Niamh McHugh and Hazel McCormack managed to come first in competition at Annaharvey Equestrian Centre, Tullamore, they also managed to come second at an event staged at Broadmeadows, Equestrian Centre, Co. Meath, thanks to an exhilarating jump-off performance from Niamh McHugh. Even though the Cross-Country in Kilkenny did not run as smoothly that year as the Show Jumping, nevertheless these athletes carried the flag proudly for St. Joseph's.

The Chef d'Equipe involved in all these great victories was Rosemary Rice. In 2006, St. Joseph's were represented at the Inter Schools Hunter Trials which took place in Ballyhale, Co Kilkenny, by Lorna Moore, Emma Wright, Clodagh Gill, Laurie Byrne and Jane Sleator. In 2011, a schools novice team made up of Eimear Daly, Megan Davitt, Jill Booker and Amy Foran took first place out of twenty participating schools in the Hoof-Prints Inter-Schools Show Jumping event that took place in Mullingar, this exceptional team repeated this win again the following weeks in Ballinasloe Co Galway and Boswell, Co Wicklow respectively and it reflected greatly on the magnificent efforts of their Chef d'Equipe Richard Davitt. Overall, 2011 was a great year for the Equestrian Club and other competitions held in CoilÓg, Co. Kildare, Boswell and Ballinasloe were attended by Sarah Hughes, Jenny Moore, Chloe Kelly, Katie Downey, Donna Cleary, Patricia Flynn, Megan Corcoran, Bronagh and Kristin Sleator. Interestingly, in an interview carried out by two students Caroline Kinahan and Emer O'Reilly for Vox, the School Magazine in 1992, the then King of Irish Show Jumping, Commandant Gerry Mullins told his young attentive interviewers:- *"half a second in show jumping is longer than any half a second in the world"*.

Equestrian Team at Twilight: from left: John Gavin, Mary-Ellen Rice, Laura McAuliffe, Aoife Farrelly.

Equestrian Team Back Row from Left: Niall Dunne, Mary-Ellen Rice, Michael O'Reilly Front: Sarah McNamee and Doreen Dowdall.

Gaelic Football

Probably more than any other sport, Gaelic Football has had a grip like attraction for both the male and female student body in the school over a very long number of years. With the introduction of physical education into school time-tables in the 1970's, more often than not these new PE classes were given over to games of Gaelic Football and Soccer, this in turn led to a class league system in the school and eventually a desire to enter the West Midland League. One of the first Gaelic Football class leagues in the school began in 1980 and had Paul Ronan, Michael McCormack, Peader Donlon, John Dillon, P.J. Brady and Enda Gavigan as captains of their respective classes and it is historically correct to report that John Dillon's class won out in the end against Paul Ronan's class in the Final of that particular year.

The West Midland League as already referred to was a relatively localised but essentially important G.A.A. league \ championship set-up that catered for schools mainly in Westmeath, Laois and Offaly and was the only level of competition available to most of the schools in those counties at the time. The Leinster Colleges competitions did exist, but were not as yet co-ordinated and full Leinster participation was still largely the preserve of the larger diocesan boarding schools not necessarily based on ability, but ordained by history, all this though was about to change.

The first outright win for the School in the West Midland League was the victory of an Under 14 football team in this competition as early as 1973 and after defeating Ard Scoil Chiaráin Clara in the semi-final proceeded to beat Kilcormac Vocational School in the Final. This glorious first for the School lined out as follows in what was then a thirteen-a-side competition:- Ernest Cleary, Thomas Reilly, Tony Byrne, Anthony Fox, Pat Joe Bradley, Micko Hyland, Noel Reidy, Donal Maher, Ger Kenny, Johnny Bradley, Aidan Dunne, Tom Fitzpatrick and Mattie Coleman, this panel also included Eugene Gaye and Jimmy Keegan in its ranks with the celebrations being concluded later that evening in Whelehan's. Interestingly, much of this team lost out in the Under 14 Hurling semi-final that same year when Ard Scoil Chiaráin exacted revenge for the earlier football defeat.

The rest of the 1970's was a barren period for football in the school but one must bear in mind that male student numbers were quite small then even in comparison to the other schools who were competing at West Midland League level. Another nine years passed before a second Under 14 football title was won in May 1982 in Tullamore at the expense of a shell shocked Ard Scoil Chiaráin Clara who had beaten Rochfortbridge by sixteen points in the earlier League stages of this competition, but were now on the end of a five point beating on the day when it mattered most. For the record the team that lined out that day in 1982 in O'Connor Park, Tullamore in which was still a thirteen-a-side competition was:- Gerry Murphy, David Bollard, Peter Leahy, Michael Corcoran, Aidan Nolan (Captain), Anthony O'Reilly, Pat Collins, Bernard Arthur, J.J. Flynn, Martin Brady, Ian Cunningham, Brendan Cocoman and Seamus Cummins from Rhode. Sub used: Declan Fennelly. That same year the Under 15 and 16 teams were not as successful; nevertheless the efforts of Michael Kennedy, Jimmy Hannon, Joseph Ennis, Brendan Leahy, Thomas MacDonagh, Gerry Feery, Mark O'Connell, Martin Henry, John Denehan, all deserve special mention. An exciting young footballer also from that era was Pat Daly who would go on to win an All-Ireland Under 21 Football medal with Offaly in 1988 coming on in the final against Cavan in a game played in Pearse, Park, Longford.

Sport more often than not played a key role in the Sisters fundraising efforts through the years whether it be for the development of the sports field or other projects being carried out in the School at the time, sport always seemed to be linked in. Back in the 1950's, these fundraisers were known as Parish Weeks. The Annals of the Convent from 1959 provide ample proof and offer an insight into the amount of hard work and effort that has always been undertaken by the Sisters in order to provide the excellent facilities they always strove for and always achieved as we read:- *"During the last week of May, a Parish Week was organised to help to raise funds to meet the debt on the new Hall. The people of the Parish were very generous in their support of the different functions. Sports were held for the children in the Convent field on Sunday 24th. May and great enthusiasm was shown by the competitors in the various events. On the following Thursday and Sunday a Social was held in the New Hall. The music was supplied by Joe Delaney and His Band. The weather was exceptionally fine during the Parish Week, and it was a great financial success, over £300 being realised"*.

"Mid-1980's: A Garryowen Rugby Player meets a Kerry Footballer!"

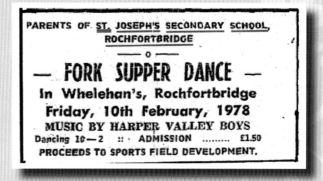

A 1978 Parents Association Fund Raiser.

As time passed, the Parish Weeks were replaced by Sports Days that by now were being organised by a very vibrant Parents Association. A highlight of these Sports Days was usually a challenge match that took place between an Under 14 team from the School and a local club that was supplying students to the School. As an example of this, one finds on Sunday May 22nd. 1983 at 4pm, St. Joseph's Under 14 footballers suffered a heavy defeat at the hands of Rhode in a game that took place in the school grounds in front of a very big crowd. According to Forum, the St. Joseph's newsletter of the time, the game was described by its biased young writer as such:- *"although we were missing Tommy Byrne, Pat Delamere, John Geoghegan and Kevin Murray, we all played exceptionally well – especially Jody Kennedy and John Daly who were running here and there for the ball. John Daly and Desmond Gorman scored our two points. Padraig Dardis played well in goals saving nearly everything, but was finally beaten by three great goals for Rhode. Thomas Dowdall, Ger Connell and Eamonn Connell played well clearing most balls that came their way. Pat Costello also played well"*.

Earlier in the year this particular Under 14 team had done quite well, but were unable to retain the West Midland League title won the previous year when going down to St. Anthony's Clara at the semi-final stage. However, in a game that had Jody Kennedy playing in the half-forward line and being described as *"the St. Anthony's defence's greatest problem"*, along with James Murphy both tried hardest on the day.

The Under 16 team of that year did not fare too badly in the West Midland League and after good wins over St. Saran's Ferbane and St. Anthony's Clara lost to Ard Scoil Chiaráin in the semi-final, but best for Rochfortbridge during that particular campaign were John Corcoran, Seamus Glennon, Anthony Maloney, Joe Gorman and Padraig Arthur.

1985 Declan Rogers – Qualified for the Leinster Under 14 Handball Final.

It was also around this time in the early 1980's, a decision was taken to change the colour of the school jerseys from green and white to blue and navy for no other reason other than to bring them into line with the predominant colours used in the trusty school uniform.

In 1984, the most successful team to represent the school were the Under 14's and after very good wins in the league stages of the West Midland League and a semi-final win over Ferbane Vocational School in the semi-final, eventually bowed out in the final to Ard Scoil Chiaráin Clara by a disappointing 2-13 to 2-2. This team was well served all year by Padraig Dardis in goals, along with Gordon Eighan, Colm Yeates, Eamon Cleary, Declan Usher, Joe Giles, John Daly, and scorer-in-chief Dessie Gorman with 3-4 in the semi-final against Ferbane. The Under 16 team that year were not as successful, and having won the competition two years previously at Under 14 level eventually lost out at the semi-final stage, having been beaten by Kilcormac Vocational School 3-4 to 1-8.

1986 Under 14 Football Team. Back Row, Left to Right: Fergal Dunne, Cathal Murphy, Declan Hogan, Enda Wright, Kenneth Gunning, Kenneth McNevin, Paul Dunning, John Moran. Front Row, Left to Right: Derek Foy, Dermot Brereton, Ian Bradley, Dermot Connell, Adrian Gill, Declan Doyle, Kevin Yeates, John Arthur, Shane Arthur.

During the rest of the 1980's, the main emphasis was placed on preparing Under 14, 15 and 16 teams for the West Midland League. In 1985, the Under 14 semi-final was contested for the second year in a row with a loss to St. Saran's Ferbane by 3-10 to 1-4 best for Rochfortbridge were Colin Cunningham, Shane Kelleghan, Michael Carley, John O'Brien, Frank Aughey and Declan Rogers who also excelled in the handball alley and qualified for the Leinster Under 14 Handball Final that same year. Again the following year at Under 14 level, Ard Scoil Chiaráin Clara proved to be our nemesis at the semi-final stage winning on a scoreline of 4-8 to 2-6. This team featured Ian Bradley, Declan Hogan, Dermot Brereton, John Moran, Paul Dunning, Fergal Dunne, Derek Foy, Dermot Connell and Enda Wright. Interestingly, in 1986 Joe Gorman and Conor Delaney were selected for Westmeath minor football and hurling teams respectively.

On the 20th. November 1987, the school was honoured by the visit of the Sam Maguire Cup in the presence of Liam Hayes, a member of the successful Meath All-Ireland winning team of the previous September. Sr. Pius looked pleased.

1987 Visit of Sam Maguire.
From Left: Joseph Giles, Tona O'Rafferty, Liam Hayes, Ursula O'Brien, Colm Arthur

1988 Under 15 Football Team.
Back Row: Left to Right: Shane Arthur, David Moore, Declan Hogan, Noel Gavin, David Bradley, Jonathon O'Connor, Alan Gavin.
Front Row: Left to Right: Michael Clarke, Dermot Malone, Kenneth Gunning (Captain), David Muldoon, Thomas Flynn, Patrick Kenny.

In 1988, the Under 14's lost a semi-final yet again to Ard Scoil Chiaráin Clara despite the best efforts of Michael Clarke, Dan Gavin, Jonathon O'Connor as captain, Dermot Malone, Joseph Loran and David Bradley.

The Under 15 team that year also went down at the semi-final stage to Ferbane Vocational School by 1-12 to 1-4, but not without a fight from David Moore, Christopher Colgan, Shane Arthur, Noel Gavin, captain Kenneth Gunning, Alan Gavin and Kenneth McNevin. In Vox magazine, 1989 was described as *"the best to date"* in the school's football history with winning the Under 14 West Midland League after an absence of seven years and getting to the now newly restructured Leinster Colleges A.I.B. Juvenile quarter-final before also losing the final of the Under 15 West Midland League. In the Leinster Colleges Under 14 quarter-final, Rochfortbridge lost to Drogheda C.B.S. after great wins over Trim Vocational School, Navan Community School and Kells C.B.S., this loss was greatly compensated for by a power-packed performance in the West Midland League Final when defeating L.S.U. Banagher by 4-13 to 0-1. This team was captained by Alan Jones along with Declan Fox, Maurice Eighan, Enda O'Rafferty, Sean Egan, Paul Briody and also included some household names of the future in David Mitchell, Damien Healy and Roy Malone. A pleasant feature of the Leinster Colleges campaign was the attendance of some parents at all the games and this support was described as being much appreciated.

The 1990's began when a rare victory was recorded at Senior Level in the West Midlands League. A combination team made of up of St. Joseph's and Mercy Kilbeggan defeated Ard Scoil Chiaráin in an absorbing Senior Championship Final played in Durrow, Co Offaly in 1990 to become holders of the Cowen Cup for the first and only time after many attempts over the years. Even though the West Midland League was now in the autumn of its existence and was being superseded by the *"fully inclusive"* Leinster Colleges, the use of *"better late than never"* could certainly have been applied in this particular case. This victory was made all the sweeter as a great friendship had already been forged between Rochfortbridge and Kilbeggan due to an Annual Senior Football game played towards the end of each school year between both schools for the Mother Philomena Cup kindly donated by Mercy Kilbeggan in her honour.

The highlight of the 1991\1992 football year was reaching the North Leinster Under 16 Final for the first time after wins over Ballymahon Secondary School, St. Saran's Ferbane and St. Mary's Edenderry, and, after a dramatic semi-final win against Marist College, Dundalk when this team edged a 4-6 to 4-5 win having been twelve points down midway through the second half, then unluckily lost this first final to Drogheda C.B.S. 1-9 to 1-3. Players that shone brightest during this ground breaking campaign were Noel Leavy, Peter Flood, Seamus Cully, Barry Pearce, Fiachra Daly, Thomas Kelly, and Damien Gavin who was to go on to captain the Westmeath Minor Football team to ultimate All-Ireland glory against Derry in 1995. The Senior Football team that year eventually succumbed to Kells Community School on a score of 2-12 to 1-6, Patrick Kenny scoring the goal, but injuries all year to Keith Oxley, Shane Donoghue, Alan Gavin and the ineligibility of Barry Collins hampered this particular campaign from the very beginning.

1989 West Midland Under 14 Football Champions. Back Row: Left to Right: Adrian Egan, Darren McKenna, Enda O'Rafferty, Jude Malone, Damien Healy, Sean Egan, Mark Dunne, Ronan Ennis, David Mulligan, Declan Fox. Front Row: Left to Right: Seamus Cully, Roy Malone, David Mitchell, Alan Jones (Captain), Patrick Kenny, Paul Briody, David Geoghegan, Maurice Eighan, Kevin Brennan.

1990 Cowen Cup Winners.
Back Row: Left to Right: Mark Staunton, Paul Seery, Shane Forde, Derek Foy, Fergal Coughlan, Paul Dunning, Dermot Brereton, Fergal Dunne, Mark Ennis, Keith Oxley.
Front Row: Left to Right: Colm Murphy, David Moore, Noel Gavin, Alan Gavin, Peter Robinson (Captain), Jonathon O'Connor, Dermot Connell, Darren McCormack, Raymond Gorman.

1995 Damien Gavin: Captains Westmeath to All-Ireland Minor Glory.

1992 Senior Football Team.
Back Row: Left to Right: Barry Pearce, Ian Jones, Darren Meehan, Keith Oxley, Mark Dunne, David Mitchell, Alan Gavin, Alan Wright and Adrian Egan.
Back Row: Left to Right: Enda O'Rafferty, Mark Geoghegan, Paul Briody, Alan Jones, Roy Malone, Jonathan O'Connor (Captain) David Muldoon and Patrick Kenny.

In 1993, the Senior Football team had a great run in the Leinster championship reaching the semi-final losing to Lucan C.B.S. 1-7 to 1-6, having recorded earlier wins over St. Fintan's Sutton, 2-6 to 0-6, St. Declan's Cabra 1-8 to 1-5, and Malahide Community School 2-7 to 1-3. The Under 16 footballers reached the North Leinster semi-final after wins over Athlone Community College and Oldcastle V.S. only to be denied by Athlone Community College whom they had already beaten in an earlier round. This team featured Alan Brady outstanding at midfield along with Dermot Kilmartin, Kenneth Berry (another member of the 1995 Westmeath All-Ireland winning panel), Darren Bannon, Ian Jones, John Jones, Emmet McDonald and Derek Griffin. The Under 14 team made history this year by winning the North Leinster Under 14 C championship for the first time with wins over Athlone Community College, Ard Scoil Chiaráin Clara, Mercy Secondary School Ballymahon,   St. Olivers Drogheda and in the North Leinster Final against Dunshaughlin Community College before losing out to Heywood Community School Co Laois in the Leinster semi-final.

As a follow on from the success of the Under 14 team in 1993, 1994 proved disappointing, yet 1995 turned out great as the Under 14 team won their group stages of the North Leinster B championship with good wins over St. Saran's Ferbane, Scoil Dara Kilcock, St. Mary's Edenderry and Scoil Mhuire Clane. Unfortunately, this good run came to an end with defeat at the hands of Drogheda C.B.S. in the North Leinster semi-final on a scoreline of 5-4 to 1-6. This team was captained and well served by Raymond Geoghegan along with James Conroy, Colm Masterson, Derek Spollen, Eoghan Hickey, Niall Brereton, Gerry Daly and David Hope who also excelled at and represented the school at handball. History was made this year though when the Under 16 football team captured the North Leinster Under 16 A championship for the first time. This was achieved with wins over St. Pat's Navan, Tullamore C.B.S. and St. Mel's Longford and even though a loss was sustained against St. Michael's Trim in the group stages, the "Bridge" reversed that result in the final beating St. Michael's by 2-7 to 1-5. This

1993 Under 16 Football Team.
Back Row: Left to Right: Niall Jones, Billy Grogan, Cathal Donoghue, Patrick Gunning, Alan Brady,
Noel Leavy, Kenneth Berry, John Jones.
Front Row: Left to Right: Eoin Daly, Ted Wright, Darren Bannon, Dermot Kilmartin, Emmet McDonald,
Ian Jones, Barry Malone, Derek Griffin.

groundbreaking Under 16 A Leinster Final was played in Navan in a game that St. David's Artane gained the upper hand in the second half to win out on a score of 0-11 to 0-8, St. Joseph's being captained by Barry Malone who was also captain of the Offaly minor football team at the same time and who would later go on to win a Leinster Senior Football Championship medal with Offaly in 1997. Other prominent members of that landmark team were Emmet Brennan, Vinnie Arthur, Eddie Doyle, Eddie Grogan, John Driver, Kevin Burke who would go on to win an All-Ireland Under 21 medal

The Offaly Connection": 1997 Barry and Roy Malone bring the Leinster Senior Football Cup to the Bridge.
From Left: Danny Reddin, Barry Malone, Denis Kelly, Roy Malone, Tony O'Sullivan, Luke Dempsey.

at midfield with Westmeath in that never to be forgotton win over Kerry in Limerick in 1999 with Barry Conroy also being a member of that historic panel. Later in the year, they were presented with their North Leinster medals in the School Canteen by Mr. Seamus Whelan, the then Chairman of the Westmeath County Board. The Senior Football team also competed in the 1995 Leinster A Championship and were very unlucky to lose narrowly to Marist College, Athlone by 0-10 to 0-9. This team featured Paul O'Connor, Ted Wright, Kevin Earley, Paul McGivney, Ciaran Leech and not forgetting Pashcal Kelleghan who would go on to star for many years in the colours of the faithful county. This year also witnessed a visit to the school by the then President of the G.A.A. Mr. Jack Boothman who spoke of the great reception he received in County Westmeath. Another relevant first for the school in 1995 was the entry of a Ladies Gaelic Football Team in the Leinster

1995 North Leinster Under 16A Champions.
Back Row: Left to Right: Barry Malone (Captain), Barry Conroy, Michael Carroll, Emmett Brennan, Paul McGivney, Vinnie Arthur, Kevin Burke, Paschal Kelleghan, Eamonn Flynn.
Front Row: Left to right: Raymond Geoghegan, Adam Nolan, Eddie Doyle, Kenneth Delaney, Eddie Grogan, John Driver.

Championships for the first time. Meanwhile, St. Joseph's had by now become a force to be reckoned with in Leinster Colleges "A" football competitions and the humble beginnings made in the West Midland League of some previous decades now had become *"un souvenir lointain"* for those long enough around who dared to think back.

The North Leinster Under 16 A Football Championship was captured again in 1997 with Keith Kavanagh captaining a side that recorded notable wins over St. Mel's Longford 2-17 to 0-5 and Marist College Athlone in the North Leinster Final 0-12 to 0-5. Unfairly, this particular Leinster Final was delayed a month with Rochfortbridge eventually going down to Good Counsel New Ross in Carlow. Despite the disappointment, this team had outstanding individuals in Padraig Leavy in goals, who was later to be the youngest member of the Westmeath Under 21 All-Ireland winning panel in 1999, others to shine were David Flynn, Thomas Keating, Anthony Murphy, Fergal McNamee, Kevin Dunne, James Nugent and Austin Bradley described in X-TRA, the school magazine of that year as a player:- *"who proved himself one of the best full forwards in Westmeath. Bradley, who was very accurate from frees and from play, notched up 1-3 and 1-4 per game"*.

The Senior Football team in 1997 recorded good progress in both League and Championship, the year began with a win over Kilbeggan in the Mother Philomena Cup and captain Cathal Donoghue collected the silverware reversing this result over Kilbeggan from the previous year. The League got off to a great start with wins over Marist Athlone, St. Saran's Ferbane, Moate Community School and Coláiste Iosagain Portarlington, before losing at the semi-final stage to St. Michael's Trim. The Championship began with a very big win over Moate Community School by 3-14 to 0-2, a headline from The Westmeath Topic that week read:- *"St. Joseph's – A force to be reckoned with"*, correctly summed up the mood.

1996 Senior Football Team.
Back Row: Left to Right: Kevin Burke, Anthony Gorman, Derek Griffin, Gerard Glennon, Barry Conroy, Barry Malone, Paschal Kelleghan, Emmet Brennan, Darren Bannon, Paul O'Connor, Cathal Malone, Cathal Donoghue.
Front Row: Left to Right: Paul McGivney, John Mitchell, Alan Plunkett, Billy Grogan, John Jones (Captain), Emmet McDonnell, Andy Glennon, Kenneth Delaney, Ciaran Leech, Ciaran Wright.

This was followed up with a win over Portmarnock Community School by 1-14 to 0-8, before eventually going down to St. Pat's Navan 2-12 to 2-7 in Navan, who later went on to capture the Leinster Championship that year. This team was ably led by Paul McGivney until injury ruled him out early in the year along with James Lynch, Jason Byrne, Kenneth Delaney, Ciaran Wright, Johnny Mitchell, Gerard Glennon and Adam Nolan.

"Anxious Supporters in Navan"
Sr. Geraldine, Martina Croghan, Eileen Alford.

The Under 14 team who were now also operating in the Leinster A Championship had a mixed season recording a good start with a win over Tullamore C.B.S. 3-12 to 1-6, before defeats to St. Pat's Navan by 4-12 to 1-9 and St. Michael's Trrim 3-9 to 2-4 in a game in which Ronan Dunbar and Joseph Bradley were both *"harshly"* dismissed. This team was also well served by Eoin Miller, Darren Kavanagh, Dermot Bradley, David Cleary, Gordon McDonnell, Damien Loran and Vincent Doherty.

The following year 1998 saw the Senior Football team contest the League Final only to go under to St.Pat's, Navan again, and although a good win was achieved in the championship over Patrician Newbridge, the quarter-final ended in defeat to Good Counsel New Ross, who although were from the *"deep south"* were by now, no strangers at all. The Under 16 team also found the going tough attempting to defend the North Leinster Championship

1997 North Leinster Under 16A Champions.
Back Row: Left to Right: Aidan Brereton, Martin O'Connor, Padraig Bennett, Kevin Dunne, Fergal Dardis, James Nugent, Padraig Leavy, Mark Brady, James Conroy, Austin Bradley, Fergal McNamee, Mr. Danny Reddin (Manager).
Middle Row: Left to Right: Brian Wright, Colin Cooney, John Gorman, Keith Kavanagh (Captain), Eoghan Hickey, Colm Masterson, David Flynn, Derek Spollen.
Front Row: Left to Right: Gerry Daly, Raymond Geoghegan, Thomas Keating, John Shaw.

won the previous year and sustained losses to St. Pat's Navan and St. Michael's Trim with Eoghan Hickey and Ronan Bennett giving their all against very stiff opposition.

The earlier part of the 2000's were not as productive as the mid to late 1990's, but then it was always going to be difficult to compete at "A" level against schools that were all male preserves, and without seeming to complain too much, it is fair to say that the effort of this particular challenge while always courageously met, never seemed to diminish over the years. It was now also proving difficult to replace a very talented crop of footballers who had just gone through the school and who subsequently went on to become outstanding club and county players in all grades for Westmeath and Offaly, and whose names will be forever remembered with great fondness in St. Joseph's. Nevertheless, life went on and in 2001 a very good young team emerged to annex an unexpected Under 14 B North Leinster football title; this group trained reluctantly in the snow and illegally during the Foot and Mouth epidemic of that year. After some great wins during the league stages of the North Leinster Championship, the North Final was eventually played due to circumstances much later than usual in April on a very blustery day in Portarlington, where Rochfortbridge just managed to hold out beating Scoil Mhuire, Clane by 5-8 to 4-7, having being eleven points ahead at half-time. However, the Leinster Final resulted in an agonising defeat to Knockbeg College, Carlow, 1-14 to 2-9. The Westmeath Examiner summed up the dejection best of all:- *"St. Joseph's Rochfortbridge were gallant runners-up in the Coca Cola Leinster Colleges Under-14 "B" Final at O'Moore Park, Portlaoise last week as a well–prepared Knockbeg College, Carlow team had enough guile and skill to emerge two point-victors on the day"*. This team was

Luke Dempsey: Managed Westmeath to All-Ireland Minor 1995 & Under-21 1999 All-Ireland Titles.

2001 Leinster Under 14B North Leinster Football Champions. A happy David Glennon lifts the trophy with Shay Hannon, Garreth Hickey and Alan Hannon in support.

1999 Westmeath: All-Ireland Under 21 Football Champions. Back Row: Kevin Burke, second from right.

captained by future Westmeath star David Glennon and featured Alan Hannon in goals who was also part of the Youth Academy at Shelbourne Football Club at the time; it also included Joe Keogh, Trevor-John Gonoud, Shay Hannon, Brian Cassidy, Ronan Foley, A.J. Murray, Darren Price, Darragh O'Connor and Noel O'Donnell. The senior team lost out that year to St. Pat's Navan in a second round game after a good win over Moate Community School in the first round. This team featured Damien Molloy in goals along with Paul Henry, Philip Sheridan, Andrew Cannon, Eoin Miller, Gordon McDonnell and Denis Glennon at midfield who would later go on to play a vital role for Westmeath Senior Footballers when they captured their first Leinster Senior Football Championship Title in 2004.

A notable first was achieved by the Senior Footballers in 2003 with the capture of the North Leinster League for the first time with wins over Boyne Community School, St. Mary's Mullingar, and St. Mel's Longford before defeating Moyne Community School, 3-4 to 1-7 in the Final with a Man of the Match performance from Stephen Bracken. With the North Leinster League secured, victories in the Leinster Senior Championship followed over St. Benildus Stillorgan and Franciscan College Gormanston which led to a quarter-final meeting with Marist College Athlone in Rochfortbridge with St. Joseph's emerging winners 1-5 to 0-5, the winning goal scored by super sub Stephen Goonery towards the end certainly managed to *"raise the roof"*. The semi-final defeat to St. Mel's after extra-time on a score 2-13 to 2-10 reversed an earlier success in the League over the same opposition and it was a source of great disappointment that a first ever Leinster Senior Final appearance was denied in such a way. This team had Stephen Gallagher in goals and along with Mark Cassidy, Gavin Hoey, Robbie Kenny, Jamie Wilson and Garreth Hickey, it also included Sean Casey, who would later go on to play Senior Football for Offaly and Conor Jordan who would star for many years for the Westmeath Senior Hurlers, none could not be faulted for their efforts in this campaign.

2003 North Leinster Senior Football League Champions.
Back Row: Left to Right: Barry Murphy, Donal Hickey, Brian Smith, Robbie Kenny, Shay Hannon, Gavin Hoey, Stephen Gallagher, Sean Casey, Conor Jordan, Mark Cassidy, Mark Conroy, Dermot Faulkner, Stephen Bracken, Mr. Luke Dempsey (Manager).
Front Row: Left to Right: Andrew Devine, David Bryan, Trevor-John Gonoud, A.J. Murray, David Glennon, Colin Connolly, Jamie Wilson, Hughie Burke, David Coyne, Ronan Foley, Kenneth Mooney.

The 2004 Senior campaign followed a similar pattern to the previous year and after a very good run in the League, the final was reached again only to suffer defeat at the hands of St. Pat's Navan in Páirc Tailteann Navan, indeed St. Pat's were to the recurring thorn affecting this side all year. After two good wins in the Championship over St. Declan's Cabra and Moate Community School, it was on to the quarter-final and a meeting again with St. Mel's of Longford where the previous year's semi-final defeat was avenged with a one point victory for St. Joseph's. The semi-final against St. Pat's Navan in St. Loman's Mullingar resulted again with victory to St. Pat's as a result of a goal in the dying minutes against the run of play after Rochfortbridge had held a comfortable lead through most of the first half. This particular team had great defenders in Jason Lynch, Hughie Burke, Michael McAdden, Brian Smith, and up front Danny Mooney, Andrew Devine, and Kenneth Casey who would go on to play Senior Football for Offaly gave their all against a St. Pat's team that was to go on to capture the All-Ireland College's Hogan Cup Title later that year. In 2005, an epic Leinster Senior Football Championship semi-final was lost by two points to eventual All-Ireland Champions Knockbeg College Carlow in Portlaoise backboned by Ronan Foley and Niall Kilcoyne. It must not be forgotten though, that most of these players had captured a North Leinster Under 14 B Title and an Under 16 A Title, (beaten by Knockbeg College, Carlow in both Leinster Finals) and that they also won North Leinster Senior League medals in 2003 during their time at St. Joseph's.

In 2006, the North Leinster Senior League was lost narrowly at the semi-final stage. In the first round of the Leinster Senior Football Championship that year victory was secured over Moate Community School 2-5 to 0-8 after a replay; this led to a second round tie which was lost to Athlone Community College 2-10 to 0-5, the campaign eventually got back on track with a win in the qualifiers over Moyne Community School by 0-13 to 1-4 before bowing out in the next round of the qualifier series 1-9 to 0-9 to Carlow Schools who edged it with a late goal, this team included Fintan Reilly, Glen O'Connell, Jack Hogan and Ronan Doyle. The following year 2007, a first round game was lost to Marist College Athlone 1-8 to 1-5 in a very wet Kinnegad; following this a qualifier was also lost to Moyne Community School at the first time of asking, who were also reversing the previous year's result. These campaigns were well served by Darren Quinn who has gone on to play in goals for Westmeath at Minor, Under 21 and Senior levels, also on board was Declan Murphy, Barry Mooney, Robert Leavy, Jamie Hayes and sharpshooter Alan Giles

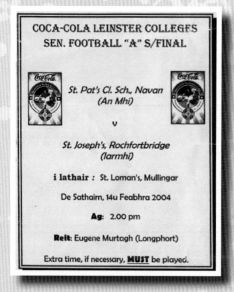

2004 "Another clash with St. Pat's"

Damien Healy: Played at Left Corner-Back in Westmeath's First Leinster Senior Football Title Win, 2004.

who notched between six and seven points from play and placed balls on each outing.

By 2008, the Under 14 Football Team was operating in the A division of Leinster Schools again and after a number of good wins in challenge matches against St. Mary's Mullingar and St. Mary's Edenderry a good win was recorded in the first round of the North Leinster Championship against Franciscan College Gormanston on a scoreline of 1-12 to 2-7. Unfortunately the remaining games were lost heavily to St. Pat's Navan and to Athlone Community College due to a last minute goal, despite the best efforts of Gary Greville, Aaron Byrne, Luke Gallagher, Wayne Leavy, Brian O'Sullivan, Cathal Burke, David Rigney and Luke Doyle. The senior footballers lost league encounters to St. Mary's Edenderry, Franciscan College Gormanston and St. Mary's Mullingar before a great one point victory was achieved over Patrician Newbridge in the first round of the Leinster Championship only to lose out in the second round again with St. Mary's Edenderry repeating their league victory in the championship only on this occasion it took a replay to separate the sides in the floodlit tie in Kinnegad. This team was captained by Robert Leavy along with Eoin Rigney who would also go on to play Senior Football with Offaly, it also included Darren Kilcoyne, Adam Browne, Daniel Riggs, Paul Lewis, Wayne Fox, Mark Conroy, Paul Carey and Eoin Gorman.

In 2009 an Under 14 team reached the North Leinster Final only to be denied by a point against St. Pat's Navan, but this year was to see a great success for the Senior Footballers as they captured the North Leinster League Title for the second time with a victory over the defending champions Athlone Community College 2-7 to 0-5 in Pairc Chiaráin Athlone. The Leinster Championship in 2009 saw victories over Coláiste Iosagain Portarlington, Marist College Athlone, St. Benildus College Dublin before losing out at the semi-final stage yet again to a very strong Good Counsel College New Ross in a game played in Timahoe Co Laois, Mark Conroy and Shane Brogan along with Paul Lewis and Cian Flynn at midfield and Jason Cully up front tried hardest. The following year, the North

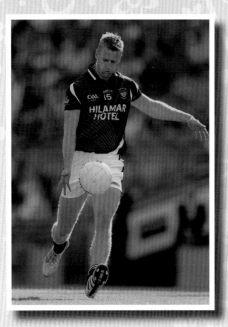

Denis Glennon: Played at Full-Forward in Westmeath's First Leinster Senior Football Title Win, 2004.

Cormac Davey: "Words of encouragement"

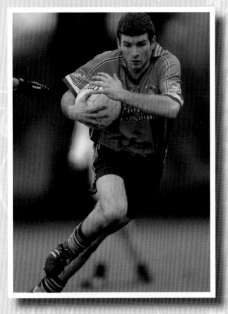

Tommy Dowling: "Gave his all, both on and off the field"

Leinster League title won the year before was lost in the Final going down to St. Mary's Mullingar by one point and the first round of the championship was lost to a very good Ardscoil Na Trionode Athy, St. Joseph's containing a very strong Offaly connection with Donal Hickey, Stephen Hannon, the McPadden twins, James and Paul along with Johnny Brickland at the heart of this campaign.

2011 Leinster Under 14A North Leinster Final. Owen Loran (22) "A study in concentration"

In 2011 another piece of history was made when the Under 14 footballers won the North Leinster A Title for the first time with emphatic wins along the way particularly against St. Mary's Mullingar in the semi-final and against Marist College Athlone in the North Leinster Final winning by a comfortable 4-14 to 1-6 in Cusack Park, Mullingar. The Leinster Final was played on the 11th March 2011 against Good Counsel New Ross Co Wexford and resulted in a 1-9 to 1-6 defeat with the winning goal coming in the fifth minute of injury time, the absence of Jack Reid through injury being particularly badly felt.

The team that lined out in that Leinster Final was as follows:- Joseph Hyland, Liam O'Reilly, Cillian Doyle, Jack Murphy, Sean Quinn, Niall McCabe, Bobby Gonoud, Ian Kilcoyne, Gavin Glennon, Mark Geoghegan, Ciaran Doyle, Evan Toner, Derek Conroy, Jack Cully, Kyle Fox with Peter Lalor replacing Derek Conroy. The Under 16 team did not live up to earlier promise as they lost to St. Pat's Navan and St. Mary's Mullingar. The Senior Team started the League campaign with a great win against St. Pat's Navan before losing to Franciscan College Gormanston, however, this result was reversed when a first round championship win was gained against the same opposition after extra-time. Confidence was high going into a second round tie against Coláiste Eoin, however, it ended in

2011 Donal O'Buachalla Manager of the Under 14A North Leinster Champions.

disappointment as the physical superiority of the Dublin team won out in the end. This team was captained by Jamie Gonoud who has starred for the Westmeath minor and Under 21 football teams in recent years; he was ably assisted by Shane Murtagh and Dermot Judge. In 2012, the Under 16 team having won their group matches against Scoil Mhuire Clane, Marist College Athlone, and Athlone Community College after extra-time eventually went down in the North Leinster Final to St. Pat's Navan by 3-14 to 1-7. They had great players in Joe Hyland in goals, Patrick Geraghty, Liam O'Reilly, Darren Giles, Graham Flood, Dylan Raleigh in a team that was captained by Shane Corcoran.

The most recent Senior Football campaign was described in Vox 2012, the student magazine as *"a season of both highs and lows"*, as after having won the Westmeath Schools Competition, a poor performance against St. Mel's Longford when a good one was needed for survival put paid to further progress in the North Leinster League. Moate Community School ended the school's involvement in the 2012 Leinster Senior Championship, but great credit must go to team captain and Meath county minor Adam Flanagan, John O'Reilly, Tomas Muldoon and Niall Cully for their efforts all year.

2011 Leinster Under 14A North Leinster Football Champions.
"Those moments of utter delight"
Standing: Left to Right: Stephen Riggs, Ciaran Doyle, Padraic Gaye, Siyabonga Nxumalo, Finbar Coyne, Ian Kilcoyne, Cathal Moran, Hugh Lyster, Jack Reid, Peter Lalor, Jack Murphy, Killian Doyle, Gavin Glennon, Ciaran McManus, Peter Fagan, Ben Hobby-Royle, Kyle Fox, Owen Loran, Liam O'Reilly.
Front Row: Left to Right: Derek Conroy, Evan Toner, Jack Cully, Bobby Gonoud, Joe Hyland, Sam Plant, Mark Geoghegan, Sean Quinn.

Ladies Gaelic Football

After many tentative steps and early promise shown throughout the early to mid 1990's, Ladies Gaelic Football eventually got up and running and began to take its proper and well earned slice of the sporting calendar from then on in the School. This appeal was in keeping with the trend countrywide as interest in Ladies Gaelic Football was spiralling upwards. In 1996 a Ladies Junior Football Team won the Westmeath Schools Final captained by Sarah Corcoran. In 1997, a Ladies Senior Football Team from St. Joseph's were crowned Leinster Vocational B Champions with players that had represented the School at all levels underage and were at the same time representing their home clubs with distinction. This campaign in 1997 began with very big wins over Mercy Kilbeggan, Moate Community School on a score of 8-10 to 5-3, next to fall was Mountmellick Community School, heavily, in the quarter-final and Blessington Community College, Co Wicklow in the semi-final, the final was played in Mountmellick against St. Aidan's Tallaght with St. Joseph's winning comfortably in the end by 4-15 to 1-5. This excellent panel was captained by Ulrika Maher and also included Anita Hyland, Sarah Graham, Louise Byrne, Karen Corcoran, Jill McQuaid, Dolores Flynn, Audrey Byrne, Sarah Corcoran, Jane Guillane, Siobhan McNamara, Andrea Maher, Julie Ann Scanlon, Lisa Earley, Yvonne Heavey, Nicola Bagnall, Sonya Quinn, Jenny McNamee, and Katrina Leogue. A highlight from 2001 was a Leinster Final appearance for the Under 16 team having secured victories over Loreto College Mullingar, Athlone Community College, Moate Community School, Mercy Secondary School Ballymahon and St. Mary's Edenderry before going down to Heywood Community School Ballinakill Co Laois in the final. After drawing with Loreto Mullingar, the senior team also in 2001 had very solid victories over Mercy Kilbeggan and Moate Community School before going down to Mercy Ballymahon in the Leinster quarter-final. These teams were best served by Alwynne Cleary, Marie Monaghan, Mary Maguire, Donna Kiernan, Aileen Leavy, Megan Glennon, Ellen Moran, Ciara Dunne, Emma Glennon, Bernadette Jessop, Anne-Marie Buckley, Emily Sweeney, Celia Gavigan, Mary Corroon and Maura O'Donoghue.

1996 Ladies Junior Football Team – Winners of the Westmeath Schools Final.
Back Row: Left to Right: Sinead Barrett, Leonie Maher, Rebecca Moody, Nicole Bagnall, Lisa Earley, Ann-Marie Corroon, Sinead Bagnall, Siobhan McNamara, Alison Plunkett, Sonya Quinn. Front Row: Left to Right: Vanessa Kenny, Mairead Mulvin, Sarah Graham, Jane Gullane, Sarah Corcoran (Captain), Yvonne Heavey, Louise Byrne, Audrey Byrne, Karen Bradley.

In 2002, a senior team made up of Caroline Burke, Hazel Bracken, Lorna Brick and captained by Mary Grogan were unlucky to lose out in the final game of the group stages of South Leinster when going down to St. Mary's Edenderry by just 1-10 to 3-3. In 2003, the Ladies Senior football team had a more successful year reaching the South Leinster semi-final with some very good victories along the way against Loreto College Mullingar and Mercy Kilbeggan. This team was captained by Martina Moran and also had Aisling Doyle, Aine Maguire, Niamh Malone, Anna Moore, Aine Weir, Joanne Harney, Nicola Murphy and Aisling Flanagan on board. After a narrow loss to St. Fergal's Rathdowney in the 2005 championship, the Senior Ladies began their campaign with a win against the same opposition in 2006 well led by captain, Xenia Wallace. This was followed by wins

2002 Sports Awards: Lorna Brick.

over Patrician College Ballyfin, a game in which Fiona Leavy who would go on to star for Westmeath scored 2-3; next to follow was a win over Coláiste Iosagáin Portarlington by 6-7 to 1-5. However, this great run ended with defeat against Coláiste Bríde, Enniscorthy where even a goal right at the end of normal time by Siobhan Loran bringing the game to extra time and Karen Mc Dermott's loss through injury was too much and Enniscorthy won out in the end by five points. Others to shine in this great run were Jackie Glennon, Cathrina Hannon, Sinead Whelehan, Laurie Byrne, Megan Brick, Colleen Gill, Christina Gahan and Karen Tracey. The Under 16 team in 2006 had a great year topping their group in the league with easy wins over Our Lady's Bower Athlone, Mountmellick Community School and Mercy

1997 Ladies Senior Football Team – Winners of the Leinster Vocational Schools B Championship.
Back Row: Left to Right: Jill McQuaid, Sarah Graham, Jane Gullane, Sonya Quinn, Anita Hyland, Yvonne Heavey,
Nicola Bagnall, Andrea Maher. Middle Row: Left to Right: Dolores Flynn, Julie-Ann Scanlon, Sarah Corcoran, Louise
Byrne, Lisa Earley, Siobhan McNamara, Jennifer McNamee. Front Row: Left to Right: Katrina Leogue,
Ulrika Maher (Captain), Audrey Byrne.

Kilbeggan before losing out to Athlone Community College in the semi-final. This team was captained by Edel Marshall and also included Siobhan Dolan, Ciara Deegan, Aoife Brady, Dawn Wallace, Aoife Hyland, Louise Darby, Ashling Hyland, Michelle Murtagh, Sarah Kiernan, Katie Deegan, Marie Morgan, Monica Seery and Maud-Annie Foley who would go on to play a central role for Westmeath at midfield when winning the All-Ireland Intermediate Championship in 2011 after a replay with Cavan winning the Player of the Match into the bargain.

This particular victory must have been a source of great pride to Geraldine Giles who during her time as a boarder in St. Joseph's played camogie and who would go on to serve for two terms as National President of the Ladies Gaelic Football Association up until 2009.

In April 2007 history was made when the Senior Team reached the All-Ireland B Final after capturing the Leinster Title for the first time with a victory over Castleknock Community School Dublin 5-12 to 0-5 in a game played in Cappagh Co Kildare. The All-Ireland semi-final resulted in a victory over Connacht champions Summerhill College Sligo, 2-10 to 4-3 in Athlone, the goals coming from Maud-Annie and Andreanna Doyle.

Maud-Annie Foley: Westmeath: All-Ireland Intermediate Medalist 2011: Player of the Match.

The All-Ireland Final resulted in a loss to Sacred Heart Clonakilty Cork by 2-9 to 1-8 with the concession of two goals either side of half-time proving decisive. After such a successful campaign, the Ladies Senior Football team found themselves playing at A level in the Leinster Senior Football Championship.

The first game of 2008 was against the then All-Ireland Champions, St. Leo's Carlow who provided very strong opposition, plus the loss of Leanne Hendley did not help the cause in this early defeat. The next game aginst St. Mary's Edenderry was lost by three points with the crossbar denying progress on three separate occasions. This team was captained by goalkeeper Claire Judge and also included Niamh Spellman, Amy Dunne, Cliona Duignan, Caitlin Mangan and Clodagh Gill. The Under 16's had a great run in 2008. The team was captained by Naomi Plunkett and had a great run recording wins over Mercy Secondary School Ballymahon by 4-12 to 3-4 and against Loreto Secondary School Navan 3-7 to 1-4 and 8-12 to 1-12 against Our Lady's Bower Athlone. The quarter-final

Geraldine Giles: National President of the Ladies Gaelic Football Association 2003-2009.

against a very strong Coláiste Iosagáin Stillorgan in Dublin had to be played without inspirational captain Naomi Plunkett this proving to be too much resulting in a loss by three points in the end. This team was well served by Joanne Fox in goals, Emma Kerrigan, Lorna Moore, Laura Kerrigan, Grace Doyle, Drew Doyle, Rachel Gallagher, Nicola Quinn, Niamh Moran and Ashling Mulleady. The Under 14's struggled in their two league games against Moate Community School and Mercy Kilbeggan, but great efforts were put in by Eimear Treacy, Frances Fallon, Lauren Kelly, Aoife Whelehan, Cliodhna Spellman, Fay Dunne, Deirdre Seery, Jean Kelly, Gemma Gorman, Sally Gorman, Rejoice Musasa, Ciara Moran, Mairead Lynam, Lisa Byrne, Shauna Smith, Fiona Battle, Nicola Burke, Caoimhe Duncan, Fiona Duignan, Niamh Murphy, Louise Eustace, Rachel Cully, Fiona Flynn, Sarah Kiernan, Rebecca Rooney, Mary Gavin, Sarah Gavin, Jennifer Connolly and Jodie Dunne.

2007 All-Ireland B Ladies Football Final. Aoife Hyland: "Those fleeting moments of utter despair".

Helena Heduan: "At the helm with St. Joseph's Ladies Footballers"

2007 All-Ireland B Ladies Football Final.
Back Row: Left to Right: Ms. Martina Croghan (Manager), Lisa Kelly, Dawn Wallace, Colleen Gill, Michelle Murtagh, Laurie Byrne, Ciara Deegan, Maud-Annie Foley, Claire Judge, Louise Darby, Aoife Hyland, Siobhan Dolan, Sarah Kiernan, Clodagh Gill, Fiona Leavy (Captain). Front Row: Left to Right: Ms. Sheila Lyster (Assistant Manager), Sinead Whelehan, Christina Gahan, Ashling Hyland, Karen Treacy, Aoife Brady, Andreanna Doyle, Leanne Hendley, Catriona Hannon, Edel Marshall, Megan Brick, Siobhan Loran, Caitlin Mangan.

The Senior Team in 2011 had a very good year despite the lack of silverware; this team was captained by Cliona Gallagher and also featured Lisa Darby, Ciara Brannock, Amie Giles, Leanne Quinn, Niamh O'Reilly and Orla Judge. The Under 16's captained by Aoife Boyle also had a very good year with wins over Moyne Community School and Mercy Secondary School Ballymahon and a loss to Moate Community School still qualified them for a quarter-final against Heywood Community School Co Laois which ended in a narrow defeat on an Astroturf surface. The highlight of the year and undoubtedly a highpoint for Ladies football in the school was the capture of the Leinster Under 14 B Championship culminating in a Leinster Final victory over St. Mary's Secondary School New Ross Co Wexford by 2-11 to 2-6. The Leinster Champions had Katie Killeen as their inspirational captain along with a string of successes throughout the year which included an 8-12 to 0-2 success over Moate Community School, and a four point winning margin in the Leinster semi-final against St. Peter's Dunboyne Co Meath. The Westmeath Topic that week as its main sports heading proudly proclaimed:- *"St. Joseph's storm their way to Leinster title"*. It went on to further state:- *"The Under 14 ladies football team from St. Joseph's Secondary School, Rochfortbridge stormed their way to Leinster glory last Monday afternoon as they overcame St. Mary's Secondary School, New Ross, Co Wexford in a thrilling and close encounter played at Dr. Cullen Park in Carlow"*. At midfield, Michaela Brady won Player of the Match for an outstanding contribution for the following reasons:- *"she was one of the main playmakers in what was truly a fantastic team performance and also scored a brilliant point in the closing stages of the first half to close the gap............Shauna Fox and Leah Kenny deserve a mention here for two outstanding displays in defence............Vicky O'Reilly's save early on in the second half proved crucial as St. Joseph's were just finding their path to victory and a goal for St. Mary's at that early stage could have been a deciding factor...........Dawn Hannon's point for St. Joseph's in the dying minutes of the game was crucial as it put just enough between the two sides to ensure that St. Mary's could not win, it was delivered with style and accuracy over the black spot"*.

2011 "Blue Heaven": Leinster Ladies Under 14B Champions.
Back Row: Left to Right: Michaela Brady, Vicky O'Reilly, Shauna Fox, Lisa Flanagan, Lauren Creamer, Alex Grennan, Aoife Holton, Shannon Lyons, Nicola Judge, Rachel O'Malley. Middle Row: Left to Right: Ms. Andrea Treanor (Manager), Megan Nolan, Nicole McPadden, Clare O'Sullivan, Rebecca Carney, Lisa Cully, Leah Kenny, Amy Cully, Dawn Hannon, Jennifer Judge, Katie Downey. Front Row: Left to Right: Katie Killeen (Captain), Mary Kerrigan, Lauren Hogan.

This Leinster Championship winning team lined up as follows:- Vicky O'Reilly, Nicole McPadden, Nicola Judge, Leah Kenny, Lisa Flanagan, Rachel O'Malley, Shauna Fox, Katie Killeen (Captain), Michaela Brady, Mary Kerrigan, Dawn Hannon, Lisa Cully, Amy Cully, Jennifer Judge, Shannon Lyons.

2012 Danni Malone:
"Another successful Westmeath Captain"

Ladies Football in the School continues to make progress, the Under 14 Team in 2012 were operating in the A Division in Leinster Colleges because of the previous years success and did excellently well eventually going down in the Leinster semi-final against a very strong St. Leo's College Carlow who are now the dominant force in Colleges football in Leinster. The senior team failed to qualify out of their group in 2012 but the efforts of Emma Treacy, Leanne Galvin, Rachel Hannon, Aoife Whelehan, Esther Harney, Tara Mulleady and Niamh McDermott cannot be overlooked. In more recent years the Westmeath Ladies County Board has introduced a series of one day blitzes in which the school continues to willingly participate in. The school also had the honour in 2012 of providing yet another winning captain for Westmeath when Danni Malone led the Westmeath Under 14 Ladies Football Team to victory in the Leinster Under 14 A Shield Final in what was a resounding victory over Offaly by 3-10 to 0-4, for the record they also claimed the Leinster Under 14 Division 2 Blitz with victories over Offaly again, Dublin and Kilkenny. Shannon Lyons was also a key member of this very successful Westmeath team.

Hurling

"Grant me O Lord, a hurler's skill, With strength of arm and speed of limb Unerring eye for the flying ball"

Hurling has always featured prominently in the School, and here again it was the West Midland League that provided the basis for competition along with a series of one day blitzes mainly aimed at First Years and organised by the Westmeath County Board usually taking place in Mullingar towards the end of the school year. The first ever hurling medals to come to the school were good ones when in 1974 the Westmeath Vocational Schools Under 16 hurlers defeated Down in the semi-final and Derry in the All-Ireland B Final in Croke Park with St. Joseph's proudly supplying four members to that All-Ireland success in Sean Reidy, Donal Maher, Anthony Fox and Ger Kenny. The first ever hurling title arrived in the school in 1983, when an Under 15 Team won the West Midland League Title defeating a strong Marist College Athlone, 2-5 to 1-4, in the final, this win compensating for the loss in the previous year's final to St. Anthony's Clara by one point.

The joy of this victory was best summed up in Forum, the School's newsletter at the time:-
"on a day when every lad who wore the green and white was a star, some exceptional performances

need mention. In particular, "Man of the Match", Conor Delaney in goals, and to the three first years, Thomas Dowdall at left-half back, Michael Nugent who had his best game yet for St. Joseph's at centre-field and John Daly at right-corner forward".

In 1988, a first year team won the North Leinster Hurling Blitz staged by St. Mary's C.B.S., Mullingar and sponsored by A.I.B. on the 18th. May of that year. This success was achieved with wins over St. Mary's, Edenderry, St. Mel's Longford and in the final against Kells C.B.S. in a game that featured a goal scored by Patrick Kenny that would grace any stage. Other members of that team included Avenil Colgan, Liam Hussey, Adrian Corcoran, Paul Briody in goals, Gerard McNamee, Alvin Mitchell and Gary McGivney.

*1988 North Leinster Colleges Hurling Blitz Champions.
Back Row: Left to Right: Avenil Colgan, Adrian Corcoran, David Muldoon, Paul Briody, Gerard McNamee, Alvin Mitchell, Mark Dunne, Patrick Kenny. Front Row: Left to Right: Garry McGivney, Alan Gavin, Kieran Farrell, Jonathon O'Connor, David Bradley, Liam Hussey, Alan Wright.*

In 1989 this particular title was retained on a sweltering hot day in Mullingar with a convincing win in the Final this time against Scoil Mhuire Clane with assured performances from Derek Sheerin, Darren Meehan, Jason Hannon and Declan Fox. In addition, Sean Egan also won the individual skills competition urged on by a supportive team on a memorable sun drenched day.

In 1997, an Under 14 team was entered into the Leinster Colleges for the first time and success was quick to arrive with victories over St. Mary's Edenderry, 6-2 to 1-1 and St. Mel's Longford 3-5 to 1-4, next to fall were Kells Community School and Dundalk Schools before Edenderry Vocational School fell in the North Leinster Final for a historic first for hurling in the school at Leinster Colleges level. This team was backboned by Rory Wright, Damien Loran, Seamus Faulkner (Captain), Adrian Gallagher, Andrew Cannon, Gordon Greville, Padraig Bennett and Brian Connaughton who would go on to hurl for many years at senior level with Westmeath. In 1999, the School entered teams in Leinster Colleges at Under 14, Under 16 and Senior levels plus a First Year team making it the busiest year in the history of hurling in the School. At senior level a great victory was achieved against Tullamore C.B.S. by 4-8 to 3-7, only to be later denied in a keenly contested quarter-final with Tullamore College emerging victorious with almost the final puck of the game. This team was captained by the excellent John Shaw from Raharney another who would go on to hurl for the Lake County for many years, the highlight of which was as a captain again, he led Westmeath to victory in the Christy Ring Cup in 2005.

The Under 16 team in 1999 was backboned by most of the members of the victorious Under 14 panel from two years previous and had a great start to the championship with wins over St. Pat's Navan and St. Joseph's Secondary School Athboy. Unfortunately, this run

1997 North Leinster Under 14 Hurling Champions.
Back Row: Left to Right: Aidan Geraghty, Ross Mealiff,
Gordon Greville, Rory Wright, Padraig Leavy, Anthony Coleman,
Nigel Graham, Christopher Glennon, John Kelly, Mr. Denis Kelly
(Manager) Middle Row: Left to Right: Philip Kelleghan, David
Mitchell, Damien Loran, Adrian Gallagher, Padraig Bennett, James
Feery, Eamon Boyle, Andrew Cannon. Front Row: Left to Right: Bobby
Troy, Shane Hoey, Seamus Faulkner (Captain), Philip Sheridan,
Mark Cole, Francis Kenny.

2005 >
John Shaw: Captained Westmeath Senior
Hurlers to Christy Ring Cup Success.

1999 Midlands First Year Hurling Champions.
Back Row: Left to Right: Conor Jordan, Ivan Oxley, Thomas Geraghty, Jamie Wilson, David Rowley, Alan
Doyle, Gavin Hoey, David Coyne, Robbie Kenny, John Connelly, Mr. Denis Kelly (Manager).
Front Row: Left to Right: Michael Malone, Drew Morgan, Padraig Kelly, Dermot Faulkner (Captain),
Patrick Darby, Gary Nolan, Brendan McAnarney, John Peppard.

came to an end in the North Leinster semi-final to defending champions Killina Presentation Secondary School Rahan 5-6 to 3-7. The Under 14 panel began training in the wet conditions of early February and with great wins over St. Mary's Edenderry, Castlepollard Vocational School, St. Mel's Longford, Tullamore College, Dunshaughlin Community College in a great semi-final before overcoming Tullamore C.B.S. in the final and adding a second North Leinster Under 14 Title to the one already won in 1997. This team was captained by Paul Kelly at full back, it could also lay claim to a splendid half back line of Enda Leonard, Declan Leech and Kenneth Earley, and up front, most of the danger came from Alan Doyle and John Conneely. The First Year team trained all year with the Under 14's and this ploy bore fruit when they triumphed in the Midlands First Year Final in Tullamore against Tullamore College 6-2 to 2-2, this team had Dermot

2005 The late Niall Keegan captains St. Joseph's to the North Leinster Juvenile Shield Final.

Faulkner as an inspirational captain; it was also excellently well served by some first-class goalkeeping all year by Thomas Geraghty, and by a never to be forgotten performance from Robbie Kenny who scored an outstanding 4-1 of his side's total in that final.

Other successful campaigns were to follow in hurling during the 1999-2000 school year. The Senior Panel fought their way to the North Leinster semi-final where they lost to eventual champions Mullingar Community College, this team found its inspiration in midfielder Niall Flanagan and from Niall Cole at centre forward. The Under 16 team fared better and after having beaten St. Pat's Navan in the semi-final, eventually lost to Tullamore College in the Final. The years between 2001-2003 on the hurling fields were relatively calm in comparison with what to come in the latter part of the decade, yet in 2004 another very good Senior Hurling Team captained by Westmeath minor Michael Malone had notable victories in the North Leinster Championship over St. Mel's Longford and St. Pat's Navan before bowing out at the semi-final stages. This team had Brian Smith another Westmeath county minor in its ranks along with Liam Quinn, John Peppard, Niall Kilcoyne, John Mooney, Kevin and Robert Reid.

When on the 19th. May 2005, the late Niall Keegan captained the Under 14 hurling team to a 4-10 to 5-5 victory over L.S.U. Banagher in O'Connor Park Tullamore, it not only completed the treble of all underage hurling titles available to the school in North Leinster, it also ushered in a period of unprecedented success previously unknown and one which continues unabated to the present day. The Westmeath Topic dedicated a full page to this latest hurling success with the headline:- *"St. Joseph's clinch North Leinster Juvenile Championship"*, it went on to exclaim:- *"St. Joseph's Rochfortbridge, clinched the North Leinster Juvenile "C" Hurling Championship at O'Connor Park in Tullamore, on Thursday May 19 last, making it a remarkable clean sweep of U-18, U-16 and U-14 titles this year"*. At centre back, captain Niall Keegan led by example and was ably assisted throughout the field by Michael Boyle in goals, Darren Kilcoyne, Mark Conroy, Kevin Morgan, Paul Carey and Robert McKeogh. The Under

16 North Leinster title was secured earlier in the year with a victory in that final over St. Finians Mullingar led by Mark Keegan and Alan Giles. The North Leinster Senior Hurling success was achieved with a win over Tullamore C.B.S. in the final starring A.J. Murray, Niall Kilcoyne and Andrew Devine. In 2006, the Senior Hurlers had a mixed season with wins over St. Pat's Navan and Athboy Community School only to lose at the semi-final stage to Boyne Community School Trim despite the best efforts of team captain Stephen Conway, Alan O'Sullivan, James Leogue, Ger Keegan and Brendan Sheridan.

It was back to winning ways again in 2007 when the Leinster Senior C Hurling Championship was captured at the expense of Scoil Aodháin Dublin marking the beginnings of a very healthy hurling rivalry that was now about to develop between St. Joseph's and a number of schools from the capital during these very prosperous years. This latest success was due to Darren Quinn, Mark Conroy, Mark Keegan, Christopher Flanagan, Andrew Doyle and Daniel Riggs. The Under 14 North Leinster Shield was also dutifully returned to the School's Trophy cabinet this year with a 3-8 to 1-5 victory over Mercy Kilbeggan in a team captained by Joey Boyle which also included Eddie Alford, Jake Byrne, Cian O'Connor and future senior captain Mark Glennon.

In 2008, the North Leinster Senior Championship saw a first round loss to Presentation Secondary School Killina, followed by victories over Tullamore College and Portlaoise C.B.S. only to be thwarted by Presentation Secondary School Killina Co Offaly at the semi-final stage, losing to this opposition becoming somewhat of a worry. For the first time since 2005 and the second time in the School's history another notable treble of North Leinster hurling titles made their way back to the school in 2009. The Under 14's won their

2005 Under 14 North Leinster Juvenile Shield Winning Team.
Back Row: Left to Right: David Kilcoyne, Niall Keegan (Captain), Kevin Morgan, Adam Shiels, Robert McKeogh, Cian Flynn, Paul Lewis.
Front Row: Left to Right: Paul Carey, Mark Conroy, Michael Boyle, Eoin O'Sullivan, Cormac Boyle, Kevin Conway, Jason Cully, Wayne Fox.

championship final with a victory over Scoil Mhuire Community School Clane Co Kildare with Shane Murtagh, Shane Farrelly and Pearce Byrne-Colgan very much to the fore. The Under 16 North Leinster Championship was regained with a win over Castlepollard Community College; this victory was down to a great effort all year by Dermot Judge. The seniors obliged and completed the treble with victory over city rivals again Scoil Chaitríona Dublin on a score of 2-14 to 2-10 to recapture the Leinster C Senior Hurling Championship for the second time in three years with Jamie Gonoud, Robbie Greville and Cillian Duggan winning medals as part of this team. In 2010, the Leinster Senior Hurling Championship was retained, this time at the expense of Naomh Colmcille Community School Dublin with a team including the youthful Steven Lynam, Jason Cully, Gerard Foley and Cormac Boyle who would go on to hurl at Minor and Under 21 levels for Westmeath. Interestingly, that year the Westmeath Schools Under 14 Championship was also won in a victory over Mercy Kilbeggan with a team that included Jason Gorman and Aaron Glynn.

The 2010-2011 season began with the Under 16 team captained by Gary Greville and featuring Alan O'Donoghue winning the North Leinster C Championship when they beat Boyne Community School in a thrilling final played in Kinnegad on a scoreline of 2-13 to 0-10, this team took a lot of inspiration from Dylan Raleigh. The senior hurling team led by Sean Deegan kept the ball rolling by capturing the North Leinster Championship beating Scoil Mhuire Clane in a close encounter 1-10 to 0-9. The Leinster semi-final victory was certainly another highpoint for hurling in the school when defeating Duiske College Graignamanagh Co Kilkenny by 1-12 to 1-8. The Leinster Final proved to be a very close affair against by now familiar opponents Scoil Chaitríona from Dublin, with St. Joseph's just winning out in the end 2-14 to 2-10 and claiming yet another Leinster Colleges Senior Hurling C Championship for the third time in the school's history. The Under 14's did not disappoint either when they won the North Leinster Colleges Final with a big win against Boyne Community School 7-18 to 2-5 thus achieving the Leinster treble for the third time. The Westmeath Topic loud in its praise wrote:- *"Doyle twins, Killian and Ciaran once again led the way for the Rochfortbridge school, scoring a massive 4-13 between them, but collectively, St. Joseph's were much better balanced and their defence kept tabs on Boyne CS throughout the match."*

Denis Kelly: Has overseen the remarkable rise of Hurling in St. Joseph's.

Ciaran and Killian Doyle: "Double trouble for every opposition in every sport"

Afterwards, there were great celebrations as Luke Byrne collected the winning trophy from Tom O'Donnell of Leinster schools". The Westmeath Schools Under 14 Championship was also retained, this time at the expense of St. Mary's C.B.S. Mullingar.

Ger Healion: In action for the Faithful County.

In 2012, the Under 14's had a mixed set of results as after victories over Dunshaughlin Community College and Boyne Community School they suffered losses to St. Peter's College Dunboyne in the group stages and to Coláiste Choilm Tullamore in the semi-final by 3-8 to 1-12 eventually bringing their Leinster Championship to an end. The Under 16's recorded wins over Moate Community School and Mercy Secondary School Kilbeggan before losing out to Killina Presentation Secondary School Co Offaly in the semi-final. Undoubtedly, the highlight in 2012 was the capture of the Leinster Colleges Senior Hurling B Championship for the first time after many years of hard work and endeavour. This very significant breakthrough was achieved after victories over St. Joseph's Cistercian Roscrea by 1-12 to 1-10 in the Rest of Leinster Final, and over Coláiste Eanna Dublin in the Leinster Final by 2-12 to 1-12. The All-Ireland semi-final against Mercy College Woodford Co Galway proved to be an easier victory than expected. On Saturday, 24th. March, 2012, all roads led to the *"stony grey soil"* of Iniskeen Co Monaghan and a meeting with St. Mary's Belfast in the All-Ireland Colleges Final, but on the day the lads from Antrim proved to be a bit stronger and seemed to have been down this particular road before. St. Joseph's were led and

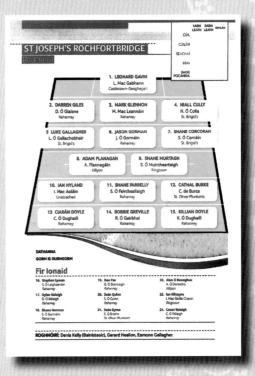

2012 All-Ireland Senior Colleges Hurling Programme.

inspired all year by their affable captain Mark Glennon and he had able hurlers alongside in Niall Cully, Adam Flanagan, Robbie Greville now playing senior hurling for Westmeath and his brother Gary until persistent injury deprived him throughout the year, all among a group who had given unstinting service to the ancient game at all levels during their time in St. Joseph's.

"No matter what way the game may go May I rest in friendship with every foe".

2012 All-Ireland Senior Colleges Hurling Finalists.
Back Row: Left to Right: Alan O'Donoghue, Steven Lynam, Adam Flanagan, Luke Gallagher, Mark Glennon (Captain), Ian Hyland, Pearce Byrne-Colgan, Shane Farrelly, Robbie Greville, Killian Doyle, Jack Cully, Daniel Fox, Darragh Duggan, Darren Giles, Sean Quinn, Ian Kilcoyne, Cathal Burke.
Front Row: Left to Right: Shane Corcoran, Shane Murtagh, Jason Gorman, Dylan Raleigh, Leonard Gavin, Niall Cully, Shane Gorman, Conor Raleigh, James Goonery, Ciaran Doyle, Daniel Greville.

Soccer

There has always been a history of Soccer in the school or to put it more accurately a history of Soccer Leagues whether they be part of physical education classes or *"big-break"* crowd-pullers usually organised by a lunch-less teacher or in some cases by students themselves. It was not uncommon in the earlier years to have two or three of these leagues run off in a school year. More recently due to an increasing variety of sports offered to students and probably also due to the ever increasing student population, these leagues are now not as much a feature of school life they once were. Yet a trip through student magazines from the late 1970's uncovers and

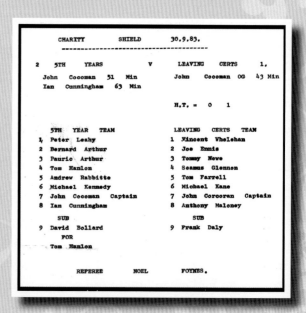

1983 The Soccer Leagues.

recaptures in many instances the excitement aroused by these domestic competitions, for example we read in one:- *"the Soccer League was a great success. There were ten teams divided into two pools. Paul Fox won Pool 1 and John Dillon won Pool 2. It was a very close and exciting Final. Both teams scored in the first five minutes, but then the game became deadlocked. At full time the score was 1-1. Extra time of fifteen minutes was played. Last kick of the game, Cully scored".*

Again, from a later school edition with similar sentiments we read:- *"the Sixth Years made their exit against the B2 team – despite the fine play of "Chuck" McDonough and John Denehan. This meant that B2 would play the winners of the A1 V 5A match in the semi-final, and it was in this match that we got the biggest surprise of the competition, whether it was post Dingle blues or maybe exhaustion from late night walking remains unanswered – but the 5A's could only look on in disbelief as John Daly raced through their defence to score the A1's second goal adding to the earlier Eamonn Cleary goal"*. It is also fair to say that since more serious soccer at competitive levels has been entered into in very recent years the success levels reached has been remarkable in this area despite the fact that many of the students on these very successful teams do not even play soccer at club level. This clearly demonstrates that with the proper coaching and expertise in place the seemingly impossible can and has become a reality.

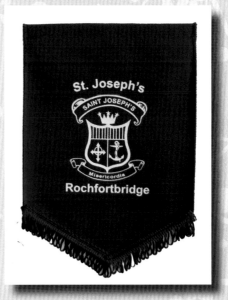

St. Joseph's represent Ireland.

In an article titled *"The Rise and Rise of Soccer in Ireland"* from Junior Journal the First Year School paper from the early 1980's, John O'Brien put forward his thoughts on the historical origins of soccer in Ireland as he saw it when he wrote:- *"Soccer was introduced into Ireland originally by members of the British Army during the time of occupation around the turn of the century. This is why soccer in Ireland was mainly played in towns and cities where British barracks were situated"*. He then went on to bemoan the fact that even though in the earlier part of the twentieth century a national thirty two county team had been set up that unfortunately did not meet the approval of all the various political viewpoints on the island eventually leading to its break-up. John finished his essay with a very insightful thought for one so young that is as relevant today as it was back then when he wished:- *"perhaps in the future we will once again have one soccer team representing the whole of Ireland"*. Another visit through the school's magazines brings a trip down memory lane which reveals a girl's soccer team taking to the field in 1984 in a series of challenge matches both home and away against Killina Presentation Secondary School Rahan with the team being formed very unexpectedly on the day before the first match! However, success came fast in this early adventure when Audrey Brennan and Co scored three goals without reply; others to shine in their soccer debuts were Colette McCormack and Eileen Gorman The return match in Rahan ended 0-0 with Dolores Gorman, Rosie Moody, Lorna O'Brien and the very impressive Margaret Slevin very much to the fore.

From that time on there is little evidence of soccer being played in the school at any competitive level, yet in 2008 a First Year soccer team participated in the Futsal Tournament that took place in the National Basketball Arena in Tallaght. Futsal is a five-a-side indoor game that promotes skill, composure and quick-thinking. That same year also marked the inclusion of a coaching course organised by the FAI in order to promote soccer in the school. This overall approach has certainly borne fruit as nowadays two out of three secondary schools take part at some level in FAI Schools Cup competitions and St. Joseph's are no exception. This is a far cry from 1968 when the FAI established the Irish Secondary Schools Football Association with only a handful of schools mainly in urban areas involved. There are now ten Cup competitions from first year through to Senior Boys and Girls that provide All Ireland winners. There are also long established representative competitions at Interprovincial and International level for both boys and girls.

St. Joseph's has now become a very serious competitor at Irish Secondary Schools Football Association (ISSFA) level and the 2010/2011 school year can rightly be described as the greatest season for soccer ever in the school with the crowning of the Under 14 team as All-Ireland Champions with Sean Quinn as captain. Having secured a win over Athlone Community College in the West Leinster League decider they then defeated Scoil Eoin Athy and Tallaght Community School which gave them a chance to claim the Leinster Champions League Title in a game which unfortunately they lost 2-0 going down to De La Salle College Dundalk, Dundalk's two goals coming in the first eleven minutes leaving no way back. They then turned their attentions towards a good run in the Cup and early wins were secured over Scoil Mhuire Strokestown Co Roscommon and Coláiste Choilm Tullamore, the turning point came with victory over Firhouse Community School Dublin, next up was a 2-0 win over former All-Ireland Champions Salesian College Cellbridge followed by a semi-final 5-3 win over Drimnagh Castle, Dublin and the Leinster Cup Final win was secured with a 5-4 penalty shoot out win following a scoreless draw against Oatlands College Stillorgan. It was then on to the All-Ireland semi-final where Munster Champions Clonmel High School Tipperary were accounted for on a 3-1 scoreline. The All-Ireland Cup Final played in Athlone on Tuesday April 12th. 2011 resulted in an unforgettable 1-0 victory over St. Gerald's Castlebar Co Mayo. St. Joseph's were All-Ireland Champions. The next day, Wednesday 13th. April, a heading stretched across the sports pages of the Irish Independent proclaiming:- *"Reid caps fine season for Joseph's"*, this article went on to capture

2011 All-Ireland Under 14 Soccer Champions & Westmeath Young Sports Stars of the Year.
Back Row: Left to Right: Kieran McManus, Jason Palmer, Joseph Hyland, Ian Kilcoyne, Killian Doyle, David Etcheri, Mark Geoghegan, Bobby Gonoud, Ciaran Doyle, Mr. Damien Rushe (Manager)
Front Row: Left to Right: Dominic Judge, Cathal Moran, Sean Quinn (Captain), Sam Plant, Jack Reid, Tony Loftus, Kaelan Hickey, Evan Toner, Peter Lalor, Finbar Coyne, Jack Murphy.

the excitement created:- *"Jack Reid bagged a sensational winner as St. Joseph's, Rochfortbridge, capped an incredible season of firsts by claiming the FAI Schools Minor Boys All-Ireland yesterday"*. The historic All-Ireland Champions line up was:- Joseph Hyland, Cathal Moran, Peter Lalor, Sean Quinn (Captain), Killian Doyle, Sam Plant, Finbar Coyne, Jack Reid, David Etcheri, Ciaran Doyle, Mark Geoghegan. Replacements: Evan Toner, Kaelan Hickey, Bobby Gonoud, Jack Murphy, Siyabonga Nuxmalo, Ian Kilcoyne, Tony Loftus, Kieran McManus, Jason Palmer and Dominic Judge.

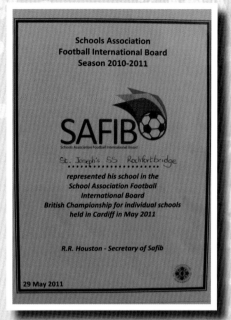

SAFIB: Schools Association Football International Board.

The already mentioned international dimension of school's soccer now came to call at the door of St. Joseph's and as All-Ireland Champions the honour of representing Ireland in the Schools Association Football International Board (SAFIB) tournament was offered and gratefully accepted. This British Isles Championship for Individual Schools was organised by the Welsh Schools F.A. that year and took place between the 27th. - 29th. May, 2011 in the Playing Fields, Treforest, University of Glamorgan. In his welcoming address to Wales, David Nickless, the Chairman of the Welsh Schools Football Association (WSFA) had this to say:- *"Congratulations to the following schools on winning through to the Championship Festival and representing their country in the event. It is a great honour for your school as the Championship is most probably the top such event in Europe for individual schools"*. The other schools competing with St. Joseph's were:- Ysgol Syr Hugh Owen Wales, Pentrehafod School Wales, Musselburgh Grammar School Scotland, St. Columb's College Northern Ireland and Richard Challenor High School England. On Friday 27th. May, St. Joseph's played Pentrehafod losing 2-1, and on Saturday defeated Syr Hugh Owen 1-0 and Richard Challenor 3-0. Yet while this was not enough to qualify them for the final, St. Joseph's were the talk of the tournament and were identified by the organisers as the best team both on and off the pitch.

English Schools Football Association.

A weekend filled with sporting memories to last a lifetime. The final icing came for this very successful team when in May they were crowned the Westmeath Examiner Junior Sports Stars of the Year for 2011.

Meanwhile, the Under 16 team in 2011 seemed to be the strongest on paper as it was littered with athleticism and skill, with players of the calibre of Luke Gallagher, Jason Gorman and Pearce Byrne-Colgan on board. The campaign started with a win over Birr Community School followed by draws against Moate Community School and Coláiste Choilm Tullamore which led to the top of the table in the West Leinster League. The semi-final meeting with St. Mel's Longford ended in a 2-0 win for St. Mel's in a game that needed extra time. Interestingly, St. Mel's went on to easily win the title and qualify for the Leinster Champions League. The Under 19 team went a step further by capturing the West Leinster League for the first time in the school's history. Having come through a difficult group, a semi-final victory was achieved against Scoil Mhuire Strokestown Co Roscommon by two goals to one; the final was won 3-1 against defending champions Moyne Community School, *"the Bridge"* being led by their inspired and athletic captain Jake Byrne. As winners of the West Leinster region, the school now represented this region in the Leinster Champions League where they were narrowly beaten 3-2 by a much fancied Coláiste Craobh Abhann Kilcoole Co Wicklow. Throughout the year, this particular success was motivated by Dwayne Lynch, Dermot Judge, Lee Wallace in goals,

"Pre-match strategies"
Sr. Pius and Jack Charlton.

Gordon O'Sullivan, Joe Guiden, Conor Slevin, Jamie Leavy, Mark Gaye, Daniel Phillips, Liam Keenan, Daniel Plant and James McGovern.

Interest was now at an all time high and 2012 began with the Under 14 First Year team having a very large panel to choose from and being entered into the Leinster Cup and the domestic West Leinster League. Unfortunately, Marist College Athlone knocked this team out of the Cup 3-2 and their involvement in the West Leinster League ended at the semi-final stage. The Under 15 team with first years Jack Hall and Matthew Rowden on board captured the West Leinster League title after topping their group and progressing to the final where they accounted for Coláiste Choilm Tullamore after a penalty shoot out, this brought them into the Leinster Champions League where minus a few players they went down to Drimnagh Castle Dublin 5-3 in the end. Later in the year, this team also had a great run in the Cup eventually going down at the semi-final stage to St. Benildus College Dublin. The Under 17 team reached the West Leinster League final going down in the end to Athlone Community College, with the Under 19's failing to retain the league title won the previous year.

Another of those international dimensions to soccer associated with St. Joseph's occurred unexpectedly during what has gone down in history as the most successful era ever for the Republic of Ireland Soccer Team and involved a friendship that developed between Sr. Pius and Jack Charlton the genial Englishman who managed the Irish Team to such unprecedented heights between 1986 and 1996. This alliance began in 1987 due to an unusual set of circumstances when Sr. Pius's name was pulled from a hat one night as the winner of a draw for an autographed football in a competition she had entered. The raffle took place in Moate. At the soccer function in Moate that evening Jack Charlton was the guest of honour and the job of announcing the winners of the Raffle fell to Jack, not surprisingly, he got into all kinds of difficulty when confronted with the pronunciation and lay out of Sr. Pius's name, however, he later confessed he knew it had to be someone in religion as he remembered a Pope by the same name. Nevertheless, this impromptu meeting led to a friendship and a regular correspondence between the two that was to see Sr. Pius at every home game that the Republic of Ireland played at Jack's request and Sr. Pius's tickets duly arrived to her a few days before each match. During those heady days, inspiration was an ingredient that this great Irish team often needed and always seemed to find from somewhere particularly in the white heat of battle. For

"Post-match analysis"
Sr. Pius and Jack Charlton.

instance, did you ever wonder what inspired Packie to dive to his right instead of to his left to save Timofte's penalty in that never to be forgotten World Cup shoot out in Genoa in 1990? Nobody seems to know. Those members of the general public not lucky enough to be privy to this great fortune looked up and thanked the heavens that warm evening that Packie had taken the correct decision and continued on with the celebrations. We thanked Sr. Pius. The value of sport.

Other Sports

Throughout the years students at St. Joseph's have excelled in a wide variety of other sports and while in some cases these sports may not have been formally organised in the school nonetheless, these students were catered for as far as was practical and competitions were entered into more often than not with remarkable heights being achieved by these participants. There is evidence both written and photographic to show that hockey and tennis were the more

1984 The late Gerry Usher: All-Ireland Under 12 Boxing Champion at 5 stone 2 lbs

favoured sports in the earlier history of the school and this was more or less very much in keeping with the convention of a girl's boarding school. These facilities just didn't happen though out of thin air, a lot of effort and expense was incurred on behalf of the Sisters to provide such facilities for these earlier students at quite considerable costs, evidence of which can be read in an extract from the Annals of the Convent in 1961 which informs us that:- *"during the year a card drive and Socials were held to help to raise funds to pay off debt on St. Joseph's. All were well supported. After Easter Roadstone Ltd. came and laid down two tennis courts for the boarders at cost £1,093.0.0".*

As there were very competitive and strong Boxing Clubs in Rochfortbridge and Tyrrellspass, we find that students in the school have fared out quite well when it comes to donning the red-padded gloves and Leinster and All-Ireland Champions have been produced. For example from Involve the student magazine of 1984 we read:- *"Michael Nugent and Gerry Usher both have won All-Ireland Juvenile titles in their respective codes and in this year's Leinster Championships others fared very well. Gordon Eighan and Martin Daly both got to the final before being beaten while Thomas Dowdall, Sean Morgan and Des Gunning put up great performances". Sean Morgan won a trip to Malta in June to fight with Connacht and Gerry Nugent got beaten in the All-Ireland Final".*

Other students who passed through the school and have excelled at boxing have included Alo Kelly and John McDonagh. In August 2012, Darragh Murray boxing out of the South Meath Club claimed the Cadet All-Ireland Title at 65 kgs in the National Stadium by defeating James Geoghegan of St. Catherine's Dublin; he added this title to two Leinster titles already won at 46 kgs and 57 kgs.

Camogie in the School has been played on and off, but it is only in very recent years that it has been properly organised. In 1993, it was decided by several students to organise a team with a view to entering the Leinster Schools Camogie Championship that September. The students involved in this first Camogie championship included:- Gemma Weir, Bernie Norris, Linda Griffith, Orla Jones, Barbara Jones, Miriam Griffith, Niamh Cunniffe, Terri Rattigan, Anne Harris, Mairead Hogan, Catherine Shaw, Lisa Connaughton, Gemma Shiels, Emer O'Reilly, Niamh Fitzsimons, Fionnuala Dunne and Denise Maguire.

In 2011 the School entered camogie teams in the Leinster Championships at Under 14 and Under 16 levels. However, 2012 has been the most successful year in camogie by far with two teams being entered into competition at Senior and Under 16 levels. The emergence of St. Brigid's Camogie Club in Rochfortbridge along with Raharney has enabled St. Joseph's to enter teams at both levels. The Under 16 team made history by capturing the Leinster Championship and bringing home the first trophy ever won by a camogie team from the school. This team was captained by Jena McKeogh and recorded victories in Leinster

1993 Camogie: Back Row: Left to Right: Gemma Weir, Bernie Norris, Linda Griffith, Orla Jones, Barbara Lanes, Miriam Griffith, Niamh Cunniffe, Terri Rattigan, Anne Harris, Mairead Hogan. Front Row: Left to Right: Catherine Shaw, Lisa Conanughton, Gemma Shiels, Emer O'Reilly, Niamh Fitzsimons, Fionnuala Dunne, Denise McGuire.

against St. Finians Mullingar, Mercy Secondary School Kilbeggan, Scoil Mhuire Trim in the semi-final before defeating Coláiste Eoin Hackettstown Carlow in the Leinster Final. The All-Ireland semi-final resulted in a victory after an epic battle over St. Aloysius Carrigtwohill Co Cork only to lose out in the Final against Mount Mercy College Cork in a game played in Templederry Co Tipperary. The Senior camogie team had also a great year with early wins over Scoil Mhuire Clane and Coláiste Naomh Mhuire Naas, leading to a semi-final victory over Coláiste Bhride Carnew Co Wicklow only to lose the Leinster Final to local rivals St. Finians Mullingar. As beaten Leinster finalists this team still qualified for an All-Ireland quarter-final where after the long journey to Belfast, St Mary's Grammar School were accounted for, the semi-final resulted in an agonising defeat to St. Mary's Secondary School Macroom Co Cork in a game played before a large crowd in Rochfortbridge.

2012: Mary Deegan: Captains Westmeath Under 16 Camogie Team to All-Ireland Glory.

This ended a very successful year for camogie in the School and with numbers interested in playing continuing to grow; more success seems just around the corner. This optimism is based on the fact that no fewer than twelve students from St. Joseph's were involved

2012: "Getting ready for the trip to Tipp"
Back Row: Left to Right: Therese Walsh, April Flanagan, Jena McKeogh, Angel Flanagan, Aine Brady, Ms. Elizabeth Shaw (Manager), Rachel O'Malley.
Middle Row: Left to Right: Megan Carroll, Anna Weir, Laura Doherty, Ashling Goss, Claire Coyne, Laura Patton, Lisa Flanagan, Kathlyn Gardiner, Shauna Fox, Leanne Darby.
Front Row: Left to Right: Sarah Kiernan, Jennifer Judge, Erin Hart, Sarah Patton, Lisa Cully, Aoife Boyle, Amy Cully, Mary Deegan, Nicola Judge, Megan Nolan.

in the Westmeath Under 16 Camogie Team that on the 26th. August 2012 defeated Armagh in the All-Ireland C Camogie Final having defeated Laois and Wicklow along the way. This team had yet another successful captain from St. Joseph's in Mary Deegan and with her from the school were Amy Cully, Lisa Cully, Lisa Flanagan, Jennifer Judge, Nicola Judge, Leah Kenny, Rachel O'Malley, Jena McKeogh, Claire Coyne, Leanne Darby and Erin Hart.

Hockey has not featured as much in recent years in the school as it did in the past, yet throughout the mid 1970's to the late 1980's, hockey teams were entered into competition at every year level into the Inter Schools Leinster League. A particularly talented group of First Years with Esther Giles and Adrienne Corcoran won the Beginners League outright in 1977 at the expense of Loreto Mullingar;

"Back to the 80's: Anyone for Hockey?"
Hillary Gaffney and Caitriona Maguire.

however, they failed to carry this form through just missing out in the final of the Fifth Year League in 1980. In an extract from Forum the then student magazine from 1982 we read:-
"The Leaving Cert hockey team have competed in the Bower Athlone, where they played Banagher, Bower, Birr, Wilson's and Loreto. They were beaten in two matches and drew in three; the 2-0 loss to Loreto was the hardest to take. However hopes are still high". From that time on, hockey seemed to disappear only to make a brief reappearance in the late 1980's with teams entered at First

2012 Westmeath: All-Ireland Under 16C Camogie Champions.
Back Row: Left to Right: Leah Kenny, Orla Daly, Susan Carey, Claire Coyne, Kelly Dalton, Lisa Flanagan, Sabina McLoughlin, Caoimhe McCrossan. Middle Row: Left to Right: Laura Varley, Ciara Griffith, Kelly Dobson, Erin Hart, Melissa McKeown, Amy Cully, Jennifer Judge, Maria Kelly, Emma Foley, Nicola Judge, Leanne Darby.
Front Row: Left to Right: Katie Heffernan, Ellie O'Reilly, Lisa Cully, Mary Deegan (Captain), Jena McKeogh, Ciara Cuskelly, Annmarie Kennedy, Sarah Kennedy, Rachel O'Malley, Aoife Corcoran.

Year and Junior levels in the Schools Leinster League. In 1989 the First Years had a great campaign which brought them to the semi-final stages of the Beginners League only to be denied by Loreto Mullingar, best players being Caroline Holdwright, Josephine Giles and Clare Leavy, the Juniors though not as successful had great contributions from Anne Marie Curran, Ann Connell and Carol Dowdall.

2006 Leinster Golf Champions.
From Left: Andrew Cunningham, John Fagan, Mrs. Fiona Burke (Manager), Gary Shaw, Kevin Metcalfe.

Another notable first in sport for the school was scaled on 27th. October 1999 when with Niall McAteer as captain along with Ronan Hogan and Michael Malone captured the Leinster Schools Senior Pitch and Putt Championship which was held in the McDonagh Pitch and Putt Course at the Curragh in Co Kildare. They staged a remarkable recovery from being two shots off the pace going into the second round, eventually ending up champions by four shots. In 2006 a team made up of Gary Shaw, Andrew Cunningham, Kevin Metcalfe and John Fagan with substitutes Aidan Fallon and Eoin Metcalfe were crowned Leinster Under 19 Golf Champions at Killeen Golf Club Co Kildare from a total of sixty six schools that started the quest for this title. Having beaten a host of top schools on their way to the final, they accounted for St. Joseph's Secondary School Drogheda and St. Michael's College Ailesbury Road Dublin on that memorable day in Co Kildare. In 2011 the School's Golf Team was made up of Conor Slevin, Joe Guiden, Ronan Purcell, Gordon O'Sullivan and Cian Burke recorded good wins over Mercy Kilbeggan and St. Finian's Mullingar but was still not enough to qualify them for the Finals as they needed to win more than twice for qualification. A Pitch and Putt Team of Conor Slevin, Jonathon Daly and Liam Metcalfe ensured an excellent outright victory in the inaugural year of the All-Ireland Secondary Schools Competition held in Tullamore with Jonathon Daly and Conor Slevin both coming in at thirteen under par and Liam Metcalfe at three under bringing in a total of twenty nine under for an eleven shot victory. Another memorable first.

For many years swimming was part of the physical education timetable and a weekly visit to the pool in Mullingar led to competitions been entered into against other schools in the area. One extremely successful meet from 1989 saw medals being won by Emma Symth, Caroline Dolan, Linda Murray, Sinead Bagnall, Maeve Wright, Elaine O'Brien, Catherine Dolan, Rebecca Maslin and Fiona Davis. The following year the intensive coaching that took place during the long winter months bore fruit when the Junior swimming team were crowned best overall school in an inter-schools swimming gala that was held in Mullingar. In 1997, the school entered both grade B and C swimming galas which took place at the Guinness Pool, Dublin and in Donaghameade Dublin respectively. In March gold was won in the Senior Girls Medley Relay swimmers as follows: Sinead Curtis, Julie Duffy, Caroline Duffy and Marie Duffy. Sinead Curtis also took silver in the Senior Girls Backcrawl. At this meet, personal bests were recorded by Bryan Fallon, Maurice Fallon, Kieran Fallon and Conor Eighan. In May of that year at the C gala in Donaghameade more honours were achieved when Caroline Duffy won silver in the Junior Girls Butterfly and Julie Duffy came third in the Inter Girls Freestyle. In 2008 Elaine Geraghty and Kevin Ronan represented the School in the Leinster A Schools Competition held in the National

Ciara Duffy: "Continues to improve her times in the USA"

Aquatic Centre in Dublin and both qualified for the All-Ireland Schools Finals which were held in Leisureland Co Galway. Both swimmers came out of the meet just short of medals but obtained personal bests on the day. In 2010, Ciara Duffy competed in the Leinster distance and graded competition winning in the Fifty Metre Freestyle and claiming silver in the Fifty Metre Backcrawl. She also swam at the ESB team's annual competition achieving two personal bests in both the 100 Metres Freestyle and 100 Metres Backcrawl and later in the Leinster Longcourse Open Competition progressing to the semi-final of the 50 Metre Freestyle.

In 1993 the school was entered in a Leinster Schools Tennis Competition for the first time with the Senior A Girls team made up of Orla Carroll, Emma Byrne, Tracey Fanning, Anne-Marie Leavy, Eileen Corroon and Fiona Dowling losing out to Mount Sackville Secondary School Dublin after an outstanding victory over Mount Temple Comprehensive School Clontarf in an earlier round. The Senior B Girls team had Imelda Byrne, Sinead Murtagh, Niamh Coyne, Louise Curran, Ruth Murtagh and Caroline Coffey. The Minor team members were Maria Fox, Muireann McCoy, Michelle Gartland, Sarah Galligan, Gillian Murphy and Gillian Egan.

1993 Junior Boys Tennis Team. Back Row: Left to Right: Michael Carroll, Thomas Larkin, Frank Gorman, John Driver.
Front Row: Left to Right: James Carroll, Clifford Flynn, Eddie Doyle.

The Boys Junior Singles Team featured Clifford Flynn, John Driver and James Carroll with the Doubles been made up of Thomas Larkin, Eddie Doyle, Frank Gorman and Trevor Thornton. In 2000 a Tennis Tournament was held for all the schools in County Westmeath and the Girls Team that was made up of Sarah Graham (Captain), Orlagh Keeney, Lorraine O'Sullivan, Susan Graham and Heidi Hill came in fourth of seven schools participating. The Boys Team made up of Sameer Kumar, Andrew Cannon, Padraig Bennett, Jamie Wilson and Daniel Mooney came third of six schools.

Interestingly, it is important to record a Boys Volleyball Team that was entered into the Junior B Volleyball All-Ireland Schools Championships in 1996. With wins over Mountmellick Community School Co Laois by two sets to one, Holy Faith Community School Rathcoole Dublin by two sets to nil and Loughrea Vocational School Co Galway by the same margin, then, unfortunately ended up losing the final narrowly to a very good Mary Immaculate Secondary School Lisdoonvarna Co Clare by two sets to one. A

1997 Junior Girls Volleyball Team.
Back Row: Left to Right: Charyn White, Maura Reegan, Martha Clancy, Aishling Sheridan, Joan Farrell. Front Row: Left to Right: Jenna Bagnall, Julianne Scanlon, Ciara Malone, Sonya Quinn, Michelle Hearnes, Nicola Morley.

great adventure that almost bore fruit. This historic team was captained by David Hope, and included Colm Masterson, James Conroy, John Algar, Michael Briody and Damien Loran; the subs were Alan Carroll, Mark Glennon, Tomas Corcoran, Niall Cole, Adrian Ennis, Edmund Hyland, Barry Dully and Padraig Harnett. In 1997 a Junior Girls Volleyball team got up and running and they trained on Tuesdays in the Sports Hall; this team was captained by Sonya Quinn and also included Martha Clancy, Michelle Hearnes and Nicola Morley.

For many years Outdoor Pursuits has afforded students the opportunity to spend a weekend away as an encouragement to become more independent and to participate in activities not normally available to them such as canoeing, surfing, hill walking, rock climbing, assault courses, absailing, wind sailing, and orienteering. These weekends usually took place around Easter and were for the most part the preserve of Third Year students and more recently Transition Year students. The usual destination for these escapades was either Delphi Adventure Centre, Connemara, Co Galway or Petersburg Outdoor Education Centre, Clonbur, Co Galway. The sheer enjoyment and value garnered from these times away has been well documented by the willing participants in vivid accounts recorded in student publications over the years with such appropriate titles as *"Sleepless in Clonbur"*, to an extract we read in Vox 1986 of one such exploit:- *"this time Groups one and two went hill walking and it was rock climbing for the rest. On the way up Ruth Shortt got stuck in the mud, losing her "welly". Frank Lynam was indeed a great help, only for him we would be half dead by now! For every little hillock we climbed Frank shouted "rest" and we all lay down as dead as do-do's"*. Again from a more recent edition we read of the same sense of adventure and fun:- *"Finally, time for our Pursuits. Some went windsurfing and canoeing (or was it swimming for most!). Others went orienteering and were handed a map and a compass, but unfortunately no-one told them they were supposed to find their way home again! After we struggled back to the centre, those who went swimming checked that all their body parts were intact, after getting out of the sub-zero water"*. In 2006,

1995 Outdoor Pursuits: "Sleepless in Clonbur"

Aisling Maher in an article titled:- *"To Hell or to Connaught"* wrote of her experiences of Outdoor Pursuits when she informed her captive audience that:- *"it's not every day you get to swing down a steep cliff into a cave, then to be told the man holding the safety rope at the top is apparently afraid of heights!"*.

In summing up, Ruth Coffey in her award winning essay *"The Value of Sport"* published in Vox Magazine 1985 attempted to establish the origins of this fixation with sport when she wrote:- *"From time immemorial games and past-times have had a strong hold on the Irish people. In ancient times when our High Kings choose Tara as their seat, to Tara each year came the cream of Ireland's athletes and warriors to join friendly issues in the Tailteann Games. Here the Fianna excelled in feats of skill and endurance, the memory of which has echoed down the centuries"*. The Sisters of Mercy in St. Joseph's both past and present have been central to all of this, for it was they who first felt the need to comply with the pressing demands for outdoor games when the convent field was levelled in the mid 1950's and the tennis courts were developed in 1961 with the Sports Hall following in 1990 all at quite considerable costs. These are the visible signs on the sporting landscape of St. Joseph's but there are other parts to this story. This work by the Sisters of providing the best possible facilities for their students was also taken on by the Parents Associations who over the years always stood up to the challenges faced with countless Field Days, Socials and Raffles and not just for much needed funds in the area of sport. These fund raising efforts were also always ongoing within the School itself and earlier accounts are fondly recalled of the many bun sales held in the old school canteen that was formerly Connell's house on the Main Street long since demolished and where you now find the Main Gate.

In more recent years the annual Sponsored Walks up Gneevebawn Hill – half-day – busier road then – different days – are just some of the fund raising efforts undertaken over the years, the others too numerous to mention. From time to time, students and teachers have even found the space and have had the consideration and thought to fund raise for many deserving external charities. Most importantly, the countless hours given by so many teachers in the promotion of sport over the years has also been central to this story, it would not have happened without them. Sport in St. Joseph's is still a work in progress, but certainly in the past it has bestowed on so many of its lucky students the talents to go forward with a sense of discipline, teamwork and optimism.

Hopefully the ability to deal with success and failure in equal measures as Ruth Coffey so movingly proposed at the beginning of this history has been taken on board, and, if this be the case, then it has been all worthwhile. The value of sport........priceless.

"Sport is something that does not matter, but it is performed as if it did.
In that contradiction lies its beauty".

Barnes, Simon (1951 -) The Spectator, 1996.

2007 All 32 County Jersey Day plus London, New York and Aussie Rules in aid of G.O.A.L.
Front Row: Left to Right: Dean Morris – Roscommon, Paul Carey – London,   Daniel Yeadon – Sligo, Caroline Keaveney – Leitrim, Eimear Noonan-Treacy – Galway, Orla Judge – Mayo, Lee Wallace – Cork, Padraig Dolan – Aussie Rules, Gary Greville –Waterford, Cliodhna Spellman – Kerry, Gemma Murphy – Limerick, Paul McPadden – Tipperary, Steven Lynam – Clare.
Middle Row: Left to Right: Martina Croghan – Roscommon, David Rigney – Kilkenny, Lisa Darby – Carlow, Anne Peppard – Meath, Gemma Davis – Kildare, Jamie Gonoud – Dublin, Gordon O'Sullivan –Wexford, Paul Metcalfe – Wicklow, Niamh Murray – Longford, Cillian Duggan – Louth, Shannon Coyne –Westmeath, Jean Kelly – Offaly.
Back Row: Left to Right: Christina Gahan – Laois, Niamh Sheridan – Cavan, Evan Gill – Antrim, Leanne Quinn – Donegal, Laura Bagnall – Monaghan, James McPadden – Tyrone, Robbie Greville – New York, Conor Slevin – Down, Cathal O'Reilly – Armagh, Shane Murtagh – Fermanagh, Mark Conroy – New York, Eoin Rigney – Derry, Finbar Murphy – Donegal.

2011 Awards night at St. Joesph's, from left to right, Eileen Alford, Thomas Dowling, Shauna Leavy, Leanne Quinn and Michéal Ó Muircheartaigh.

In October, 2012. Darragh Murray won a Bronze Medal for Ireland at the European Schoolboys Boxing Championships held in Anapa, Russia.

~ CHAPTER 46 ~
LEAVING CERT CLASS PHOTOS
2001-2012

Education

Class
Photos

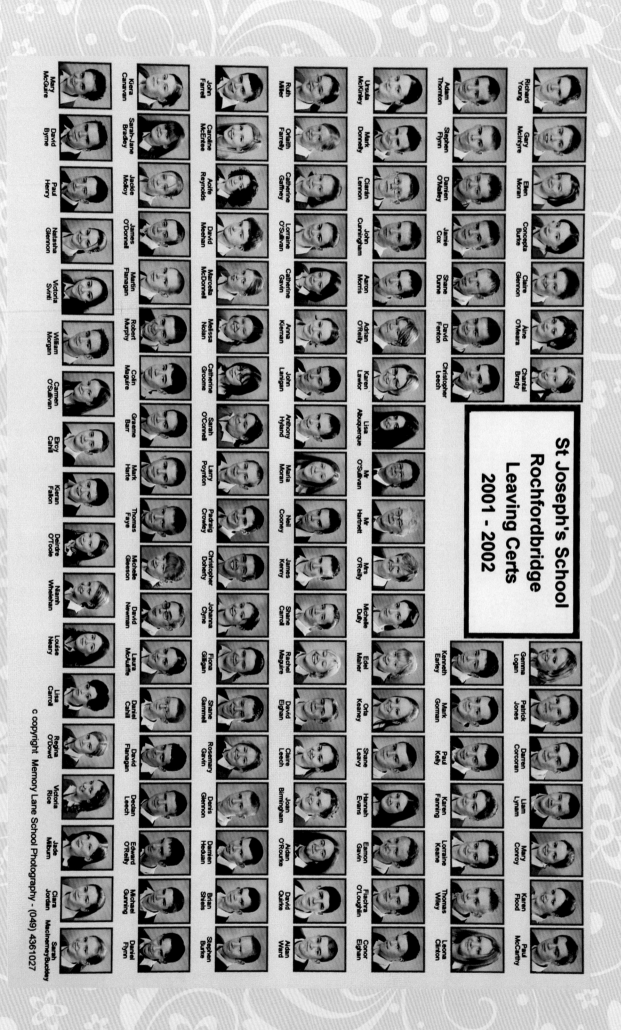

St Joseph's School
Rochfordbridge
Leaving Certs
2001 - 2002

Richard Young, Gary McIntyre, Eilen Moran, Concepta Burke, Áine O'Meara, Chantal Brady

Adam Thornton, Stephen Flynn, Damien O'Malley, Jamie Cox, Shane Dunne, David Fenton, Christopher Leech

Ursula McKinley, Mark Donnelly, Ciaran Lennon, John Cunningham, Aaron Morris, Adrian O'Reilly, Karen Lawlor, Lisa Albuquerque, Mr O'Sullivan, Mr Hartnett, Mrs O'Reilly, Michele Duly, Edel Maher, Orla Kearney, Shane Leavy, Joan Birmingham, Aidan O'Rourke, David Quirke, Aidan Ward

Ruth Miller, Catherine Gaffney, Lorraine O'Sullivan, Catherine Gavin, Anna Kiernan, John Lanigan, Anthony Hyland, Maria Moran, Neil Cooney, James Kenny, Shane Carroll, Rachel Maguire, David Eighan, Claire Leech, Rosemary Gavin, Declan Leech, Damien Hedian, Michael Gunning

Orlaith Farrelly, Caroline McEntee, Aoife Reynolds, David Meehan, Marcella McDonnell, Melissa Nolan, Catherine Groome, Sarah O'Connell, Larry Poynton, Padraig Crowley, Christopher Doherty, Johanna Clyne, Fiona Gilligan, Shane Gammell, Rosemary Gavin, Denis Glennon, Brian Shiels, Stephen Burke

John Farrell, Stephen Flynn...

Kenneth Earley, Mark Gorman, Paul Kelly, Shane Evans, Hannah Evans, Eamon Gavin, Fiachra O'Loughlin, Conor Eighan

Gemma Logan, Patrick Jones, Darren Corcoran, Liam Lynam, Mary Conroy, Karen Flood, Paul McCarthy

Mark Hante, Thomas Faye, Michael Gleeson, David Newman, Laura McAuliffe, Daniel Cahill, David Flanagan, Declan Leech, Edward O'Reilly, Michael Gunning

Ruth Miller, Catherine Farrelly, Lorraine O'Sullivan

Graeme Barr, Mark Hante, Thomas Faye

Kiera Canavan, Sarah-Jane Bradley, Jackie McEvoy, James O'Donnell, Martin Flanagan, Robert Murphy, Colin Maguire, Eroy Cahill, Kieran Fallon, Deirdre O'Toole, Niamh Whelehan, Louise Neary, Lisa Carroll, Regina O'Dowd, Victoria Rice, Jade Milburn, Ciara Jordan

Mary McGuire, David Byrne, Paul Henry, Natasha Glennon, Victoria Svirril, William Morgan, Carmen O'Sullivan

Paddy Kelly, Karen Fanning, Lorraine Keane, Eamon Gavin

Liam Lynam, Mary Conroy, Karen Flood, Thomas Wiley, Leona Clinton

Daniel Cahill, David Flanagan, Victoria Rice, Jade Milburn, Daniel Flynn

Sarah MacInerney/Buckley

c copyright Memory Lane School Photography - (049) 4361027

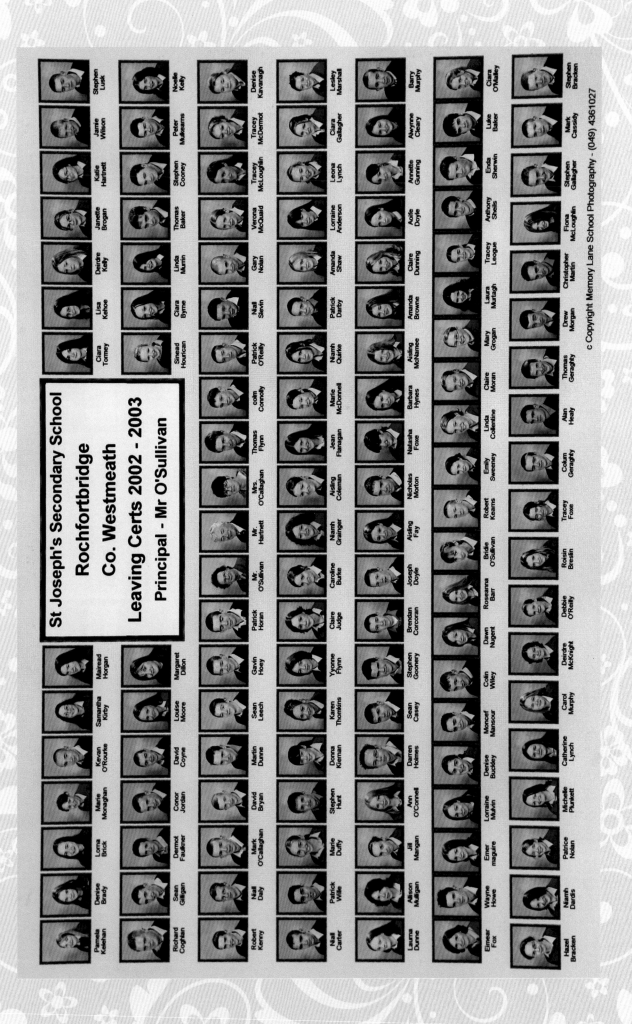

St Joseph's Secondary School
Rochfortbridge
Co. Westmeath
Leaving Certs 2002 - 2003
Principal - Mr O'Sullivan

c Copyright Memory Lane School Photography - (049) 4361027

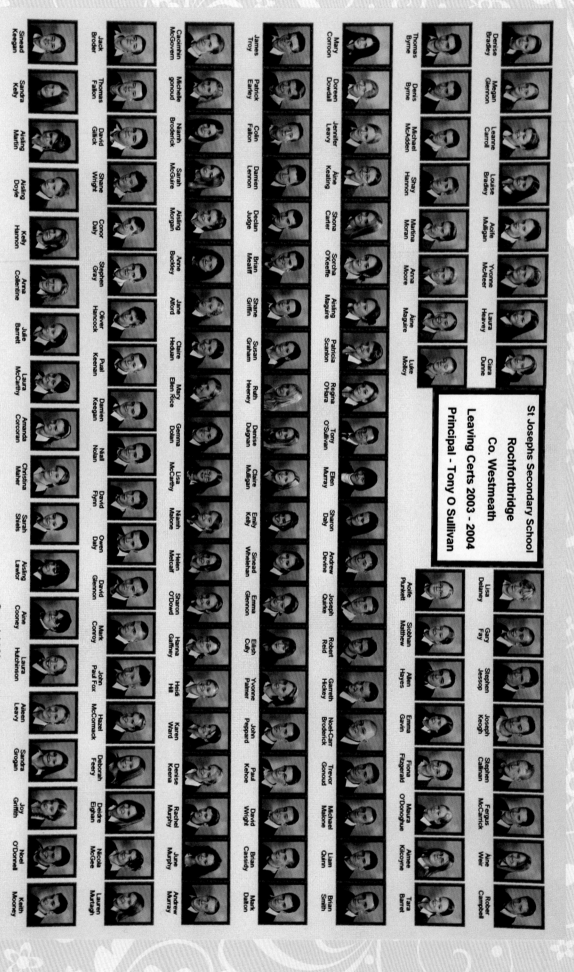

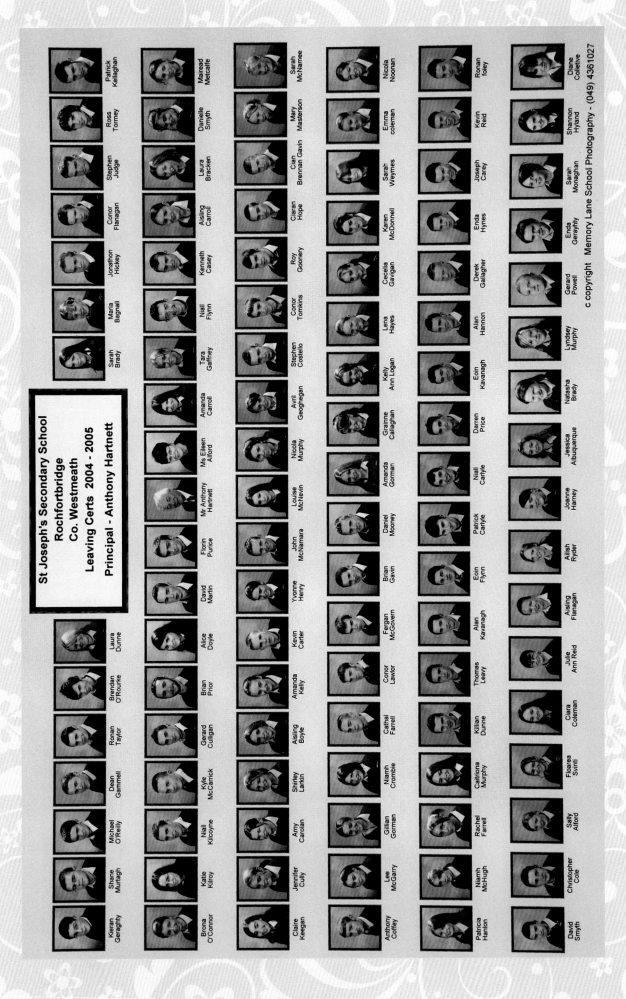

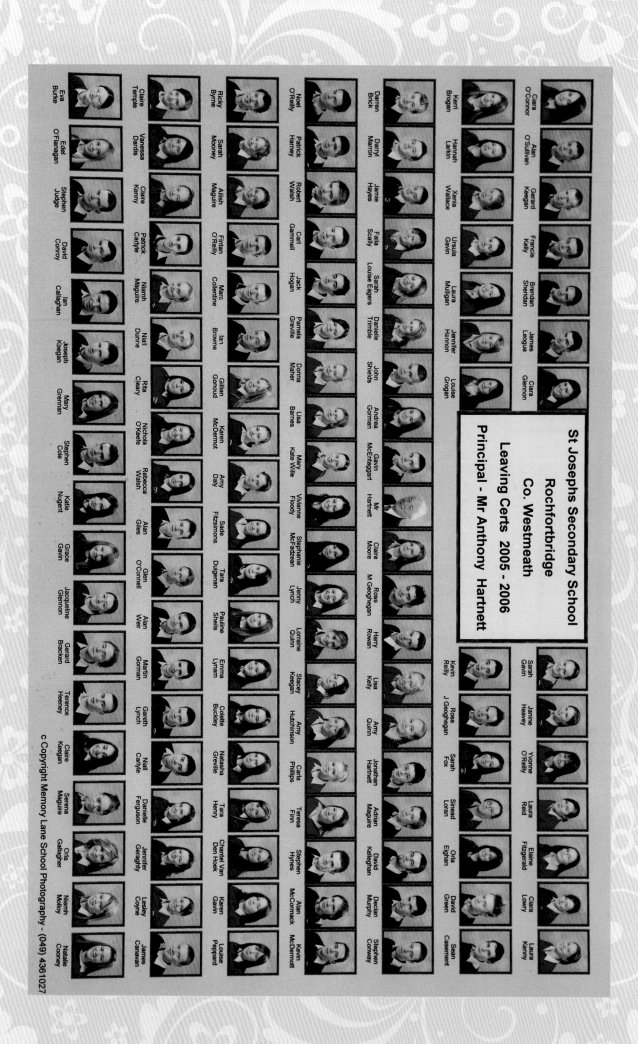

St Josephs Secondary School
Rochfortbridge
Co. Westmeath
Leaving Certs 2005 - 2006
Principal - Mr Anthony Hartnett

© Copyright Memory Lane School Photography - (049) 4361027

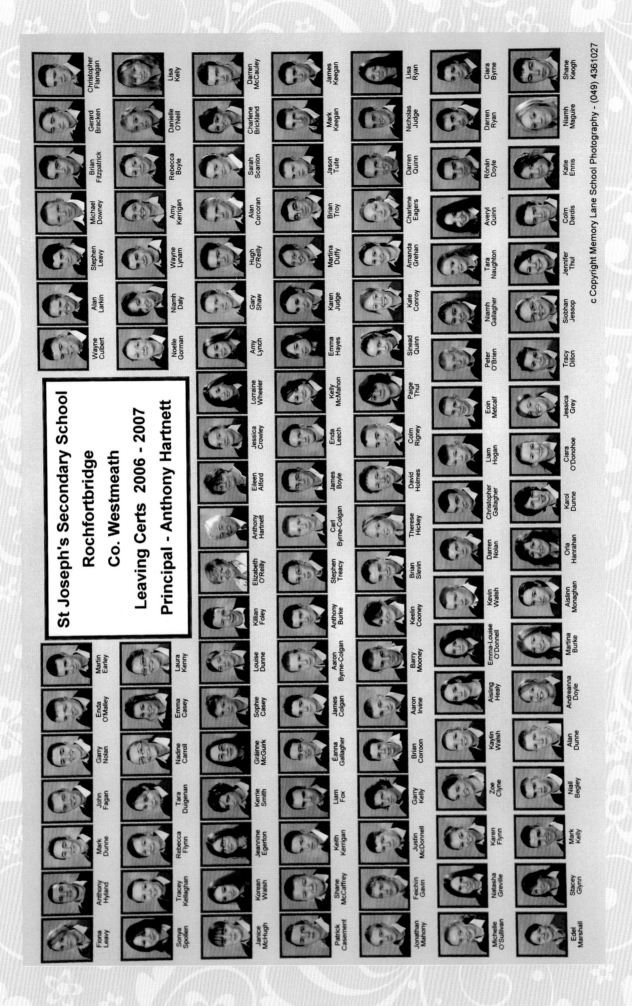

St Joseph's Secondary School
Rochfortbridge
Co. Westmeath
Leaving Certs 2006 - 2007
Principal - Anthony Hartnett

Fiona Leavy, Sonya Spollen, Janice McHugh, Patrick Casement, Jonathan Mahony, Michelle O'Sullivan, Edel Marshall

Anthony Hyland, Tracey Kellaghan, Korean Walsh, Shane McCaffrey, Feichin Gavin, Natasha Greville, Stacey Glynn

Mark Dunne, Rebecca Flynn, Jeannine Egerton, Keith Kerrigan, Justin McDonnell, Karen Flynn, Mark Kelly

John Fagan, Tara Duigenan, Kerrie Smith, Liam Fox, Garry Kelly, Zoe Clyne, Niall Begley

Garry Nolan, Nadine Carroll, Gráinne McGuirk, Eanna Gallagher, Brian Corroon, Kaylin Walsh, Alan Dunne

Enda O'Malley, Emma Casey, Sophie Casey, James Colgan, Aaron Irvine, Aisling Healy, Andreanna Doyle

Martin Earley, Laura Kenny, Louise Dunne, Aaron Byrne-Colgan, Barry Mooney, Emma-Louise O'Donnell, Martina Burke

Lorraine Wheeler, Jessica Crowley, Eileen Alford, Anthony Hartnett, Elizabeth O'Reilly, Killian Foley, Keelin Cooney, Kevin Walsh, Aislinn Monaghan, Oria Hanrahan

Kelly McMahon, Enda Leech, James Boyle, Carl Byrne-Colgan, Stephen Treacy, Anthony Burke, Barry Mooney, Darren Nolan, Christopher Gallagher, Karol Dunne

Paige Thul, Colm Rigney, David Holmes, Therese Hickey, Brian Slevin, Keelin Cooney, Ciara O'Donohoe, Liam Hogan, Jessica Grey

Wayne Culbert, Alan Larkin, Stephen Leavy, Michael Downey, Brian Fitzpatrick, Gerard Bracken, Christopher Flanagan

Noelle Gorman, Niamh Daly, Wayne Lynam, Amy Kerrigan, Rebecca Boyle, Danielle O'Neill, Lisa Kelly

Amy Lynch, Gary Shaw, Hugh O'Reilly, Alan Corcoran, Sarah Scanlon, Charlene Brickland, Darren McCauley

Emma Hayes, Karen Judge, Martina Duffy, Brian Troy, Jason Tuite, Mark Keegan, James Keegan

Sinead Quinn, Kate Conroy, Amanda Grehan, Charlene Eagers, Darren Quinn, Nicholas Judge, Lisa Ryan

Peter O'Brien, Niamh Gallagher, Tara Naughton, Averyl Quinn, Darren Quinn, Rónán Doyle, Darren Ryan, Ciara Byrne

Tracy Dillon, Siobhan Jessop, Jennifer Thul, Colm Dardis, Katie Ennis, Niamh Maguire, Shane Keogh

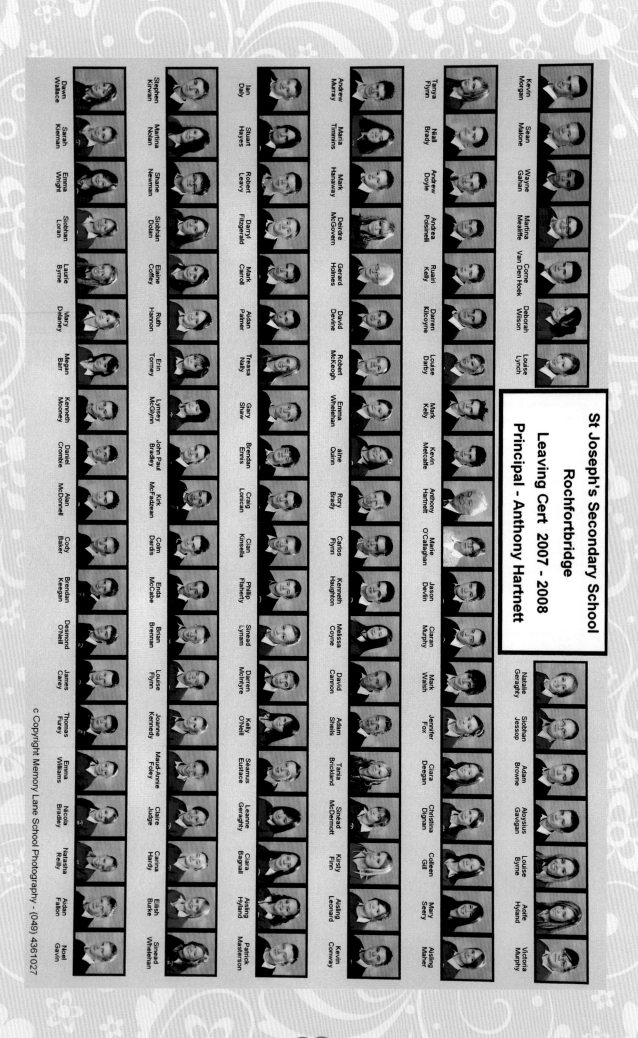

St Joseph's Secondary School
Rochfortbridge
Leaving Cert 2007 - 2008
Principal - Anthony Hartnett

Kevin Morgan, Sean Malone, Wayne Gahan, Martina Mealiffe, Corie Van Den Hoek, Deborah Wilson, Louise Lynch

Tanya Flynn, Niall Brady, Andrew Doyle, Andrea Polsinelli, Ruairi Kelly, Darren Kilcoyne, Louise Darby, Mark Kelly, Kevin Metcalfe, Anthony Hartnett, Marie O'Callaghan, Jason Devlin

Andrew Murray, Maria Timmins, Mark Hanaway, Deirdre McGovern, Gerard Holmes, David Devine, Robert McKeogh, Emma Whelehan, aine Quinn, Rory Brady, Carlos Flynn, Kenneth Haughton, Melissa Coyne, David Cannon, Adam Sheils, Tania Brickland, Sinead McDermott, Kirsty Finn, Aisling Leonard, Kevin Conway

Ian Daly, Stuart Hayes, Robert Leavy, Darryl Fitzgerald, Mark Carroll, Aidan Palmer, Treasa Nally, Gary Shaw, Brendan Ennis, Craig Lorican, Cian Kinsella, Philip Flaherty, Sinead Lynam, Darren McIntyre, Kelly O'Neill, Seamus Eustace, Leanne Geraghty, Ciara Bagnall, Aisling Hyland, Patrick Masterson

Stephen Kirwan, Martina Nolan, Shane Newman, Siobhan Dolan, Elaine Coffey, Ruth Hannon, Erin Tormey, Lynsey McGlynn, John Paul Bradley, Kirk McFadzean, Colm Dardis, Enda McCabe, Brian Brennan, Louise Flynn, Joanne Kennedy, Maud-Anne Foley, Claire Judge, Carina Hardy, Eilish Burke, Sinead Whelehan

Dawn Wallace, Sarah Kiernan, Emma Wright, Siobhan Loran, Laurie Byrne, Mary Delaney, Megan Barr, Kenneth Mooney, Daniel Crombie, Alan McDonnell, Cody Baker, Brendan Keegan, Desmond O'Neill, James Carey, Thomas Furey, Emma Williams, Nicola Bradley, Natasha Reilly, Aidan Fallon, Noel Gavin

Natalie Geraghty, Siobhan Jessop, Adam Browne, Aloysius Gavigan, Louise Byrne, Aoife Hyland, Victoria Murphy

Jennifer Fox, Ciara Deegan, Christina Dignan, Colleen Gill, Mary Seery, Aisling Maher

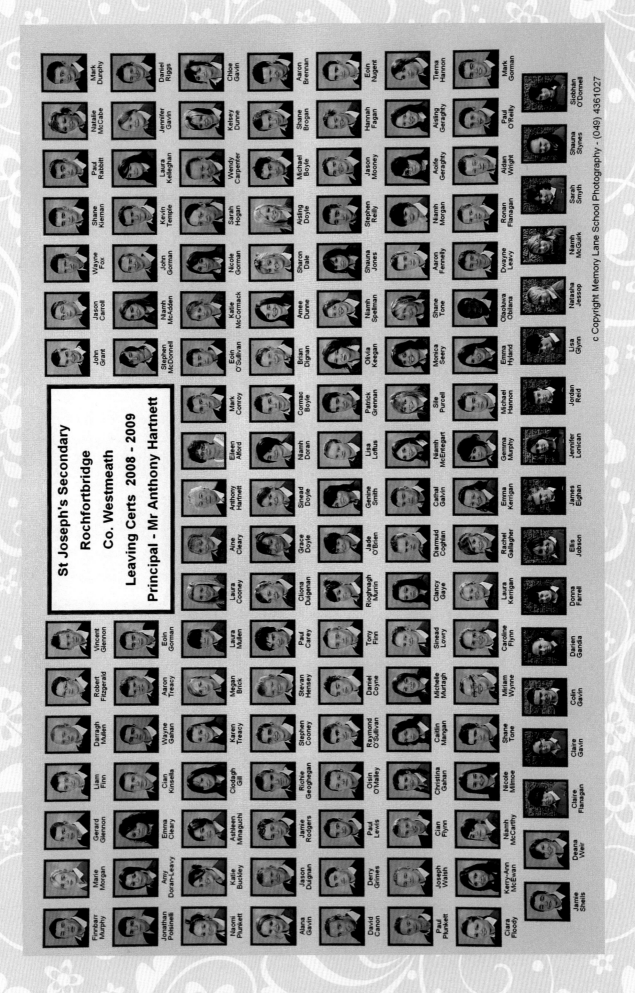

St Joseph's Secondary
Rochfortbridge
Co. Westmeath
Leaving Certs 2008 - 2009
Principal - Mr Anthony Hartnett

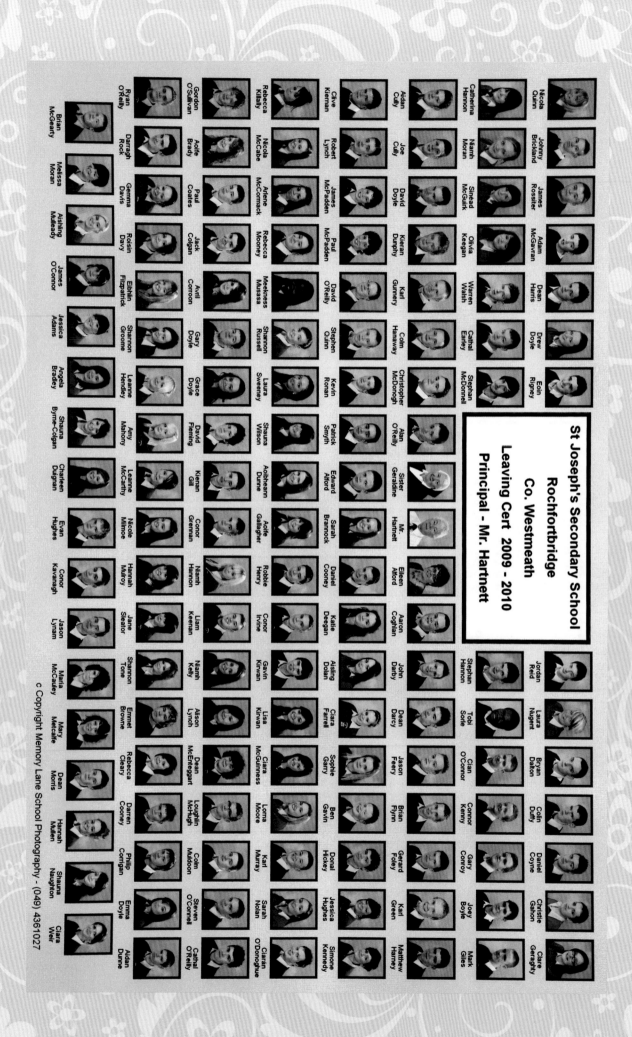

St Joseph's Secondary School
Rochfortbridge
Co. Westmeath
Leaving Cert 2009 - 2010
Principal - Mr. Hartnett

Nicola Quinn, Johnny Brickland, James Rossiter, Adam McGavran, Drew Doyle, Eoin Rigney

Catherina Hannon, Niamh Moran, Sinead McGuirk, Olivia Keegan, Warren Walsh, Dean Harris

Aidan Cully, Joe Cully, David Doyle, Kieran Dunphy, Karl Gunney, Cathal Earley, Stephan McDonnell

Clive Kieran, Robert Lynch, James McPadden, Paul McPadden, David O'Reilly, Stephen Quinn, Christopher McDonogh, Alan O'Reilly

Rebecca Killally, Nicola McCabe, Arlene McCormack, Rebecca Mooney, Meekness Mussasa, Shannon Russell, Laura Sweeney, Shauna Wilson, Sister Geraldine, Mr. Hartnett, Eileen Alford

Gordon O'Sullivan, Aoife Brady, Paul Coates, Jack Colgan, Avril Corroon, Gary Doyle, Grace Doyle, David Fleming, Kieran Gill, Conor Grennan, Hannah Mulroy, Liam Keenan, Niamh Kelly

Ryan O'Reilly, Darragh Rock, Gemma Davis, Roisin Davy, Elbhlin Fitzpatrick, Shannon Groome, Leanne Hendley, Amy Mahony, Leanne McCarthy, Nicole Milmoe, Niamh Hannon, Conor Irvine

Brian McGearty, Melissa Moran, Aishling Mulleady, James O'Connor, Jessica Adams, Angela Bradley, Shauna Byrne-Colgan, Charleen Duignan, Evan Hughes, Conor Kavanagh, Jason Lynam, Jane Sleator

Patrick Smyth, Edward Alford, Aoife Gallagher, Sarah Brannock, Robbie Henry, Conor Irvine, Daniel Cooney, Katie Deegan, Aaron Coghlan

Kevin Ronan, Aoibheann Dunne

Colin Hanaway

Gavin Kirwan, Lisa Kirwan, Ciara McGuinness, Lorna Moore, Karl Murray, Sarah Nolan, Ciaran O'Donoghue

Shannon Tone, Emmet Browne, Rebecca Cleary, Dean McEnteggart, Darren Cooney, Philip Corrigan, Steven O'Connell, Aidan Dunne

Maria McCauley, Mary Metcalfe, Dean Morris, Hannah Mullen, Loughlin McHugh, Colm Muldoon, Cathal O'Reilly

Shauna Naughton, Clara Weir

Niamh Kelly, Alison Lynch

Ailsing Dolan, Ciara Farrell, Sophie Garry, Ben Gavin, Donal Hickey, Jessica Hughes, Simone Kennedy

John Darby, Dean Darcy, Jason Feery, Brian Flynn, Gerard Foley, Gary Conroy, Karl Green, Matthew Harney

Stephan Hannon, Tobi Sorle, Cian O'Connor, Connor Kenny

Jordan Reid, Laura Nugent, Bryan Dalton, Colin Duffy, Daniel Coyne, Joey Boyle, Mark Giles, Christie Gahon, Clare Geraghty

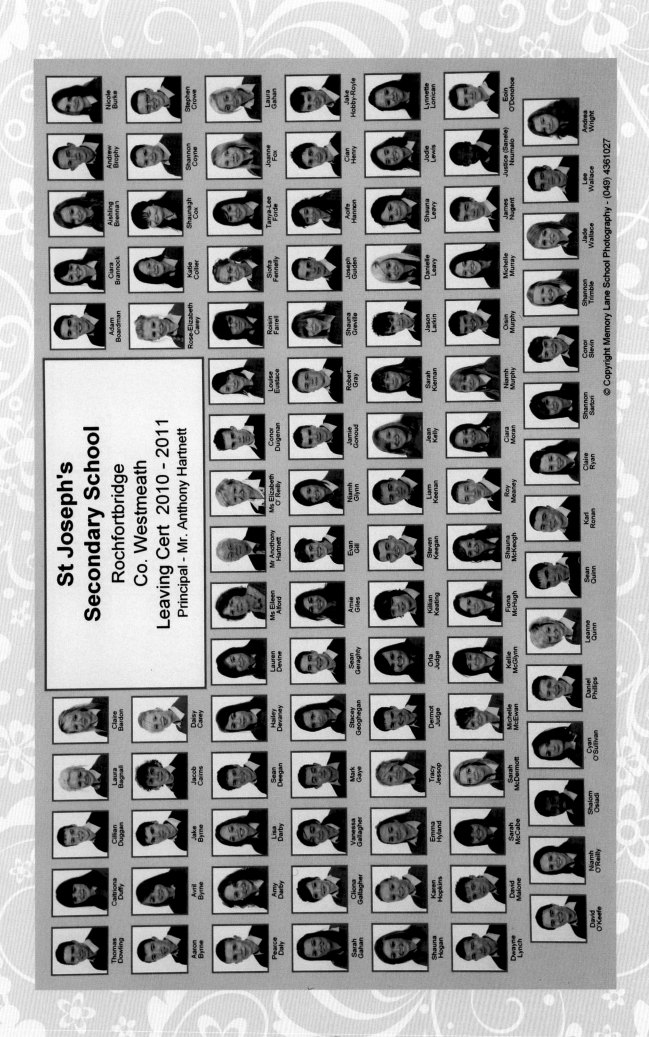

St Joseph's Secondary School

Rochfortbridge
Co. Westmeath
Leaving Cert 2010 - 2011
Principal - Mr. Anthony Hartnett

Nicole Burke, Andrew Brophy, Aishling Brennan, Ciara Brannock, Adam Boardman, Claire Bardon, Laura Bagnall, Cillian Duggan, Catriona Duffy, Thomas Dowling

Stephen Crowe, Shannon Coyne, Shaunagh Cox, Katie Collier, Rose-Elizabeth Carey, Daisy Carey, Jacob Cairns, Jake Byrne, Avril Byrne, Aaron Byrne

Laura Gahan, Joanne Fox, Tanya-Lee Forde, Siofra Fennelly, Roisin Farrell, Louise Eustace, Conor Duigenan, Ms Elizabeth O'Reilly, Mr Anothony Hartnett, Ms Eileen Alford, Lauren Devine, Hailey Devaney, Sean Deegan, Lisa Darby, Amy Darby, Pearce Daly

Jake Hobby-Royle, Cian Henry, Aofie Hannon, Joseph Guiden, Shauna Greville, Robert Gray, Jamie Gonoud, Niamh Glynn, Evan Gill, Amie Giles, Sean Geraghty, Stacey Geoghegan, Mark Gaye, Vanessa Gallagher, Cliona Gallagher, Sarah Gahan

Lynnette Lonican, Jodie Lewis, Shauna Leavy, Danielle Leavy, Jason Larkin, Sarah Kiernan, Jean Kelly, Liam Keenan, Steven Keegan, Killian Keating, Orla Judge, Dermot Judge, Tracy Jessop, Emma Hyland, Karen Hopkins, Shauna Hogan

Eoin O'Donohoe, Justice (Sanele) Nxumalo, James Nugent, Michelle Murray, Oisin Murphy, Niamh Murphy, Ciara Moran, Roy Meaney, Shauna McKeogh, Fiona McHugh, Kellie McGlynn, Michelle McEwan, Sarah McDermott, Sarah McCabe, David Malone, Dwayne Lynch

Andrea Wright, Lee Wallace, Jade Wallace, Shannon Trimble, Conor Slevin, Shannon Sartori, Claire Ryan, Karl Ronan, Sean Quinn, Leanne Quinn, Daniel Phillips, Cyan O'Sullivan, Shalom Osiadi, Niamh O'Reilly, David O'Keefe

St Joseph's Secondary School
Rochfortbridge
Leaving Cert 2011 - 2012
Principal - Ms Eileen Alford

~ CHAPTER 47 ~

APPENDICES

CENSUS OF IRELAND 1901. RESIDENTS OF A HOUSE 26 IN CASTLELOST (CASTLELOST, WESTMEATH) - CONVENT OF MERCY ROCHFORTBRIDGE									
Surname	**Fore-name**	**Age**	**Sex**	**Relation to head**	**Religion**	**Birth-place**	**Occupation**	**Literacy**	**Marital Status**
O'Neill	Mary Stanislaus	56	F	Head of Community	Roman Catholic	Dublin City	Superior of Community	Read and write	Not Married
Hackett	Mary Magdalen	60	F	Member of Community	Roman Catholic	Co Tipperary	Sister of Mercy	Read and write	Not Married
Wyer	Mary Agnes	57	F	Member of Community	Roman Catholic	Co Westmeath	Sister of Mercy	Read and write	Not Married
Nangle	Mary Angela	46	F	Member of Community	Roman Catholic	Co Westmeath	Sister of Mercy	Read and write	Not Married
Coffy	Mary Hacogue	40	F	Member of Community	Roman Catholic	Co Westmeath	Sister of Mercy	Read and write	Not Married
Fitzpatrick	Mary Columba	41	F	Member of Community	Roman Catholic	Co Westmeath	Sister of Mercy	Read and write	Not Married
O'Gorman	Mary Josephine	29	F	Member of Community	Roman Catholic	Co Donegal	Sister of Mercy	Read and write	Not Married
Byrne	Mary Teresa	25	F	Member of Community	Roman Catholic	Co Westmeath	Sister of Mercy	Read and write	Not Married
Lambe	Bridget	28	F	Servant	Roman Catholic	Co Westmeath	Cook - Servant-Dom	Read and write	Not Married
Flood	Lizzie	18	F	Servant	Roman Catholic	Co Meath	Laundress-Servant-Domestic	Read and write	Not Married
Coleman	Esther	14	F	Servant	Roman Catholic	Co Westmeath	Scullery Maid - Domestic Servant	Read and write	Not Married

RESIDENTS OF A HOUSE 7.2 IN CASTLELOST (CASTLELOST, WESTMEATH)

Surname	Fore-name	Age	Sex	Religion	Birth-place	Occup-ation	Literacy	Marital Status	Specified Illnesses
Cronin	Ellen Mary Jane	38	F	Roman Catholic	Co Cork	Teacher	Read and write	Not Married	Deaf and Dumb
Mc Eneaney	Catherine	20	F	Roman Catholic	Co Louth	Teacher	Read and write	Not Married	-
Waters	Teresa	18	F	Roman Catholic	Co Louth	Pupil	Read and write	Not Married	Deaf and Dumb
Farrelly	Bridget	18	F	Roman Catholic	Co Meath	Pupil	Read and write	Not Married	Deaf and Dumb
Maloney	Elizabeth	17	F	Roman Catholic	Co Galway	Pupil	Read and write	Not Married	Deaf and Dumb
O Reilly	Mary Catherine	17	F	Roman Catholic	Co Cavan	Pupil	Read and write	Not Married	Deaf and Dumb
Mc Weeney	Bridget	17	F	Roman Catholic	Co Leitrim	Pupil	Read and write	Not Married	-
Grant	Maggie	16	F	Roman Catholic	Co Meath	Pupil	Read and write	Not Married	Deaf and Dumb
Ryan	Margaret	16	F	Roman Catholic	Co Tipperary	Pupil	Read and write	Not Married	Deaf and Dumb
Coyne	Geraldine	16	F	Roman Catholic	London	Pupil	Read and write	Not Married	Deaf and Dumb
Egan	Catherine	15	F	Roman Catholic	Co Westmeath	Pupil	Read and write	Not Married	Deaf and Dumb
Bracken	Elizabeth	15	F	Roman Catholic	King's Co	Pupil	Read and write	Not Married	Deaf and Dumb
Lally	Catherine	15	F	Roman Catholic	Co Galway	Pupil	Read and write	Not Married	Deaf and Dumb
Connolly	Mary	14	F	Roman Catholic	Arran Isles	Pupil	Read and write	Not Married	Deaf and Dumb
Mc Loughlin	Teressa	14	F	Roman Catholic	Derry City	Pupil	Read and write	Not Married	Deaf and Dumb
O' Reilly	Catherine	14	F	Roman Catholic	Co Longford	Pupil	Read and write	Not Married	Deaf and Dumb
Egan	Elizabeth	13	F	Roman Catholic	Co Westmeath	Pupil	Read and write	Not Married	Deaf and Dumb
Kelly	Catherine	13	F	Roman Catholic	Co Kildare	Pupil	Read and write	Not Married	Deaf and Dumb
Fitzgerald	Bridget	11	F	Roman Catholic	Co Kerry	Pupil	Read and write	Not Married	Deaf and Dumb
Coyne	Mary Teresa	11	F	Roman Catholic	London	Pupil	Read and write	Not Married	Deaf and Dumb
Boylan	Catherine	11	F	Roman Catholic	Co Westmeath	Pupil	Read and write	Not Married	Deaf and Dumb
Moore	Margaret	3	F	Roman Catholic	Limerick City	Pupil	Cannot read	Not Married	Deaf and Dumb
Mc Laughlin	Catherine	7	F	Roman Catholic	Derry City	Pupil	Read and write	Not Married	Deaf and Dumb
Sheridan	Mary	12	F	Roman Catholic	Co Westmeath	Pupil	Read and write	Not Married	Dumb
Sheridan	Catherine	9	F	Roman Catholic	Co Westmeath	Pupil	Read and write	Not Married	Dumb
Kelly	Jane	9	F	Roman Catholic	Co Louth	Pupil	Cannot read	Not Married	Dumb

RESIDENTS OF A HOUSE 7.2 IN CASTLELOST (CASTLELOST, WESTMEATH)

CENSUS OF IRELAND 1901. RESIDENTS OF A HOUSE 7.1 IN CASTLELOST (CASTLELOST, WESTMEATH) ST. JOSEPH'S INSTITUTE FOR THE DEAF AND DUMB.

Surname	Forename	Age	Sex	Relation to head	Religion	Birthplace	Occupation	Literacy	Marital Status
Smith	Mary Gertrude	25	F	Proprietors	Roman Catholic	Co Meath	Sister of Mercy	Read and write	Not Married
O' Kelly	Mary Antonio	22	F	Proprietors	Roman Catholic	Co Kerry	Sister of Mercy	Read and write	Not Married
Gherity	Mary	50	F	Servant	Roman Catholic	Co Westmeath	Domestic Servant - Cook	Read and write	Widow
Lambe	Mary	25	F	Servant	Roman Catholic	Co Westmeath	Domestic Servant - Laundress	Read and write	Not Married

CENSUS OF IRELAND 1911. RESIDENTS OF A HOUSE 8.1 IN ROCHFORT BRIDGE TOWN (THIS IS CALLED `CASTLELOST' THE SAME AS NO. 1, ON ENUMERATION ABSTRACT BUT ROCHFORT BRIDGE TOWN ON THE PRINTED LIST) (CASTLELOST, WESTMEATH)

THE DEAF AND DUMB INSTITUTE.

Surname	Forename	Age	Sex	Religion	Birthplace	Occupation	Literacy	Marital Status	Specified Illnesses
Glynn	Mary	46	F	Roman Catholic	W Meath	Pupil	Cannot Read	Single	Deaf and Dumb
Walshe	Emily	39	F	Roman Catholic	Co Dublin	Pupil	Cannot Read	Single	Deaf and Dumb
Grant	Maggie	26	F	Roman Catholic	Meath	Pupil	Read and write	Single	Deaf and Dumb
McWeeney	Bridget	23	F	Roman Catholic	Leitrim	Pupil	Read and write	Single	Deaf and Dumb
Fitzgerald	Bride	23	F	Roman Catholic	Kerry	Pupil	Read and write	Single	Deaf and Dumb
Maguire	Mary	25	F	Roman Catholic	Meath	Pupil	Read and write	Single	Deaf and Dumb
Boylan	Kathleen	20	F	Roman Catholic	W Meath	Pupil	Read and write	Single	Deaf and Dumb
Sheridan	Katie	21	F	Roman Catholic	W Meath	Pupil	Read and write	Single	Deaf Only
Mullins	Julia	20	F	Roman Catholic	-	Pupil	Read and write	Single	Deaf and Dumb
Reynolds	Annie	20	F	Roman Catholic	Leitrim	Pupil	Read and write	Single	Deaf and Dumb
Fitzsimons	Rose	20	F	Roman Catholic	Meath	Pupil	Read and write	Single	Deaf and Dumb
McLoughlin	Kathleen	18	F	Roman Catholic	Derry	Pupil	Read and write	Single	Deaf and dumb
Lennon	Lissie	18	F	Roman Catholic	Cavan	Pupil	Read and write	Single	Deaf and Dumb
Kirby	Nellie	16	F	Roman Catholic	Limerick	Pupil	Read and write	Single	Deaf and Dumb
Moore	Madge	16	F	Roman Catholic	Limerick	Pupil	Read and write	Single	Deaf and Dumb
Maloney	Mary A	16	F	Roman Catholic	Kerry	Pupil	Read and write	Single	Deaf and Dumb

Surname	Forename	Age	Sex	Religion	Birthplace	Occupation	Literacy	Marital Status	Specified Illnesses
McGroder	Rosanna	16	F	Roman Catholic	Fermanagh	Pupil	Read and write	Single	Deaf and Dumb
Murphy	Mary B	16	F	Roman Catholic	Meath	Pupil	Read and write	Single	Deaf and Dumb
Delemere	Katie	14	F	Roman Catholic	W Meath	Pupil	Read and write	Single	Deaf Only
Connor	Mary	15	F	Roman Catholic	Galway	Pupil	Read and write	Single	Deaf and Dumb
Hope	Kathleen	10	F	Roman Catholic	W Meath	Pupil	Read and write	Single	Deaf and Dumb
Kelliher	Mary	12	F	Roman Catholic	Kerry	Pupil	Read and write	Single	Deaf and Dumb
Doyle	Ellen	12	F	Roman Catholic	Kerry	Pupil	Read and write	Single	Deaf and Dumb
Gallagher	Rita	11	F	Roman Catholic	Donegal	Pupil	Read and write	Single	Deaf and Dumb
Williams	Birdie	11	F	Roman Catholic	Tipperary	Pupil	Read and write	Single	Deaf Only
Torde	Bridget	11	F	Roman Catholic	Galway	Pupil	Read and write	Single	Deaf and Dumb
Maguire	Teresa	10	F	Roman Catholic	W Meath	Pupil	Cannot Read	Single	Deaf and Dumb
Feeney	Kathleen	8	F	Roman Catholic	W Meath	Pupil	Cannot Read	Single	Deaf and Dumb
Kelly	Mary A	7	F	Roman Catholic	Galway	Pupil	Cannot Read	Single	Deaf and Dumb
Flynn	Mary	6	F	Roman Catholic	King's Co	Pupil	Cannot Read	Single	Dumb Only
Mulvey	Bridget	18	F	Roman Catholic	W Meath	Pupil	Cannot Read	Single	Dumb Only

CENSUS OF IRELAND 1911. RESIDENTS OF A HOUSE 23 IN ROCHFORT BRIDGE TOWN (THIS IS CALLED `CASTLELOST' THE SAME AS NO. 1, ON ENUMERATION ABSTRACT BUT ROCHFORT BRIDGE TOWN ON THE PRINTED LIST) (CASTLELOST, WESTMEATH)

CONVENT OF MERCY.

Surname	Fore-name	Age	Sex	Relation to head	Religion	Birth-place	Occup-ation	Liter-acy	Irish Lang-uage	Marital Status
Smith	Gertrude	37	F	Superior	Roman Catholic	Co Meath	Sister of Mercy	Read and write	-	Single
Hackett	Magdalen	74	F	Assistant	Roman Catholic	Tipperary	Sister of Mercy	Read and write	-	Single
ONeill	Mary Stainslans	69	F	Assistant	Roman Catholic	Dublin	Sister of Mercy	Read and write	-	Single
Wyer	Agnes	69	F	Assistant	Roman Catholic	Kings Co	Sister of Mercy	Read and write	-	Single
Coffy	Alacoque	53	F	Assistant	Roman Catholic	Westmeath	Sister of Mercy	Read and write	-	Single
Fitzpatrick	Columba	56	F	Assistant	Roman Catholic	Westmeath	Sister of Mercy	Read and write	-	Single
Byrne	Teresa	38	F	Assistant	Roman Catholic	Westmeath	Sister of Mercy	Read and write	-	Single
Moone	Mary	29	F	Assistant	Roman Catholic	Westmeath	Sister of Mercy	Read and write	English and Irish	Single
Lambe	Brigid	38	F	Servant	Roman Catholic	Westmeath	Cook Domestic Servant	Read and write	-	Single
Cahill	Rose Anne	39	F	Servant	Roman Catholic	Cavan	Domestic Servant	Read and write	-	Single
OBrien	Alice	16	F	Servant	Roman Catholic	Louth	Domestic Servant	Read and write	-	Single

BREAKDOWN OF FUNDS RAISED
TO BUILD THE CONVENT CHAPEL 1920-1923

Event	£	s	d.
Parish Collection	379	7	0
Féte	254	7	0
Races in Gibbonstown	170	18	0
Football	21	0	0
Raffle	98	0	0
Collected by Miss Mullaly and Dr. Stanley	50	0	0
Charity Sermon	125	0	0
Collected from			
Bishop and Priests	1200	0	0
Convents	40	0	0
Total	2338	12	0
Later Collections			
Seculars	875	0	0
Races in 1921 and 1922	204	10	0
Concert in 1923	98	0	0
Various	73	0	0
Total	3500	0	0

APPROXIMATE COSTS FOR WIRING IN THE DIFFERENT CONVENT BUILDINGS BY THE ESB IN 1950.

Area	£	s	d.[1]
Convent	613	10	0
St. Josephs	301	5	0
National Schools	60	0	0
Farm Yard	16	0	0
Pump (St. Josephs)	46	0	0
Pump (in grounds)	44	0	0
Hall & D.E. Classroom	70	0	0
Sub – Total	1150	15	0
Fittings etc.			
Cooker	30	10	0
Imersion groups	26	00	0
Toaster	2	11	0
Iron	1	13	6
Fire	3	16	0
Chapel parlour fittings – Brooks Ltd.	11	10	6
Sub – Total	76	1	0
	1150	15	0
Total	1,226	16	0

1. In old imperial currencey which lasted until 1971, the letters £,s,d stood for pounds shillings and pence. There were twelve pence in a shilling and twenty shillings in a pound. Decimal currency replaced the imperial.

ACKNOWLEDGEMENTS

Anita Farrell	Dermot Bennett
Ann Buckley Jnr.	Nuala Lawlor
Anne Carey	Breda O'Connell
Annette Farrell	Máire L'Estrange
Bernie Bradley	Rosemary Rice
Brigid Keegan	Ann Hannon
Carmel O'Sullivan	Rita Clarke
Caroline Kelleher	Marie Therése Kilmartin
Deirdre Grace	Joe Lyster
Denis Kelly	Luke Dempsey
Dodie Gallagher	Fionnuala Dunne
Frances Flynn	Sr. Rosario Shaw
Liz Deegan(Fox)	Sheamus Kiernan
Luke Dempsey	Lorraine Kelly Polgar
Martina Croghan	Olive Gray (Kelly)
Mary Mooney	Bernadette McCarthy (Eggerton)
Pádraig Nolan	Niamh Broderick
Pascal Dunne	Mary Manning
Philomena Geraghty	Bernadette Bagnall
Ruth and William Kelleghan	Elizabeth Shaw
Seán Ennis	Robbie Kenny
Sheila Lyster	Mary Frances
Sr. Geraldine Coyne	Dympna Quinn
Sr. Pius Doran	Margaret Smith
Sr. Regina O'Reilly	Marie Goonery
Tom Kiernan	Ann Healy(Corrigan)
Geraldine Farrell	Shirley McCormack
Collette Buckley	Sheila Gill
Anne Keegan	Sheamus Casey
Tom Hanlon	Fionnuala Gorman
Brendan Nugent.	Timmy McAuliffe
Nora Ryan	Shona Nolan
Donal O'Buachalla	Mary Daly
Ger Kenny	Fr. Michael Kilmartin
Mary Daly	Oliver Egan
Cormac Davey	Adrian Lee
Mary Fox(Mooney)	Lorna Dunne(Mooney)
Joan Gorman	Sr. Dolores Carroll
Mary Murphy	Dermot O'Rourke

BIBLIOGRAPHY

Published Works

Caitríona Clear, *Nuns in nineteenth century lreland* (Dublin, Washinglon D.C, 1987),

Donald H. Akenson, *The Irish Education Experiment, The National System of Education in the Nineteenth Century*(London, Toronto(1970).

Patrick J. Corish, David Sheehy, *Records of the Irish Catholic Church,* (Dublin, 2001).

Caitríona Clear, *Walls Within Walls* (Dublin, Washington D.C.), 1987.

Anthony Cogan, *The Diocese of Meath, Ancient and Modern* (Dublin, 1867).

Leo Daly, *Titles* (Mullingar, 1980).

Daniel Dunne, Andrew Doyle, *Blessing nd Rededication of the Church of the Sacred Heart Meedin* (Mullingar, 1983).

Samuel Lewis, *Topographical Dictionary of lreland* (Baltimore 1837)

Country LifeMagazine. June 1961.

Sr. M. Gertrude, *A Valiant Woman* (Sydney, 1925).

The Parliamentary Gazeteer of Ireland. (Dublin, London and Edinburgh, 1846).

Olive Curran, (ed.), *History of the Diocese of Meath 1860-1993* (3 Vols, Dublin, 1995.

John Brady , *A short history af the parishes of the diocese of Meath* (Navan, 1937).

John Coolahan, *Irish Education: Its History and Stucture* (Dublin 1981).

Irish Monthly, May 1931.

Patrick J. Dowling *The hedge schools of lreland'* (Cork' 1968).

Timothy Corcoran, *Educational Systems in Ireland from the close of the middle ages,*(Dublin 1928).

Marquess of Londonderry (ed.),*Memoirs and Correspondence of Viscount Castlereagh*(London, 1848,9).

Graham Balfour, *The Educational System of Great Britain and lreland* (Oxford; Clarendon Press. 1903).

Paul Connell, *Parson, Priest and Master, National Educatian in Co. Meath, 1824-41*(Dublin,1995).

Patrick J. Corish, *The Irish Catholic Experience: A Historical Survey*(Dublin, 1985).

Norman Atkinson, *A History of Educational Institutions* (Dublin, 1969).

Mount Carmel Centenary Book 1875-1975, (Australia 1975).

Gabriel Flynn, 'Bishop Thomas Nulty and the lrish Land Question' in *Riocht na Midhe*, vol. iii, no. 4 (1985-86).

Mary C. Sullivan, *Catherine McAuley and the tradition of Mercy* (Cambridge University Press,(1995).

John Magee, *The Canon Rogers Memorial Lecture*; The Master; A social History of the Irish Nationol Teacher 1831-1921, p.14, delivered at St. Joseph's College of Education Belfast, on 2 November 1982.

M. Raphael Consedine, *Listening Journey*(Victoria Australia, 1983).

F.Byrne, *History of the Catholic Church in South Australia,*(Melbourne. 1896).

Urban Corrigan,*The achievements of Catholic education in Australia*(Sydney., 1937).

Ronald Fogarty, *Cathotic Education in Australia 1806-1905* (2 vols. Loodon, New York 1957).

Patrick Francis Cardinal Moran, *History of the Catholic Church in Australia*(Sydney, no date but circa 1896).

McMillan (ed.). *The Wilcannia historical Society Guide Book.*

Booklet on the History of Wilcannia and White Cliffs, pp 28-29 (Author and Title Unknown.).

The Town and Country Journal Sydney, 18 Aug. 1888.

Catholic Directory of Australia 1891-1902: Diocese of Wilcannia.

The Advocate, Sydney, 28 July 1894.

Desmond Bowen, *The Protestant Crusade in lreland l800-1870, A Study of Protestant-Catholic Relations between the Act of Union and disestablishment* (Belfast, 1978).

Roland B. Savage, *Catherine McAuley* (Dublin 1995),

Oliver Egan, *Tyrrellspass Past and Present*, (Kildare, 1986).

Peter J. Dooley, *The Dooleys of Fartullagh in Riocht na Midhe,* Journal of the Meath Archaeological and Historical Society, Vol. III no.4(1992-1993).

Paul Walsh, *The placenames of Westmeath.*

Kathleen Wright, *Light from the bridge, 2003.*

Kuno Meyer, *The Life of Colmán of Lynn*, Ed. Leo Daly, (Dublin 1999).

Rev. Dr. *W.Moran, Friarstown, House of Refuge in na Midhe*(1961 Vol II, no.2).

Public Record Office of Northern Ireland. Education Facsimiles 101-120, *The Penal Laws*.

W.P.Burke, *Irish Priests in Penal Time, 1660-1760* (1914).

Irish Ecclesiastcal Record 1876, Registry of Irish Priests Anno, 1704.

Caesar Otway,*A Tour in Connaught, (1839).*

Beneath Cathedral Towers - Mullingar (2009).

Stephen Darby, *Ballybryan......a step back in time*(Offaly Topic 1995).

St. Joseph's School Journals, *Vox, Involve* and *The Leaving Cert Books*.

Other Sources

The census of lreland for the year 1891: showing the area, population ond the number of houses; Occupations, religion ond education,Vol. 1., Province of Leinster, County ofWestmeath, H.C.1890-1891.

The census af lreland 1881: Pt.l.Showing the area, popalation area number of houses;Occupations, religion and education,Vo11l. Province of Leinster County ofWestmeath, H.C.1872, (C.662) lxvii.

The Royal Commission on the condition of the poorer classes in lreland. Supplement to the First Report of the Commissioners, H.C.1836 xxxii.

Appendix to the second report to the commissioners of Educational Inquiry (Parochial Abstracts) H.C. 1826-1827(12), xii, pp 786-789.

The Census of lreland l861,pt.ii, report and tables on ages and education vol. i. H.C. 1863 (3204-1) lvi.

First report of the commissioners of Irish education inquiry, pp 1-881, H.C.1825 (400) xii, pp l-997.

Second report pp 1-133I,H.C. 1826-7.

Third report pp 3-32, H.C. 1826-7 (13), xiii, pp 1- 155.

Fourth Report... pp 3-202, H.C.1826-7 (89), xiii, pp 156-358.

Fifth Report...pp 3- 26,H.C. 1826-7 (441), xiii, pp 359-84.

Sixth Report...pp. 3-116, H.C. 1826-7(442), xiii, pp. 385- 500.

Seventh Report...pp.3-36, H.C.1826-7 (443), xiii pp. 501-36.

Eight Report...pp 3-461, H.C.1826-7 (509), xiii, pp 537-998.

Ninth Report...pp 3-138, H.C.1826-7 (516), xiii.

Eighteenth Report of the Commissioners of National Education in Ireland for the year 1851, p.xlvii[1852], H.C. 1852-3.

The National Archives Files

N./A. 1/89 folio 122.

N.A./2/134 folio 184-185.

N./A. 1/89 folio 122.

N.A./2/134 folio 184-185.

N./A. 1/89 folio 122.

N.A. Ed 9/23596.

N.A. Ed9/23942.

N.A. Ed 2/135 folio l60.

N.A. Ed. 9/9419.

N.A. Ed. 9/12369..

N.A. Ed 2/134 folio 184-185

N.A. Ed. 9/6935.

N.A. Ed2/134-185.

N.A. Ed 9/11762

N.A. Ed. 9/6035.

Manuscript Sources

Survey of the Plantation measure of the estate of George Rochfort in Castlelost in the Barony of Fartullagh in 1783. N.A.

Survey of part of the Town and Lands of Begarsbidge, the estate of Gustavus Rochfort Esq. 1823. N.A.

Ann Bennett, *A History of the parish af Rochfortbridge and its people in the ruineteenth century)*. This minor thesis was submitted in part fulfillment for the requirements of the B.A. examination, Maynooth, 1975.

The Register of the Sisters of Mercy, Wilcannia-Forbes Congregation Australia. Supplied by Sister M Ryan, Australia.

The Annals of the Sisters of Mercy, Rochfortbridge.

The Annals of the Sisters of Mercy, Tullamore.

Diary of Bishop Dunne, 1887-1892. Archives of Diocese of Wilcannia-Forbes, copy in the Archives of the Sisters of Mercy, Wilcannia Forbes Congregation.

Views expressed by Mr. W.J. Taylor, Coolabah, in a letter to Mr. Tony Lawler MHR, 24 Nv. 1898. Notes supplied by Sr. M.Ryan, Australia. Copy given to WFMA by Miss Gwen Rowe, White Cliffs History Group.

Letters written by Sr.M.Paul Fielding to her Sister, Maria Fielding Kelleghan and her daughter Sr. Antonia Kelleghan between 1897 and 1901. Letters in the possession of Billy and Ruth Kelleghan, Killucan, Co. Westmeath.

Letter written by the Dept. Of Education in 1952, to Sr. M.Magdalene Claffey, giving temporary Secondary Status as Secondar School to St. Joseph's. Letter in St. Joseph's School archives.

Letter written by Dr. Kyne, to Garda, Patrick O'Reilly, Tyrrellspass, with reference to the possibility of admitting boys as students to St. Josephs.(1962). Letter in the possession of Sr. Regina O'Reilly, Convent of Mercy, Trim, Co. Meath.

Photos, Newspaper extracts and miscellaneous sources in the possession of Michael Curran, Gibbonstown, Rochfortbridge.

Newspaper Sources

The Times(1875), undated newspaper article in the possession of the Sisters of Mercy, Rochfortbridge.

Newspaper cutting dated 1862 in possession of Ml. Curran Gibbonstown, Rochfortbridge

*The Freemans Journal,*Sydney, 1862 (undated extract).

The Freemans Journal, Sydney, 17 March, 1894.

The Freemans Journal, Sydney, 2 Dec. 1902.

The Freemans Journal Sydney, 2 December, 1905

Westmeath Journal, 13th Jan. 1831.

The Westmeath Examiner, 25th Feb. 1905.

Westmeath Examiner (31st March 1906).

Westmeath Examiner (14th Aprl, 1906).

Westmeath Examiner (5th of May 1928).

Westmeath Examiner (30th June 1962).

Westmeath Examiner (11th October 1962).

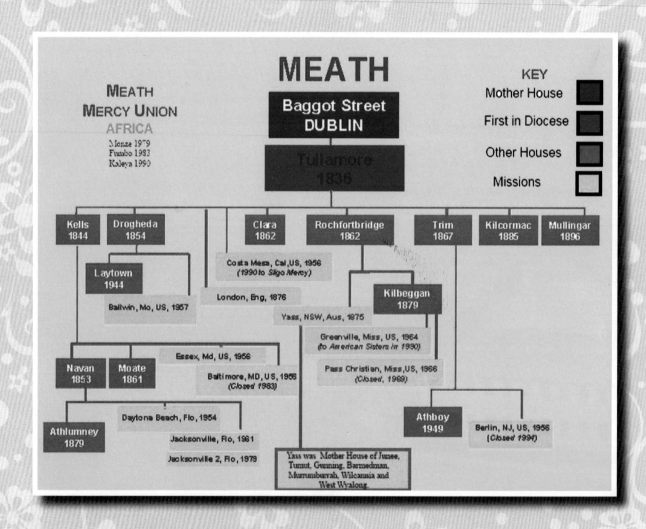

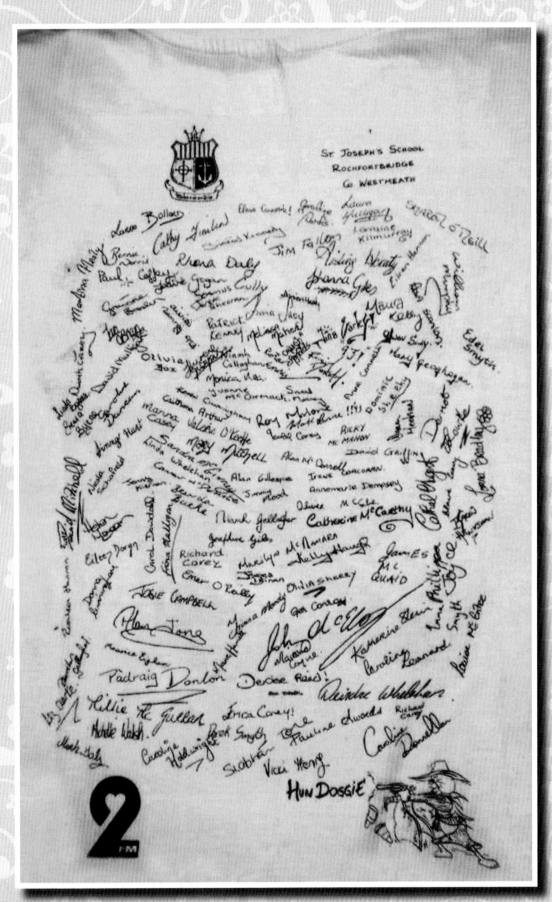

Dermot O'Rourke's tee-shirt signed by the Leaving Cert Class of 1993.

Aerial View taken in the village of the Fertile fields are, the Convent Grounds, the new and the old - St. Joseph's Secondary School, the Convent of Mercy in the centre, behind the Church and The new Convent Primary School in the far distance. The photo was taken around 1986, prior to the renovation of the Parish Church of the Immaculate Conception.